EVERYDAY Mutts

By Patrick McDonnell

Andrews McMeel
Publishing, LLC

Kansas City

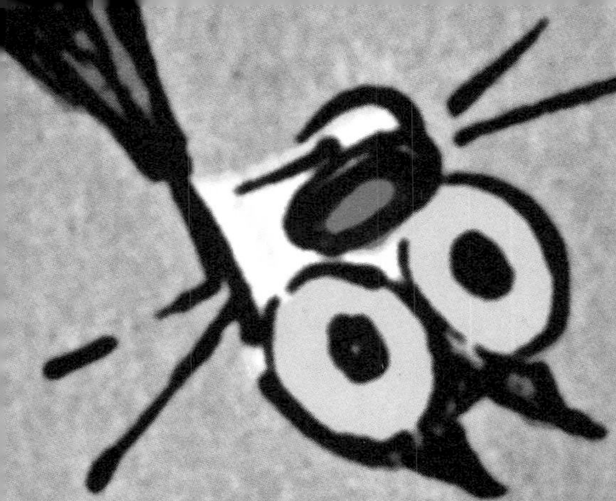

Other Books by Patrick McDonnell

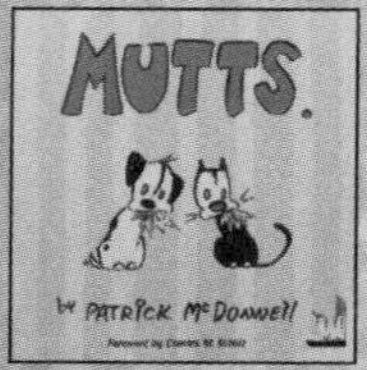
MUTTS.
Mutts

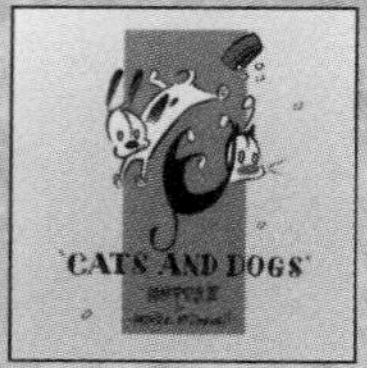
CATS AND DOGS
Cats and Dogs: Mutts II

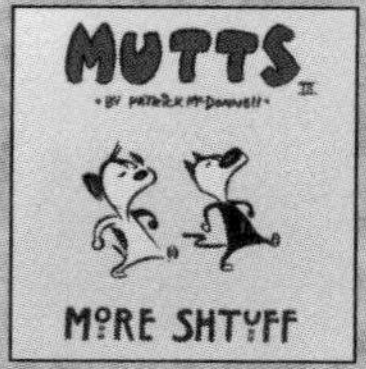
MUTTS
MORE SHTUFF
More Shtuff: Mutts III

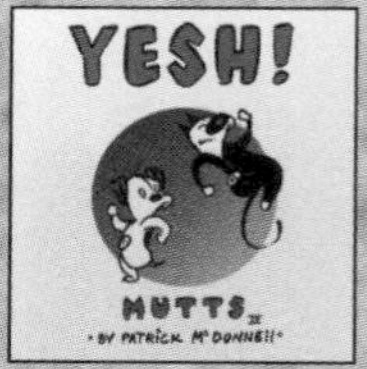
YESH!
MUTTS
Yesh!: Mutts IV

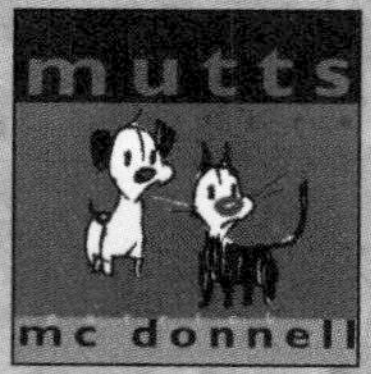
mutts
mc donnell
Our Mutts: Five

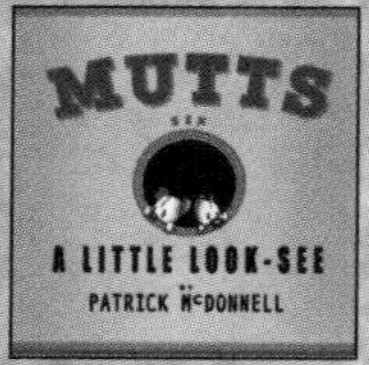
MUTTS
A LITTLE LOOK-SEE
PATRICK McDONNELL
A Little Look-See: Mutts VI

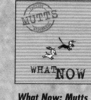

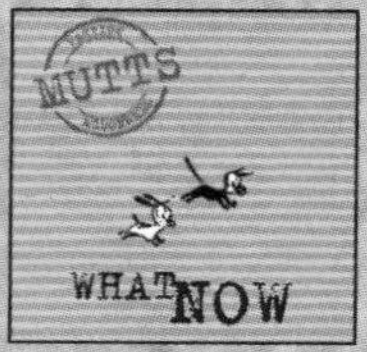
MUTTS
WHAT NOW
What Now: Mutts VII

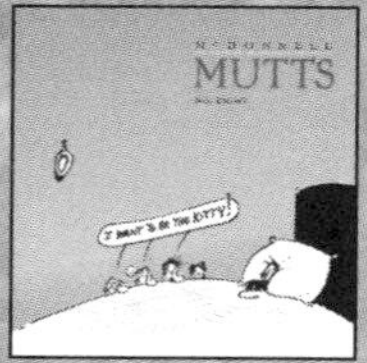
MUTTS
I Want to Be the Kitty: Mutts No. Eight

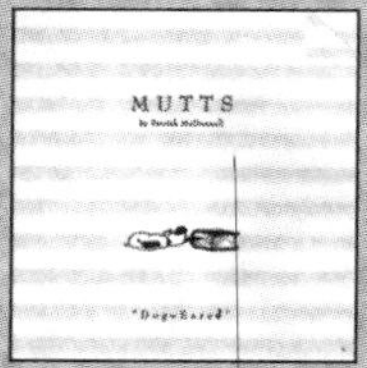
MUTTS
Dog-Eared: Mutts IX

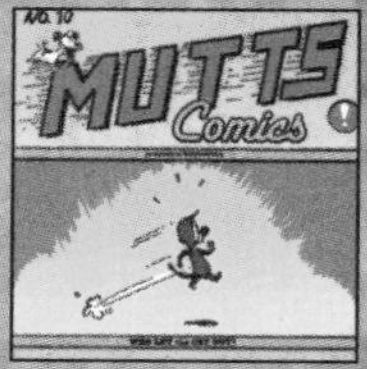
MUTTS
Comics
Who Let the Cat Out?: Mutts X

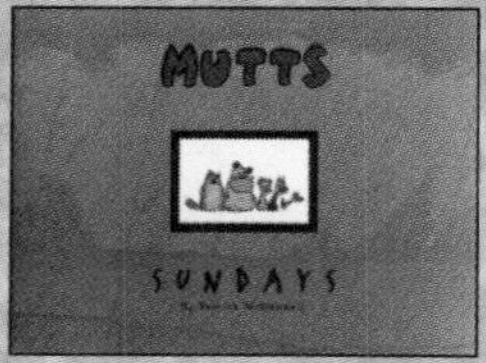
MUTTS
SUNDAYS
Mutts Sundays

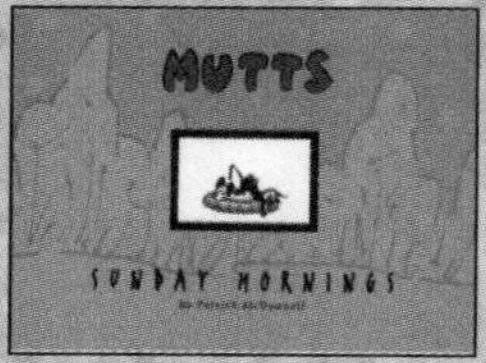
MUTTS
SUNDAY MORNINGS
Mutts Sunday Mornings

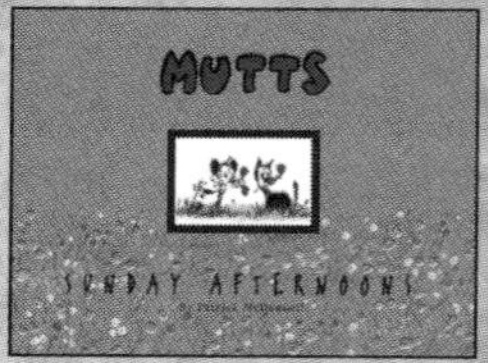
MUTTS
SUNDAY AFTERNOONS
Mutts Sunday Afternoons

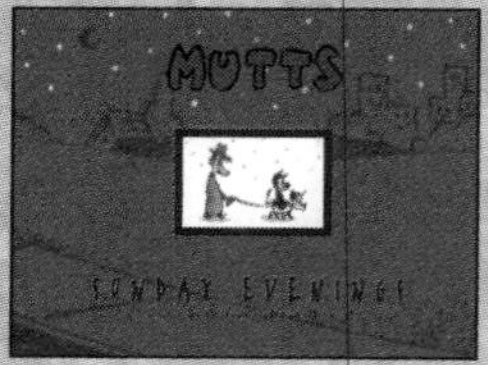
MUTTS
SUNDAY EVENINGS
Mutts Sunday Evenings

For information, write Andrews McMeel Publishing, LLC, an Andrews McMeel Universal company, 4520 Main Street, Kansas City, Missouri 64111.

07 08 09 10 BAM 10 9 8 7 6 5 4 3 2

ISBN-13: 978-0-7407-6197-3
ISBN-10: 0-7407-6197-8

Library of Congress Control Number: 2006925987

Everyday Mutts is printed on recycled paper.

Mutts can be found on the Internet at www.muttscomics.com.

www.andrewsmcmeel.com

www.barkandsmile.com

Other Books by Kim Levin

Pawfiles • *Hound for the Holidays* (with John O'Neill)
Growing Up (with John O'Neill) • *Dogma* (with Erica Salmon) • *Why We Love Cats*
Why We Love Dogs • *Why We Really Love Dogs* • *Dogs Are Funny*
Dogs Love . . . • *Working Dogs: Tales from Animal Planet's K-9 to 5 World*
Cattitude (with Christine Montaquila) • *Erin Go Bark* (with John O'Neill)
For the Love You Give (with John O'Neill)

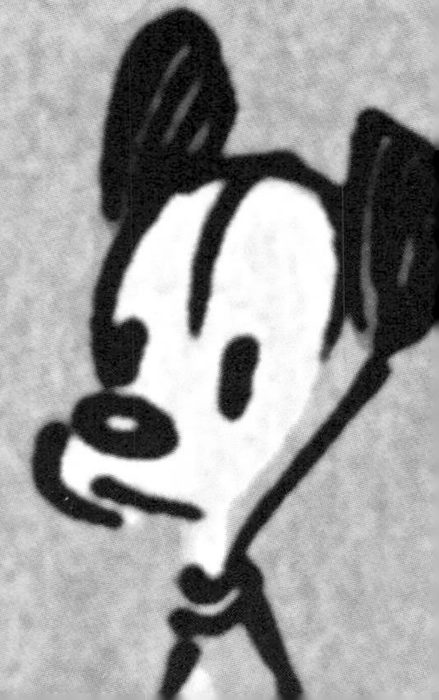

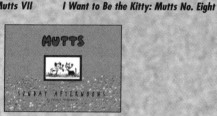

THIS LATEST MUTTS COLLECTION CONTAINS ABOUT A YEAR'S
WORTH OF NEW COMIC STRIPS, BOTH DAILY AND SUNDAY.
I'VE ALSO INCLUDED SOME OF MY SKETCHBOOK PAGES,
A FEW SPECIALTY DRAWINGS, AND A COUPLE PHOTOGRAPHS.
IT'S A TREASURY OF WHAT I DO EVERY DAY.

AND YES, THAT'S "MY EARL" ON THE COVER. HE'S JUST
TURNED SEVENTEEN, AND STILL EAGERLY GREETS THE WORLD WITH
UNABASHED LOVE AND JOY. IT'S WHAT HE DOES EVERY DAY.

THANKS FOR SPENDING SOME TIME WITH MUTTS.

PATRICK McDONNELL

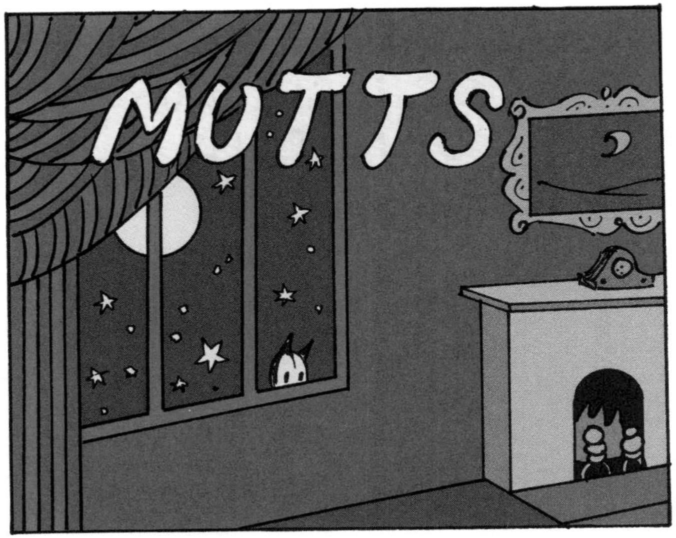
MUTTS

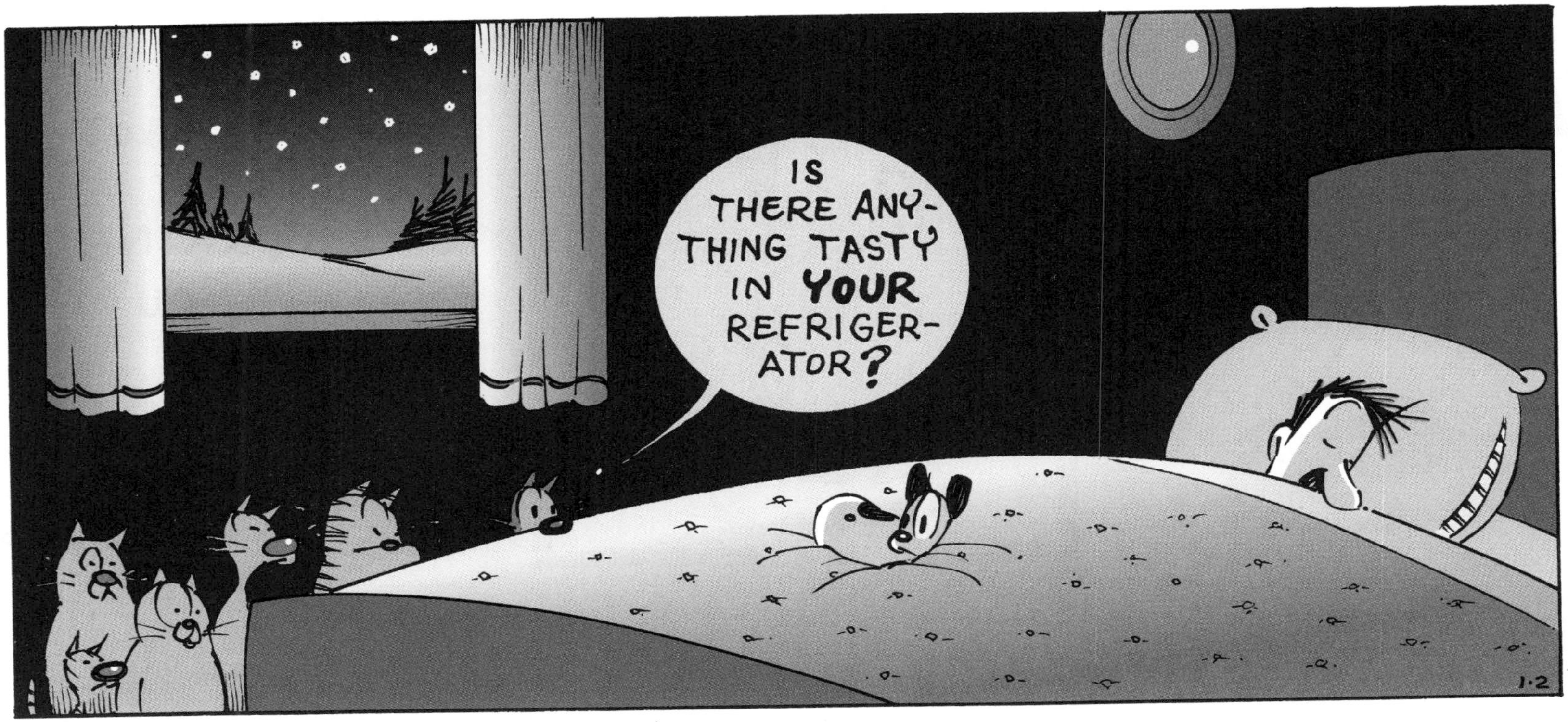
IS THERE ANY-THING TASTY IN YOUR REFRIGER-ATOR?
1·2

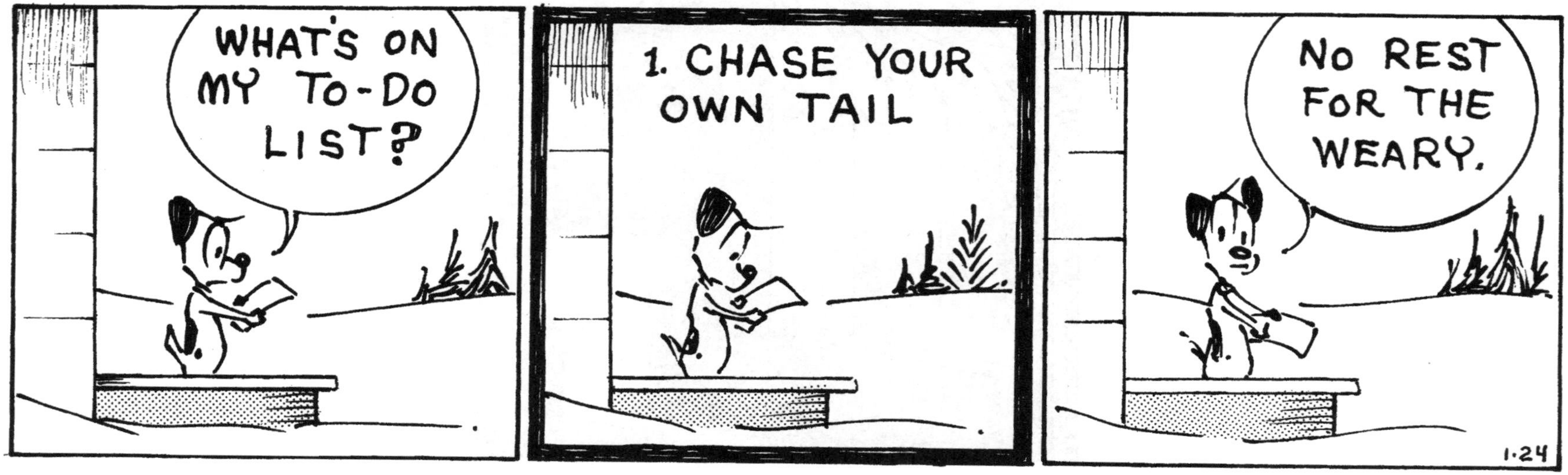
WHAT'S ON MY TO-DO LIST?
1. CHASE YOUR OWN TAIL
NO REST FOR THE WEARY.
1·24

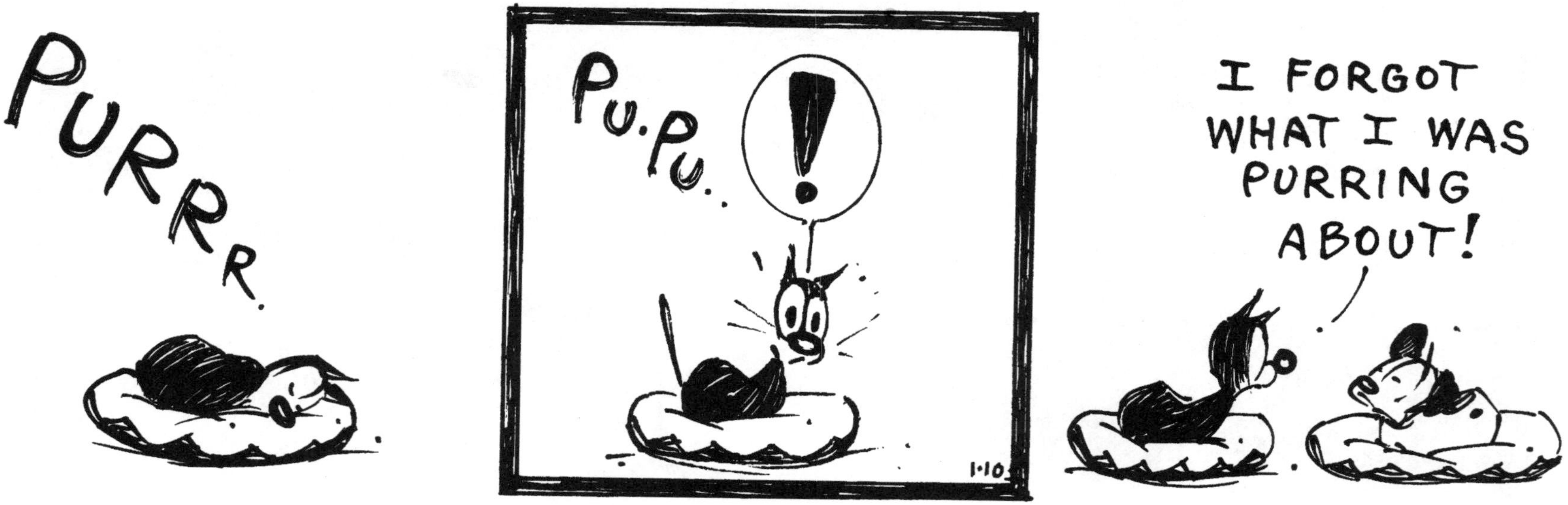
PURRRR.
PU.PU...
!
1·10
I FORGOT WHAT I WAS PURRING ABOUT!

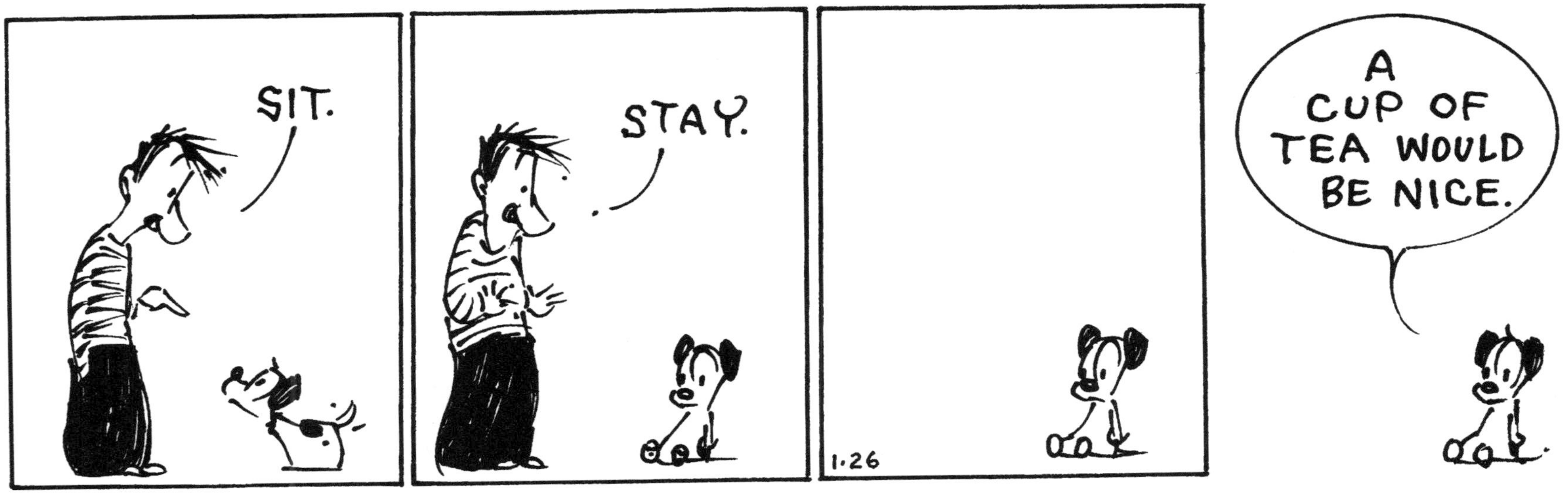
SIT.
STAY.
1.26
A CUP OF TEA WOULD BE NICE.

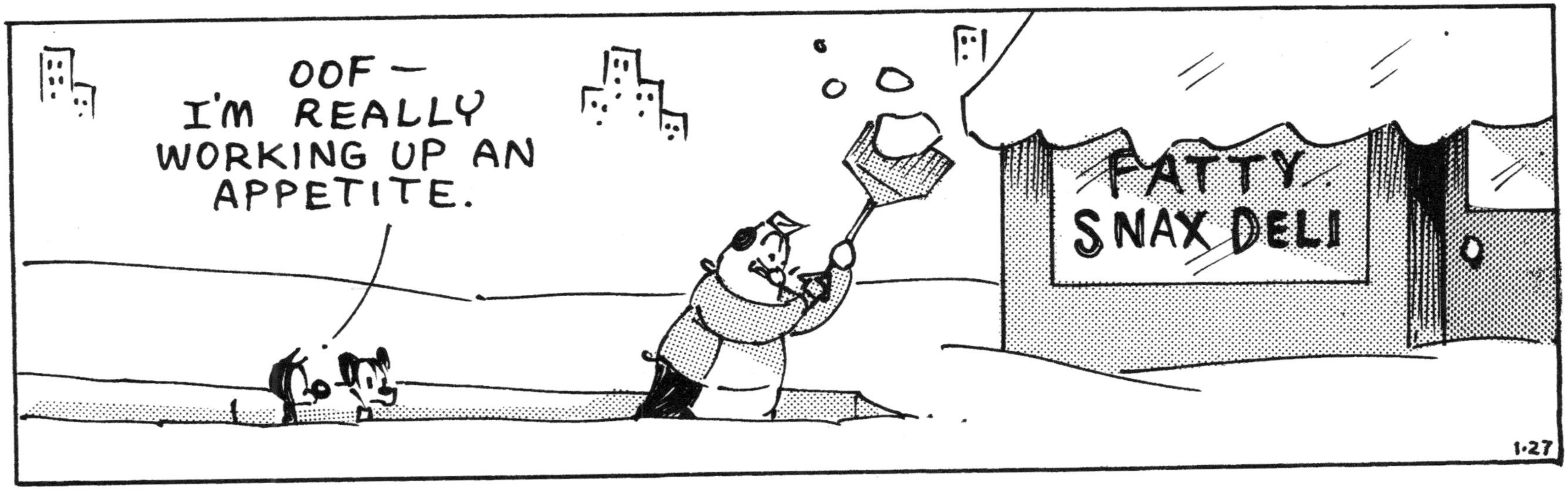
OOF — I'M REALLY WORKING UP AN APPETITE.
FATTY SNAX DELI
1.27

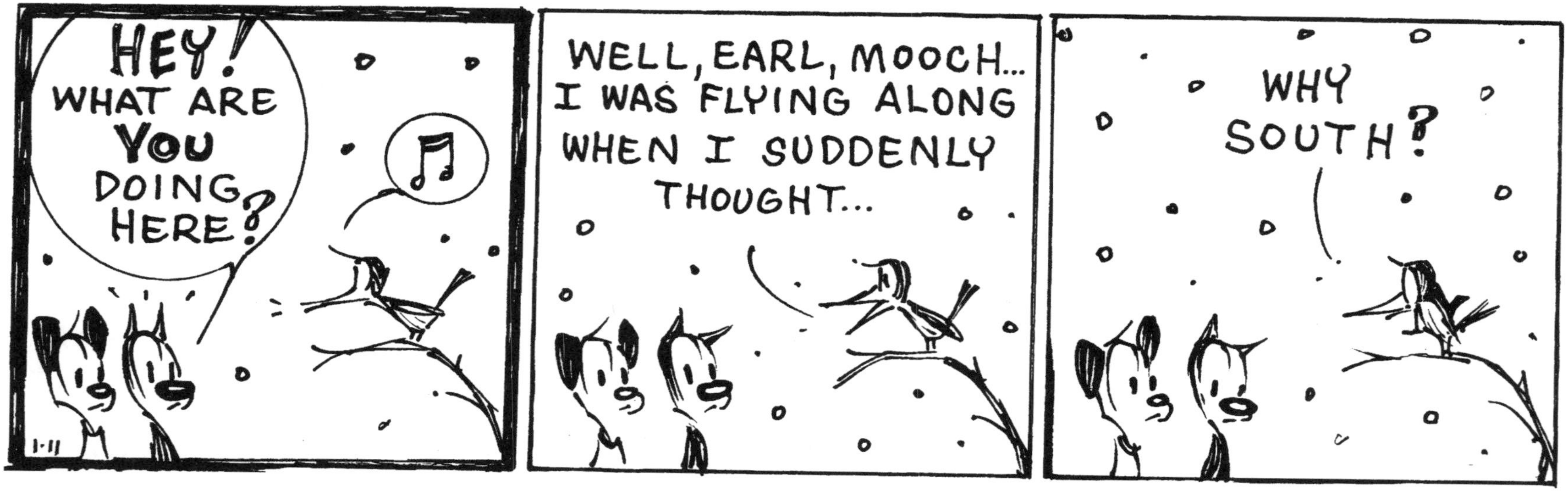
HEY! WHAT ARE YOU DOING HERE?
1·11
WELL, EARL, MOOCH... I WAS FLYING ALONG WHEN I SUDDENLY THOUGHT...
WHY SOUTH?

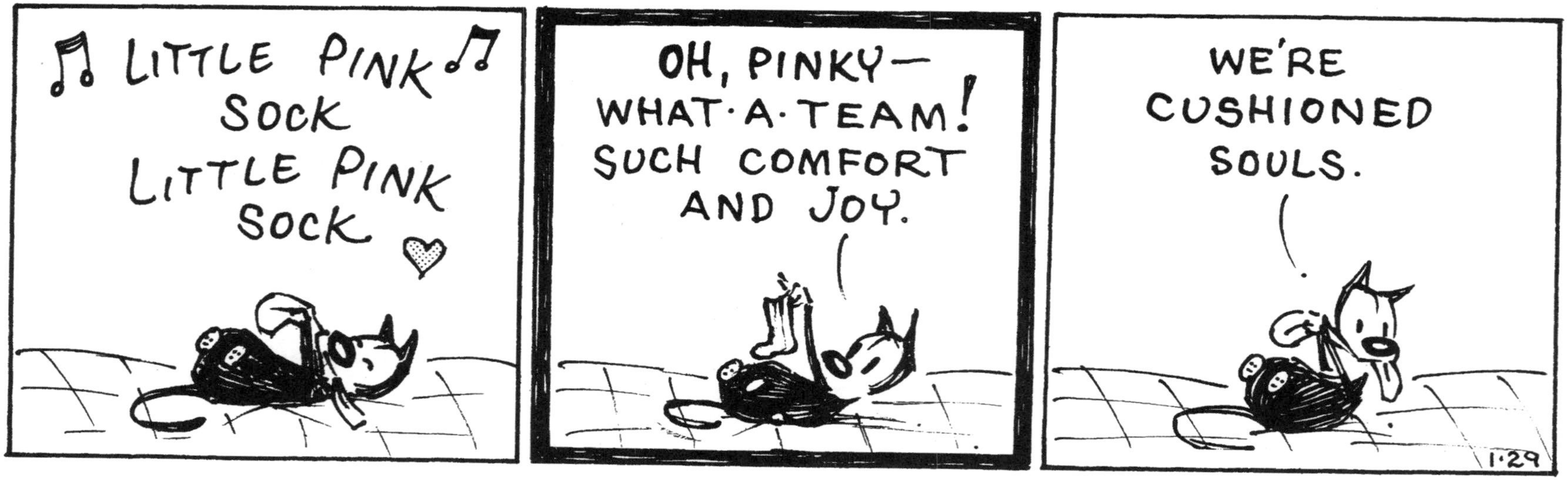
LITTLE PINK SOCK LITTLE PINK SOCK
OH, PINKY— WHAT·A·TEAM! SUCH COMFORT AND JOY.
WE'RE CUSHIONED SOULS.
1·29

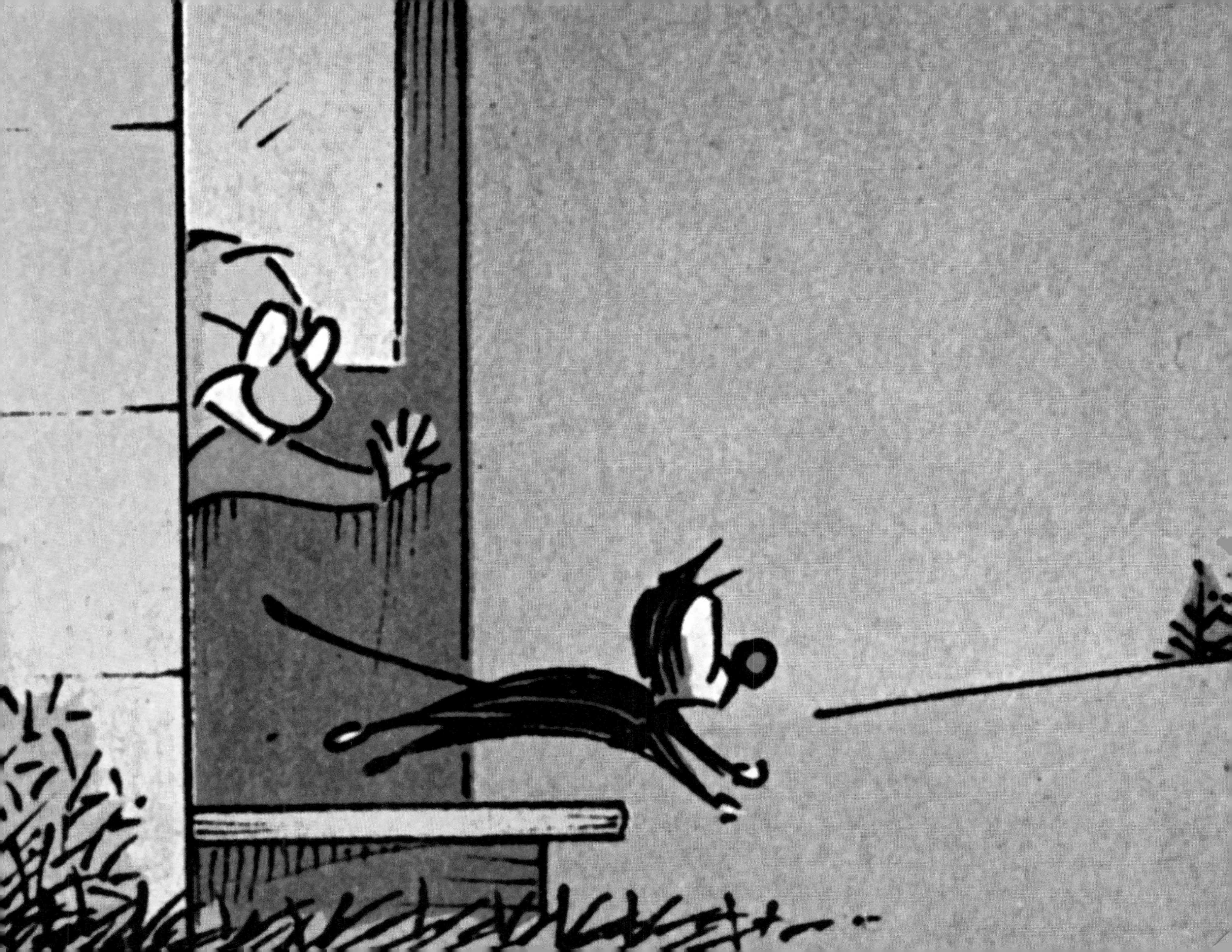

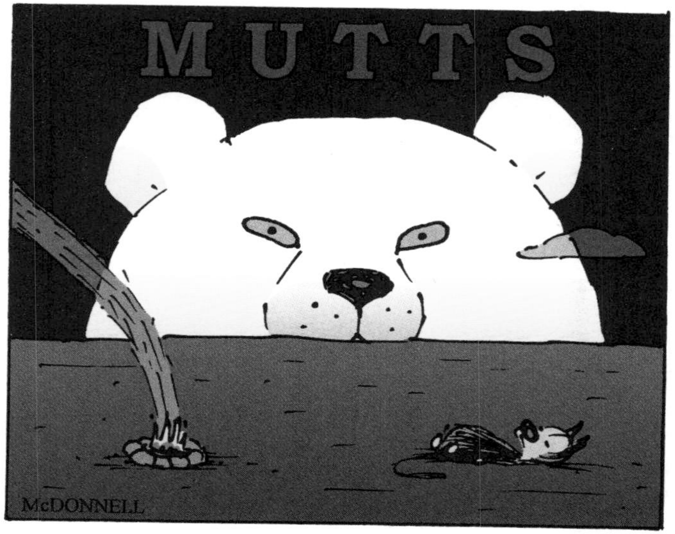
MUTTS
McDONNELL

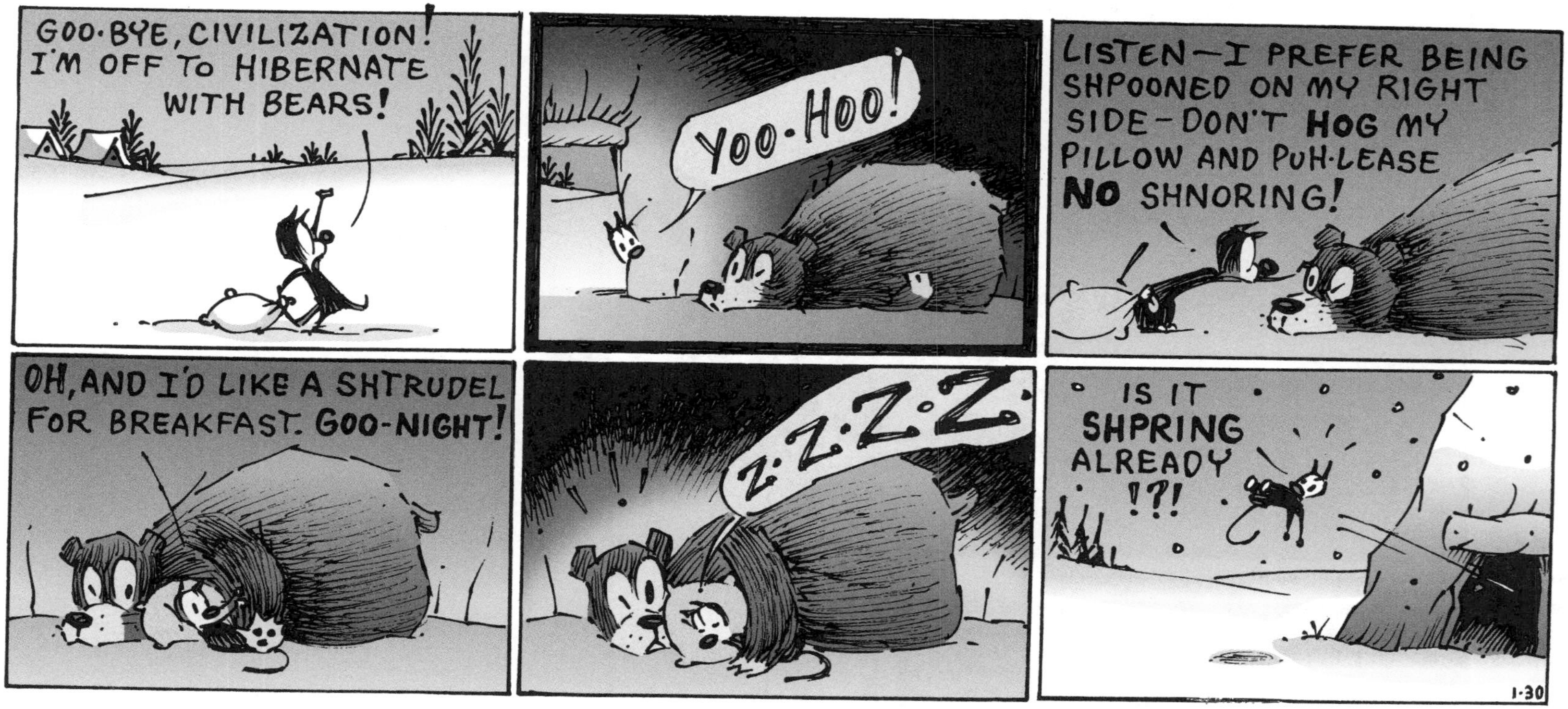
GOO·BYE, CIVILIZATION! I'M OFF TO HIBERNATE WITH BEARS!
YOO·HOO!
LISTEN—I PREFER BEING SHPOONED ON MY RIGHT SIDE—DON'T HOG MY PILLOW AND PUH·LEASE NO SHNORING!
OH, AND I'D LIKE A SHTRUDEL FOR BREAKFAST. GOO-NIGHT!
Z·Z·Z·Z
IS IT SHPRING ALREADY !?!
1·30

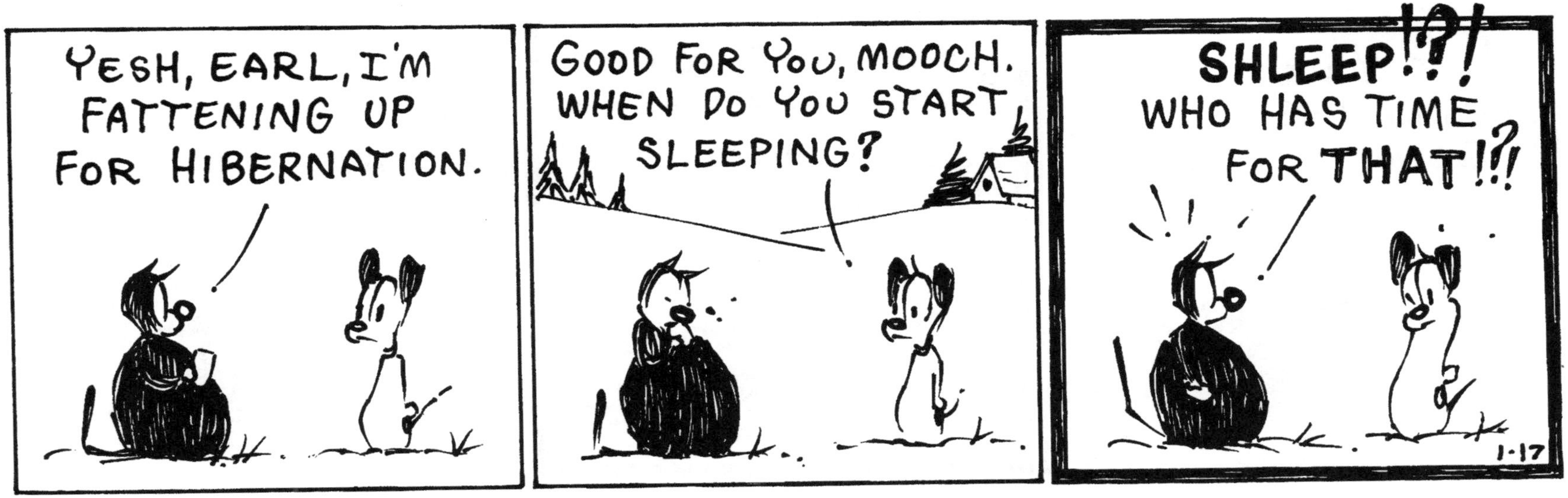
YESH, EARL, I'M FATTENING UP FOR HIBERNATION.
GOOD FOR YOU, MOOCH. WHEN DO YOU START SLEEPING?
SHLEEP!?! WHO HAS TIME FOR THAT!?!
1-17

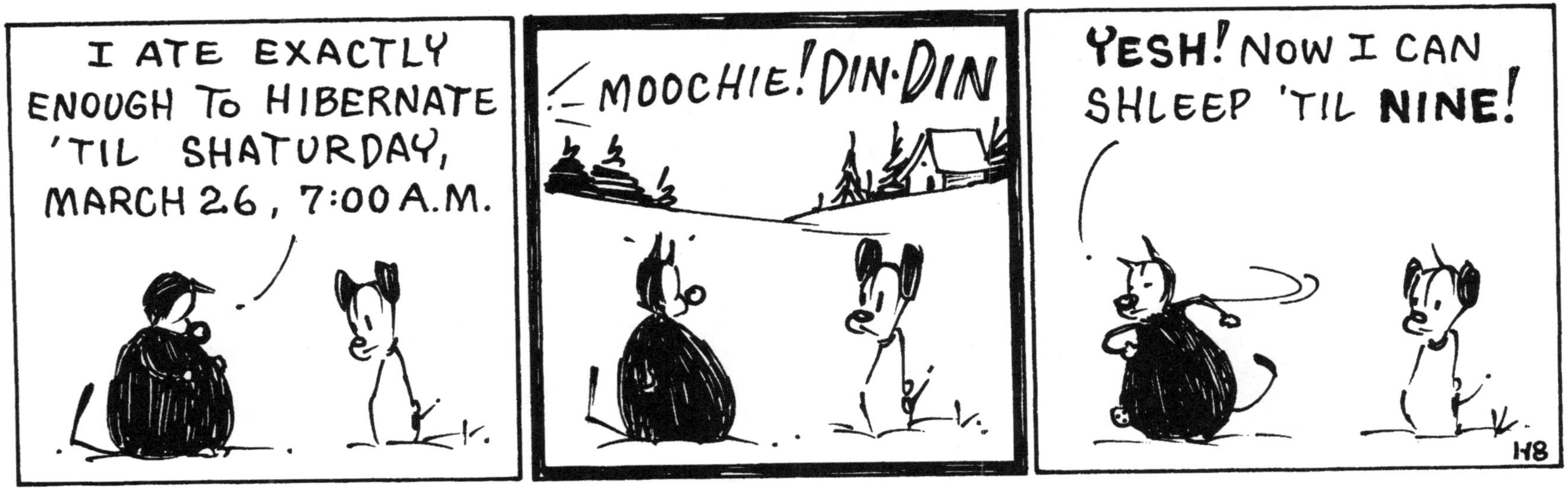
I ATE EXACTLY ENOUGH TO HIBERNATE 'TIL SHATURDAY, MARCH 26, 7:00 A.M.
MOOCHIE! DIN-DIN
YESH! NOW I CAN SHLEEP 'TIL NINE!
1-18

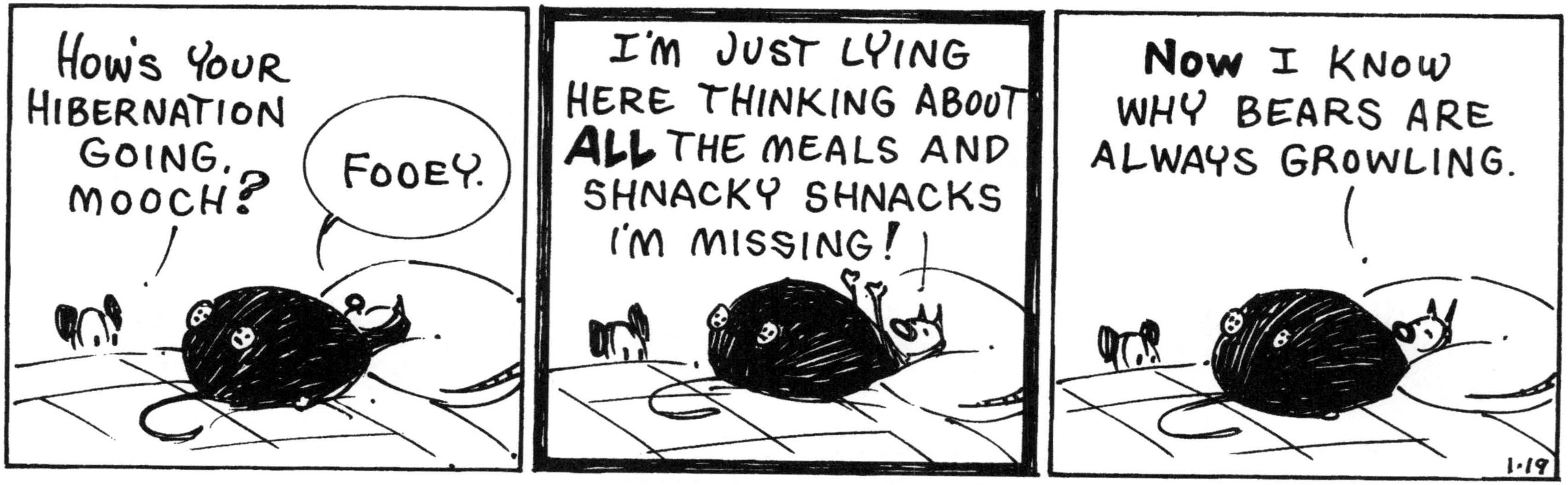
HOW'S YOUR HIBERNATION GOING, MOOCH?
FOOEY.
I'M JUST LYING HERE THINKING ABOUT ALL THE MEALS AND SHNACKY SHNACKS I'M MISSING!
NOW I KNOW WHY BEARS ARE ALWAYS GROWLING.
1.19

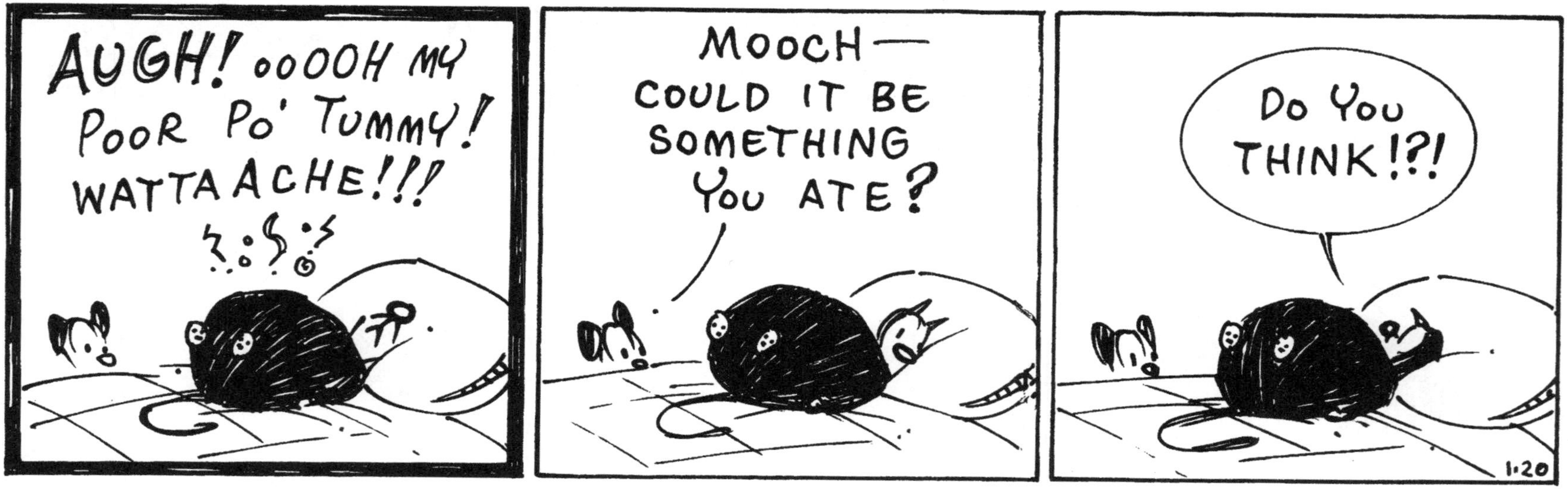
AUGH! OOOOH MY POOR PO' TUMMY! WATTA ACHE!!!
MOOCH— COULD IT BE SOMETHING YOU ATE?
DO YOU THINK!?!
1.20

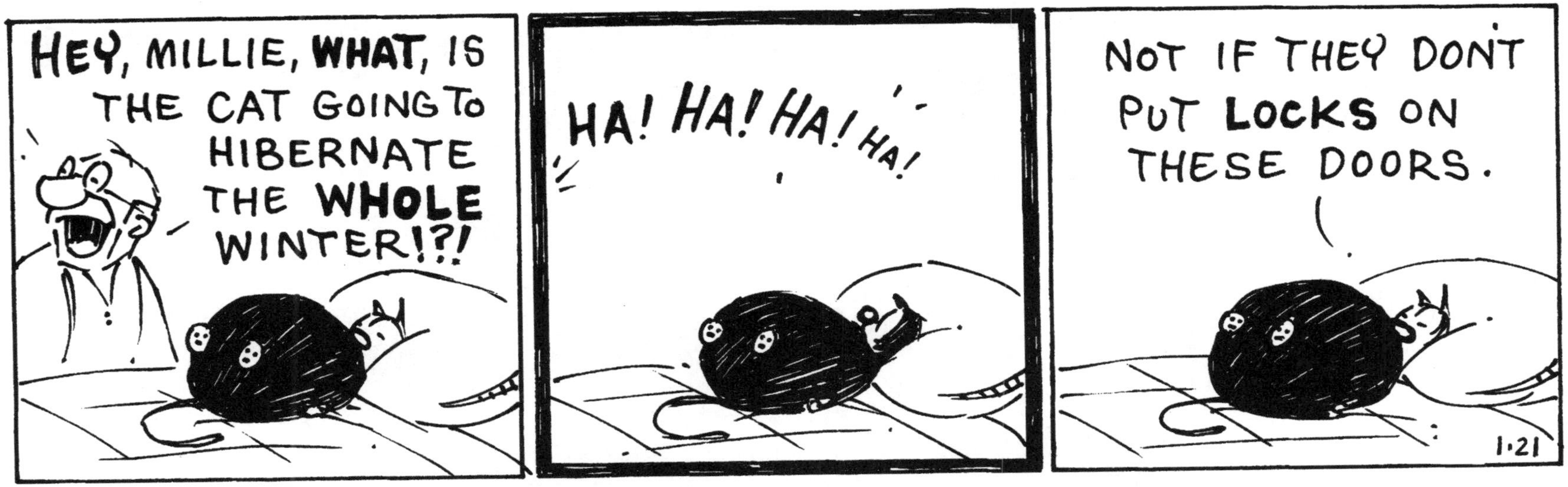
HEY, MILLIE, **WHAT**, IS THE CAT GOING TO HIBERNATE THE **WHOLE** WINTER!?!
HA! HA! HA! HA!
NOT IF THEY DON'T PUT **LOCKS** ON THESE DOORS.
1·21

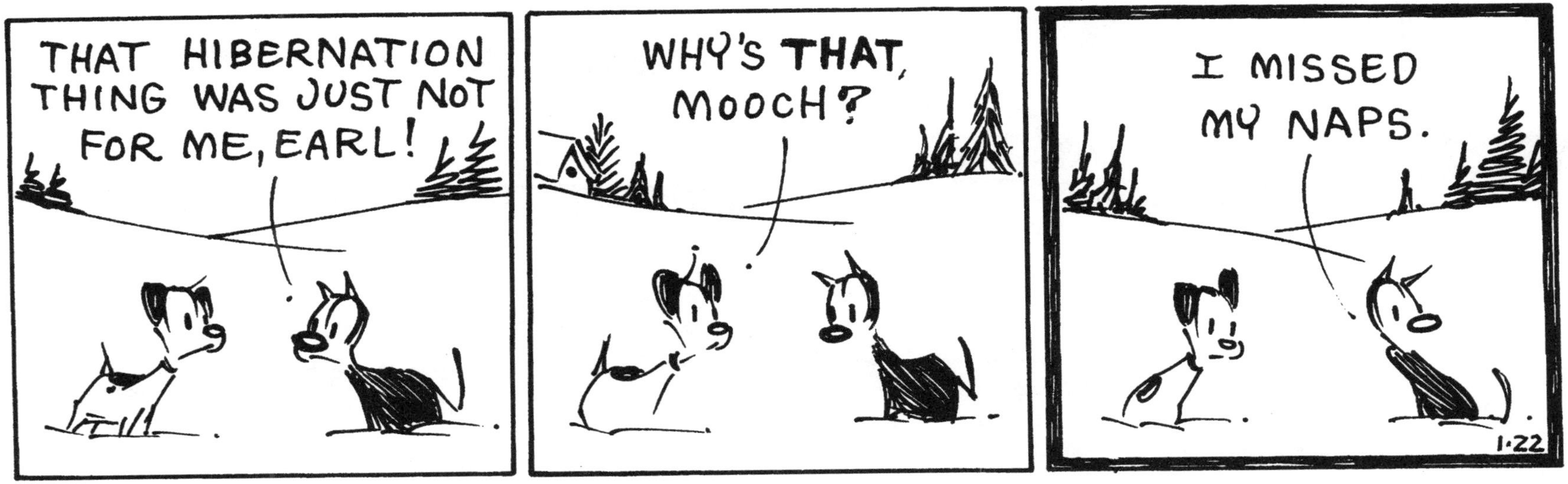
THAT HIBERNATION THING WAS JUST NOT FOR ME, EARL!
WHY'S **THAT**, MOOCH?
I MISSED MY NAPS.
1·22

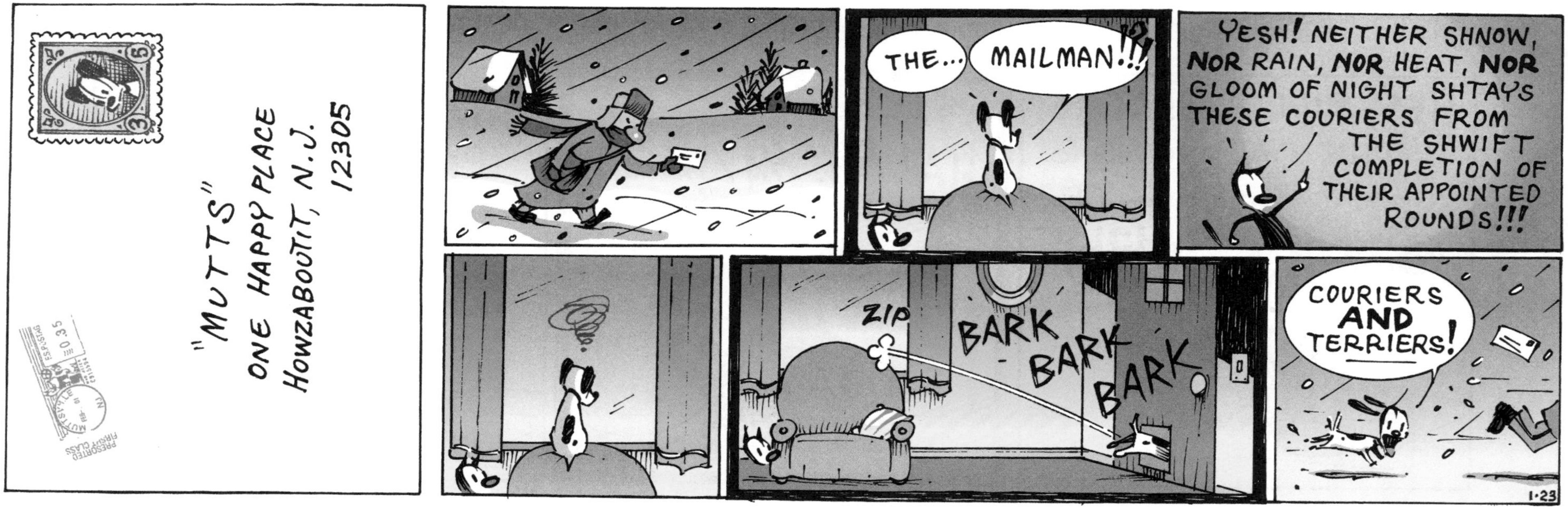
"MUTTS"
ONE HAPPY PLACE
HOWZABOUTIT, N.J.
12305
THE...
MAILMAN!!!
YESH! NEITHER SHNOW, NOR RAIN, NOR HEAT, NOR GLOOM OF NIGHT SHTAYS THESE COURIERS FROM THE SHWIFT COMPLETION OF THEIR APPOINTED ROUNDS!!!
ZIP
BARK
BARK
BARK
COURIERS AND TERRIERS!
1·23

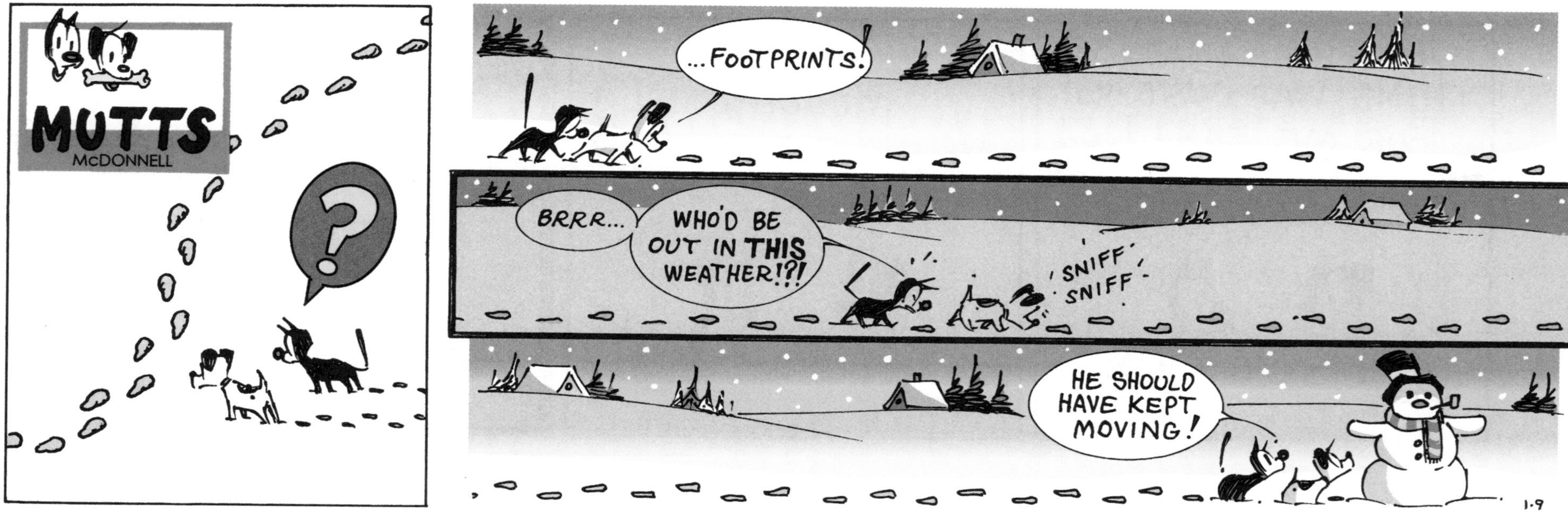
MUTTS
McDONNELL
?
...FOOTPRINTS!
BRRR...
WHO'D BE OUT IN THIS WEATHER!?!
SNIFF
SNIFF
HE SHOULD HAVE KEPT MOVING!
1·9

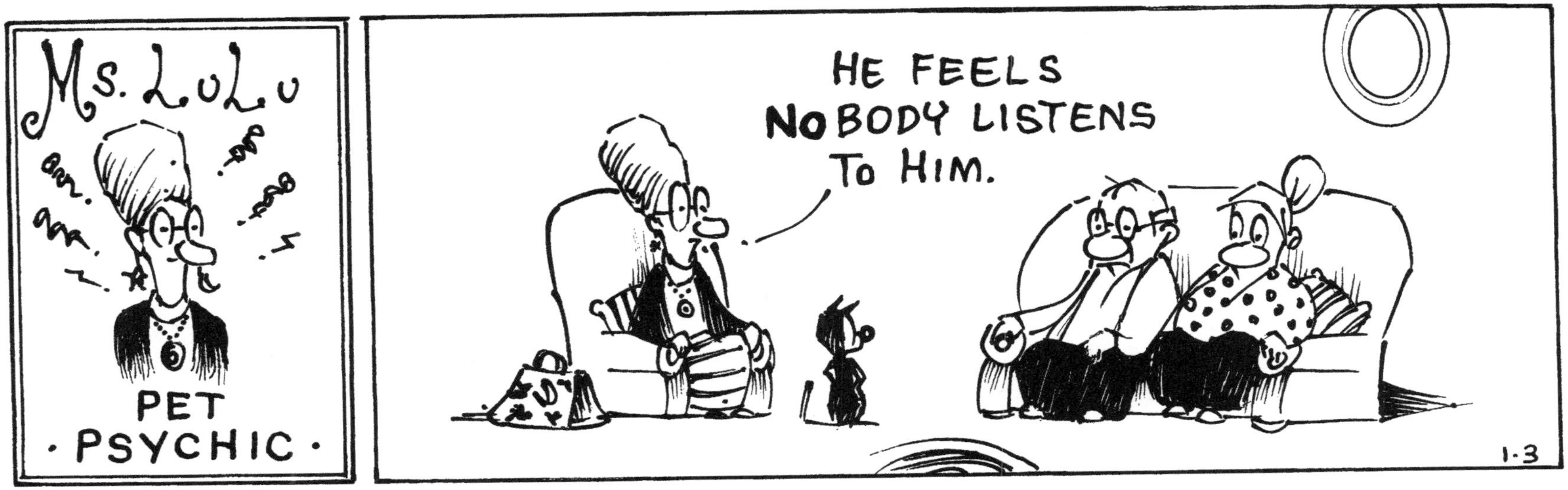
Ms. LuLu
PET
·PSYCHIC·
HE FEELS **NO**BODY LISTENS TO HIM.
1·3

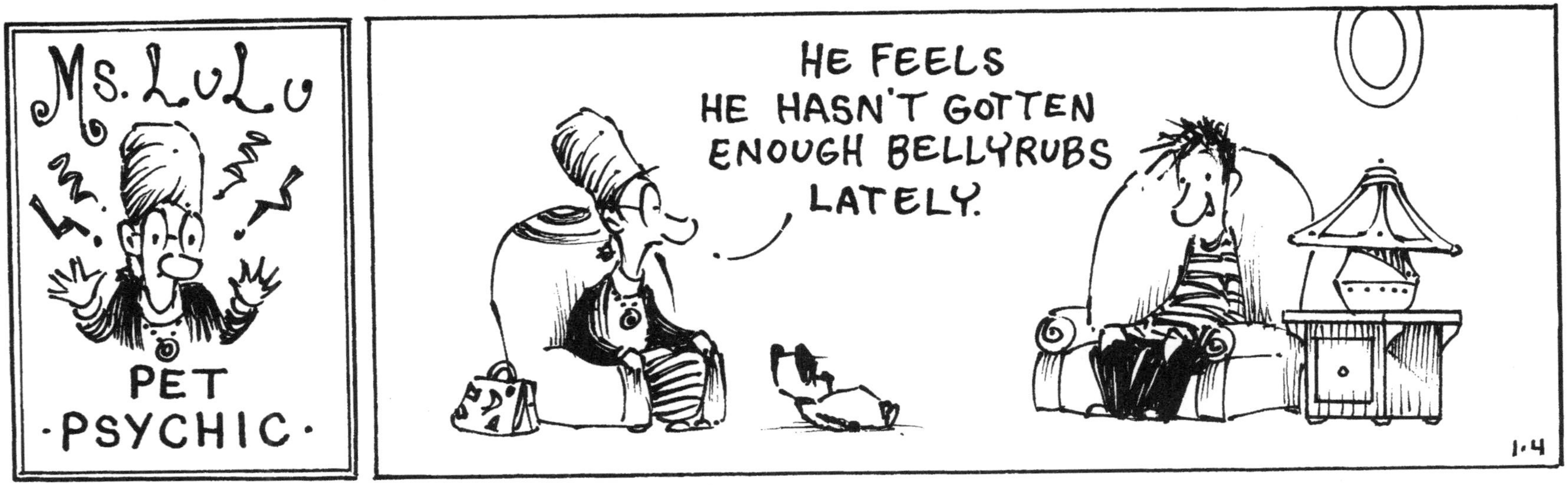
Ms. LuLu
PET
·PSYCHIC·
HE FEELS HE HASN'T GOTTEN ENOUGH BELLYRUBS LATELY.
1·4

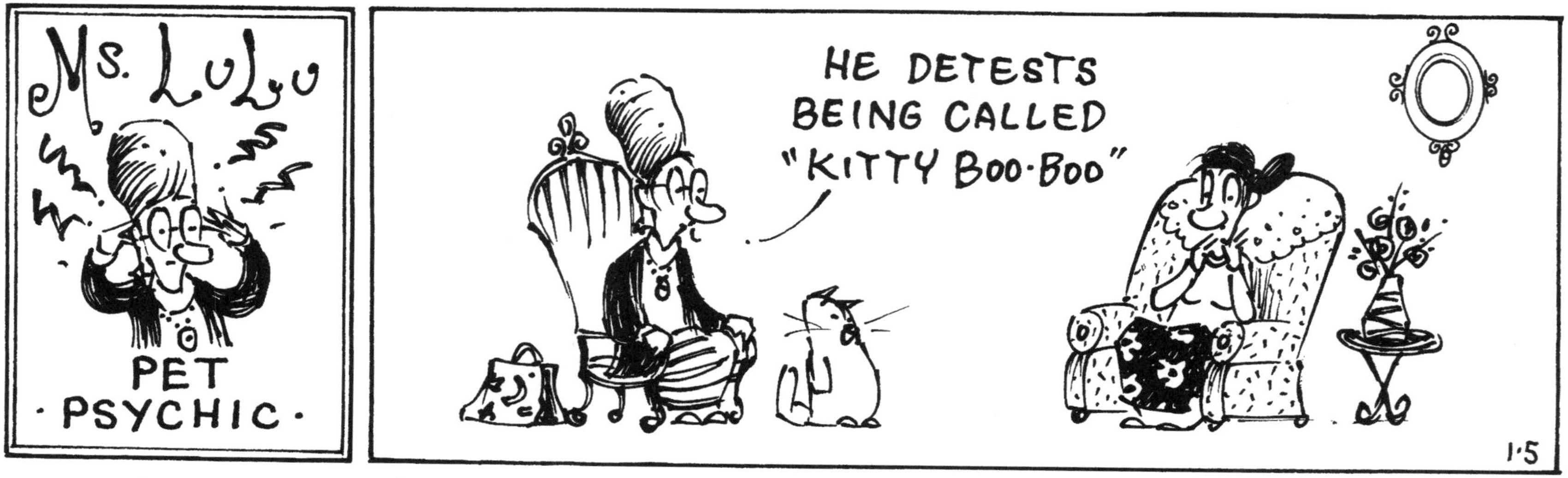
Ms. LuLu
PET
·PSYCHIC·
HE DETESTS BEING CALLED "KITTY BOO-BOO"
1·5

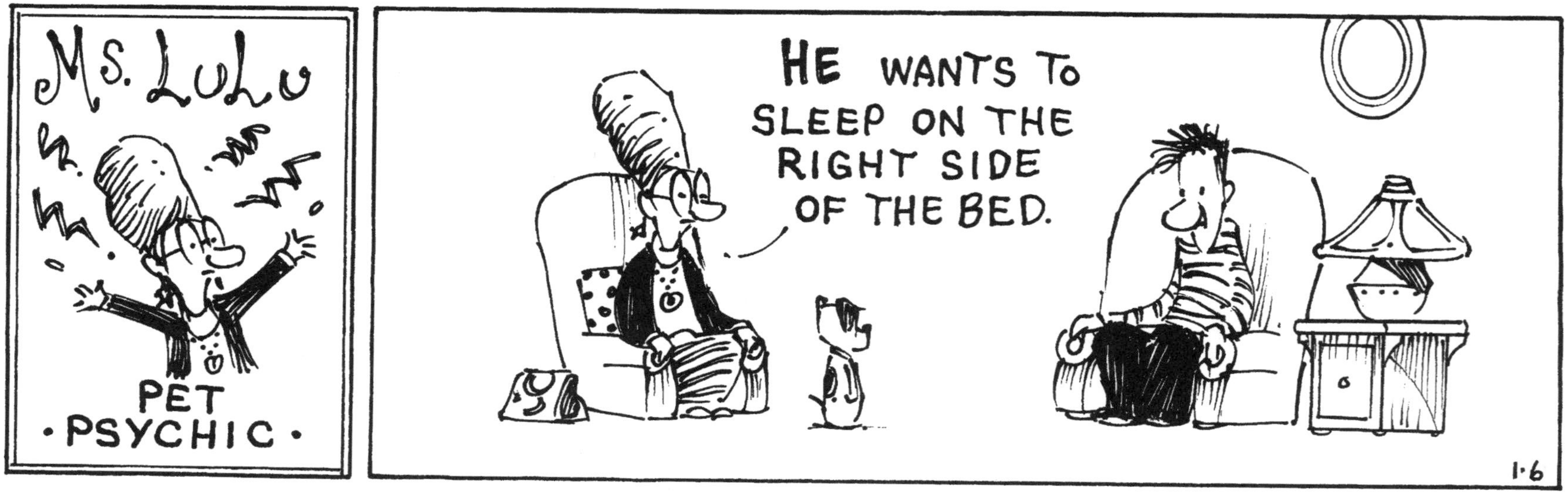
Ms. LuLu
PET
·PSYCHIC·
HE WANTS TO SLEEP ON THE RIGHT SIDE OF THE BED.
1·6

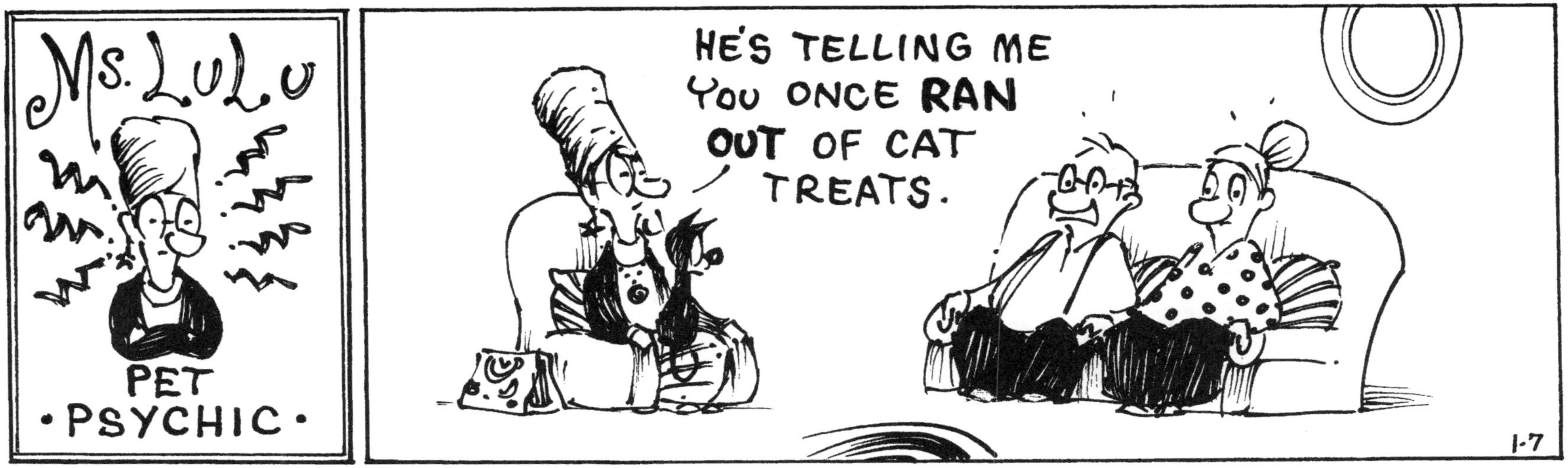
Ms. LuLu
PET
•PSYCHIC•
HE'S TELLING ME YOU ONCE **RAN OUT** OF CAT TREATS.
1-7

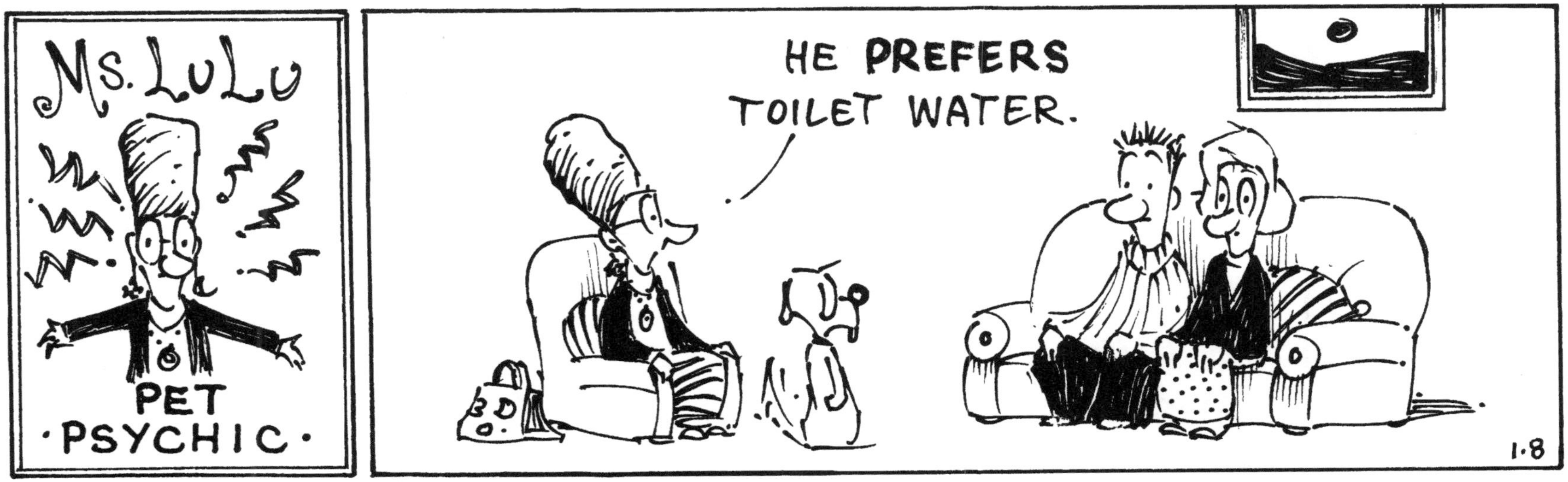
Ms. LuLu
PET
•PSYCHIC•
HE **PREFERS** TOILET WATER.
1-8

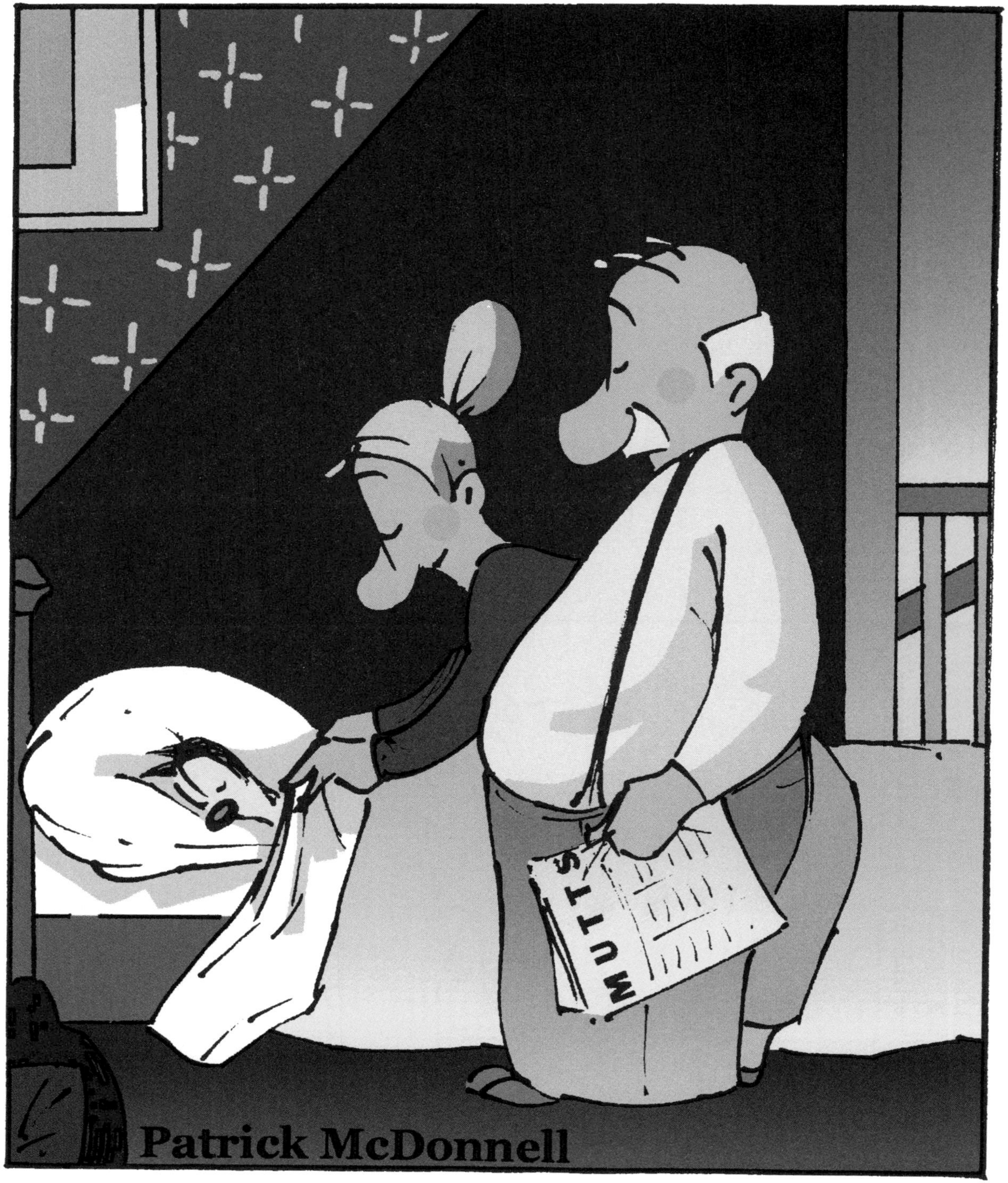
MUTTS
Patrick McDonnell

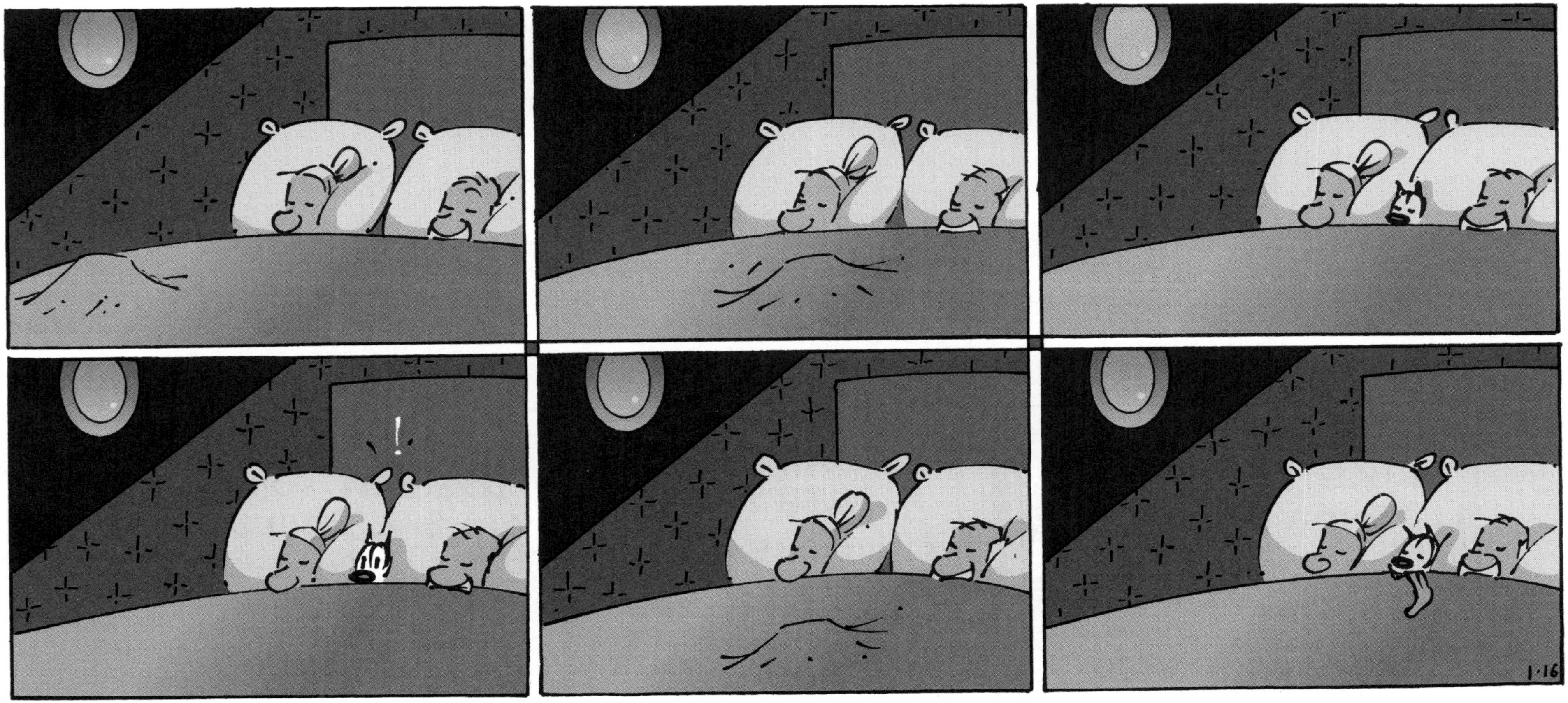
!
1·16

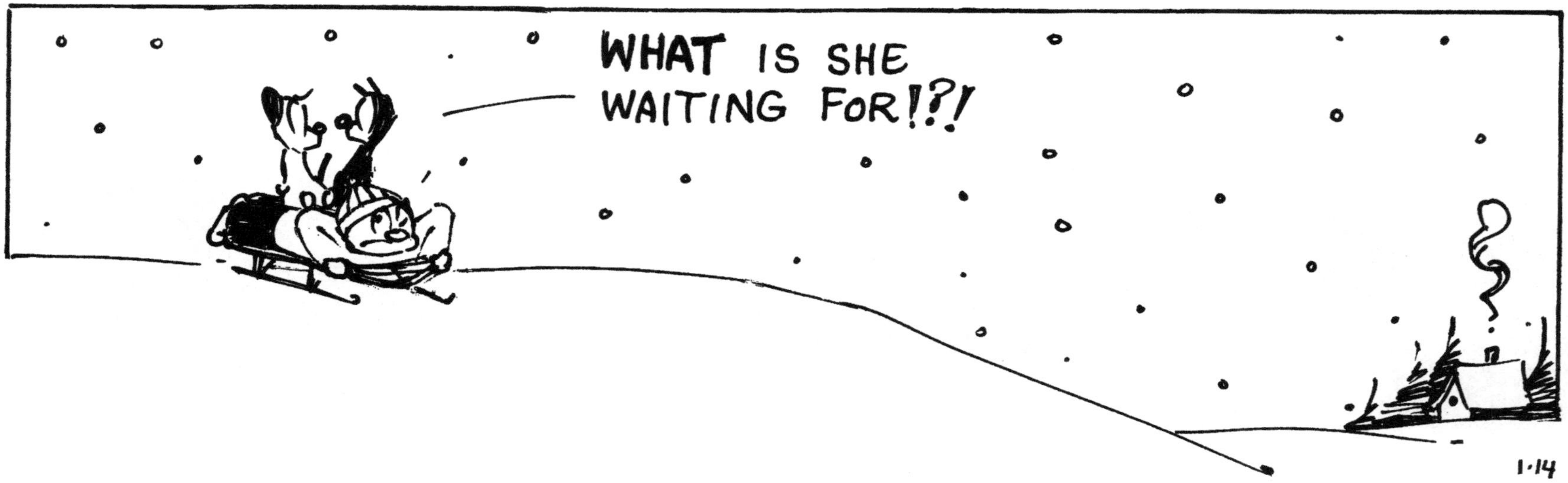
WHAT IS SHE WAITING FOR!?!
1·14

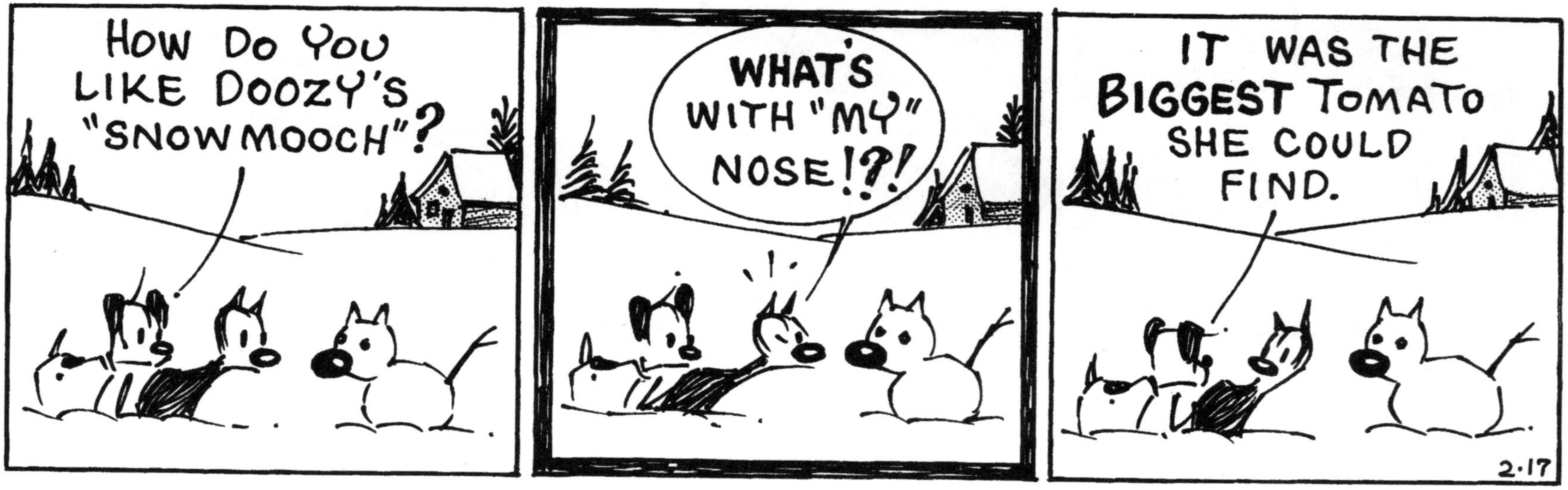
HOW DO YOU LIKE DOOZY'S "SNOWMOOCH"?
WHAT'S WITH "MY" NOSE!?!
IT WAS THE BIGGEST TOMATO SHE COULD FIND.
2·17

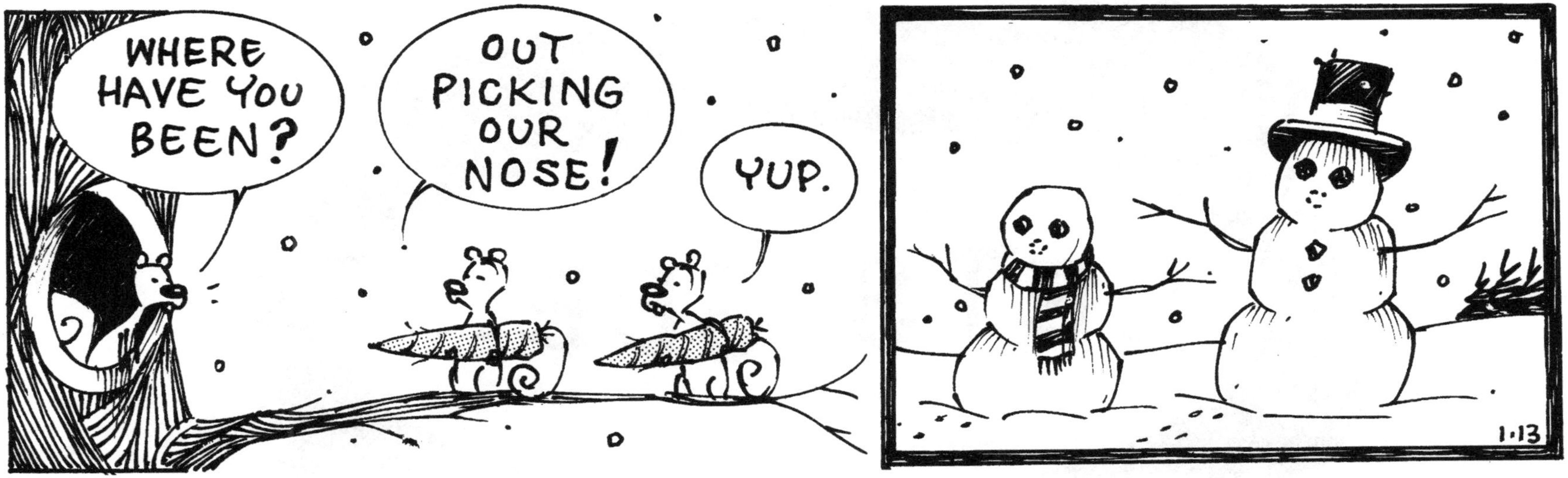
WHERE HAVE YOU BEEN?
OUT PICKING OUR NOSE!
YUP.
1·13

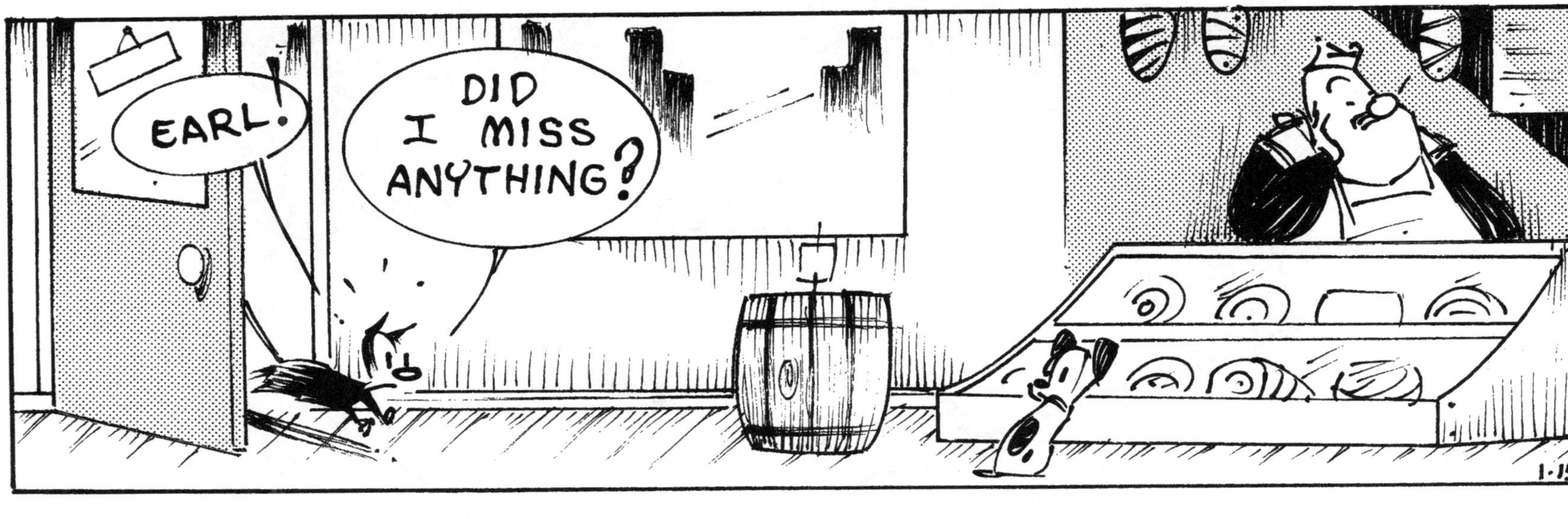
EARL!
DID I MISS ANYTHING?
1·15

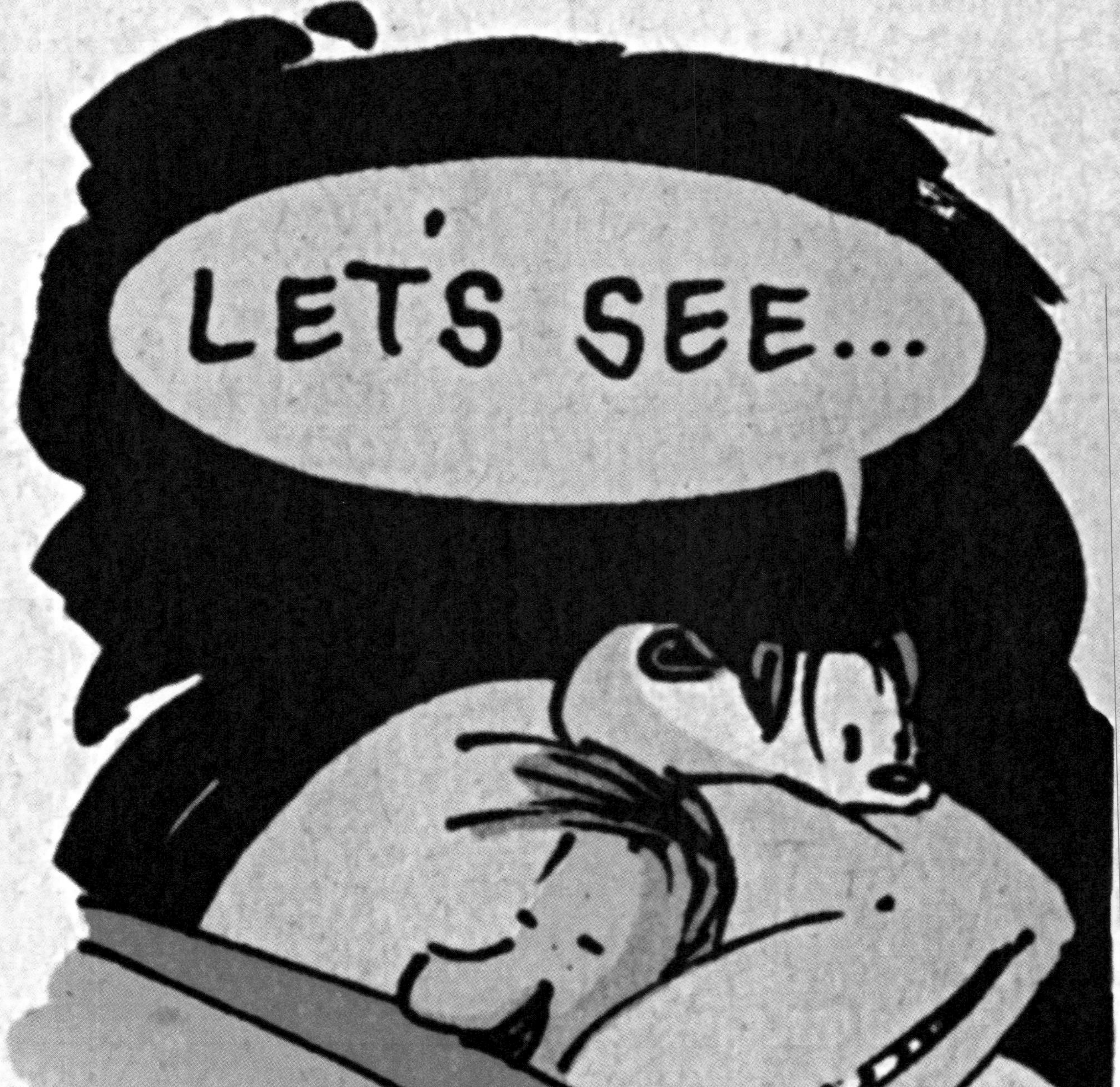
LET'S SEE...

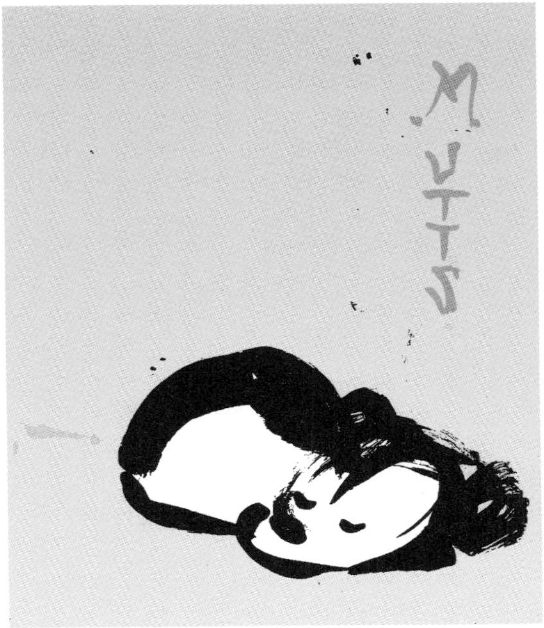
MUTTS

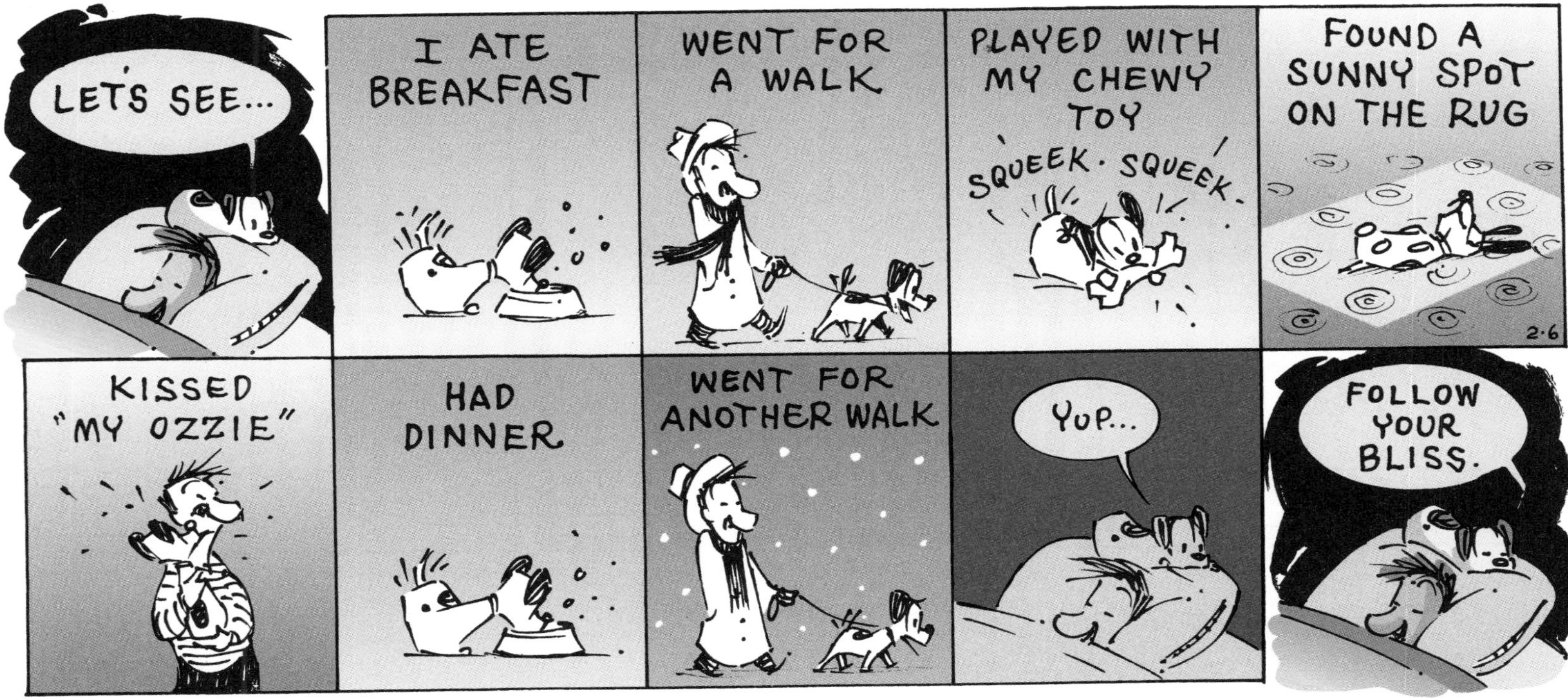
LET'S SEE...
I ATE BREAKFAST
WENT FOR A WALK
PLAYED WITH MY CHEWY TOY
SQUEEK · SQUEEK
FOUND A SUNNY SPOT ON THE RUG
2·6
KISSED "MY OZZIE"
HAD DINNER
WENT FOR ANOTHER WALK
YUP...
FOLLOW YOUR BLISS.

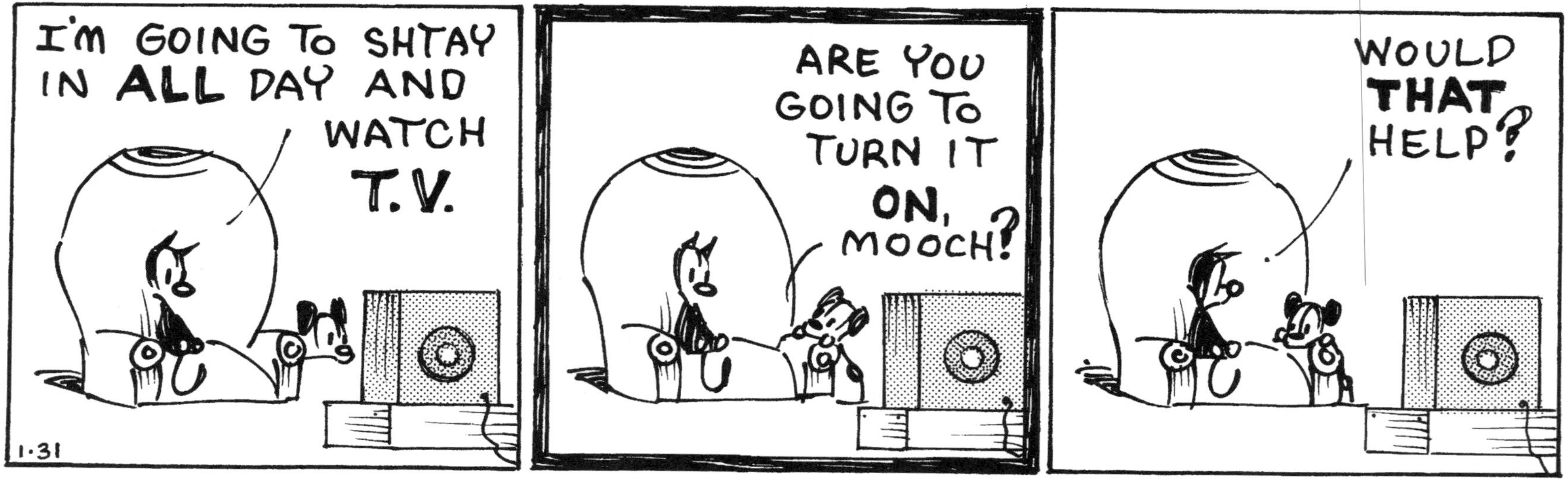
I'M GOING TO SHTAY IN ALL DAY AND WATCH T.V.
1·31
ARE YOU GOING TO TURN IT ON, MOOCH?
WOULD THAT HELP?

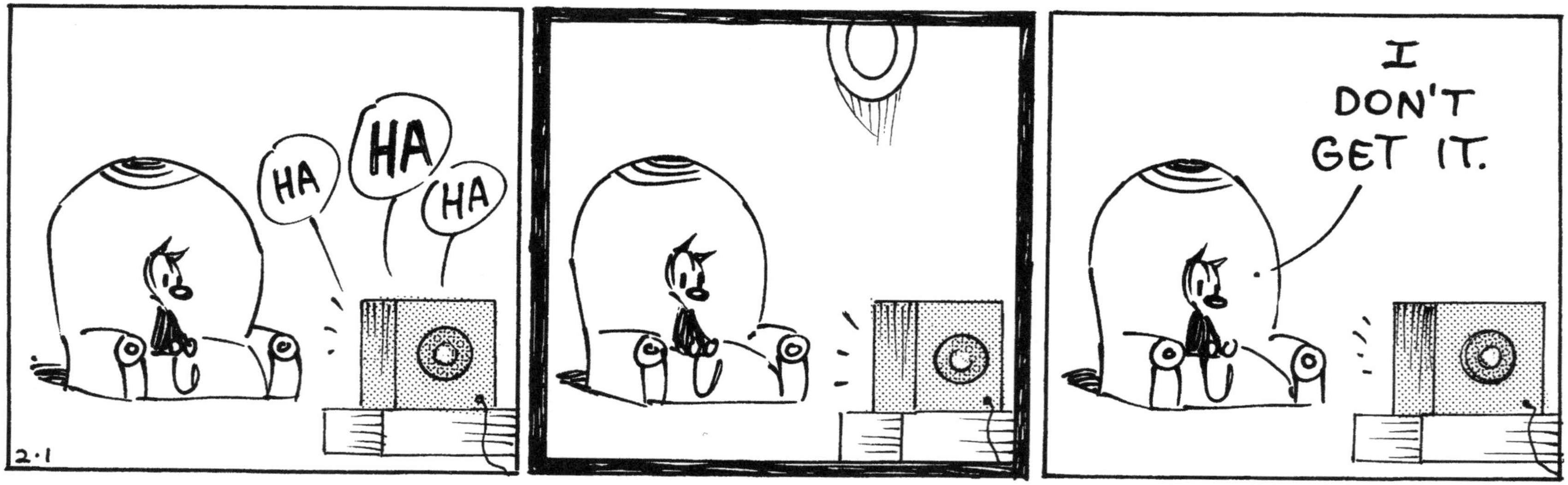
HA
HA
HA
2·1
I DON'T GET IT.

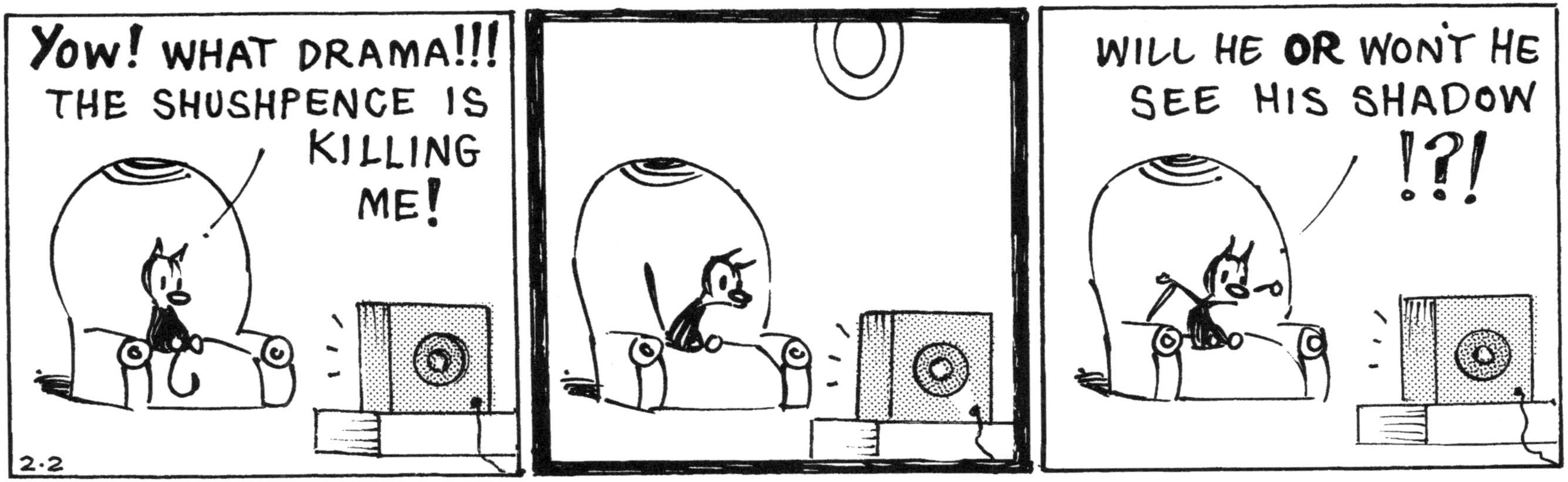
YOW! WHAT DRAMA!!! THE SHUSHPENCE IS KILLING ME!
WILL HE OR WON'T HE SEE HIS SHADOW !?!
2·2

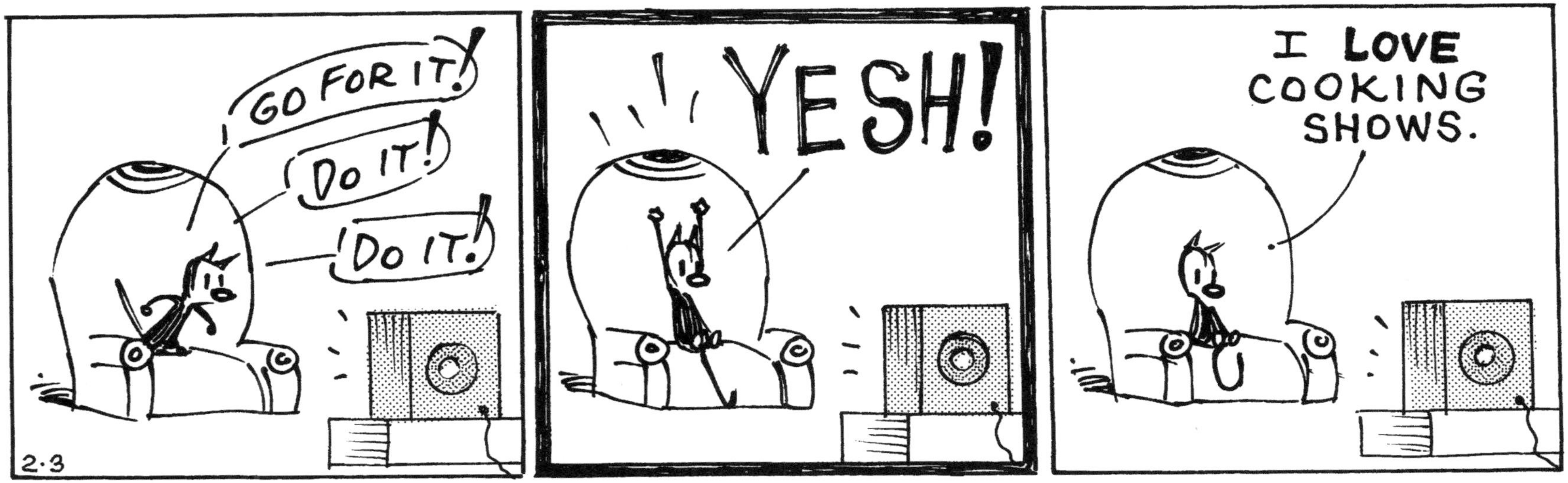
GO FOR IT!
DO IT!
DO IT!
YESH!
I LOVE COOKING SHOWS.
2·3

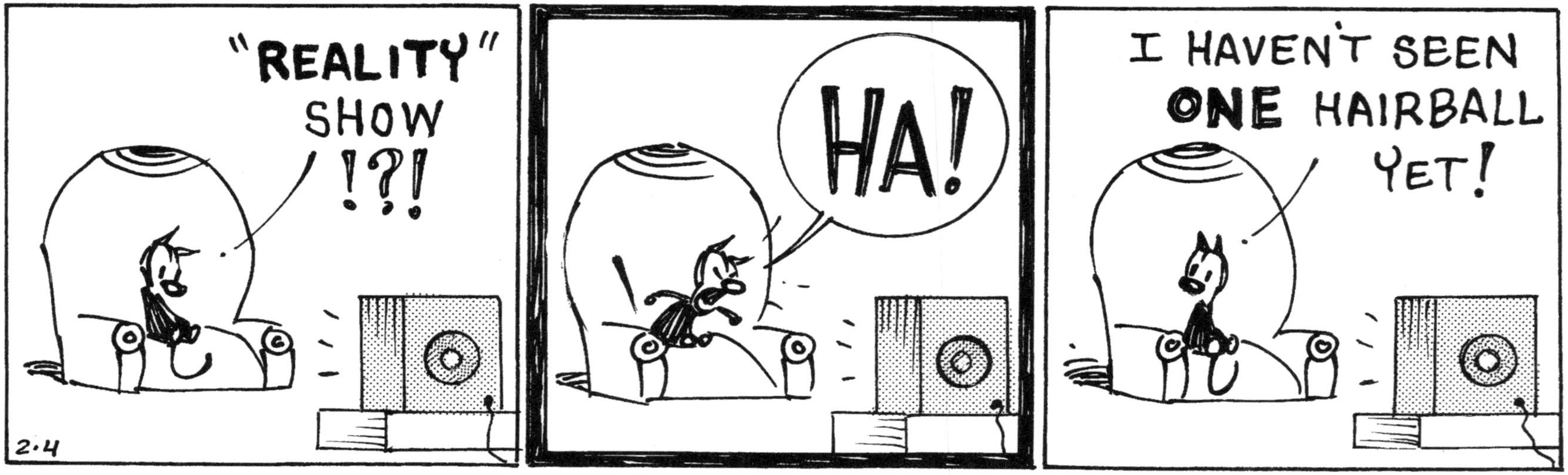
"REALITY" SHOW !?!
HA!
I HAVEN'T SEEN ONE HAIRBALL YET!
2·4

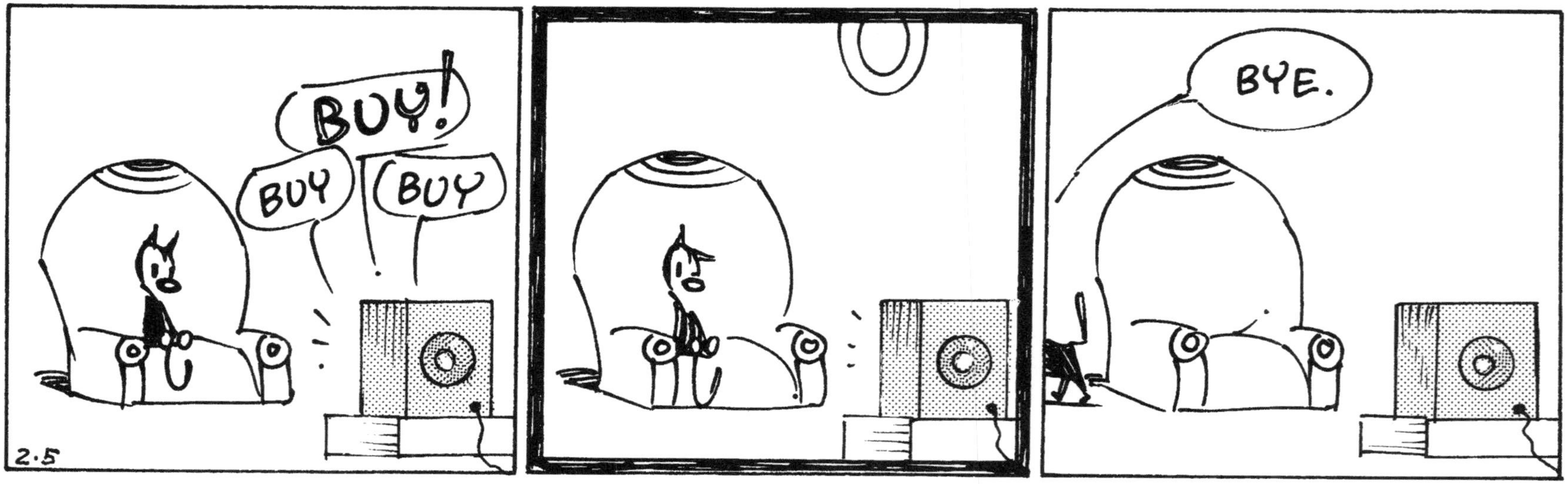
BUY!
BUY
BUY
BYE.
2·5

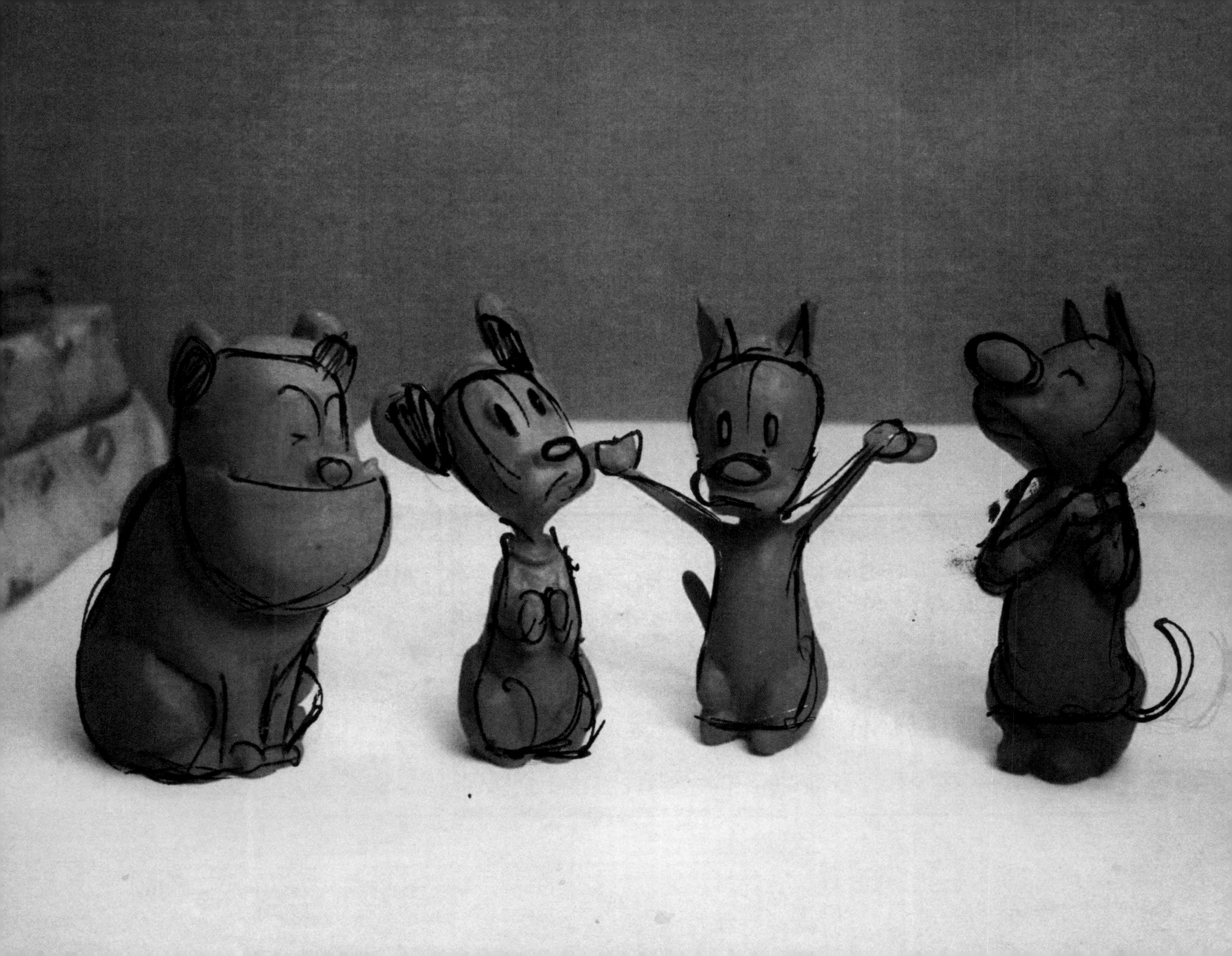

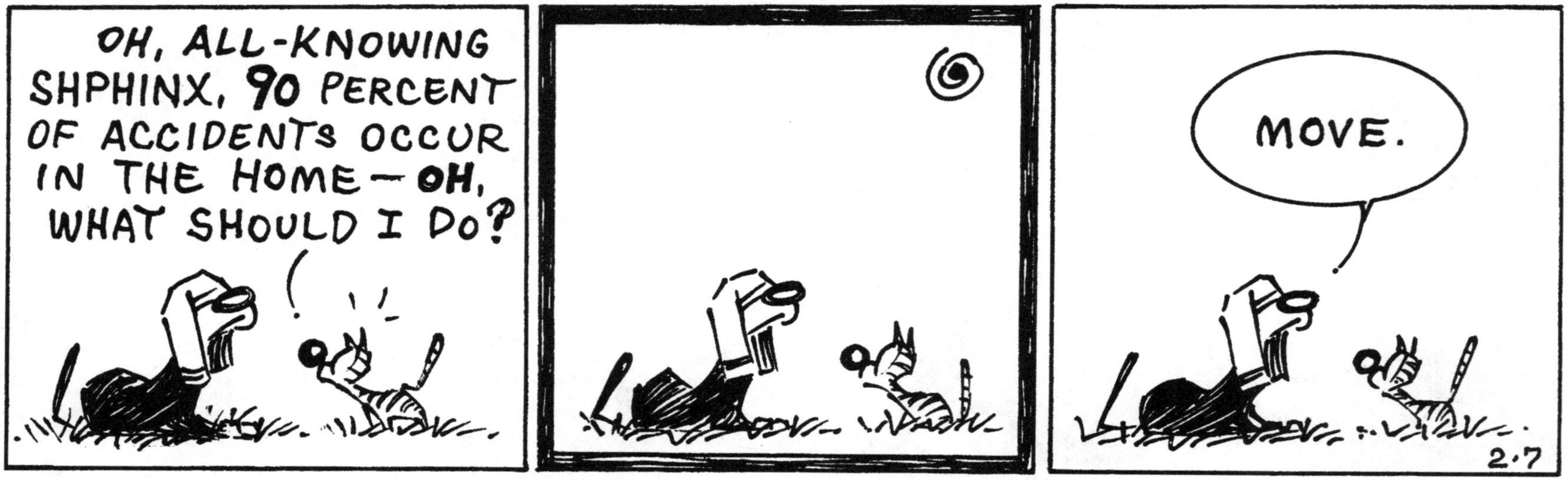
OH, ALL-KNOWING SHPHINX, 90 PERCENT OF ACCIDENTS OCCUR IN THE HOME—OH, WHAT SHOULD I DO?
MOVE.
2·7

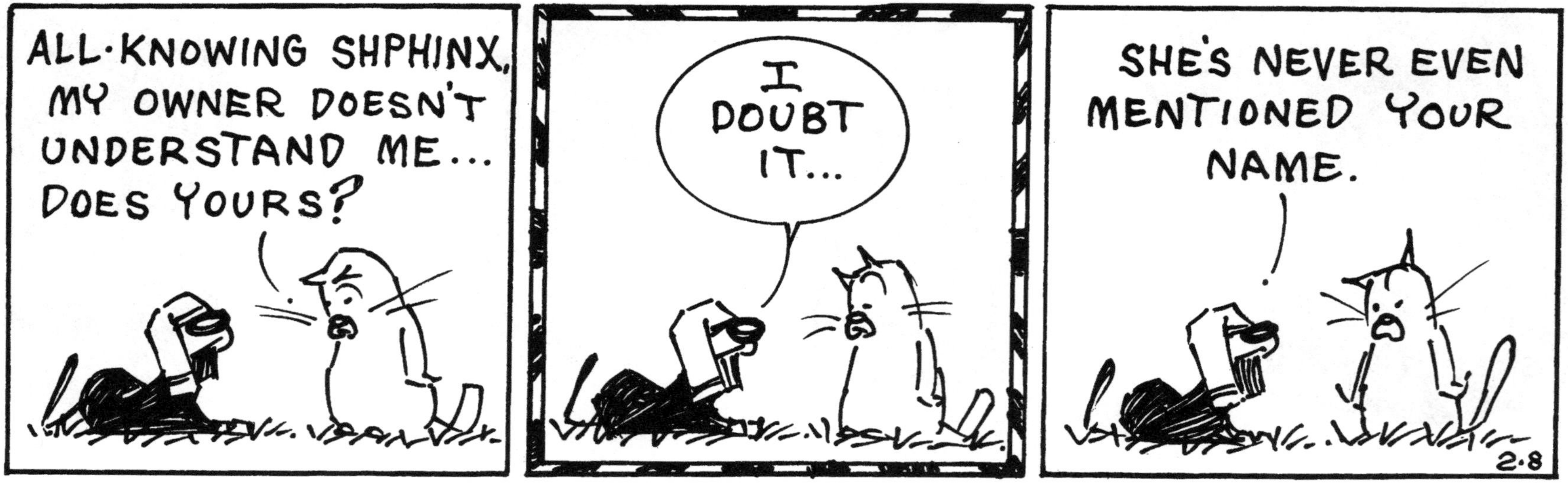
ALL·KNOWING SHPHINX, MY OWNER DOESN'T UNDERSTAND ME... DOES YOURS?
I DOUBT IT...
SHE'S NEVER EVEN MENTIONED YOUR NAME.
2·8

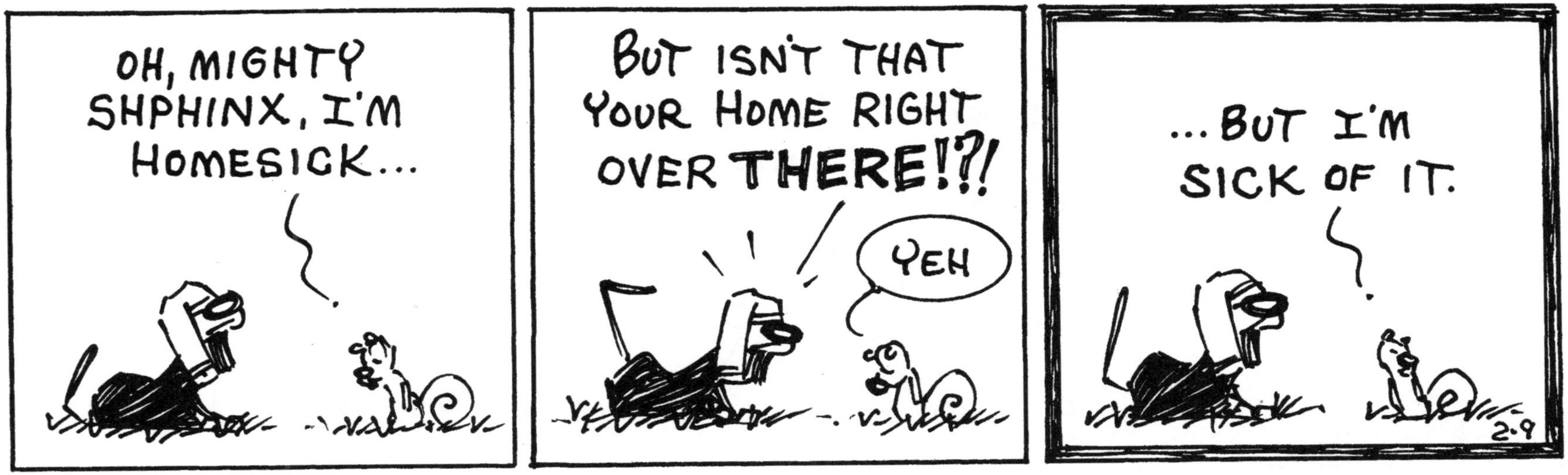
OH, MIGHTY SHPHINX, I'M HOMESICK...
BUT ISN'T THAT YOUR HOME RIGHT OVER THERE!?!
YEH
...BUT I'M SICK OF IT.
2·9

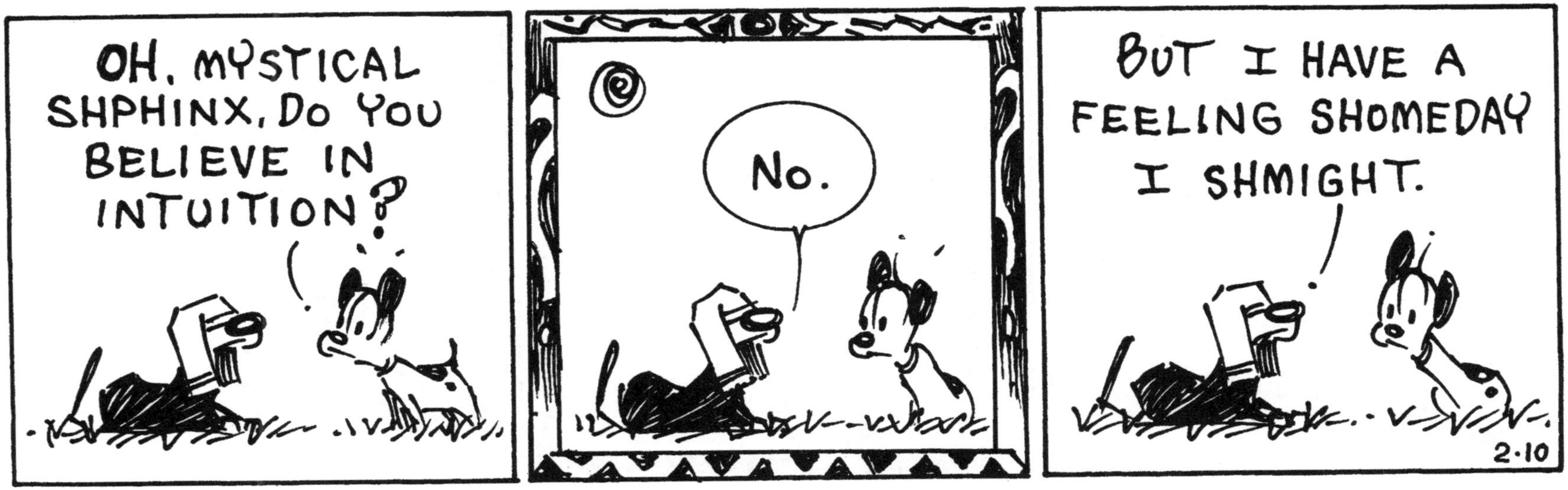
OH, MYSTICAL SHPHINX, DO YOU BELIEVE IN INTUITION?
NO.
BUT I HAVE A FEELING SHOMEDAY I SHMIGHT.
2·10

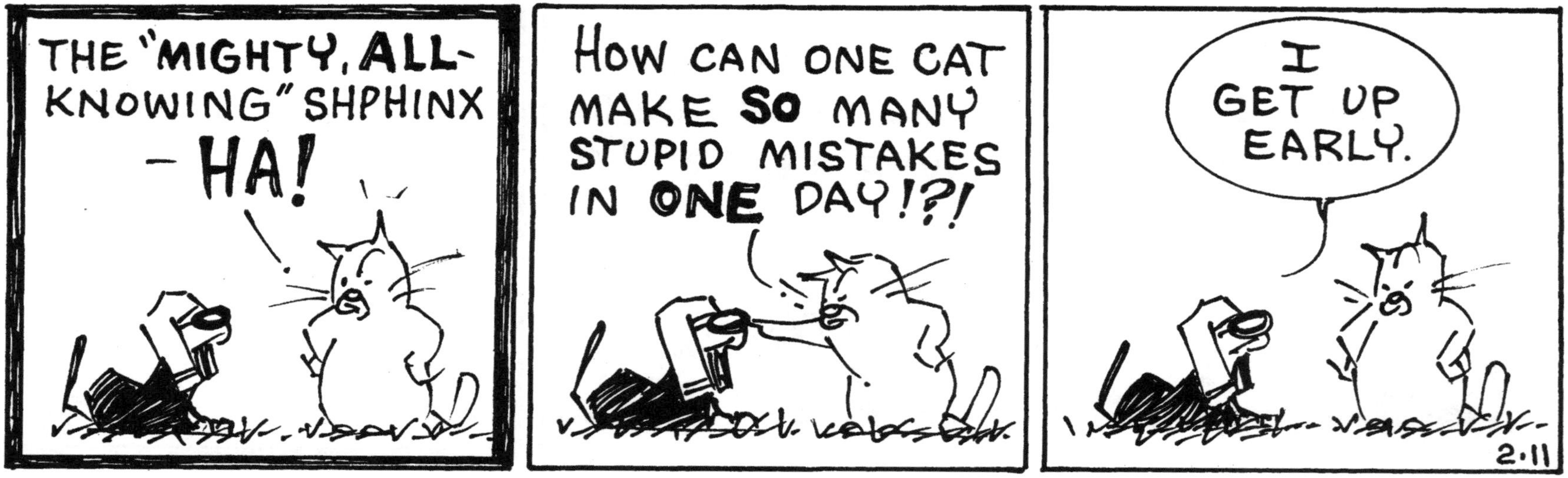
THE "MIGHTY, ALL-KNOWING" SHPHINX
- HA!
HOW CAN ONE CAT MAKE SO MANY STUPID MISTAKES IN ONE DAY!?!
I GET UP EARLY.
2·11

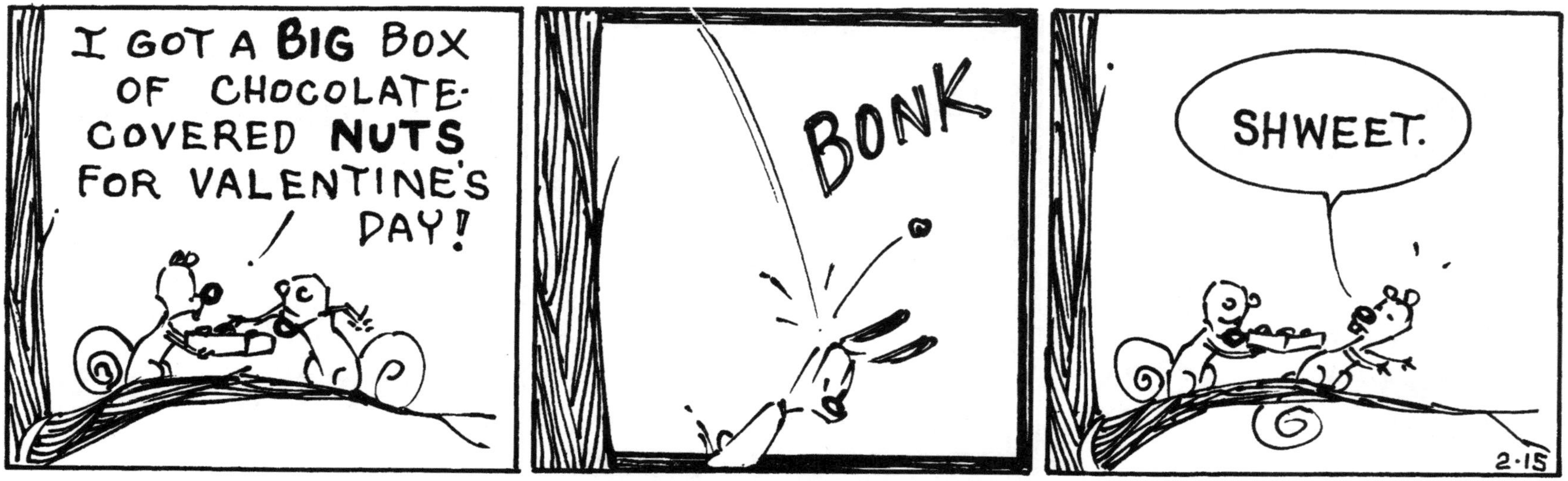
I GOT A BIG BOX OF CHOCOLATE-COVERED NUTS FOR VALENTINE'S DAY!
BONK
SHWEET.
2·15

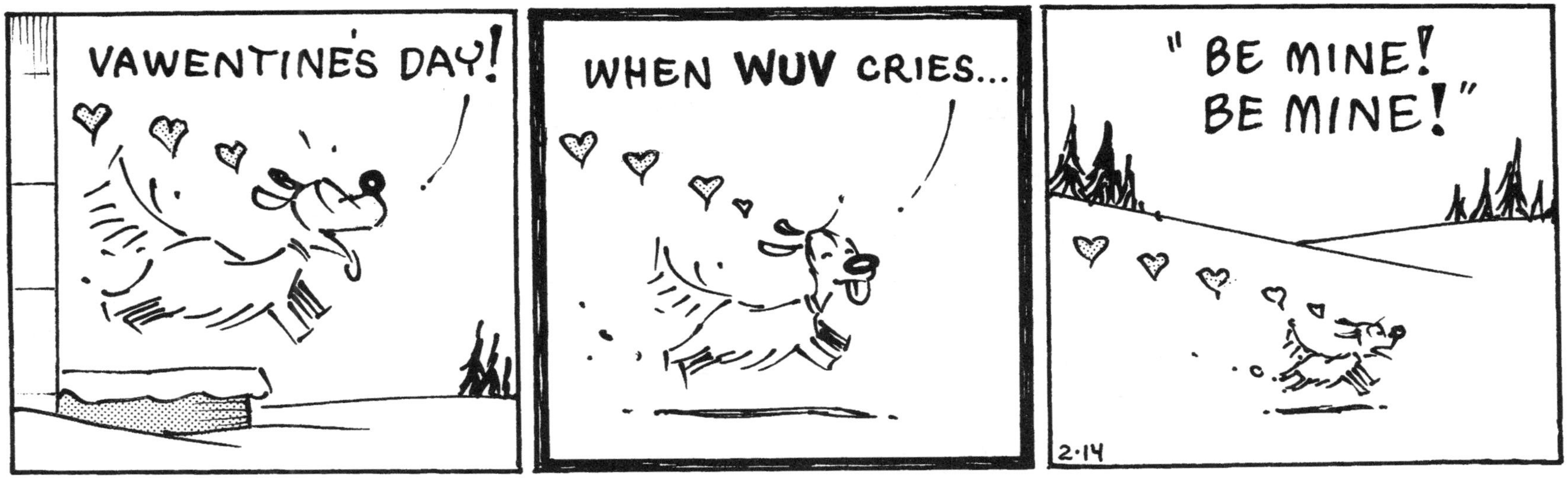
VAWENTINE'S DAY!
WHEN WUV CRIES...
"BE MINE! BE MINE!"
2·14

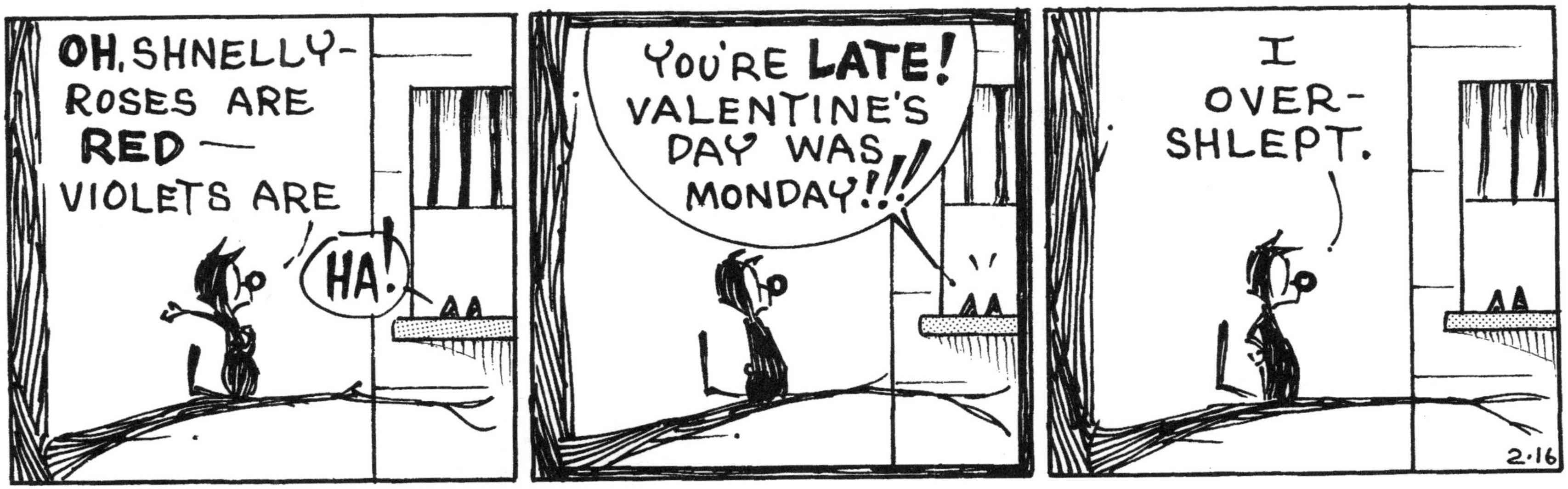
OH, SHNELLY- ROSES ARE RED — VIOLETS ARE
HA!
YOU'RE LATE! VALENTINE'S DAY WAS MONDAY!!!
I OVER-SHLEPT.
2·16

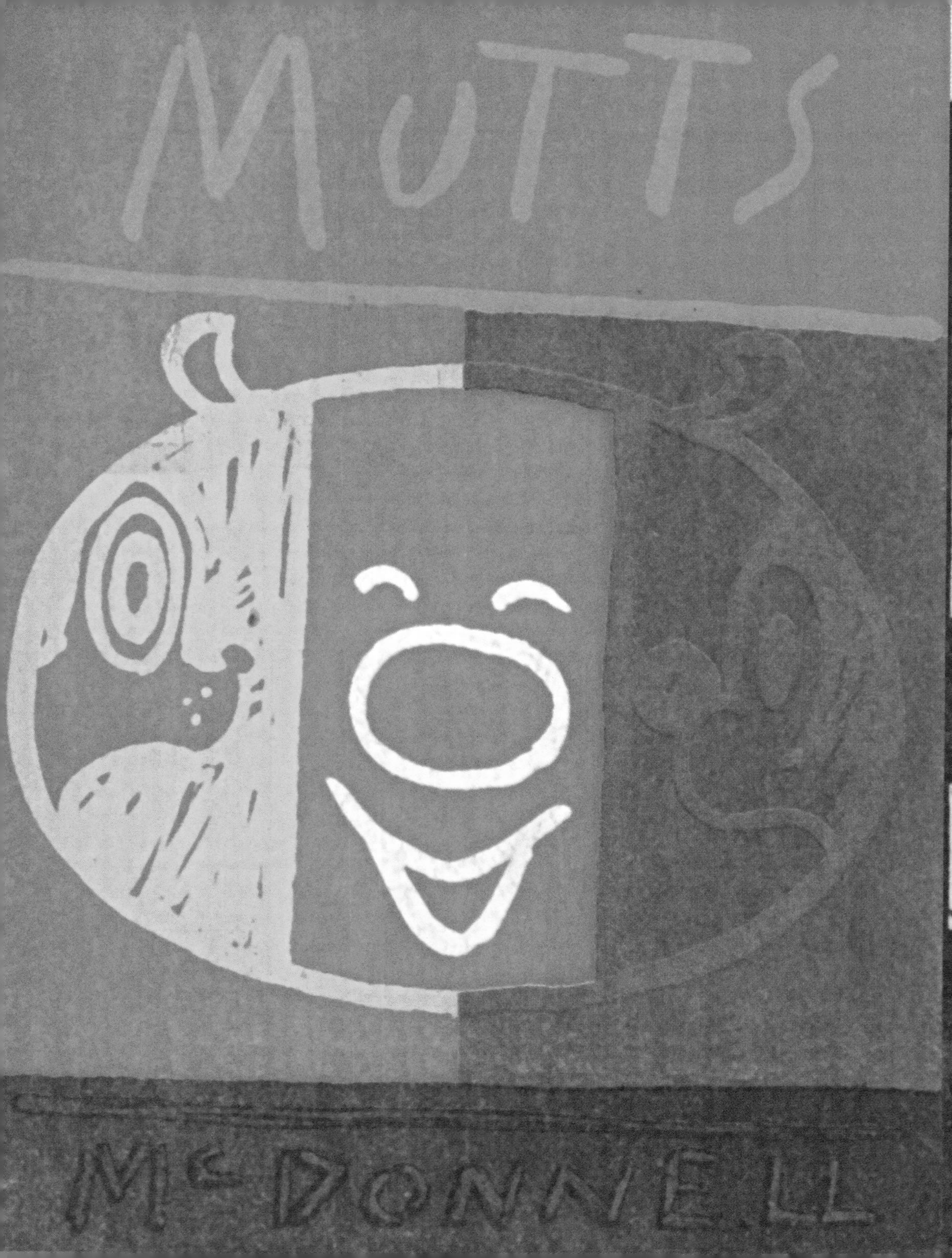
MUTTS
McDONNELL

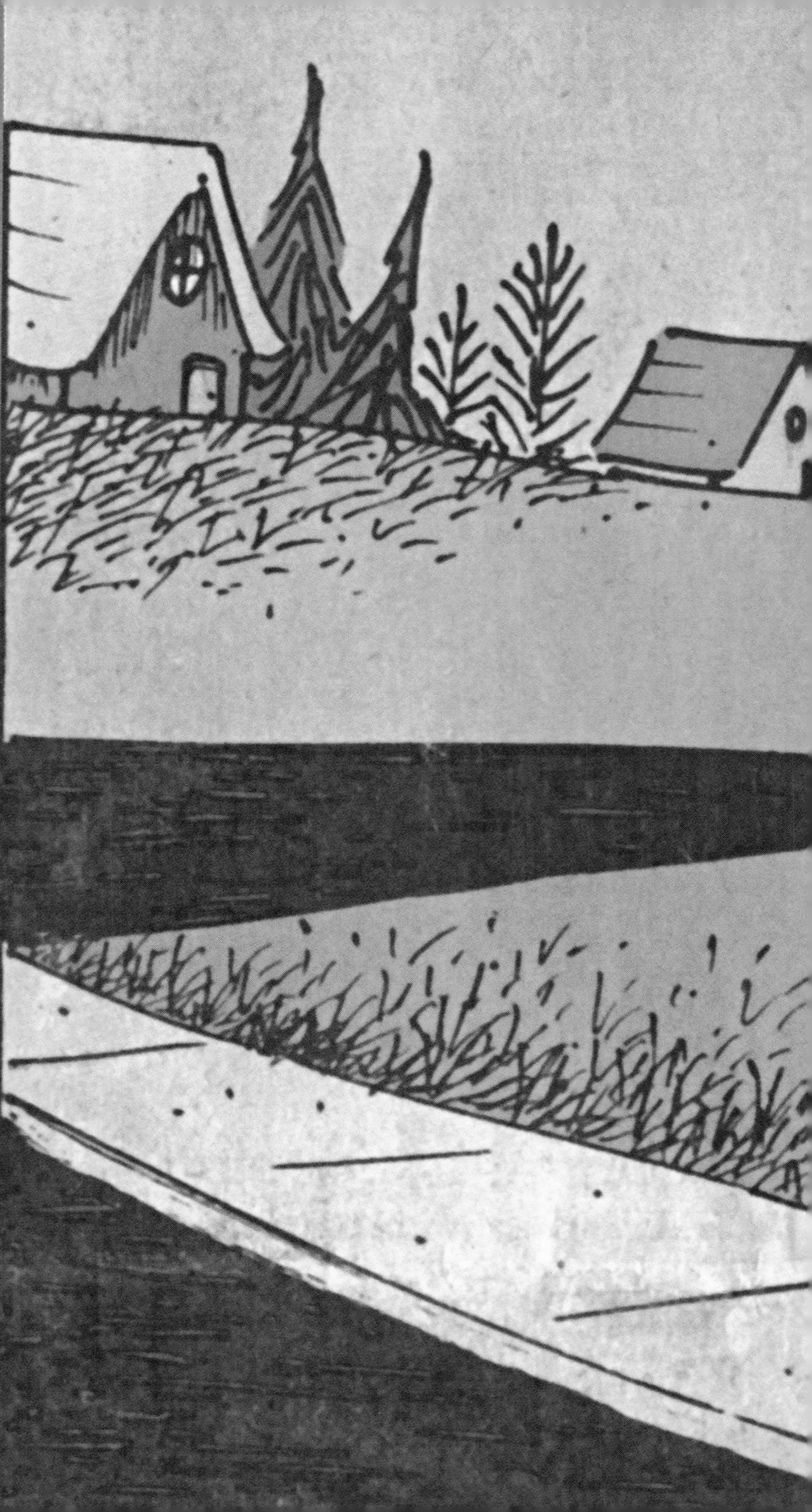

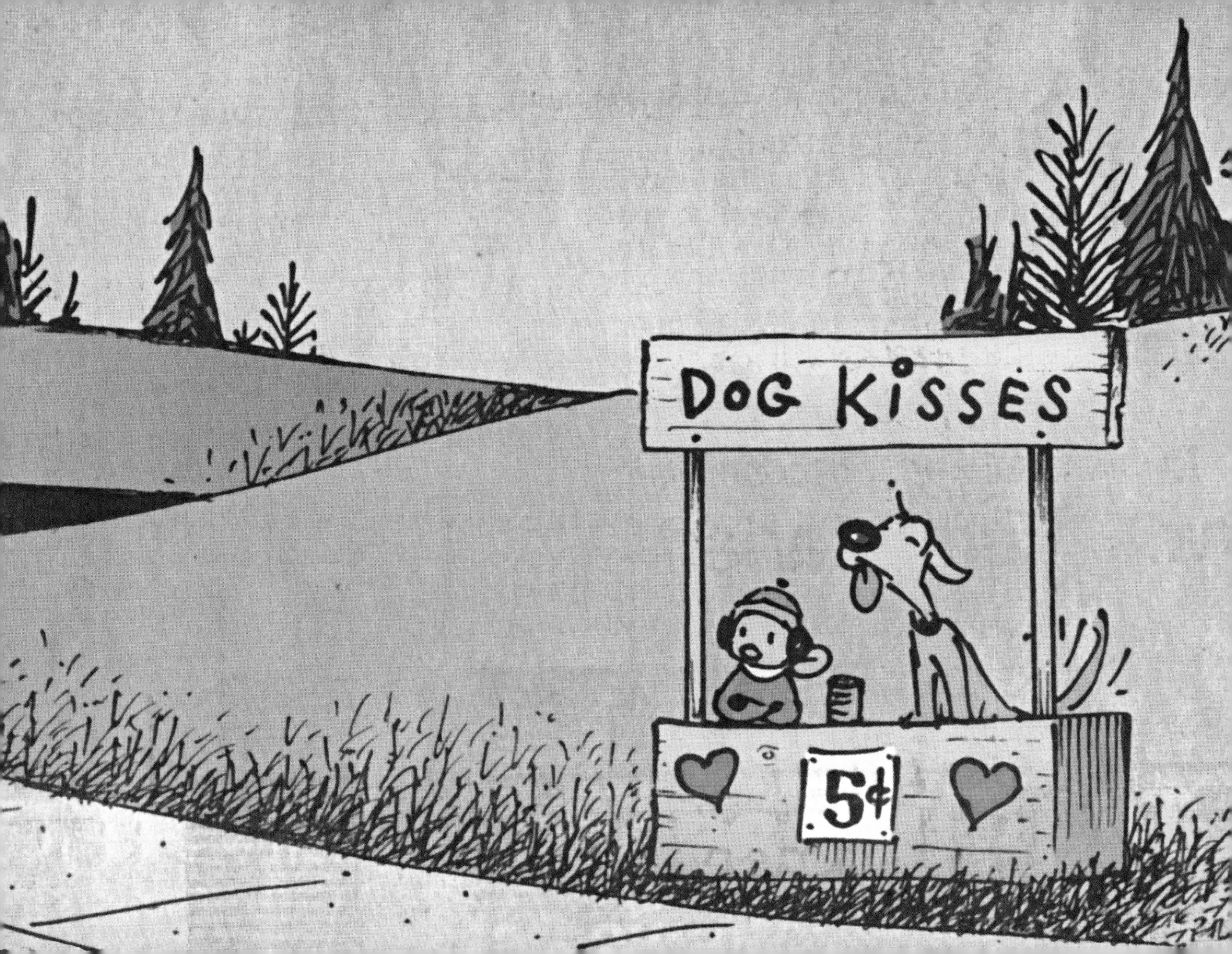
DOG KISSES
5¢

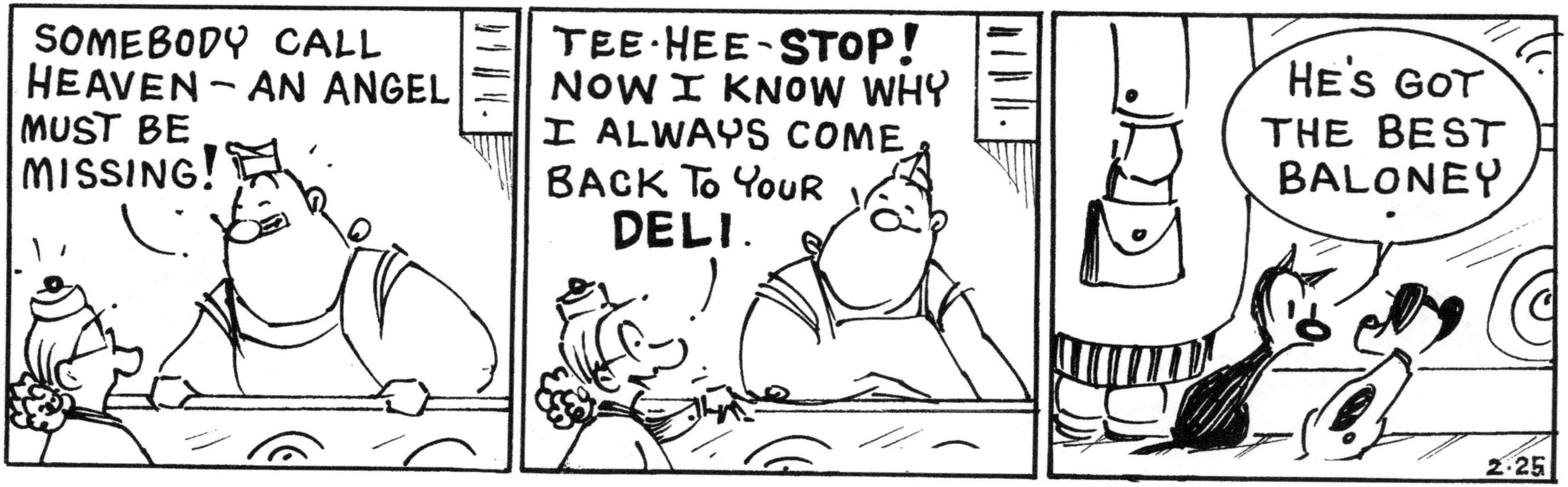
SOMEBODY CALL HEAVEN – AN ANGEL MUST BE MISSING!
TEE-HEE-STOP! NOW I KNOW WHY I ALWAYS COME BACK TO YOUR DELI.
HE'S GOT THE BEST BALONEY
2·25

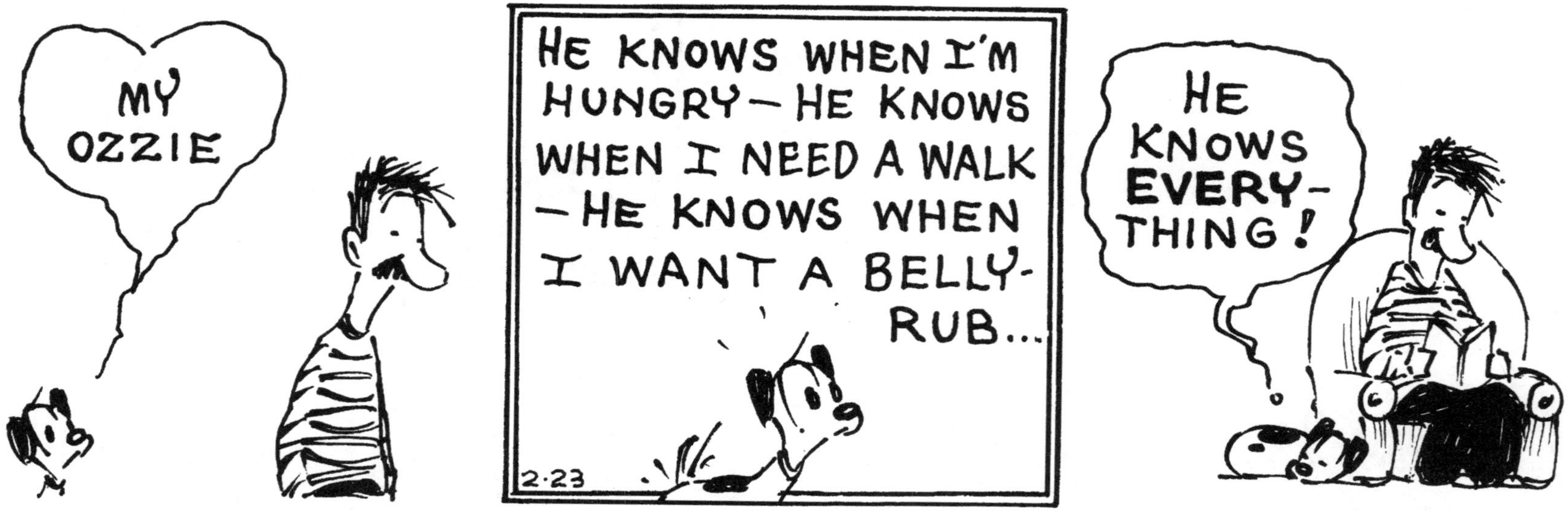
MY OZZIE
HE KNOWS WHEN I'M HUNGRY – HE KNOWS WHEN I NEED A WALK – HE KNOWS WHEN I WANT A BELLY-RUB...
2·23
HE KNOWS EVERY-THING!

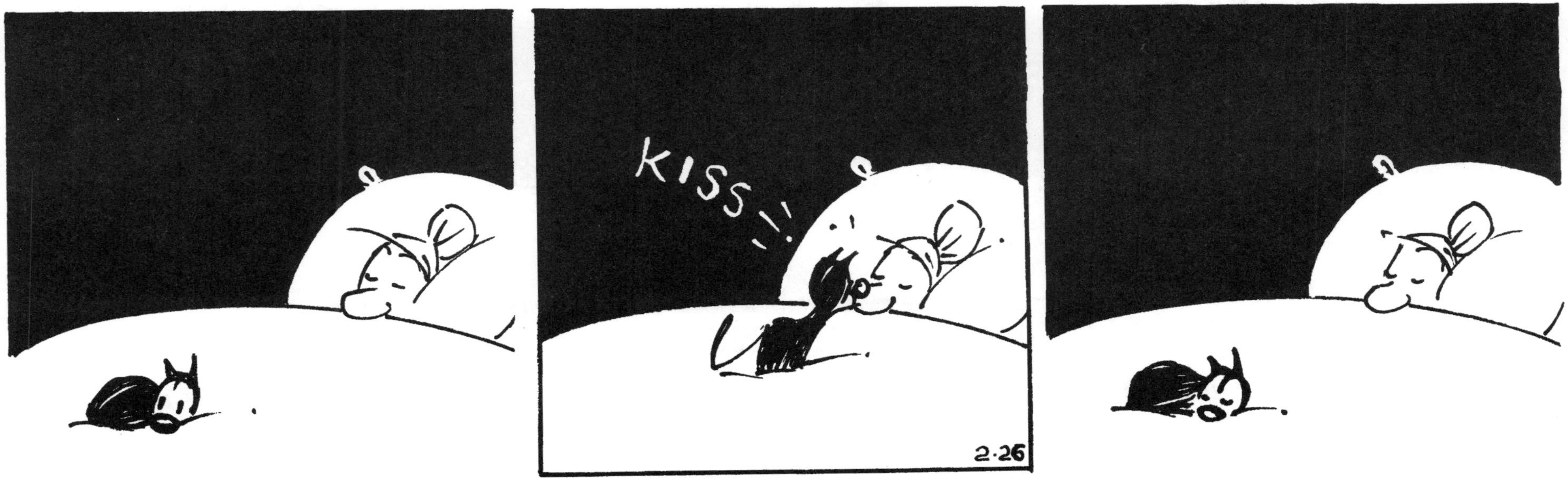
KISS !!
2·26

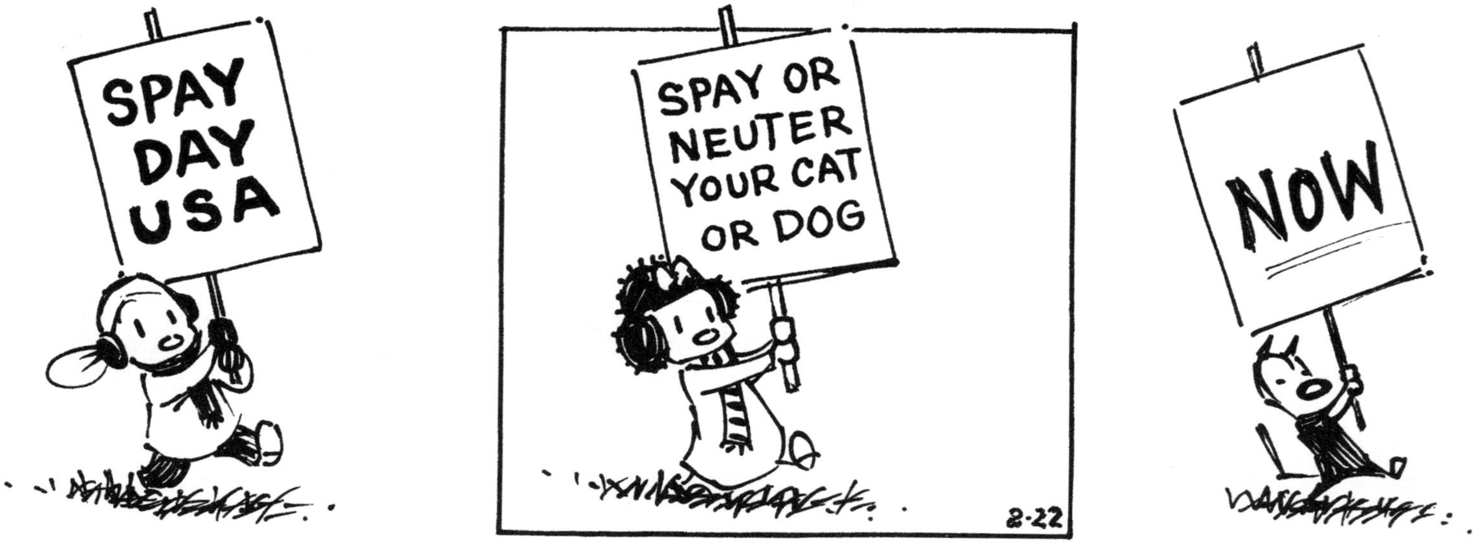
SPAY DAY USA
SPAY OR NEUTER YOUR CAT OR DOG
NOW
2·22

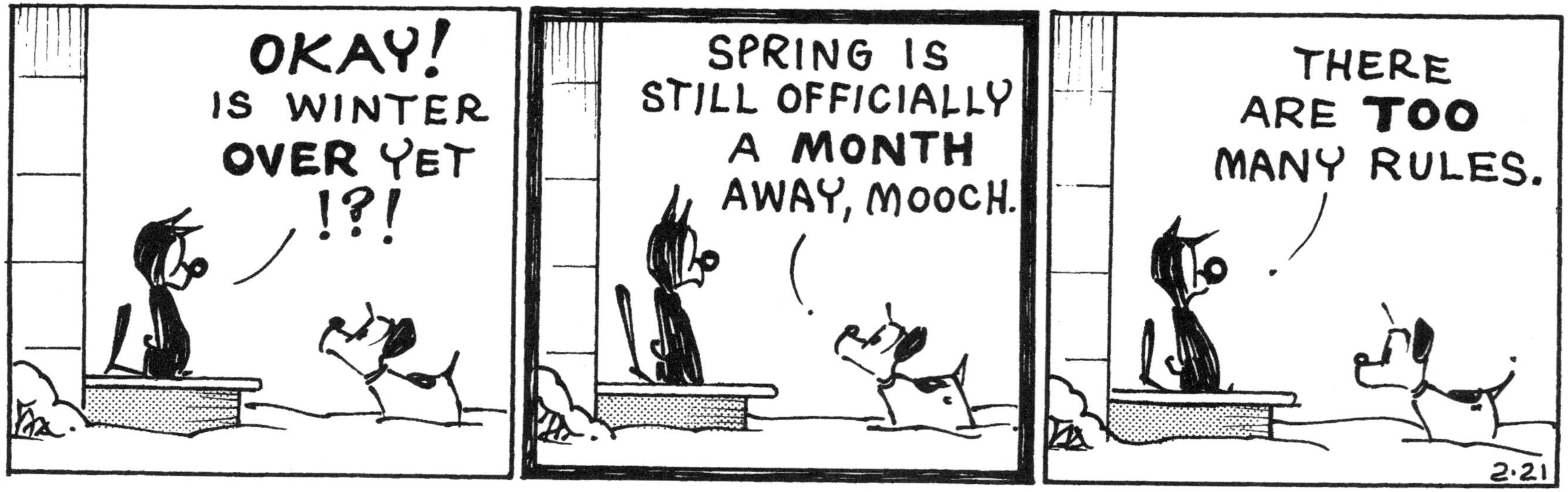
OKAY! IS WINTER OVER YET !?!
SPRING IS STILL OFFICIALLY A MONTH AWAY, MOOCH.
THERE ARE TOO MANY RULES.
2·21

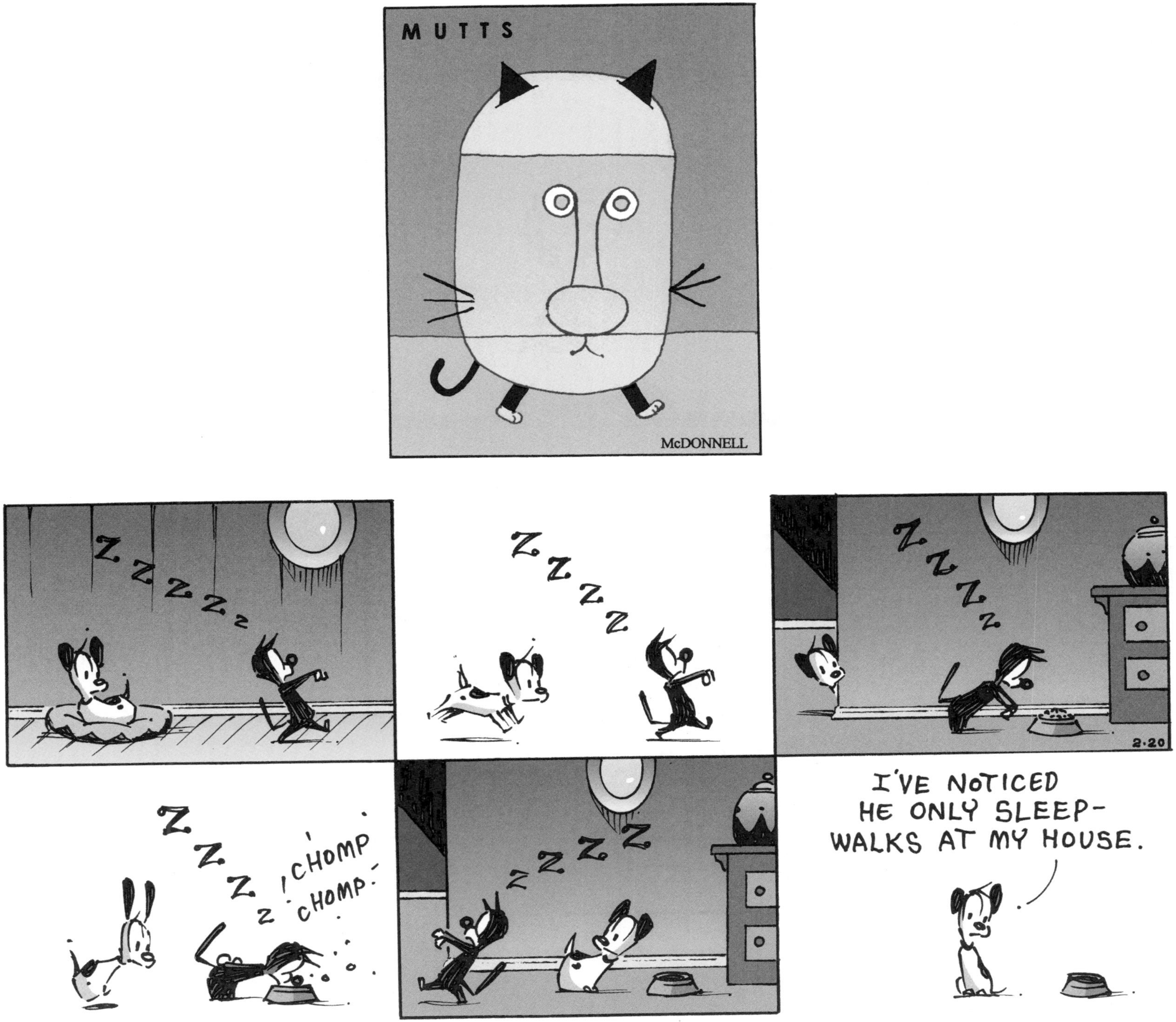
MUTTS
McDONNELL
Z Z Z Z Z z
Z Z Z Z
Z Z Z Z z
2·20
Z Z Z z
CHOMP
CHOMP
z Z Z Z
I'VE NOTICED
HE ONLY SLEEP-
WALKS AT MY HOUSE.

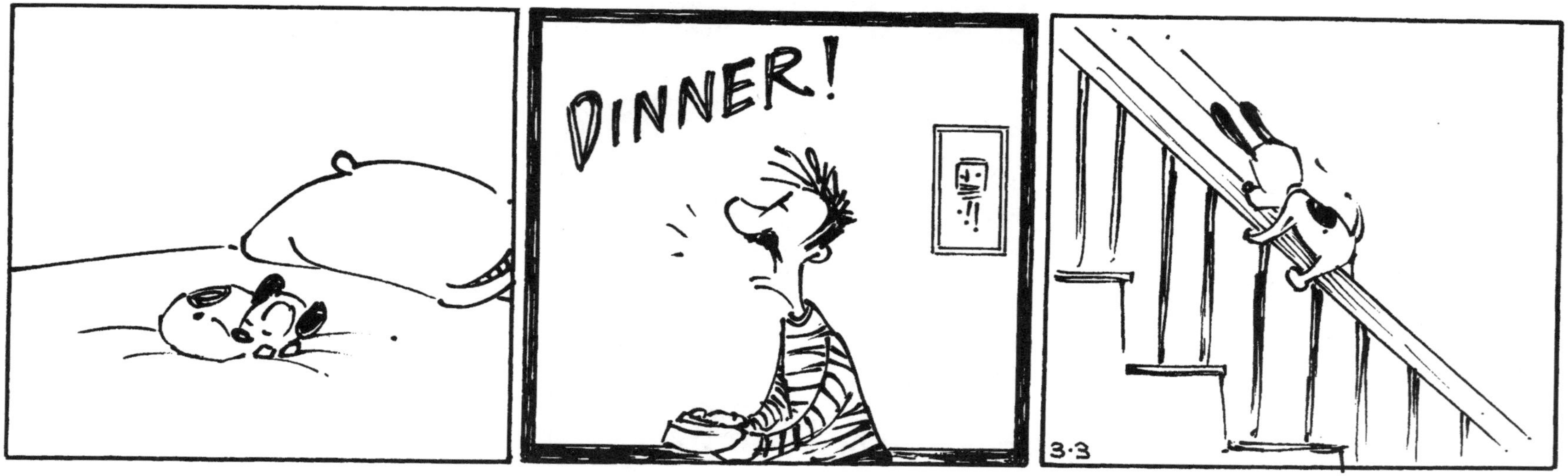
DINNER!
3·3

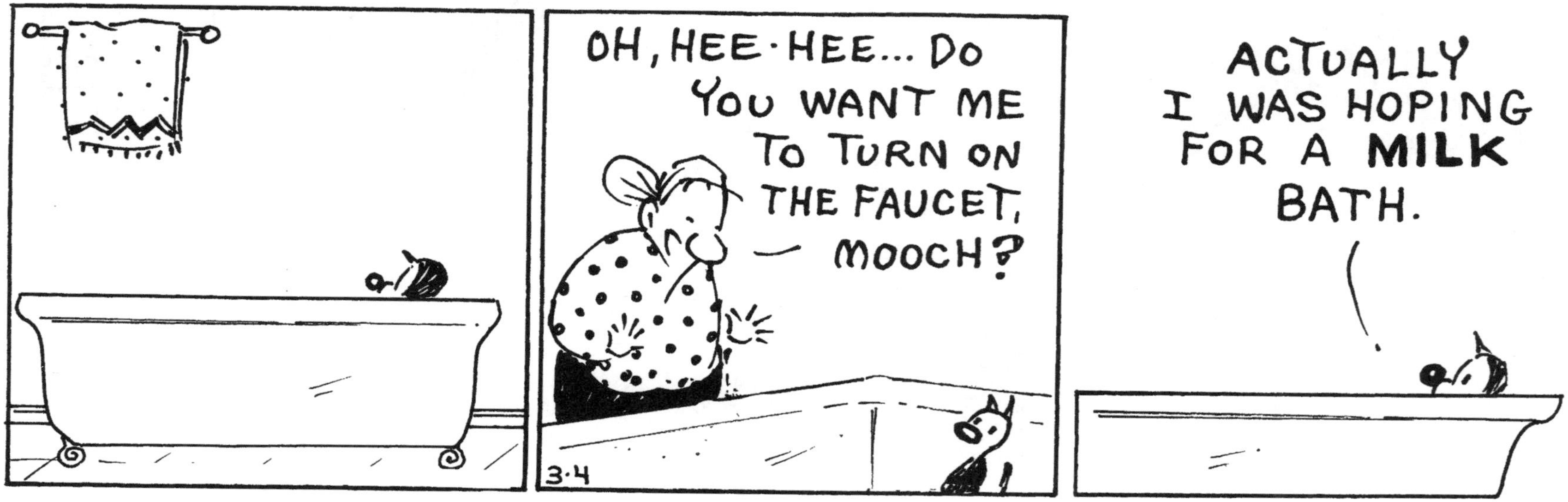
OH, HEE·HEE... DO YOU WANT ME TO TURN ON THE FAUCET, MOOCH?
ACTUALLY I WAS HOPING FOR A **MILK** BATH.
3·4

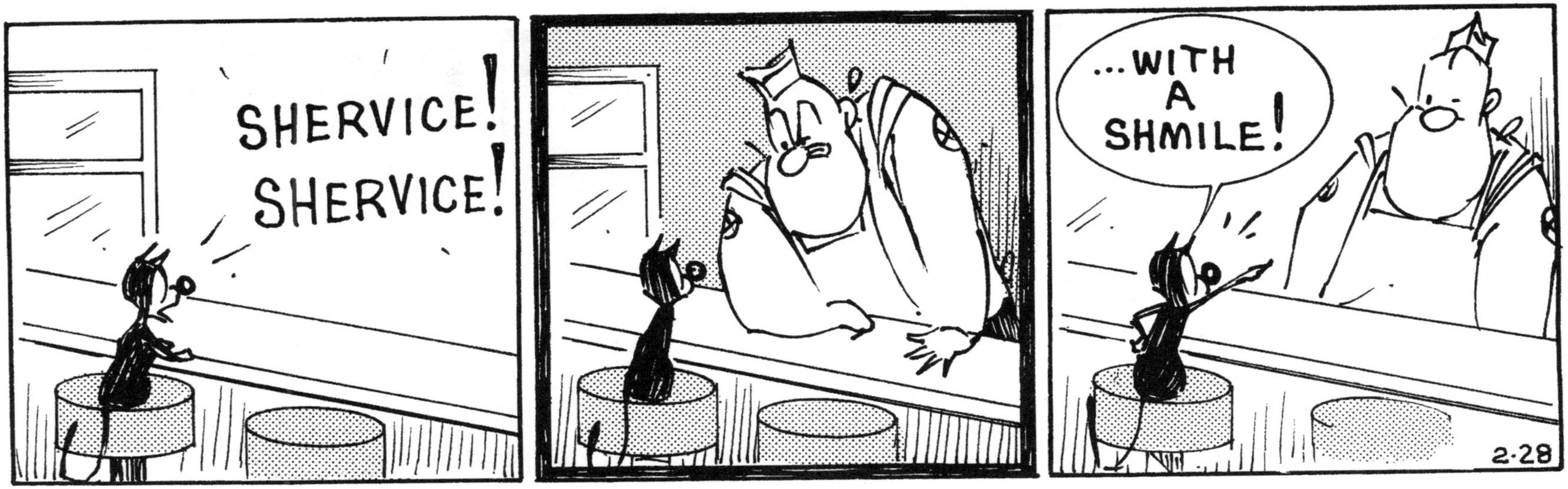

SHERVICE! SHERVICE!
...WITH A SHMILE!
2·28

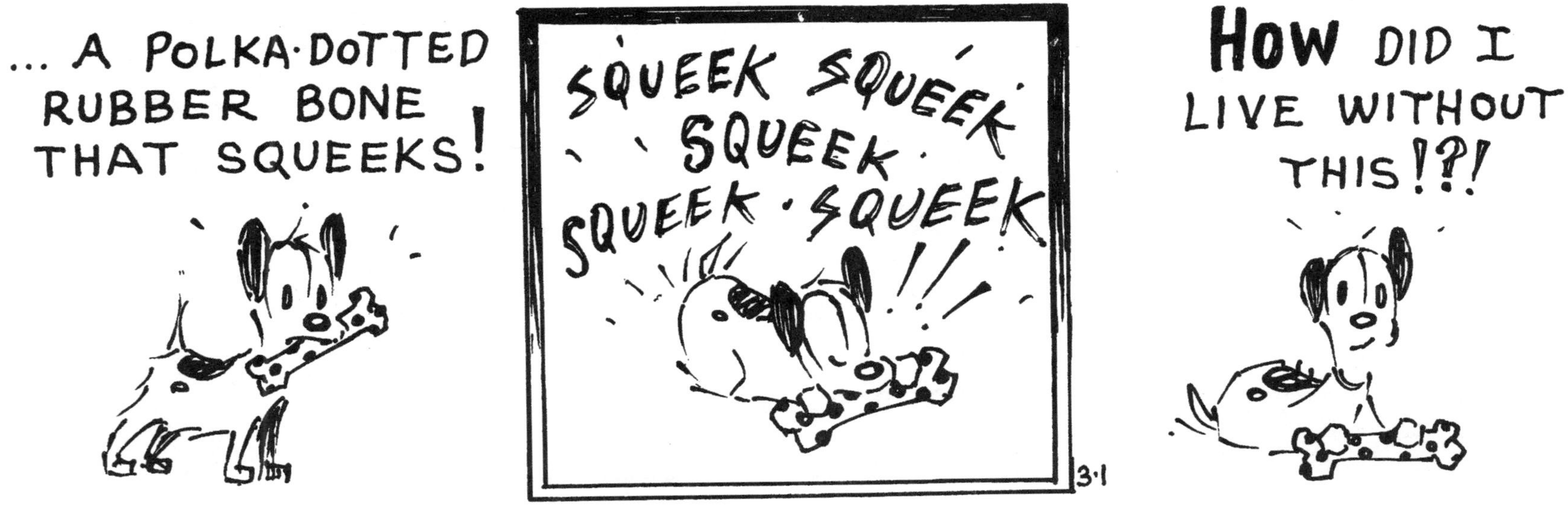

... A POLKA·DOTTED RUBBER BONE THAT SQUEEKS!
SQUEEK SQUEEK SQUEEK SQUEEK · SQUEEK
3·1
HOW DID I LIVE WITHOUT THIS!?!

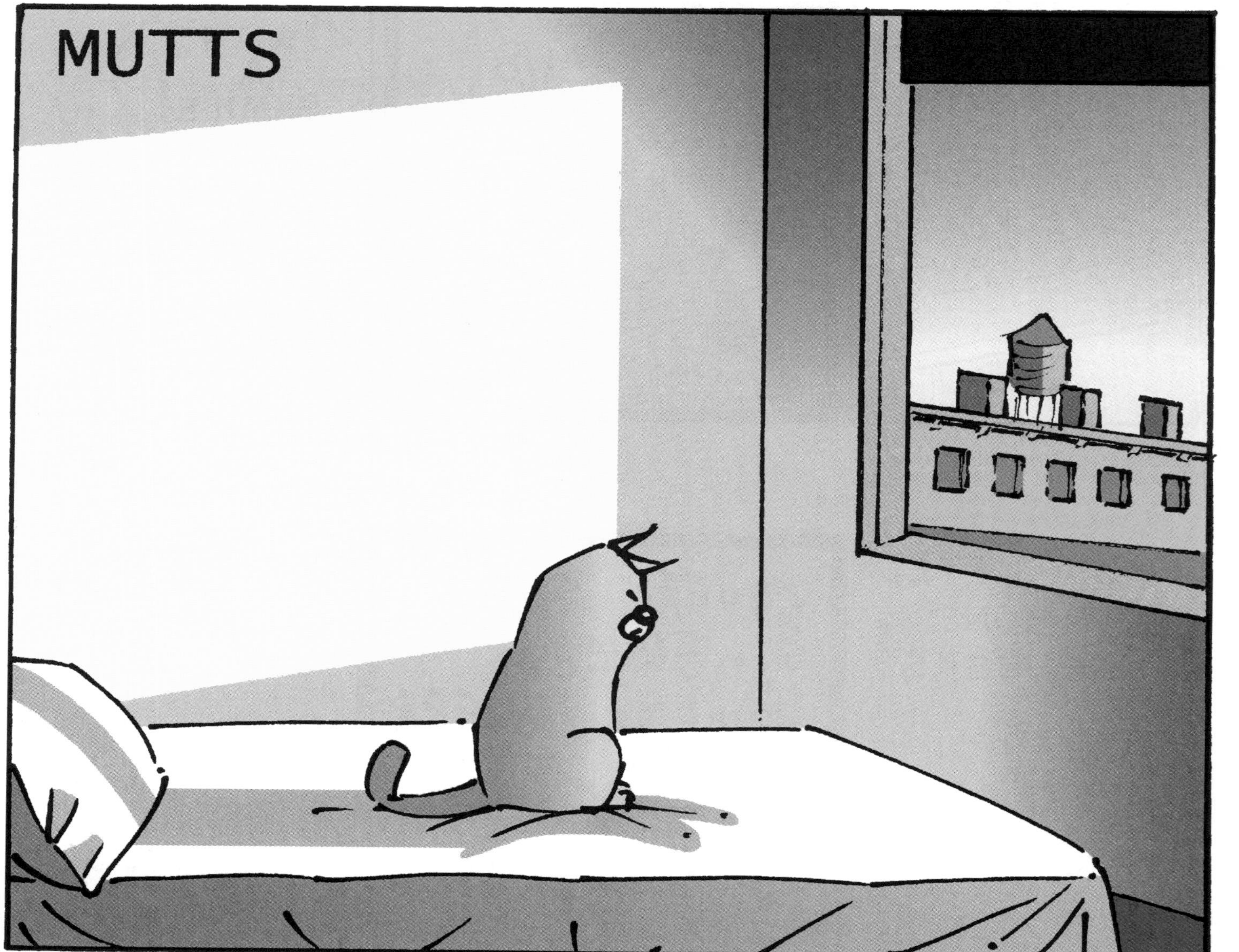
MUTTS

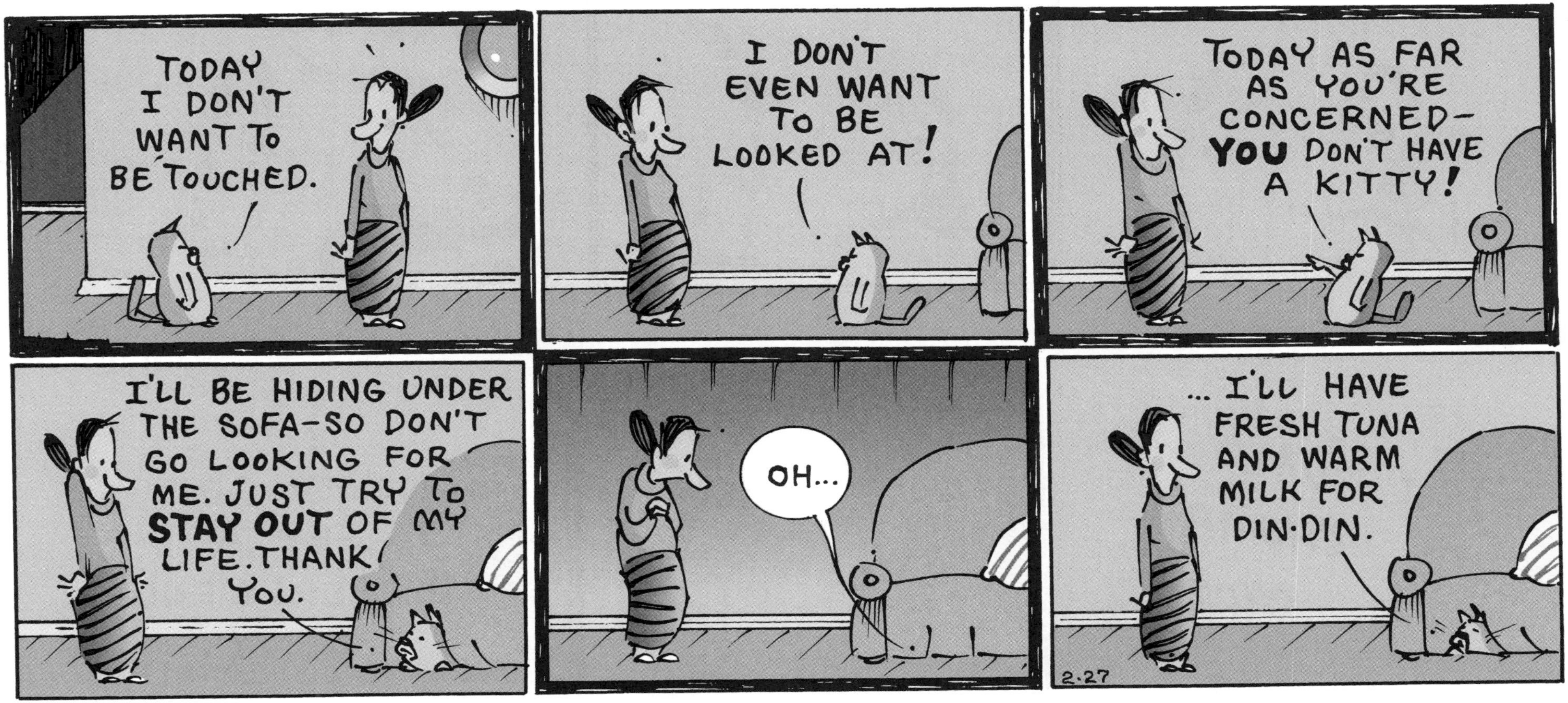
TODAY I DON'T WANT TO BE TOUCHED.
I DON'T EVEN WANT TO BE LOOKED AT!
TODAY AS FAR AS YOU'RE CONCERNED- **YOU** DON'T HAVE A KITTY!
I'LL BE HIDING UNDER THE SOFA-SO DON'T GO LOOKING FOR ME. JUST TRY TO **STAY OUT** OF MY LIFE. THANK YOU.
OH...
...I'LL HAVE FRESH TUNA AND WARM MILK FOR DIN·DIN.
2·27

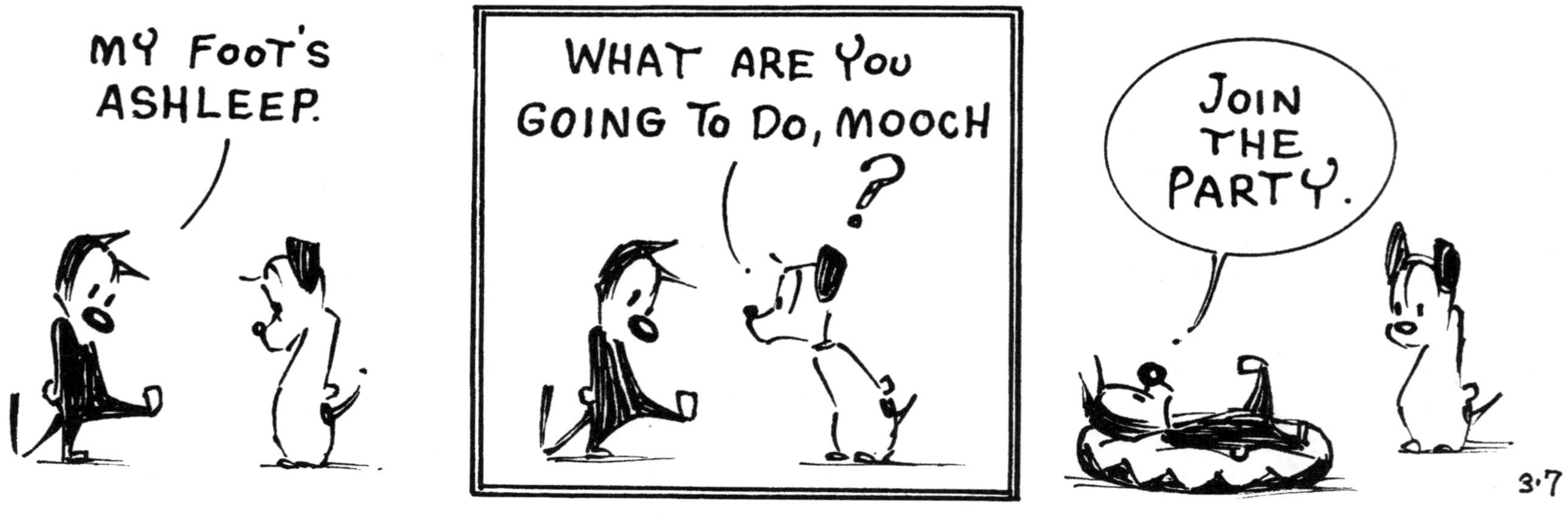
MY FOOT'S ASHLEEP.
WHAT ARE YOU GOING TO DO, MOOCH?
JOIN THE PARTY.
3·7

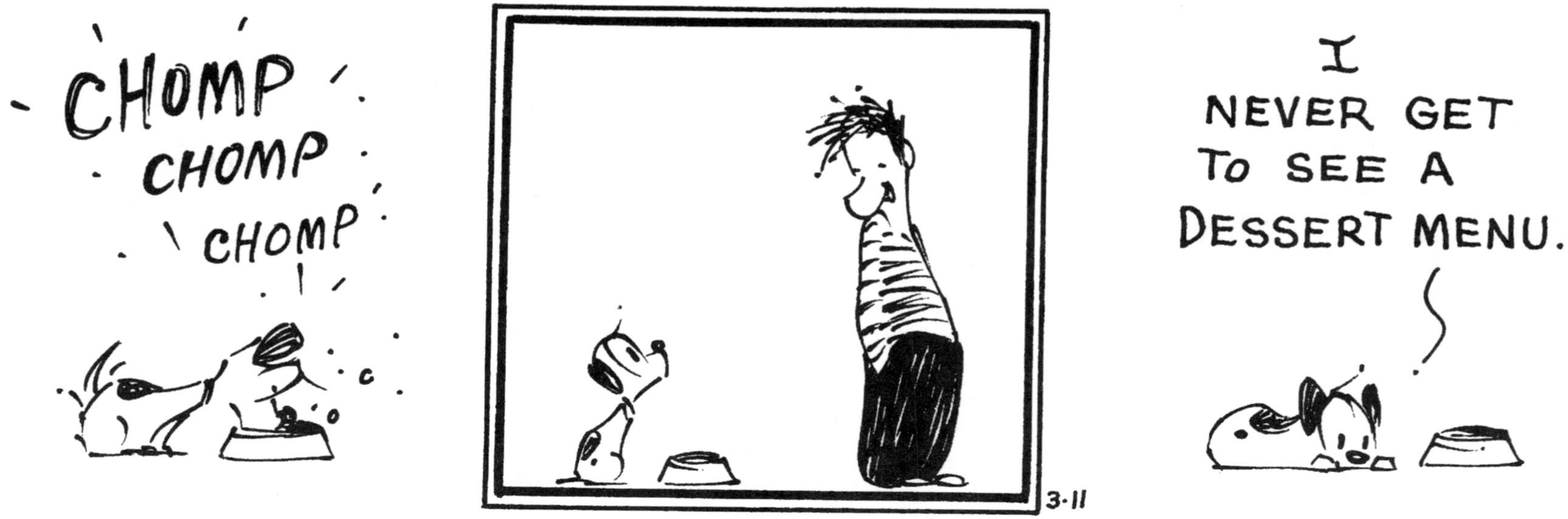
CHOMP CHOMP CHOMP
I NEVER GET TO SEE A DESSERT MENU.
3·11

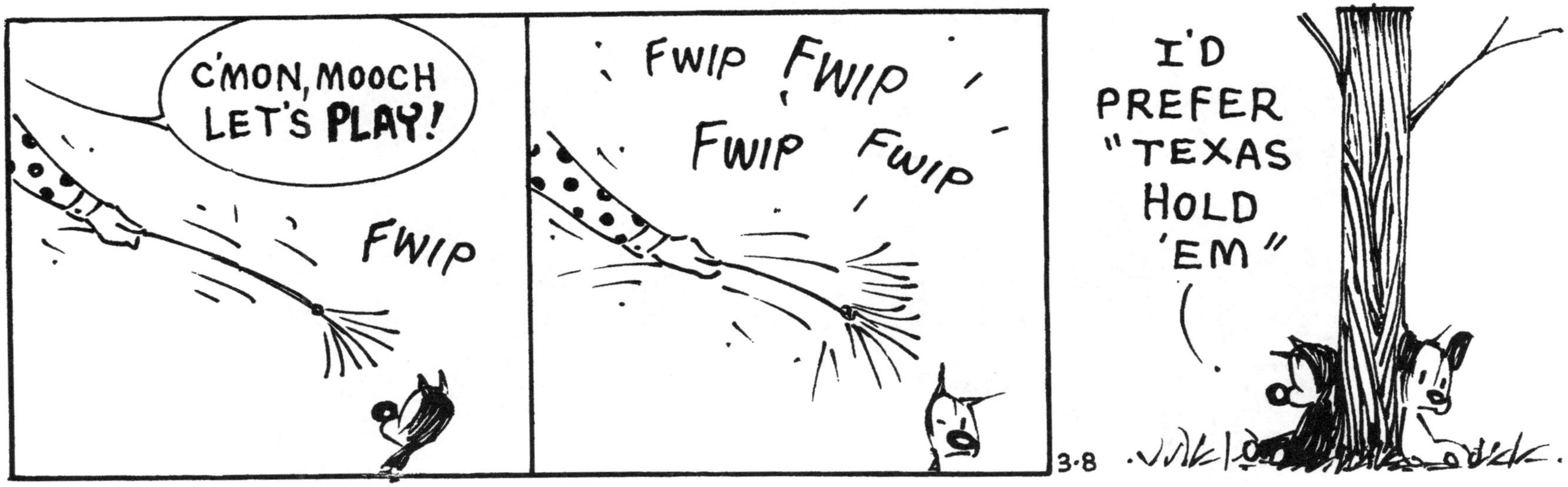
C'MON, MOOCH
LET'S PLAY!
FWIP
FWIP FWIP
FWIP FWIP
I'D PREFER "TEXAS HOLD 'EM"
3·8

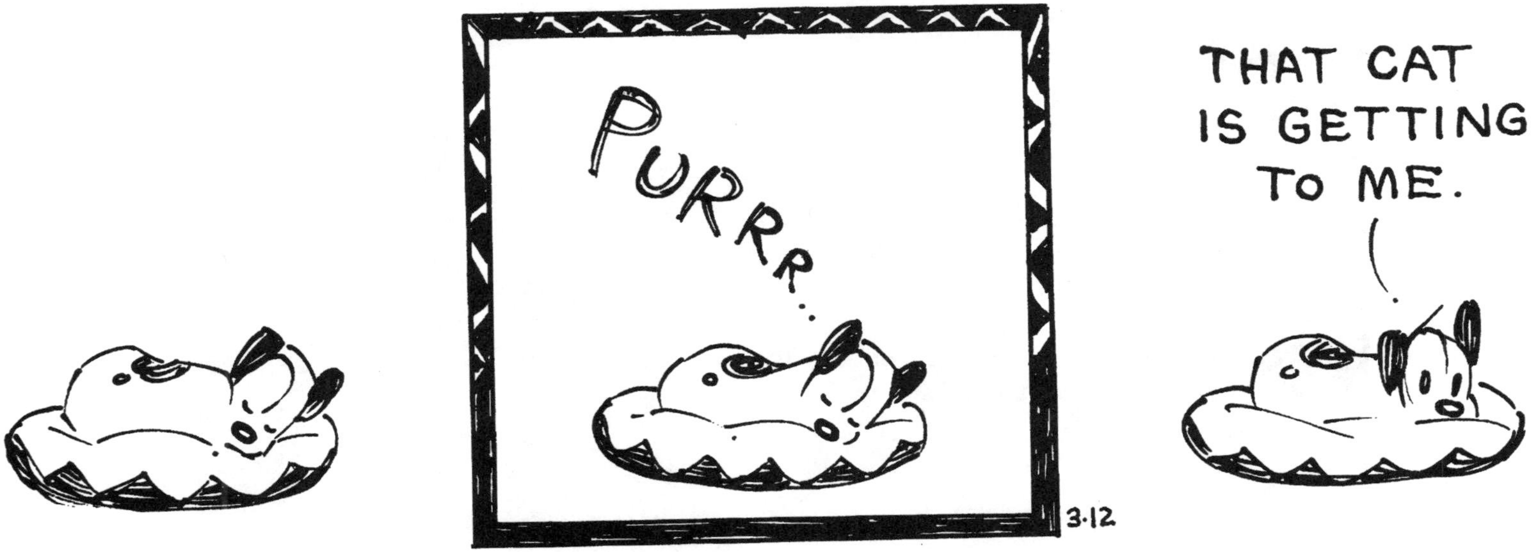
PURRR...
THAT CAT IS GETTING TO ME.
3·12

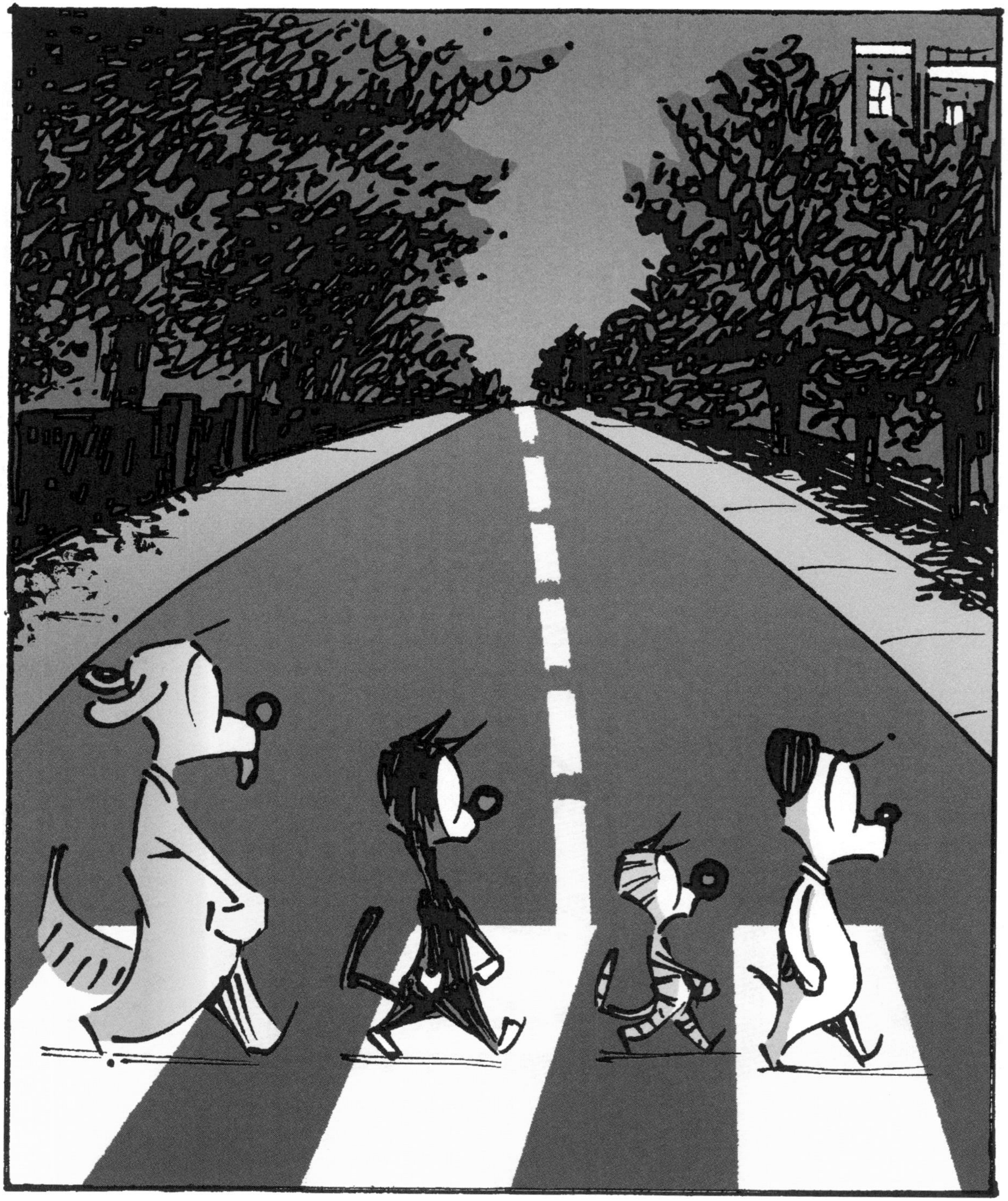

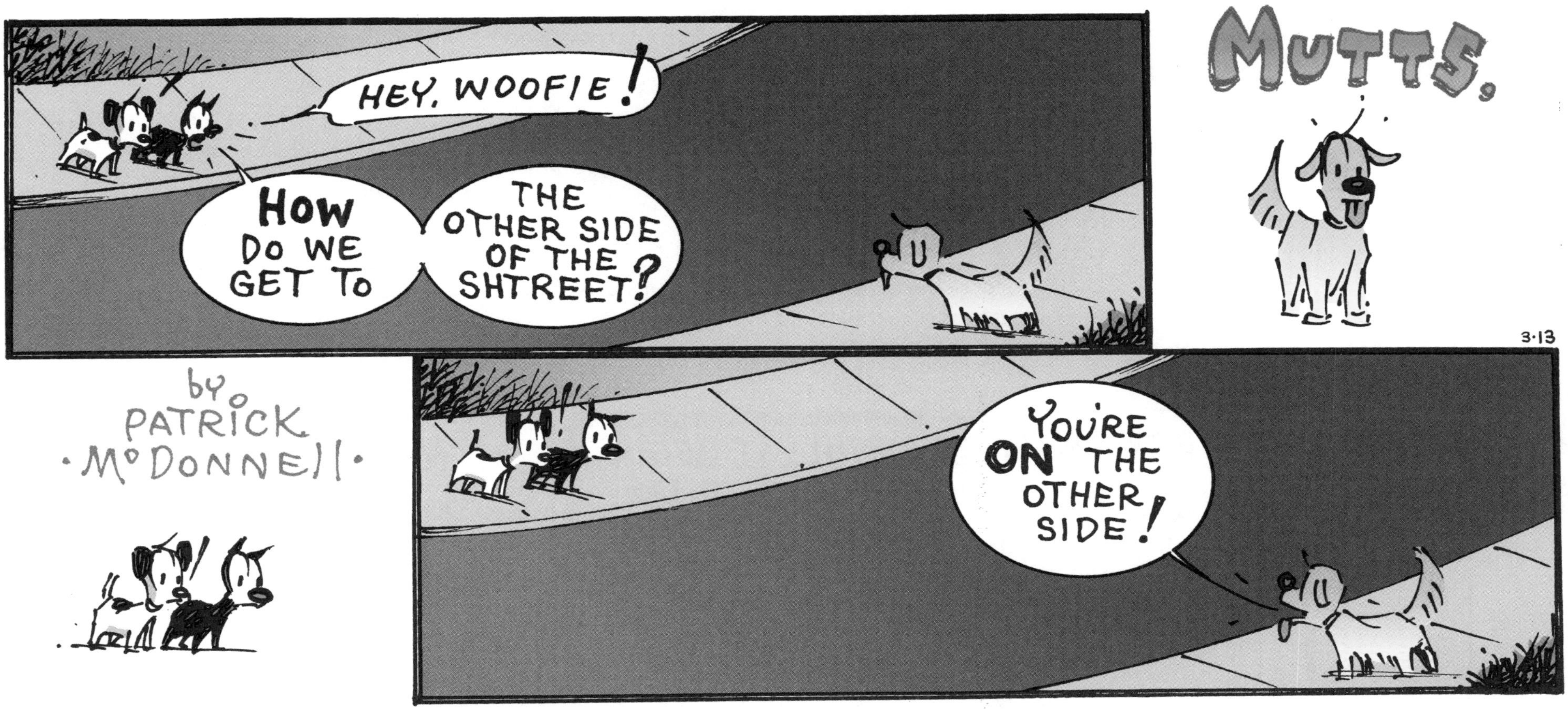
MUTTS.
by PATRICK McDONNELL
3·13
HEY, WOOFIE!
HOW DO WE GET TO
THE OTHER SIDE OF THE SHTREET?
YOU'RE ON THE OTHER SIDE!

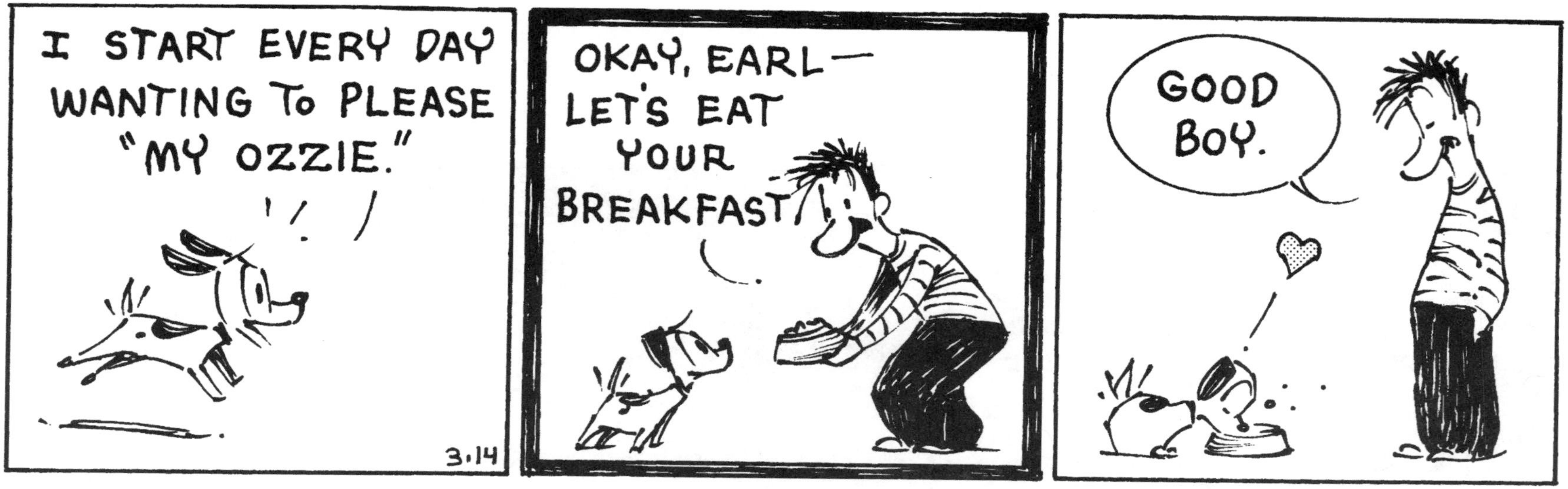
I START EVERY DAY WANTING TO PLEASE "MY OZZIE."
3.14
OKAY, EARL— LET'S EAT YOUR BREAKFAST
GOOD BOY.

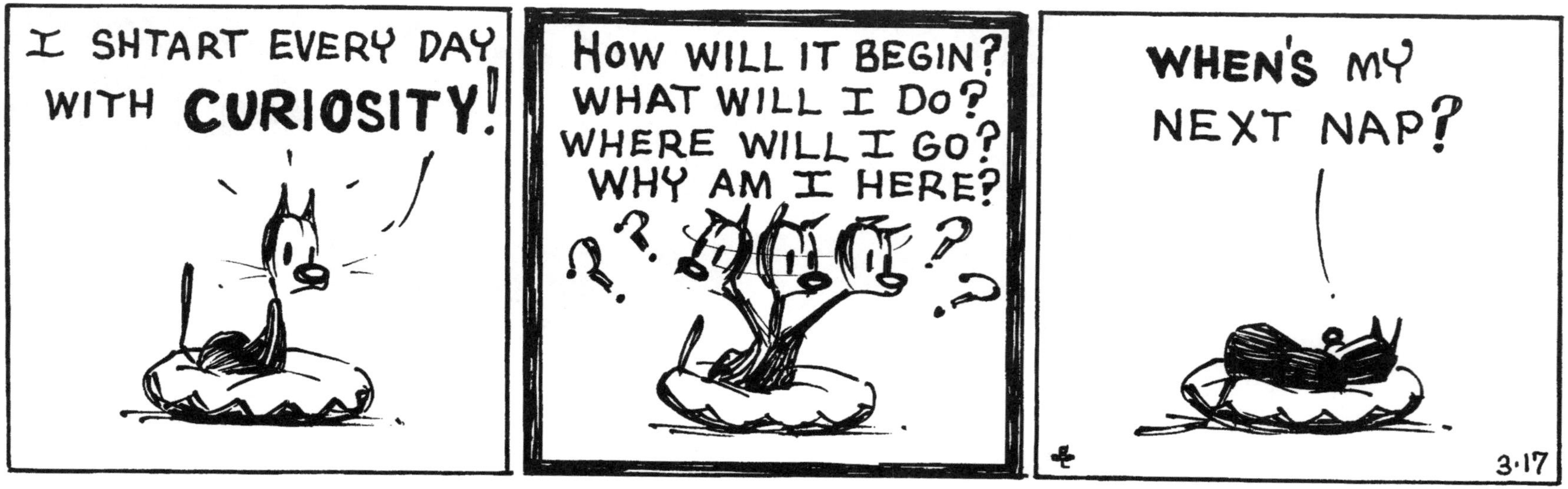
I SHTART EVERY DAY WITH CURIOSITY!
HOW WILL IT BEGIN?
WHAT WILL I DO?
WHERE WILL I GO?
WHY AM I HERE?
WHEN'S MY NEXT NAP?
3.17

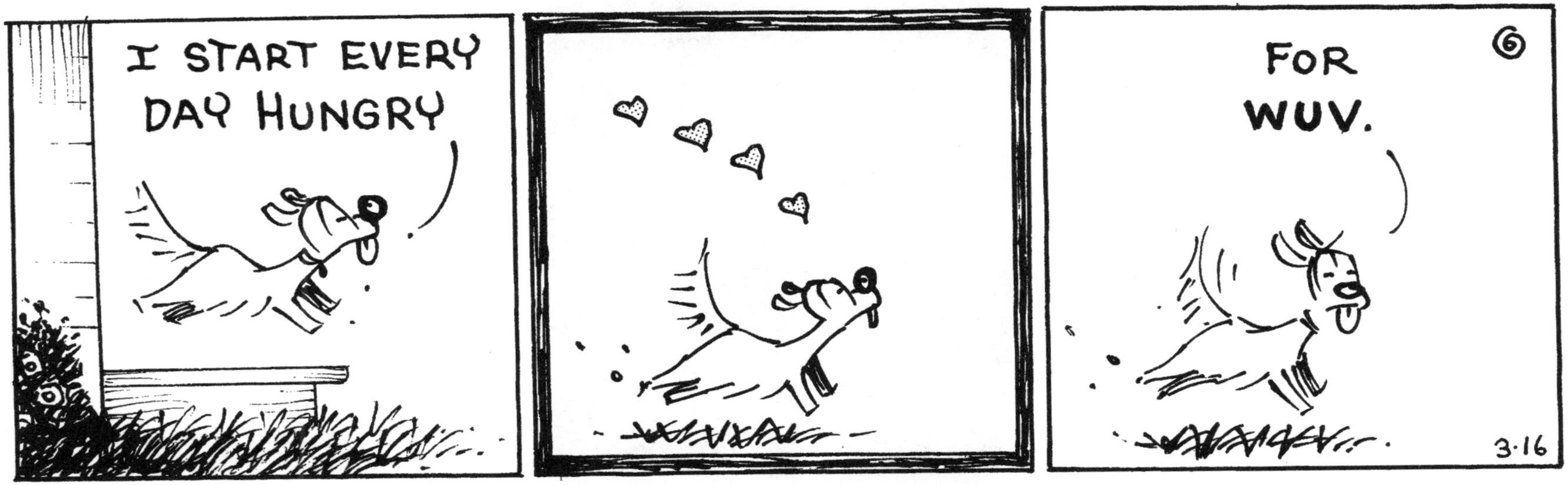
I START EVERY DAY HUNGRY
FOR WUV.
3·16

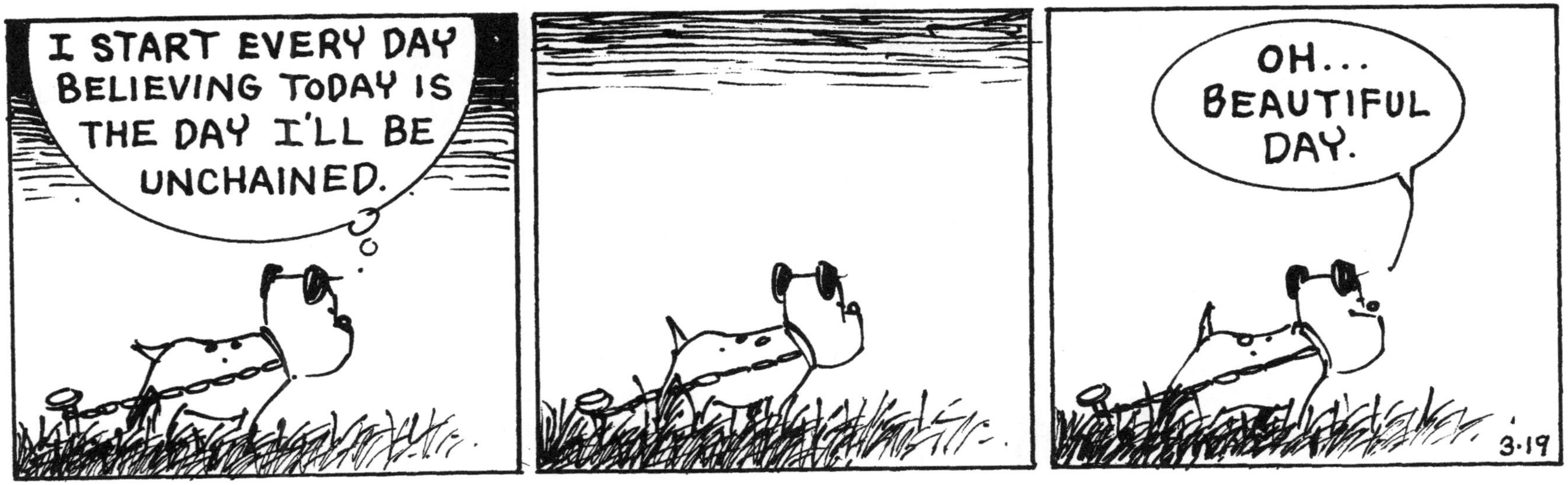
I START EVERY DAY BELIEVING TODAY IS THE DAY I'LL BE UNCHAINED.
OH... BEAUTIFUL DAY.
3·19

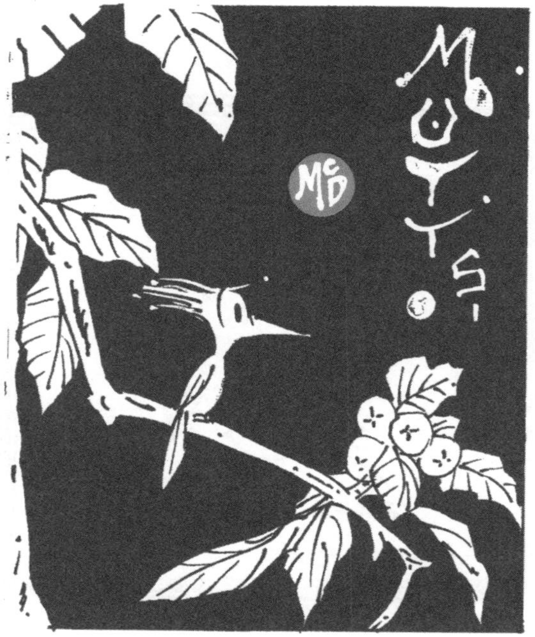

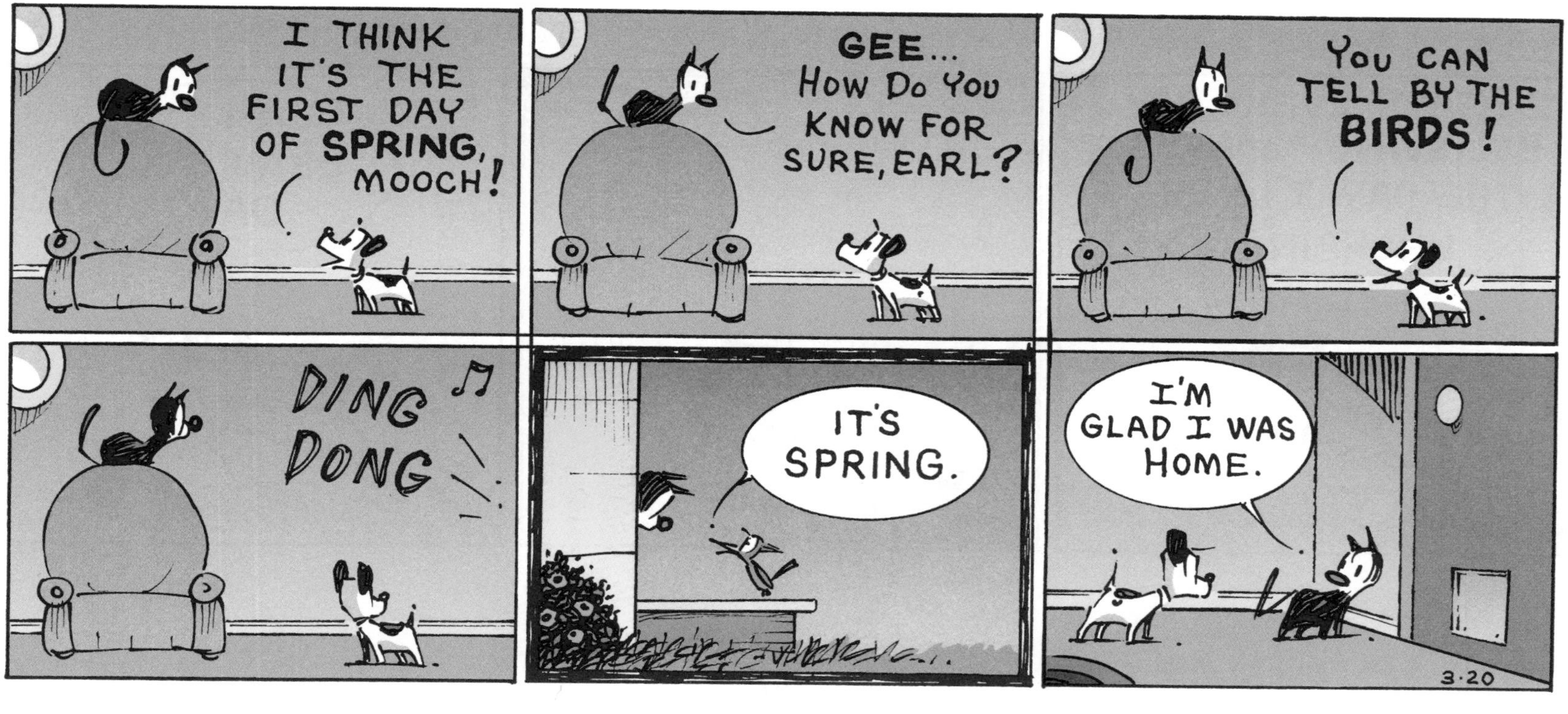

I THINK IT'S THE FIRST DAY OF SPRING, MOOCH!
GEE... HOW DO YOU KNOW FOR SURE, EARL?
YOU CAN TELL BY THE BIRDS!
DING DONG
IT'S SPRING.
I'M GLAD I WAS HOME.
3·20

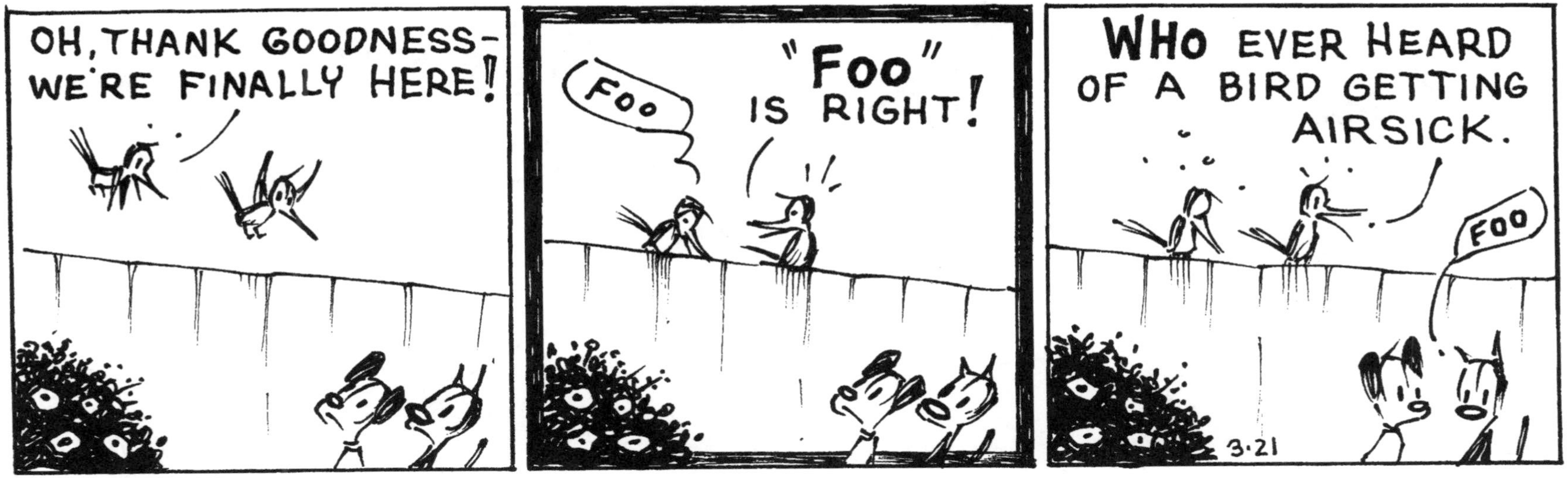
OH, THANK GOODNESS-
WE'RE FINALLY HERE!
FOO
"FOO" IS RIGHT!
WHO EVER HEARD OF A BIRD GETTING AIRSICK.
FOO
3·21

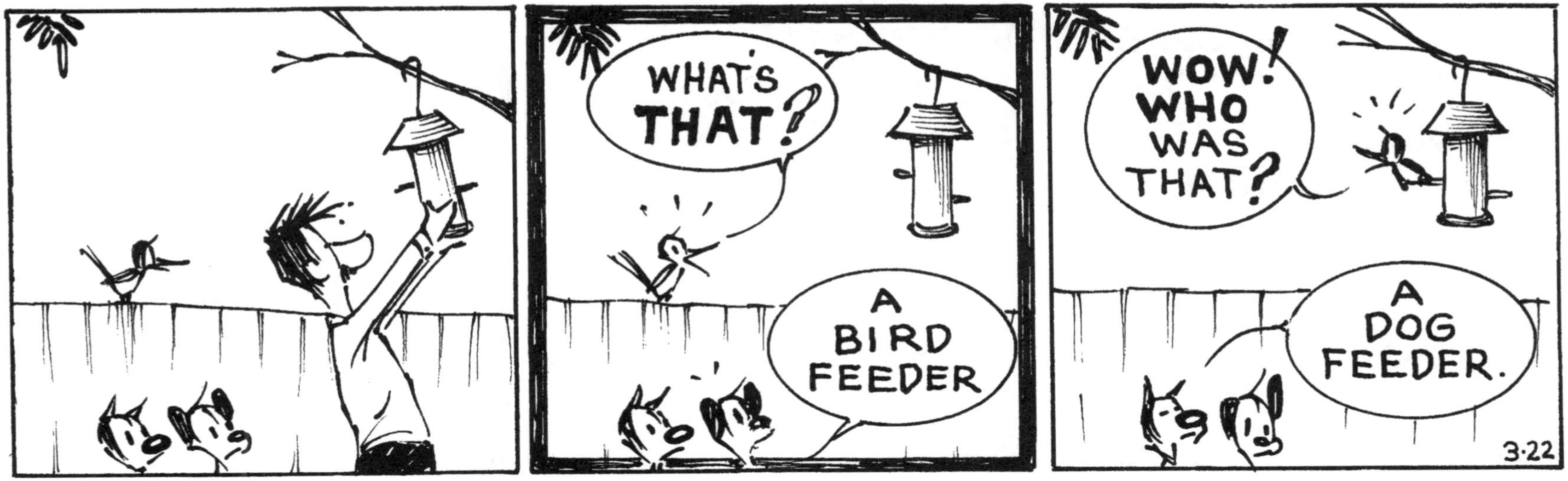
WHAT'S THAT?
A BIRD FEEDER
WOW! WHO WAS THAT?
A DOG FEEDER.
3·22

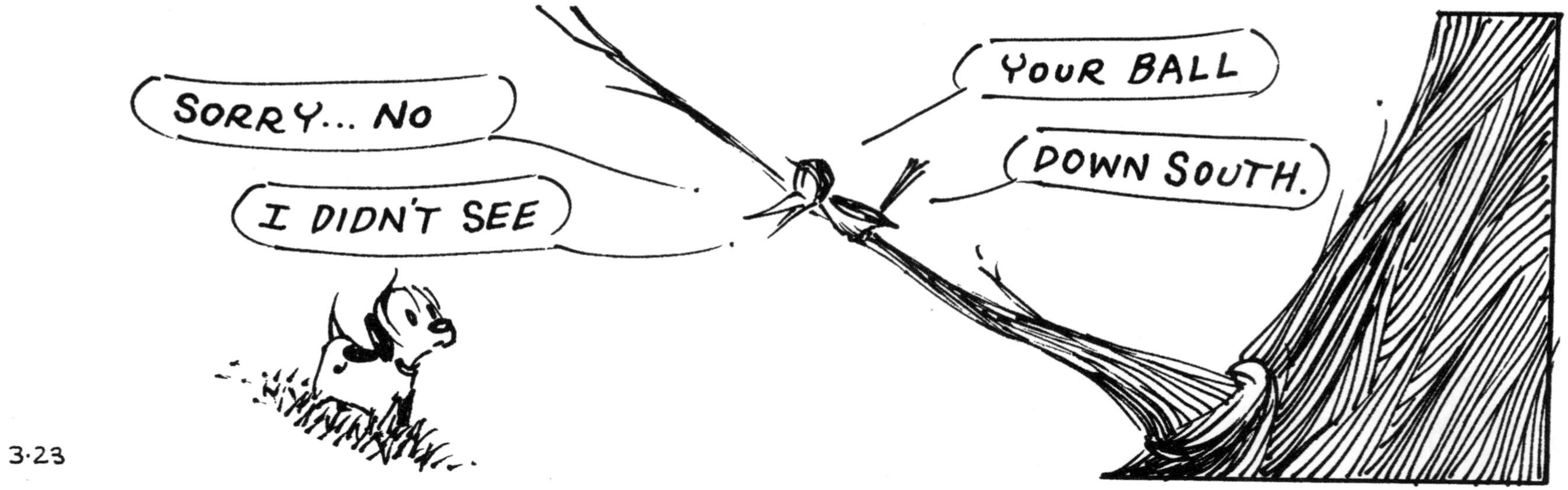
SORRY... NO
I DIDN'T SEE
YOUR BALL
DOWN SOUTH.
3·23

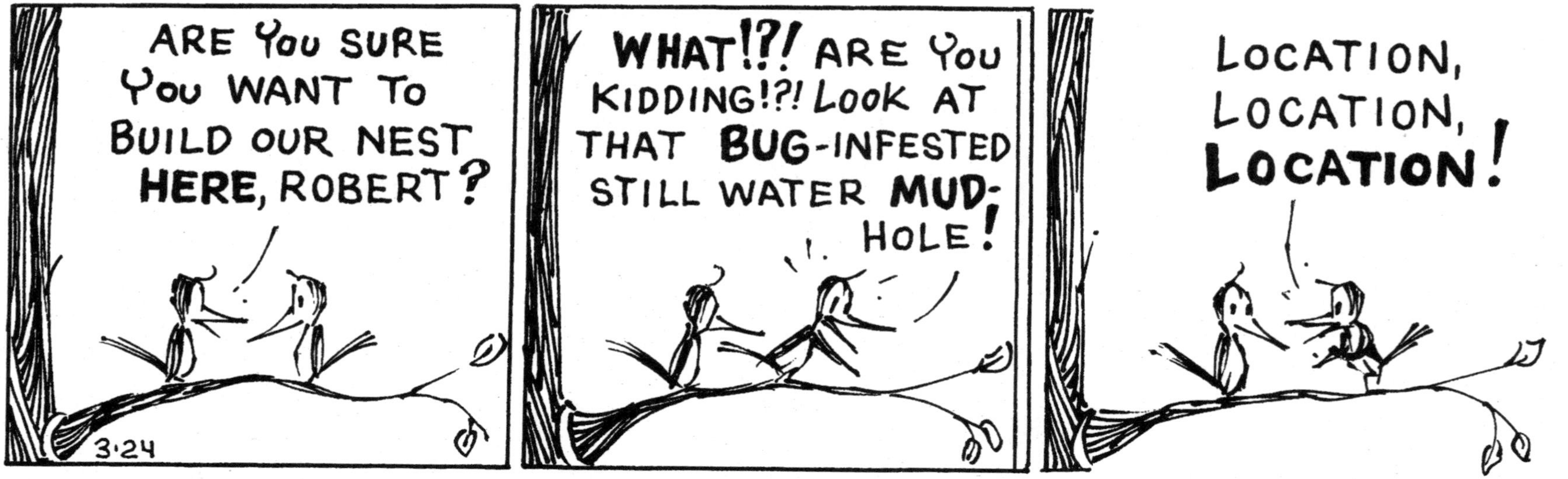
ARE YOU SURE YOU WANT TO BUILD OUR NEST HERE, ROBERT?
3·24
WHAT!?! ARE YOU KIDDING!?! LOOK AT THAT BUG-INFESTED STILL WATER MUD-HOLE!
LOCATION, LOCATION, LOCATION!

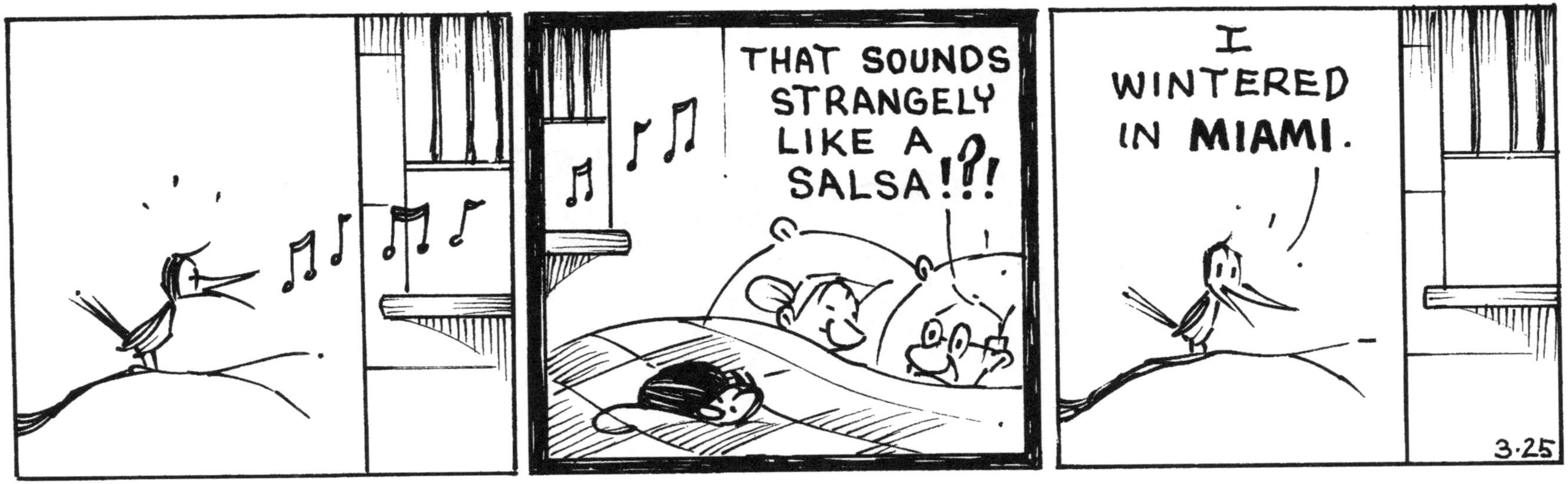
THAT SOUNDS STRANGELY LIKE A SALSA!?!
I WINTERED IN **MIAMI**.
3·25

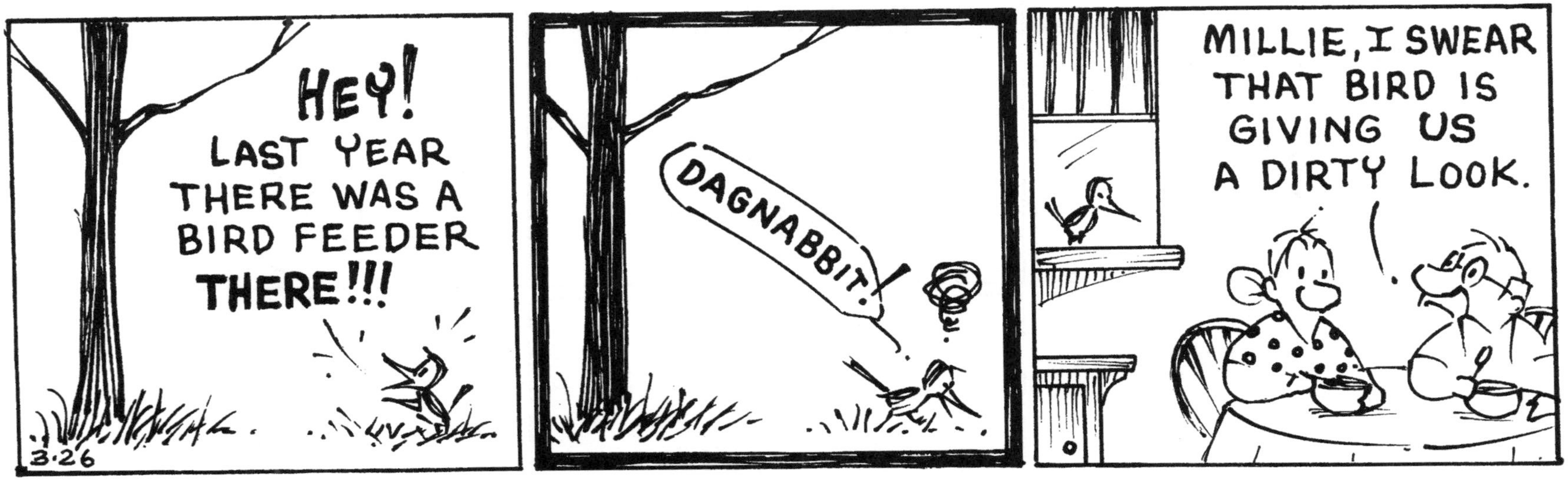
HEY! LAST YEAR THERE WAS A BIRD FEEDER **THERE**!!!
3·26
DAGNABBIT!
MILLIE, I SWEAR THAT BIRD IS GIVING US A DIRTY LOOK.

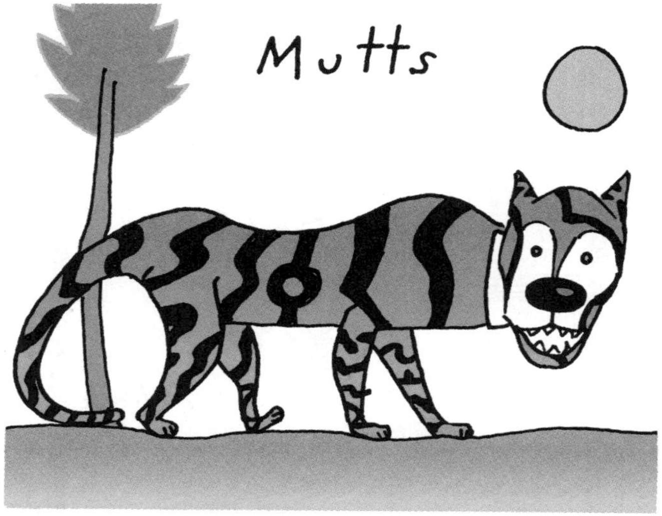
Mutts

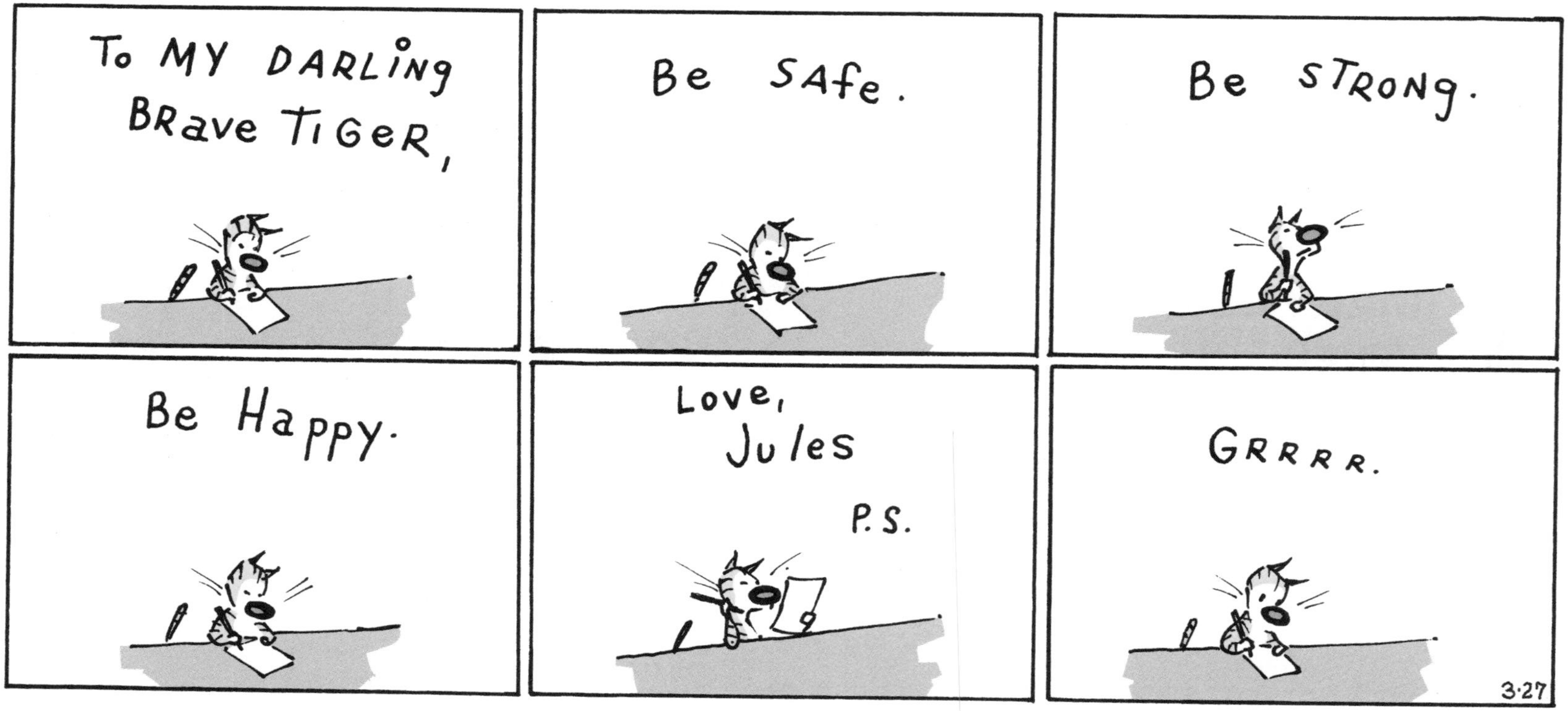
To MY DARLING BRAVE TIGER,
Be SAFE.
Be STRONG.
Be Happy.
Love, Jules
P.S.
GRRRR.
3·27

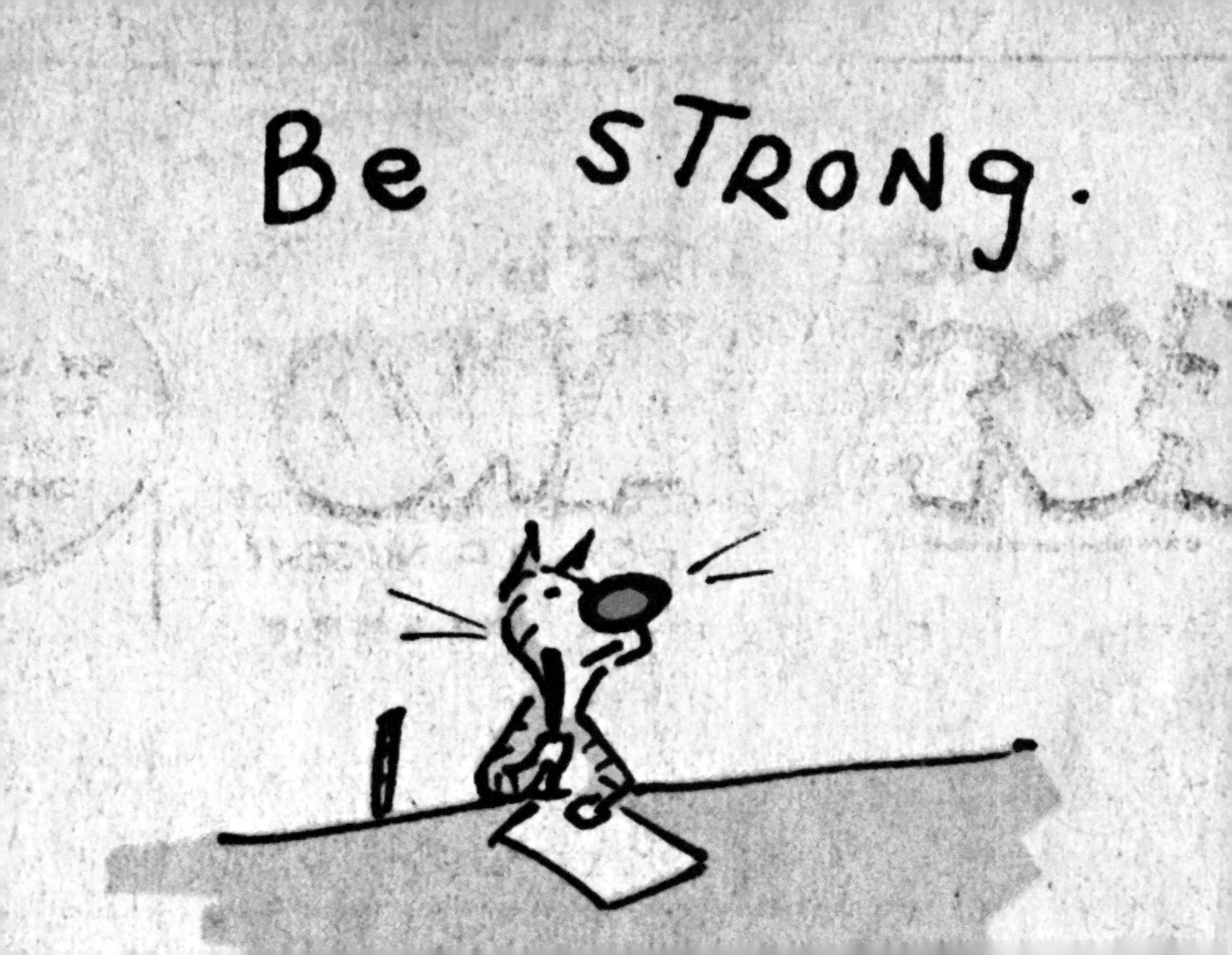
Be STRONG.

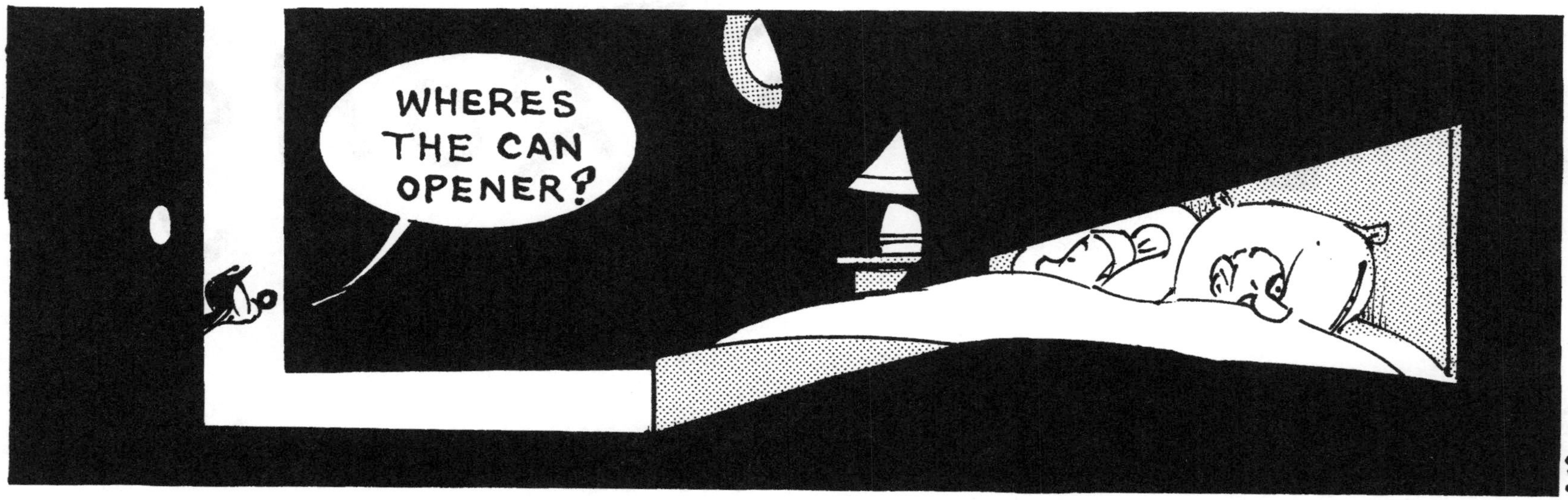
WHERE'S THE CAN OPENER?
3·29

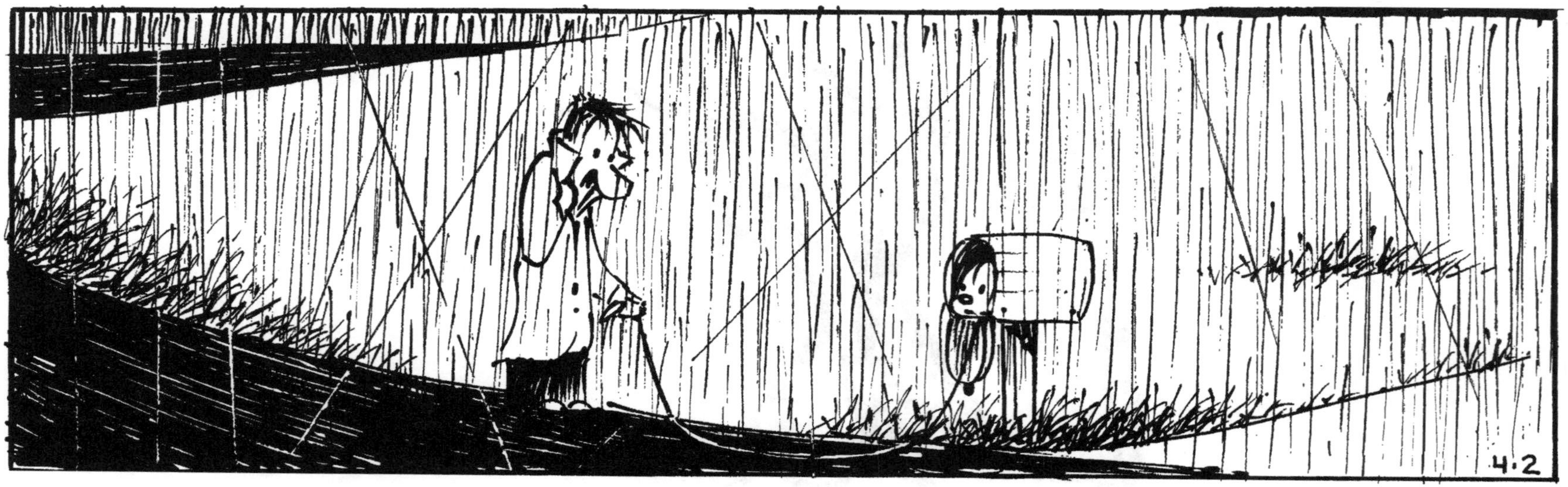
4·2

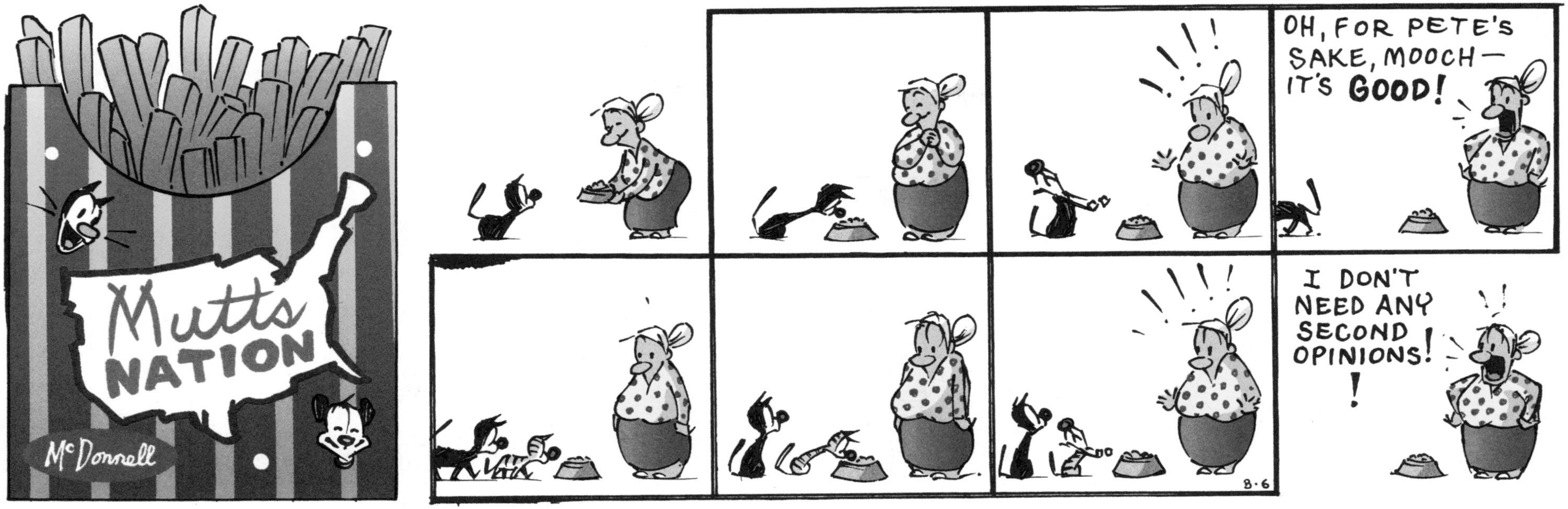
Mutts
NATION
McDonnell
OH, FOR PETE'S SAKE, MOOCH— IT'S GOOD!
I DON'T NEED ANY SECOND OPINIONS!
8·6

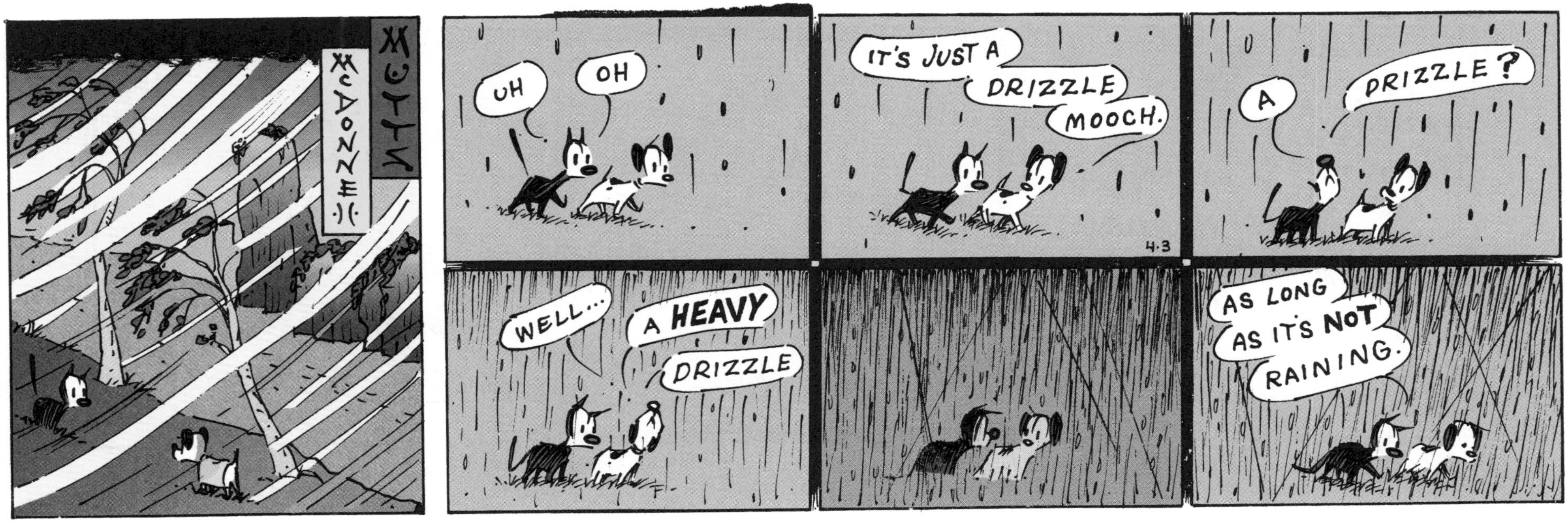
MUTTS
McDONNELL
UH
OH
IT'S JUST A
DRIZZLE
MOOCH.
4·3
A
DRIZZLE?
WELL...
A HEAVY
DRIZZLE
AS LONG
AS IT'S NOT
RAINING.

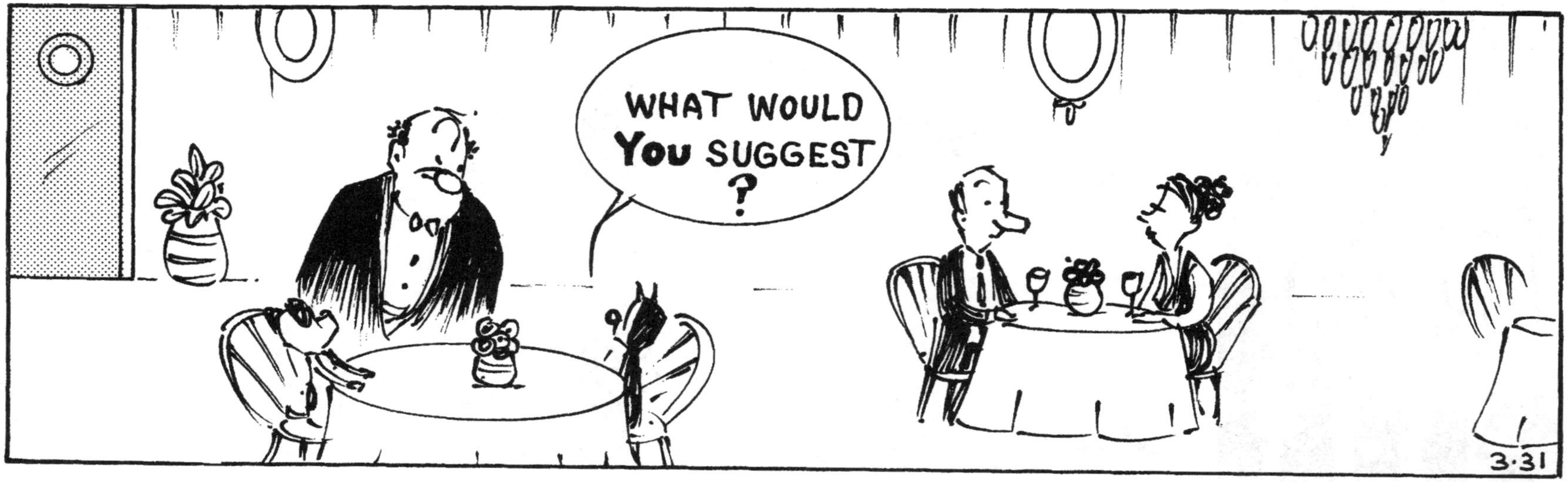
WHAT WOULD YOU SUGGEST ?
3·31

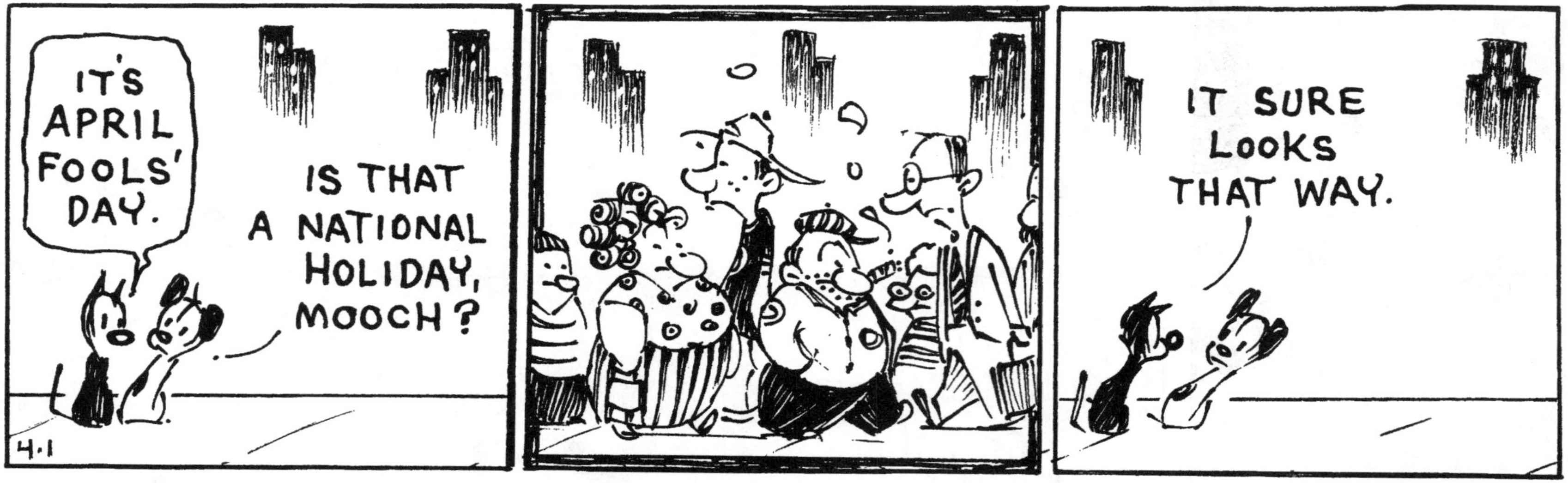
IT'S APRIL FOOLS' DAY.
IS THAT A NATIONAL HOLIDAY, MOOCH?
4·1
IT SURE LOOKS THAT WAY.

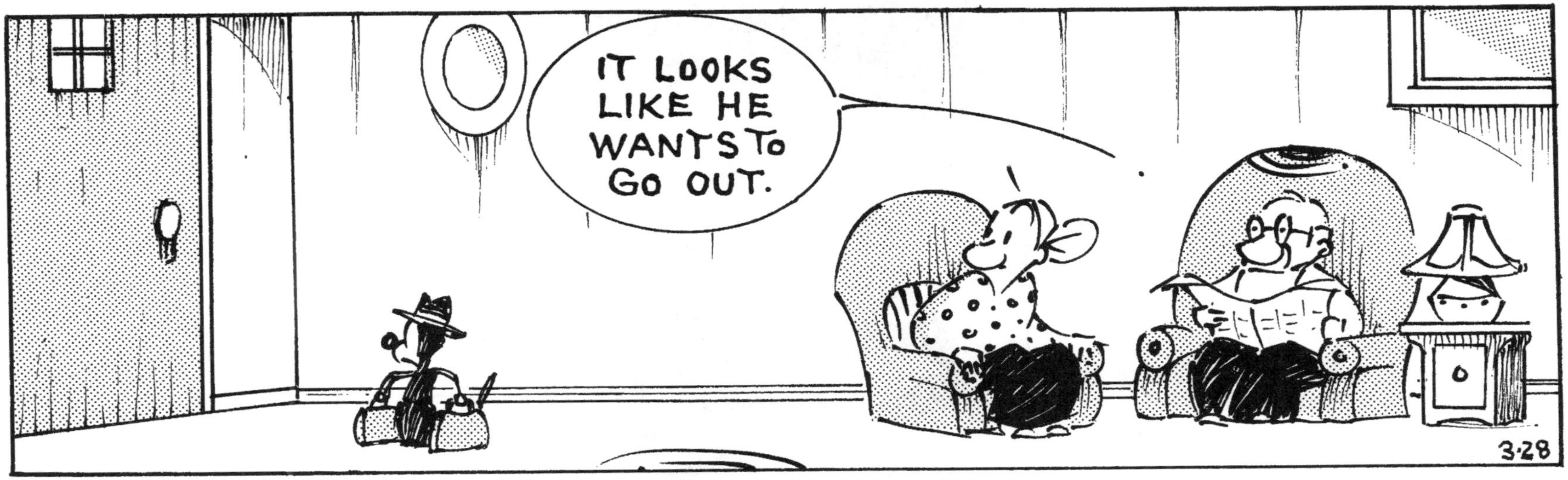
IT LOOKS LIKE HE WANTS TO GO OUT.
3·28

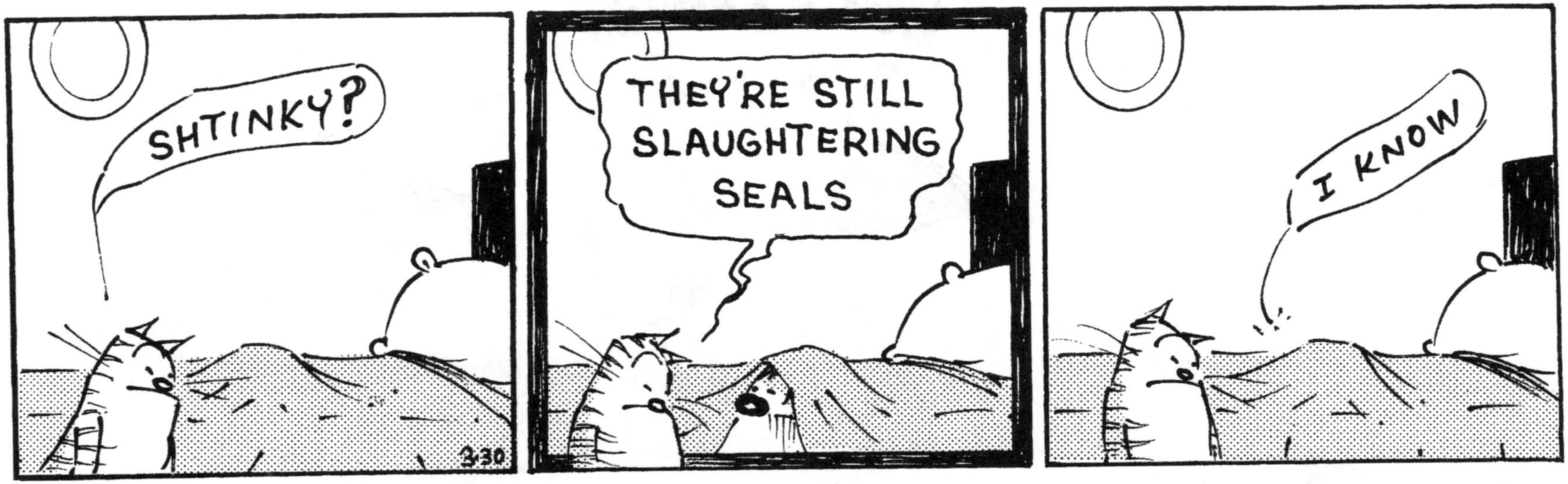
SHTINKY?
3·30
THEY'RE STILL SLAUGHTERING SEALS
I KNOW

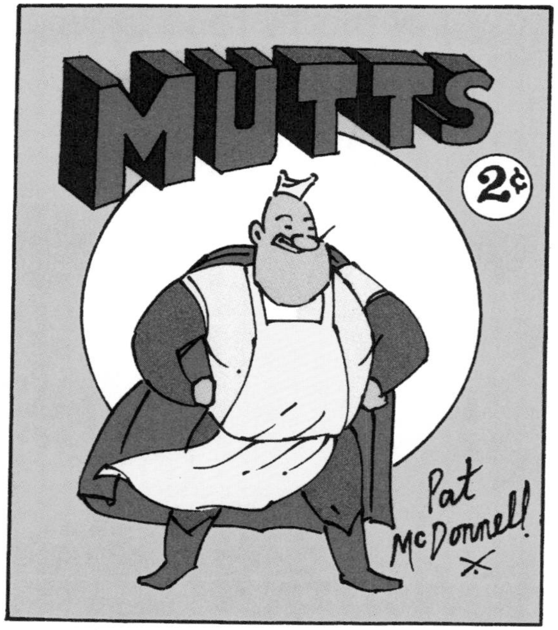
MUTTS
2¢
Pat McDonnell

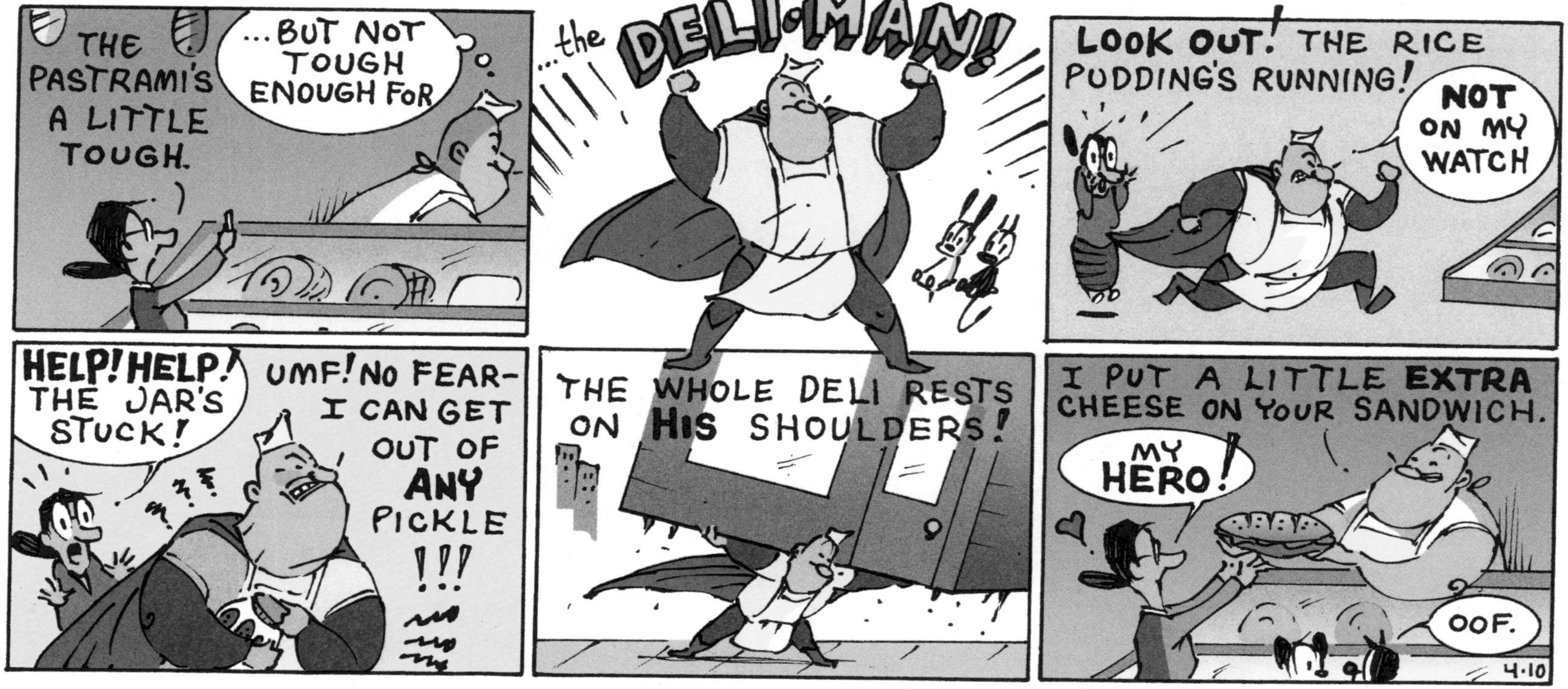
THE PASTRAMI'S A LITTLE TOUGH.
...BUT NOT TOUGH ENOUGH FOR
...the DELI·MAN!
LOOK OUT! THE RICE PUDDING'S RUNNING!
NOT ON MY WATCH
HELP! HELP! THE JAR'S STUCK!
UMF! NO FEAR- I CAN GET OUT OF ANY PICKLE !!!
THE WHOLE DELI RESTS ON HIS SHOULDERS!
I PUT A LITTLE EXTRA CHEESE ON YOUR SANDWICH.
MY HERO!
OOF.
4·10

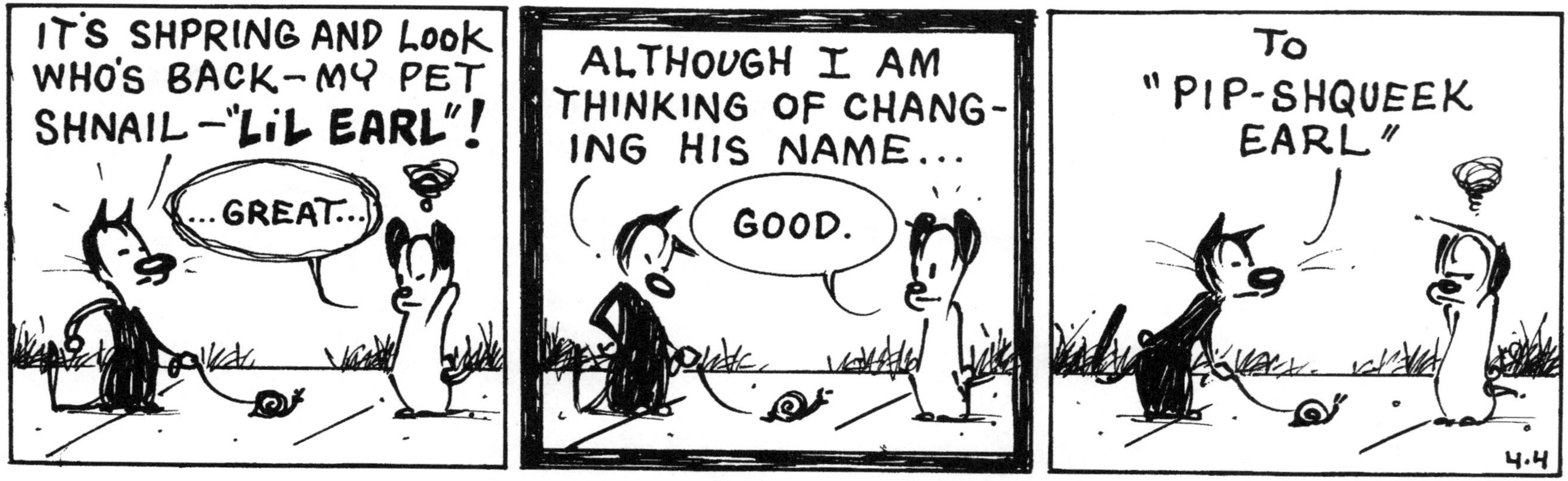
IT'S SHPRING AND LOOK WHO'S BACK–MY PET SHNAIL–"LI'L EARL"!
...GREAT...
ALTHOUGH I AM THINKING OF CHANG-ING HIS NAME...
GOOD.
TO "PIP-SHQUEEK EARL"
4.4

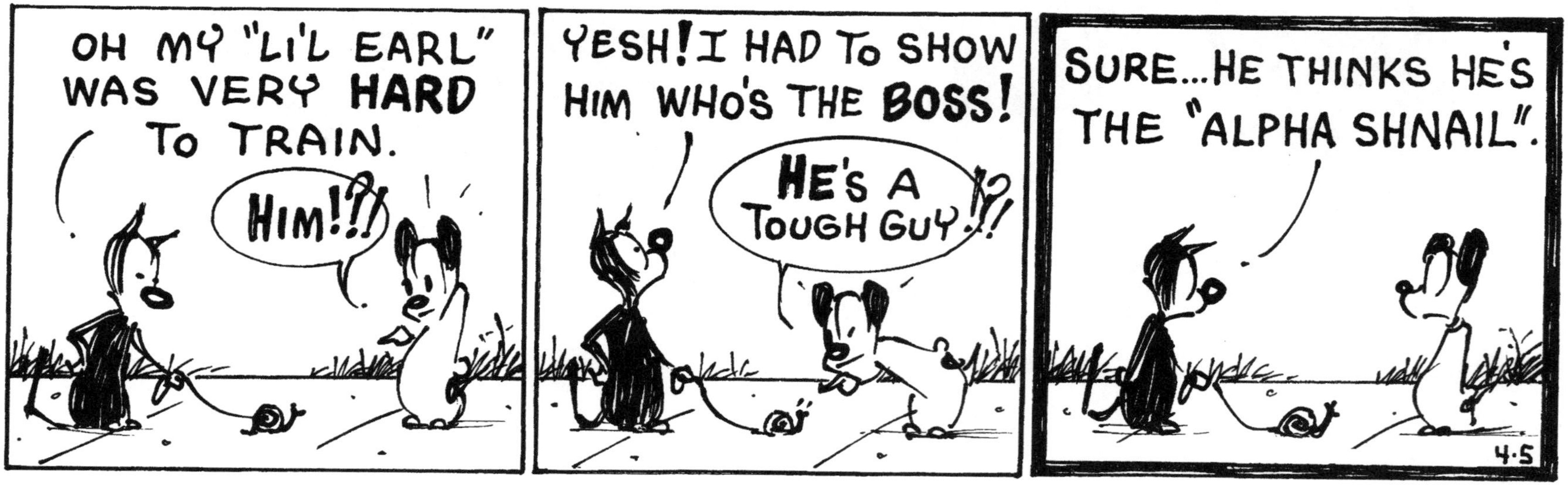
OH MY "LI'L EARL" WAS VERY HARD TO TRAIN.
HIM!?!
YESH! I HAD TO SHOW HIM WHO'S THE BOSS!
HE'S A TOUGH GUY?!
SURE...HE THINKS HE'S THE "ALPHA SHNAIL".
4.5

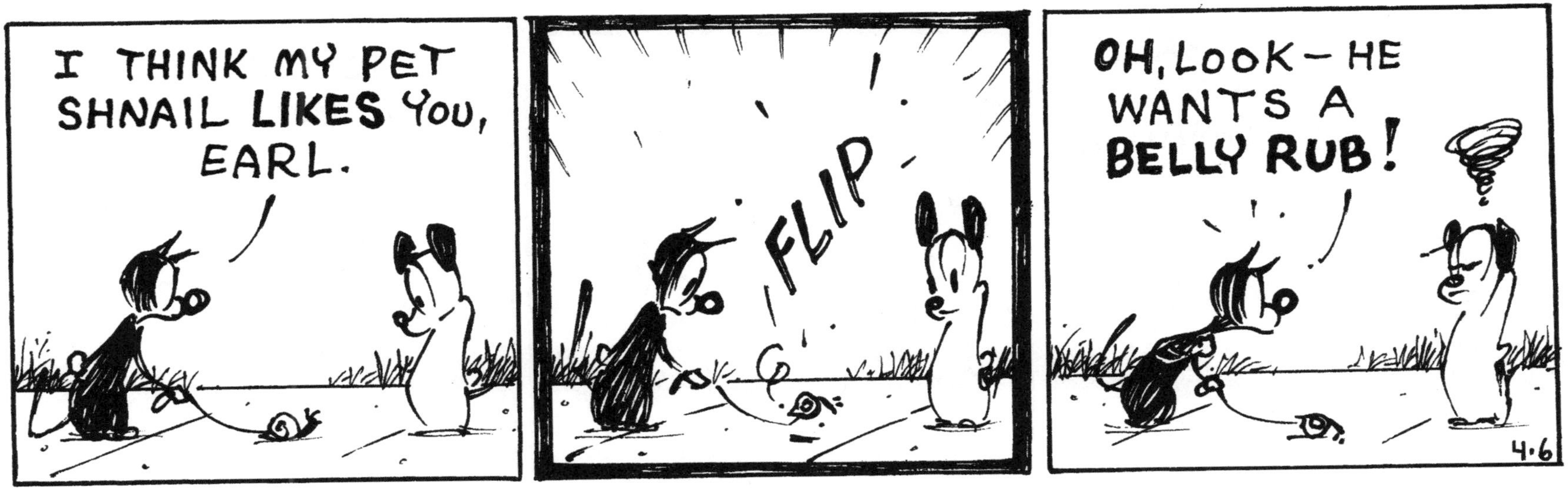
I THINK MY PET SHNAIL LIKES YOU, EARL.
FLIP
OH, LOOK—HE WANTS A BELLY RUB!
4·6

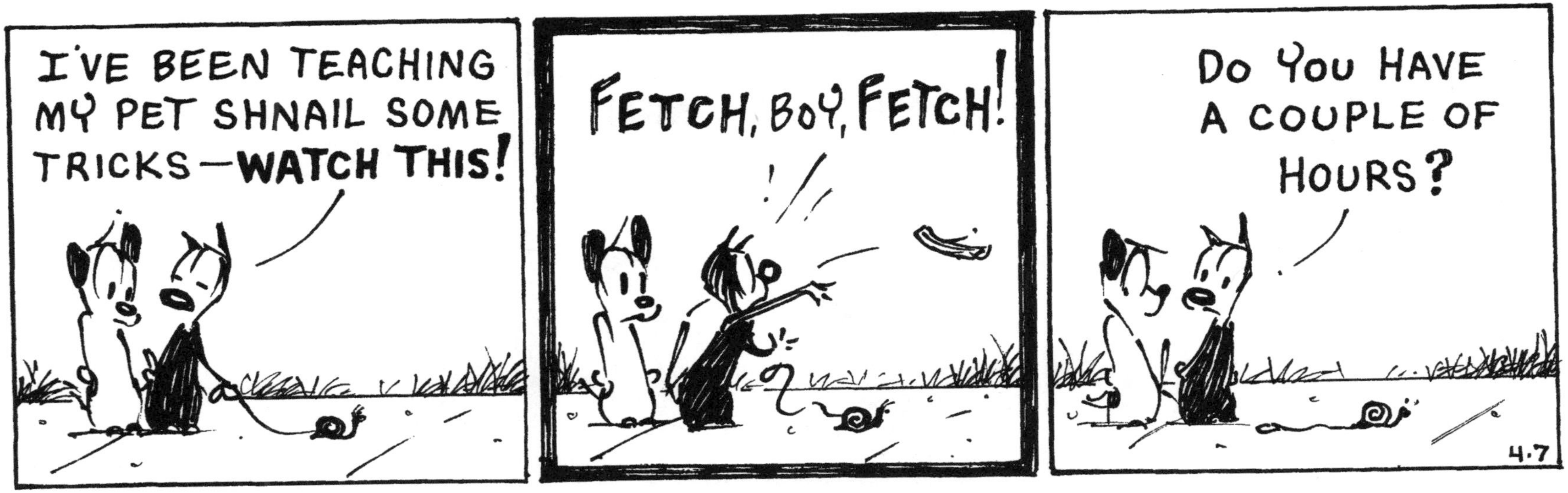
I'VE BEEN TEACHING MY PET SHNAIL SOME TRICKS—WATCH THIS!
FETCH, BOY, FETCH!
DO YOU HAVE A COUPLE OF HOURS?
4·7

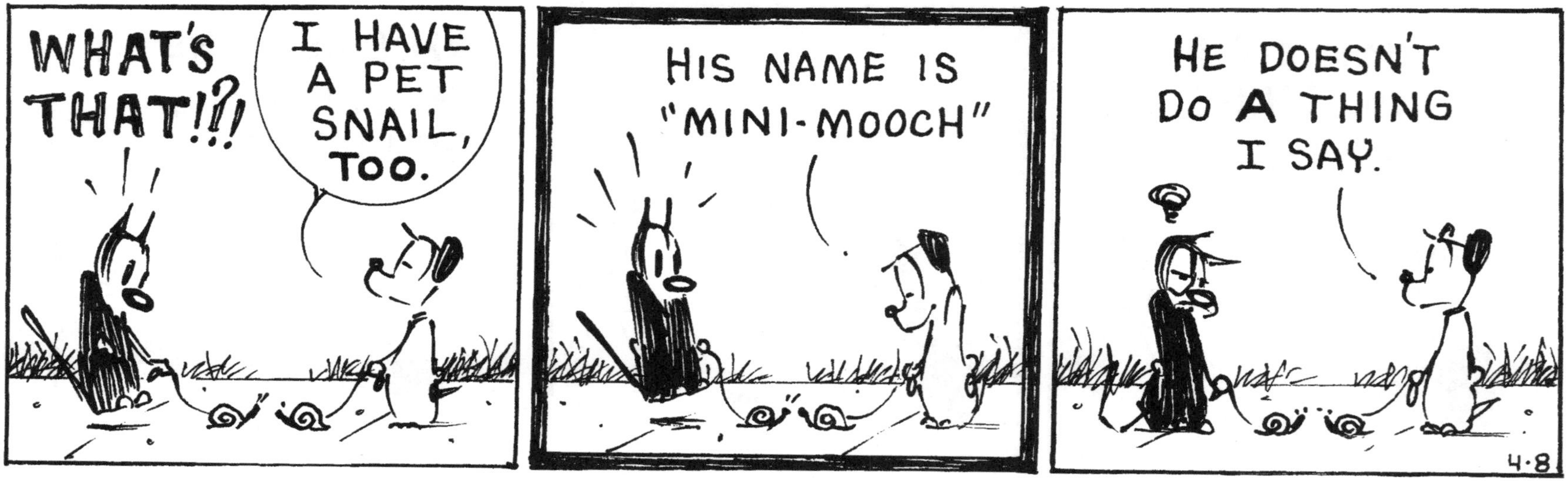
WHAT'S THAT!?!
I HAVE A PET SNAIL, TOO.
HIS NAME IS "MINI-MOOCH"
HE DOESN'T DO A THING I SAY.
4·8

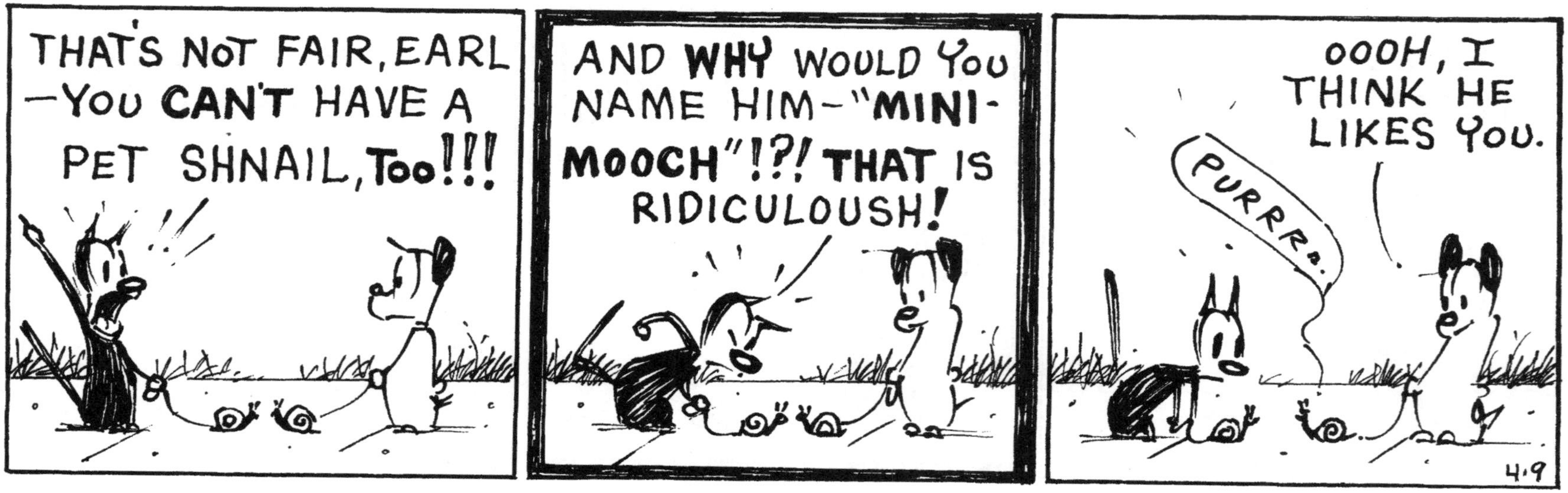
THAT'S NOT FAIR, EARL —YOU CAN'T HAVE A PET SHNAIL, TOO!!!
AND WHY WOULD YOU NAME HIM—"MINI-MOOCH"!?! THAT IS RIDICULOUSH!
PURRRR.
OOOH, I THINK HE LIKES YOU.
4·9

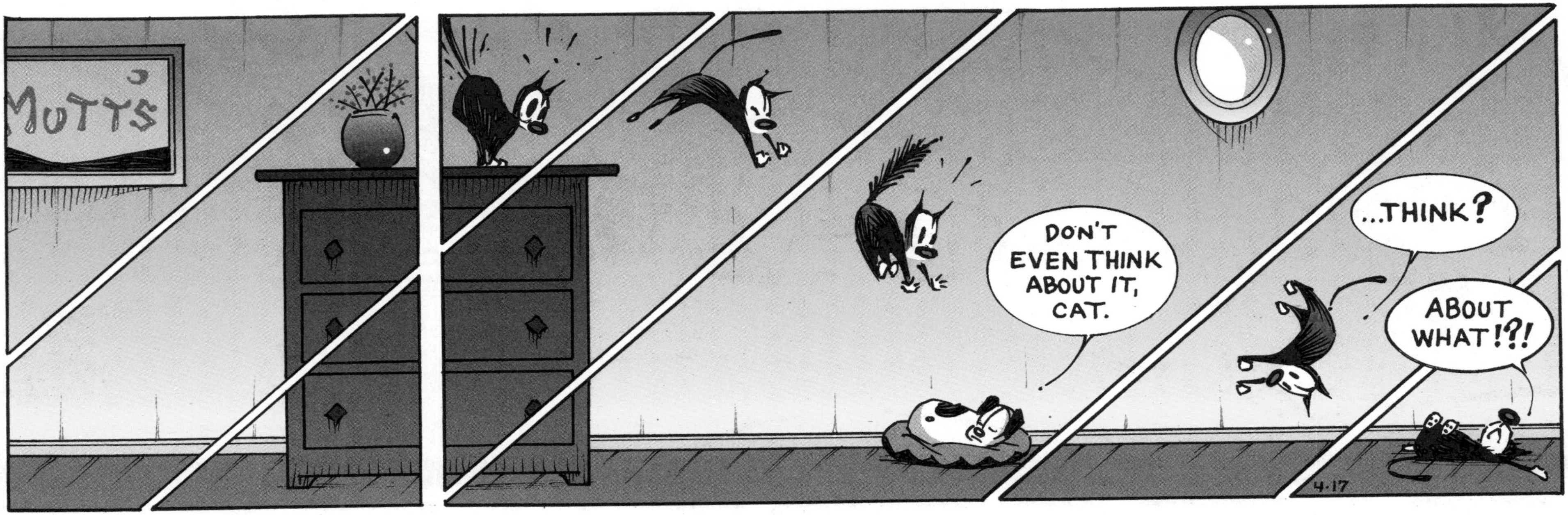
MUTTS
DON'T EVEN THINK ABOUT IT, CAT.
...THINK?
ABOUT WHAT!?!
4·17

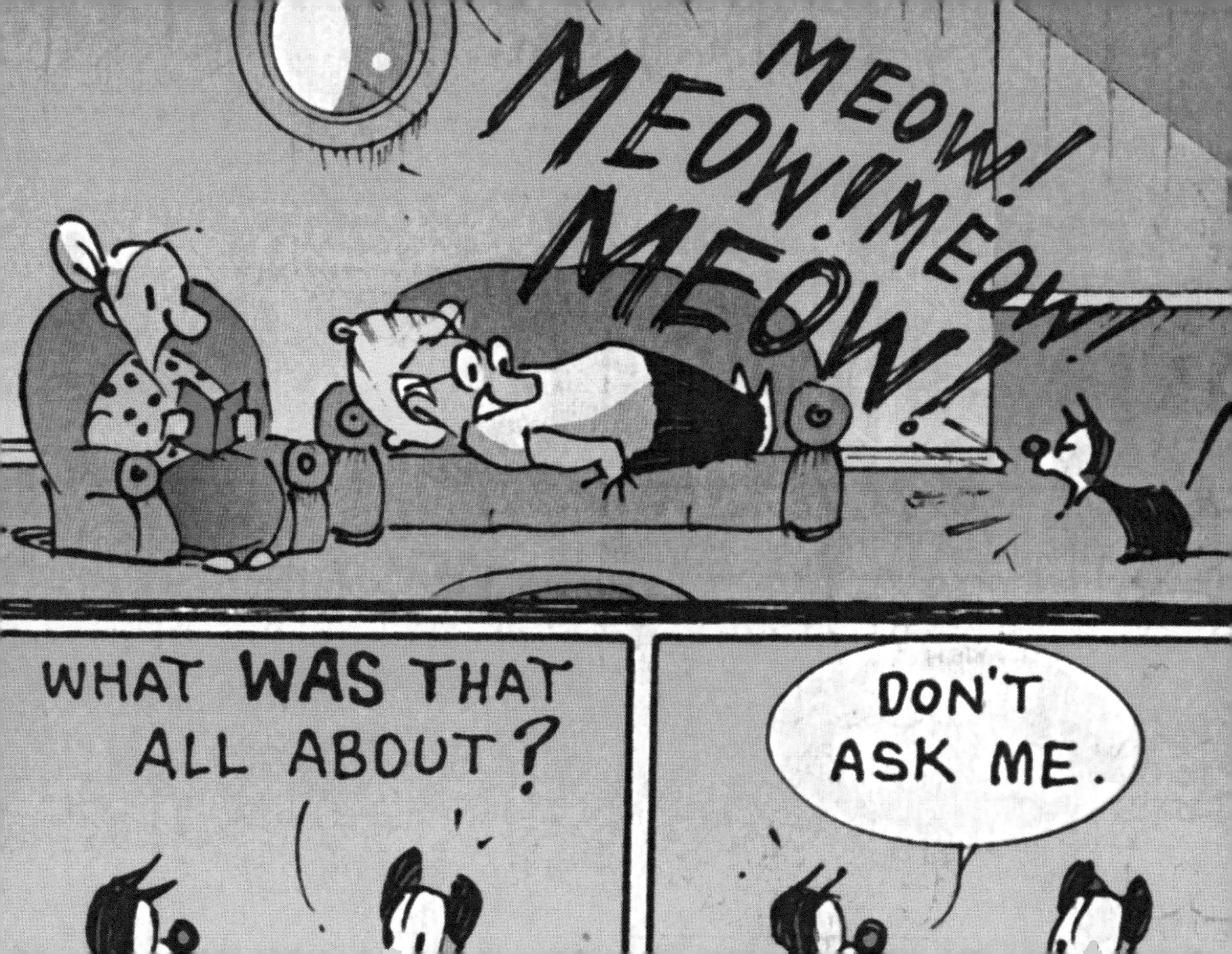
MEOW! MEOW! MEOW! MEOW!
MEOW!
WHAT WAS THAT ALL ABOUT?
DON'T ASK ME.

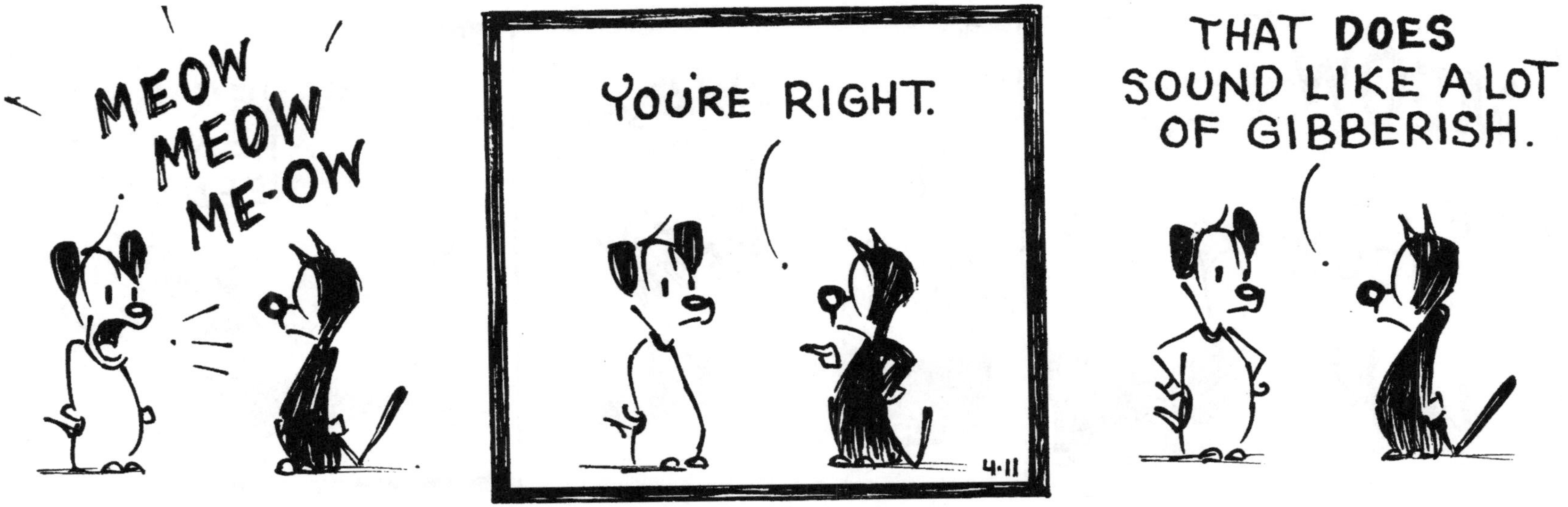
MEOW
MEOW
ME-OW
YOU'RE RIGHT.
THAT **DOES** SOUND LIKE A LOT OF GIBBERISH.
4-11

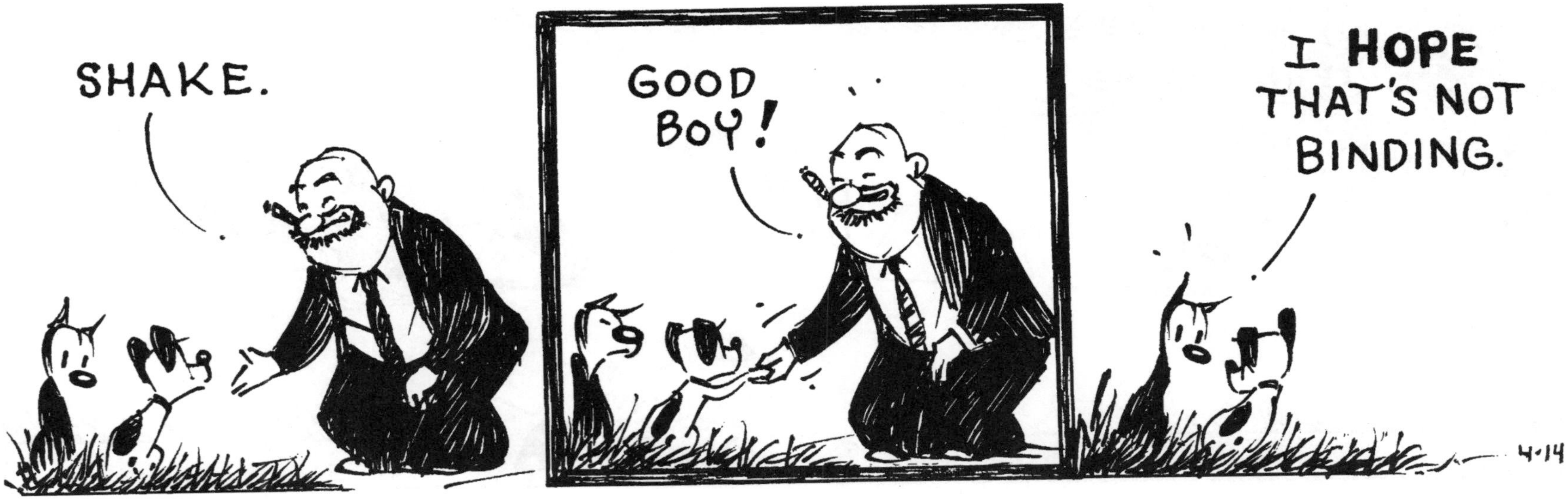
SHAKE.
GOOD BOY!
I **HOPE** THAT'S NOT BINDING.
4-14

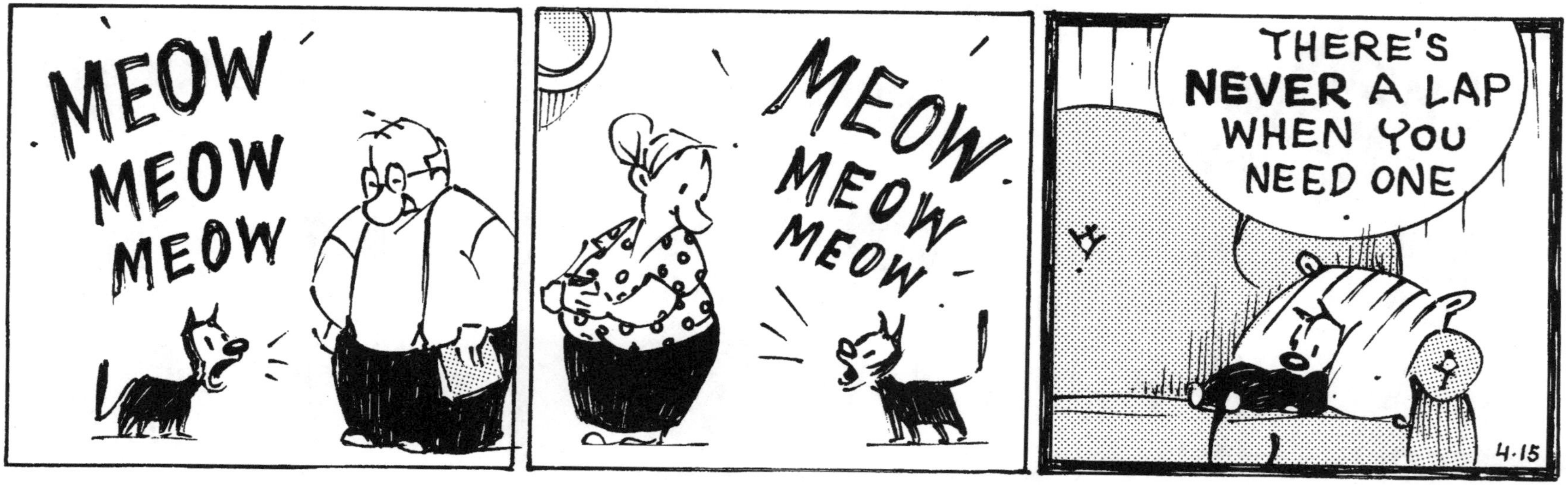
MEOW
MEOW
MEOW
MEOW
MEOW
MEOW
THERE'S **NEVER** A LAP WHEN YOU NEED ONE
4.15

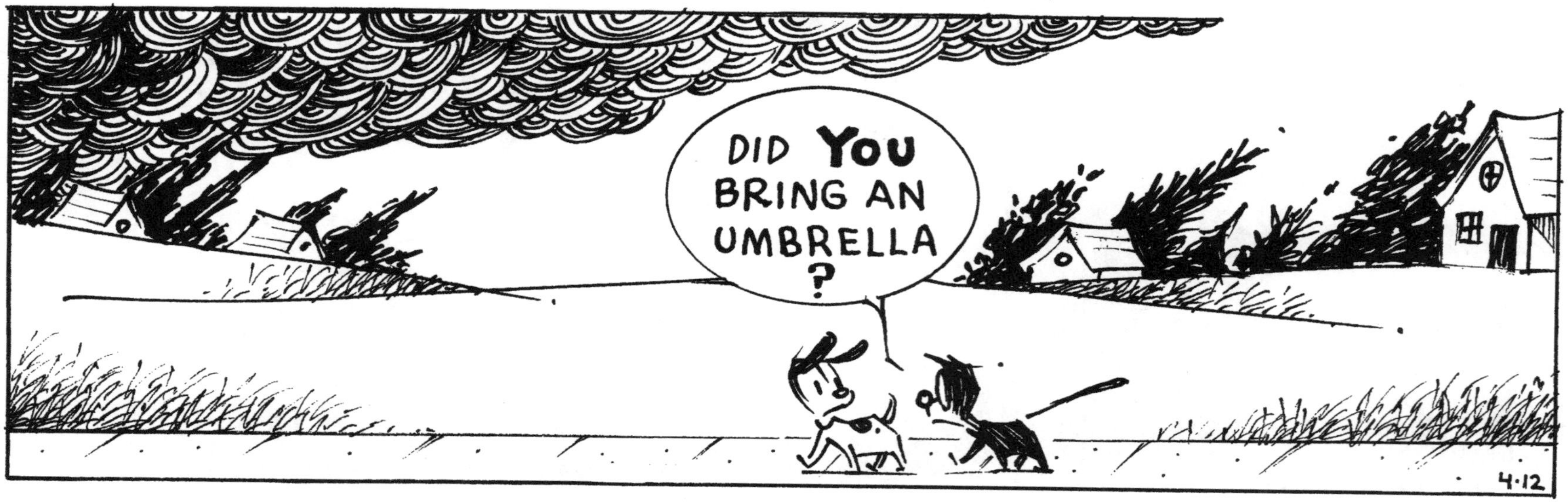
DID **YOU** BRING AN UMBRELLA ?
4.12

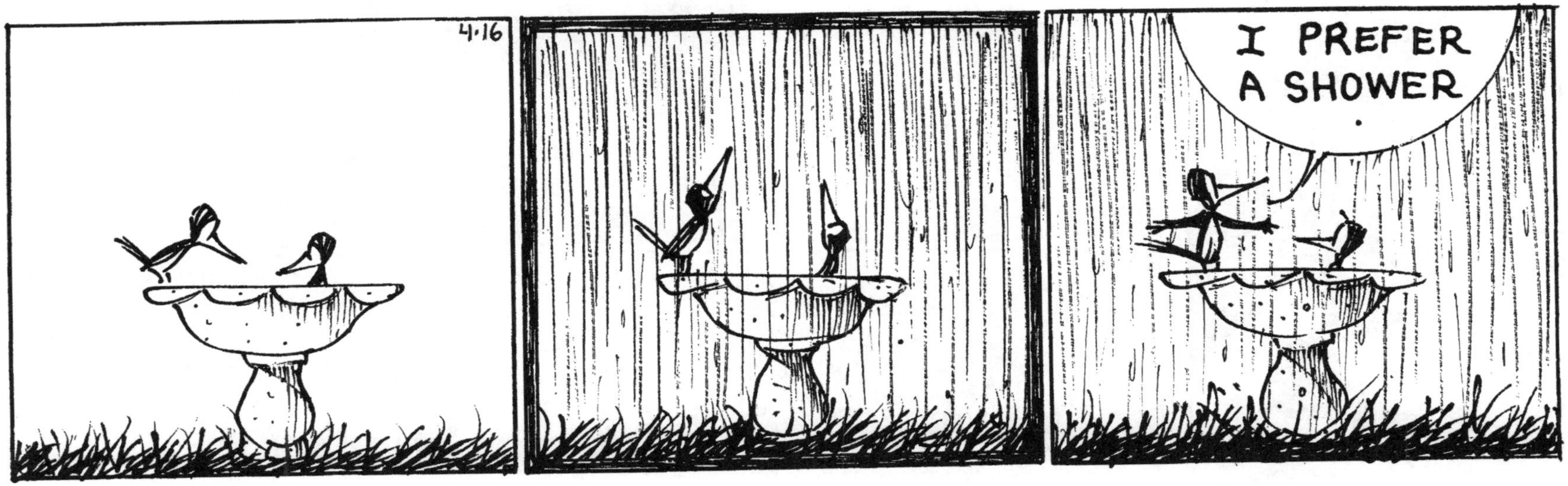
4.16
I PREFER A SHOWER.

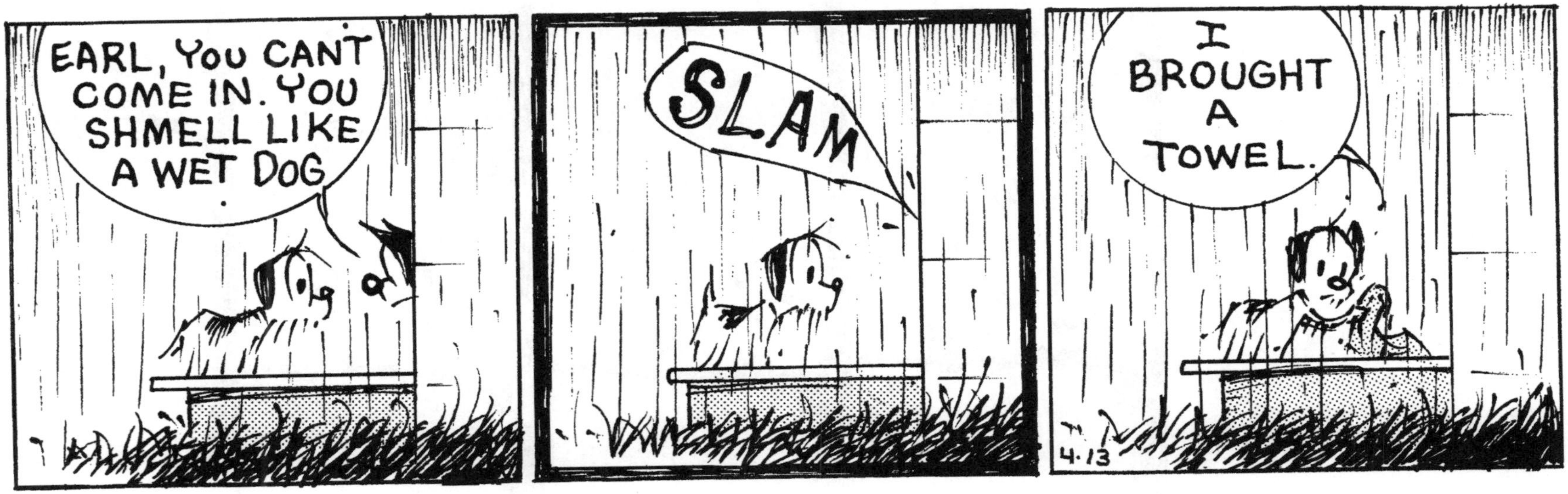
EARL, YOU CAN'T COME IN. YOU SHMELL LIKE A WET DOG.
SLAM
I BROUGHT A TOWEL.
4.13

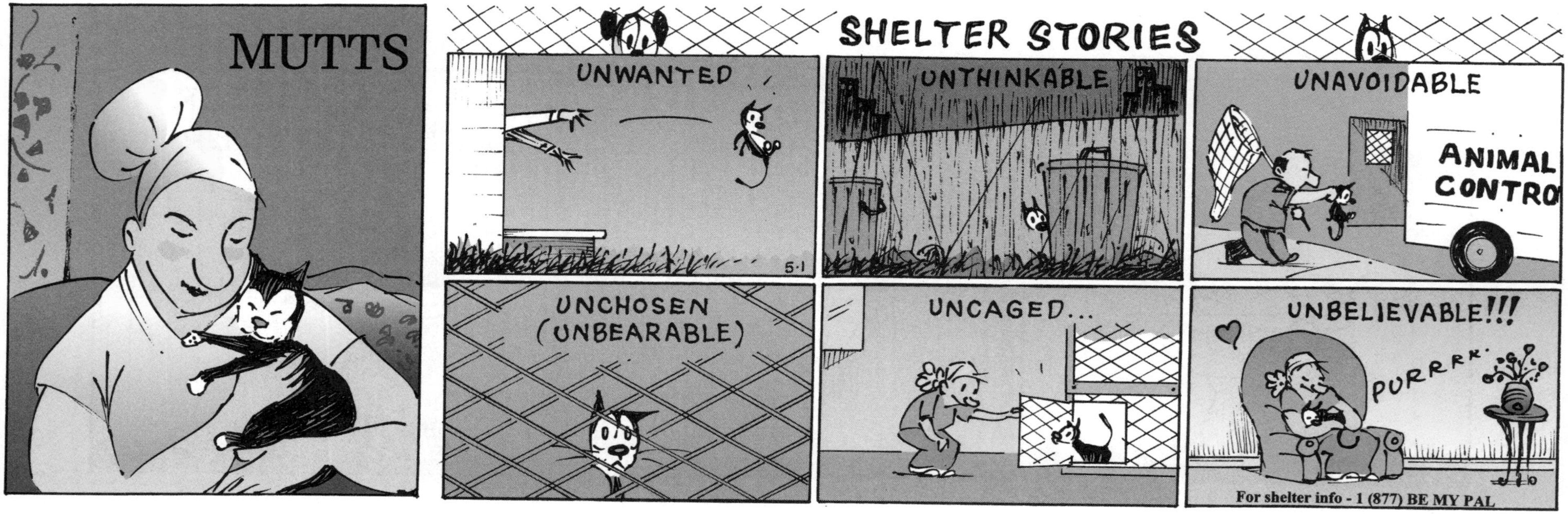
MUTTS
SHELTER STORIES
UNWANTED
5·1
UNTHINKABLE
UNAVOIDABLE
ANIMAL CONTRO
UNCHOSEN (UNBEARABLE)
UNCAGED...
UNBELIEVABLE!!!
PURRRR.
For shelter info - 1 (877) BE MY PAL

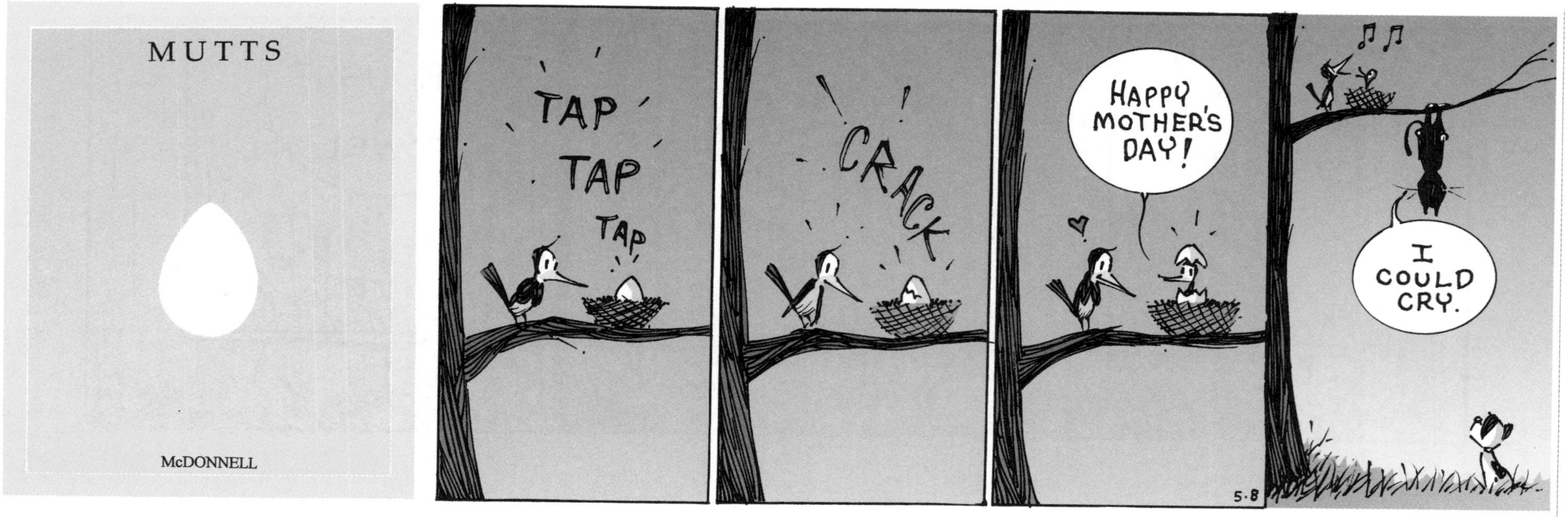
MUTTS
McDONNELL
TAP
TAP
TAP
CRACK
HAPPY MOTHER'S DAY!
5·8
I COULD CRY.

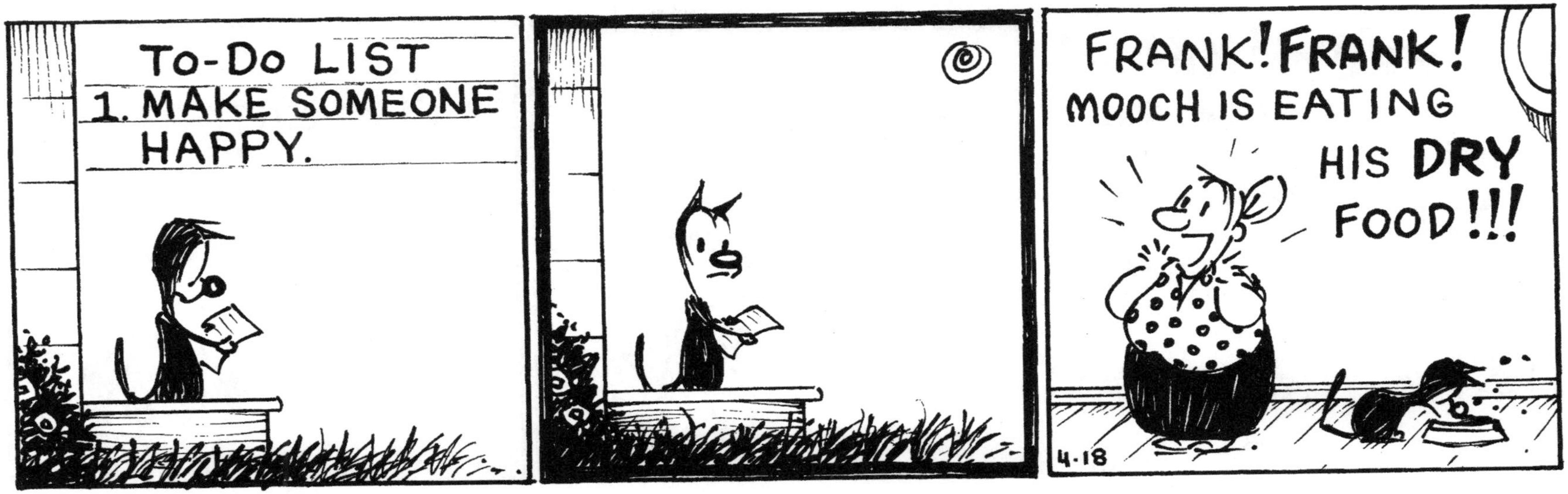
To-Do LIST
1. MAKE SOMEONE HAPPY.
FRANK! FRANK! MOOCH IS EATING HIS DRY FOOD!!!
4.18

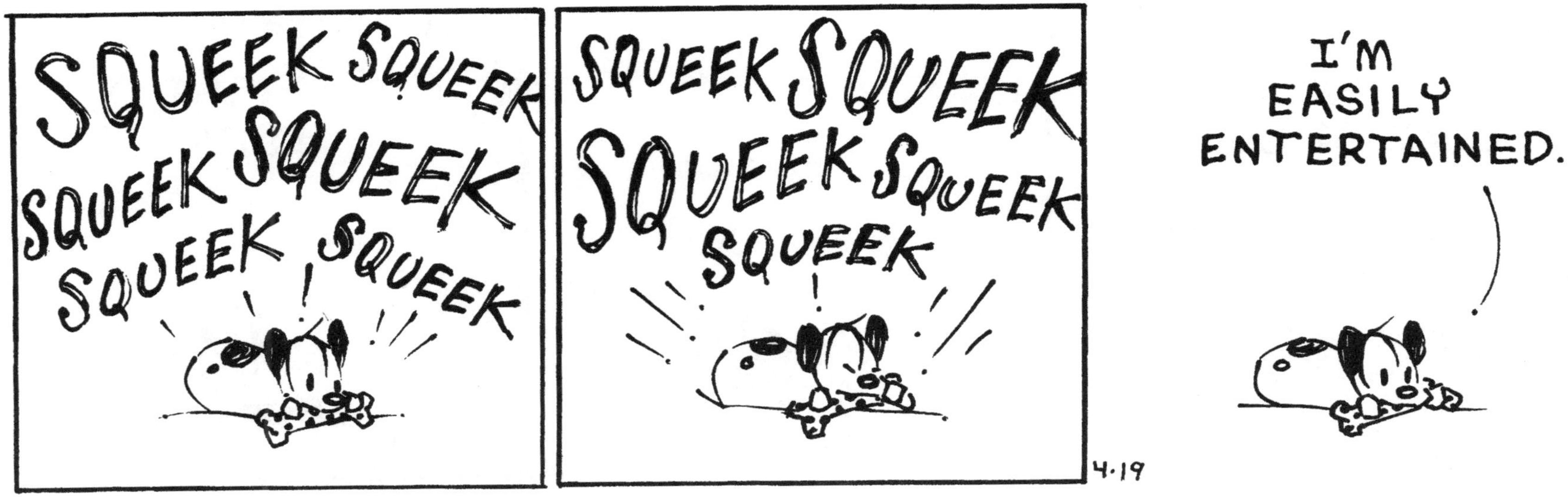
SQUEEK SQUEEK
SQUEEK SQUEEK
SQUEEK SQUEEK
SQUEEK SQUEEK
SQUEEK SQUEEK SQUEEK
SQUEEK
I'M EASILY ENTERTAINED.
4.19

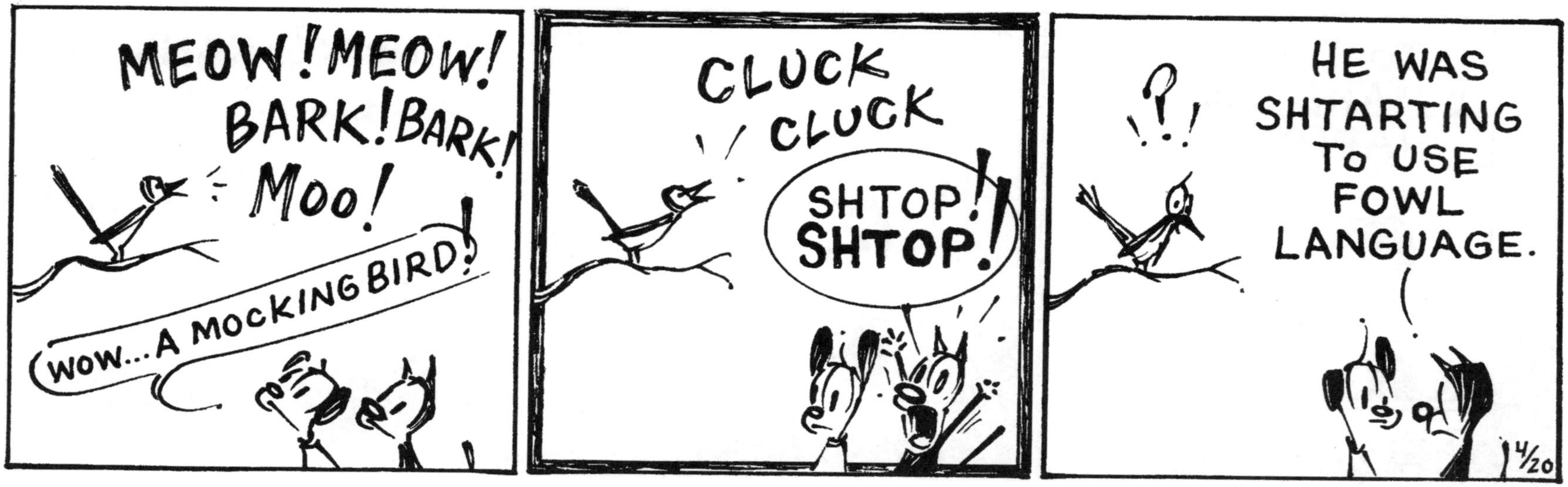
MEOW! MEOW!
BARK! BARK!
Moo!
WOW... A MOCKINGBIRD!
CLUCK
CLUCK
SHTOP! SHTOP!
HE WAS SHTARTING To USE FOWL LANGUAGE.
4/20

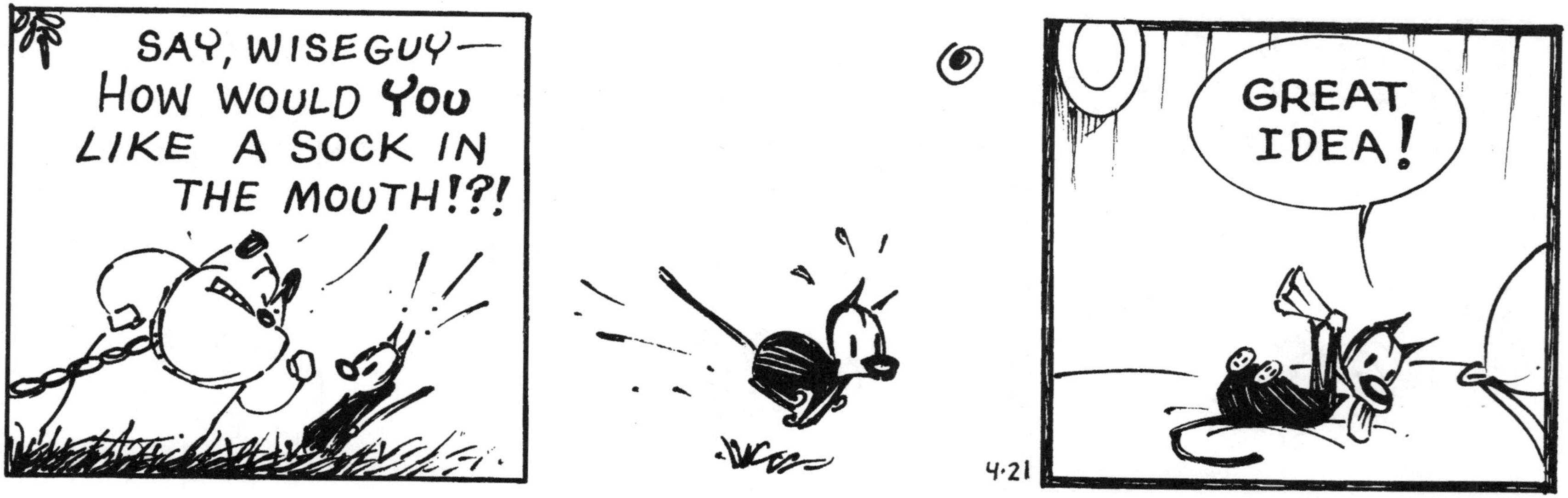
SAY, WISEGUY— HOW WOULD YOU LIKE A SOCK IN THE MOUTH!?!
4·21
GREAT IDEA!

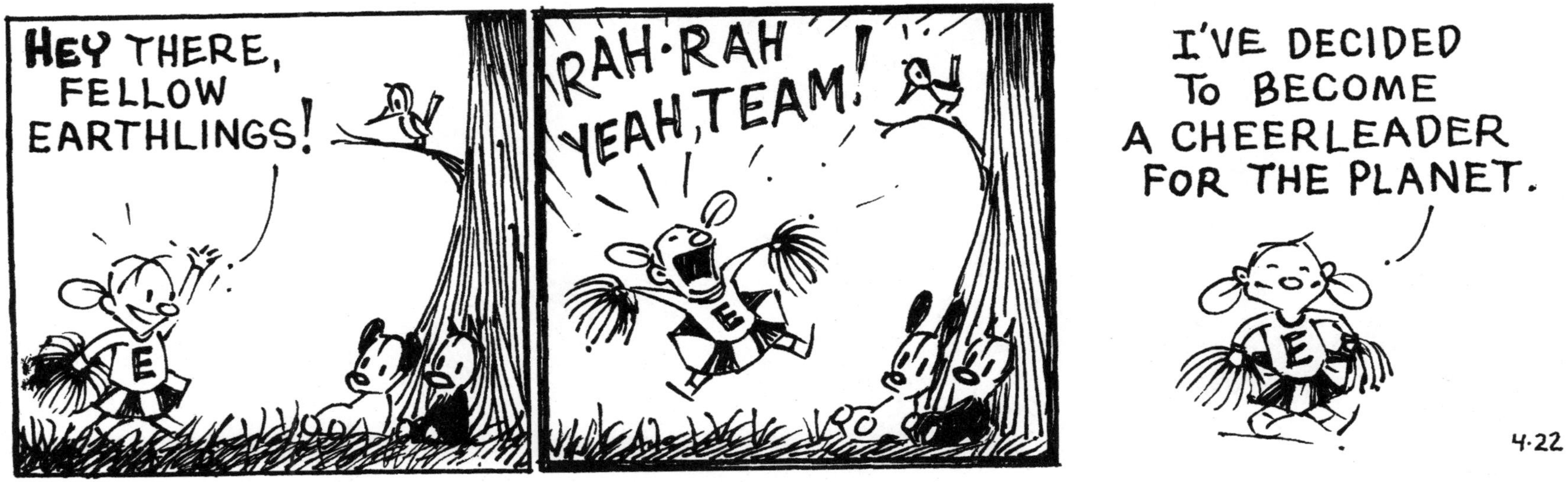
HEY THERE, FELLOW EARTHLINGS!
RAH·RAH YEAH, TEAM!
I'VE DECIDED TO BECOME A CHEERLEADER FOR THE PLANET.
4·22

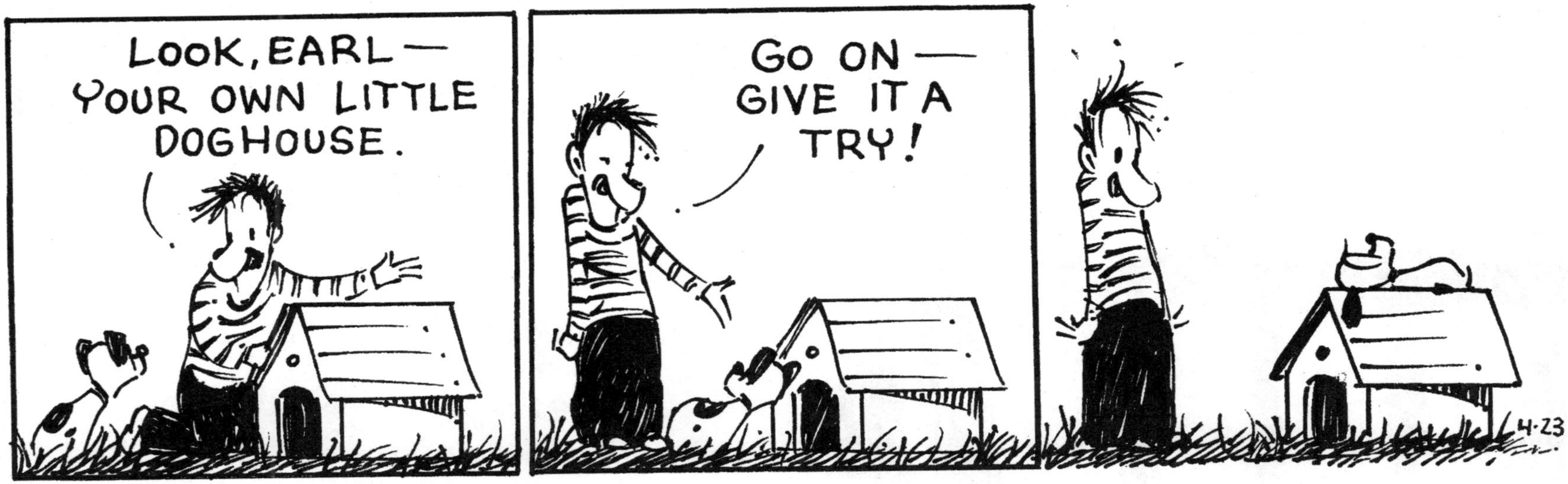
LOOK, EARL— YOUR OWN LITTLE DOGHOUSE.
GO ON— GIVE IT A TRY!
4·23

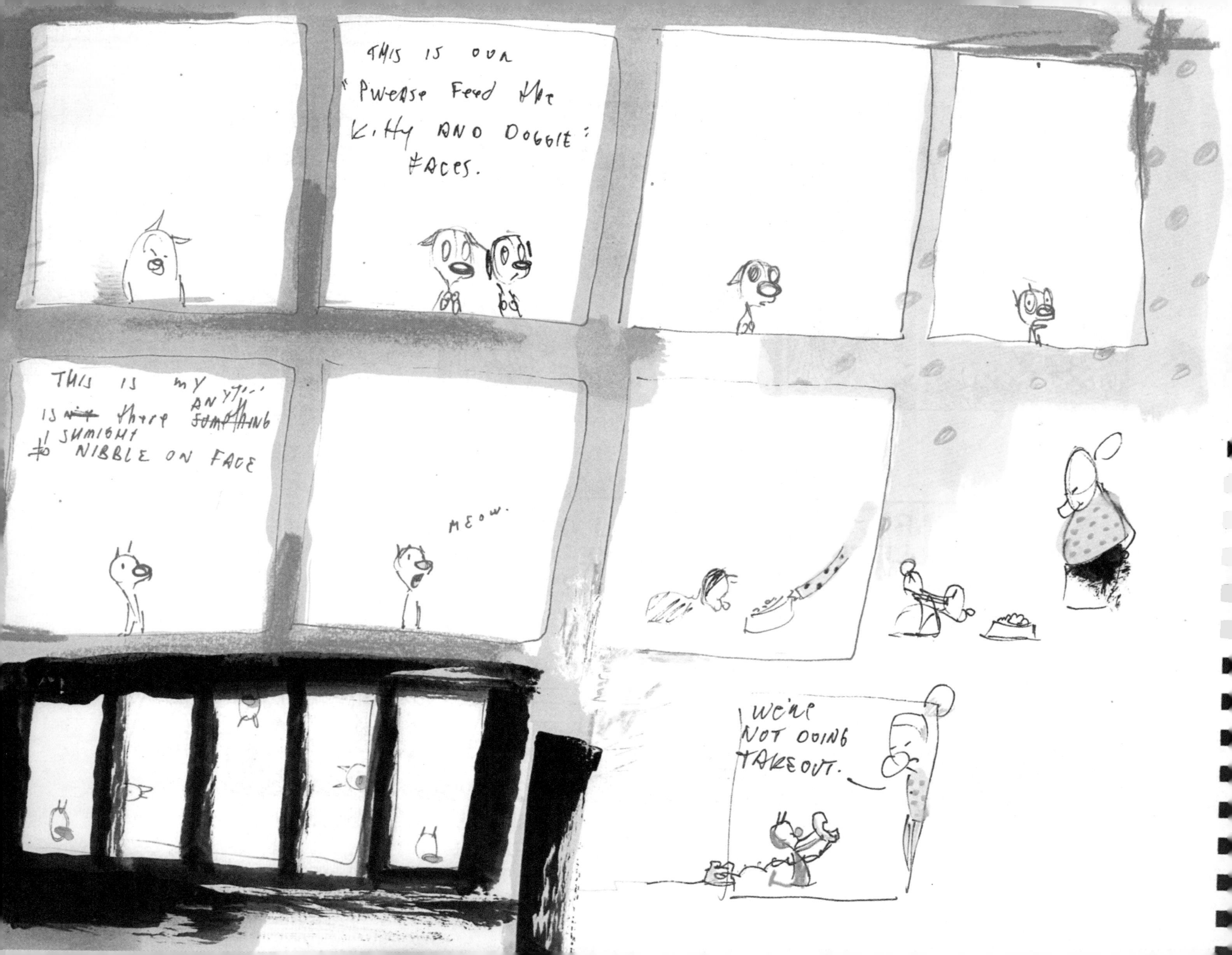
THIS IS OUR "PWEASE FEED THE KITTY AND DOGGIE" FACES.
THIS IS MY
IS THERE ANYTHING
TO NIBBLE ON FACE
MEOW.
WE'RE NOT DOING TAKEOUT.

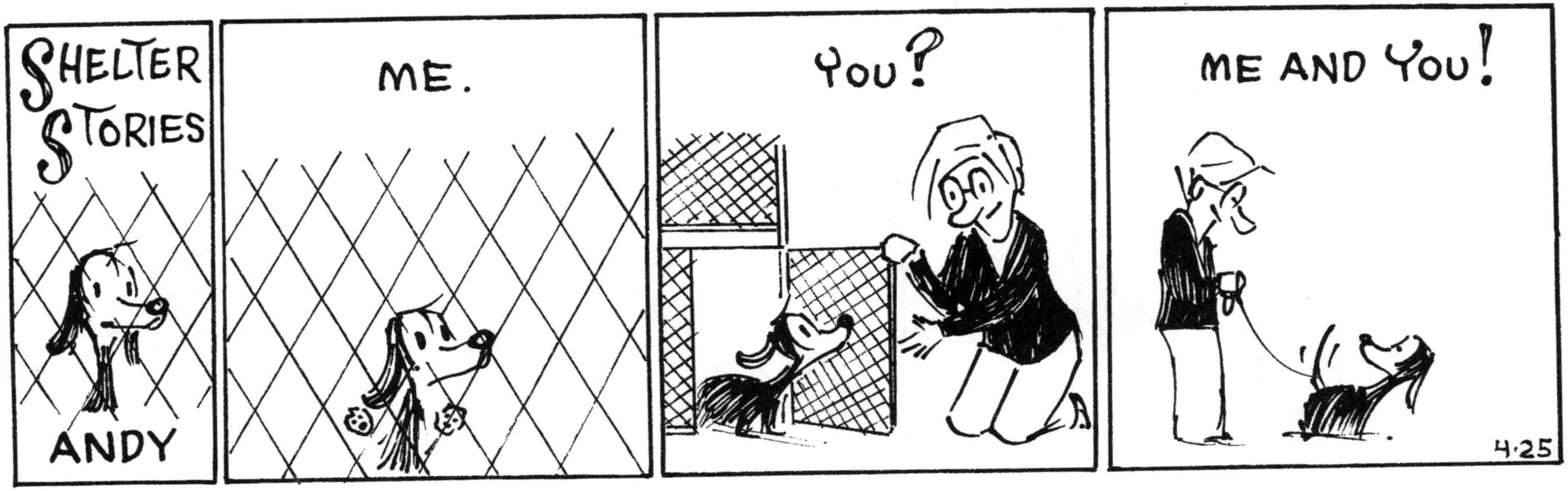
SHELTER STORIES
ANDY
ME.
YOU?
ME AND YOU!
4·25

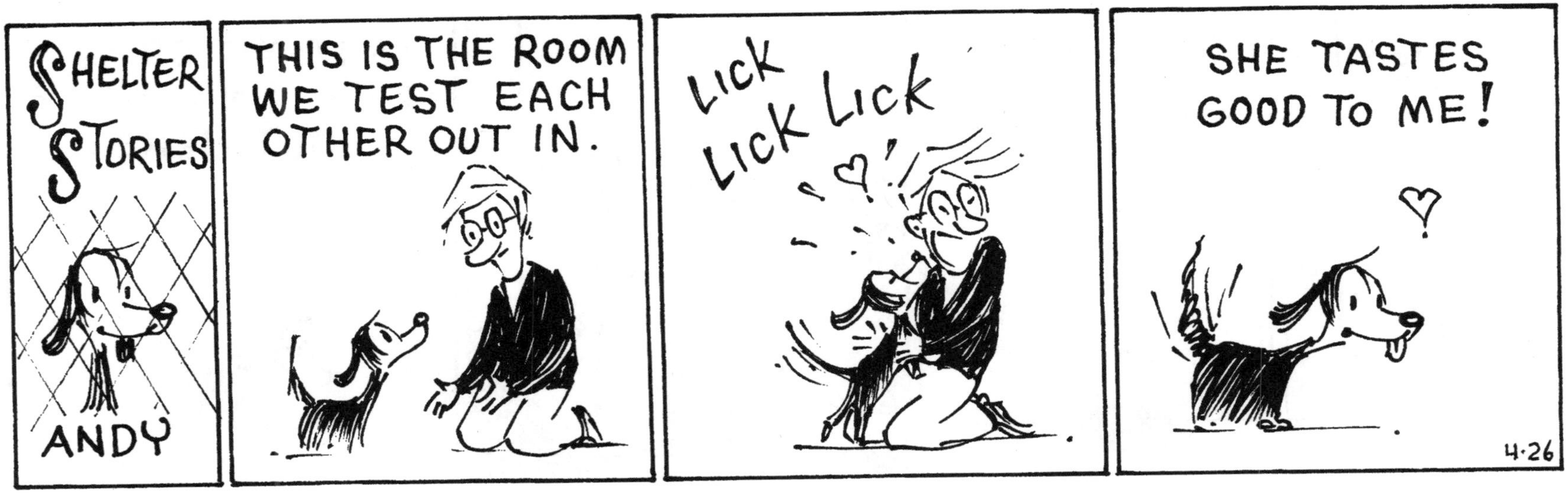
SHELTER STORIES
ANDY
THIS IS THE ROOM WE TEST EACH OTHER OUT IN.
LICK LICK LICK
SHE TASTES GOOD TO ME!
4·26

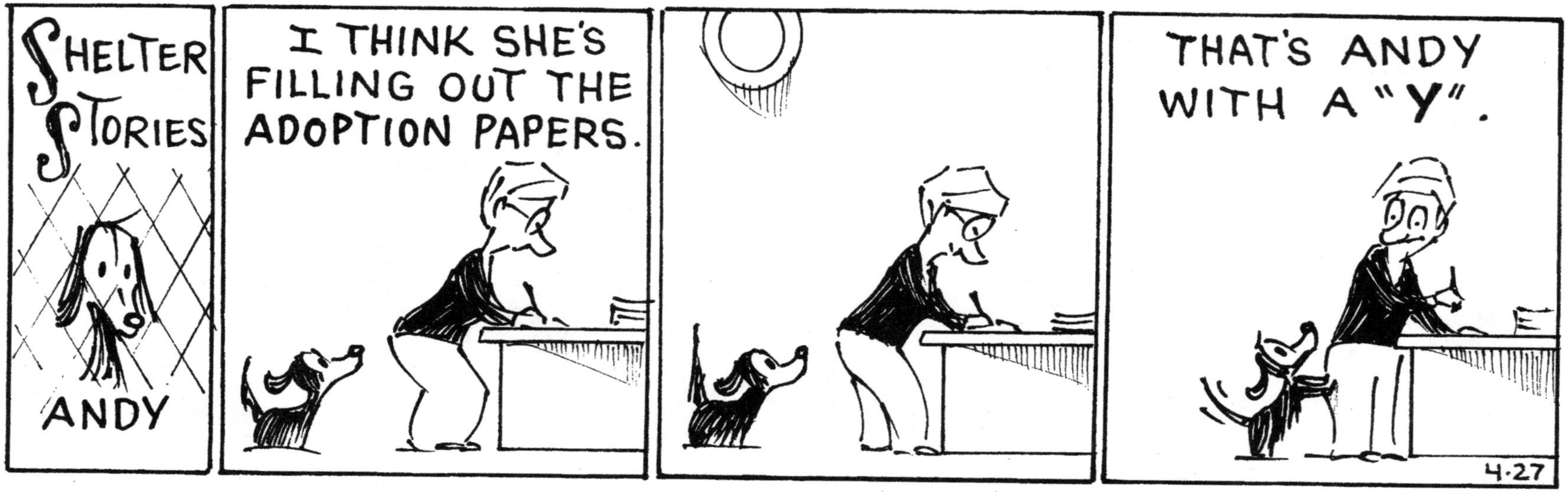
SHELTER STORIES
ANDY
I THINK SHE'S FILLING OUT THE ADOPTION PAPERS.
THAT'S ANDY WITH A "Y".
4·27

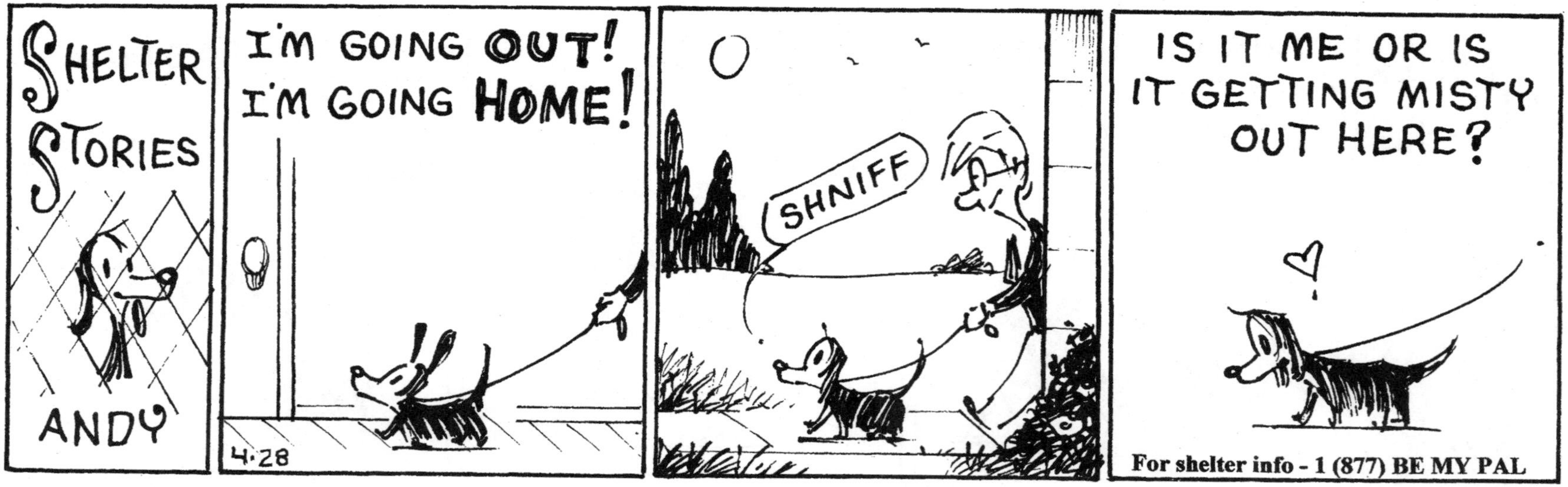
SHELTER STORIES
ANDY
I'M GOING OUT! I'M GOING HOME!
4·28
SHNIFF
IS IT ME OR IS IT GETTING MISTY OUT HERE?
For shelter info - 1 (877) BE MY PAL

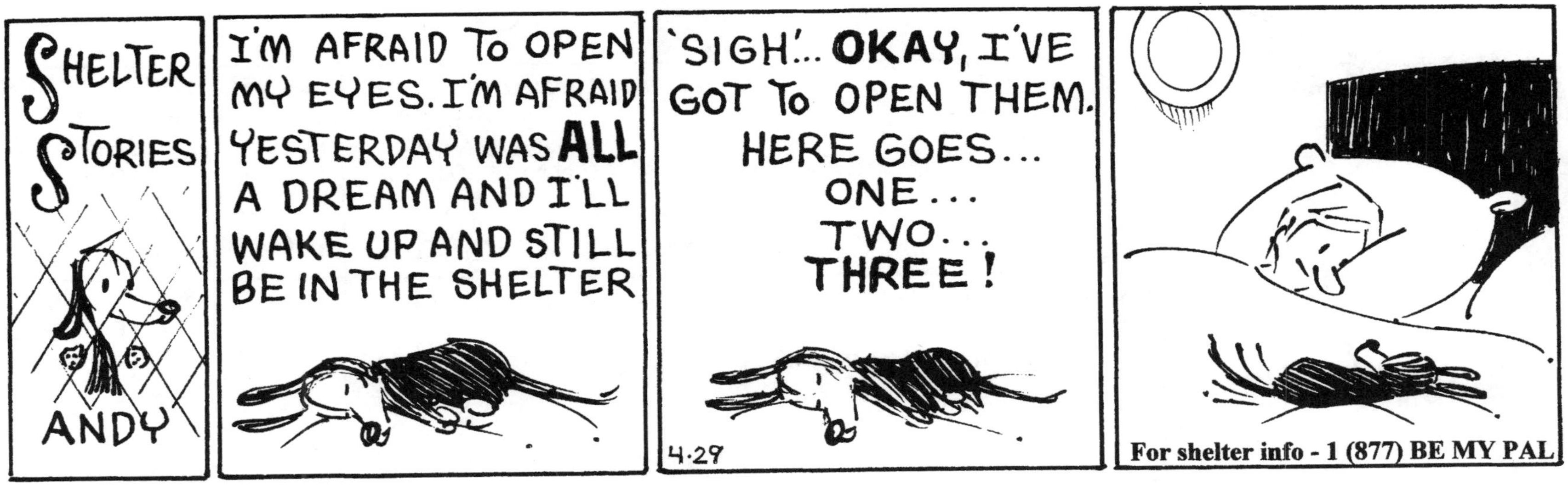
SHELTER STORIES
ANDY
I'M AFRAID TO OPEN MY EYES. I'M AFRAID YESTERDAY WAS ALL A DREAM AND I'LL WAKE UP AND STILL BE IN THE SHELTER
`SIGH'... OKAY, I'VE GOT TO OPEN THEM. HERE GOES... ONE... TWO... THREE!
4·29
For shelter info - 1 (877) BE MY PAL

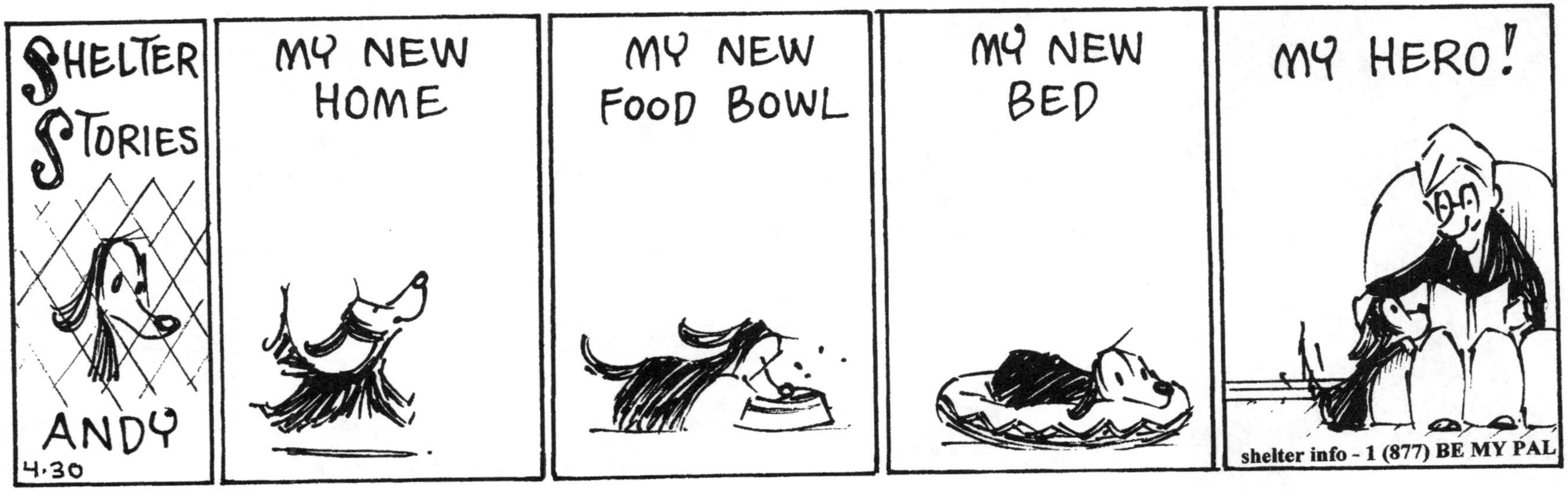
SHELTER STORIES
ANDY
4·30
MY NEW HOME
MY NEW FOOD BOWL
MY NEW BED
MY HERO!
shelter info - 1 (877) BE MY PAL

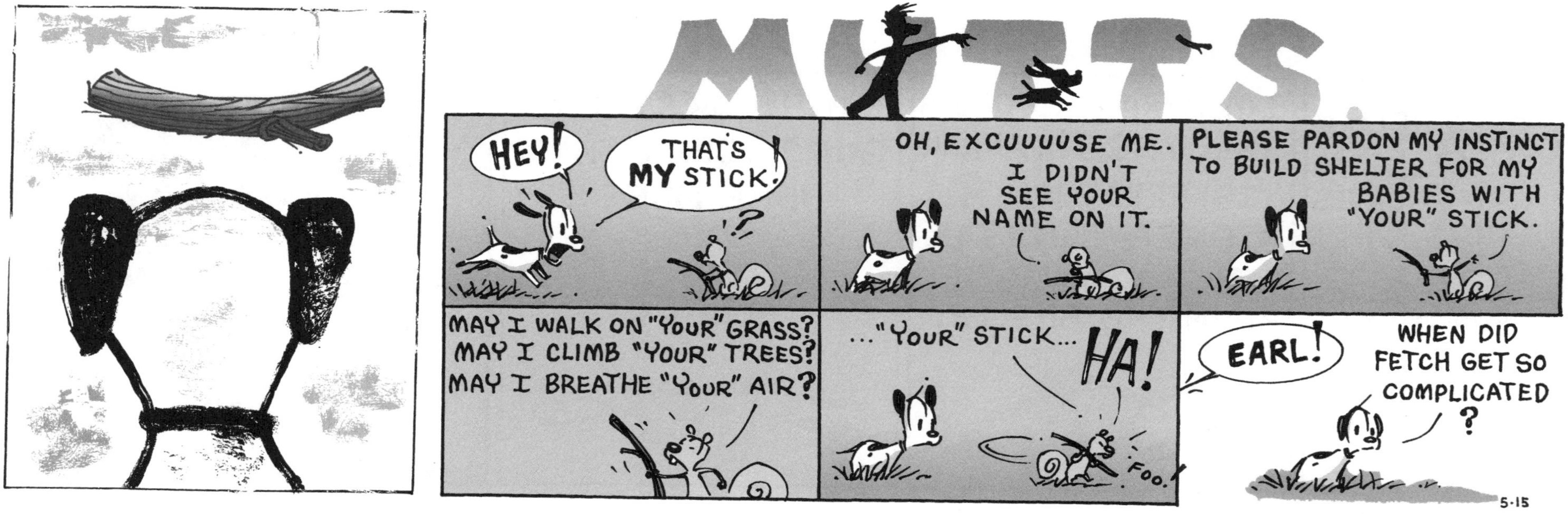
MUTTS.
HEY!
THAT'S MY STICK!
OH, EXCUUUUSE ME.
I DIDN'T SEE YOUR NAME ON IT.
PLEASE PARDON MY INSTINCT TO BUILD SHELTER FOR MY BABIES WITH "YOUR" STICK.
MAY I WALK ON "YOUR" GRASS? MAY I CLIMB "YOUR" TREES? MAY I BREATHE "YOUR" AIR?
..."YOUR" STICK... HA!
FOO.
EARL!
WHEN DID FETCH GET SO COMPLICATED?
5-15

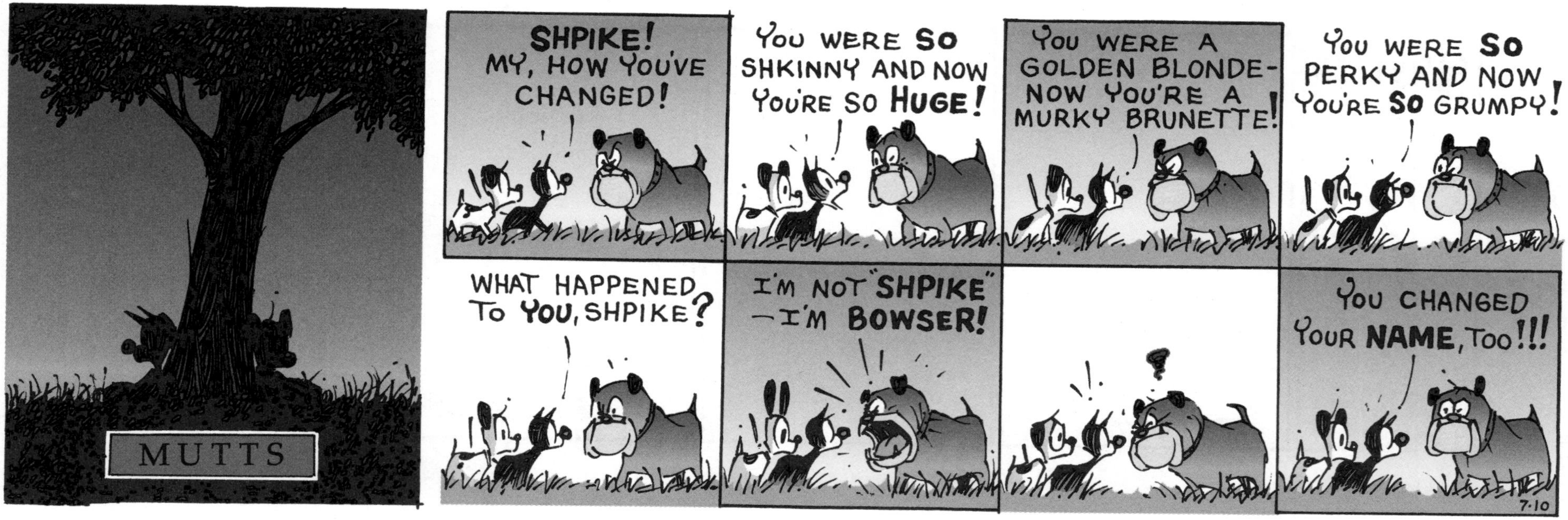
MUTTS
SHPIKE! MY, HOW YOU'VE CHANGED!
YOU WERE SO SHKINNY AND NOW YOU'RE SO HUGE!
YOU WERE A GOLDEN BLONDE- NOW YOU'RE A MURKY BRUNETTE!
YOU WERE SO PERKY AND NOW YOU'RE SO GRUMPY!
WHAT HAPPENED TO YOU, SHPIKE?
I'M NOT "SHPIKE" —I'M BOWSER!
YOU CHANGED YOUR NAME, TOO!!!
7-10

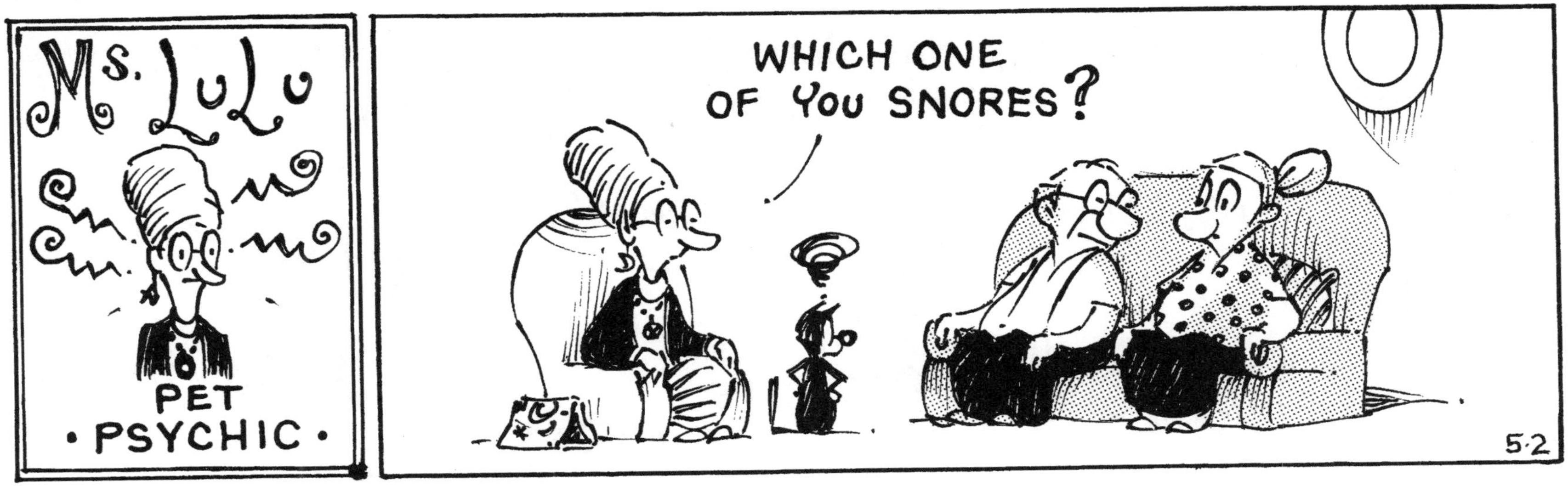
Ms. LuLu
PET
• PSYCHIC •
WHICH ONE OF YOU SNORES?
5·2

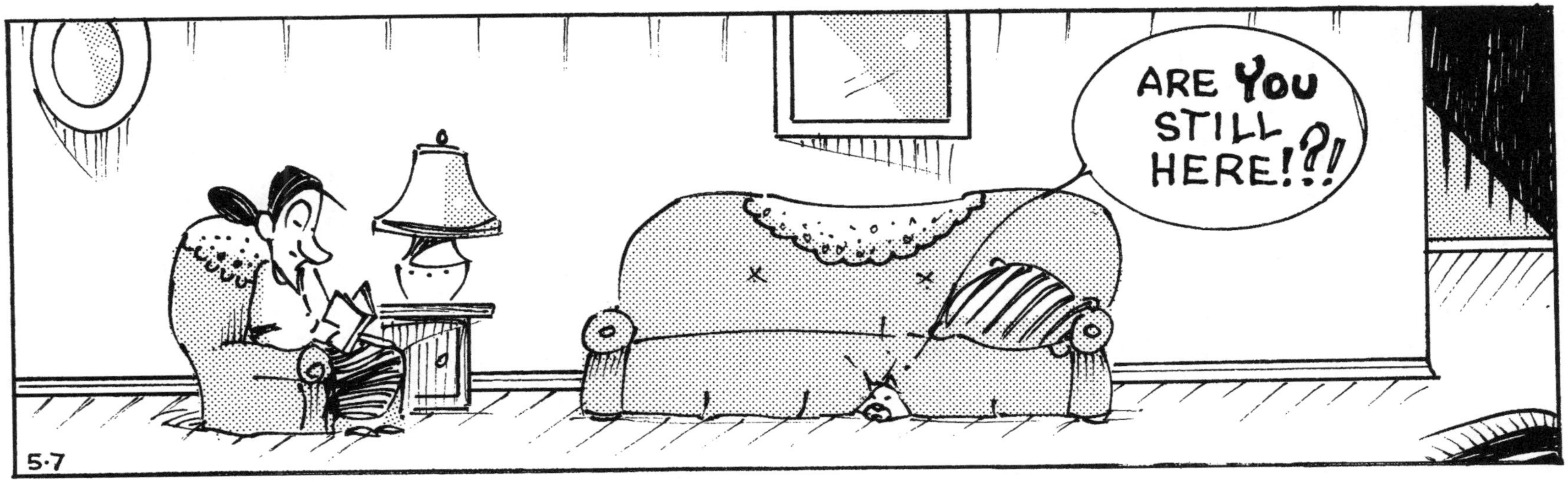
ARE YOU STILL HERE!?!
5·7

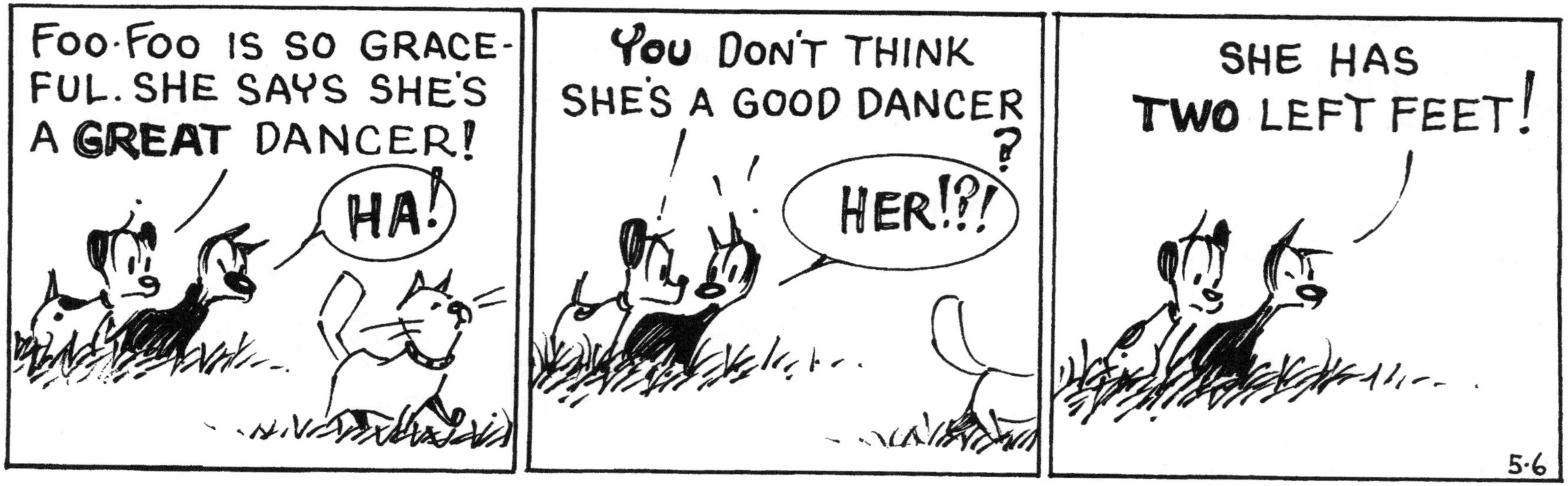
FOO·FOO IS SO GRACE-FUL. SHE SAYS SHE'S A GREAT DANCER!
HA!
YOU DON'T THINK SHE'S A GOOD DANCER?
HER!?!
SHE HAS TWO LEFT FEET!
5·6

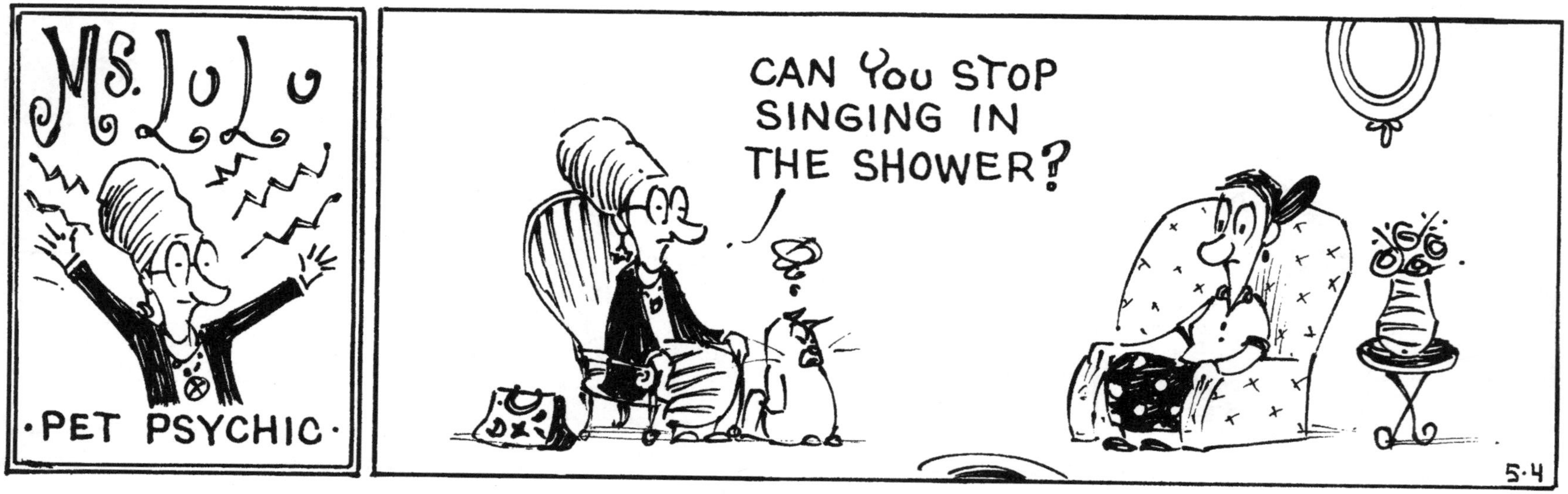
MS. LULU
·PET PSYCHIC·
CAN YOU STOP SINGING IN THE SHOWER?
5·4

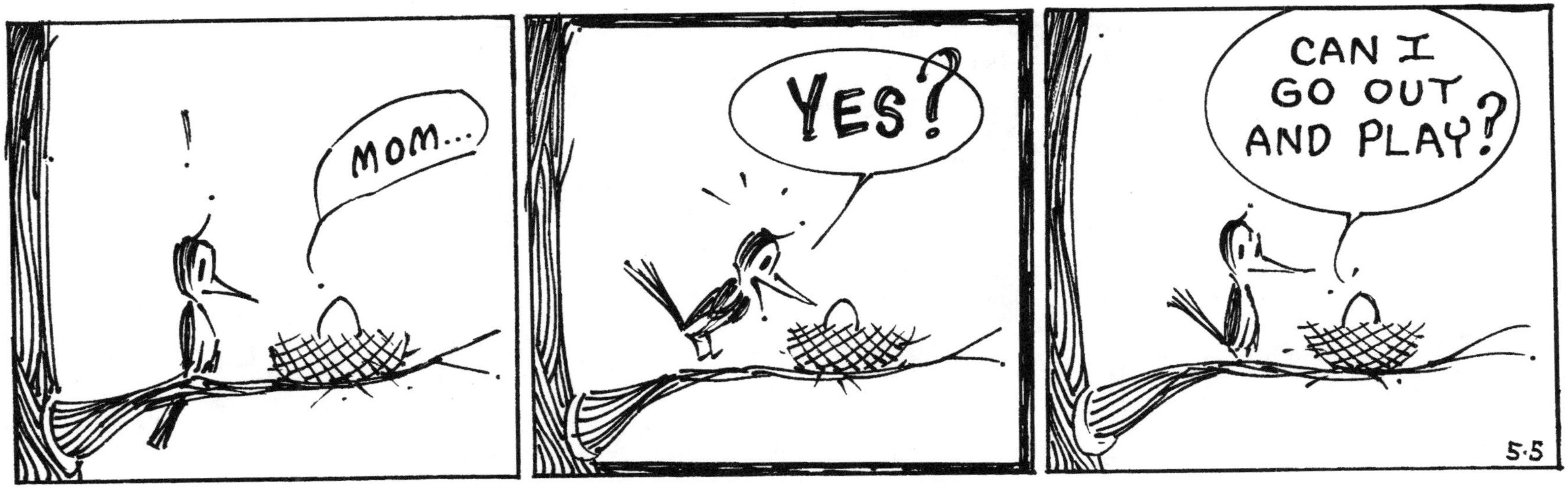
MOM...
YES?
CAN I GO OUT AND PLAY?
5·5

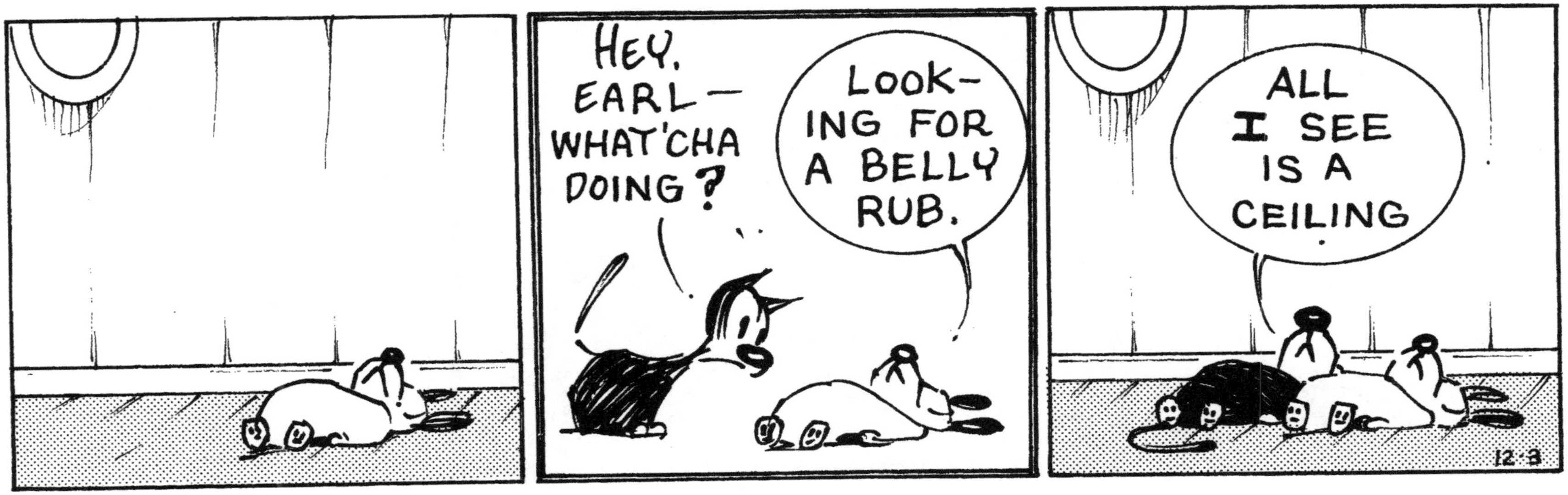
HEY, EARL— WHAT'CHA DOING?
LOOK-ING FOR A BELLY RUB.
ALL I SEE IS A CEILING
12·3

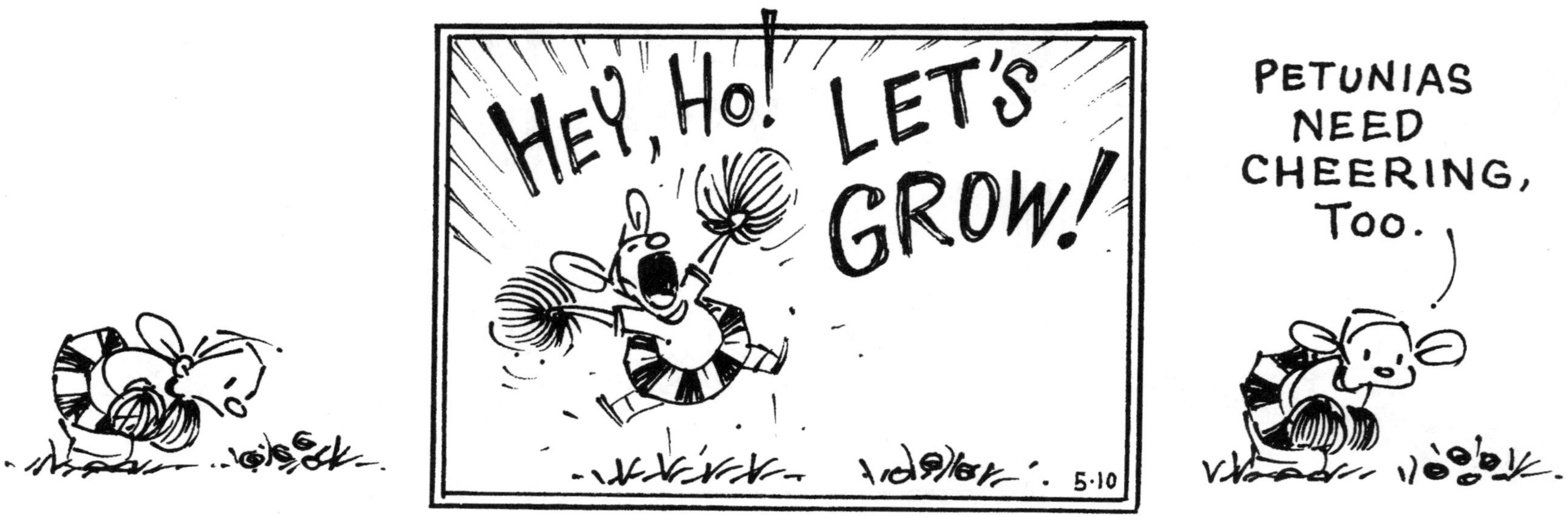
HEY, HO! LET'S GROW!
PETUNIAS NEED CHEERING, TOO.
5·10

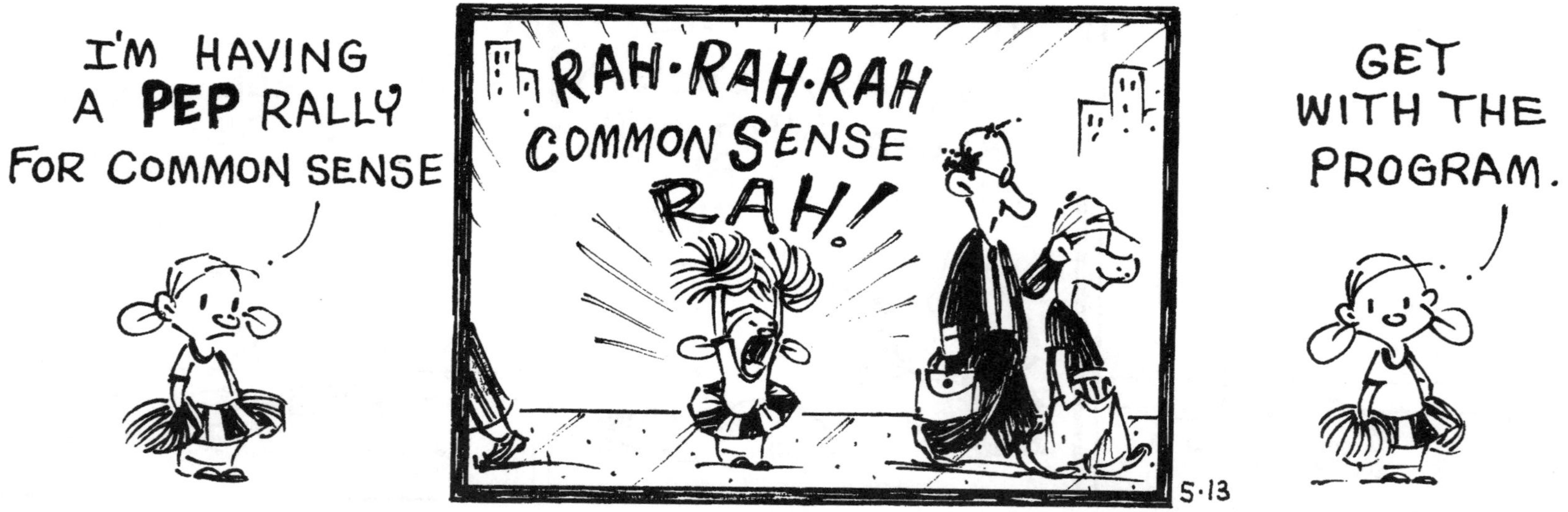
I'M HAVING A PEP RALLY FOR COMMON SENSE
RAH·RAH·RAH COMMON SENSE RAH!
GET WITH THE PROGRAM.
5·13

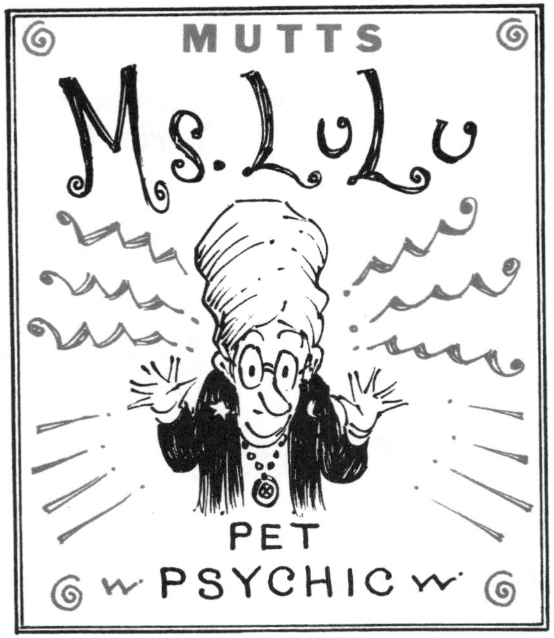
MUTTS
Ms. LuLu
PET
PSYCHIC

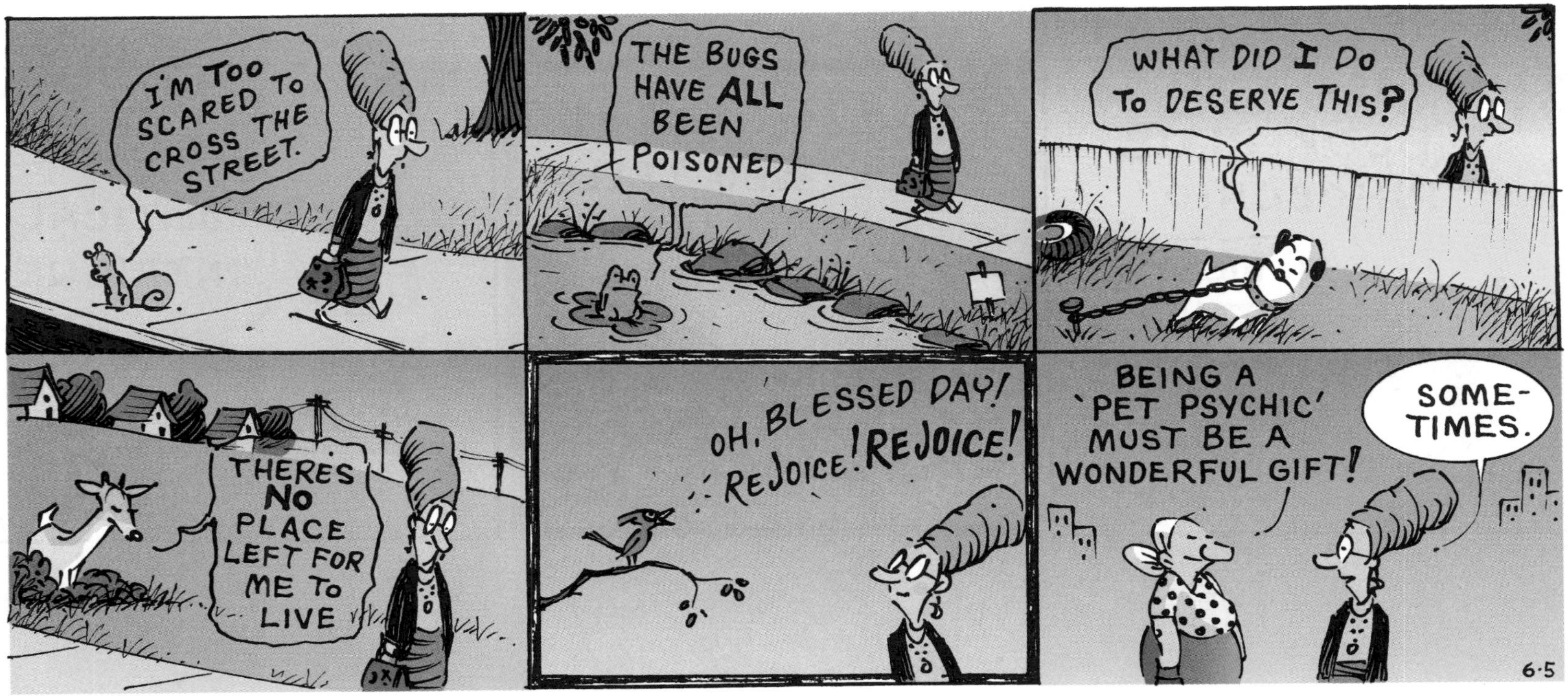
I'M TOO SCARED TO CROSS THE STREET.
THE BUGS HAVE ALL BEEN POISONED
WHAT DID I DO TO DESERVE THIS?
THERES NO PLACE LEFT FOR ME TO LIVE
OH, BLESSED DAY! REJOICE! REJOICE!
BEING A 'PET PSYCHIC' MUST BE A WONDERFUL GIFT!
SOME-TIMES.
6·5

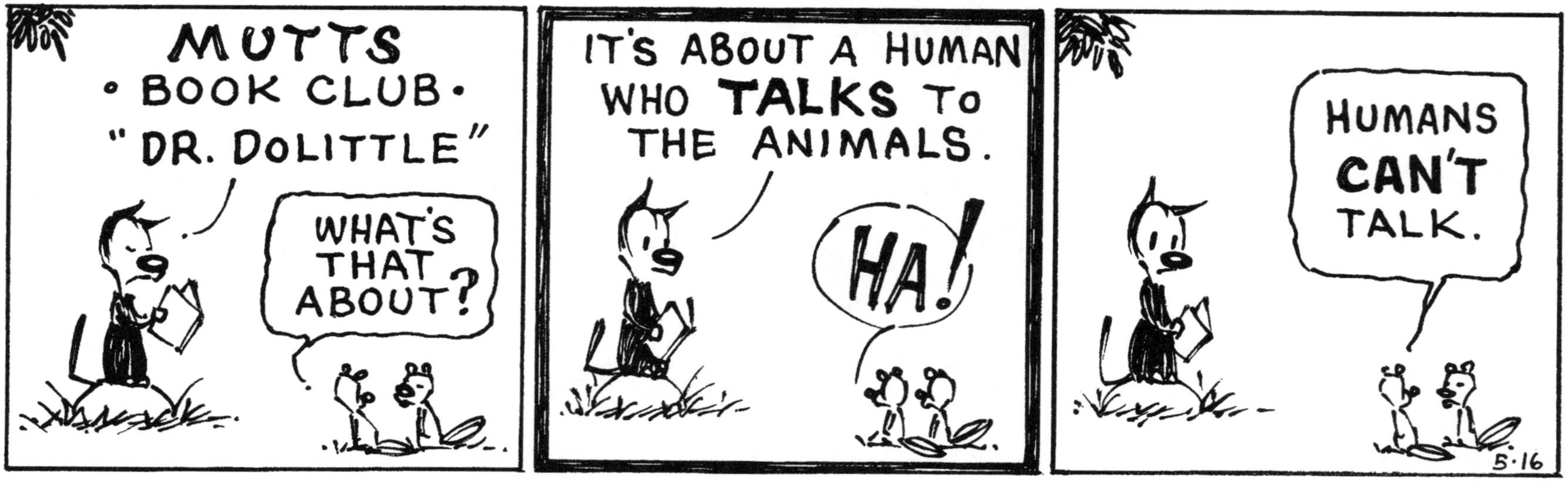
MUTTS
• BOOK CLUB •
"DR. DOLITTLE"
WHAT'S THAT ABOUT?
IT'S ABOUT A HUMAN WHO TALKS TO THE ANIMALS.
HA!
HUMANS CAN'T TALK.
5·16

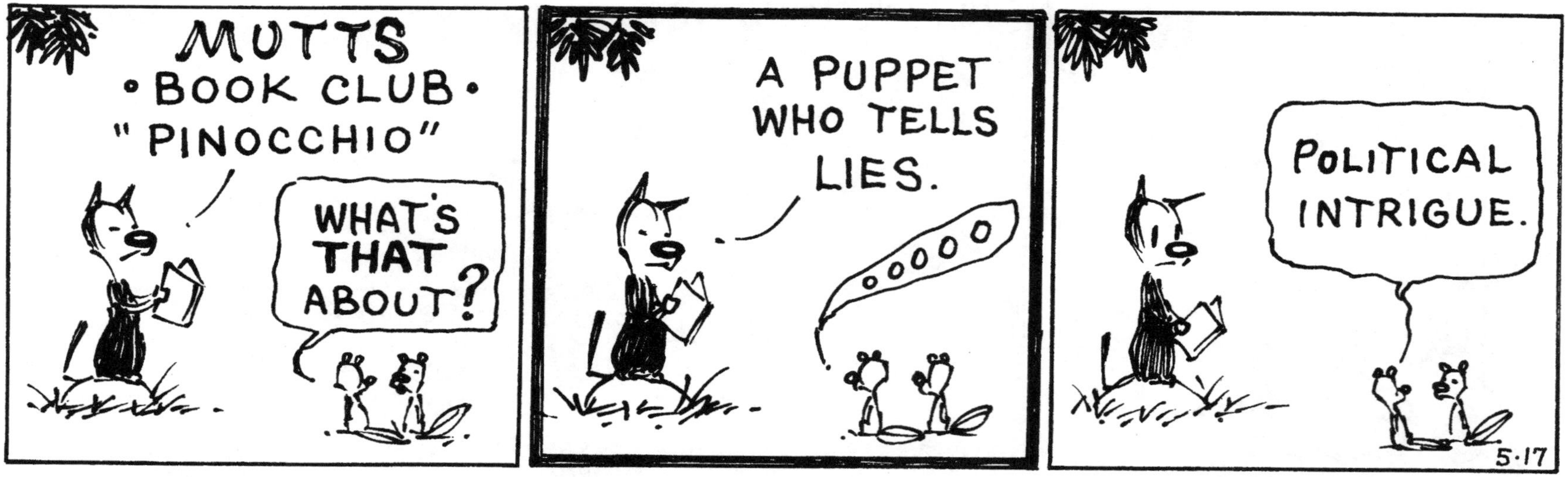
MUTTS
• BOOK CLUB •
"PINOCCHIO"
WHAT'S THAT ABOUT?
A PUPPET WHO TELLS LIES.
OOOOO
POLITICAL INTRIGUE.
5·17

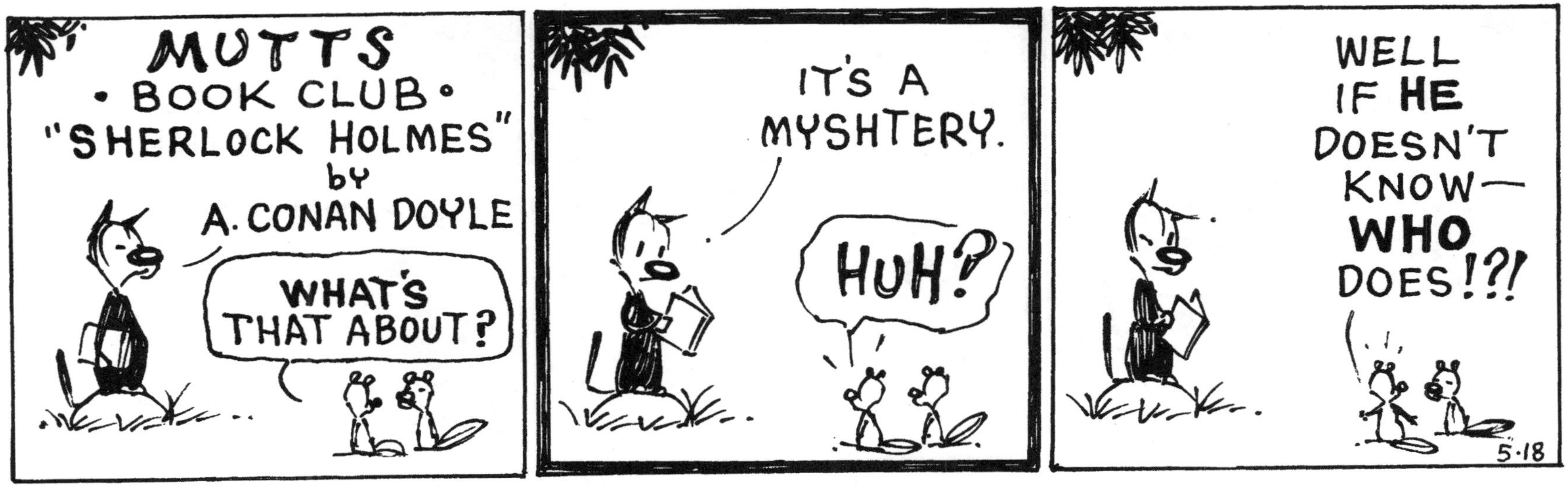
MUTTS
• BOOK CLUB •
"SHERLOCK HOLMES"
by
A. CONAN DOYLE
WHAT'S THAT ABOUT?
IT'S A MYSHTERY.
HUH?
WELL IF HE DOESN'T KNOW— WHO DOES!?!
5·18

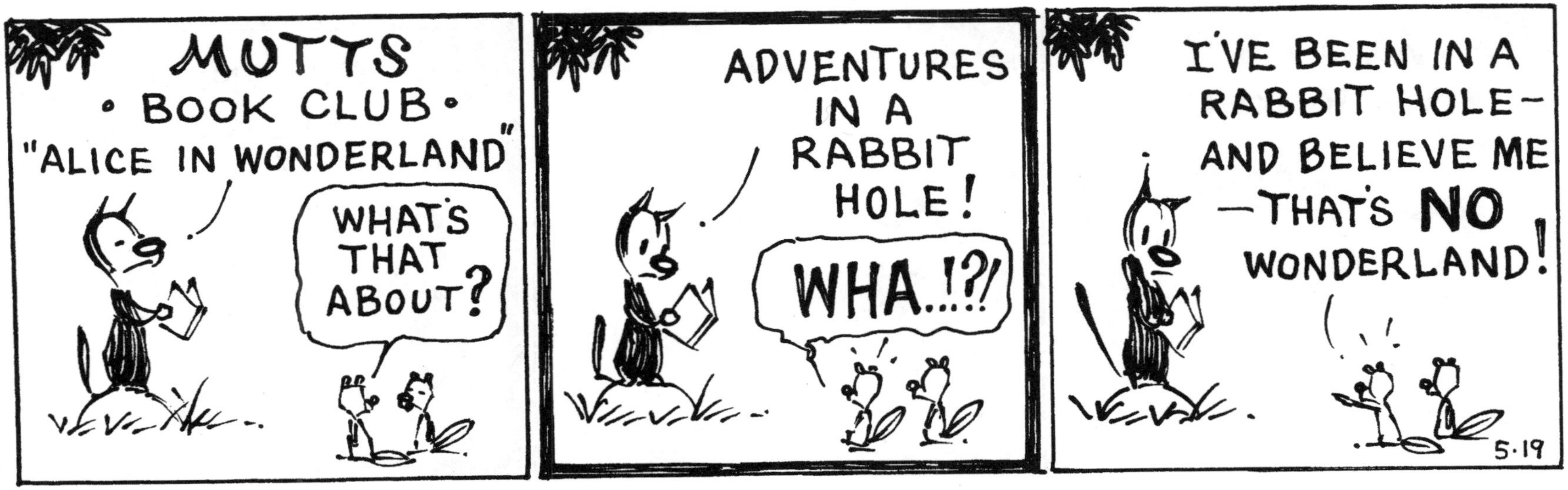
MUTTS
• BOOK CLUB •
"ALICE IN WONDERLAND"
WHAT'S THAT ABOUT?
ADVENTURES IN A RABBIT HOLE!
WHA..!?!
I'VE BEEN IN A RABBIT HOLE— AND BELIEVE ME —THAT'S NO WONDERLAND!
5·19

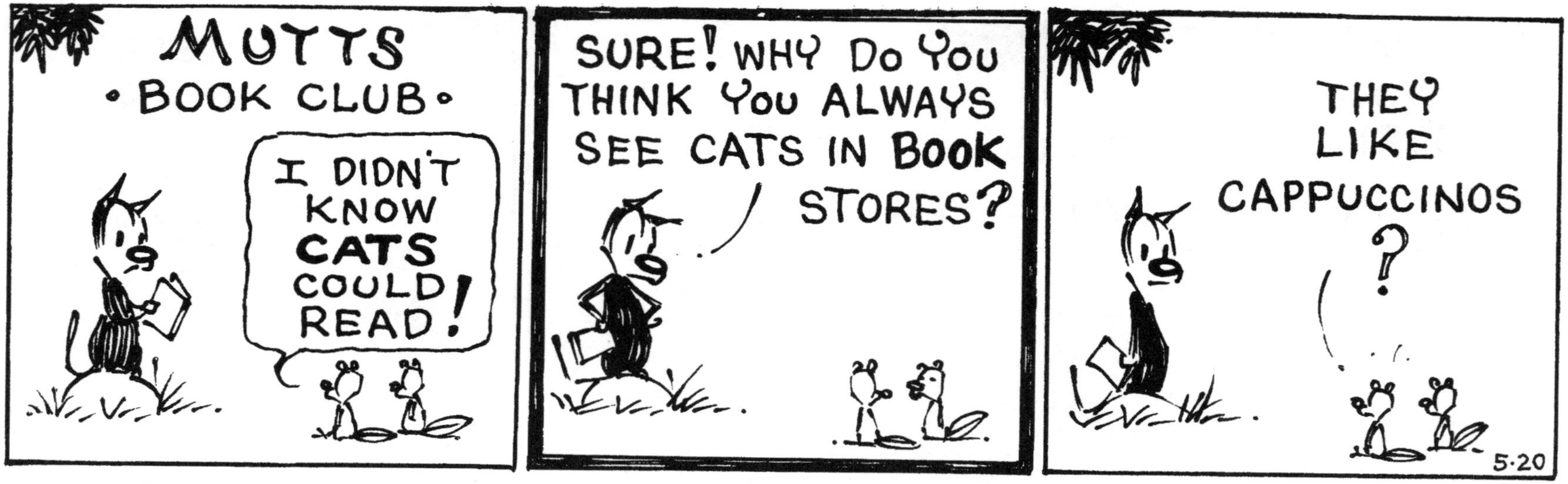
MUTTS
• BOOK CLUB •
I DIDN'T KNOW CATS COULD READ!
SURE! WHY DO YOU THINK YOU ALWAYS SEE CATS IN BOOK STORES?
THEY LIKE CAPPUCCINOS
?
5·20

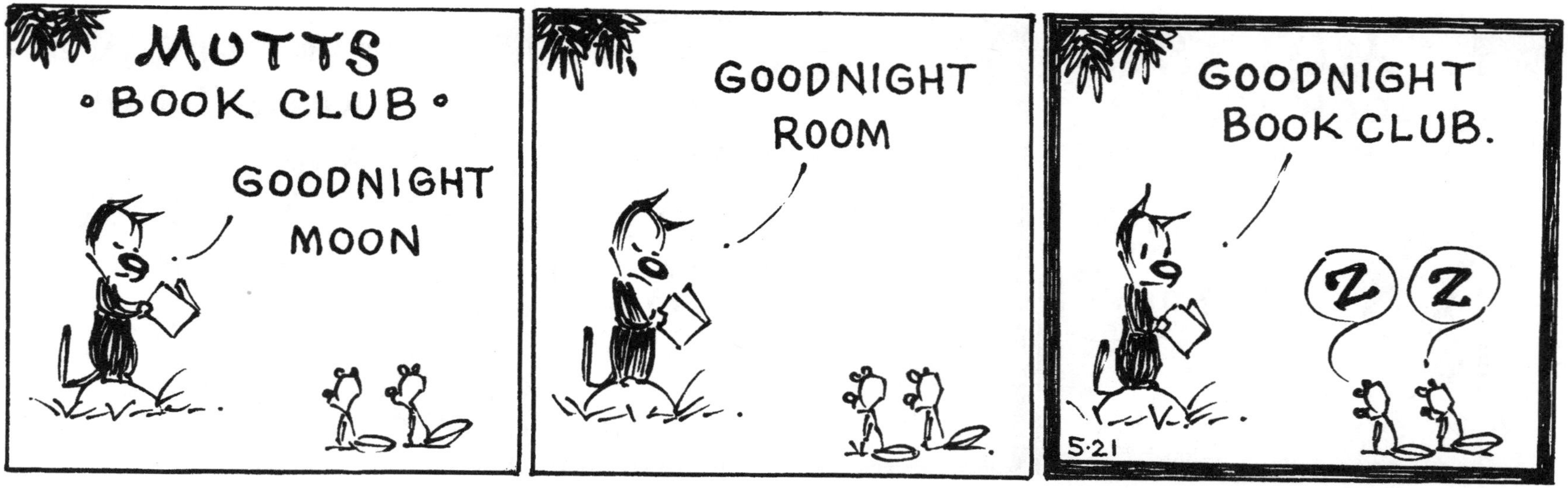
MUTTS
• BOOK CLUB •
GOODNIGHT MOON
GOODNIGHT ROOM
GOODNIGHT BOOK CLUB.
Z
Z
5·21

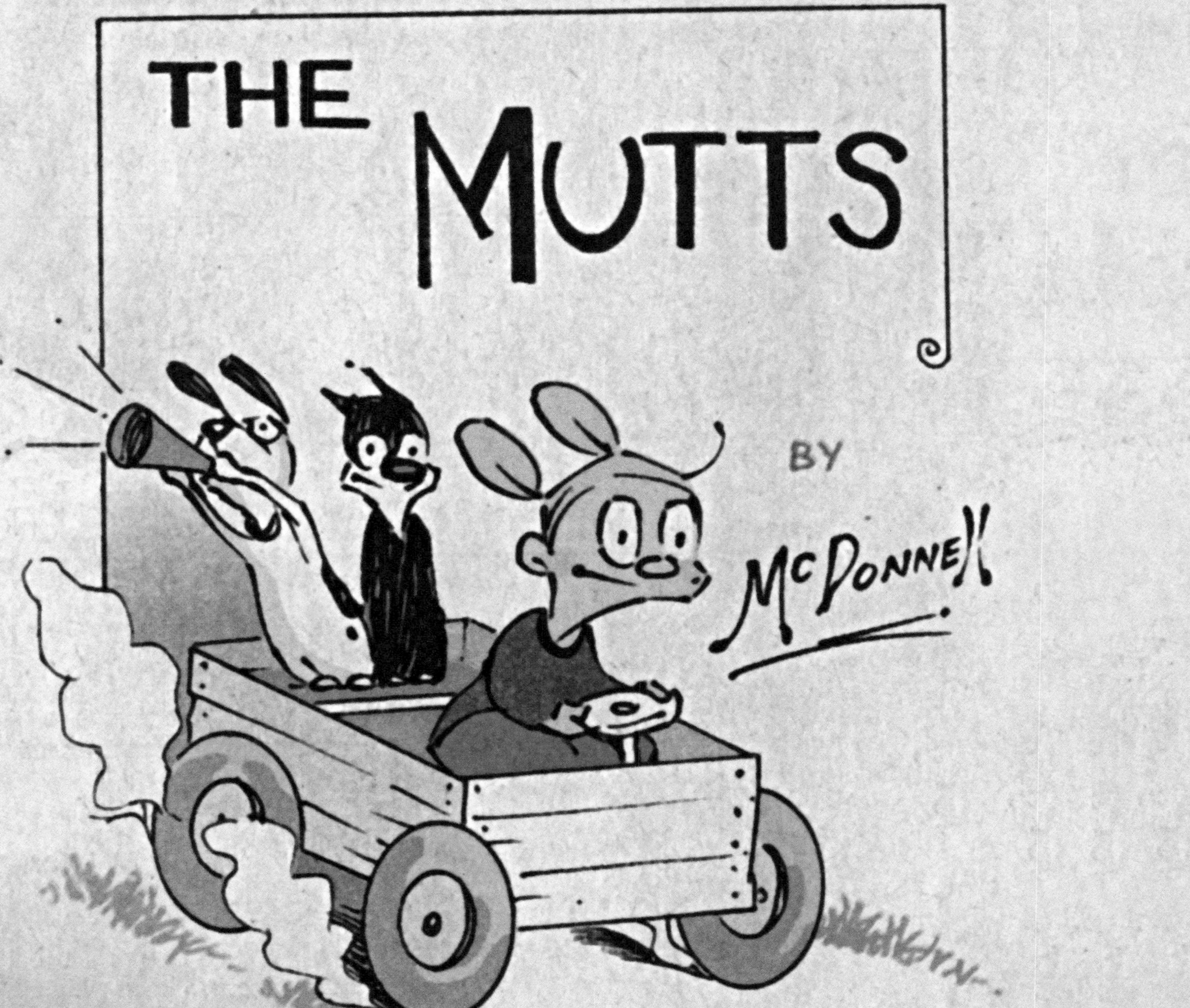
THE MUTTS
BY
McDONNELL

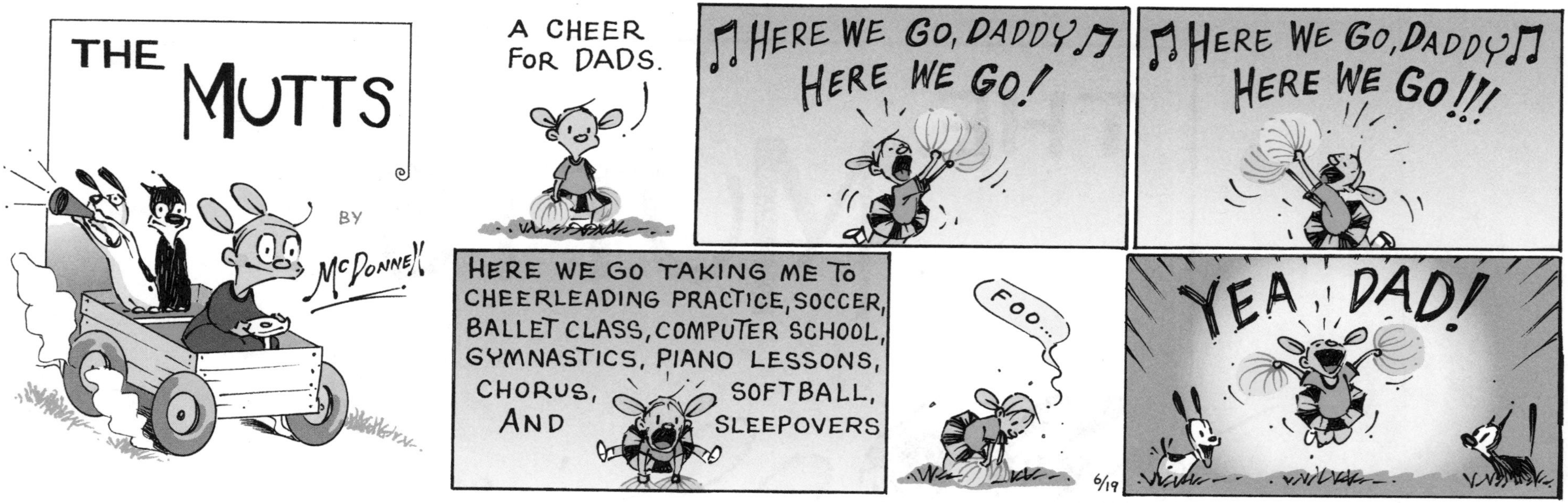
THE MUTTS
BY
McDONNELL
A CHEER FOR DADS.
♫ HERE WE GO, DADDY ♫ HERE WE GO!
♫ HERE WE GO, DADDY ♫ HERE WE GO!!!
HERE WE GO TAKING ME TO CHEERLEADING PRACTICE, SOCCER, BALLET CLASS, COMPUTER SCHOOL, GYMNASTICS, PIANO LESSONS, CHORUS, SOFTBALL, AND SLEEPOVERS
FOO...
6/19
YEA, DAD!

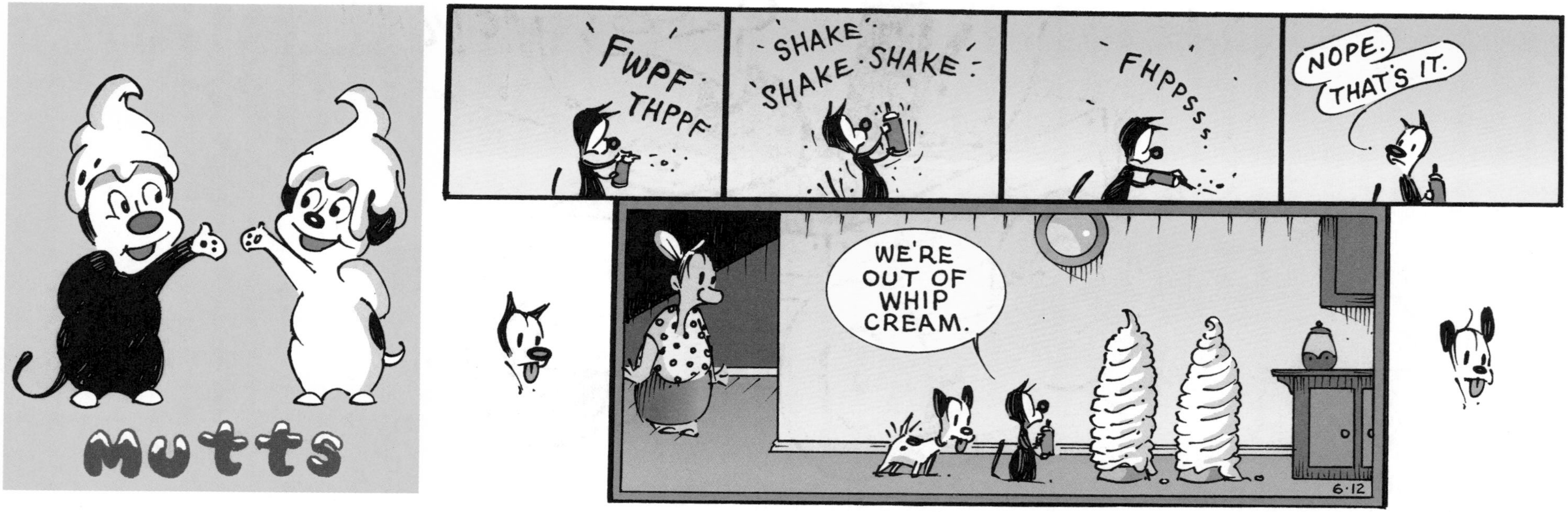
Mutts
FWPF THPPF
SHAKE SHAKE SHAKE
FHPPSSS
NOPE. THAT'S IT.
WE'RE OUT OF WHIP CREAM.
6·12

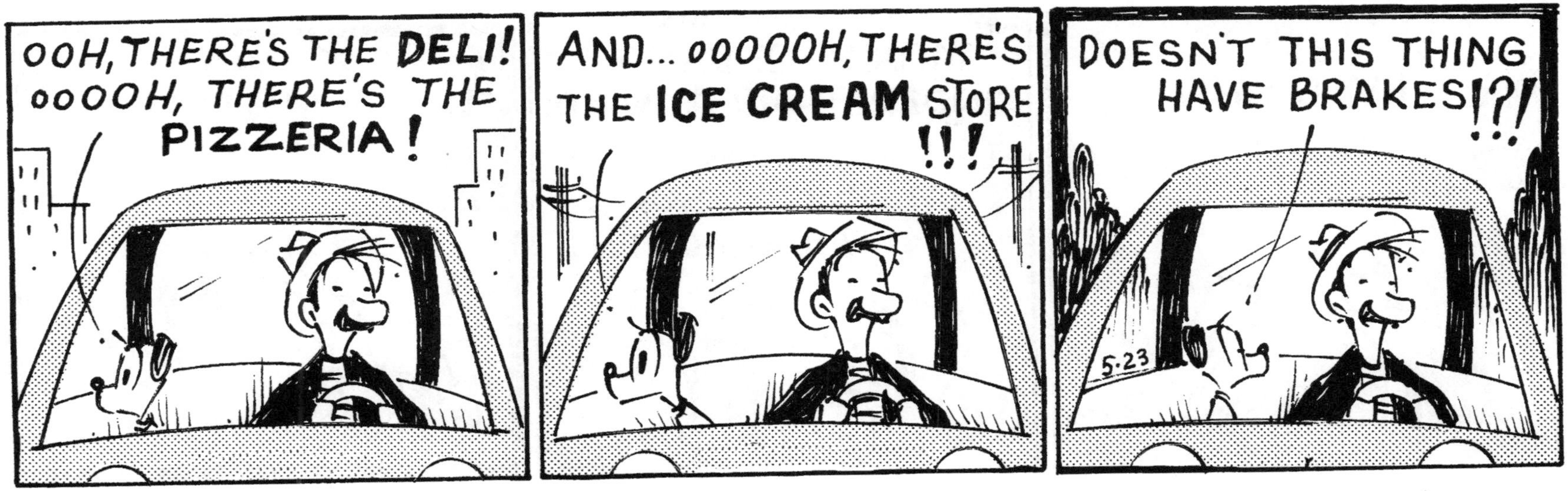
OOH, THERE'S THE DELI! OOOOH, THERE'S THE PIZZERIA!
AND... OOOOOH, THERE'S THE ICE CREAM STORE!!!
DOESN'T THIS THING HAVE BRAKES!?!
5-23

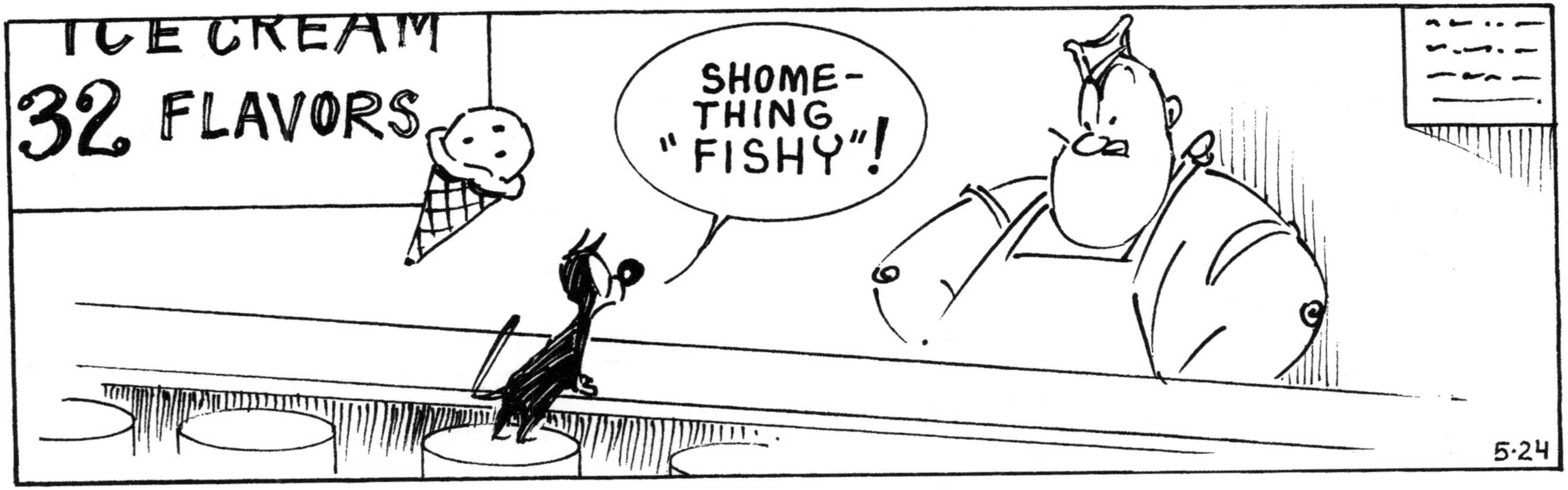
ICE CREAM
32 FLAVORS
SHOME-THING "FISHY"!
5-24

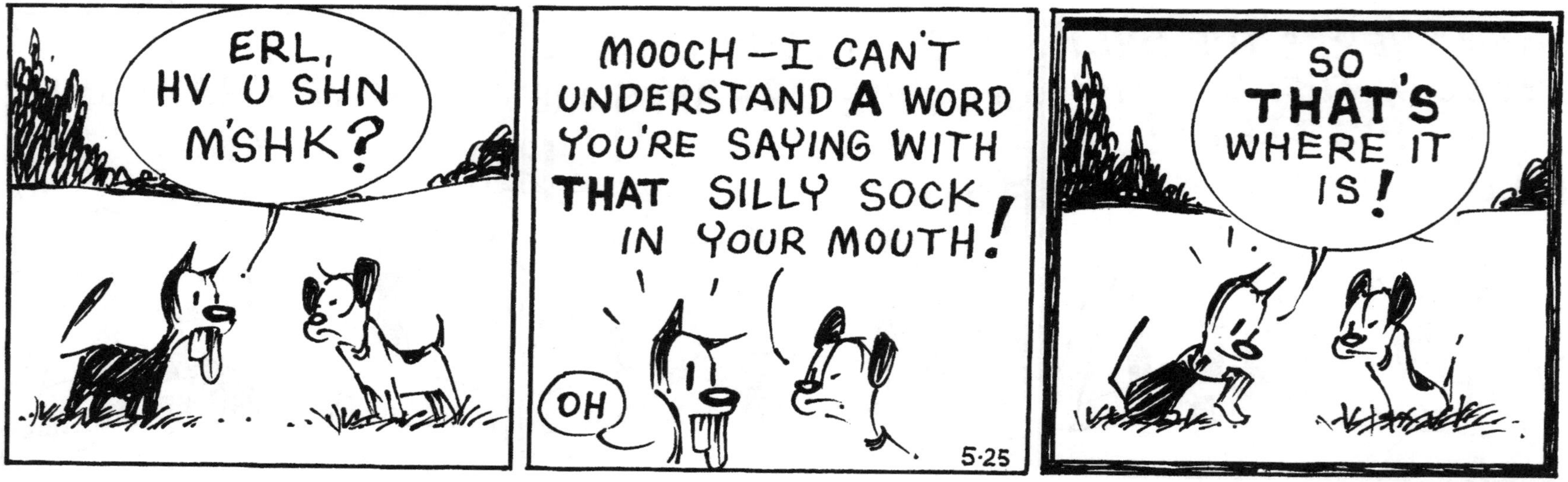
ERL, HV U SHN M'SHK?
MOOCH—I CAN'T UNDERSTAND **A** WORD YOU'RE SAYING WITH **THAT** SILLY SOCK IN YOUR MOUTH!
OH
5·25
SO **THAT'S** WHERE IT IS!

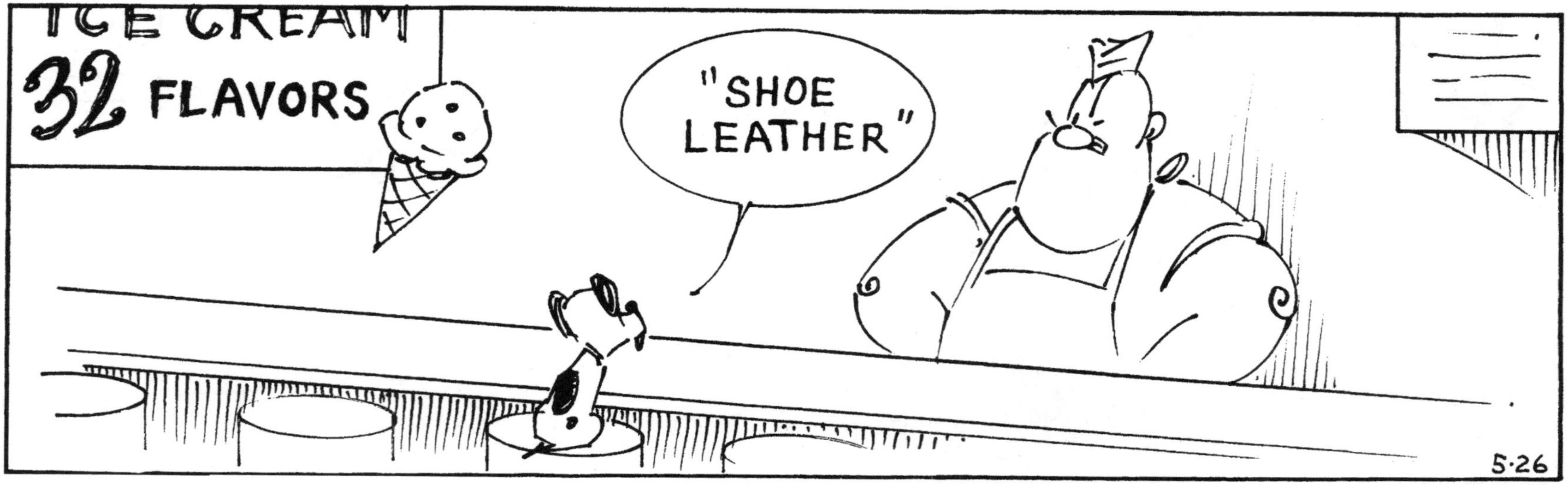
ICE CREAM
32 FLAVORS
"SHOE LEATHER"
5·26

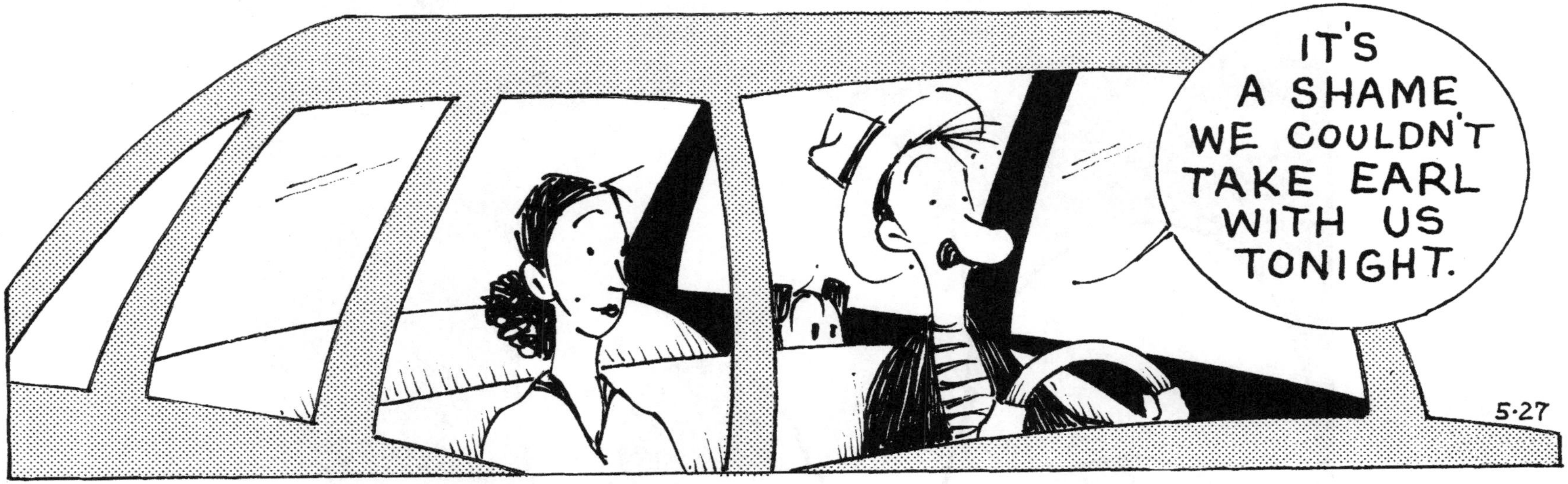
IT'S A SHAME WE COULDN'T TAKE EARL WITH US TONIGHT.
5·27

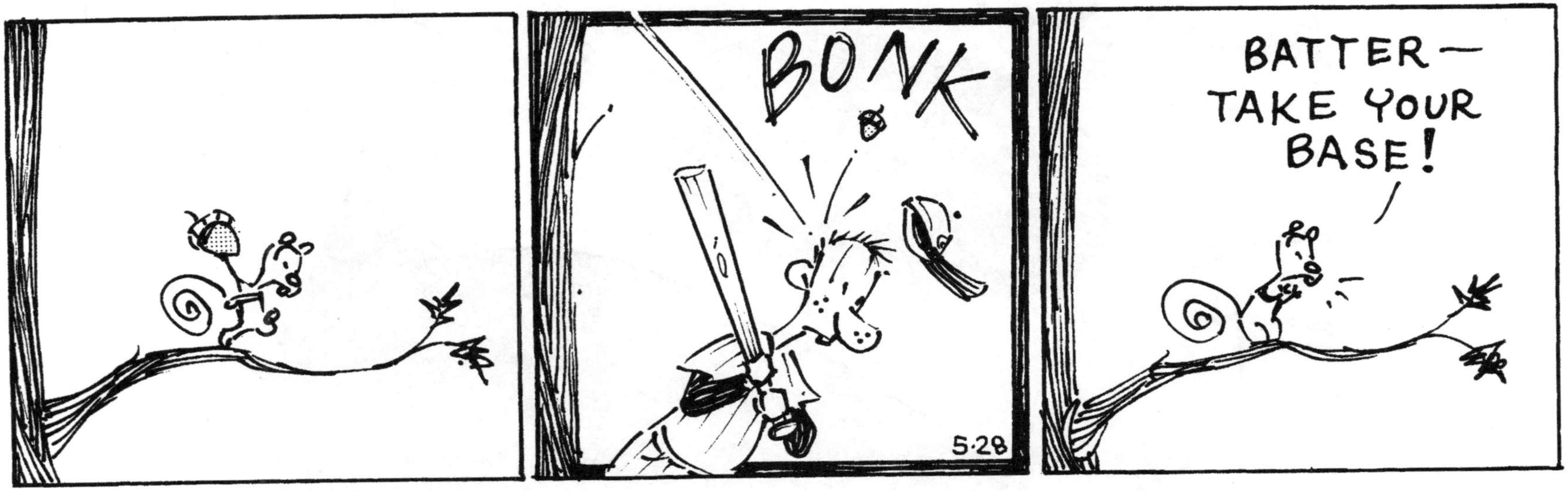
BONK
5·28
BATTER — TAKE YOUR BASE!

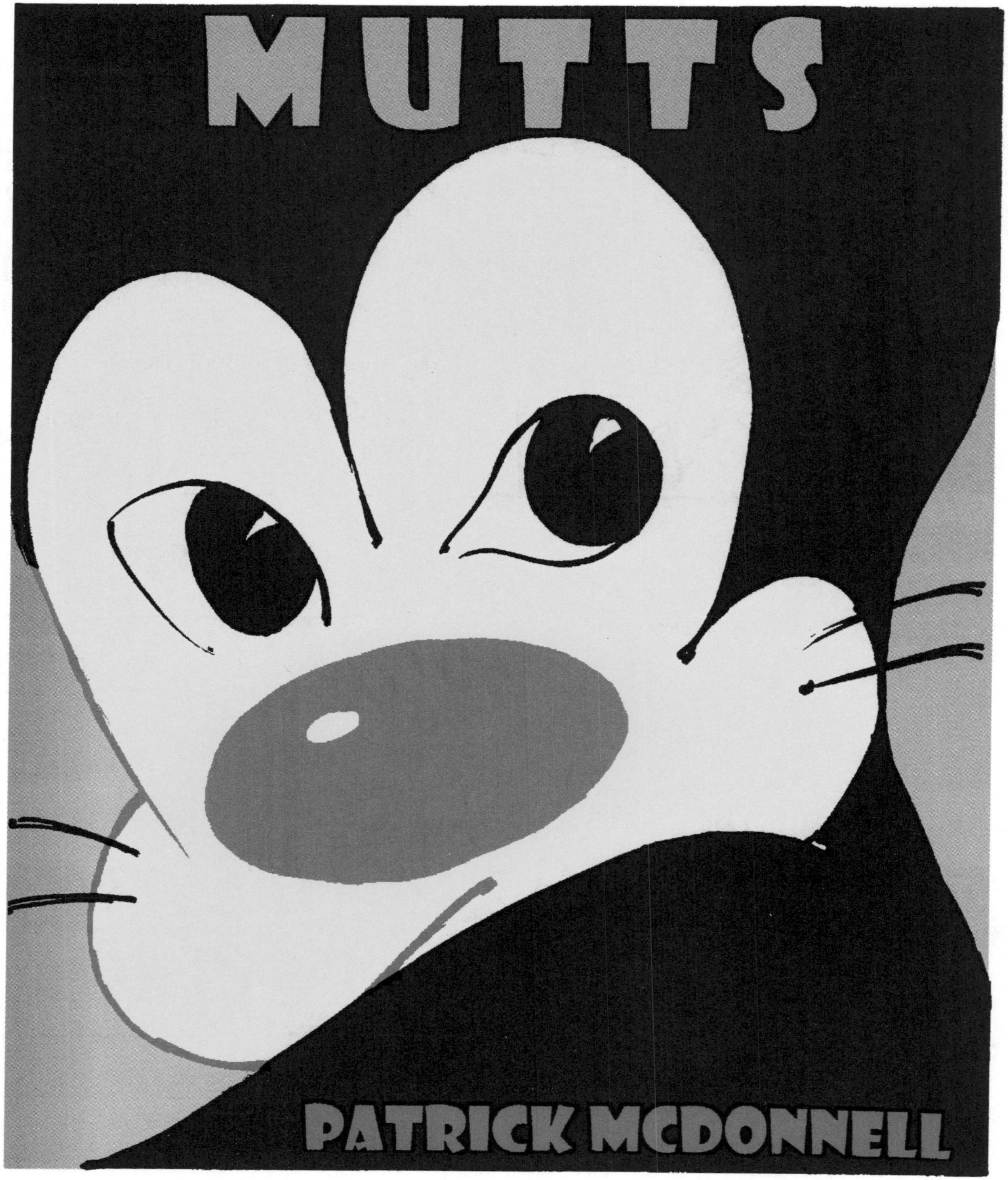
MUTTS
PATRICK MCDONNELL

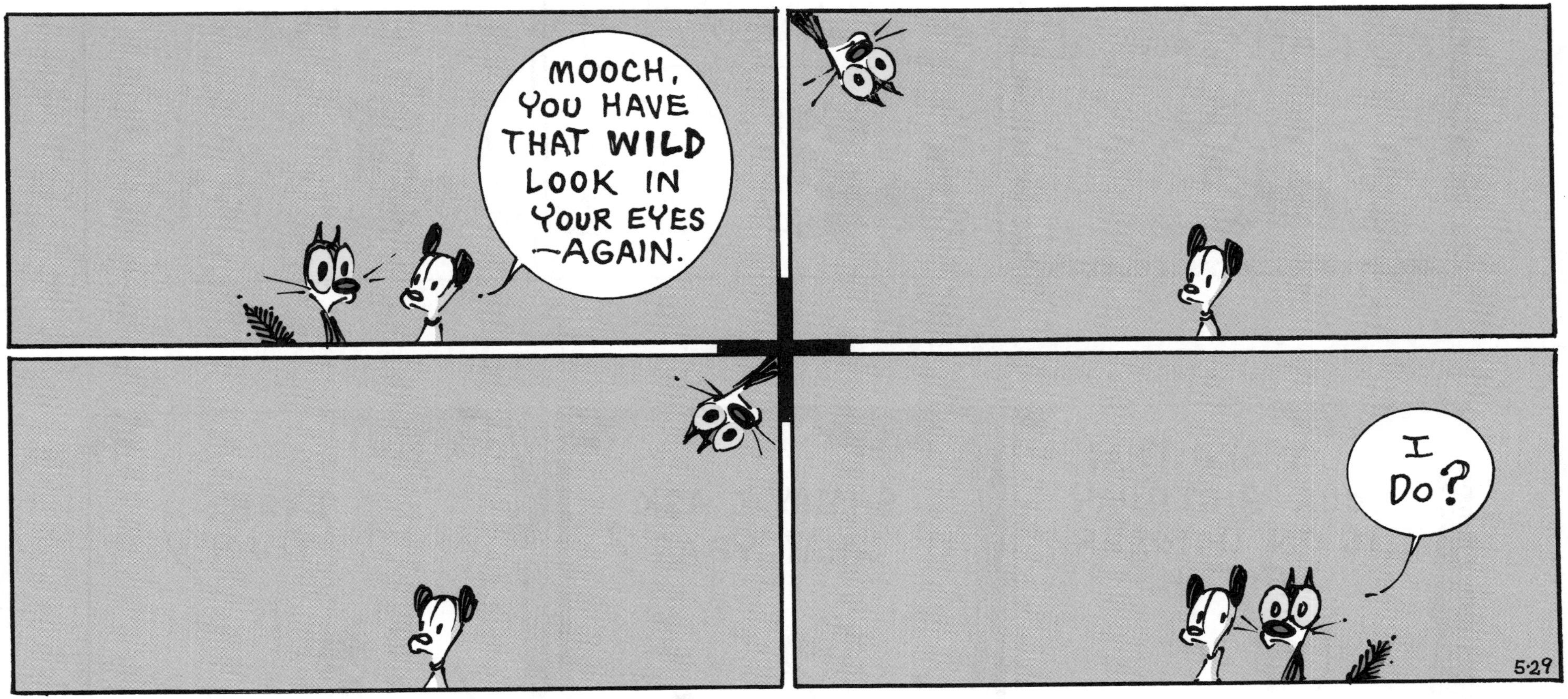
MOOCH, YOU HAVE THAT WILD LOOK IN YOUR EYES —AGAIN.
I DO?
5·29

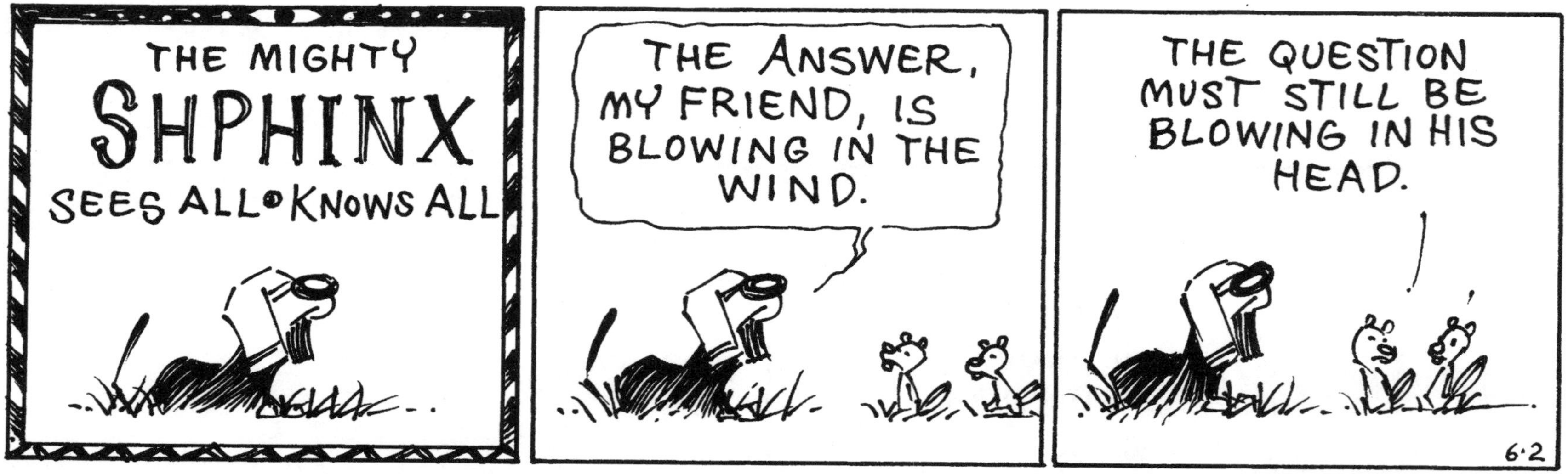
THE MIGHTY SHPHINX SEES ALL • KNOWS ALL
THE ANSWER, MY FRIEND, IS BLOWING IN THE WIND.
THE QUESTION MUST STILL BE BLOWING IN HIS HEAD.
6·2

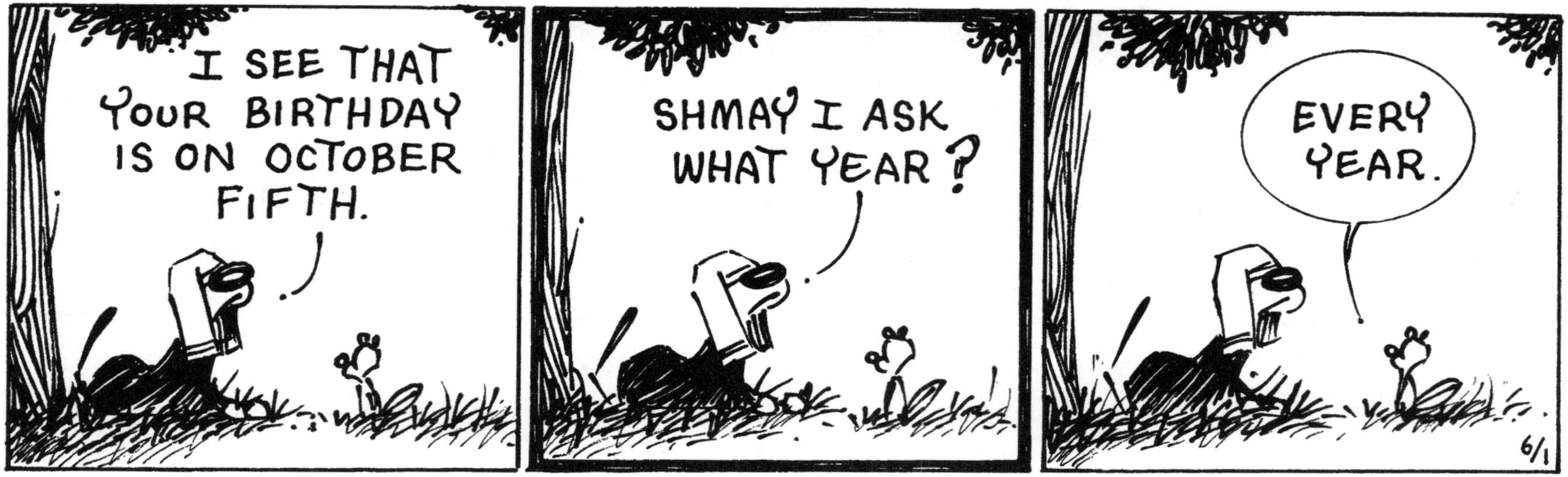
I SEE THAT YOUR BIRTHDAY IS ON OCTOBER FIFTH.
SHMAY I ASK WHAT YEAR?
EVERY YEAR.
6/1

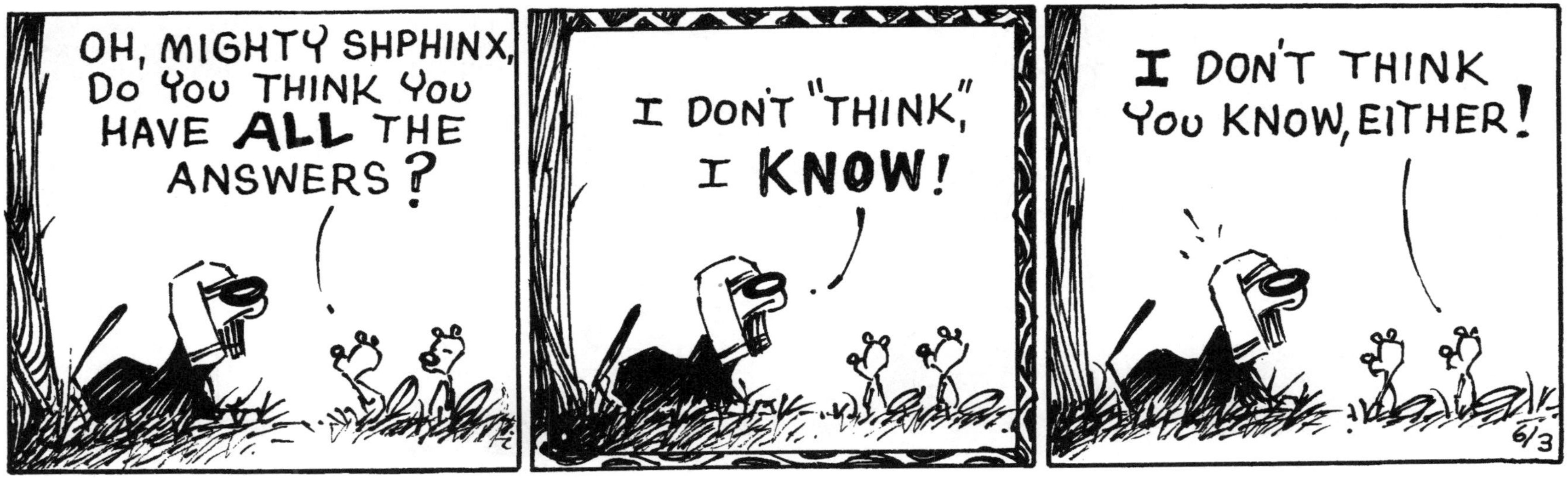
OH, MIGHTY SHPHINX, DO YOU THINK YOU HAVE ALL THE ANSWERS?
I DON'T "THINK," I KNOW!
I DON'T THINK YOU KNOW, EITHER!
6/3

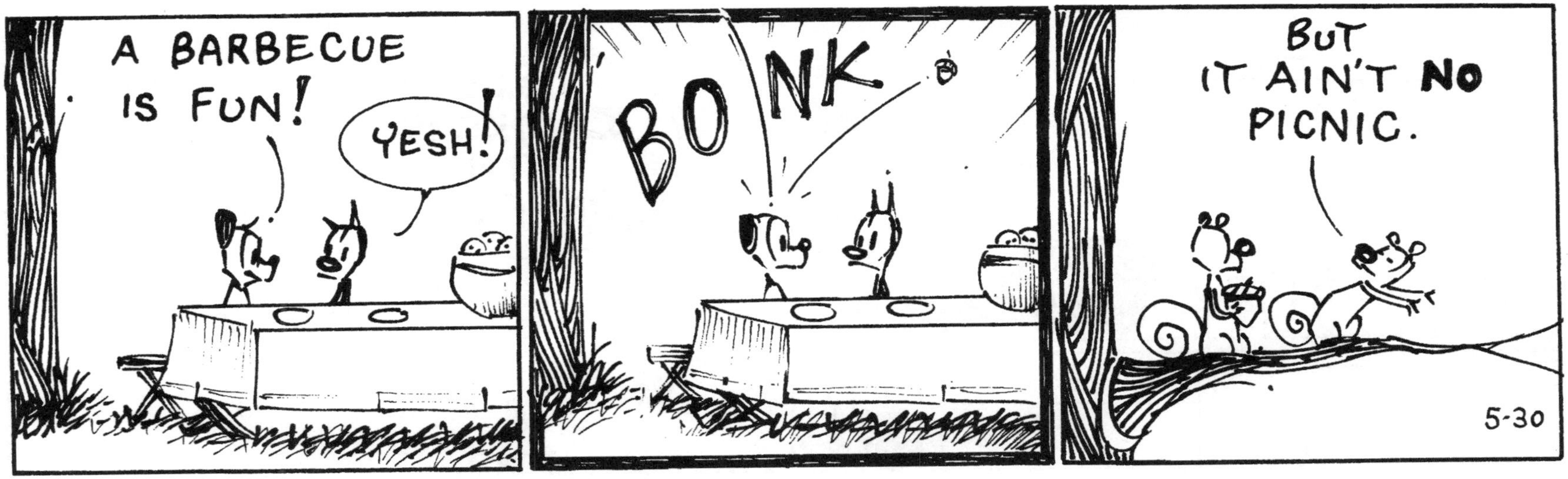
A BARBECUE IS FUN!
YESH!
BONK
BUT IT AIN'T NO PICNIC.
5-30

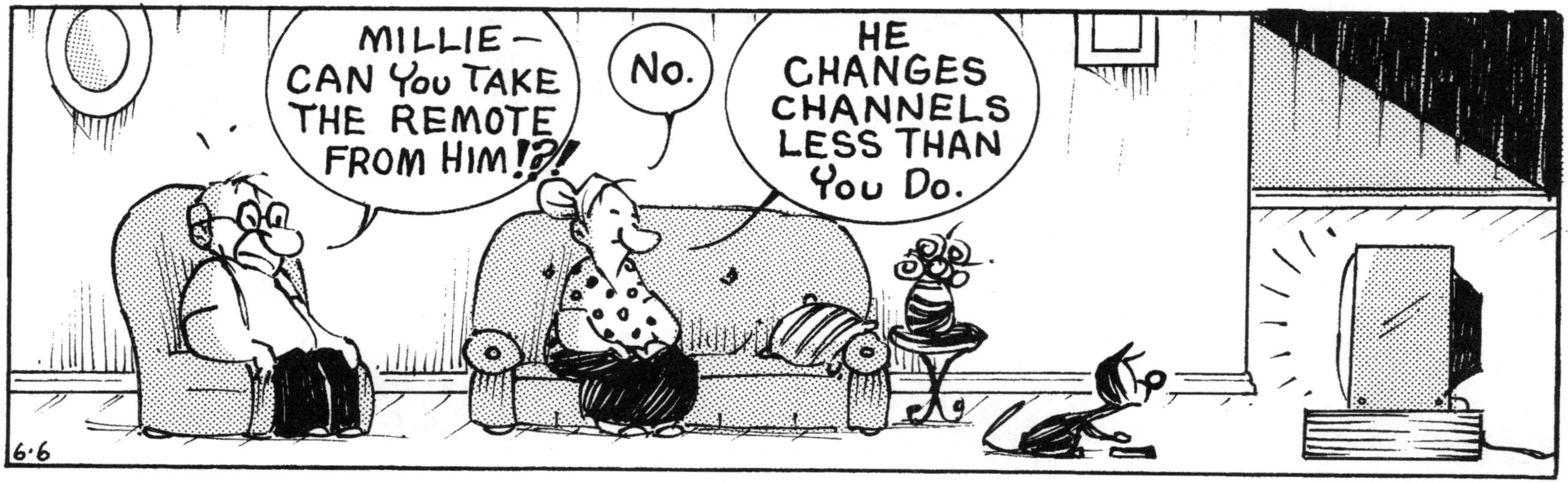
MILLIE— CAN YOU TAKE THE REMOTE FROM HIM!?!
No.
HE CHANGES CHANNELS LESS THAN YOU DO.
6·6

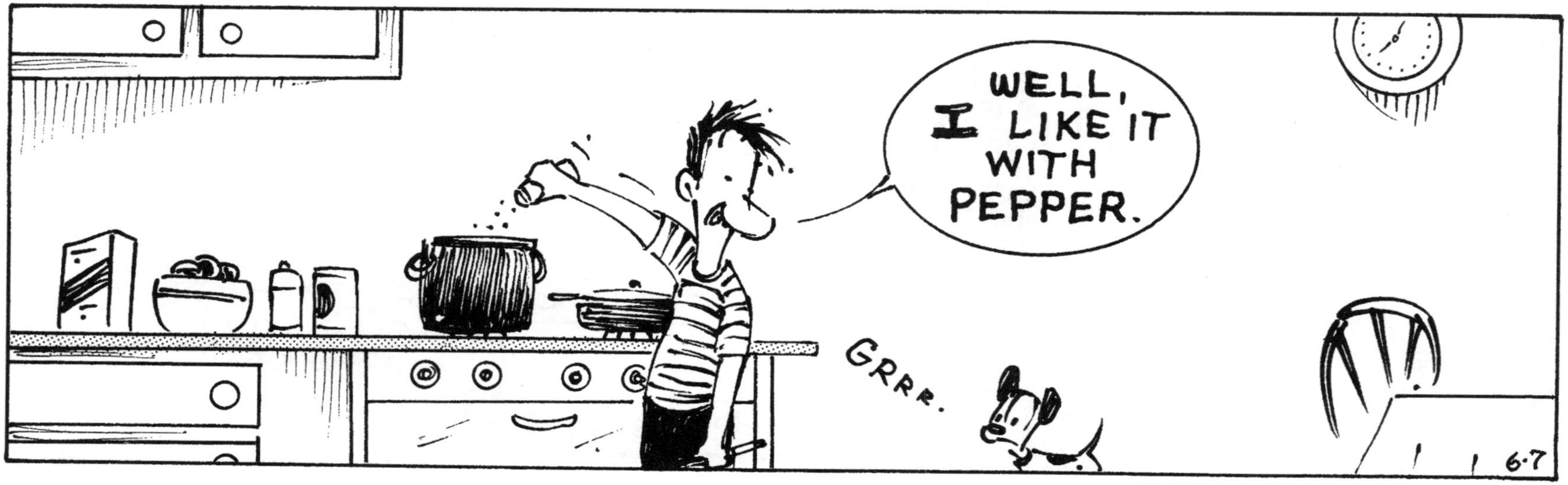
WELL, I LIKE IT WITH PEPPER.
GRRR.
6·7

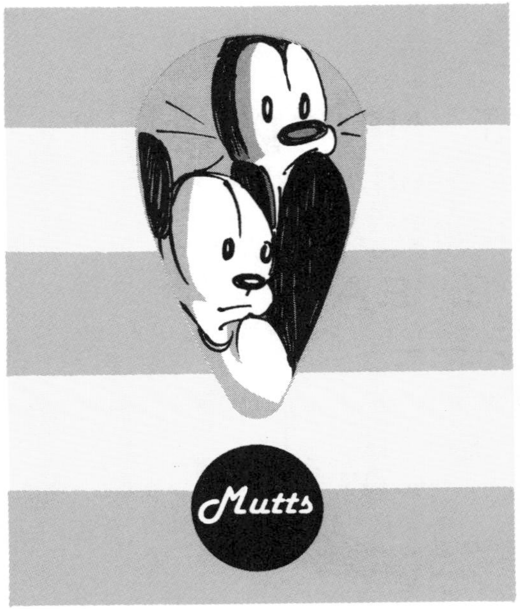
Mutts

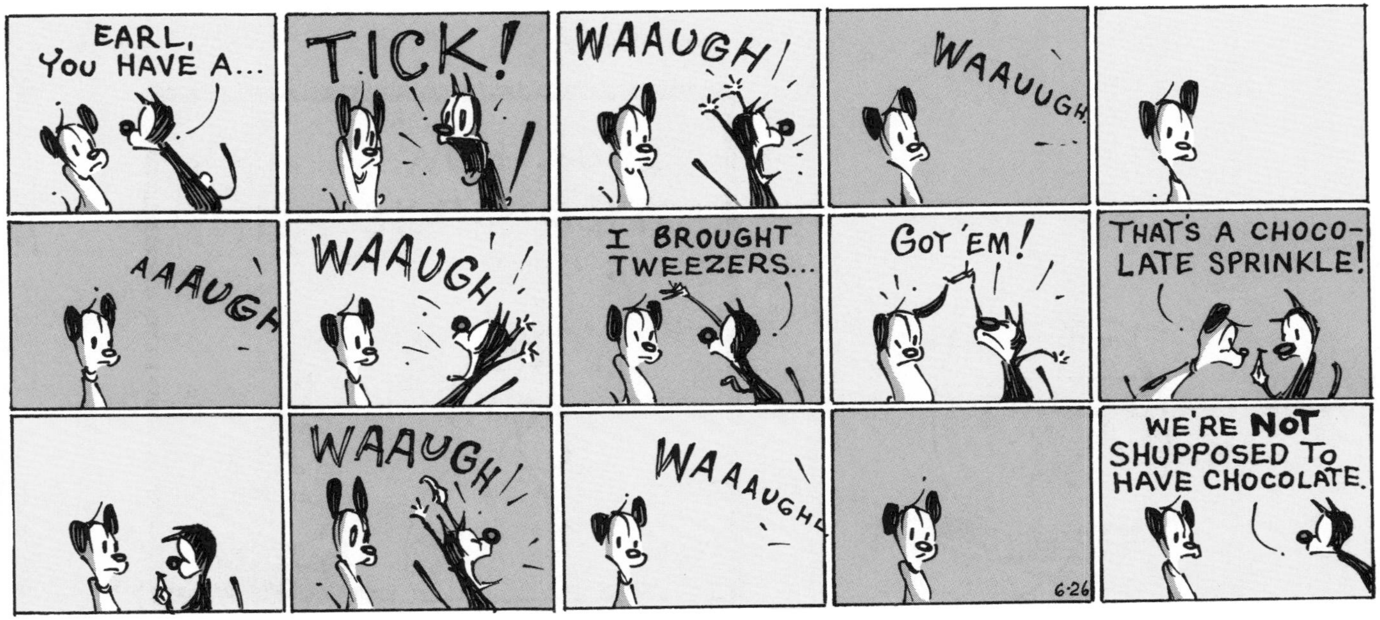
EARL, YOU HAVE A...
TICK!
WAAUGH
WAAUUGH
AAAUGH
WAAUGH
I BROUGHT TWEEZERS...
GOT 'EM!
THAT'S A CHOCO-LATE SPRINKLE!
WAAUGH
WAAAUGHL
6·26
WE'RE NOT SHUPPOSED TO HAVE CHOCOLATE.

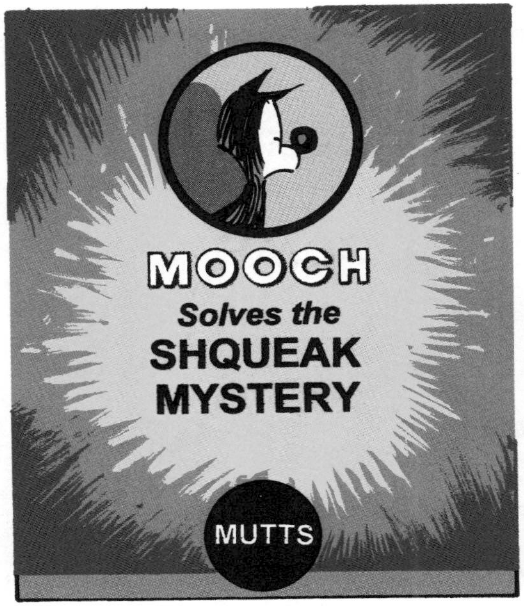
MOOCH
Solves the
SHQUEAK
MYSTERY
MUTTS

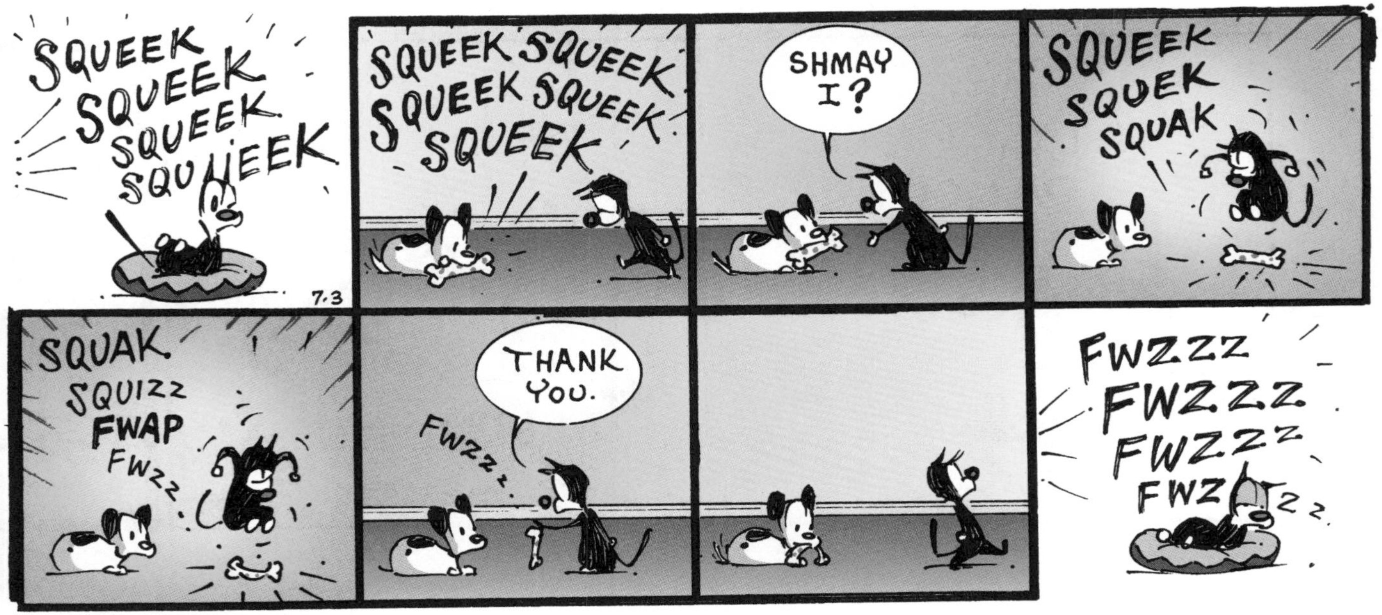
SQUEEK SQUEEK SQUEEK SQUEEK
7·3
SQUEEK SQUEEK SQUEEK SQUEEK SQUEEK
SHMAY I?
SQUEEK SQUEK SQUAK
SQUAK SQUIZZ FWAP FWZZ
FWZZZ
THANK YOU.
FWZZZ FWZZZ FWZZZ FWZ ZZ

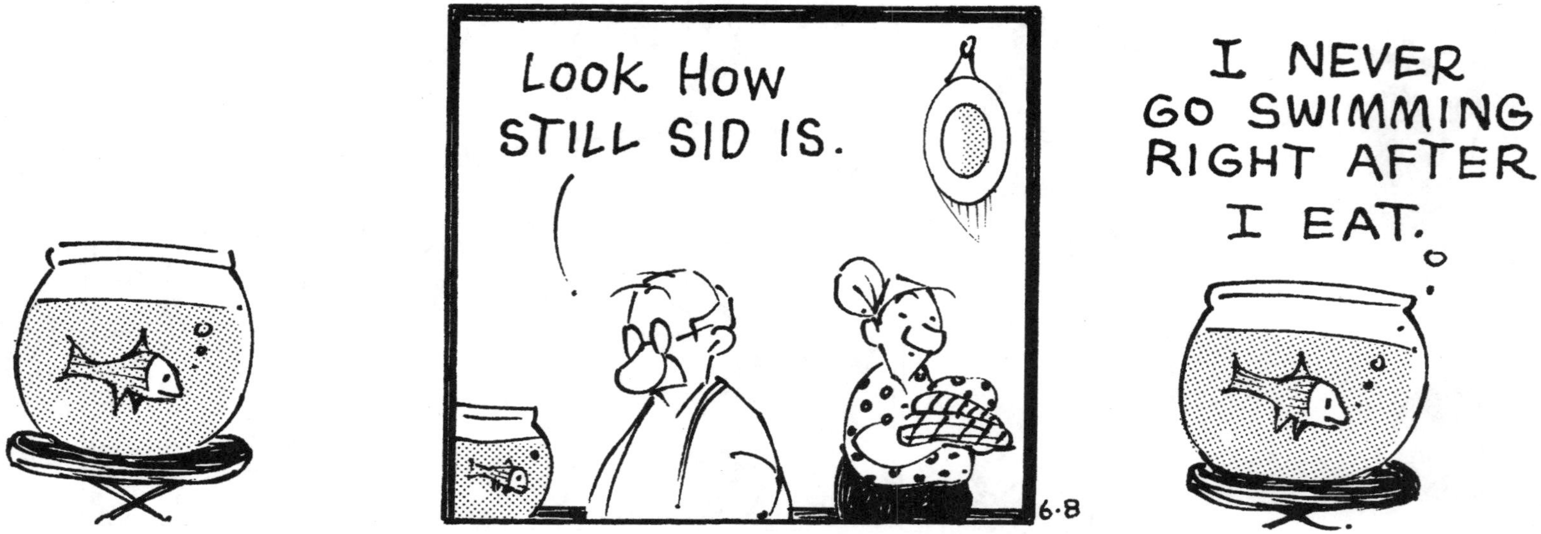
LOOK HOW STILL SID IS.
I NEVER GO SWIMMING RIGHT AFTER I EAT.
6·8

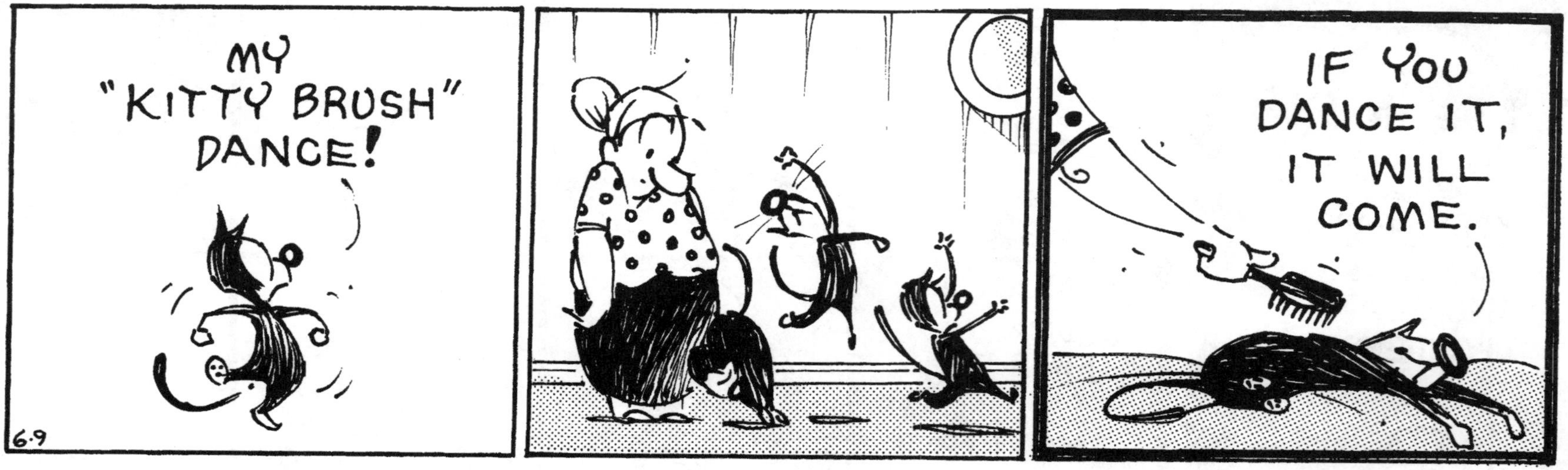
MY "KITTY BRUSH" DANCE!
6·9
IF YOU DANCE IT, IT WILL COME.

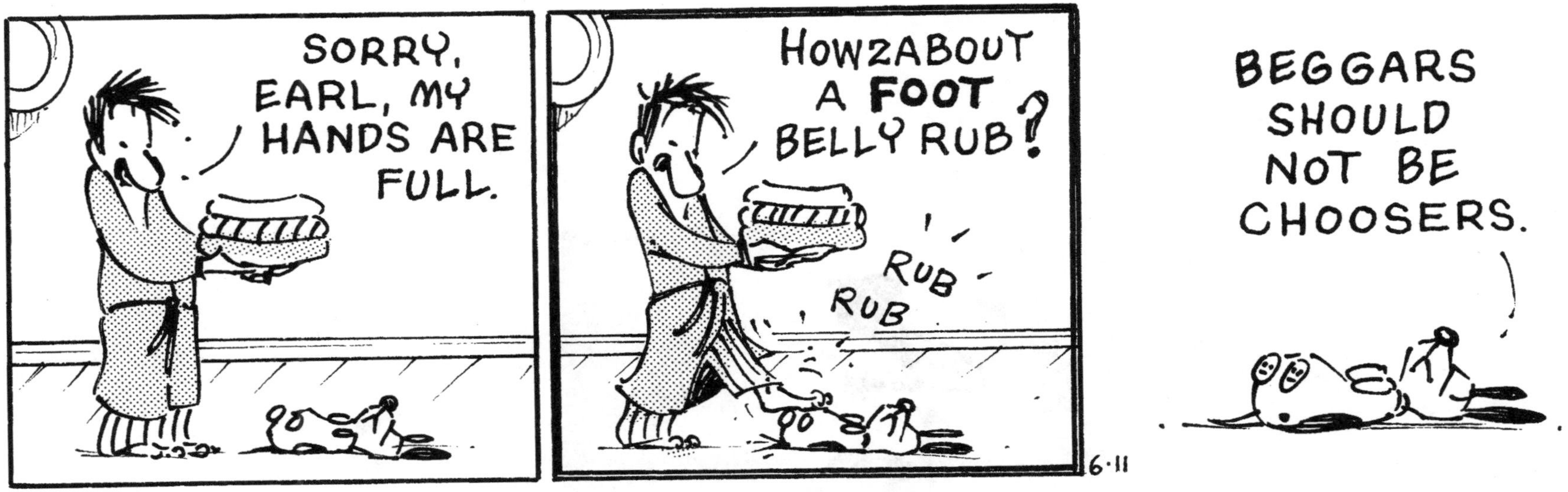
SORRY, EARL, MY HANDS ARE FULL.
HOWZABOUT A FOOT BELLY RUB?
RUB RUB
BEGGARS SHOULD NOT BE CHOOSERS.
6·11

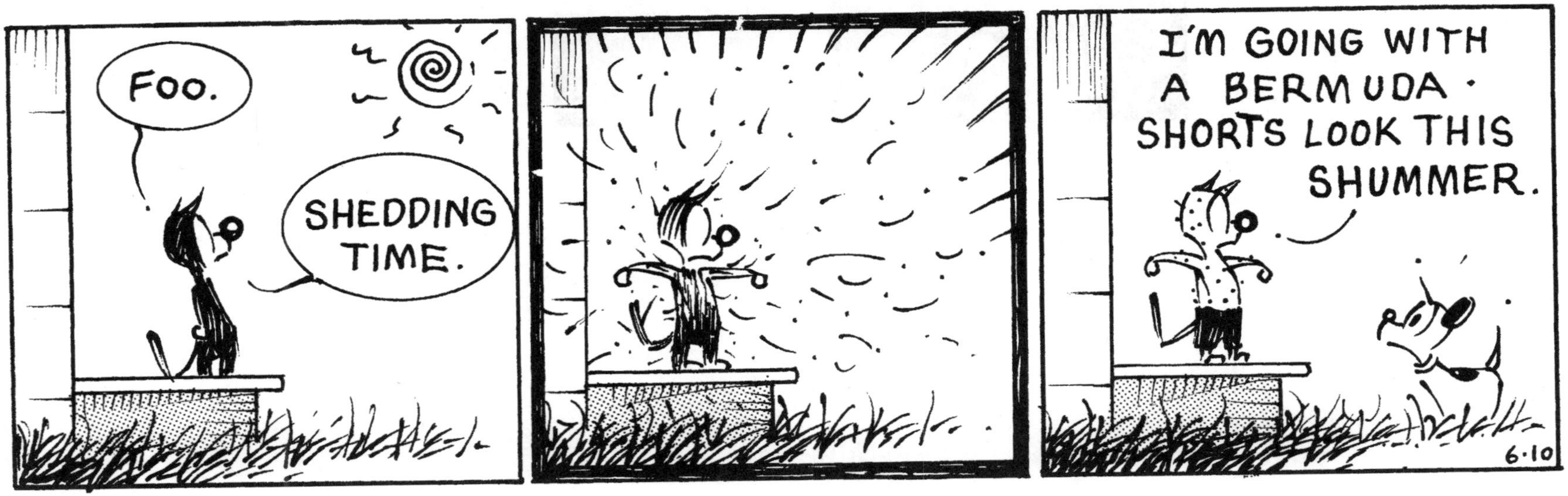
FOO.
SHEDDING TIME.
I'M GOING WITH A BERMUDA-SHORTS LOOK THIS SHUMMER.
6·10

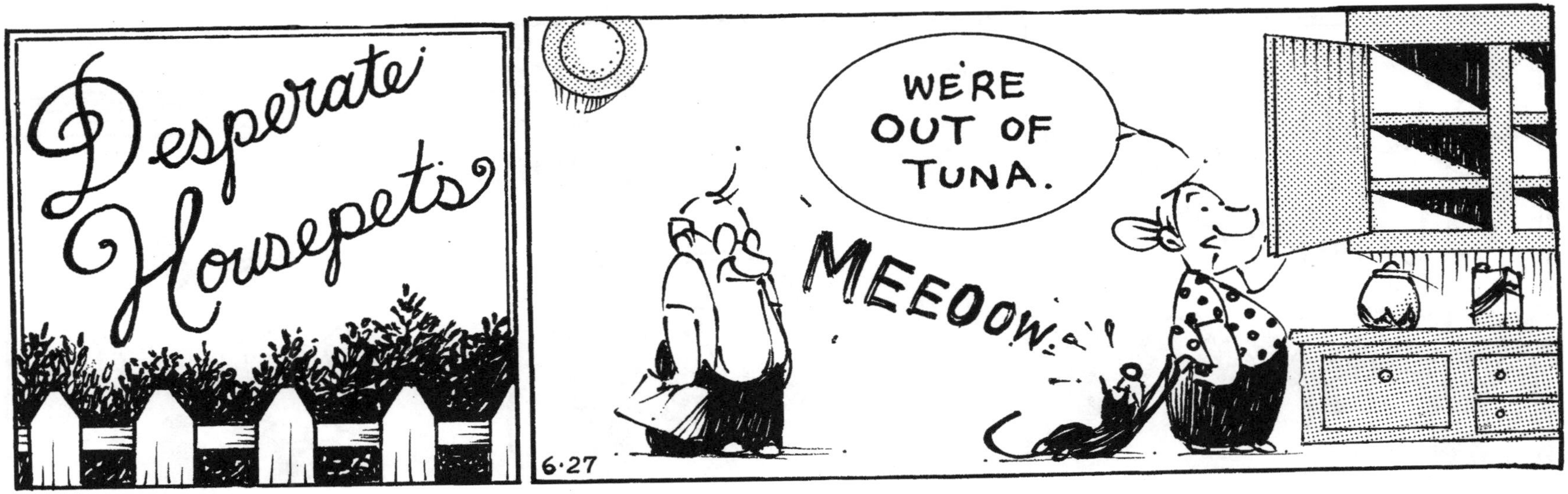
Desperate Housepets
WE'RE OUT OF TUNA.
MEEOOW
6·27

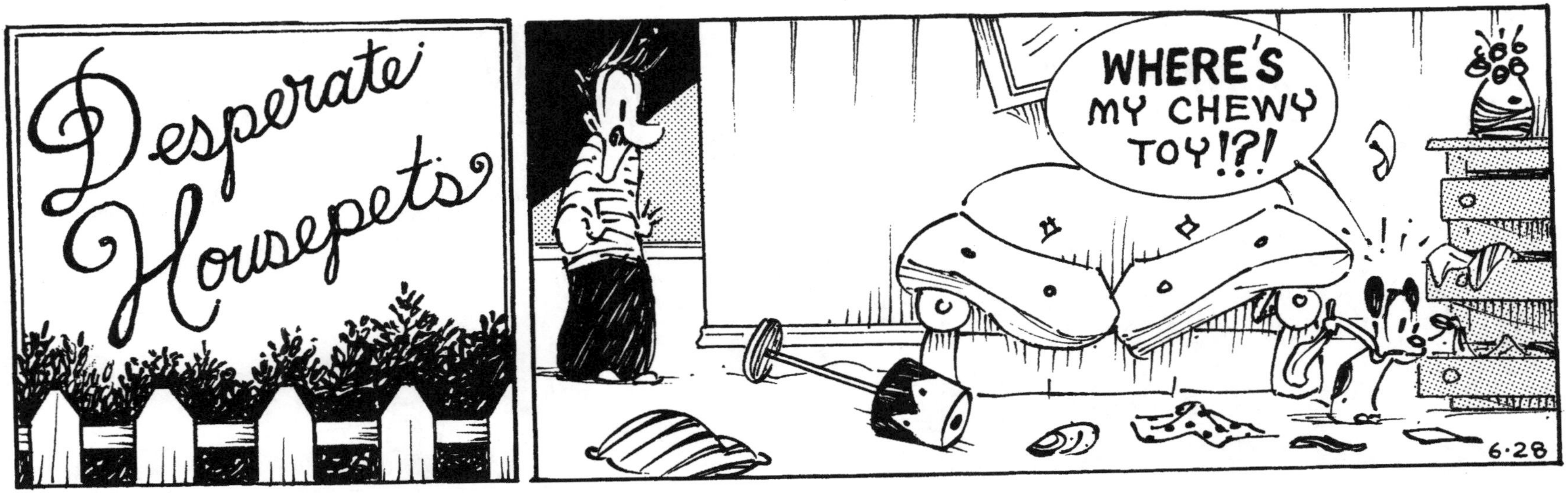
Desperate Housepets
WHERE'S MY CHEWY TOY!?!
6·28

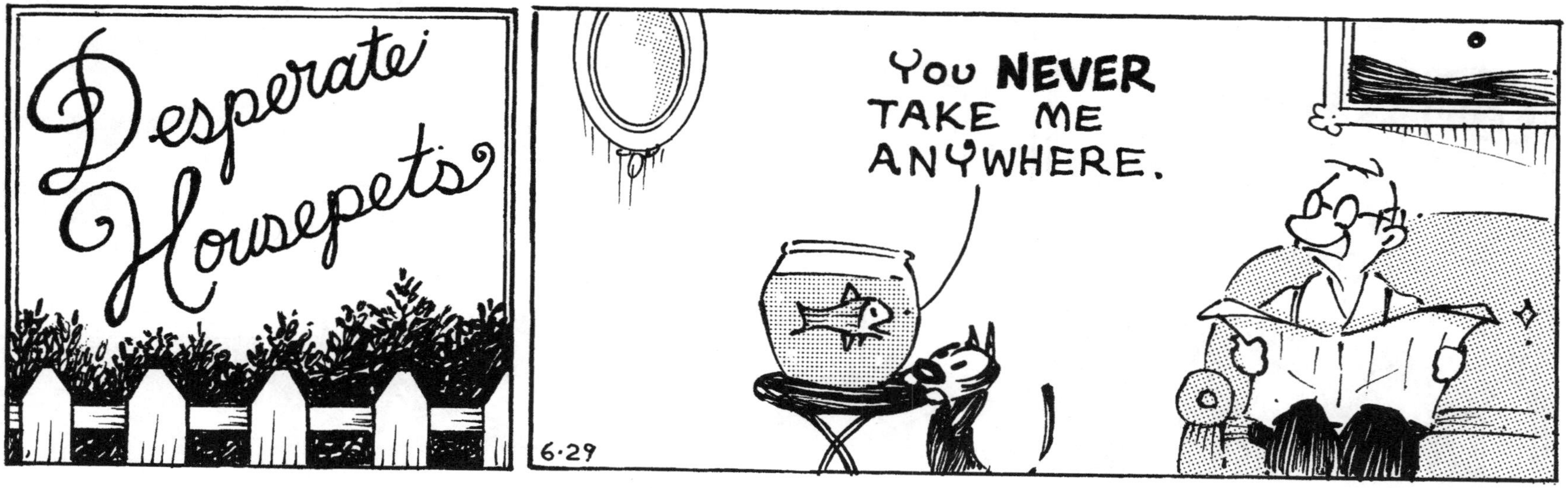
Desperate Housepets
6·29
You NEVER TAKE ME ANYWHERE.

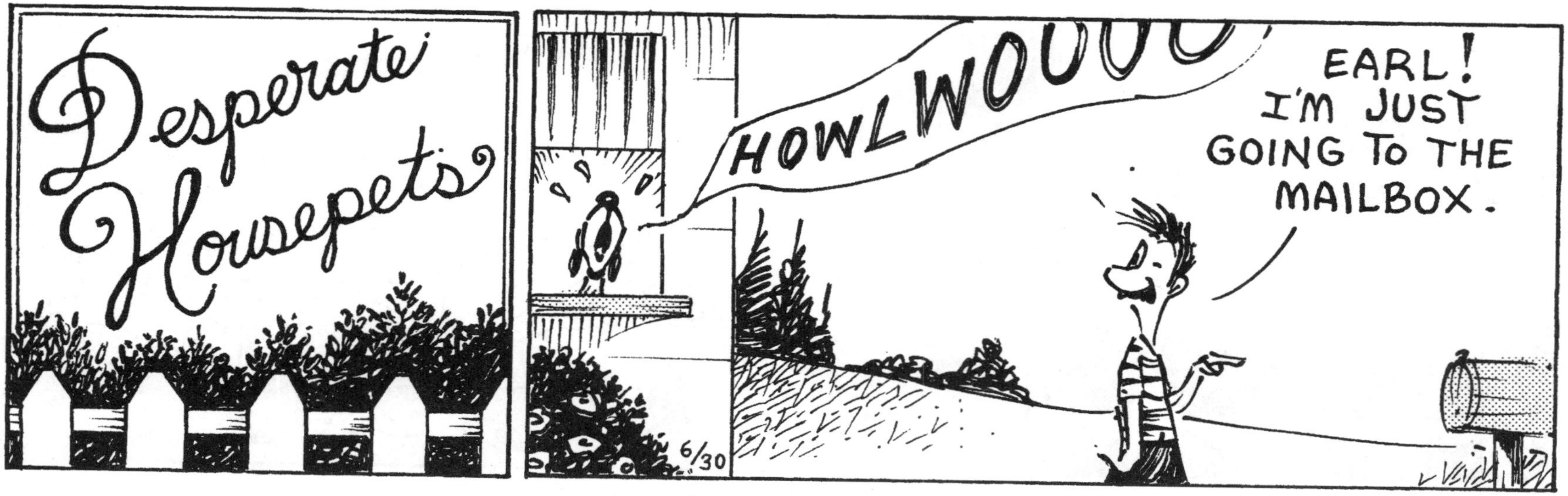
Desperate Housepets
6/30
HOWLWOOOO
EARL! I'M JUST GOING TO THE MAILBOX.

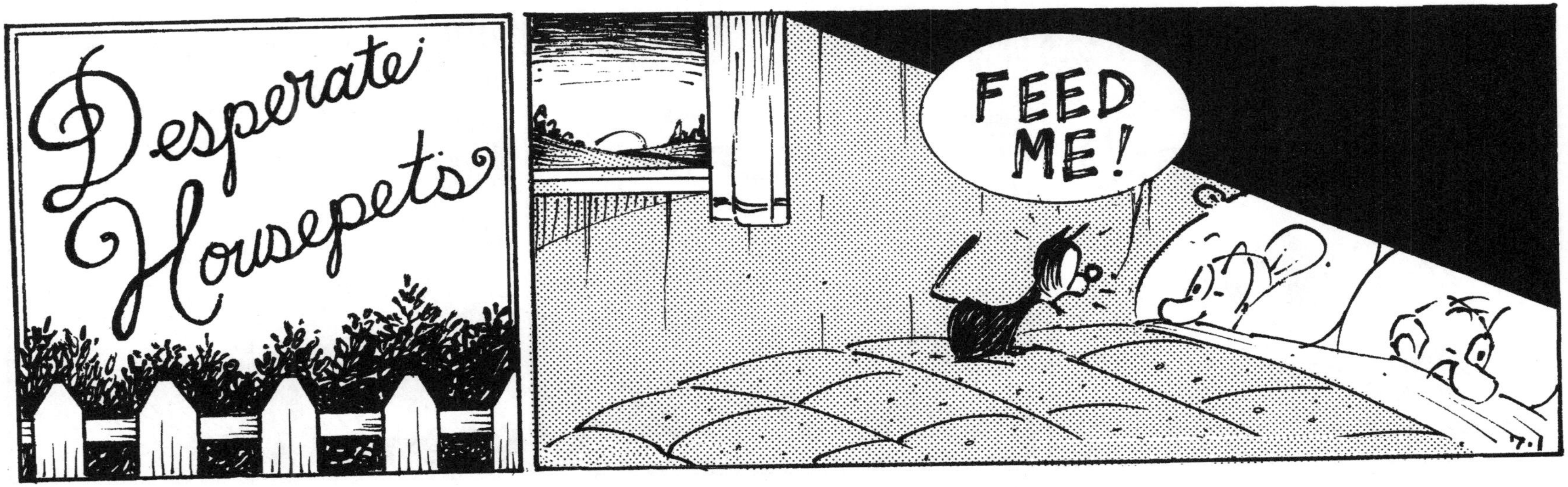
Desperate Housepets
FEED ME!
7.1

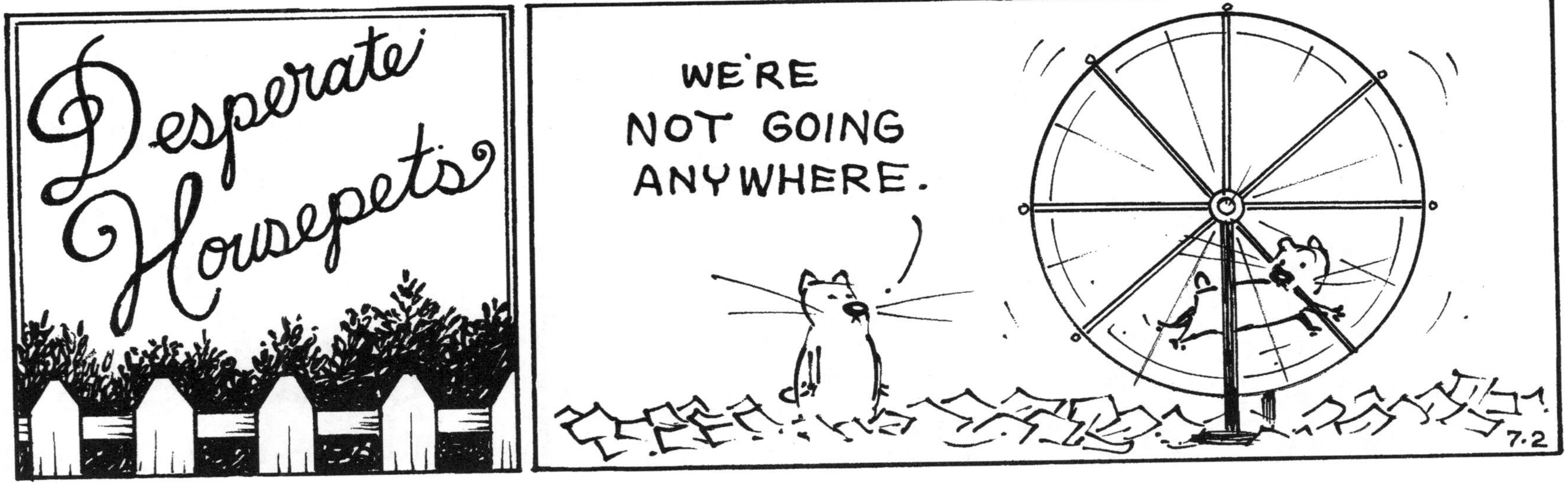
Desperate Housepets
WE'RE NOT GOING ANYWHERE.
7.2

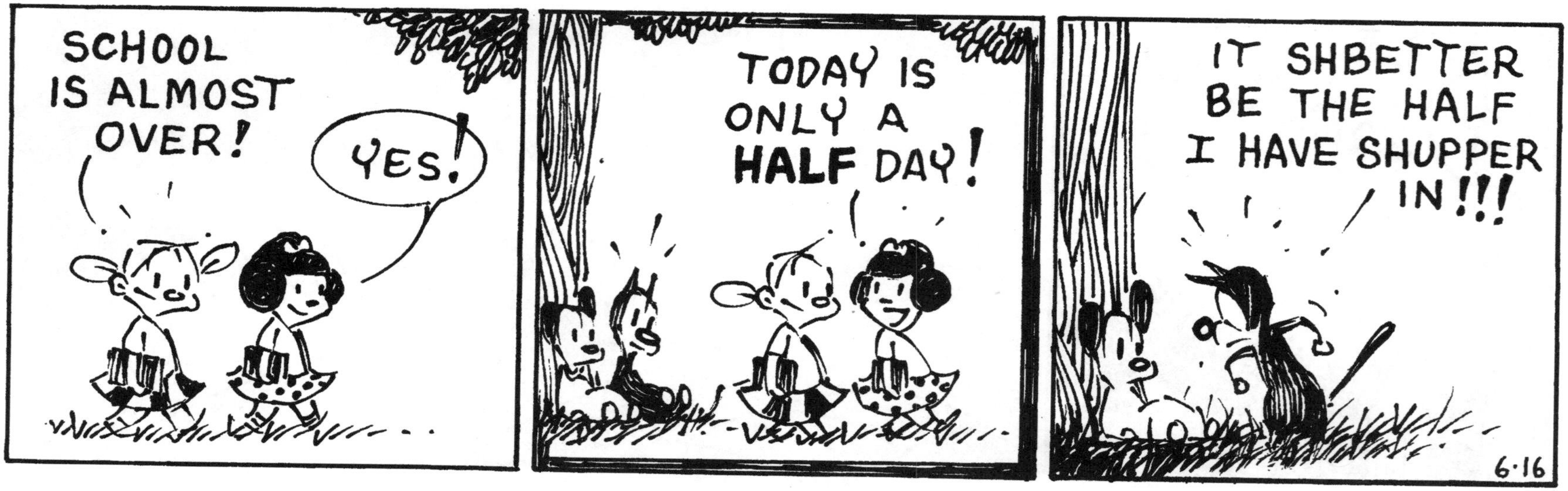
SCHOOL IS ALMOST OVER!
YES!
TODAY IS ONLY A HALF DAY!
IT SHBETTER BE THE HALF I HAVE SHUPPER IN!!!
6·16

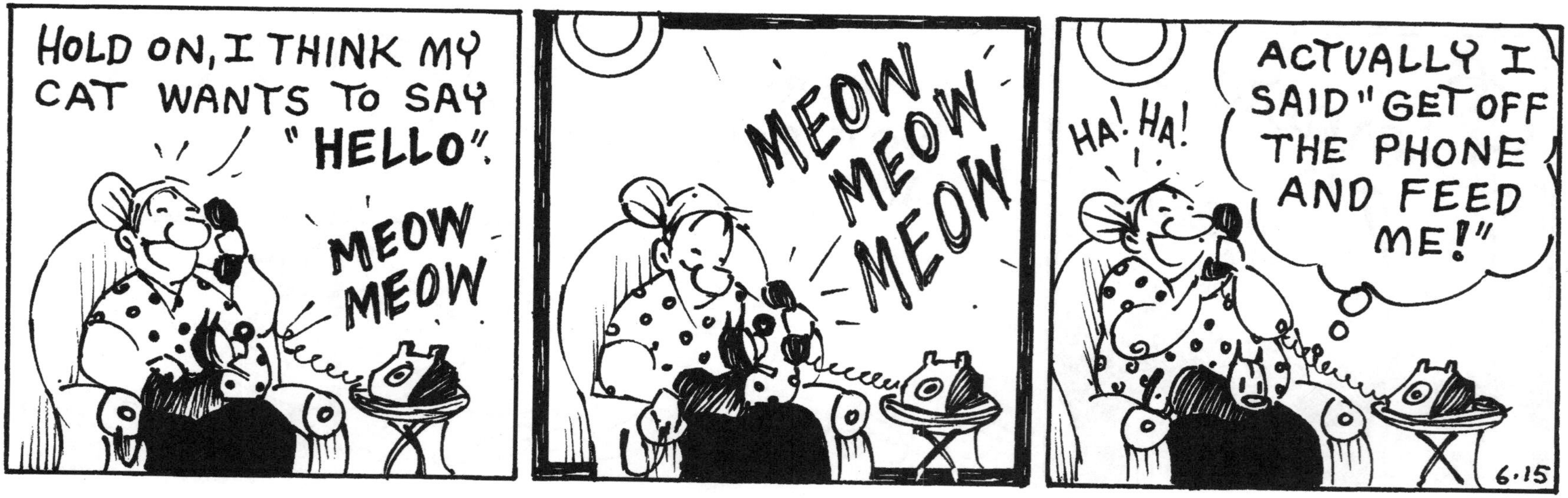
HOLD ON, I THINK MY CAT WANTS TO SAY "HELLO".
MEOW MEOW
MEOW MEOW MEOW
HA! HA!
ACTUALLY I SAID "GET OFF THE PHONE AND FEED ME!"
6·15

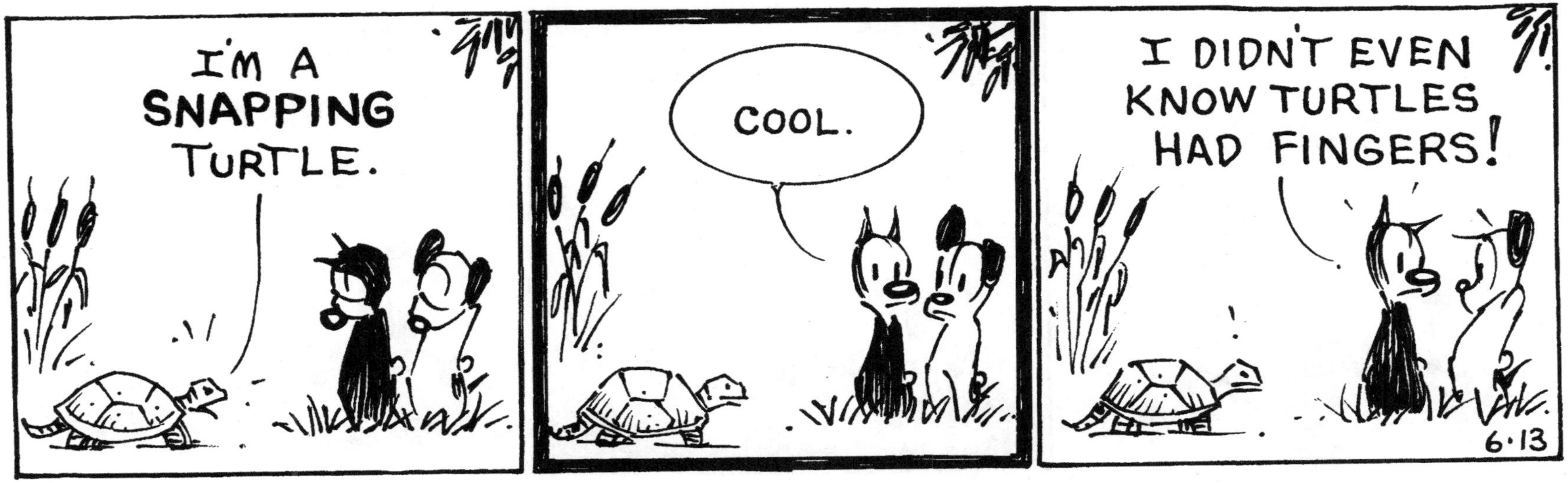
I'M A SNAPPING TURTLE.
COOL.
I DIDN'T EVEN KNOW TURTLES HAD FINGERS!
6·13

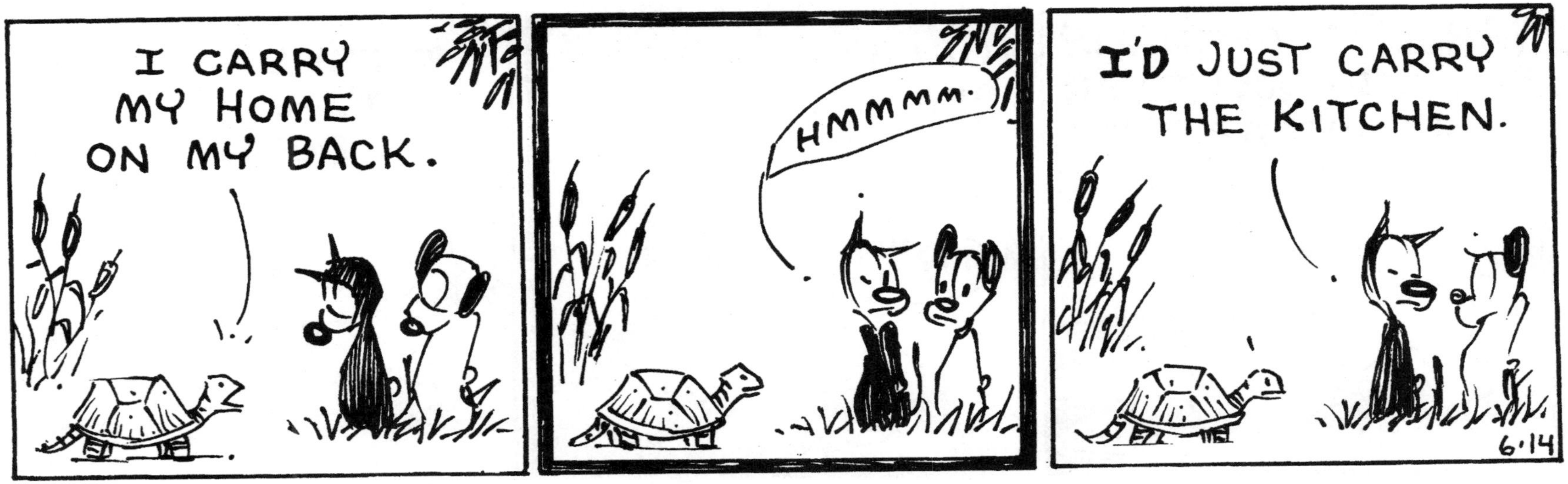
I CARRY MY HOME ON MY BACK.
HMMMM.
I'D JUST CARRY THE KITCHEN.
6·14

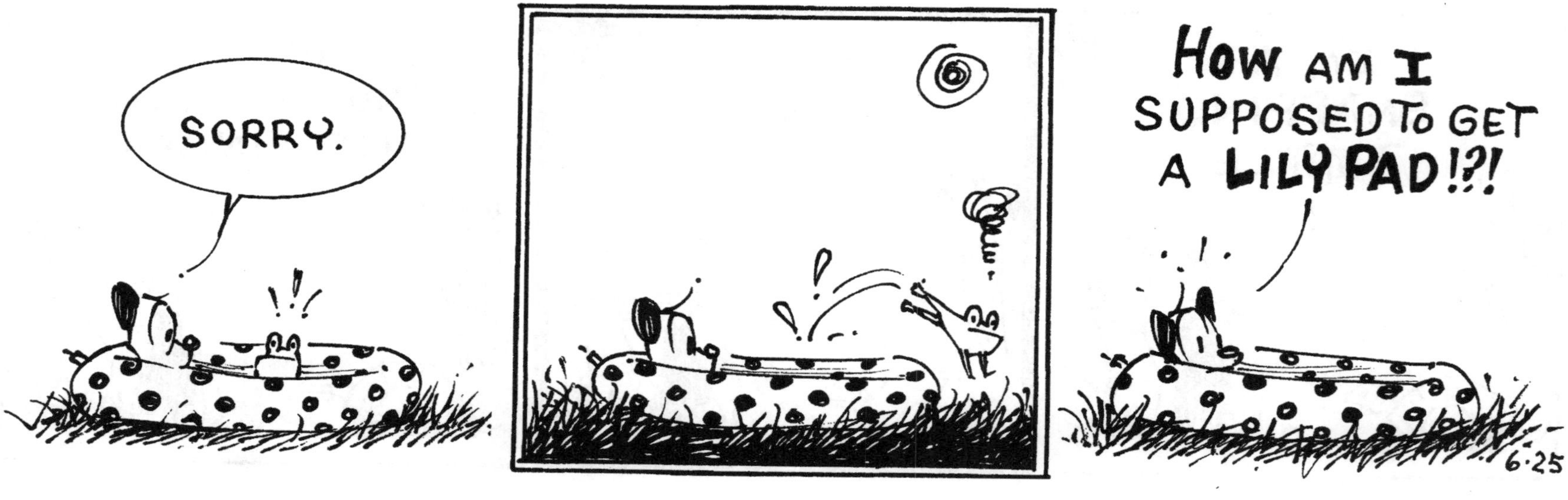
SORRY.
HOW AM I SUPPOSED TO GET A LILY PAD!?!
6·25

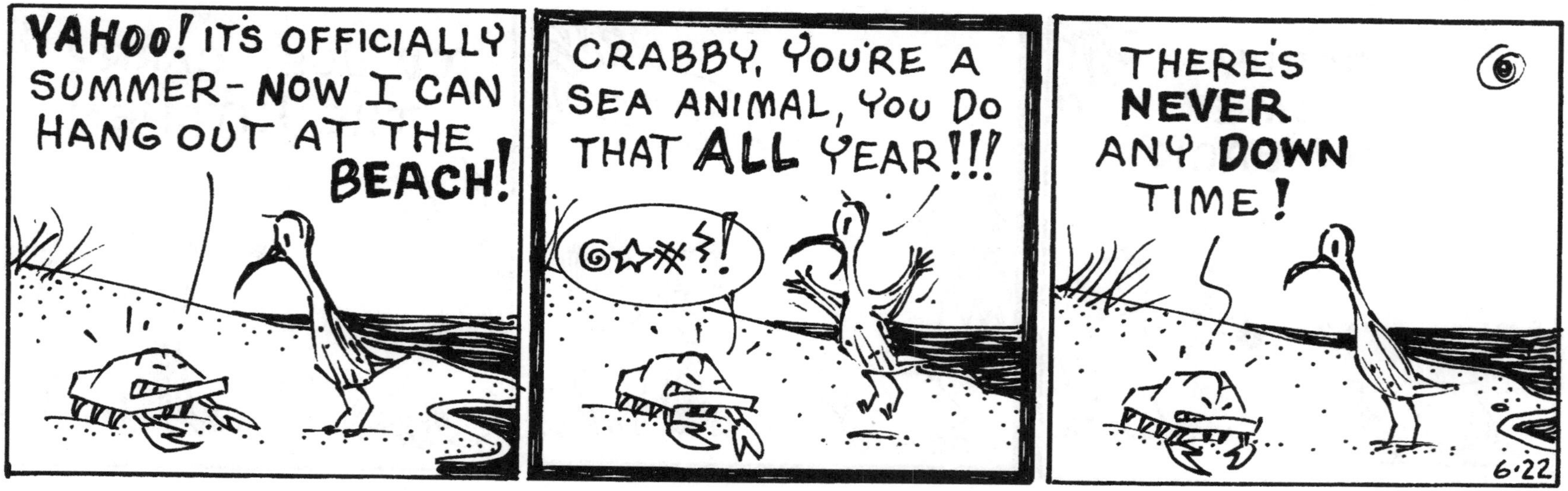
YAHOO! IT'S OFFICIALLY SUMMER- NOW I CAN HANG OUT AT THE BEACH!
CRABBY, YOU'RE A SEA ANIMAL, YOU DO THAT ALL YEAR!!!
THERE'S NEVER ANY DOWN TIME!
6·22

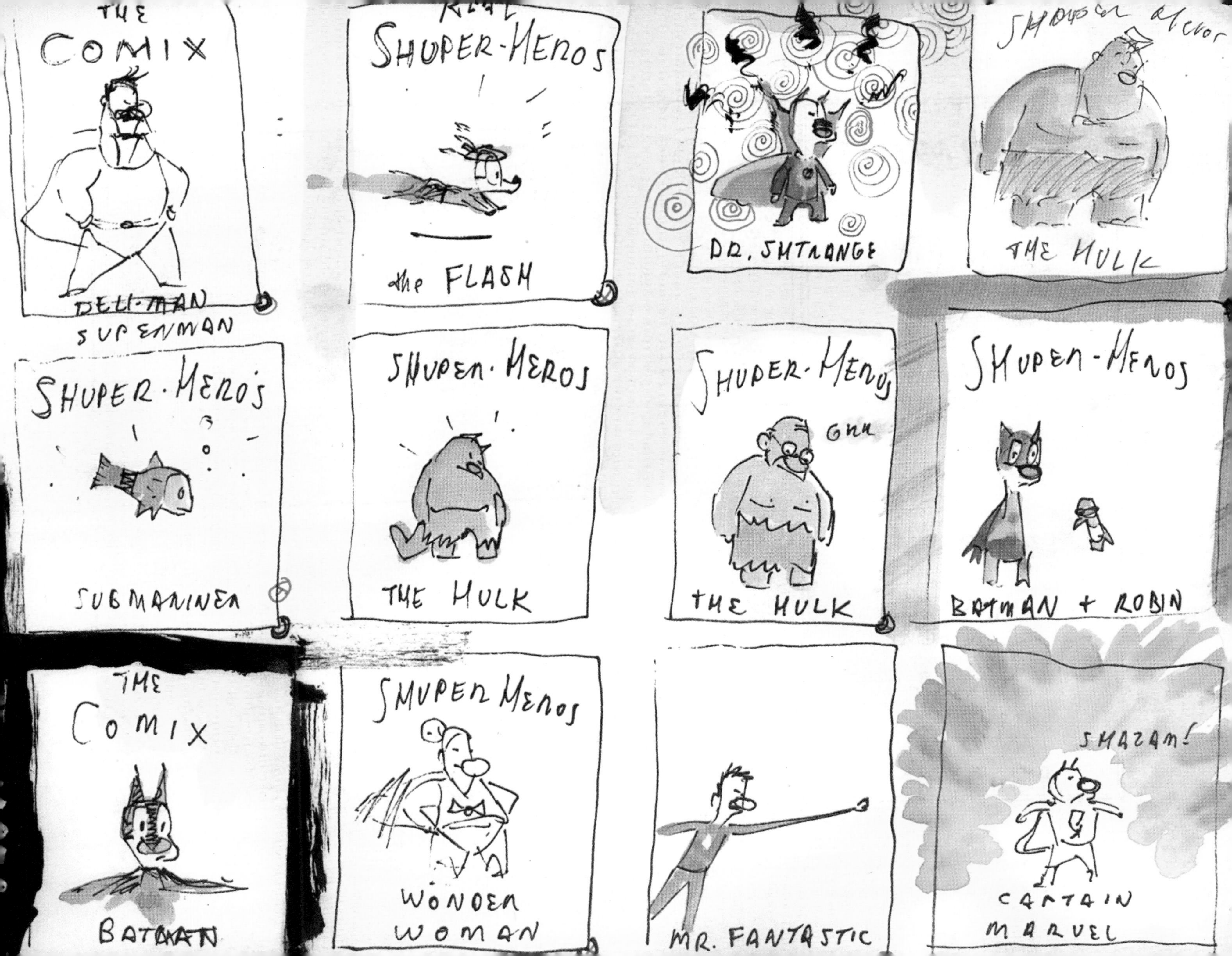
THE COMIX
SUPERMAN
REAL SHUPER-HEROS
the FLASH
DR. SHTRANGE
THE HULK
SHUPER-HERO'S
SUBMARINER
SHUPER-HEROS
THE HULK
SHUPER-HEROS
GRR
THE HULK
SHUPER-HEROS
BATMAN + ROBIN
THE COMIX
BATMAN
SHUPER HEROS
WONDER WOMAN
MR. FANTASTIC
SHAZAM!
CAPTAIN MARVEL

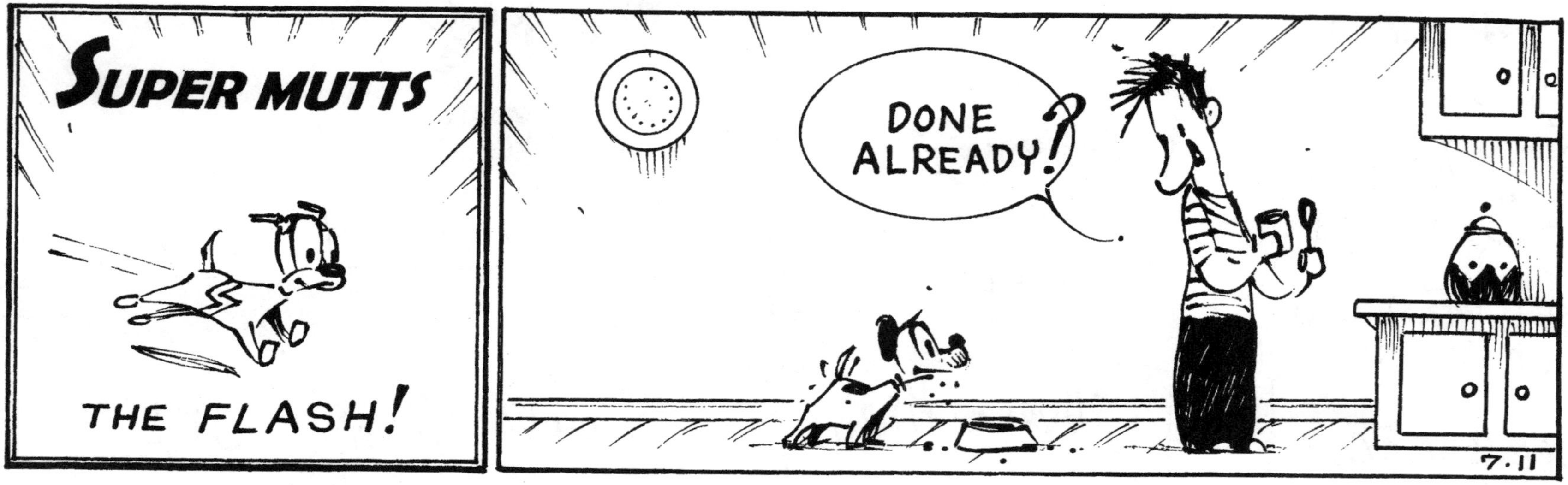
SUPER MUTTS
THE FLASH!
DONE ALREADY?!
7·11

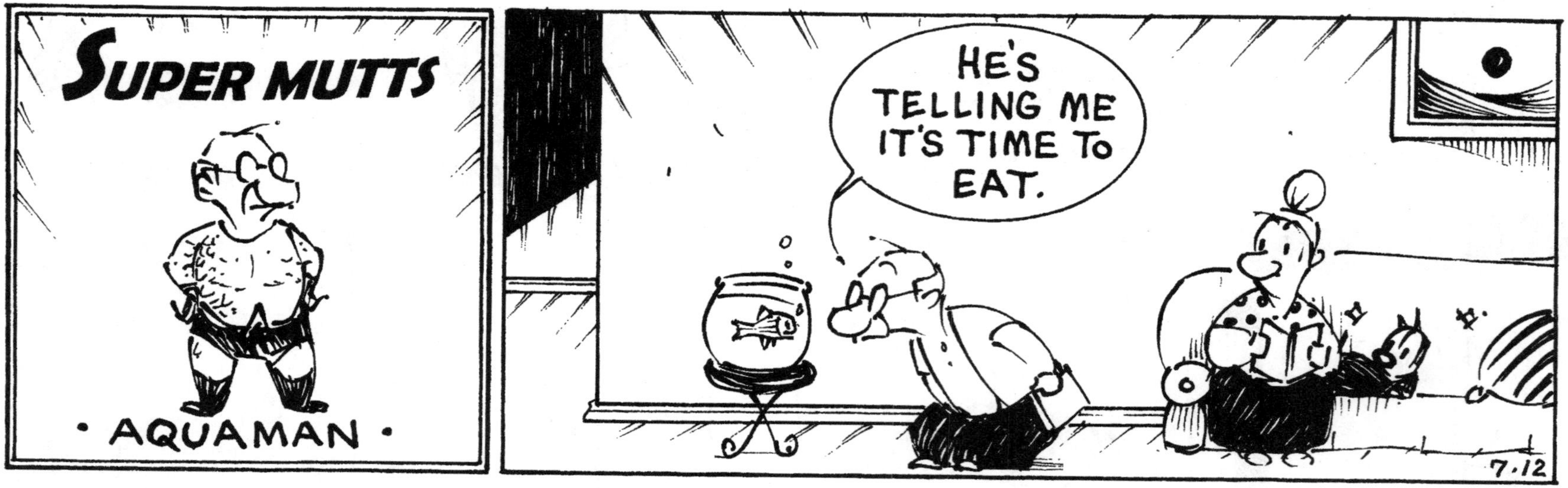
SUPER MUTTS
· AQUAMAN ·
HE'S TELLING ME IT'S TIME TO EAT.
7·12

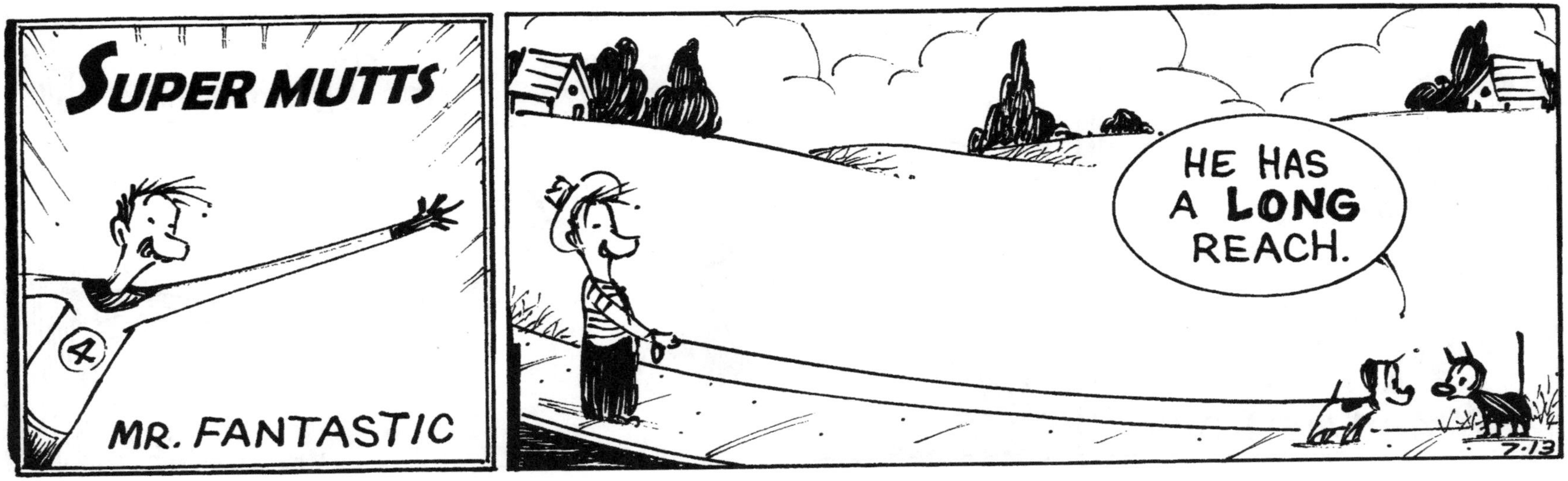
SUPER MUTTS
4
MR. FANTASTIC
HE HAS A **LONG** REACH.
7.13

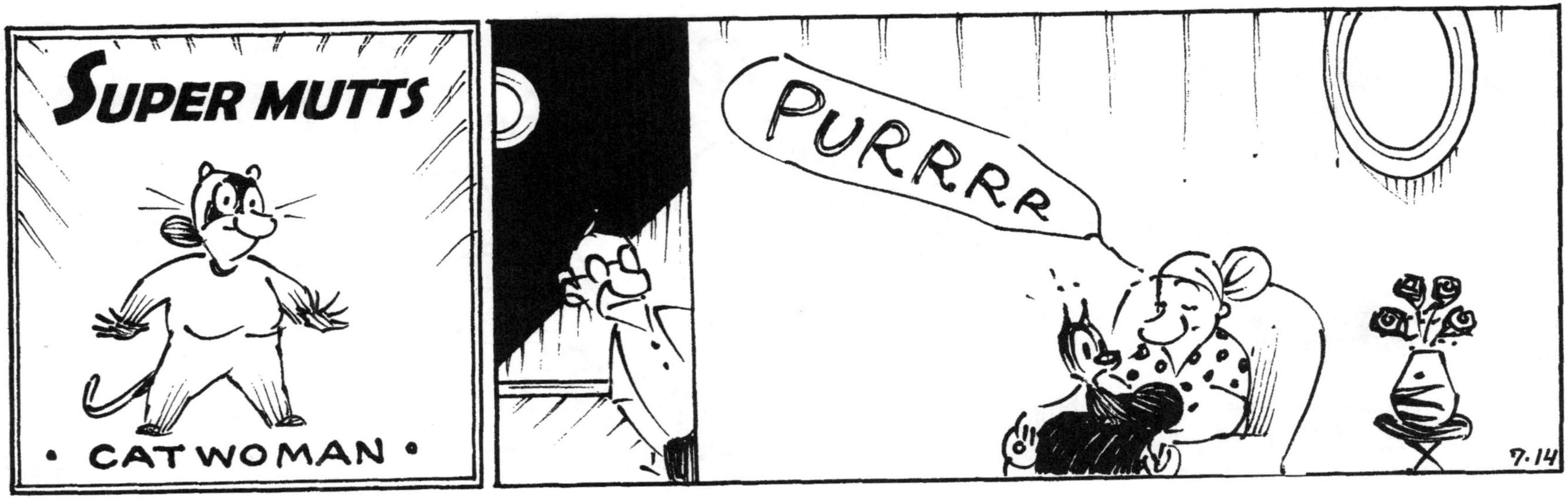
SUPER MUTTS
• CATWOMAN •
PURRRRR
7.14

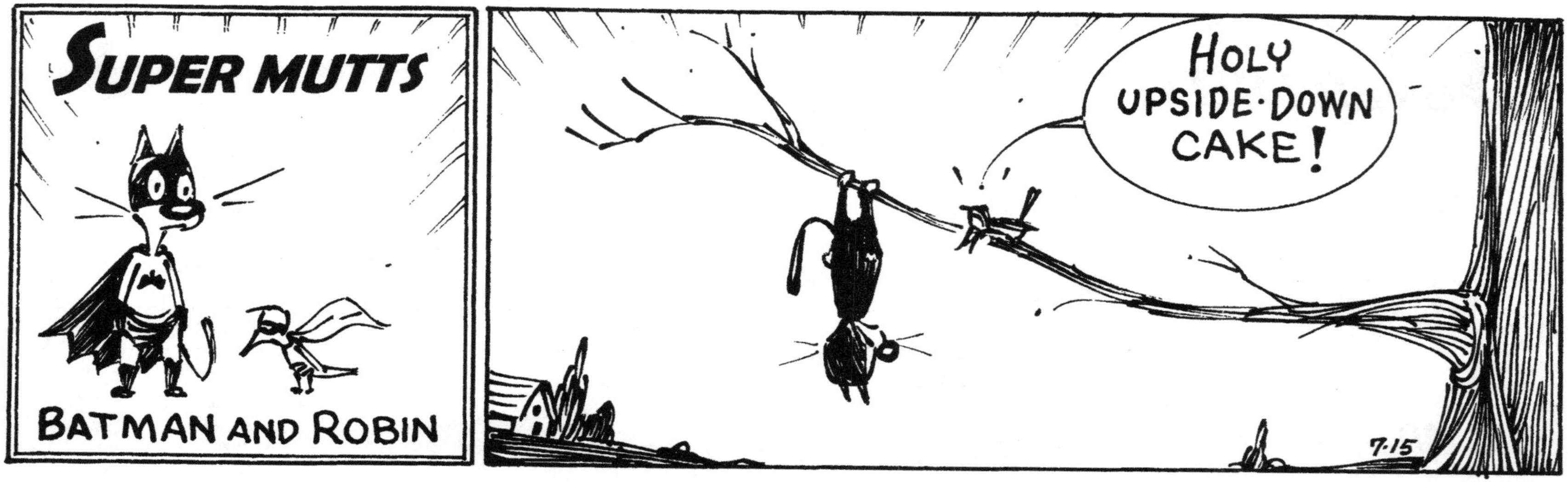
SUPER MUTTS
BATMAN AND ROBIN
HOLY UPSIDE-DOWN CAKE!
7·15

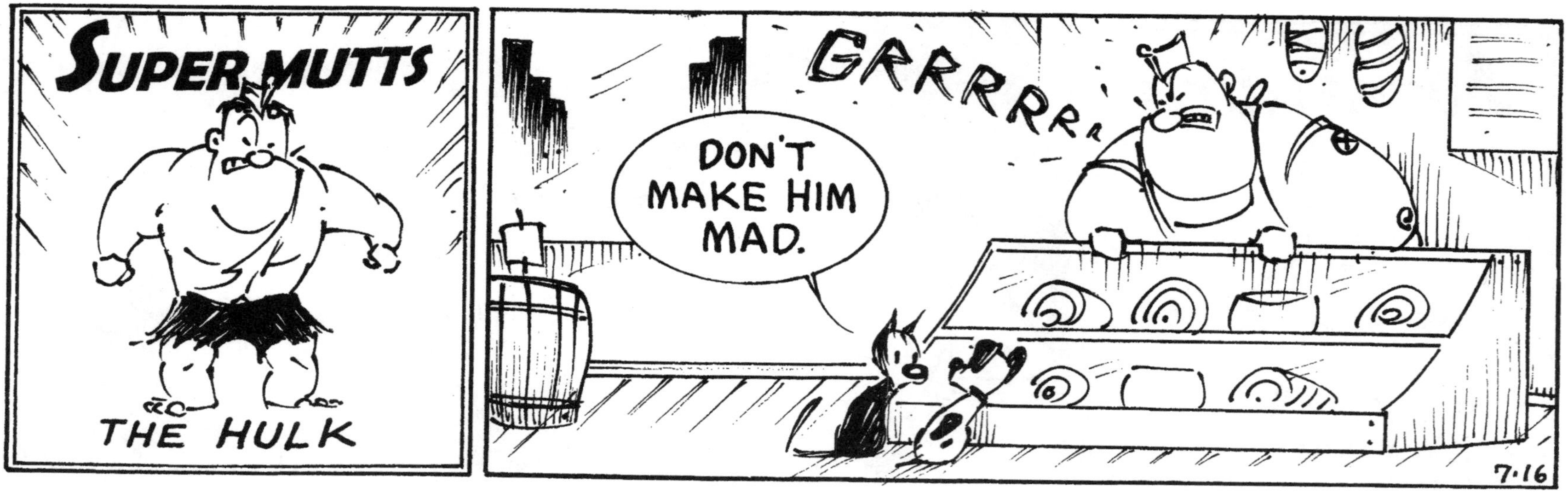
SUPER MUTTS
THE HULK
GRRRRRR
DON'T MAKE HIM MAD.
7·16

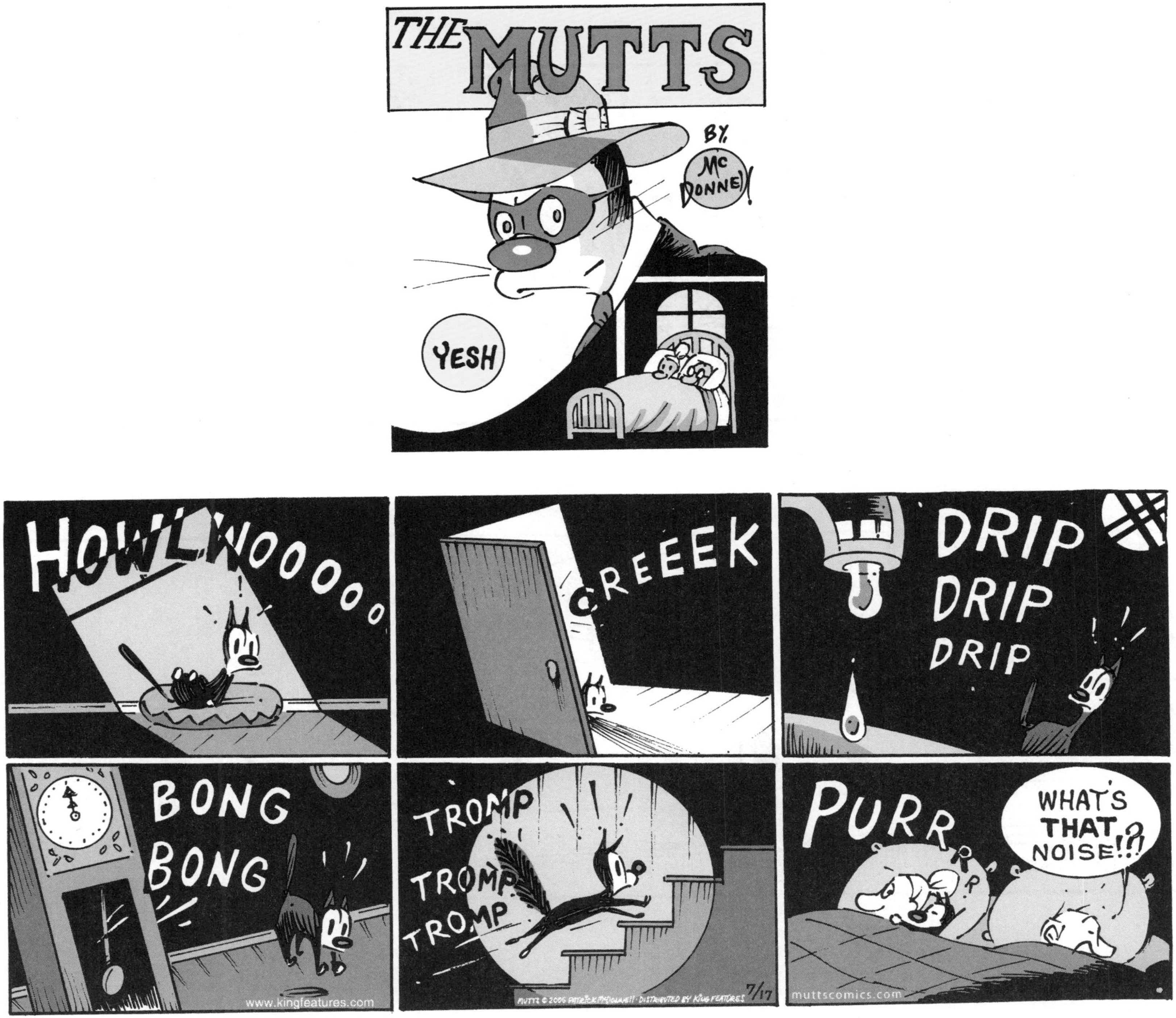
THE MUTTS
BY. MC DONNELL
YESH
HOWL WOOOOOO
CREEEK
DRIP
DRIP
DRIP
BONG
BONG
TROMP
TROMP
TROMP
PURRRRR
WHAT'S THAT NOISE!?!
www.kingfeatures.com
MUTTS © 2005 PATRICK McDONNELL · DISTRIBUTED BY KING FEATURES 7/17
muttscomics.com

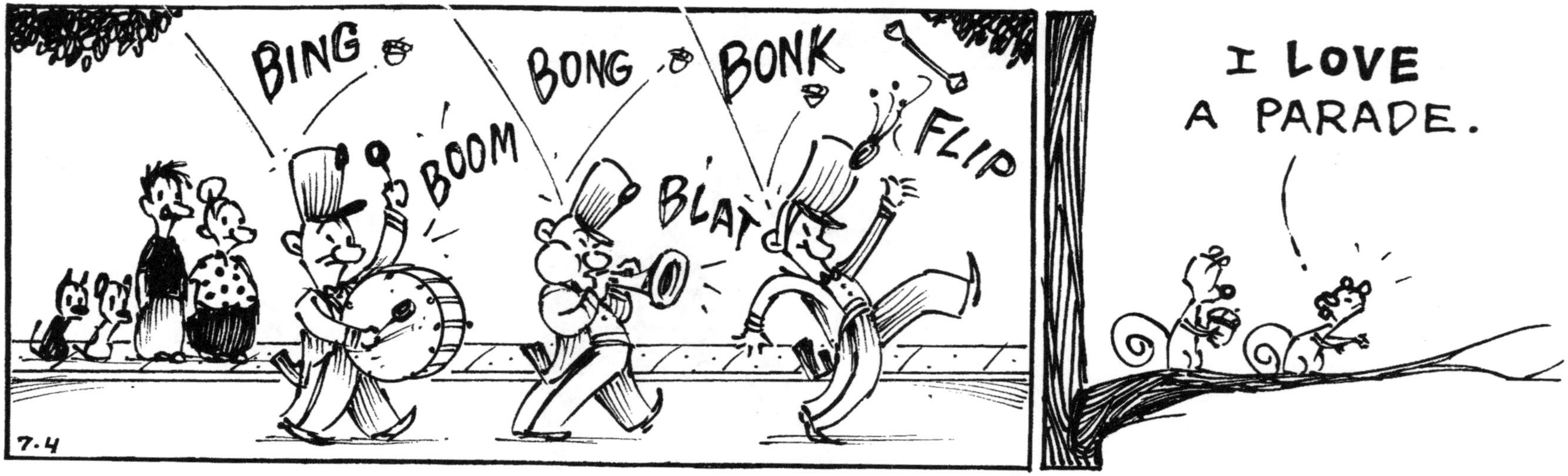
BING
BONG
BONK
BOOM
BLAT
FLIP
7·4
I LOVE A PARADE.

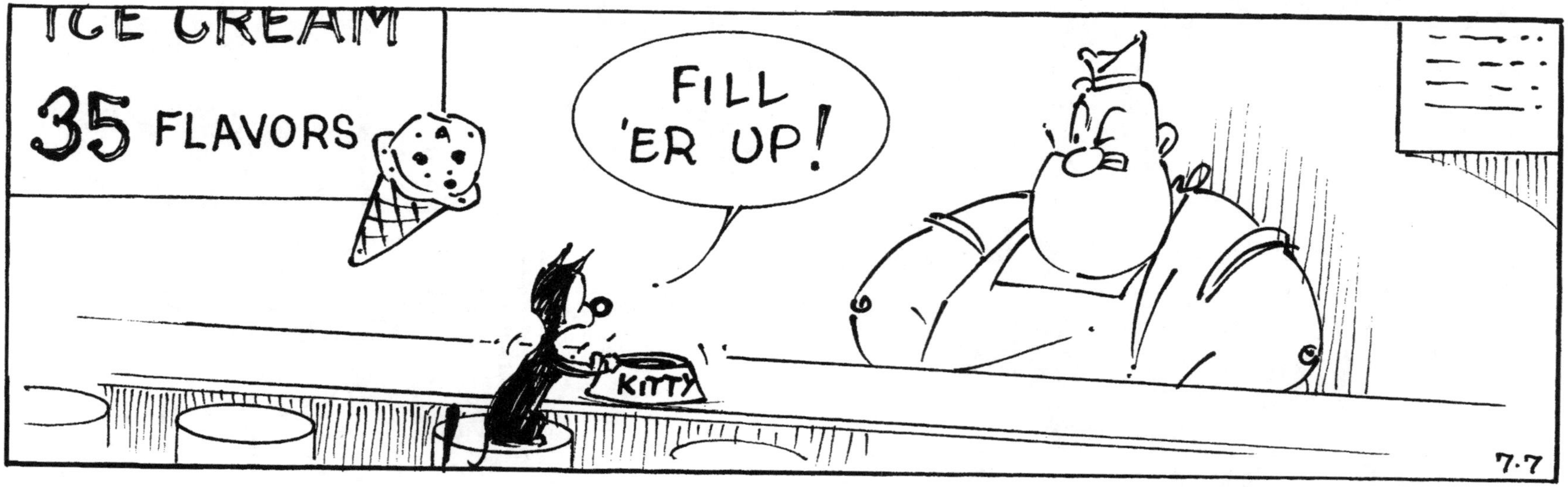
ICE CREAM
35 FLAVORS
FILL 'ER UP!
KITTY
7·7

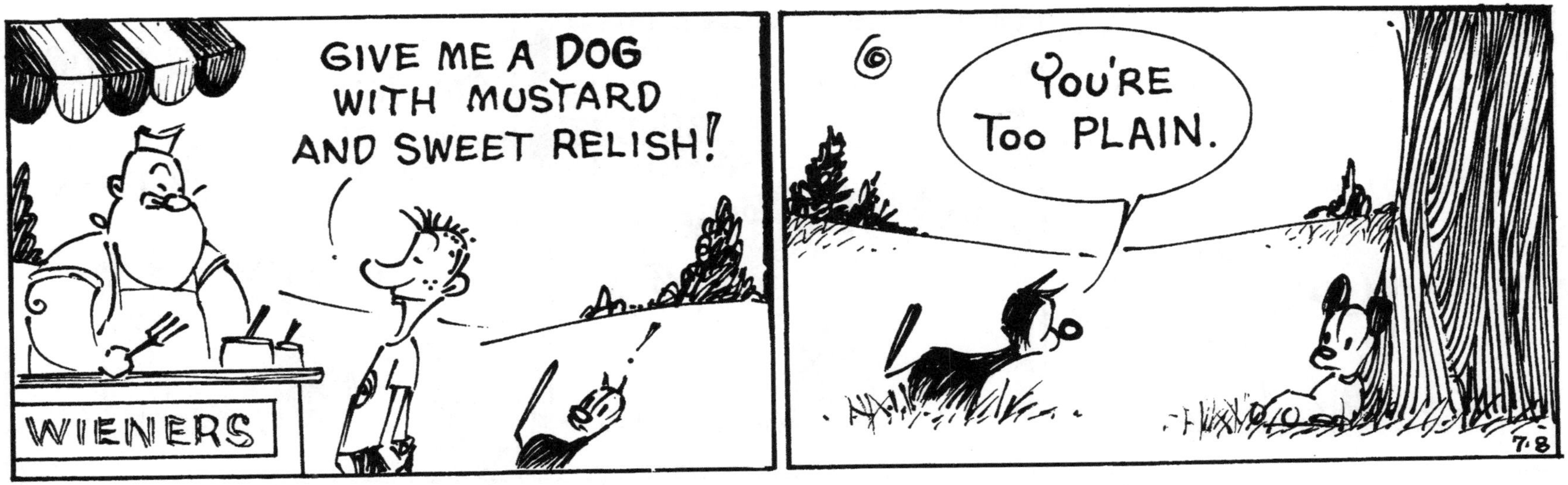
GIVE ME A DOG WITH MUSTARD AND SWEET RELISH!
WIENERS
YOU'RE Too PLAIN.
7·8

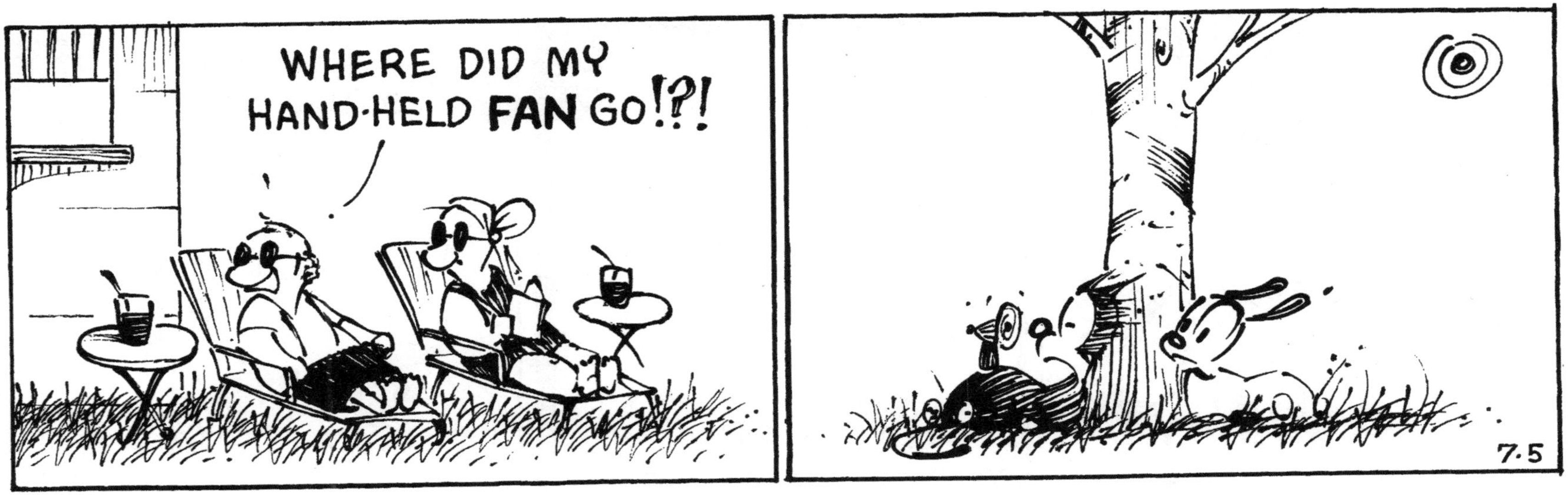
WHERE DID MY HAND-HELD FAN GO!?!
7·5

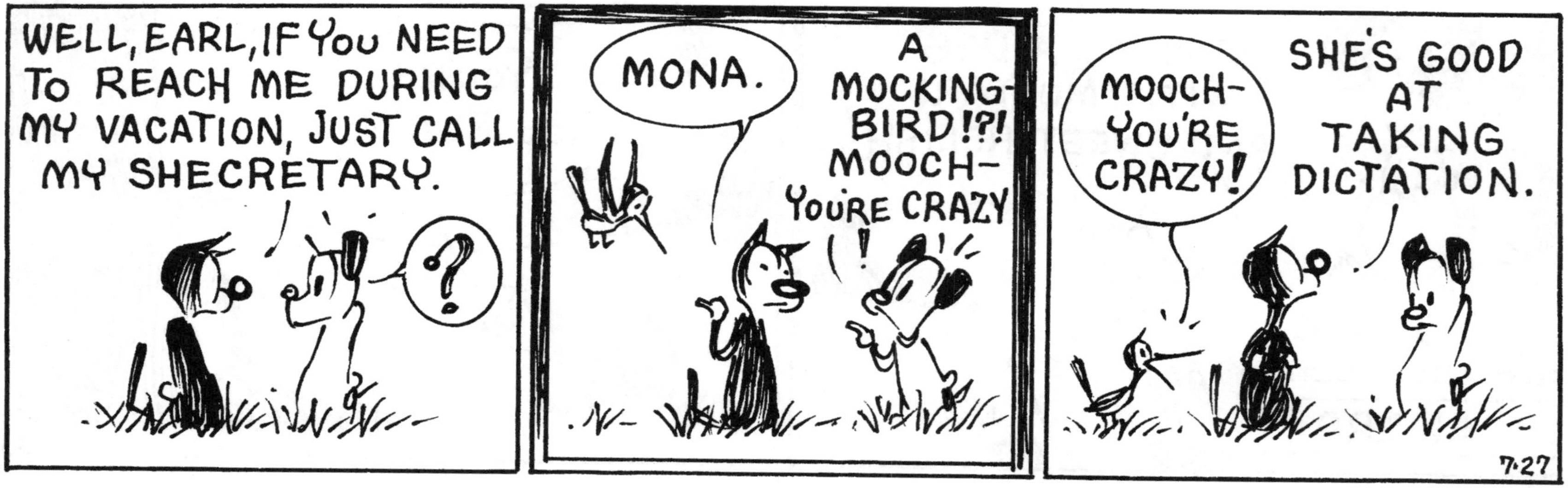
WELL, EARL, IF YOU NEED TO REACH ME DURING MY VACATION, JUST CALL MY SHECRETARY.
?
MONA.
A MOCKING-BIRD!?! MOOCH- YOU'RE CRAZY
MOOCH- YOU'RE CRAZY!
SHE'S GOOD AT TAKING DICTATION.
7·27

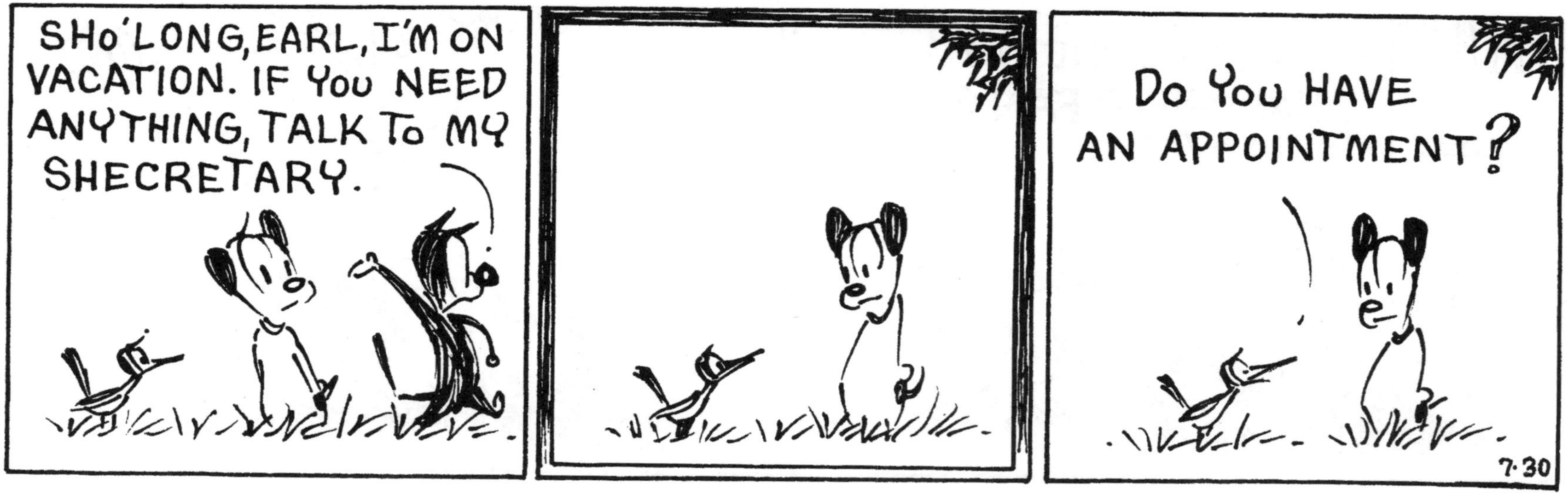
SHO'LONG, EARL, I'M ON VACATION. IF YOU NEED ANYTHING, TALK TO MY SHECRETARY.
DO YOU HAVE AN APPOINTMENT?
7·30

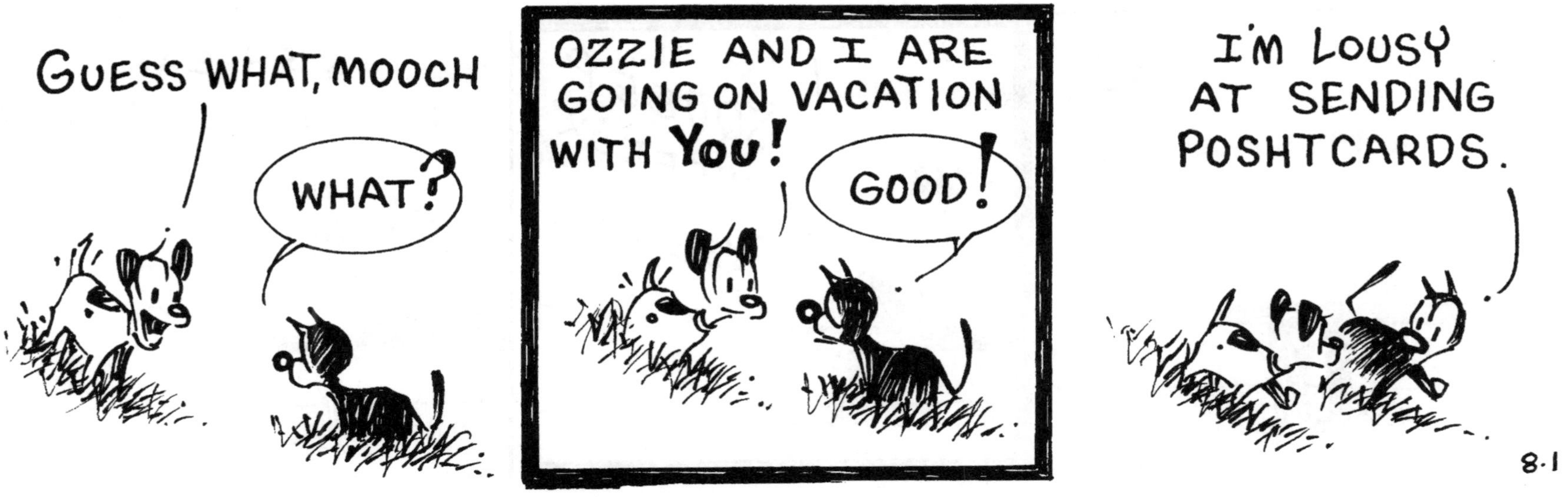
GUESS WHAT, MOOCH
WHAT?
OZZIE AND I ARE GOING ON VACATION WITH YOU!
GOOD!
I'M LOUSY AT SENDING POSHTCARDS.
8·1

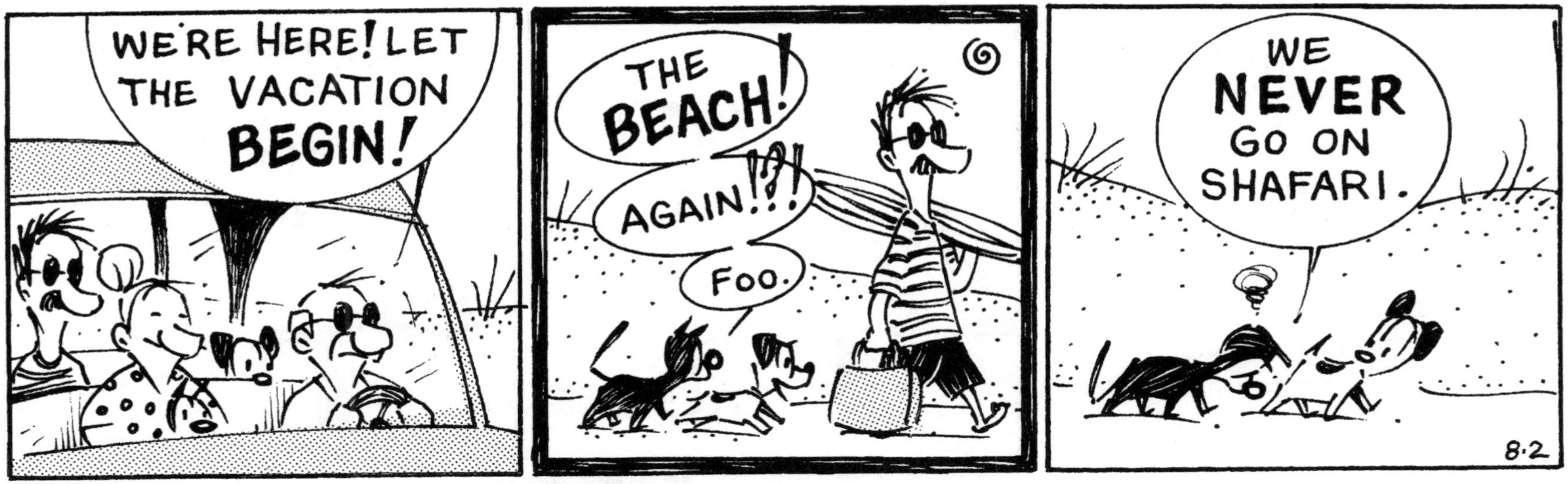
WE'RE HERE! LET THE VACATION BEGIN!
THE BEACH!
AGAIN!?!
FOO.
WE NEVER GO ON SHAFARI.
8·2

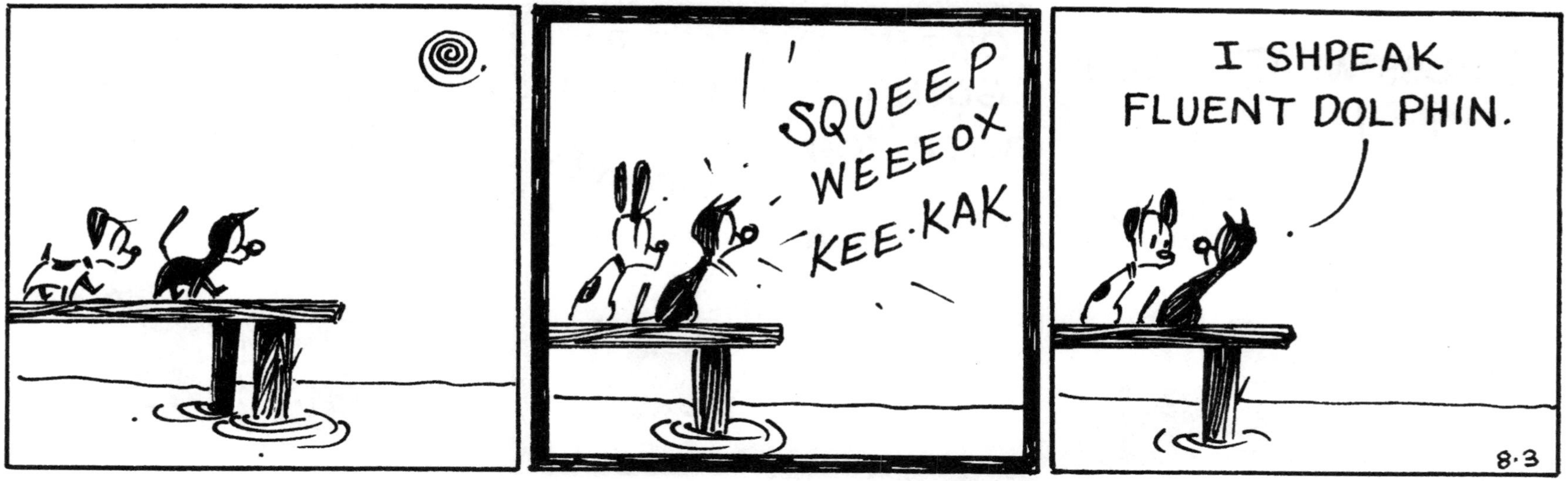
SQUEEP
WEEEOX
KEE·KAK
I SHPEAK FLUENT DOLPHIN.
8·3

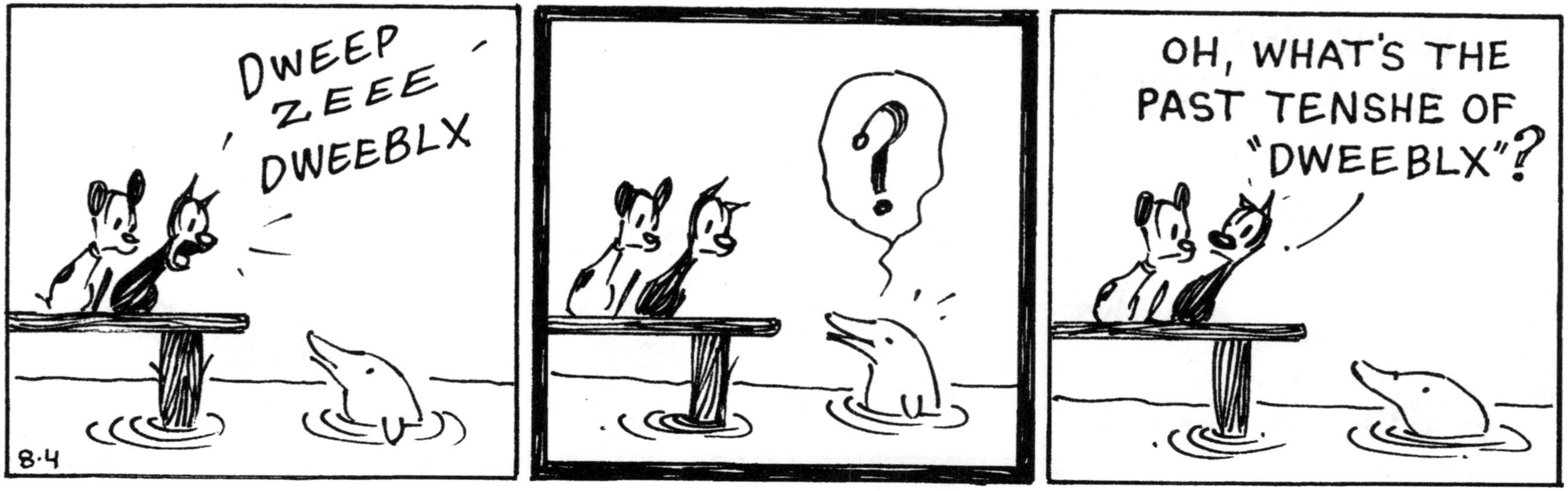
DWEEP
ZEEE
DWEEBLX
8·4
?
OH, WHAT'S THE PAST TENSHE OF "DWEEBLX"?

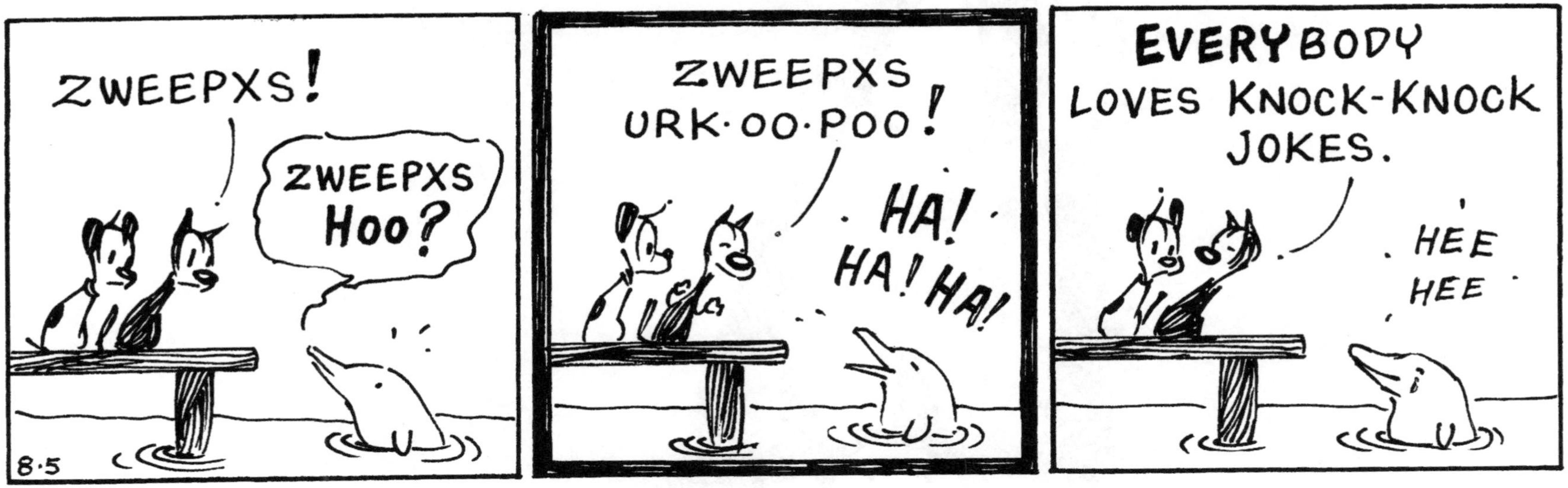
ZWEEPXS!
ZWEEPXS HOO?
8·5
ZWEEPXS URK·OO·POO!
HA! HA! HA!
EVERYBODY LOVES KNOCK-KNOCK JOKES.
HEE HEE

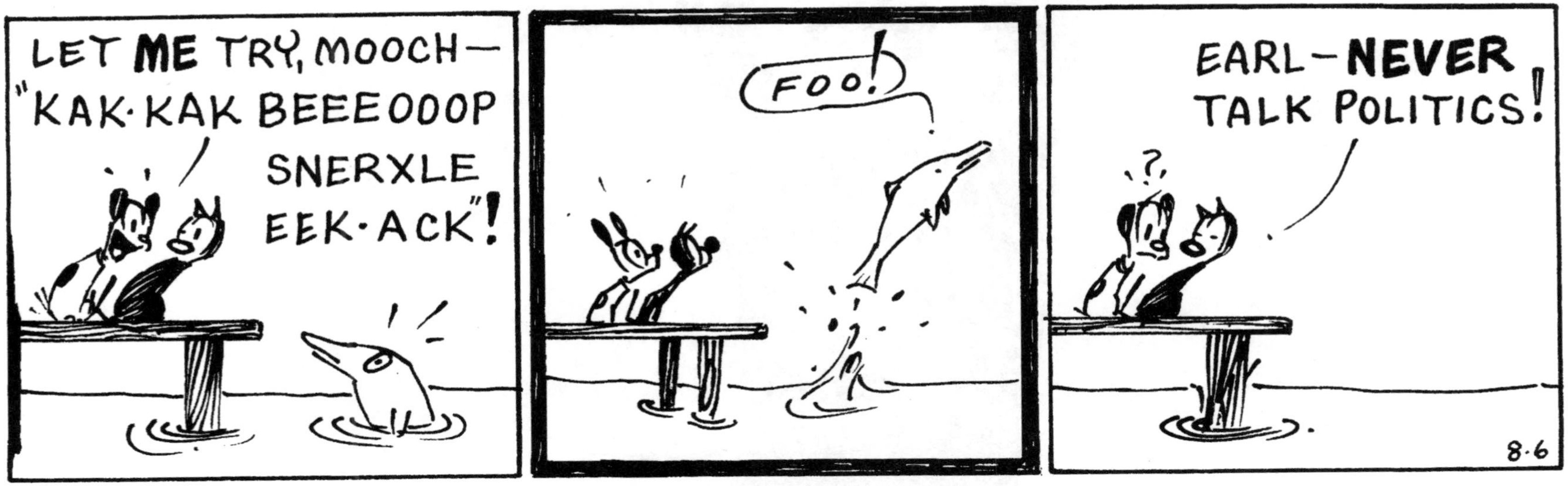
LET ME TRY, MOOCH—
"KAK·KAK BEEEOOOP SNERXLE EEK·ACK"!
FOO!
EARL—NEVER TALK POLITICS!
?
8·6

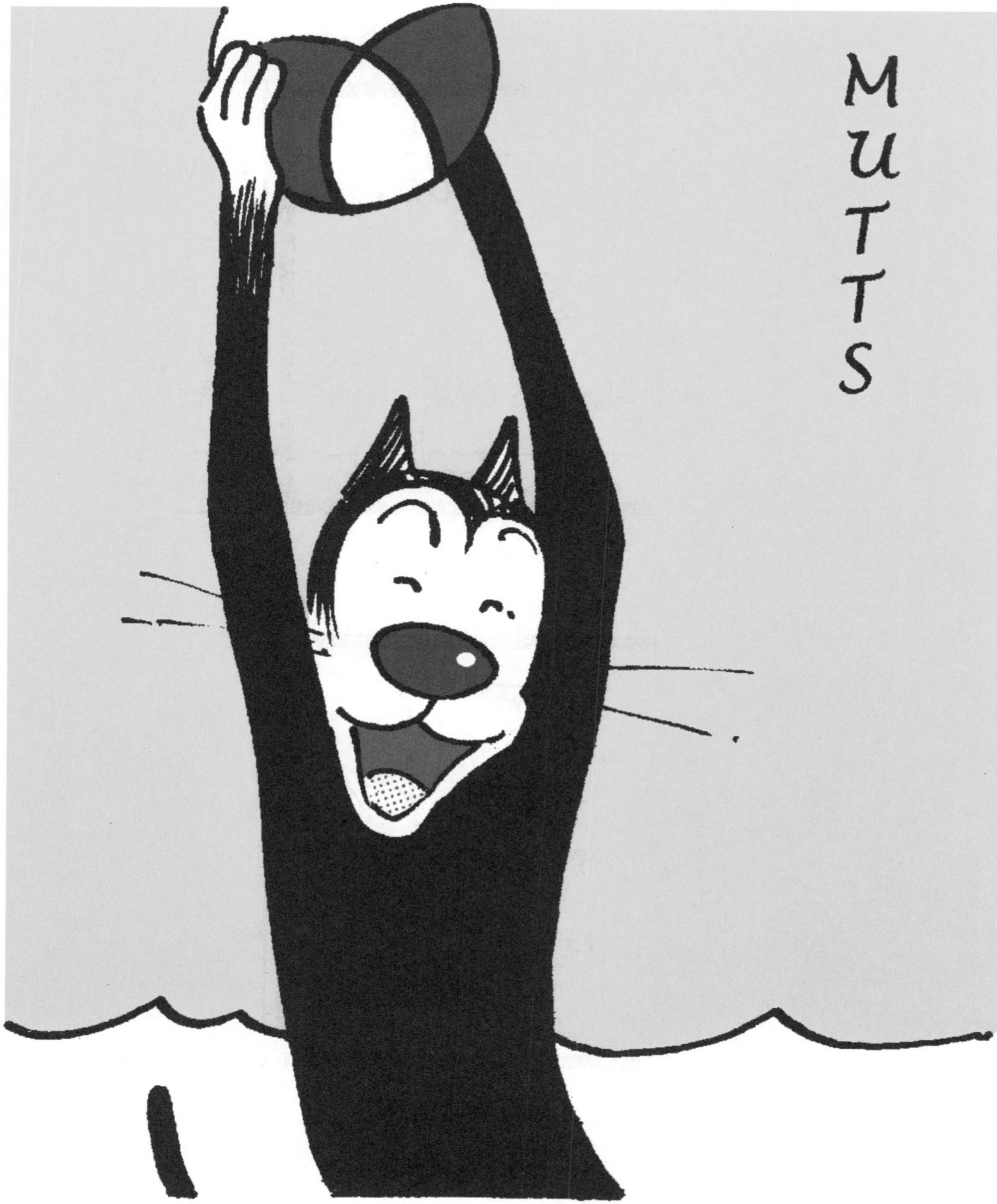
MUTTS

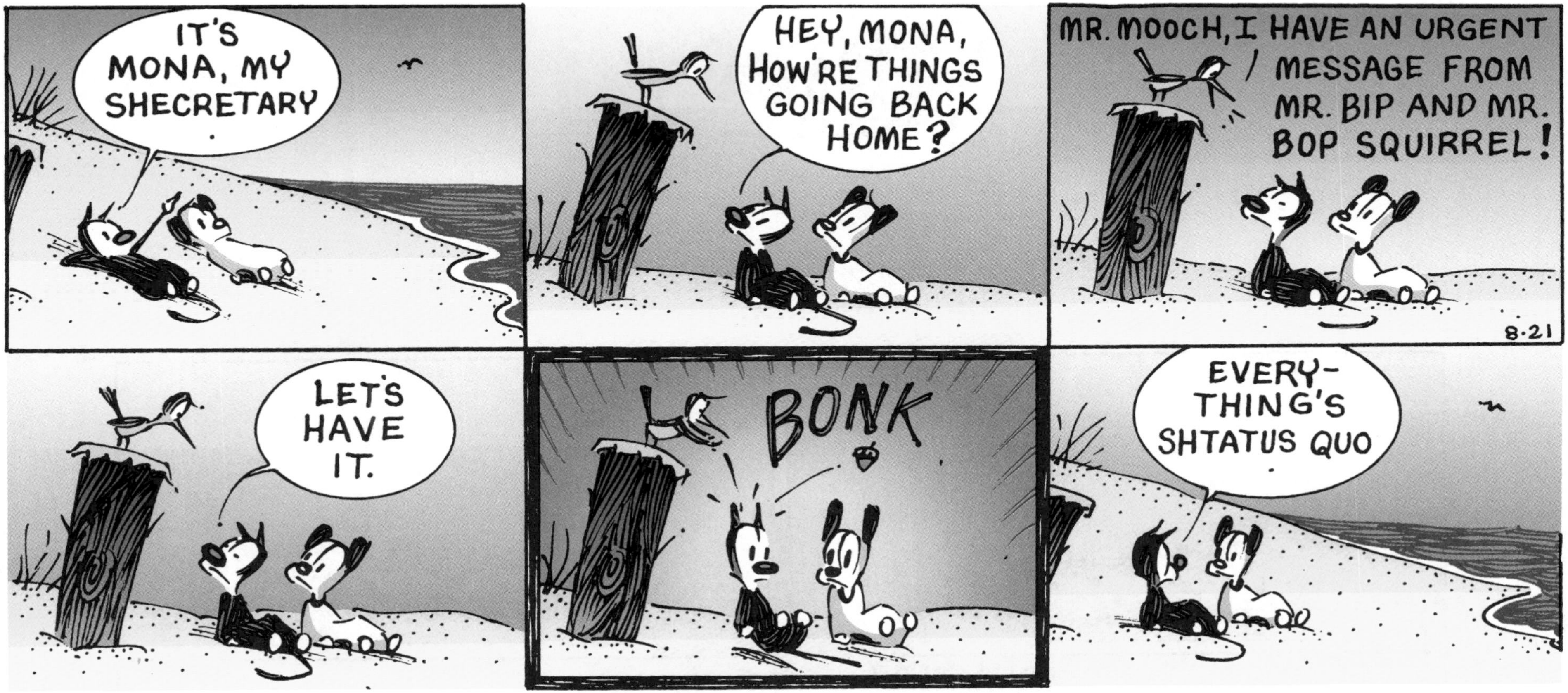
IT'S MONA, MY SHECRETARY
HEY, MONA, HOW'RE THINGS GOING BACK HOME?
MR. MOOCH, I HAVE AN URGENT MESSAGE FROM MR. BIP AND MR. BOP SQUIRREL!
8·21
LET'S HAVE IT.
BONK
EVERY-THING'S SHTATUS QUO

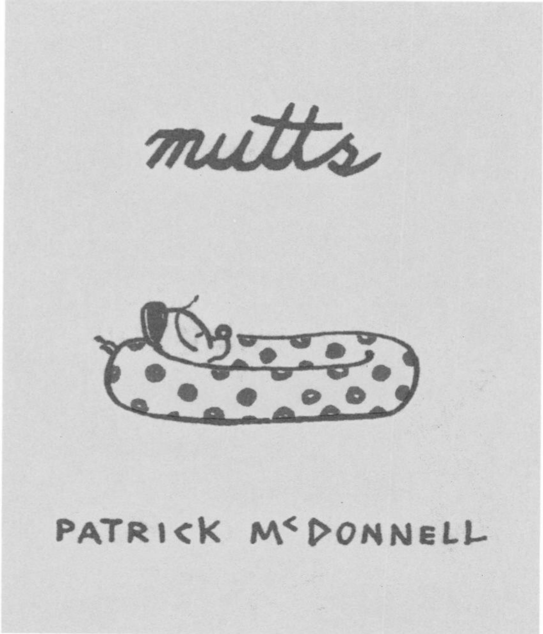
mutts
PATRICK McDONNELL

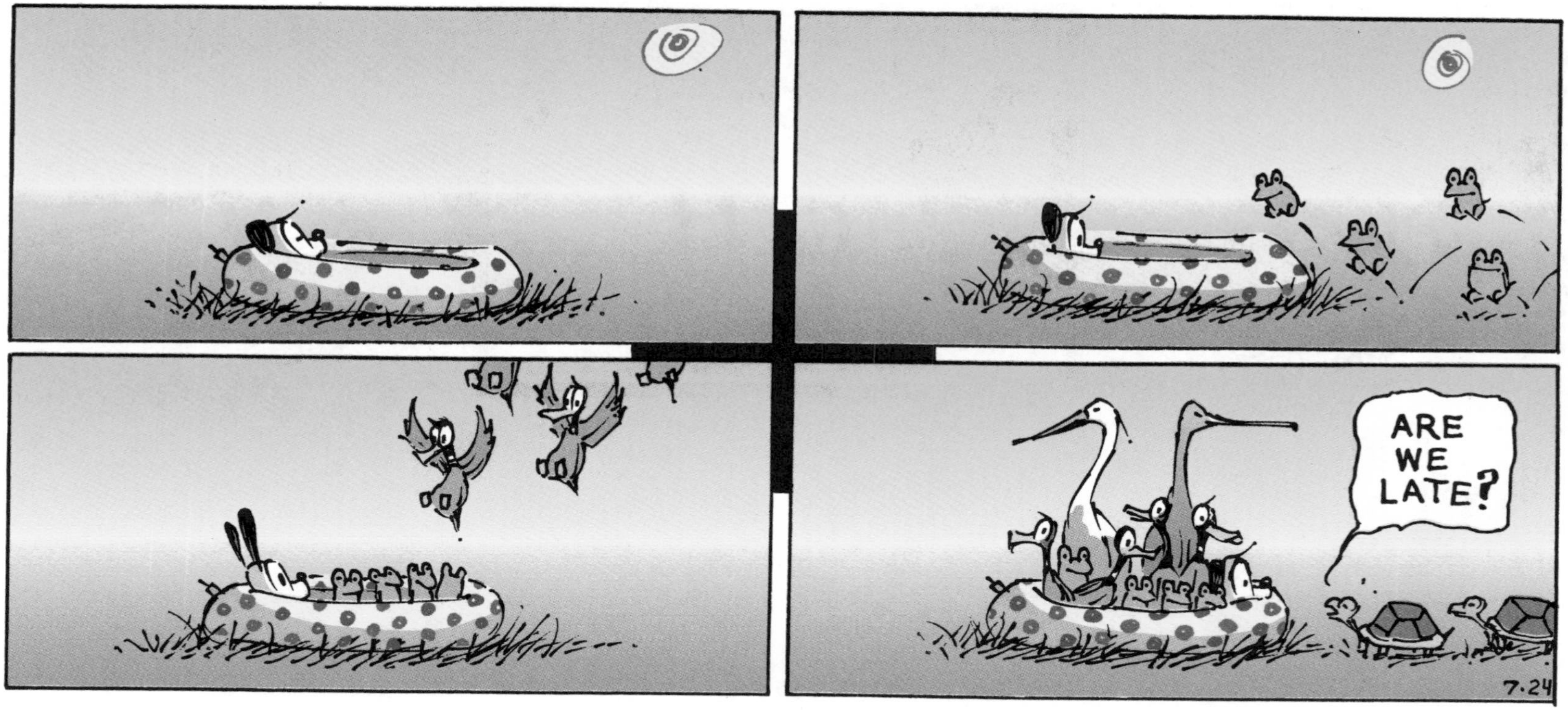
ARE WE LATE?
7.24

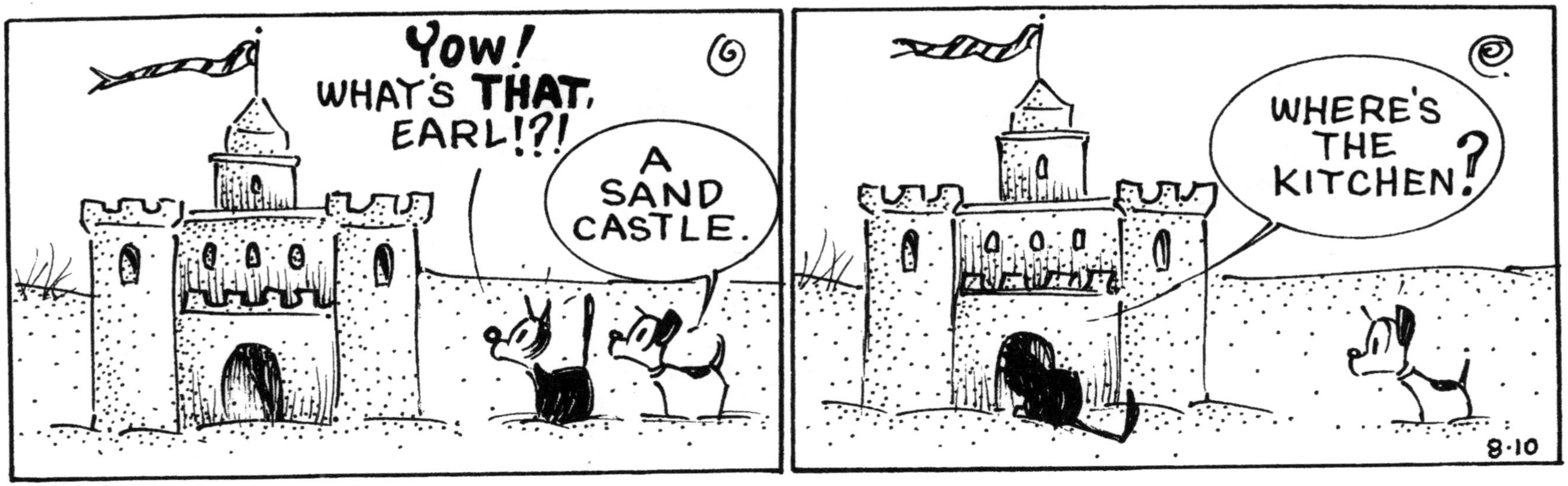
YOW! WHAT'S THAT, EARL!?!
A SAND CASTLE.
WHERE'S THE KITCHEN?
8·10

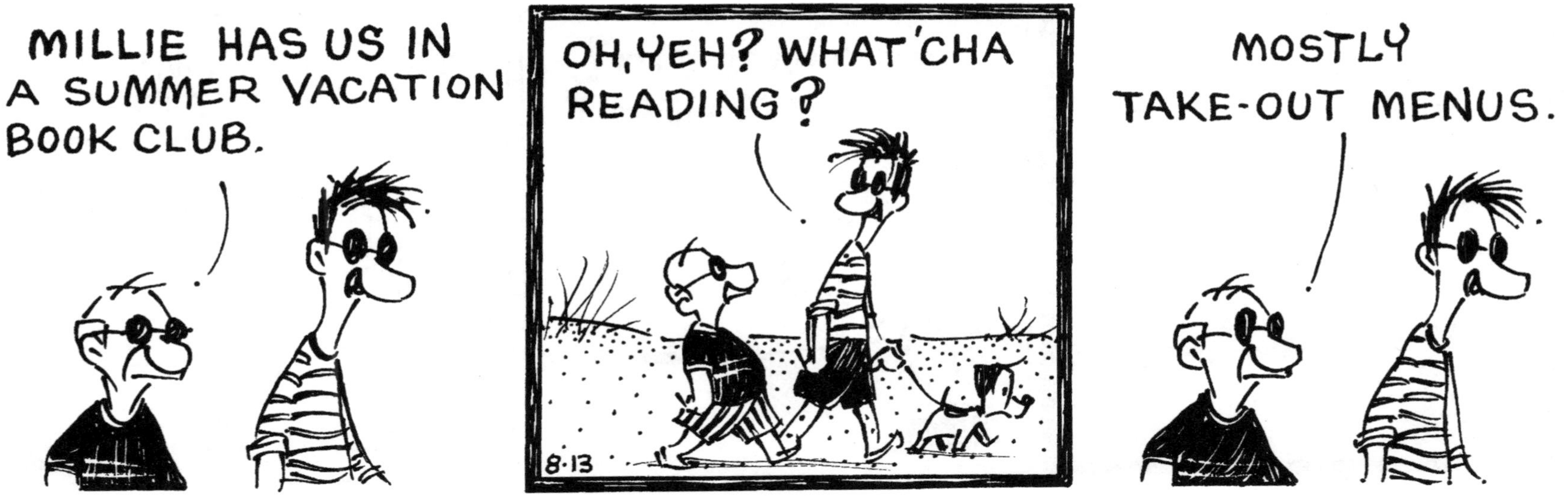
MILLIE HAS US IN A SUMMER VACATION BOOK CLUB.
OH, YEH? WHAT'CHA READING?
8·13
MOSTLY TAKE-OUT MENUS.

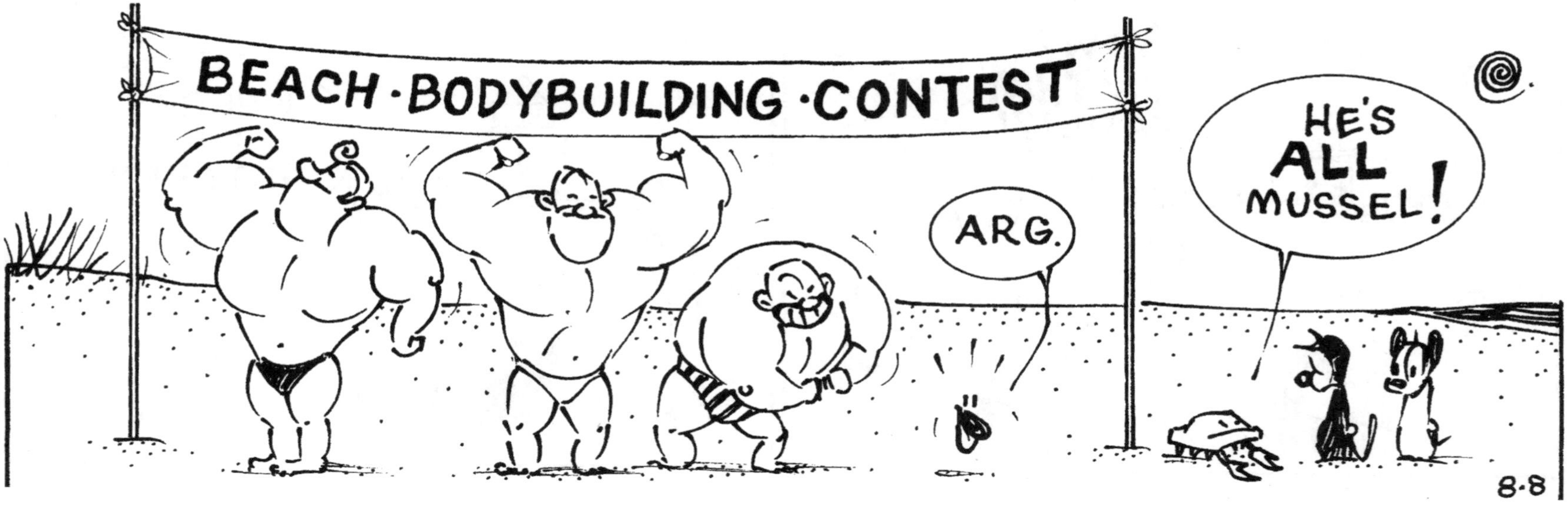
BEACH · BODYBUILDING · CONTEST
ARG.
HE'S ALL MUSSEL!
8·8

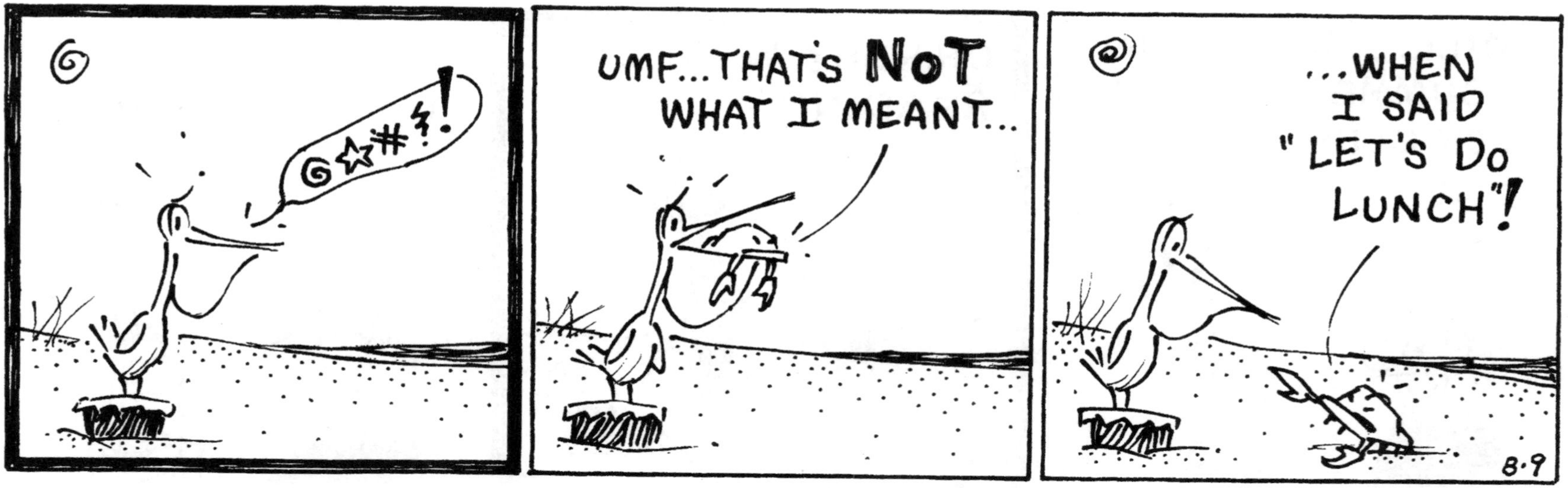
G☆#‡!
UMF...THAT'S NOT WHAT I MEANT...
...WHEN I SAID "LET'S DO LUNCH"!
8·9

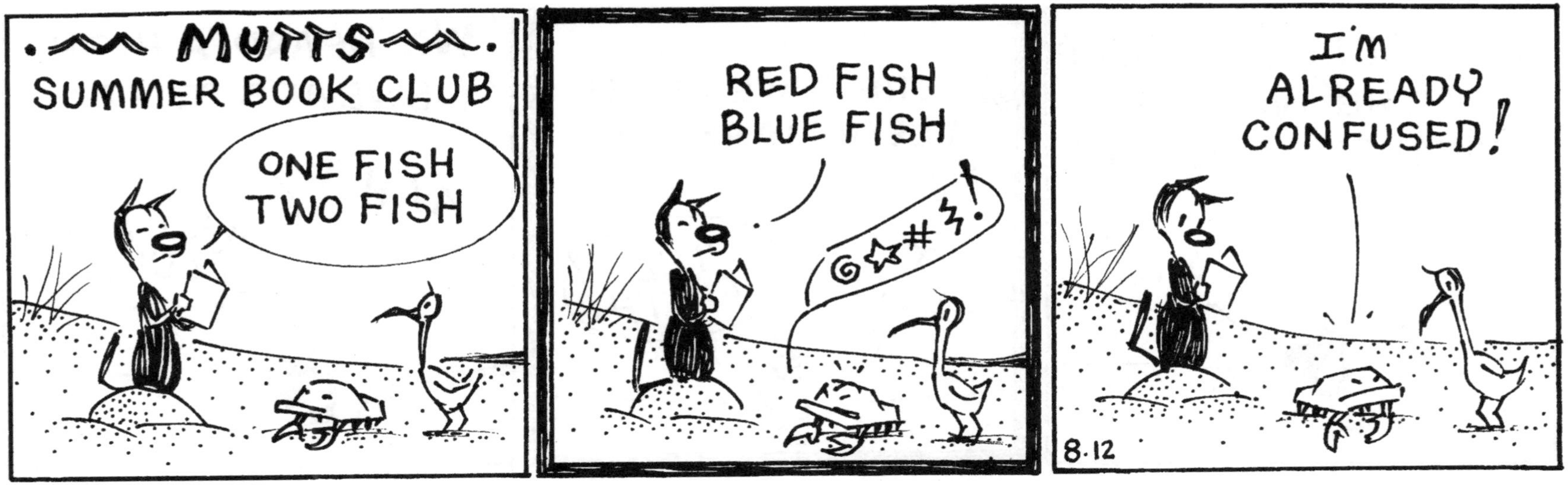
MUTTS
SUMMER BOOK CLUB
ONE FISH TWO FISH
RED FISH BLUE FISH
I'M ALREADY CONFUSED!
8.12

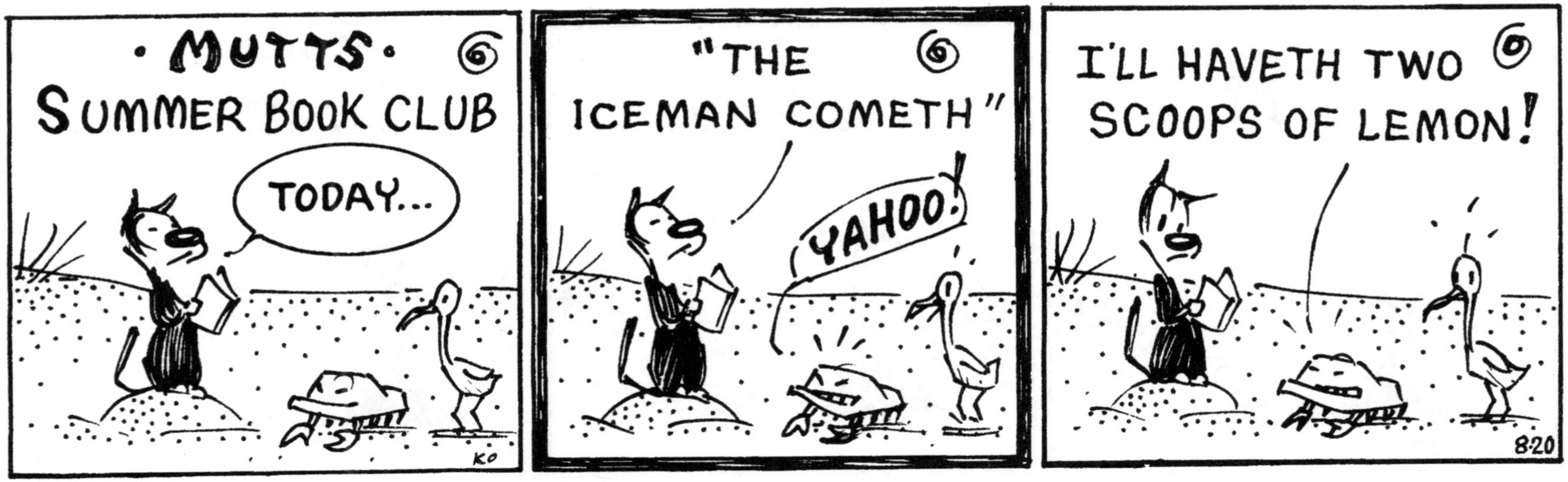
MUTTS
SUMMER BOOK CLUB
TODAY...
"THE ICEMAN COMETH"
YAHOO!
I'LL HAVETH TWO SCOOPS OF LEMON!
8·20

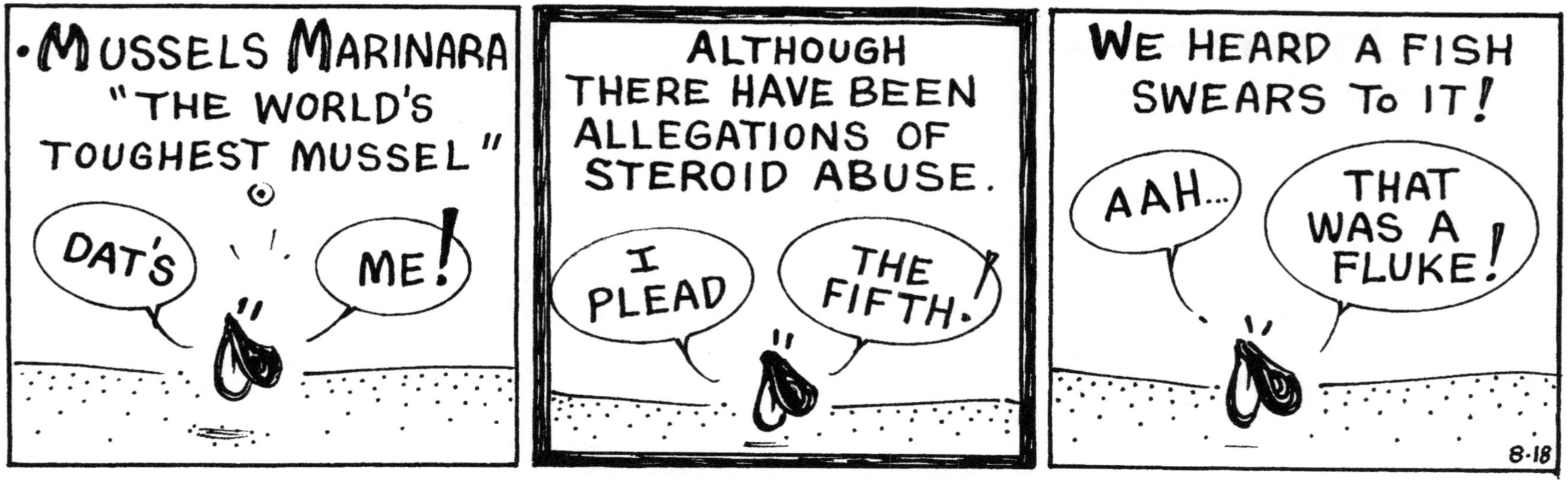
• MUSSELS MARINARA "THE WORLD'S TOUGHEST MUSSEL"
DAT'S
ME!
ALTHOUGH THERE HAVE BEEN ALLEGATIONS OF STEROID ABUSE.
I PLEAD
THE FIFTH.!
WE HEARD A FISH SWEARS TO IT!
AAH...
THAT WAS A FLUKE!
8·18

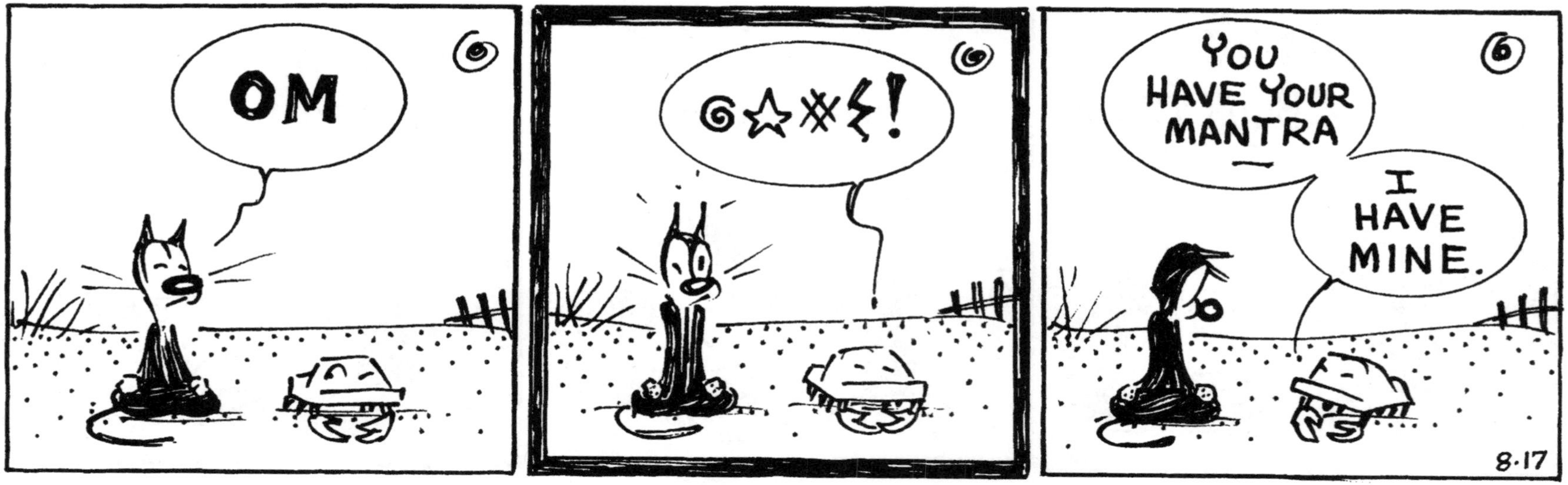
OM
I HAVE MINE.
8·17

CRABBY THEATRE
MUTTS.
SERIES
No. ONE
2¢

DID I EVER TELL YA ABOUT MY TIME ON THE S.S. LILLY MAE...
IT WAS RUN BY A FUNNY-TALKING, ONE-EYED SAILOR WITH A STRONG HANKERING FOR SPINACH...
AND FOR HIS GIRLFRIEND —WHO WAS AS THIN AS AN EEL...
7.31
HIS CREW WAS A GOON, A JEEP, AND SOME WIMP (ONE OF THE JONES BOYS) WHO THOUGHT I WAS LUNCH!
ARG!
OH, CRABBY— I DON'T BELIEVE A WORD!!!
IT WAS IN ALL THE NEWSPAPERS.

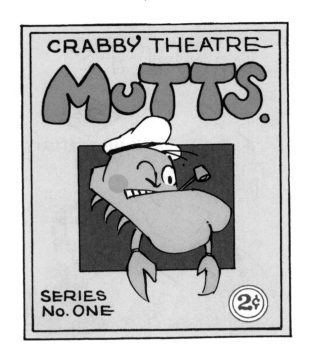

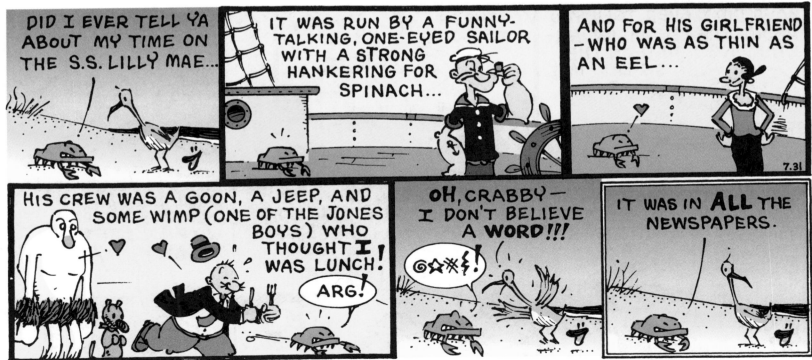

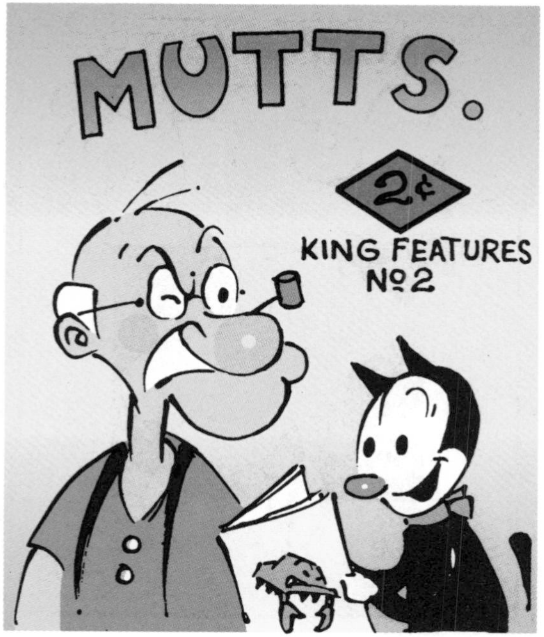
MUTTS.
2¢
KING FEATURES
Nº2

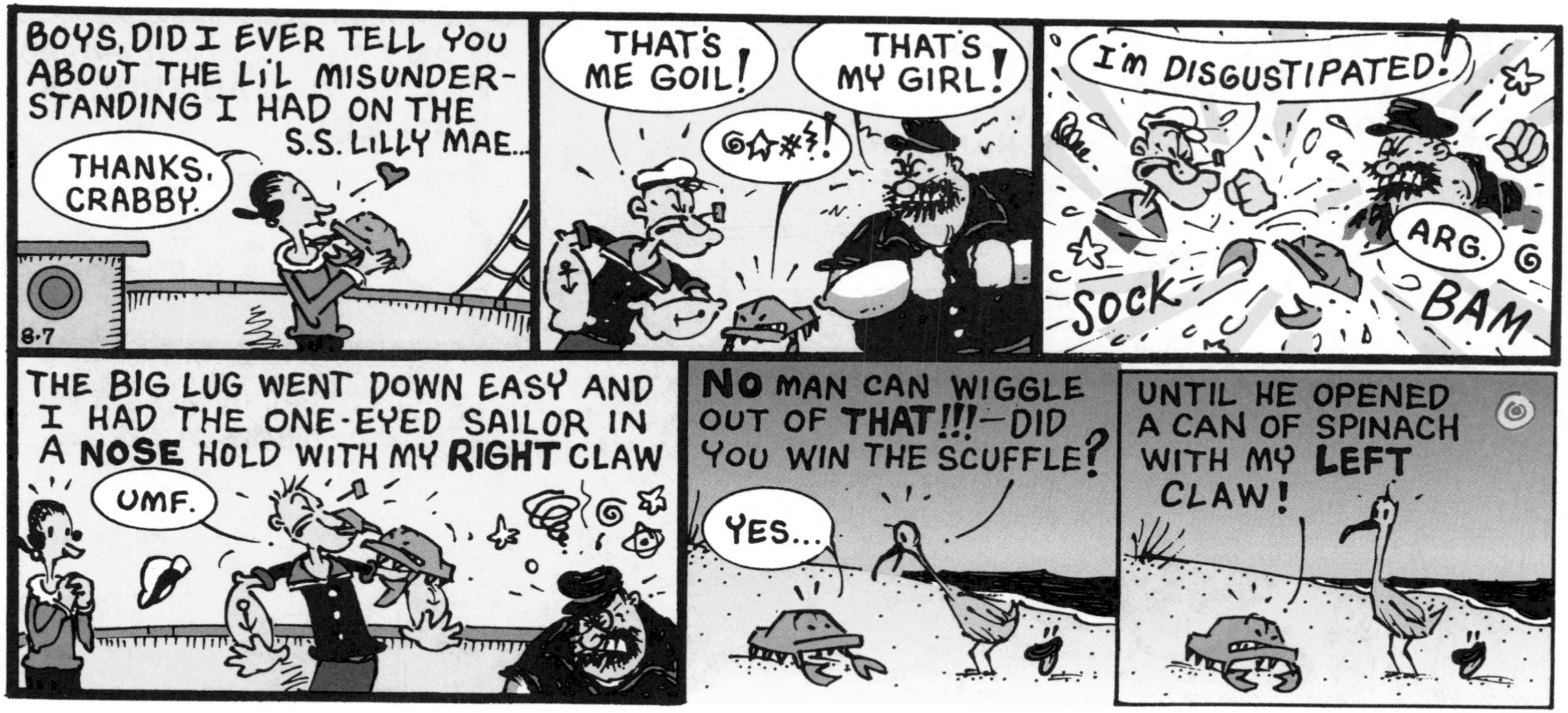
BOYS, DID I EVER TELL YOU ABOUT THE LI'L MISUNDERSTANDING I HAD ON THE S.S. LILLY MAE...
THANKS, CRABBY.
8·7
THAT'S ME GOIL!
THAT'S MY GIRL!
I'M DISGUSTIPATED!
ARG.
SOCK
BAM
THE BIG LUG WENT DOWN EASY AND I HAD THE ONE-EYED SAILOR IN A NOSE HOLD WITH MY RIGHT CLAW
UMF.
NO MAN CAN WIGGLE OUT OF THAT!!!—DID YOU WIN THE SCUFFLE?
YES...
UNTIL HE OPENED A CAN OF SPINACH WITH MY LEFT CLAW!

CRABBY THEATRE
STARRING
MUTTS
MCD.
No. 3

THE ONE-EYED SAILOR AND I BECAME BEST PALS...
ARF
ARF
WE SET SAIL ON MANY EXCITING ADVENTURES...
ARG.
WHY, WE EVEN RULED AN ISLAND TOGETHER-SPINACHOVIA! WE HAD IT ALL...
BUT OF COURSE, ALL GOOD THINGS COME TO AN END.
WHY?!
8·14
SOON I WAS CRABBING ABOUT EVERYTHING AND I WAS ASKED TO JUMP SHIP.
YOU BLEW IT, CRABBY!
WELL, IF I LEARNED ONE THING FROM THAT GREAT MAN, IT WAS...
I @☆#$! AM WHAT I @☆#$! AM.

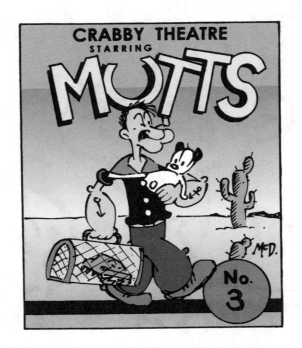

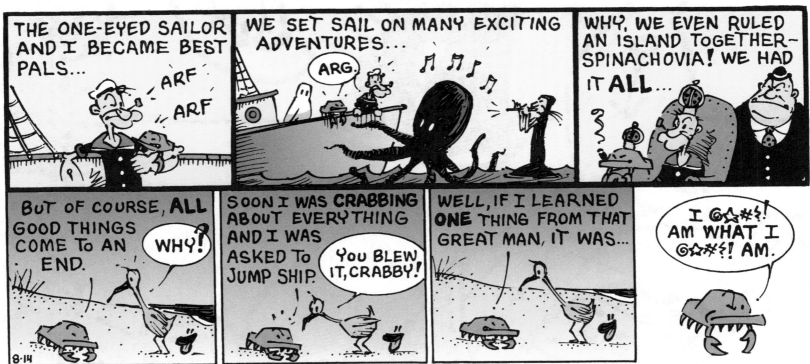

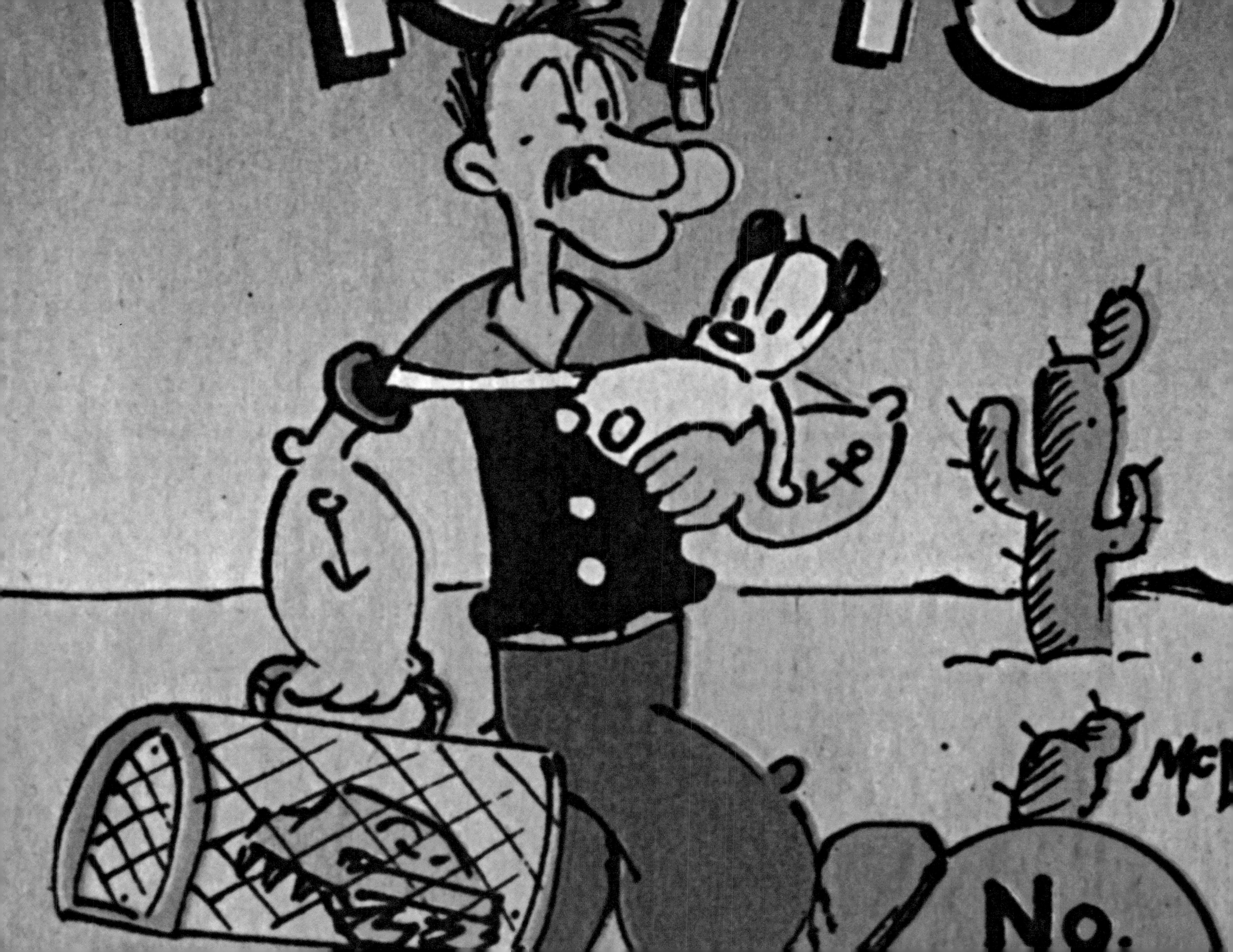
No.

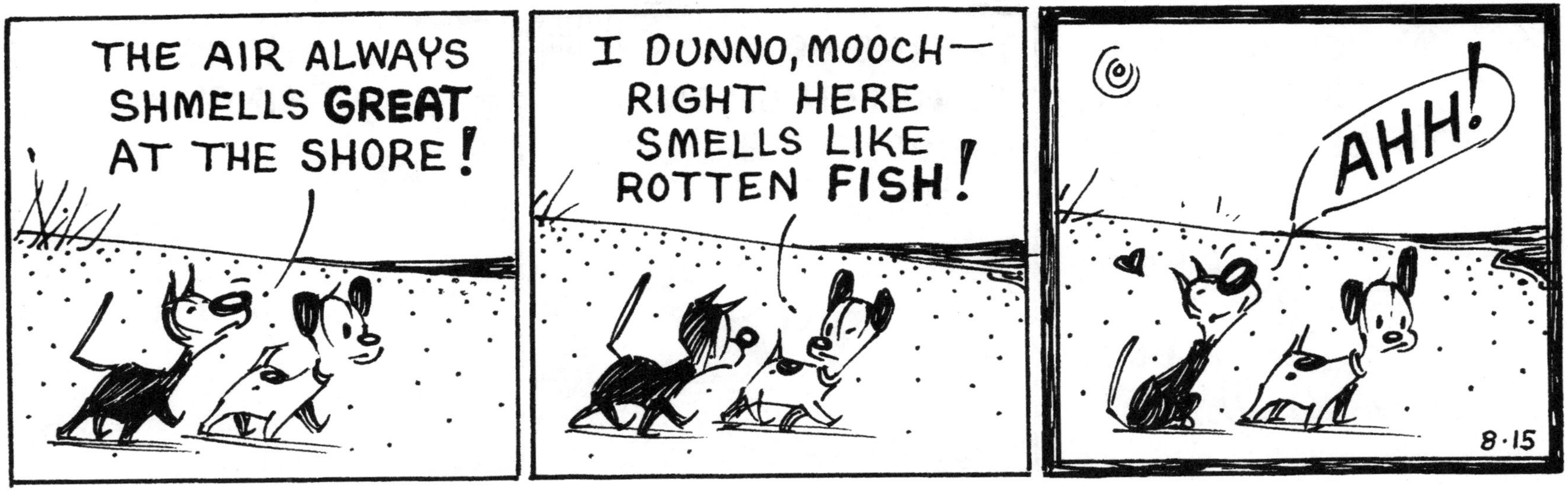
THE AIR ALWAYS SHMELLS GREAT AT THE SHORE!
I DUNNO, MOOCH— RIGHT HERE SMELLS LIKE ROTTEN FISH!
AHH!
8·15

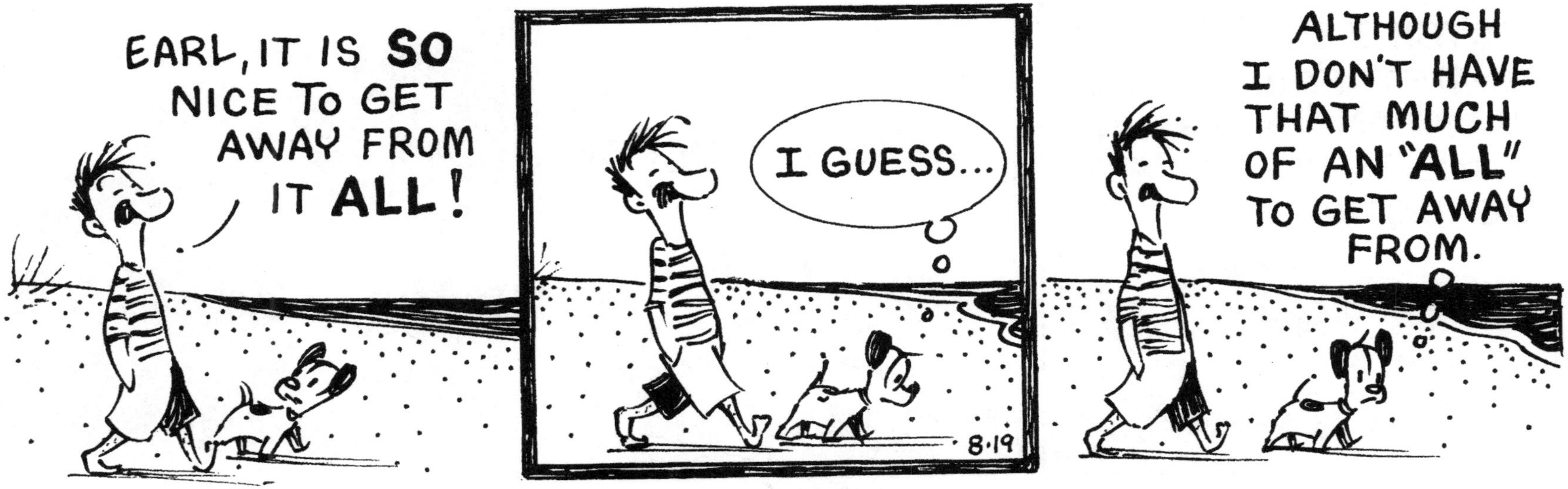
EARL, IT IS SO NICE TO GET AWAY FROM IT ALL!
I GUESS...
8·19
ALTHOUGH I DON'T HAVE THAT MUCH OF AN "ALL" TO GET AWAY FROM.

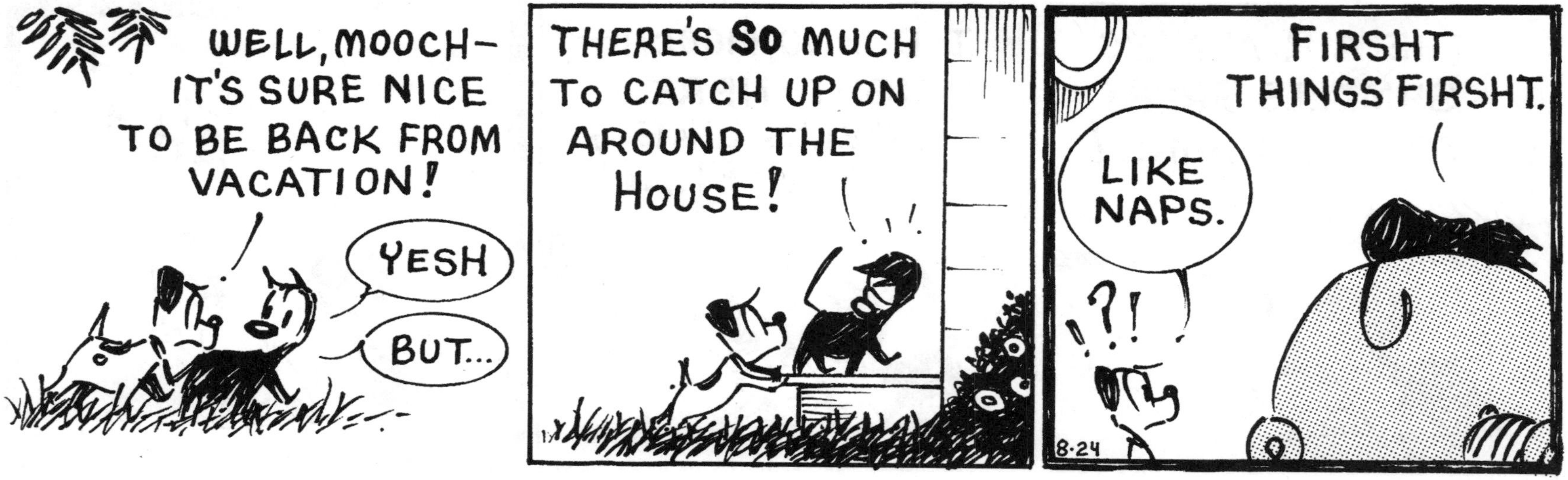
WELL, MOOCH–
IT'S SURE NICE TO BE BACK FROM VACATION!
YESH
BUT...
THERE'S SO MUCH TO CATCH UP ON AROUND THE HOUSE!
FIRSHT THINGS FIRSHT.
LIKE NAPS.
?!
8·24

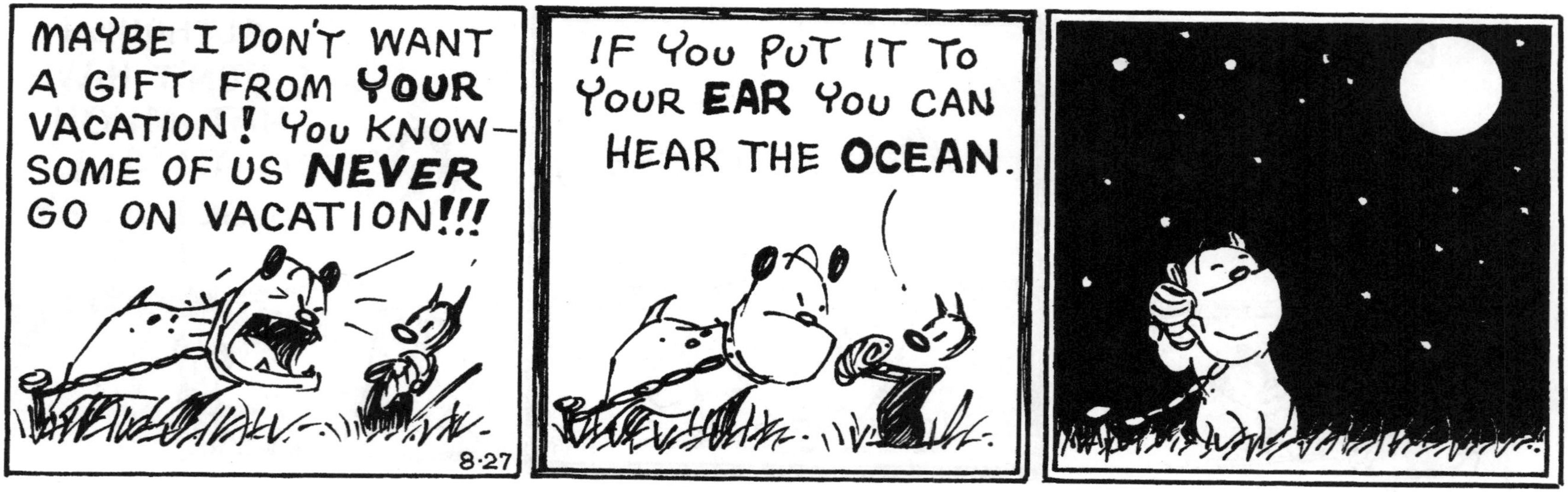
MAYBE I DON'T WANT A GIFT FROM YOUR VACATION! YOU KNOW– SOME OF US NEVER GO ON VACATION!!!
8·27
IF YOU PUT IT TO YOUR EAR YOU CAN HEAR THE OCEAN.

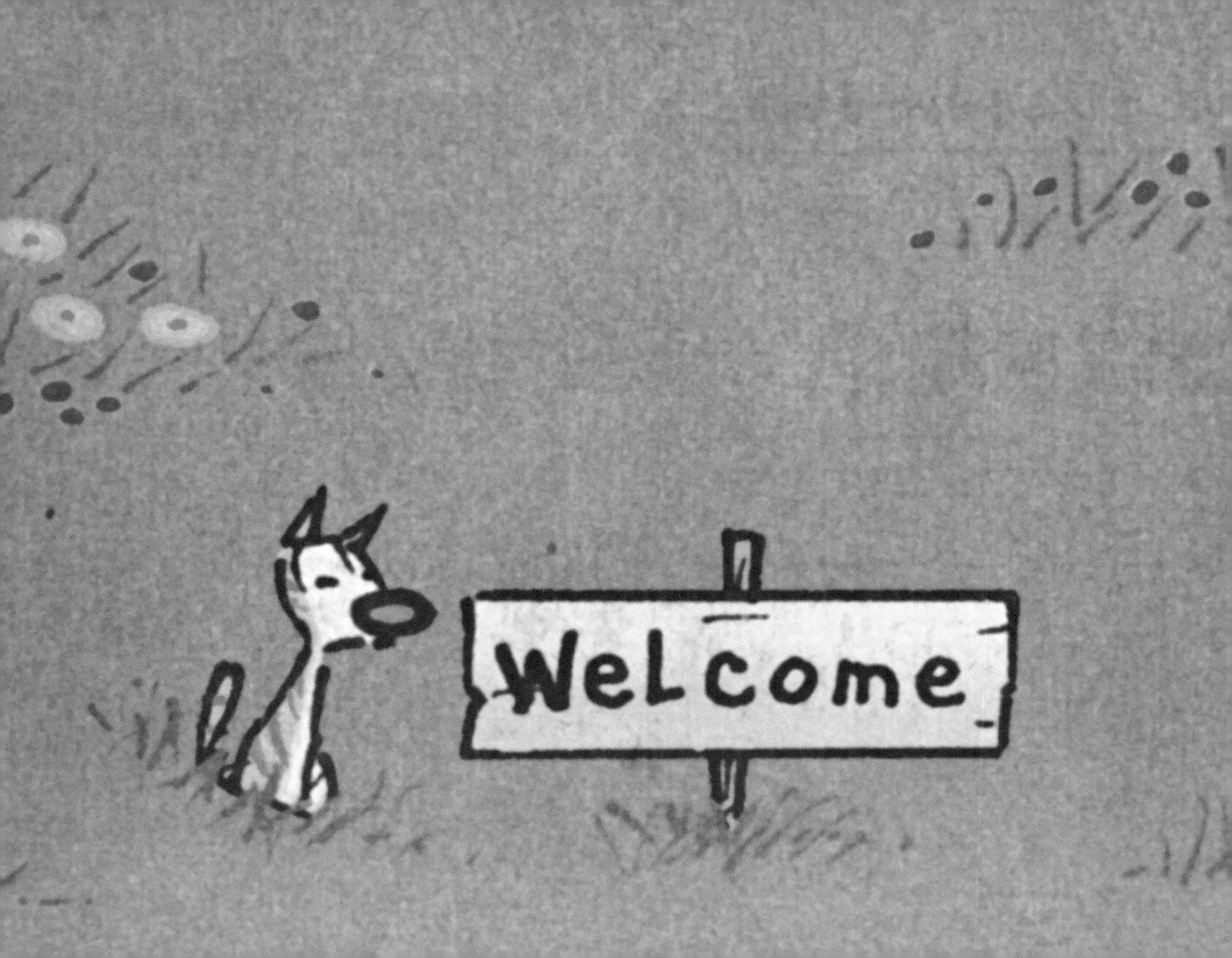
Welcome

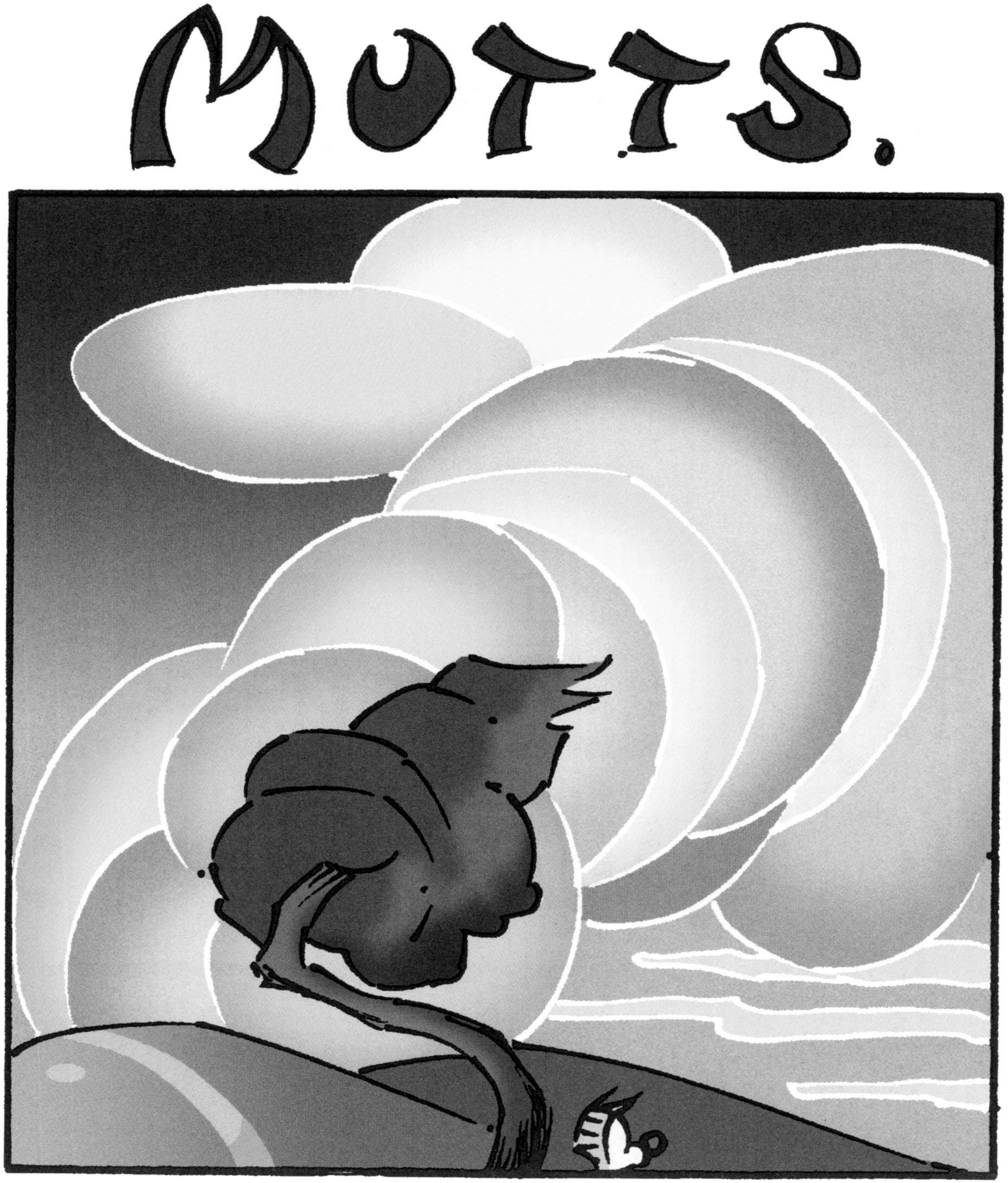
MUTTS.

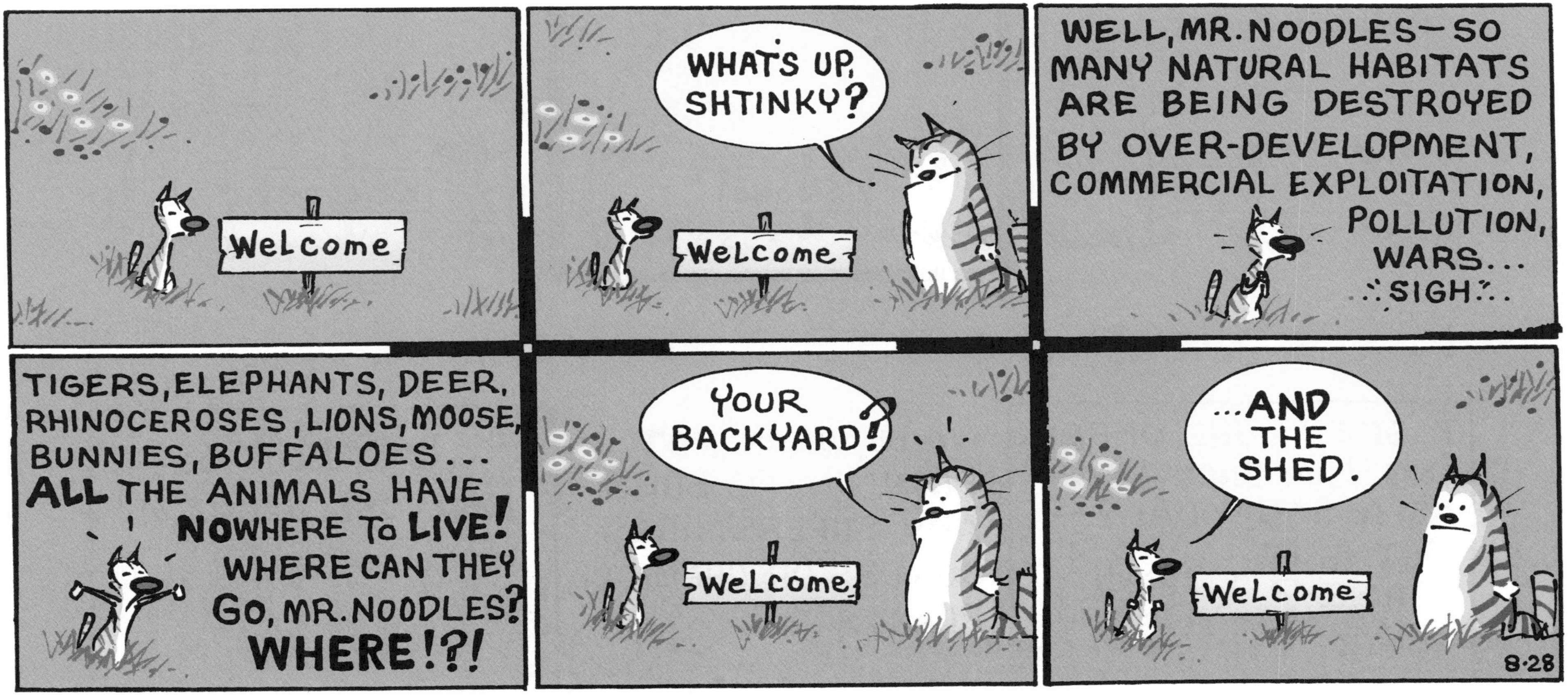
Welcome
WHAT'S UP, SHTINKY?
Welcome
WELL, MR. NOODLES— SO MANY NATURAL HABITATS ARE BEING DESTROYED BY OVER-DEVELOPMENT, COMMERCIAL EXPLOITATION, POLLUTION, WARS... SIGH...
Welcome
TIGERS, ELEPHANTS, DEER, RHINOCEROSES, LIONS, MOOSE, BUNNIES, BUFFALOES... ALL THE ANIMALS HAVE NOWHERE TO LIVE! WHERE CAN THEY GO, MR. NOODLES? WHERE!?!
YOUR BACKYARD?!
Welcome
...AND THE SHED.
Welcome
8·28

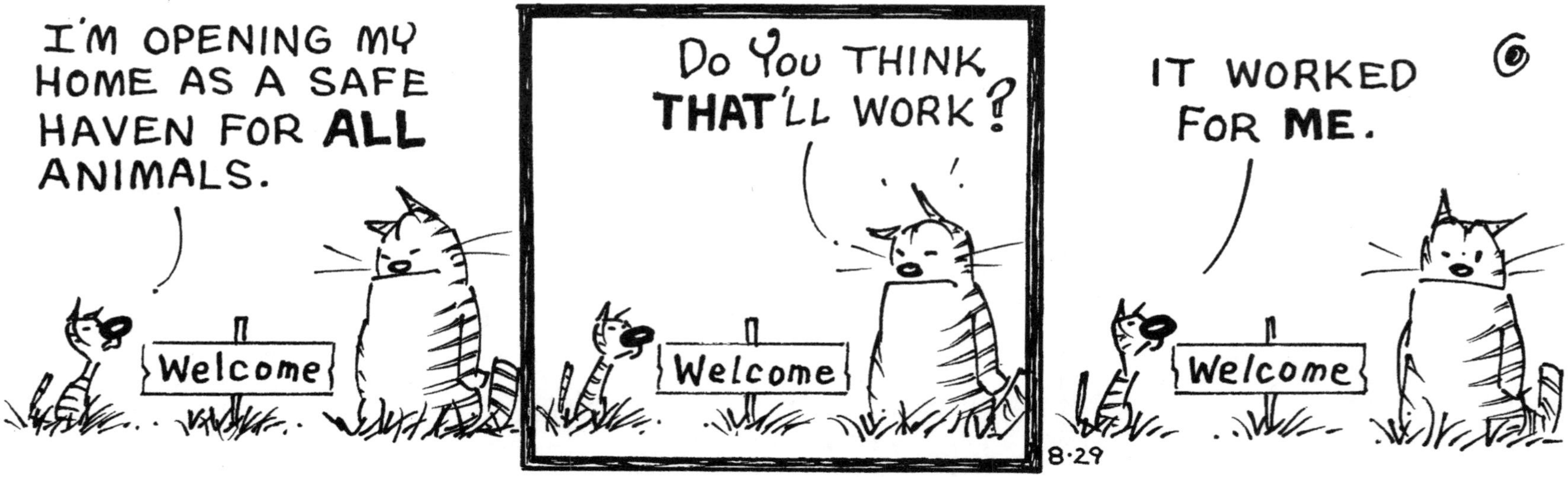
I'M OPENING MY HOME AS A SAFE HAVEN FOR **ALL** ANIMALS.
Welcome
DO YOU THINK **THAT**'LL WORK?
Welcome
IT WORKED FOR **ME**.
Welcome
8·29

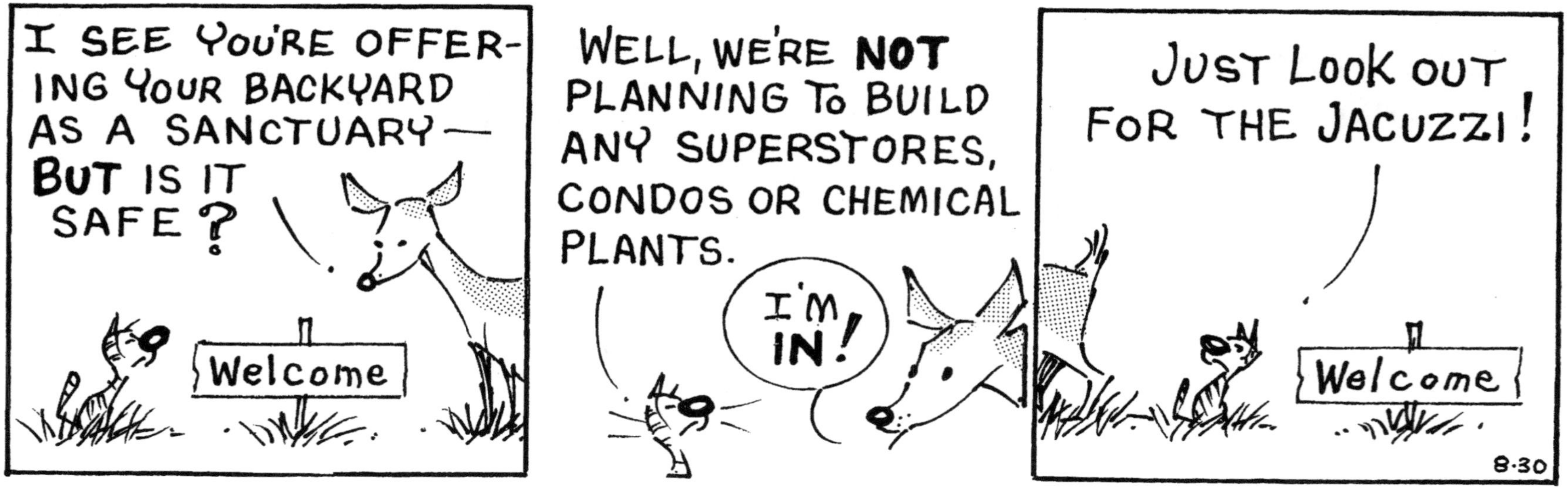
I SEE YOU'RE OFFERING YOUR BACKYARD AS A SANCTUARY— **BUT** IS IT SAFE?
Welcome
WELL, WE'RE **NOT** PLANNING TO BUILD ANY SUPERSTORES, CONDOS OR CHEMICAL PLANTS.
I'M **IN**!
JUST LOOK OUT FOR THE JACUZZI!
Welcome
8·30

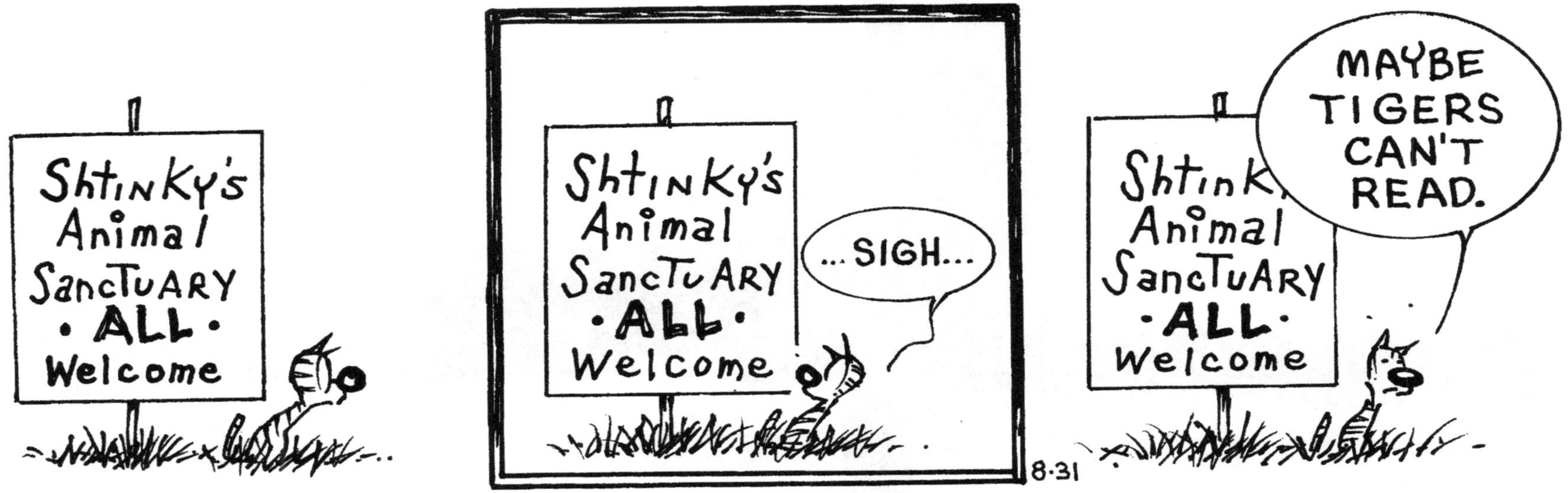
Shtinky's Animal Sanctuary • ALL • Welcome
Shtinky's Animal Sanctuary • ALL • Welcome
...SIGH...
Shtinky's Animal Sanctuary • ALL • Welcome
MAYBE TIGERS CAN'T READ.
8·31

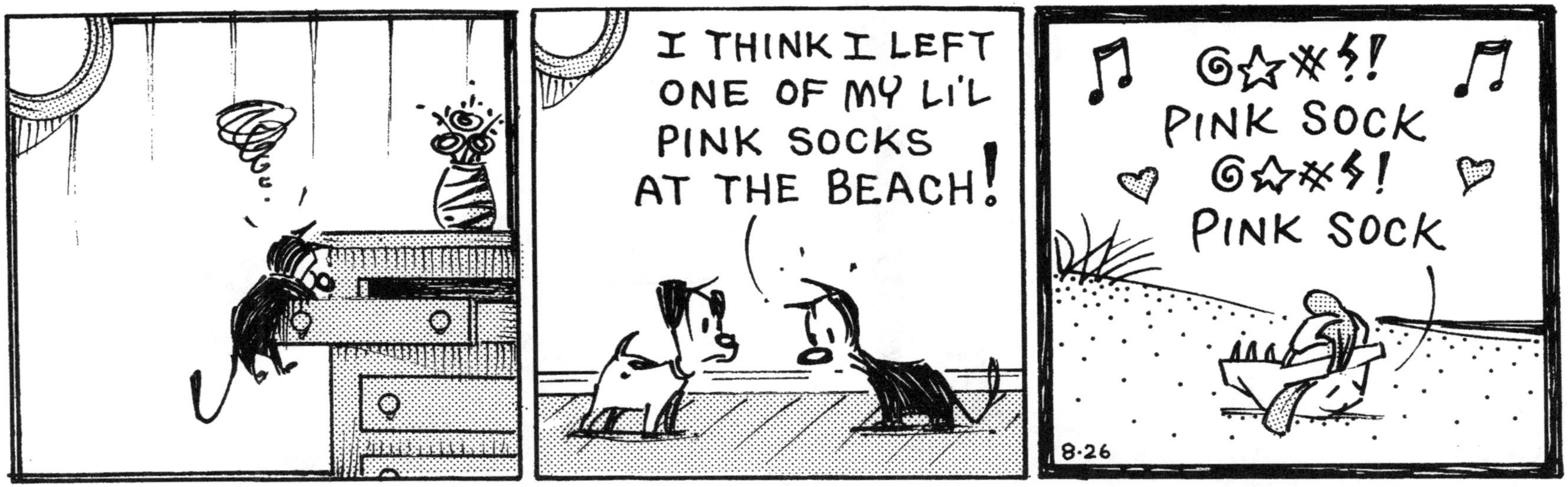
I THINK I LEFT ONE OF MY LI'L PINK SOCKS AT THE BEACH!
PINK SOCK
PINK SOCK
8·26

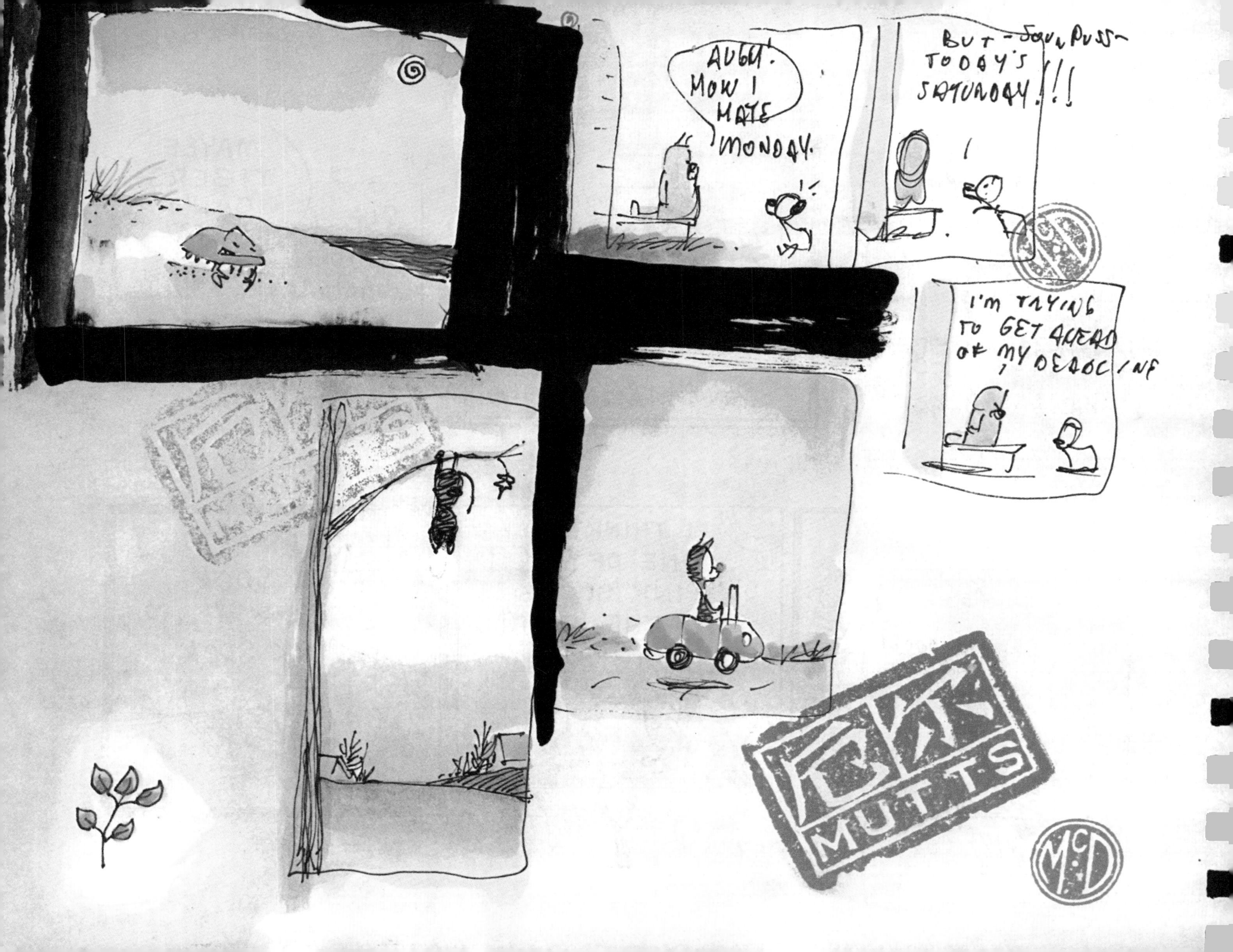
AUGH! NOW I HATE MONDAY.
BUT - SOURPUSS - TODAY'S SATURDAY!!!
I'M TRYING TO GET AHEAD OF MY DEADLINE
MUTTS
McD

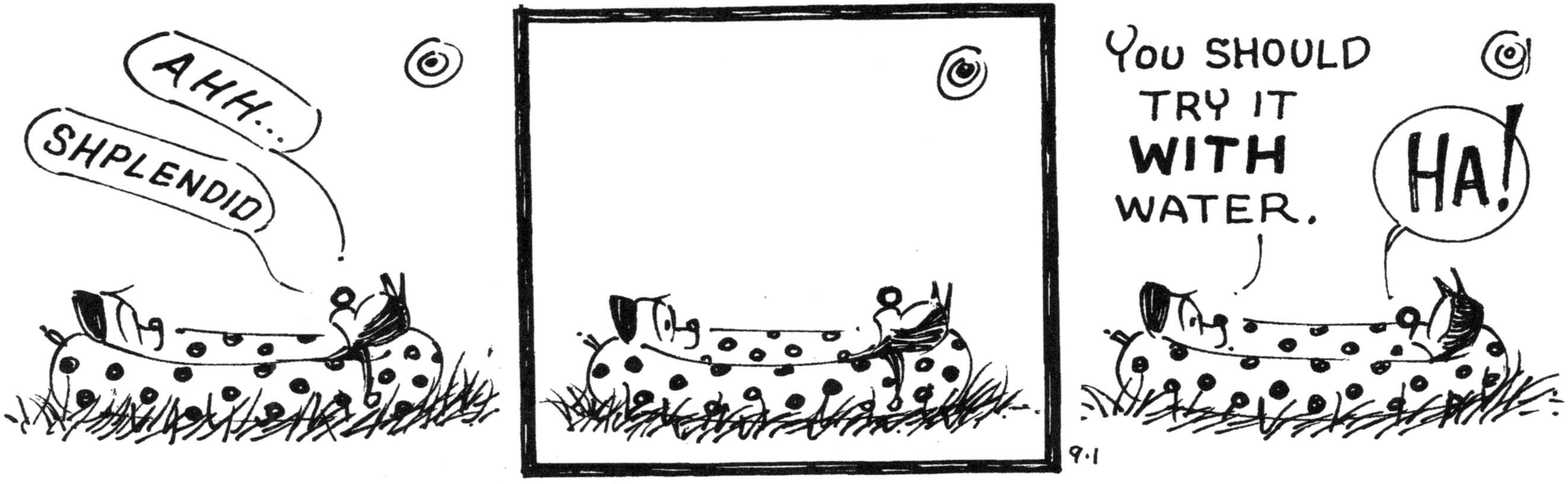
AHH...
SHPLENDID
YOU SHOULD TRY IT WITH WATER.
HA!
9·1

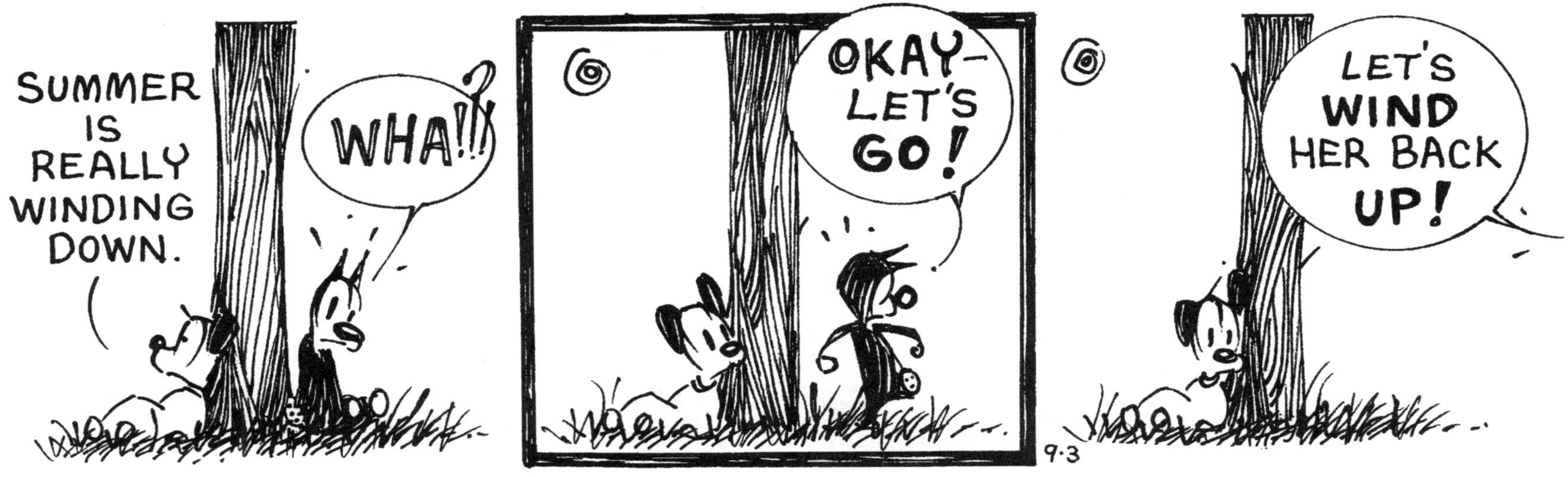
SUMMER IS REALLY WINDING DOWN.
WHA!?!
OKAY- LET'S GO!
LET'S WIND HER BACK UP!
9·3

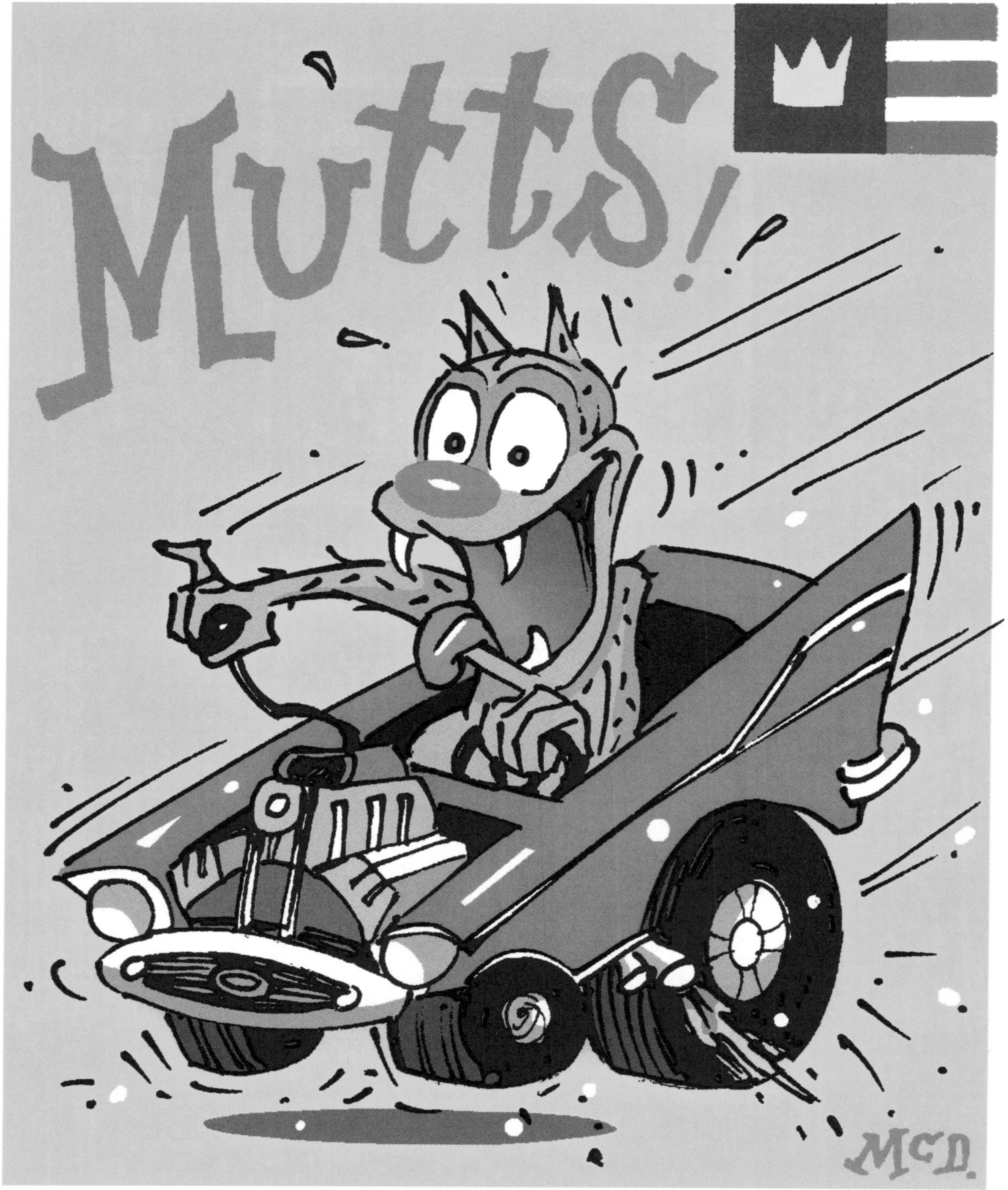
MUTTS!
McD.

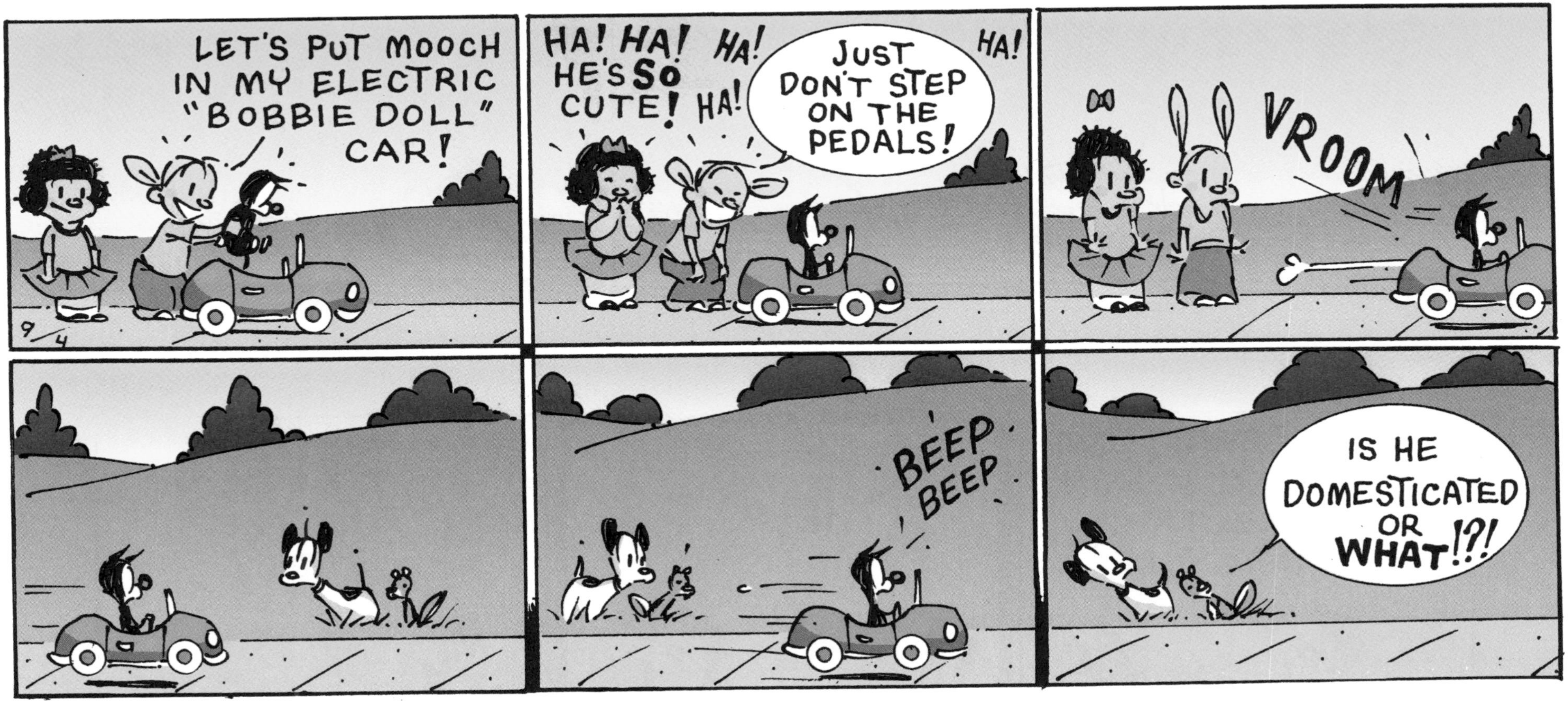
LET'S PUT MOOCH IN MY ELECTRIC "BOBBIE DOLL" CAR!
9/4
HA! HA! HA! HE'S SO CUTE! HA! HA!
JUST DON'T STEP ON THE PEDALS!
VROOM
BEEP BEEP
IS HE DOMESTICATED OR WHAT!?!

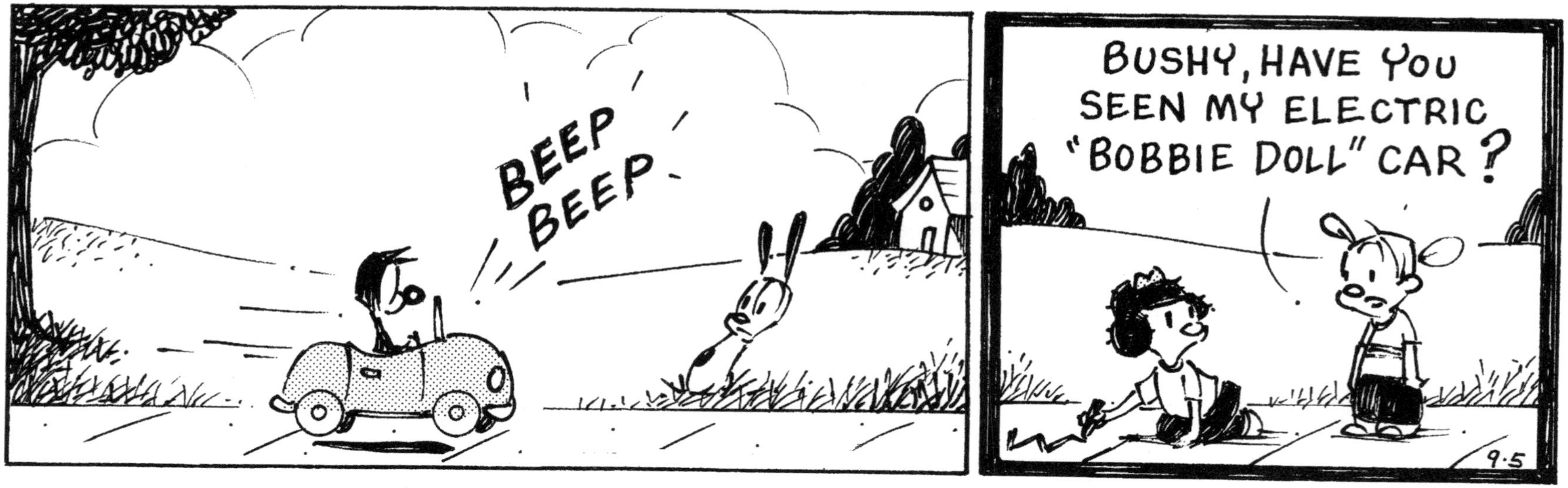
BEEP
BEEP
BUSHY, HAVE YOU SEEN MY ELECTRIC "BOBBIE DOLL" CAR?
9·5

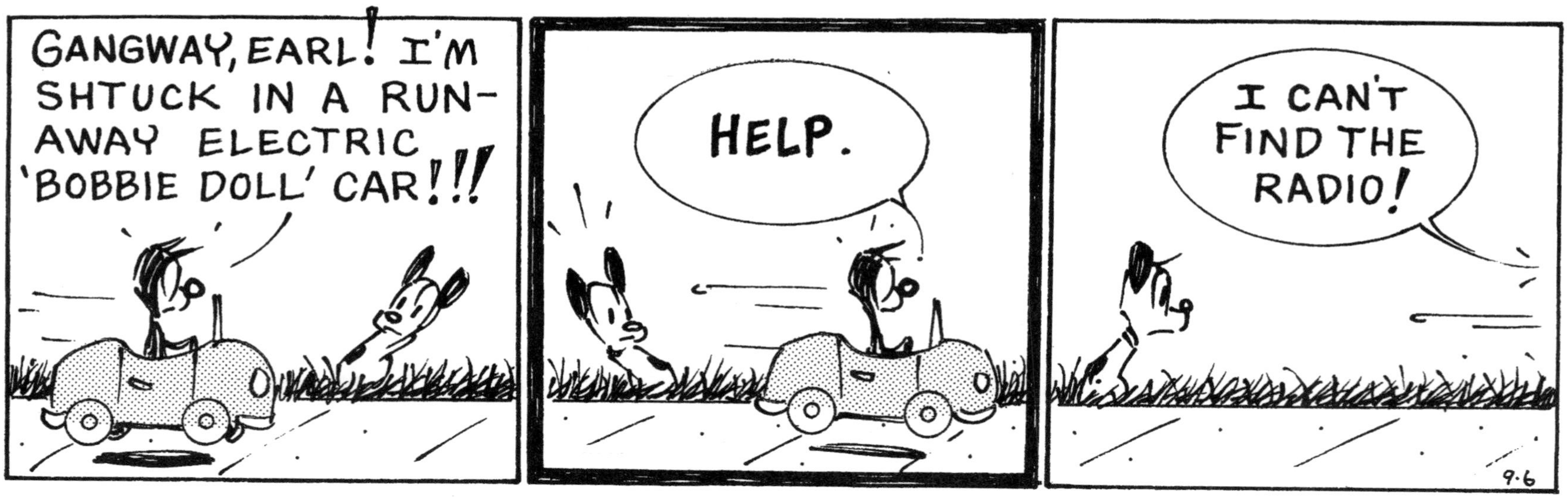
GANGWAY, EARL! I'M SHTUCK IN A RUN-AWAY ELECTRIC 'BOBBIE DOLL' CAR!!!
HELP.
I CAN'T FIND THE RADIO!
9·6

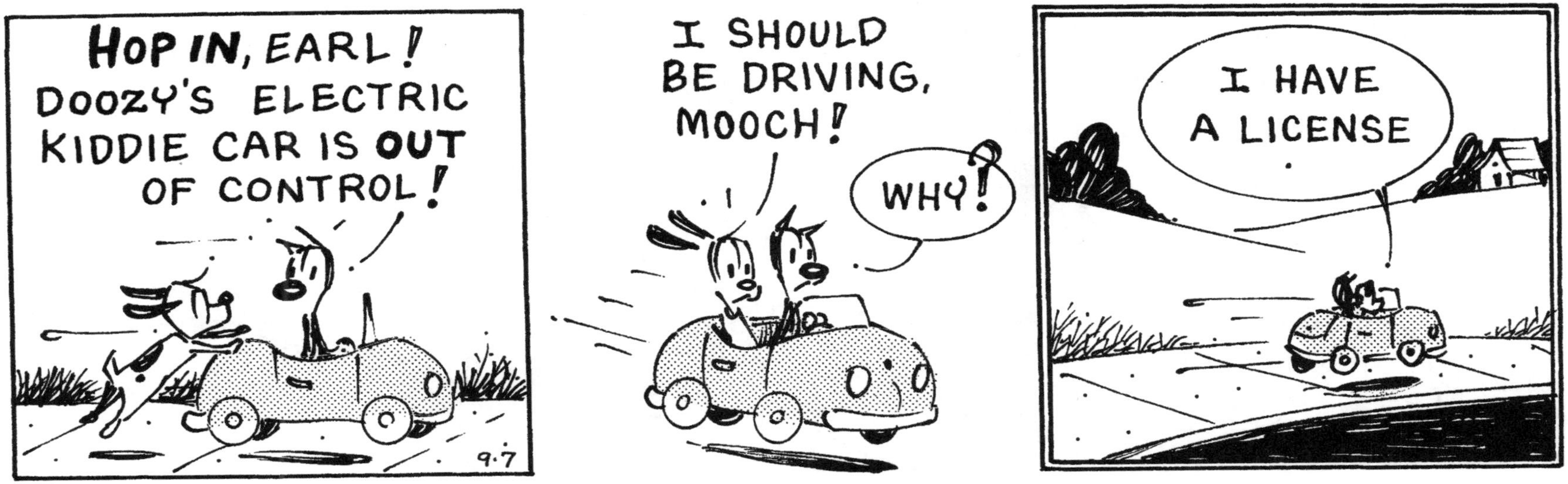
HOP IN, EARL! DOOZY'S ELECTRIC KIDDIE CAR IS OUT OF CONTROL!
9·7
I SHOULD BE DRIVING, MOOCH!
WHY?!
I HAVE A LICENSE

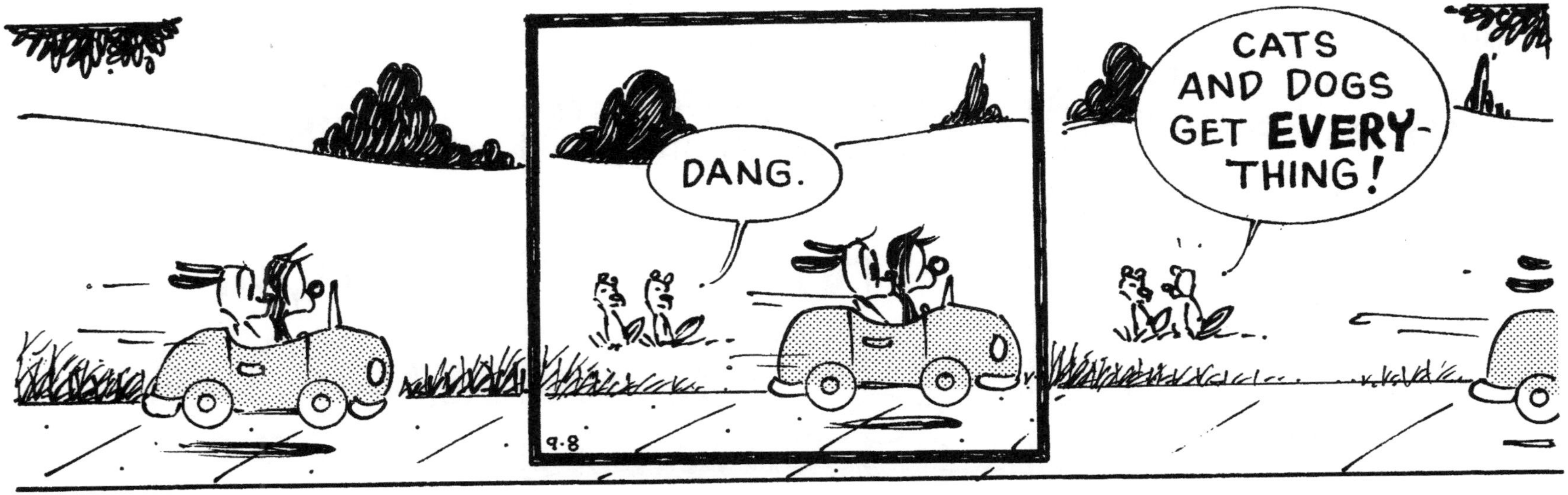
DANG.
9·8
CATS AND DOGS GET EVERY-THING!

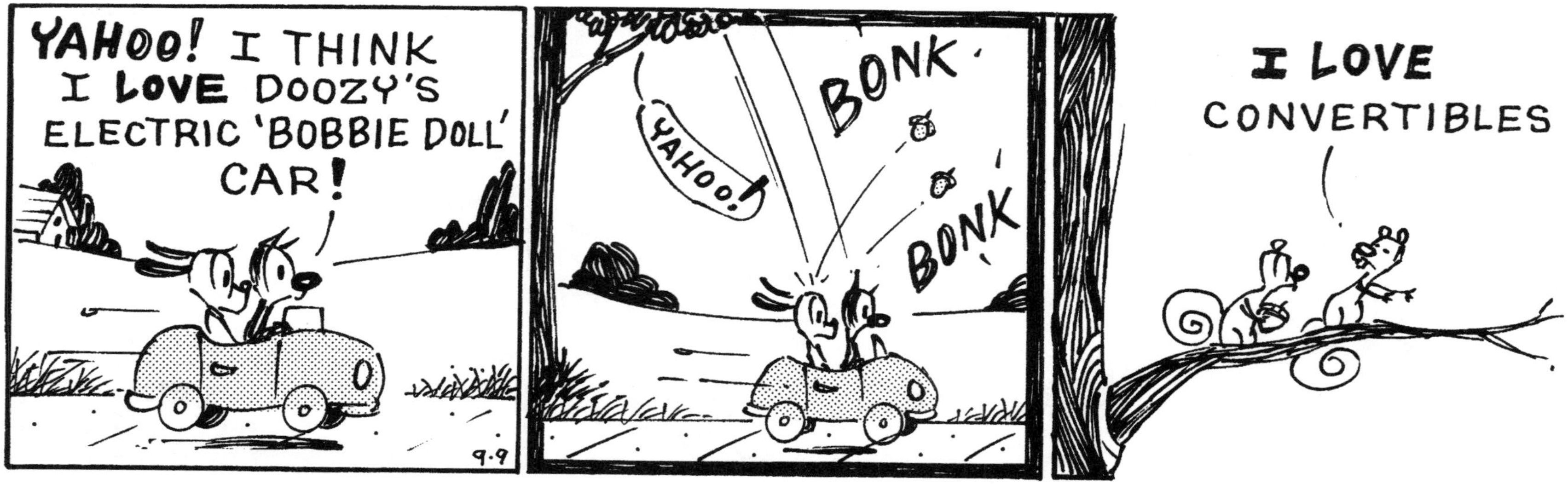
YAHOO! I THINK I LOVE DOOZY'S ELECTRIC 'BOBBIE DOLL' CAR!
9·9
YAHOO!
BONK
BONK
I LOVE CONVERTIBLES

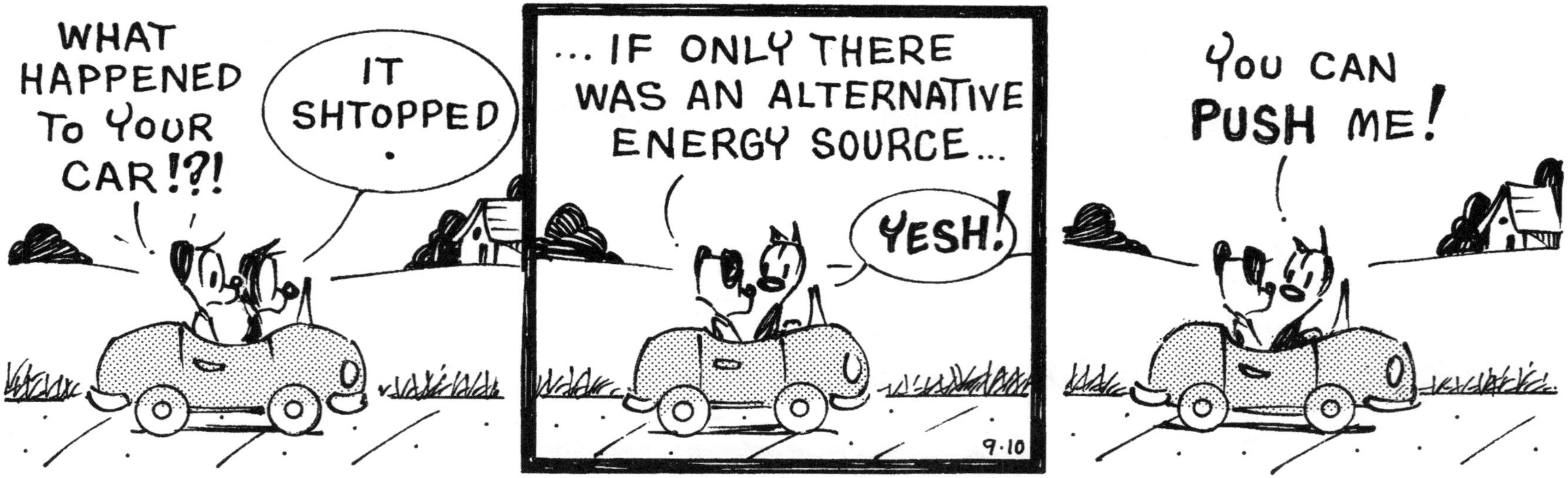
WHAT HAPPENED TO YOUR CAR!?!
IT SHTOPPED.
...IF ONLY THERE WAS AN ALTERNATIVE ENERGY SOURCE...
YESH!
9·10
YOU CAN PUSH ME!

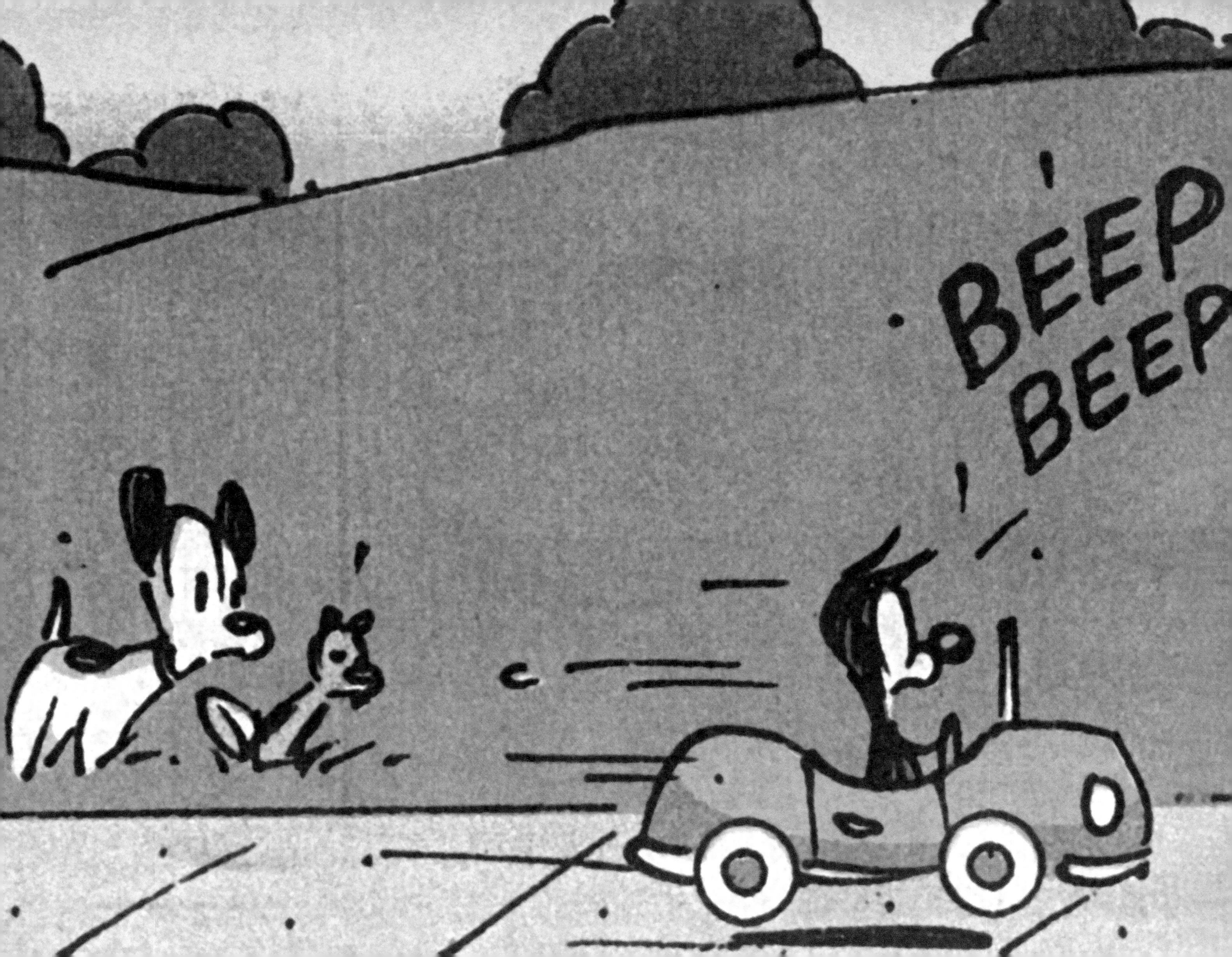
BEEP
BEEP

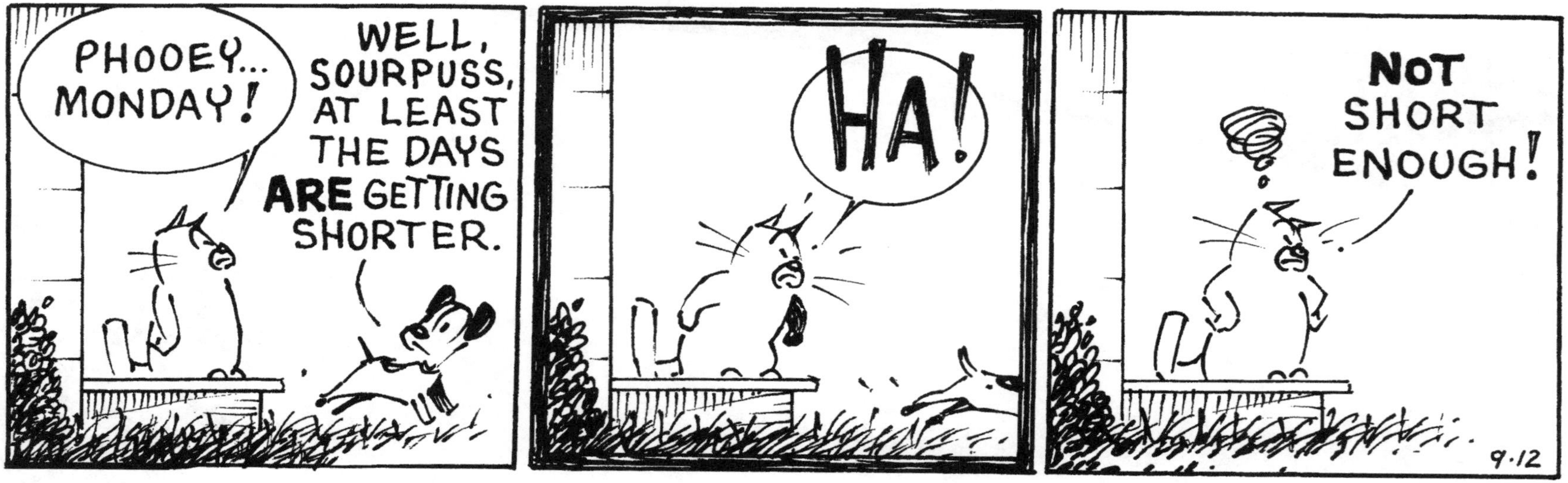
PHOOEY... MONDAY!
WELL, SOURPUSS, AT LEAST THE DAYS ARE GETTING SHORTER.
HA!
NOT SHORT ENOUGH!
9-12

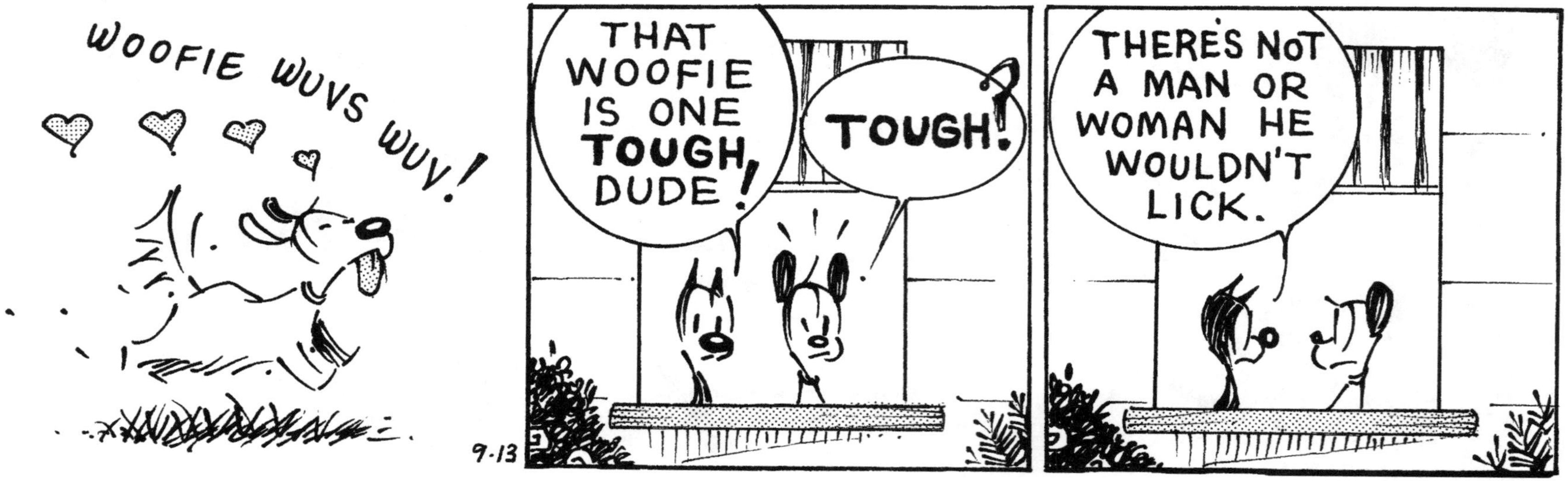
WOOFIE WUVS WUV!
9-13
THAT WOOFIE IS ONE TOUGH DUDE!
TOUGH?!
THERE'S NOT A MAN OR WOMAN HE WOULDN'T LICK.

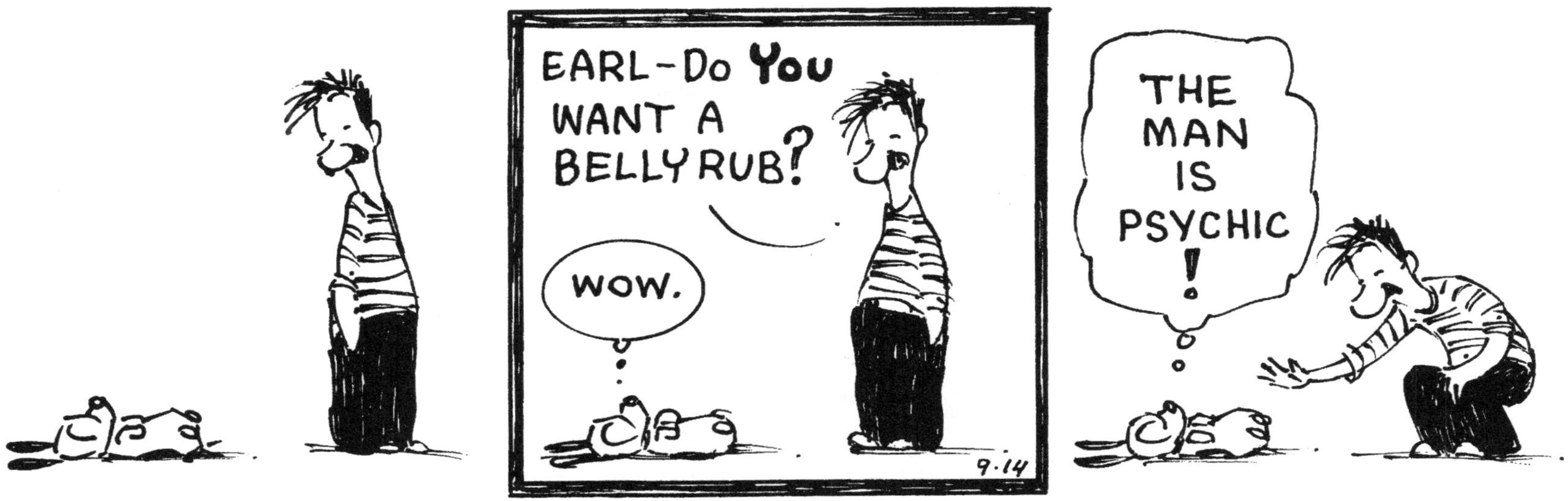
EARL-Do YOU WANT A BELLY RUB?
WOW.
THE MAN IS PSYCHIC!
9·14

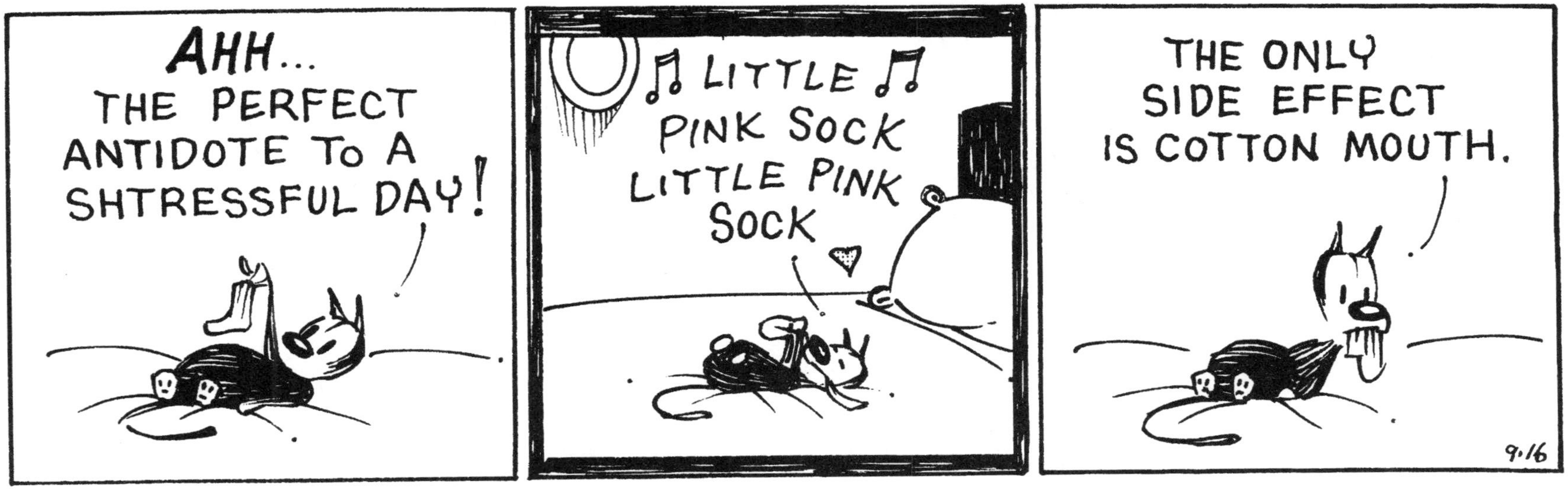
AHH... THE PERFECT ANTIDOTE To A SHTRESSFUL DAY!
♫ LITTLE ♫ PINK SOCK LITTLE PINK SOCK
THE ONLY SIDE EFFECT IS COTTON MOUTH.
9·16

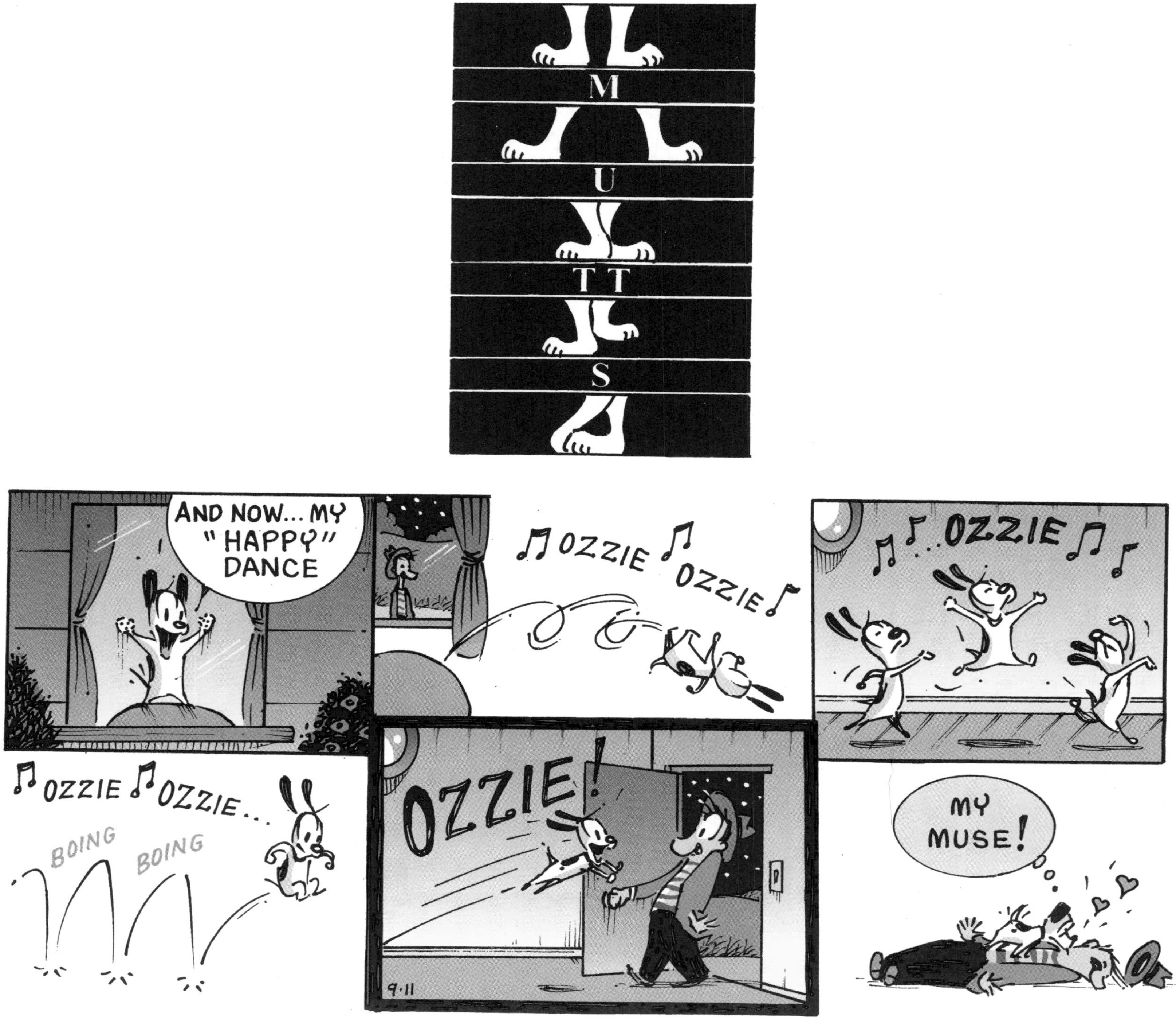
MUTTS
AND NOW... MY "HAPPY" DANCE
OZZIE OZZIE OZZIE
...OZZIE
OZZIE OZZIE...
BOING
BOING
OZZIE!
9·11
MY MUSE!

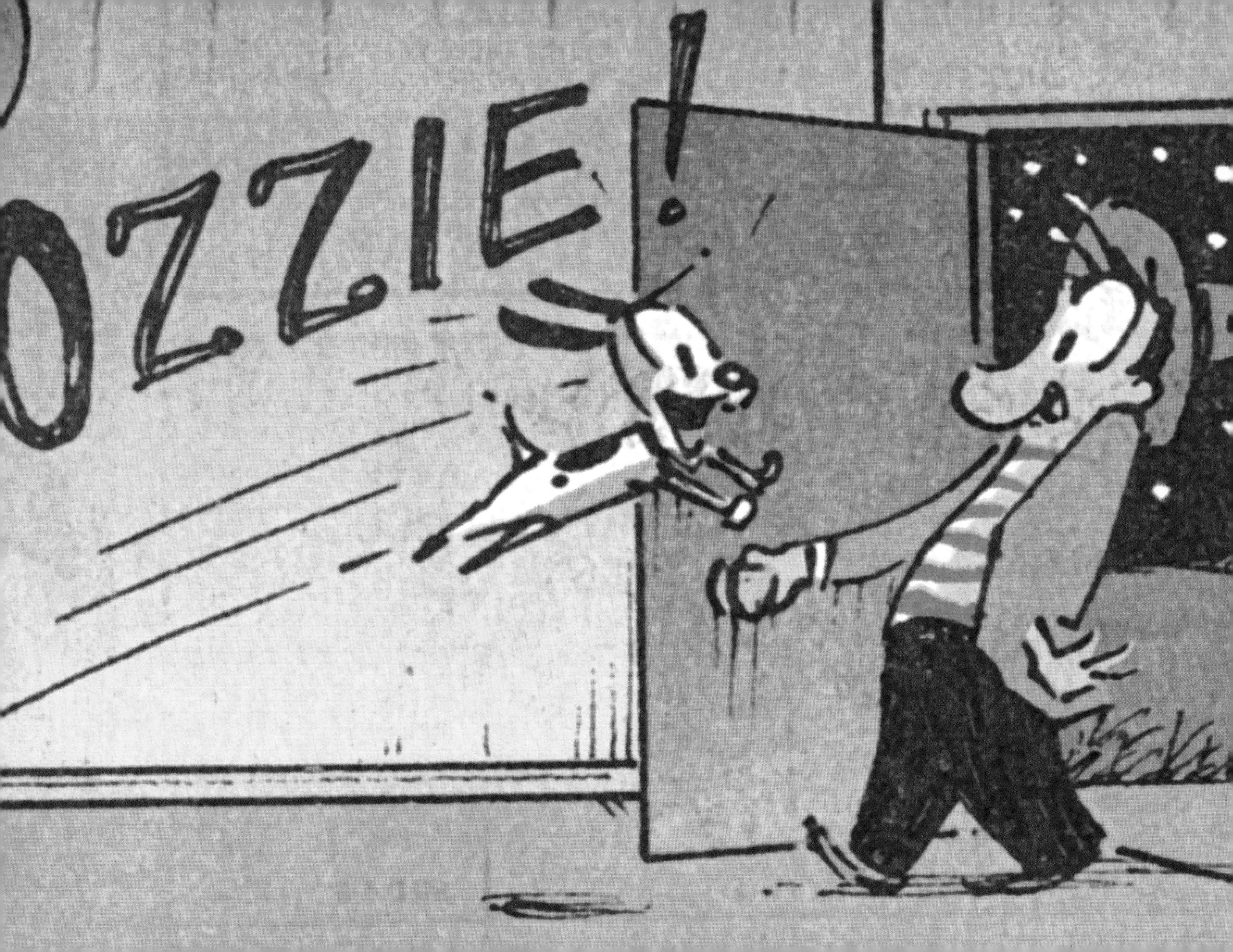
OZZIE!

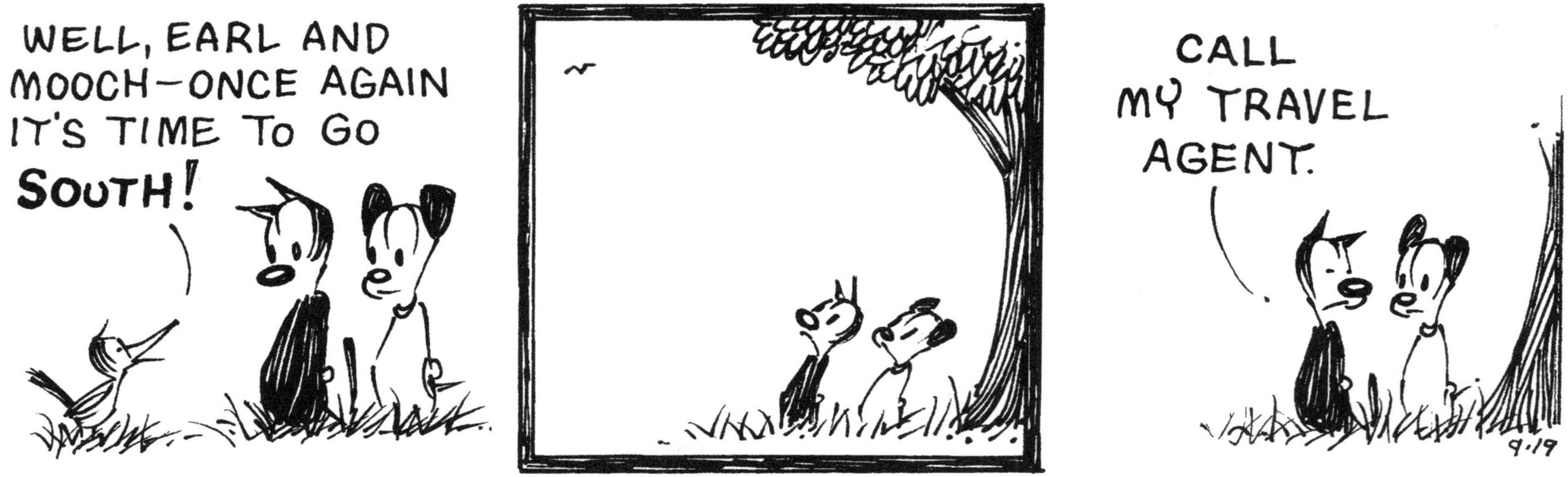
WELL, EARL AND MOOCH—ONCE AGAIN IT'S TIME TO GO **SOUTH**!
CALL MY TRAVEL AGENT.
9·19

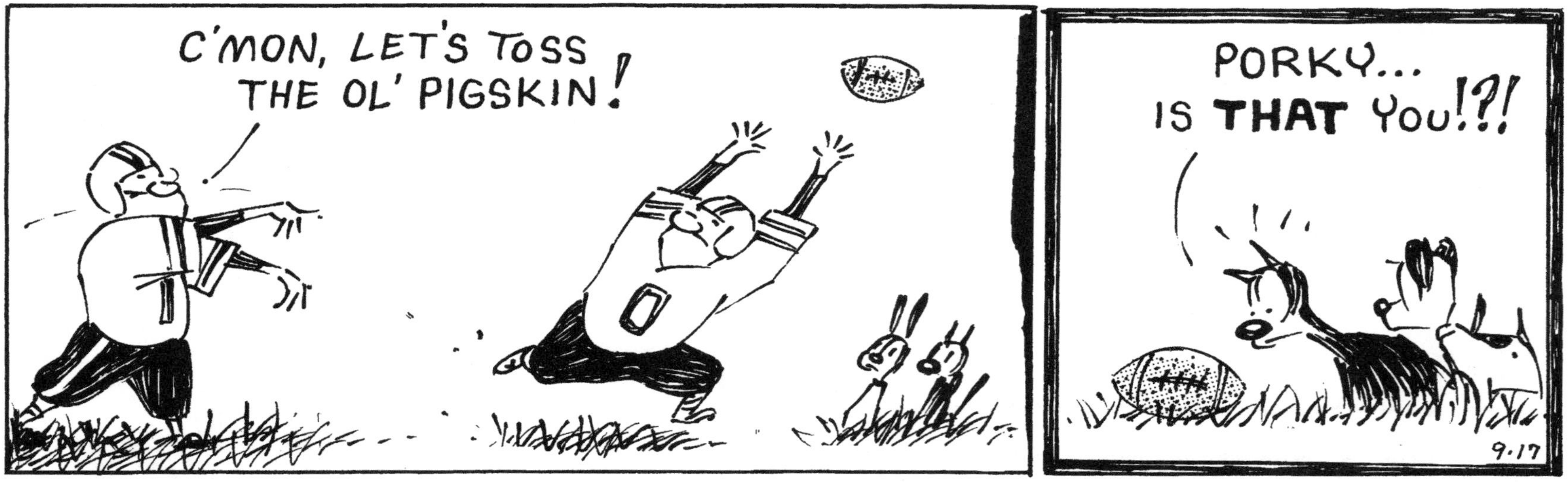
C'MON, LET'S TOSS THE OL' PIGSKIN!
PORKY... IS **THAT** YOU!?!
9·17

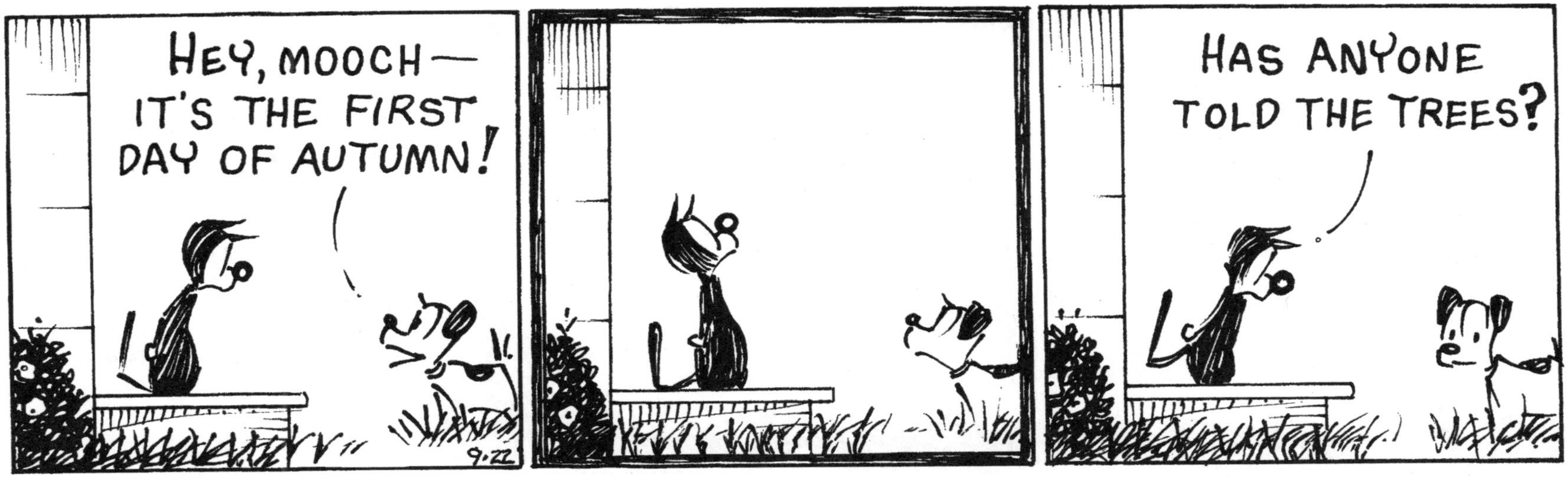
HEY, MOOCH—
IT'S THE FIRST DAY OF AUTUMN!
HAS ANYONE TOLD THE TREES?
9.22

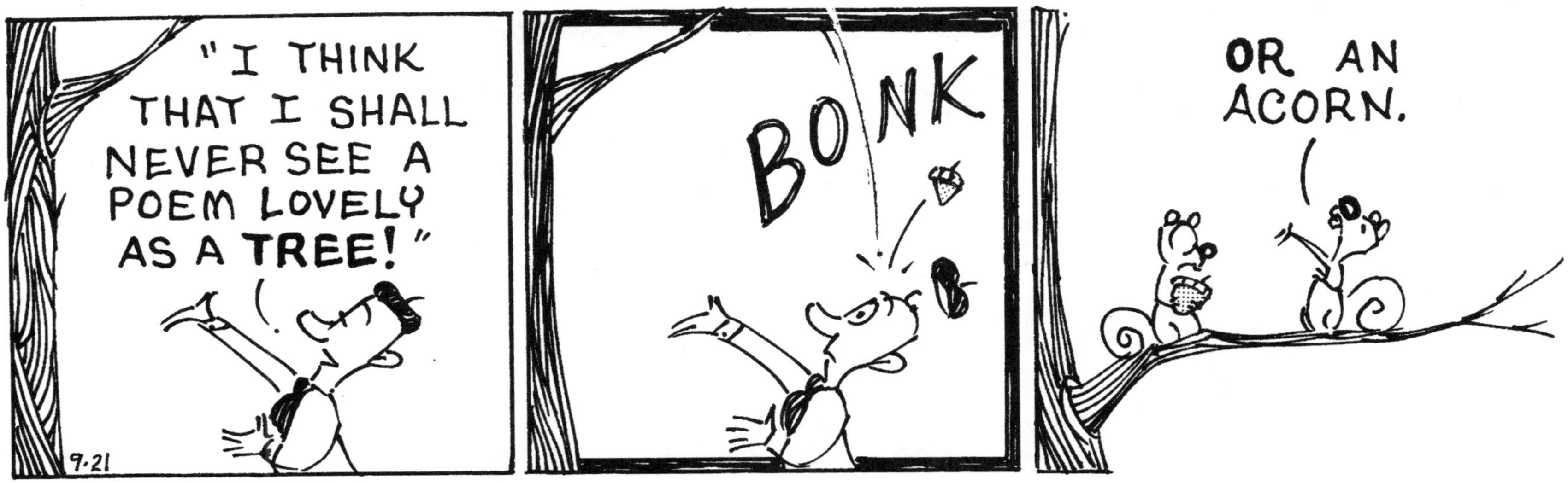
"I THINK THAT I SHALL NEVER SEE A POEM LOVELY AS A TREE!"
9.21
BONK
OR AN ACORN.

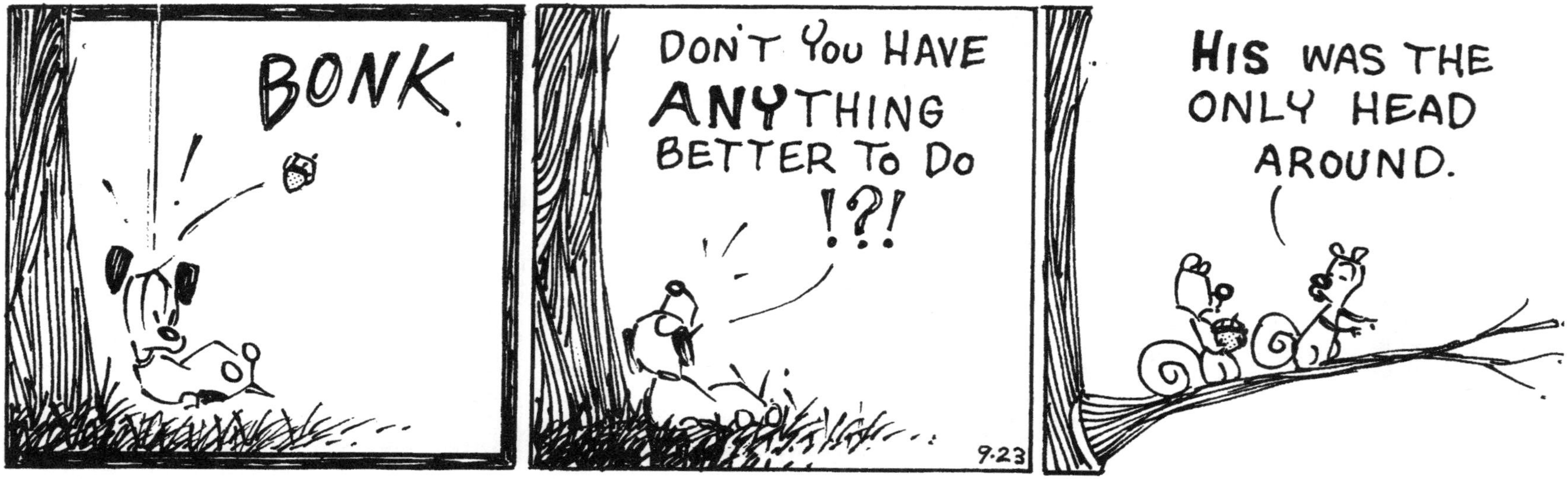
BONK
DON'T YOU HAVE ANYTHING BETTER TO DO !?!
HIS WAS THE ONLY HEAD AROUND.
9·23

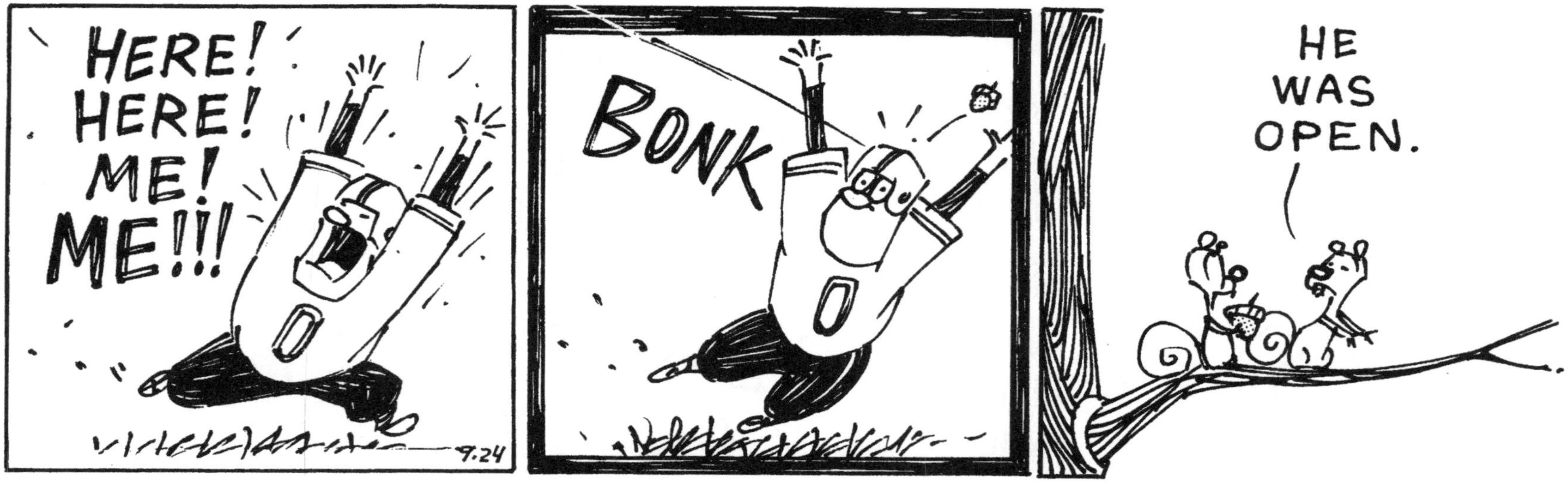
HERE! HERE! ME! ME!!!
9·24
BONK
HE WAS OPEN.

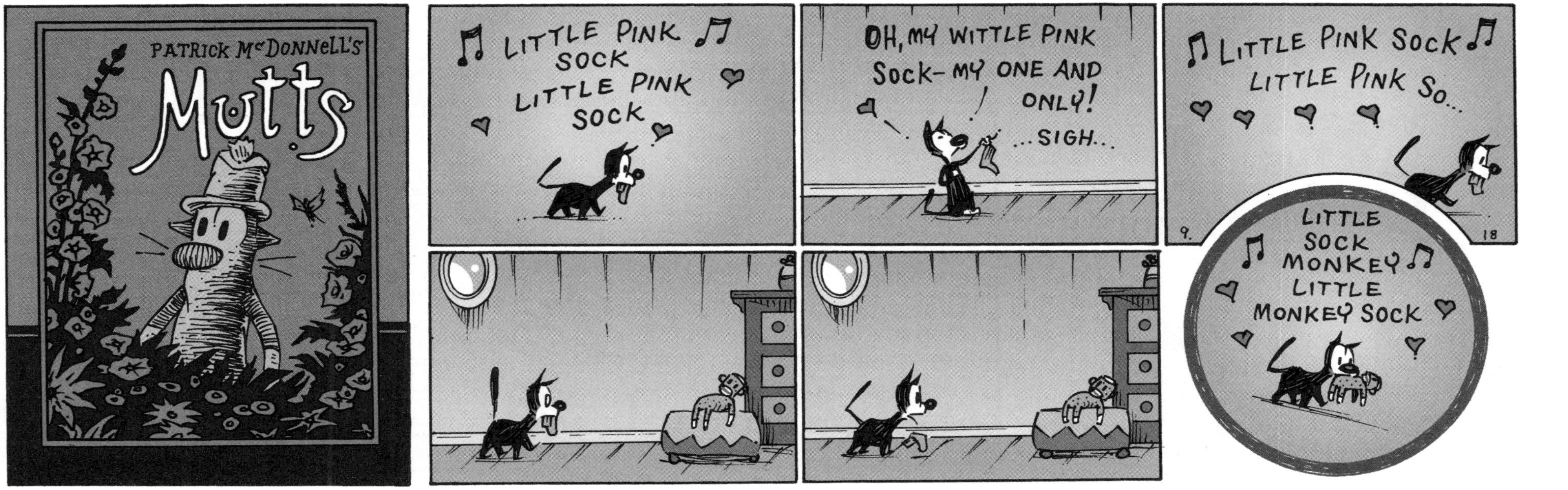
PATRICK McDONNELL'S
Mutts
♫ LITTLE PINK SOCK LITTLE PINK SOCK ♫
OH, MY WITTLE PINK SOCK- MY ONE AND ONLY!
...SIGH...
♫ LITTLE PINK SOCK ♫ LITTLE PINK SO...
9. 18
♫ LITTLE SOCK MONKEY ♫ LITTLE MONKEY SOCK

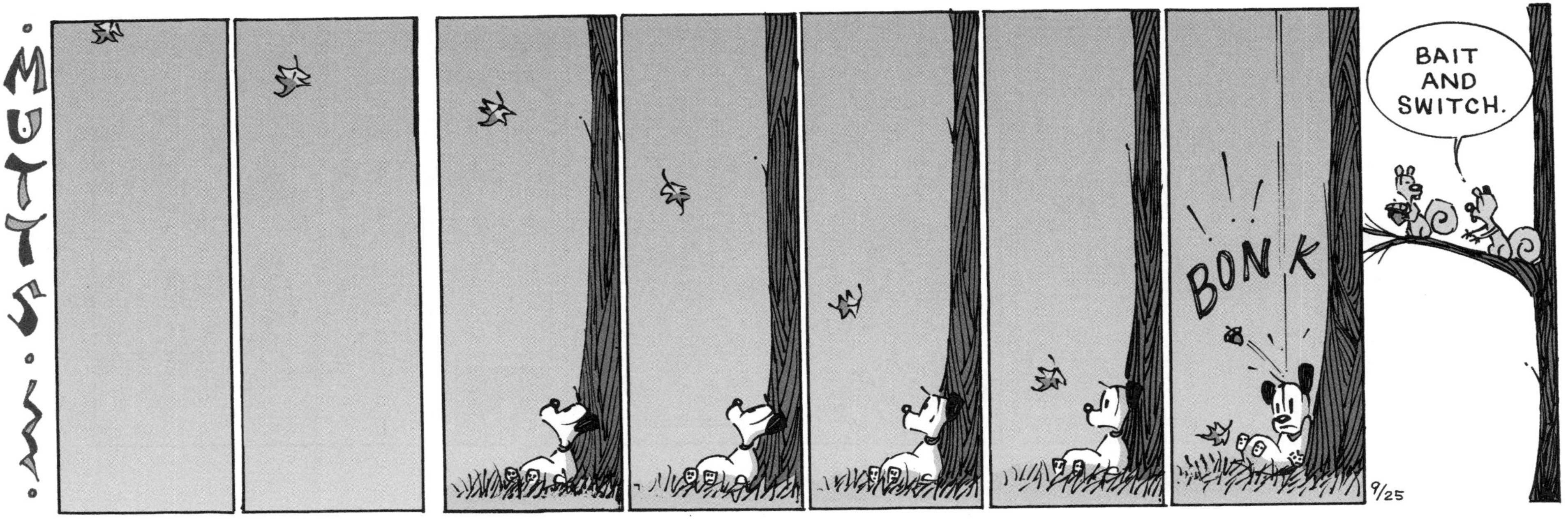
MUTTS
BONK
9/25
BAIT AND SWITCH.

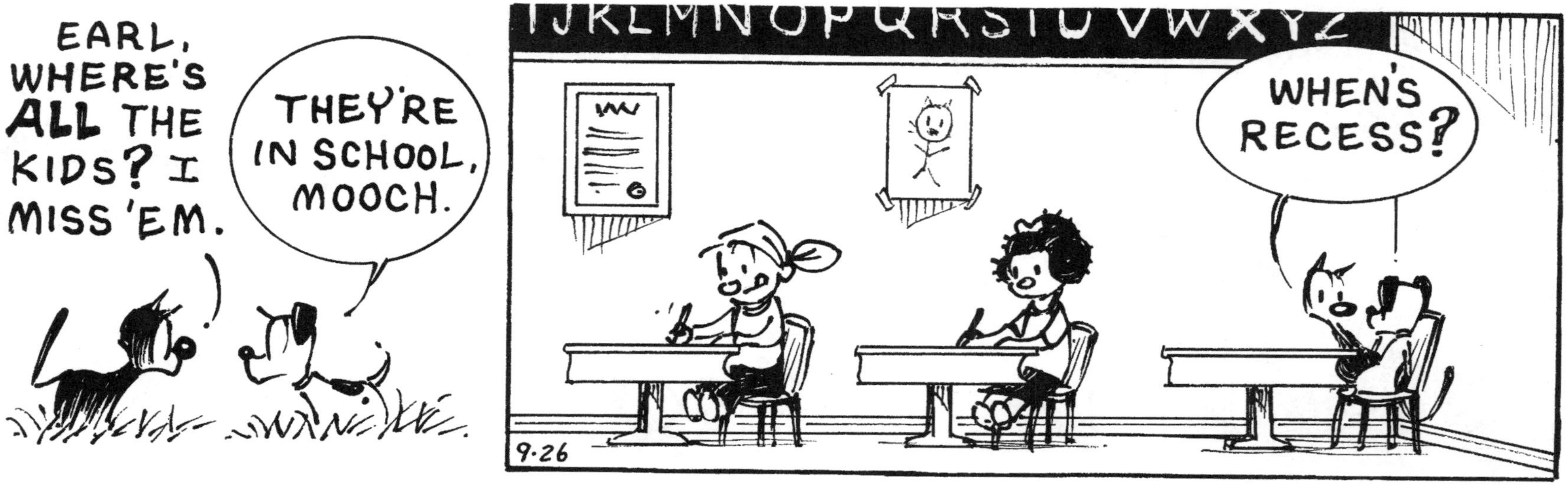
EARL, WHERE'S **ALL** THE KIDS? I MISS 'EM.
THEY'RE IN SCHOOL, MOOCH.
IJKLMNOPQRSTUVWXYZ
WHEN'S RECESS?
9·26

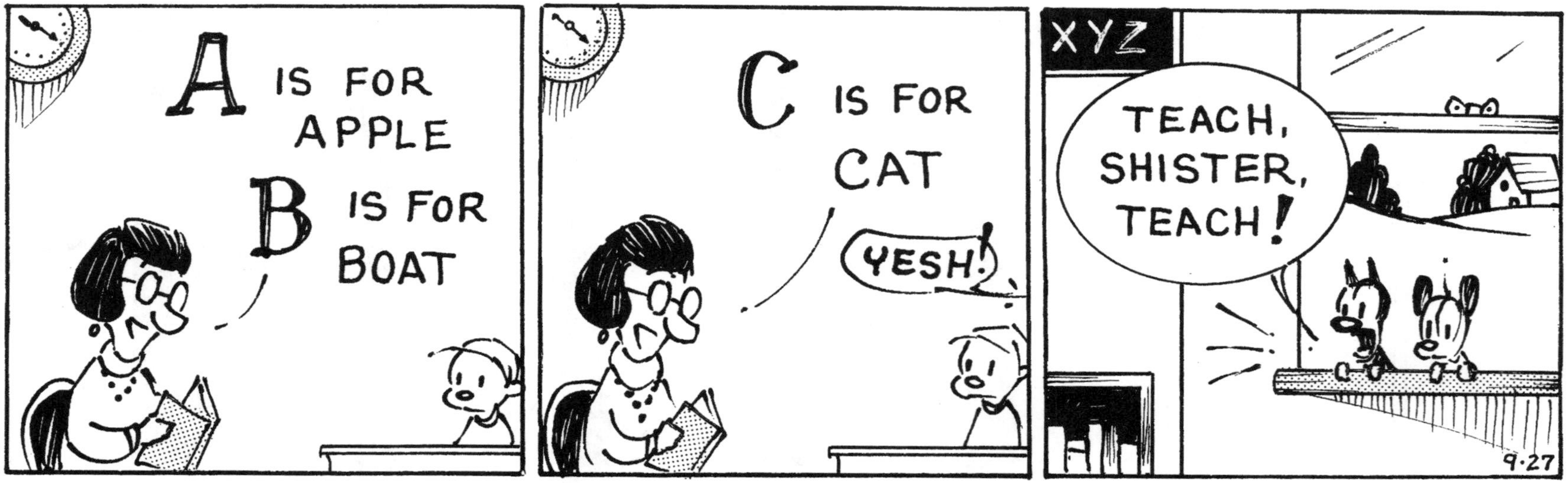
A IS FOR APPLE
B IS FOR BOAT
C IS FOR CAT
YESH!
XYZ
TEACH, SHISTER, TEACH!
9·27

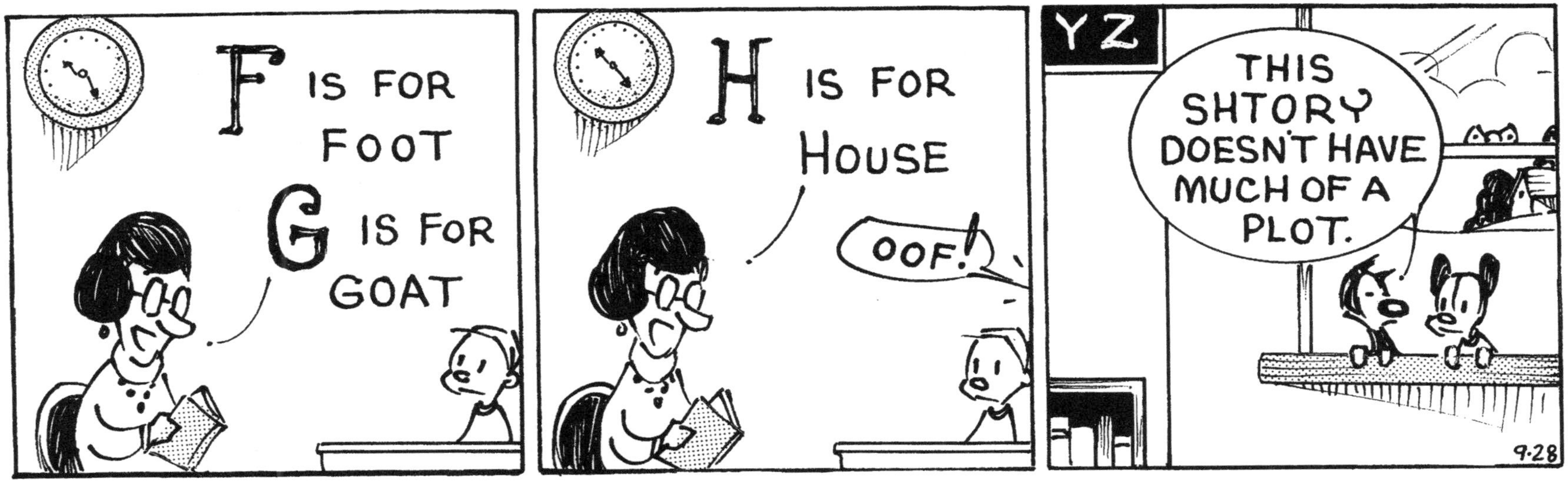
F IS FOR FOOT
G IS FOR GOAT
H IS FOR HOUSE
OOF!
YZ
THIS SHTORY DOESN'T HAVE MUCH OF A PLOT.
9-28

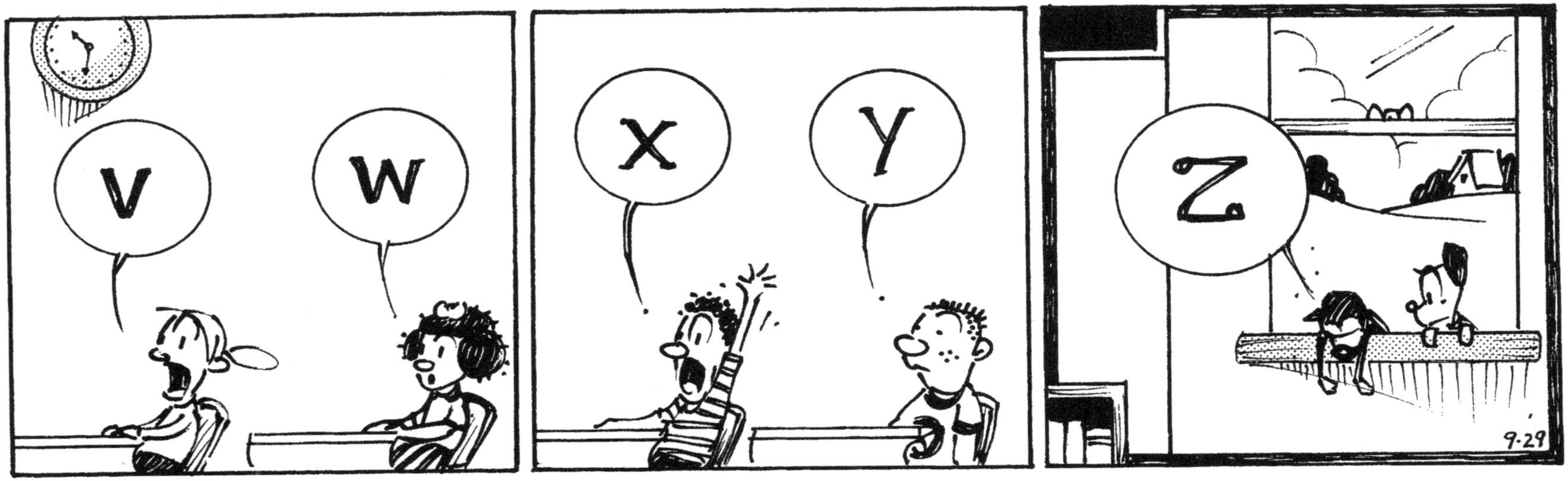
V
W
X
Y
Z
9-29

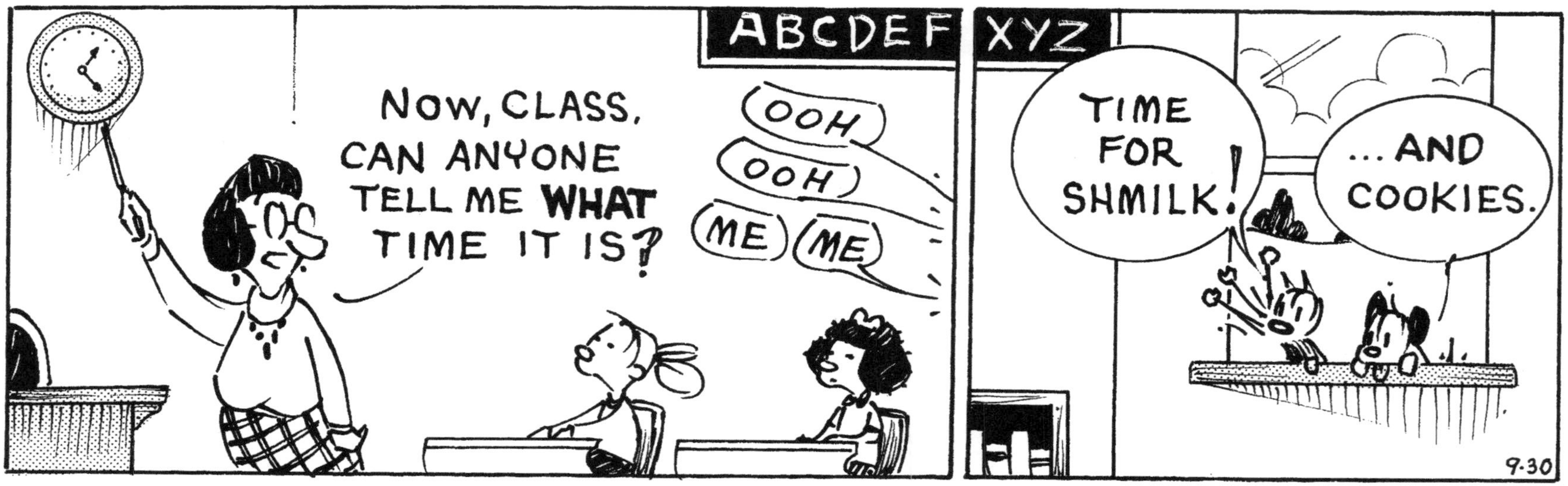
ABCDEF XYZ
NOW, CLASS, CAN ANYONE TELL ME **WHAT** TIME IT IS?
OOH
OOH
ME
ME
TIME FOR SHMILK!
...AND COOKIES.
9·30

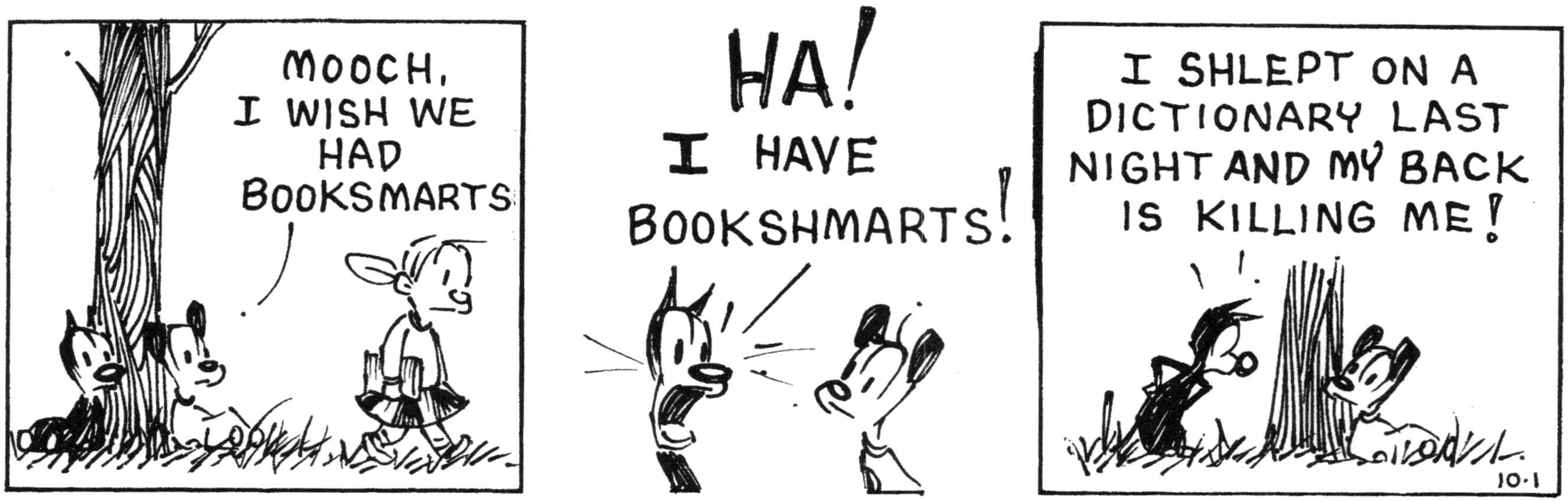
MOOCH, I WISH WE HAD BOOKSMARTS.
HA! I HAVE BOOKSHMARTS!
I SHLEPT ON A DICTIONARY LAST NIGHT AND MY BACK IS KILLING ME!
10·1

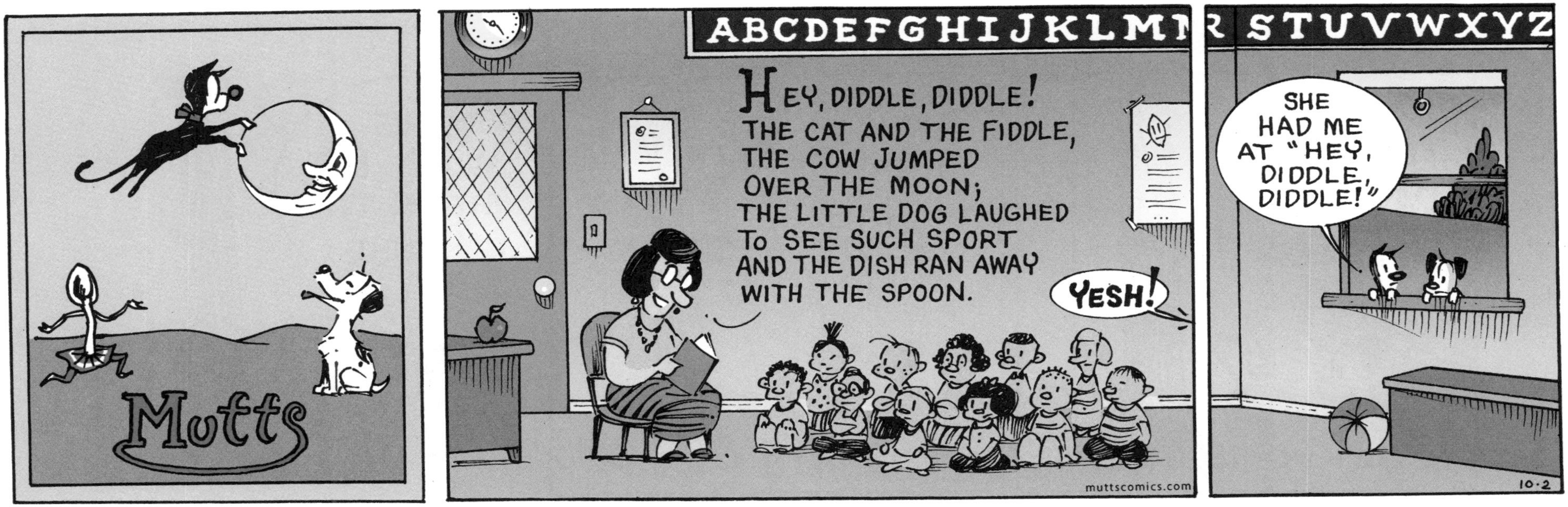
Mutts
ABCDEFGHIJKLM
STUVWXYZ
HEY, DIDDLE, DIDDLE! THE CAT AND THE FIDDLE, THE COW JUMPED OVER THE MOON; THE LITTLE DOG LAUGHED TO SEE SUCH SPORT AND THE DISH RAN AWAY WITH THE SPOON.
YESH!
SHE HAD ME AT "HEY, DIDDLE, DIDDLE!"
muttscomics.com
10·2

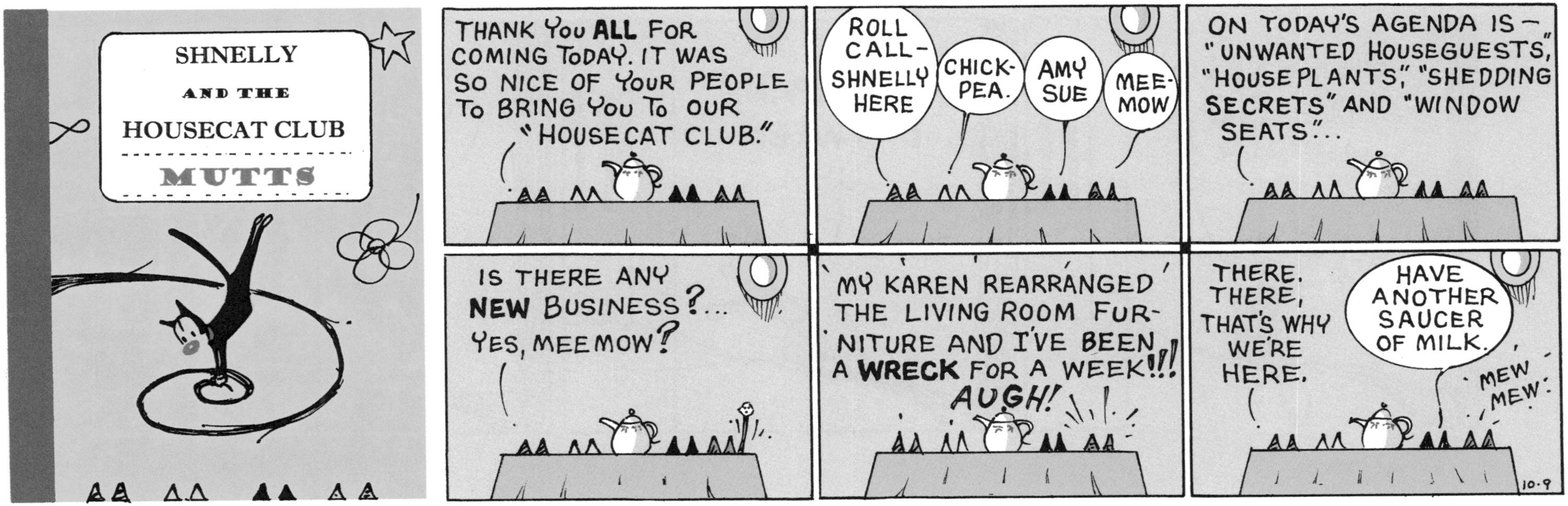
SHNELLY
AND THE
HOUSECAT CLUB
MUTTS
THANK YOU ALL FOR COMING TODAY. IT WAS SO NICE OF YOUR PEOPLE TO BRING YOU TO OUR "HOUSECAT CLUB."
ROLL CALL- SHNELLY HERE
CHICK-PEA.
AMY SUE
MEE-MOW
ON TODAY'S AGENDA IS - "UNWANTED HOUSEGUESTS," "HOUSE PLANTS," "SHEDDING SECRETS" AND "WINDOW SEATS."...
IS THERE ANY NEW BUSINESS?... YES, MEEMOW?
MY KAREN REARRANGED THE LIVING ROOM FUR-NITURE AND I'VE BEEN A WRECK FOR A WEEK!!!
AUGH!
THERE, THERE, THAT'S WHY WE'RE HERE.
HAVE ANOTHER SAUCER OF MILK.
MEW MEW
10·9

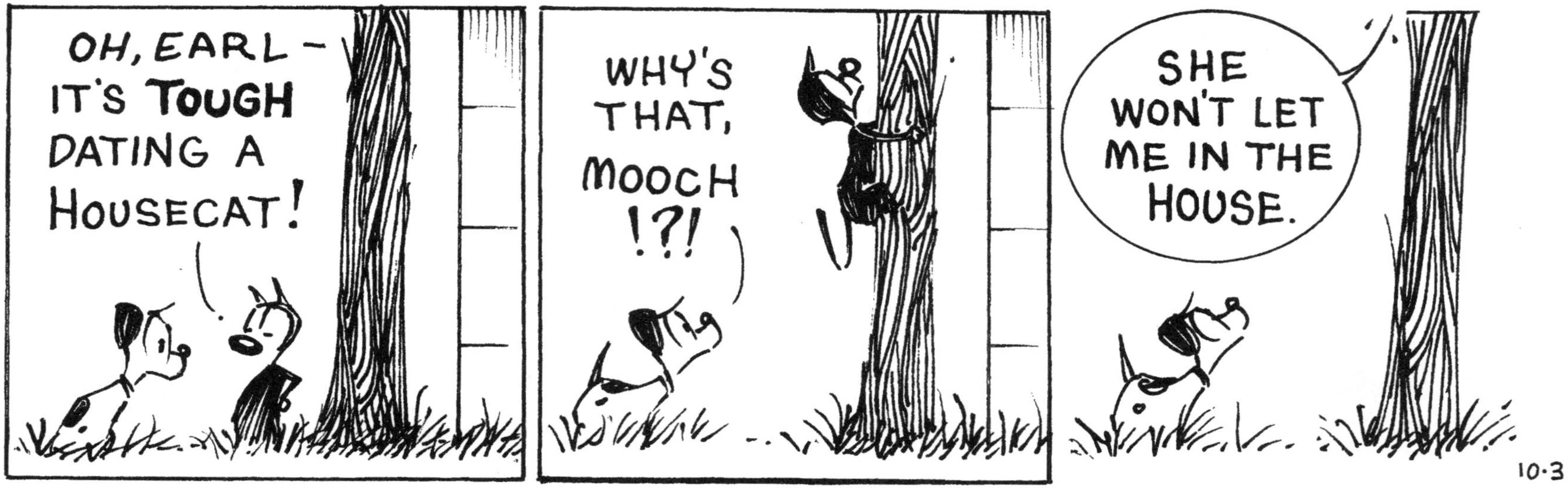
OH, EARL - IT'S **TOUGH** DATING A HOUSECAT!
WHY'S THAT, MOOCH !?!
SHE WON'T LET ME IN THE HOUSE.
10·3

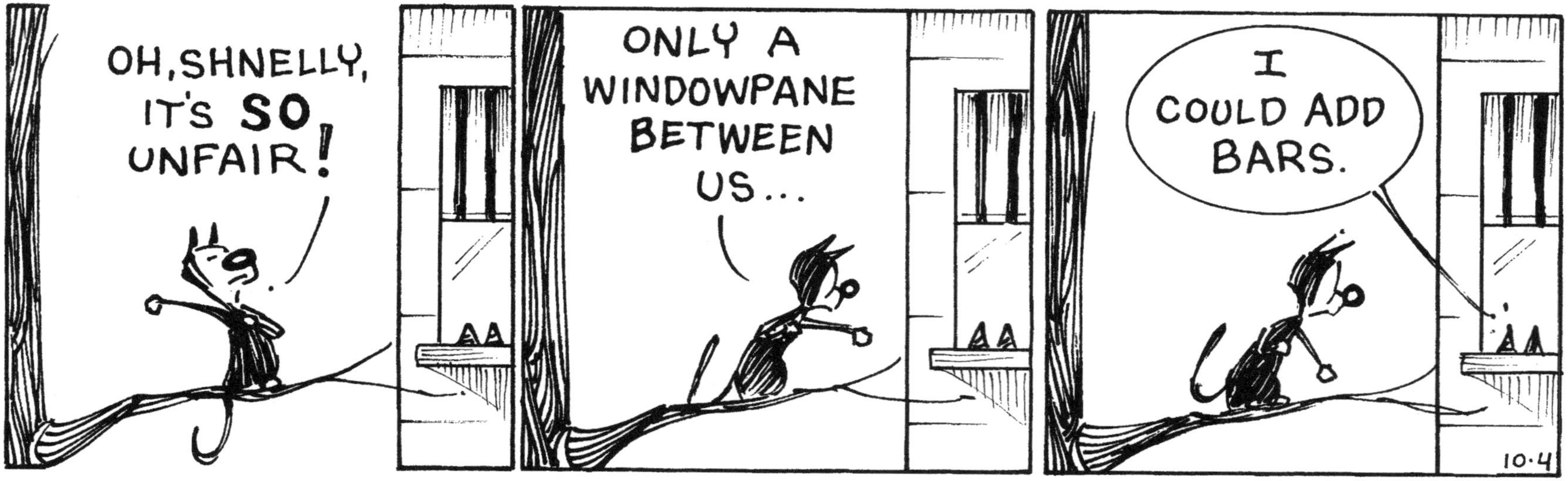
OH, SHNELLY, IT'S **SO** UNFAIR!
ONLY A WINDOWPANE BETWEEN US...
I COULD ADD BARS.
10·4

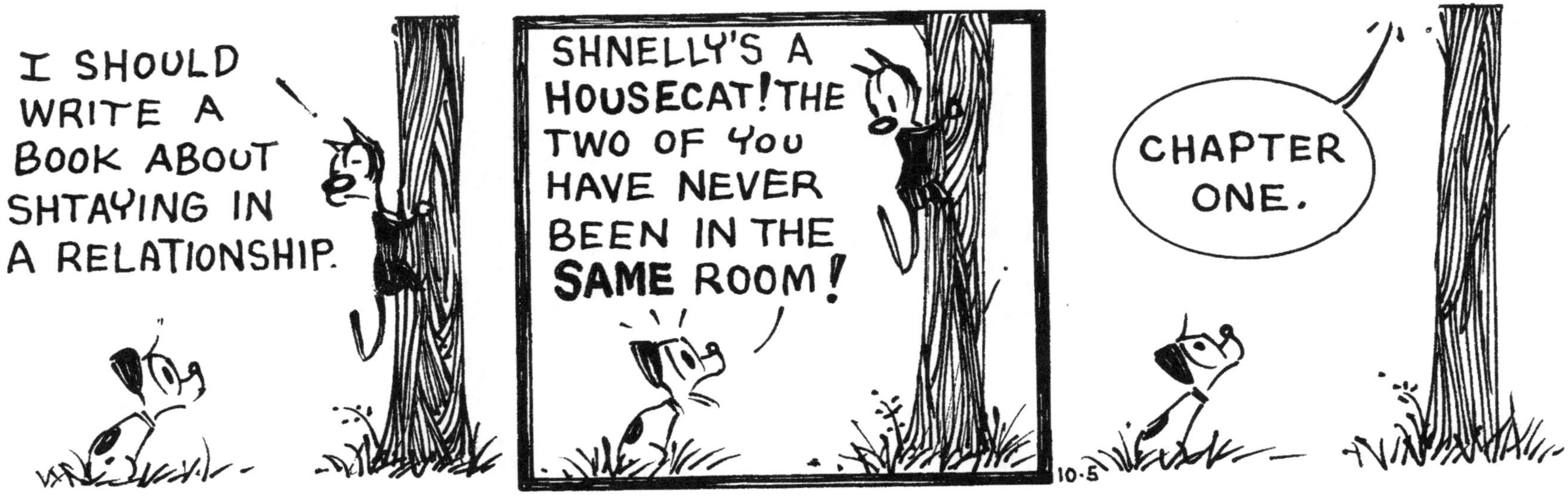
I SHOULD WRITE A BOOK ABOUT SHTAYING IN A RELATIONSHIP.
SHNELLY'S A HOUSECAT! THE TWO OF YOU HAVE NEVER BEEN IN THE SAME ROOM!
CHAPTER ONE.
10·5

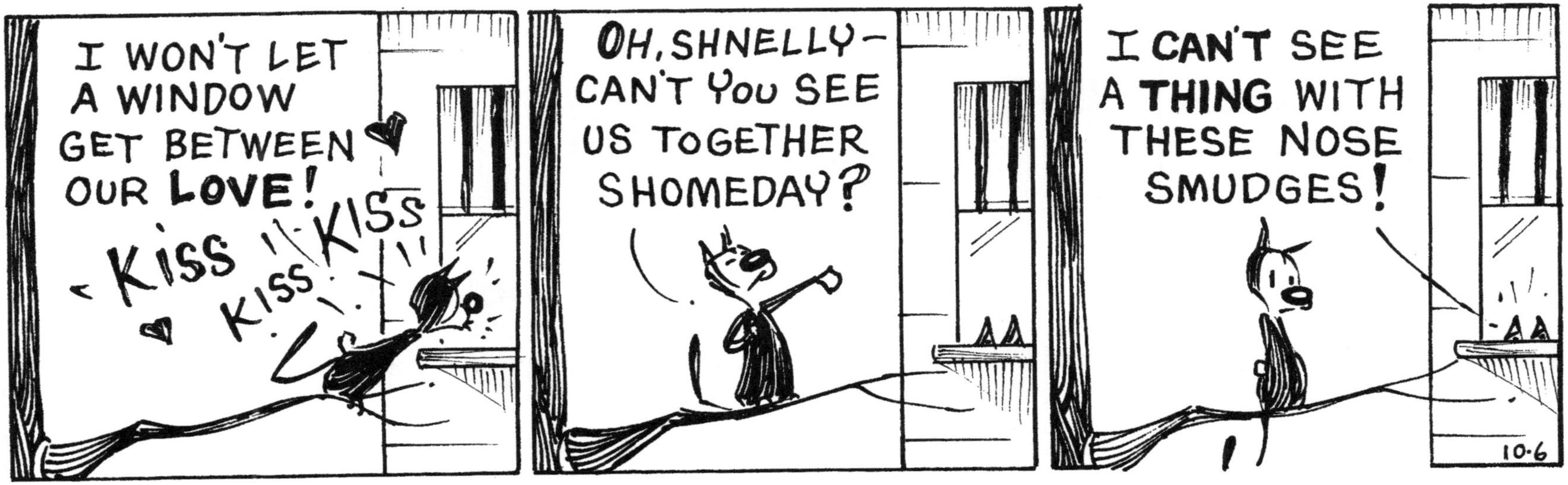
I WON'T LET A WINDOW GET BETWEEN OUR LOVE!
KISS
KISS
KISS
OH, SHNELLY- CAN'T YOU SEE US TOGETHER SHOMEDAY?
I CAN'T SEE A THING WITH THESE NOSE SMUDGES!
10·6

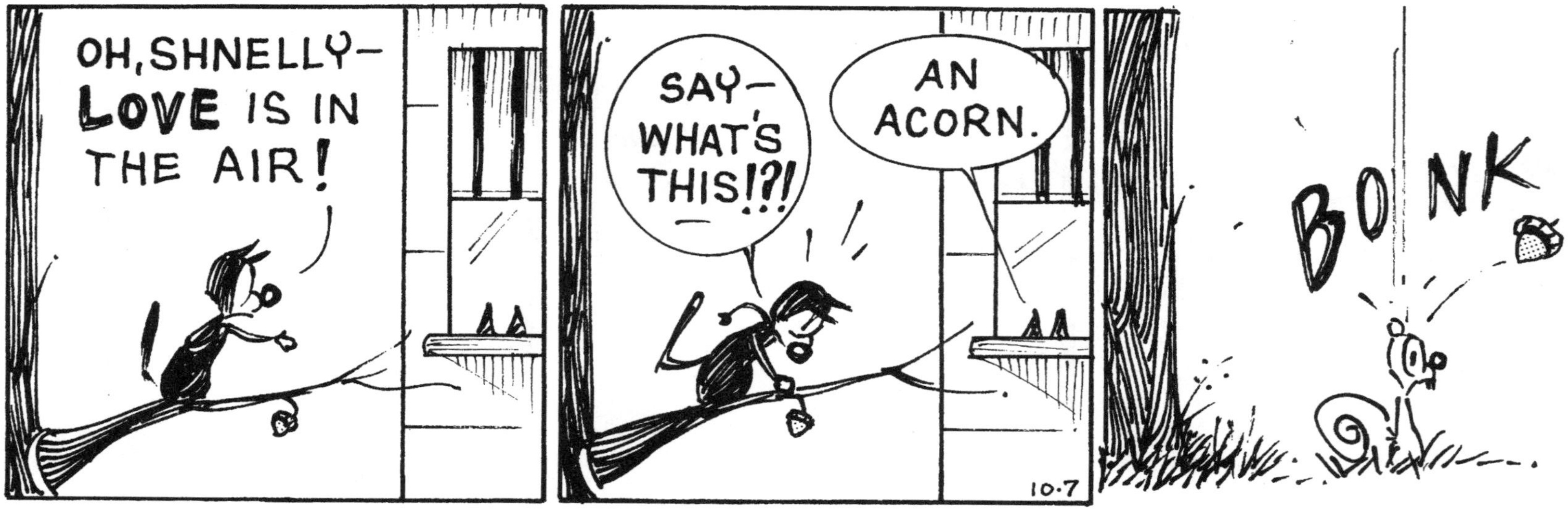
OH, SHNELLY-
LOVE IS IN THE AIR!
SAY-WHAT'S THIS!?!
AN ACORN.
10·7
BONK

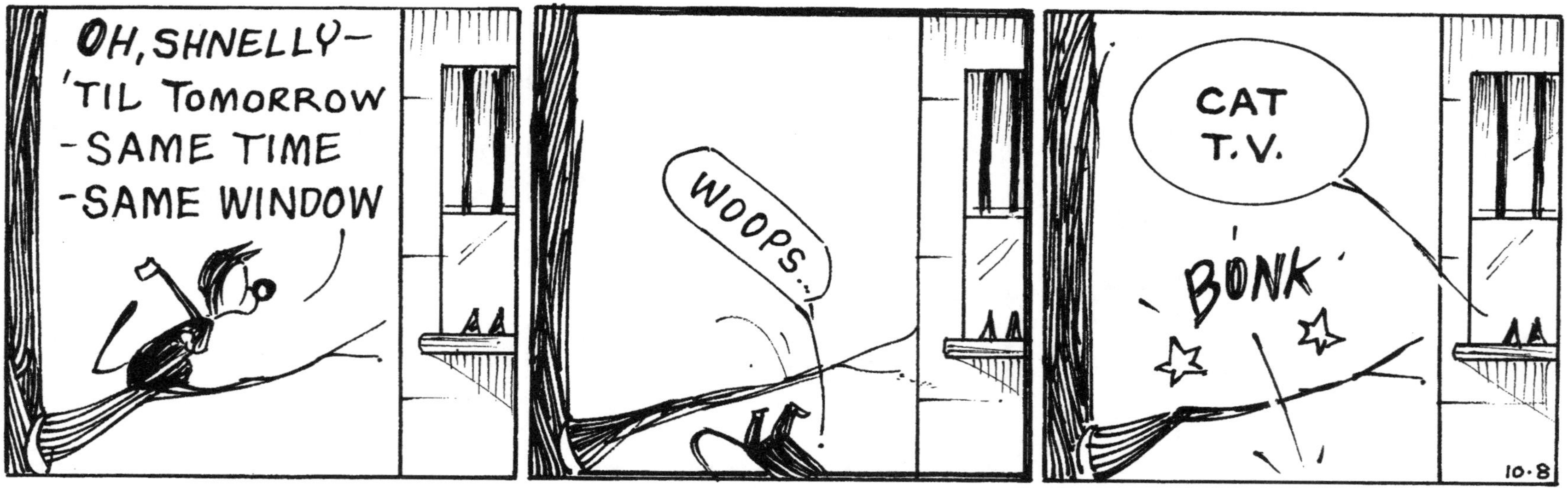
OH, SHNELLY-
'TIL TOMORROW -SAME TIME -SAME WINDOW
WOOPS..
CAT T.V.
BONK
10·8

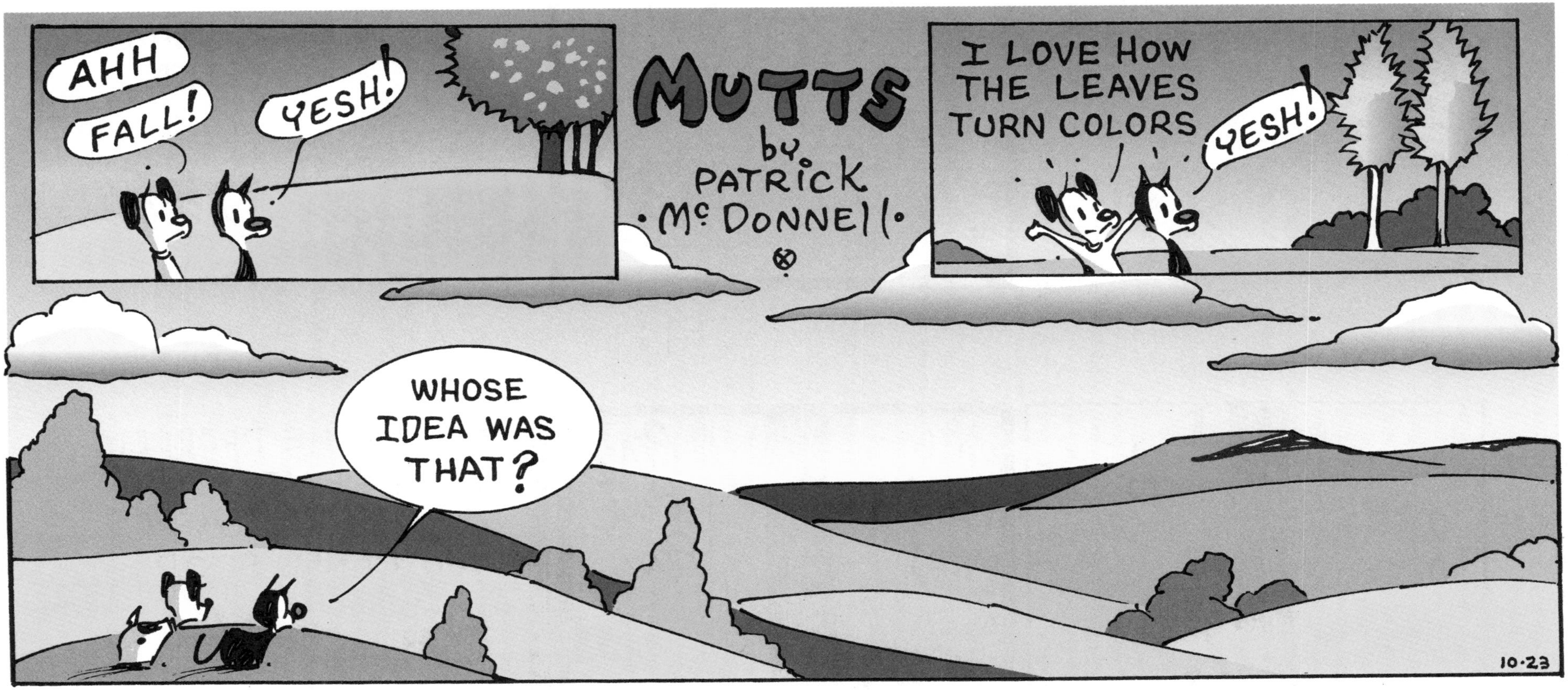
AHH
FALL!
YESH!
MUTTS
by PATRICK McDONNELL
I LOVE HOW THE LEAVES TURN COLORS
YESH!
WHOSE IDEA WAS THAT?
10·23

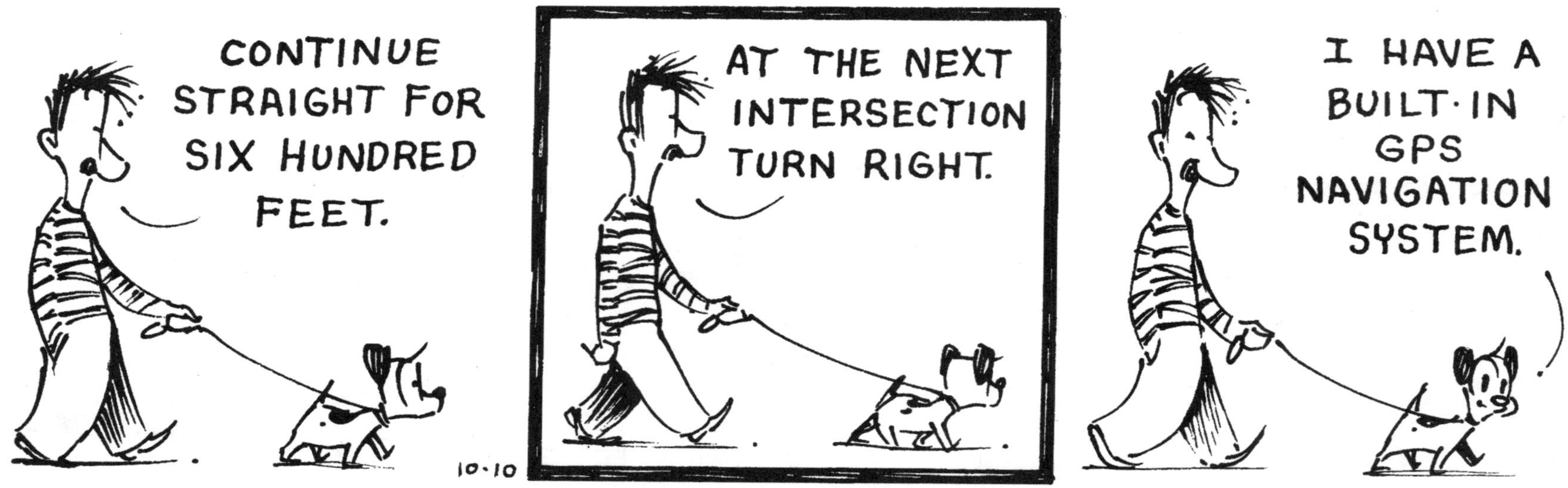
CONTINUE STRAIGHT FOR SIX HUNDRED FEET.
AT THE NEXT INTERSECTION TURN RIGHT.
I HAVE A BUILT-IN GPS NAVIGATION SYSTEM.
10-10

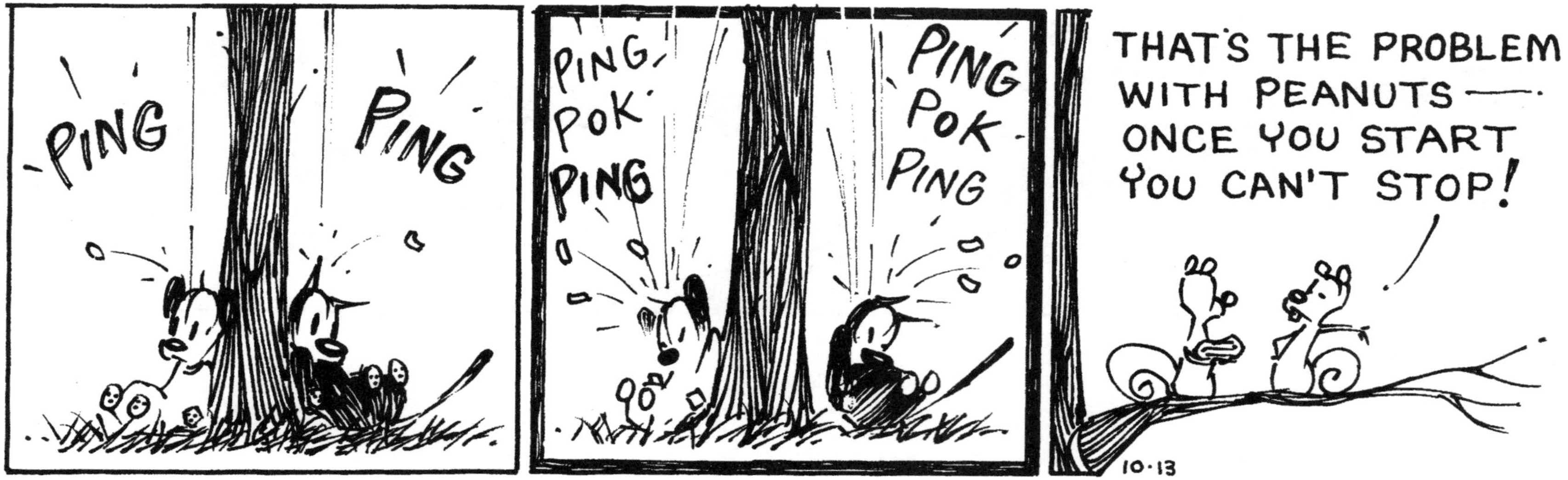
PING
PING
PING POK PING
PING POK PING
THAT'S THE PROBLEM WITH PEANUTS — ONCE YOU START YOU CAN'T STOP!
10-13

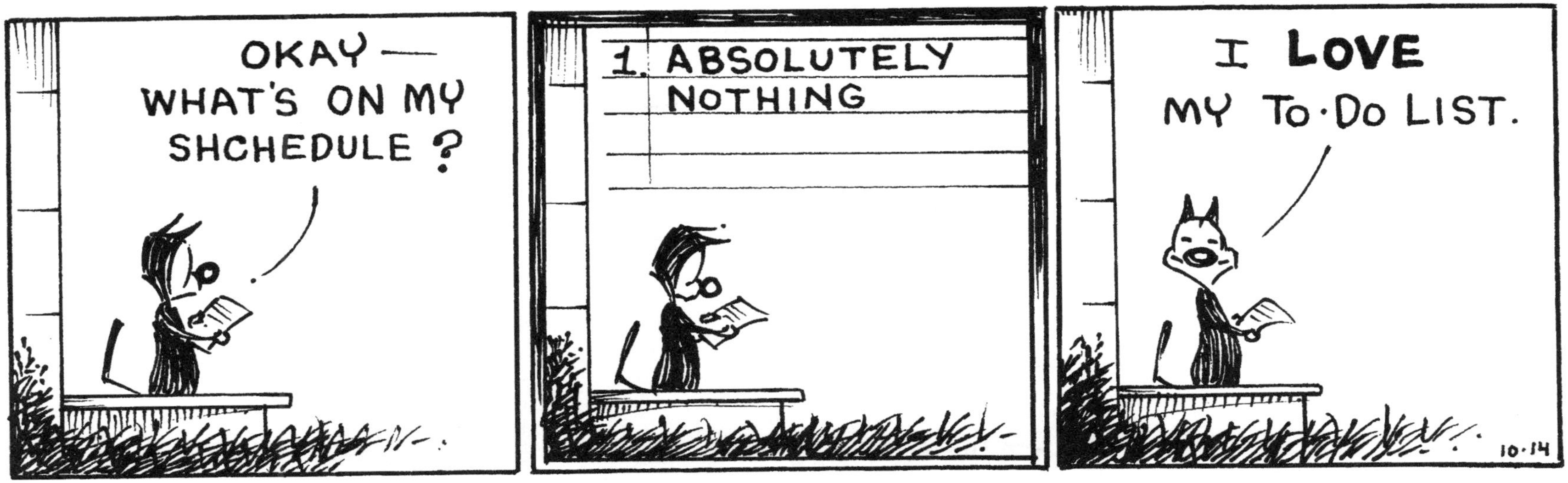
OKAY— WHAT'S ON MY SHCHEDULE?
1. ABSOLUTELY NOTHING
I LOVE MY TO·DO LIST.
10·14

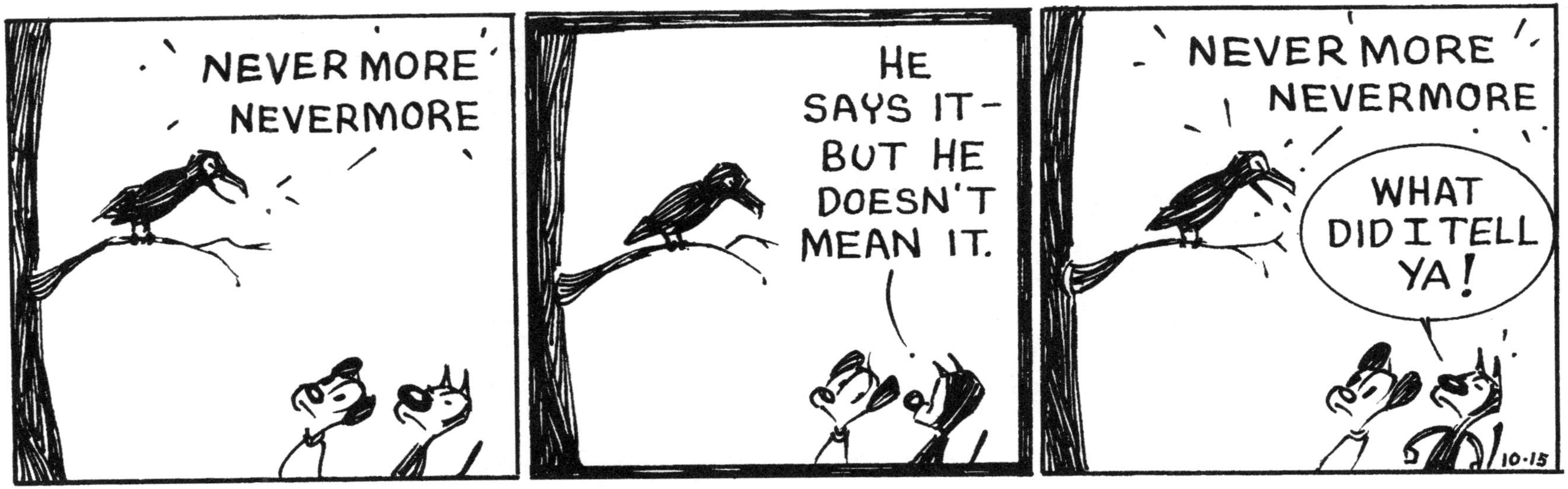
NEVERMORE NEVERMORE
HE SAYS IT— BUT HE DOESN'T MEAN IT.
NEVERMORE NEVERMORE
WHAT DID I TELL YA!
10·15

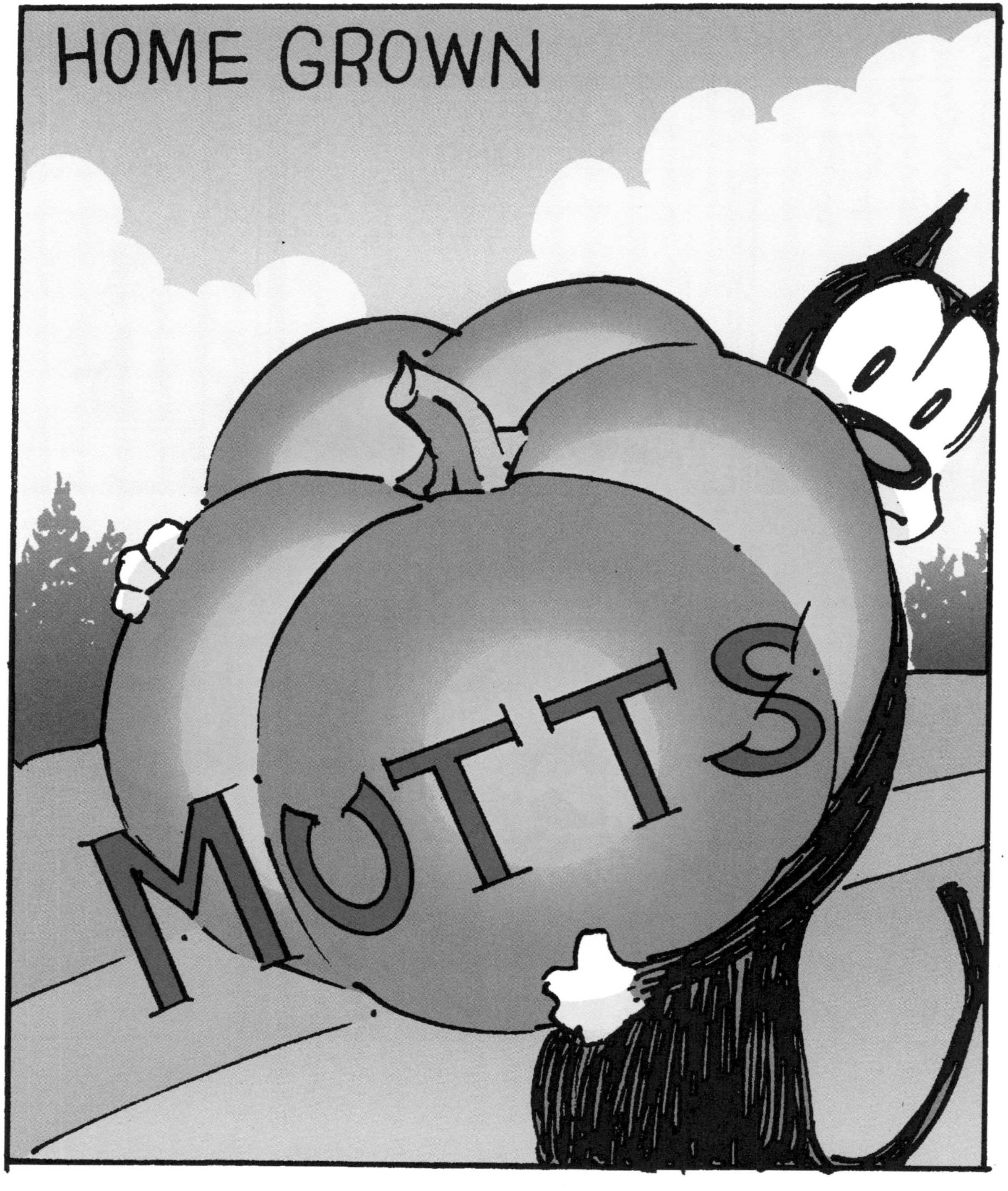
HOME GROWN
MUTTS

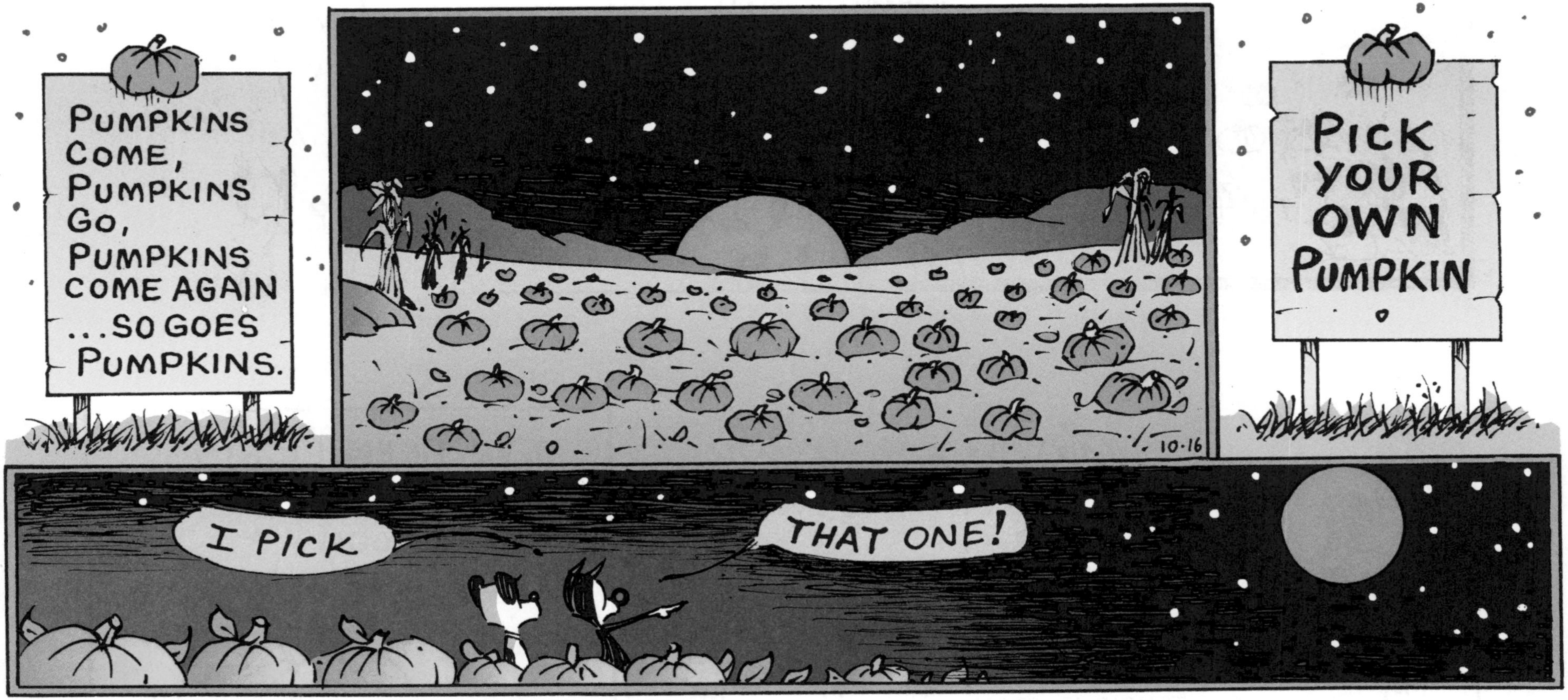
PUMPKINS COME, PUMPKINS GO, PUMPKINS COME AGAIN ...SO GOES PUMPKINS.
10·16
PICK YOUR OWN PUMPKIN
I PICK
THAT ONE!

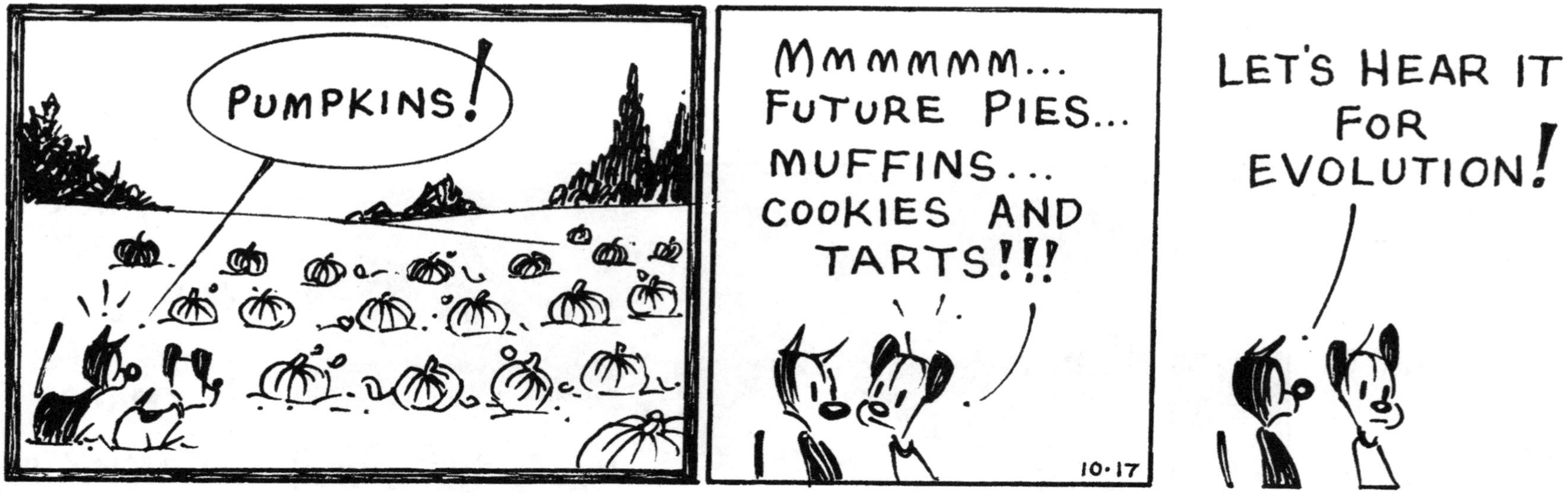
PUMPKINS!
MMMMMM... FUTURE PIES... MUFFINS... COOKIES AND TARTS!!!
10·17
LET'S HEAR IT FOR EVOLUTION!

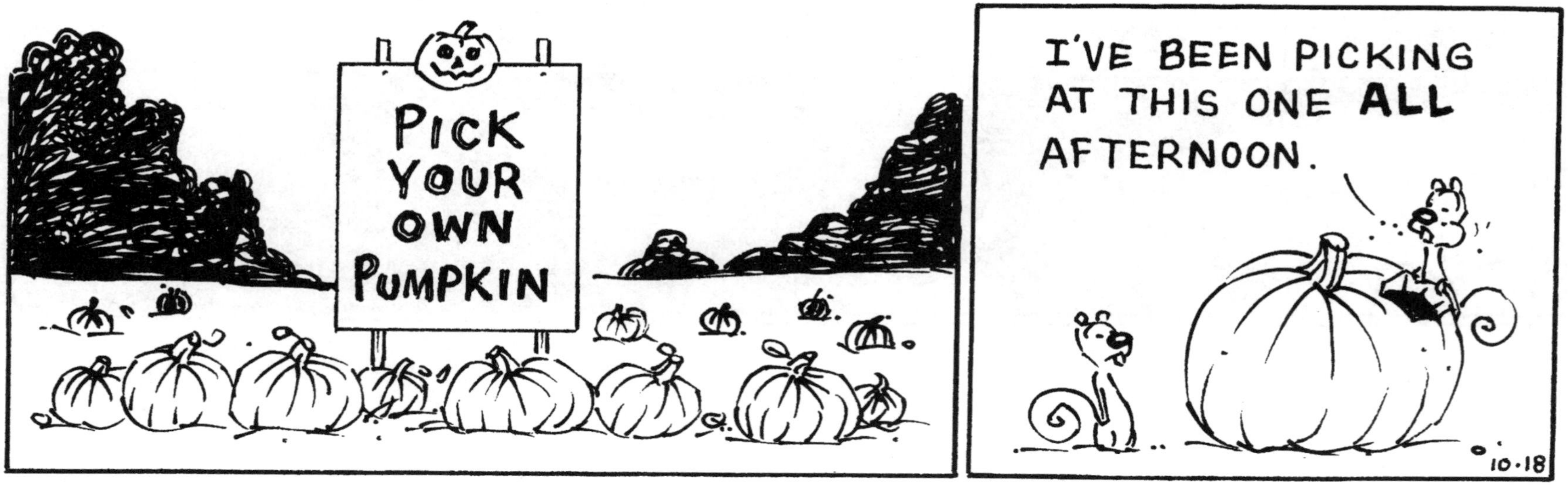
PICK YOUR OWN PUMPKIN
I'VE BEEN PICKING AT THIS ONE ALL AFTERNOON.
10·18

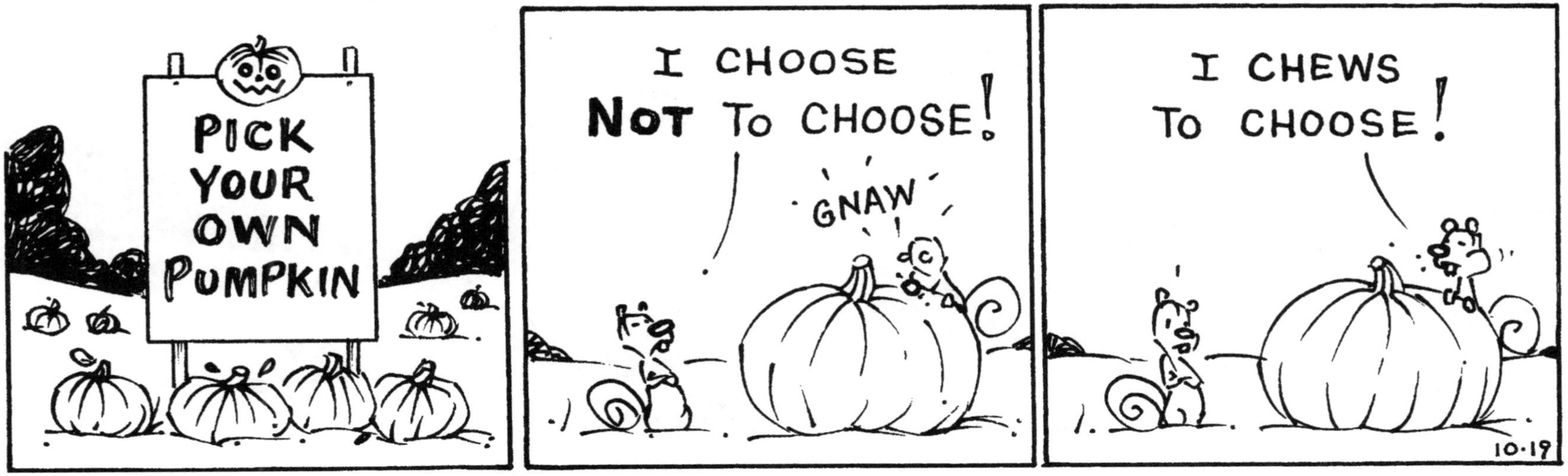
PICK YOUR OWN PUMPKIN
I CHOOSE NOT TO CHOOSE!
GNAW
I CHEWS TO CHOOSE!
10·19

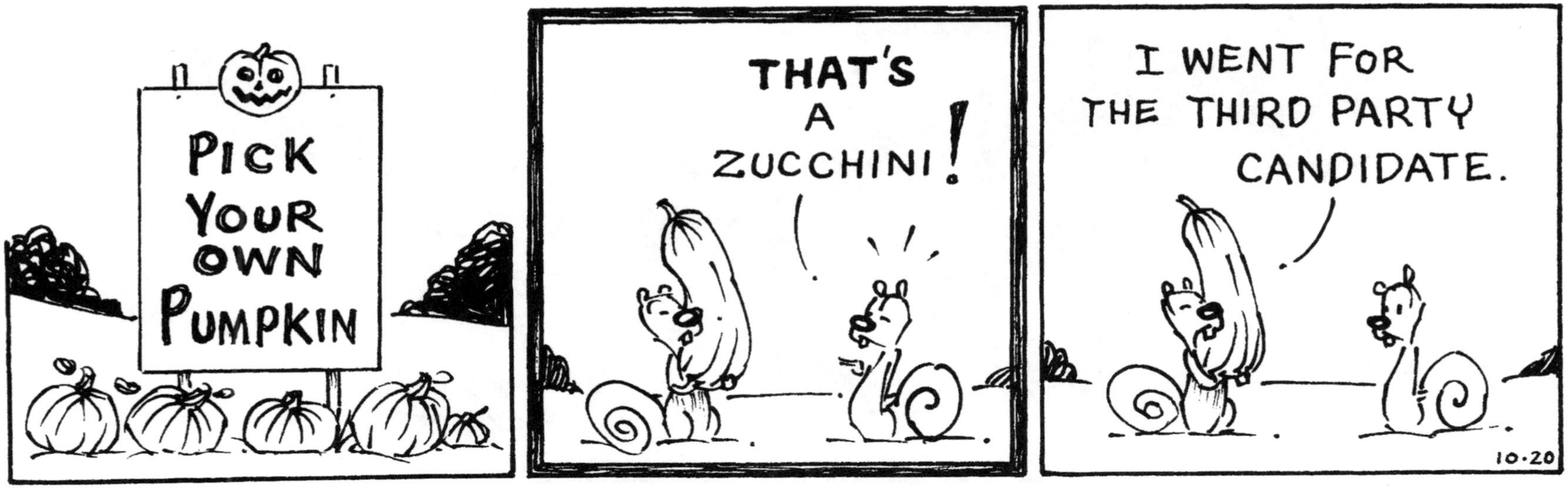
PICK YOUR OWN PUMPKIN
THAT'S A ZUCCHINI!
I WENT FOR THE THIRD PARTY CANDIDATE.
10·20

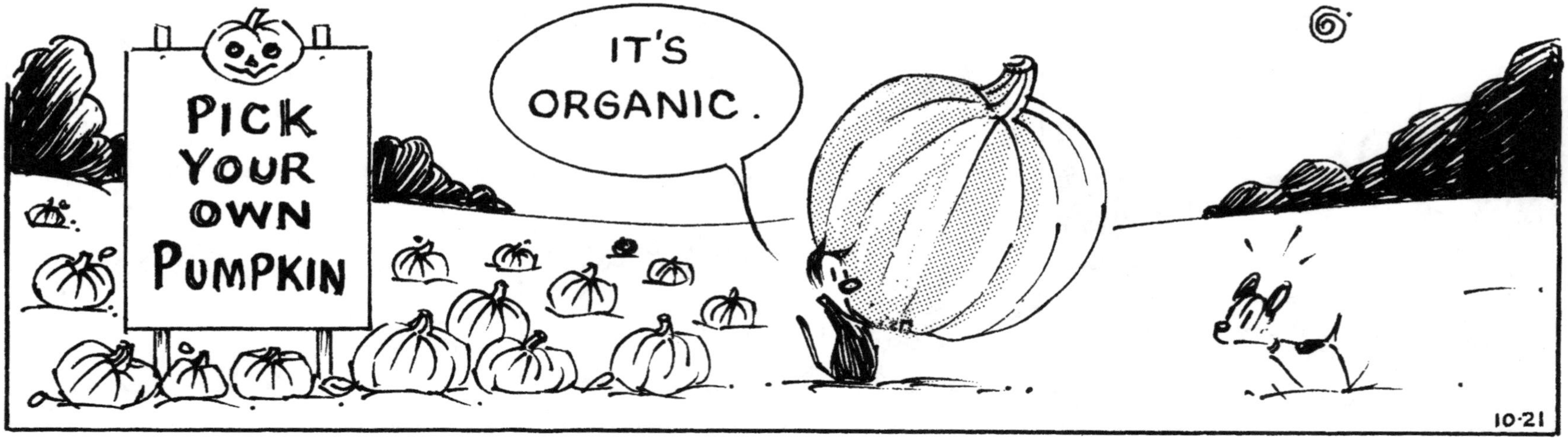
PICK YOUR OWN PUMPKIN
IT'S ORGANIC.
10·21

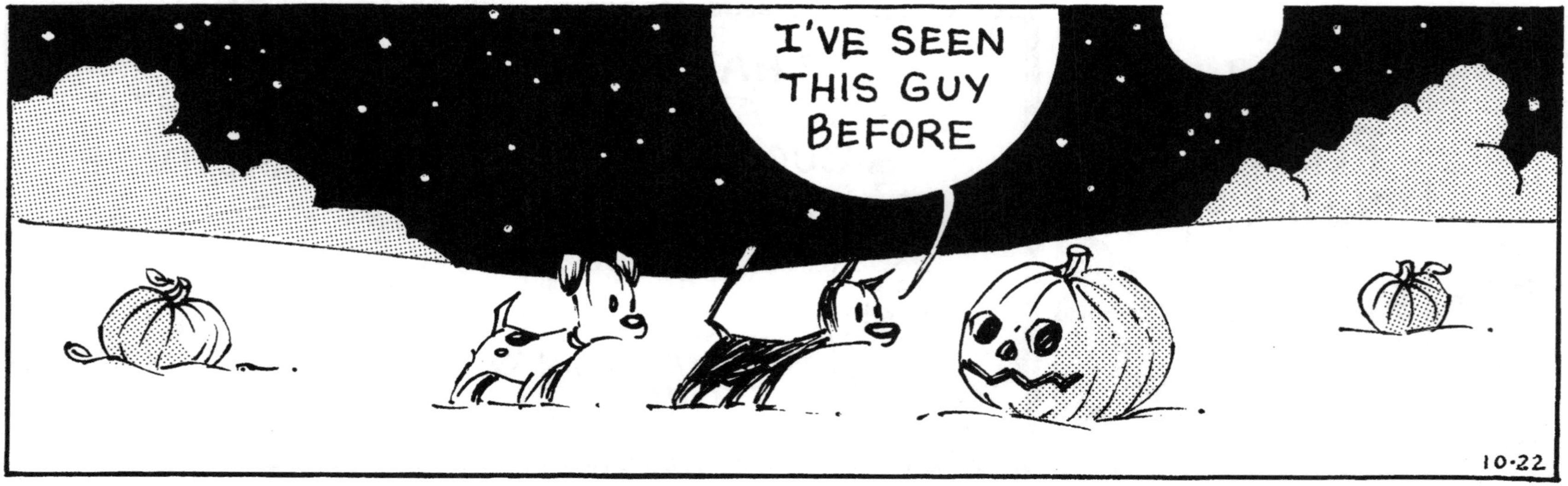
I'VE SEEN THIS GUY BEFORE
10·22

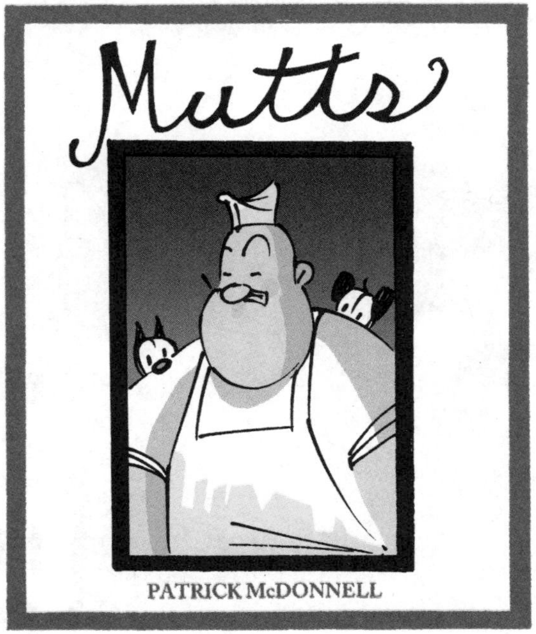
Mutts
PATRICK McDONNELL

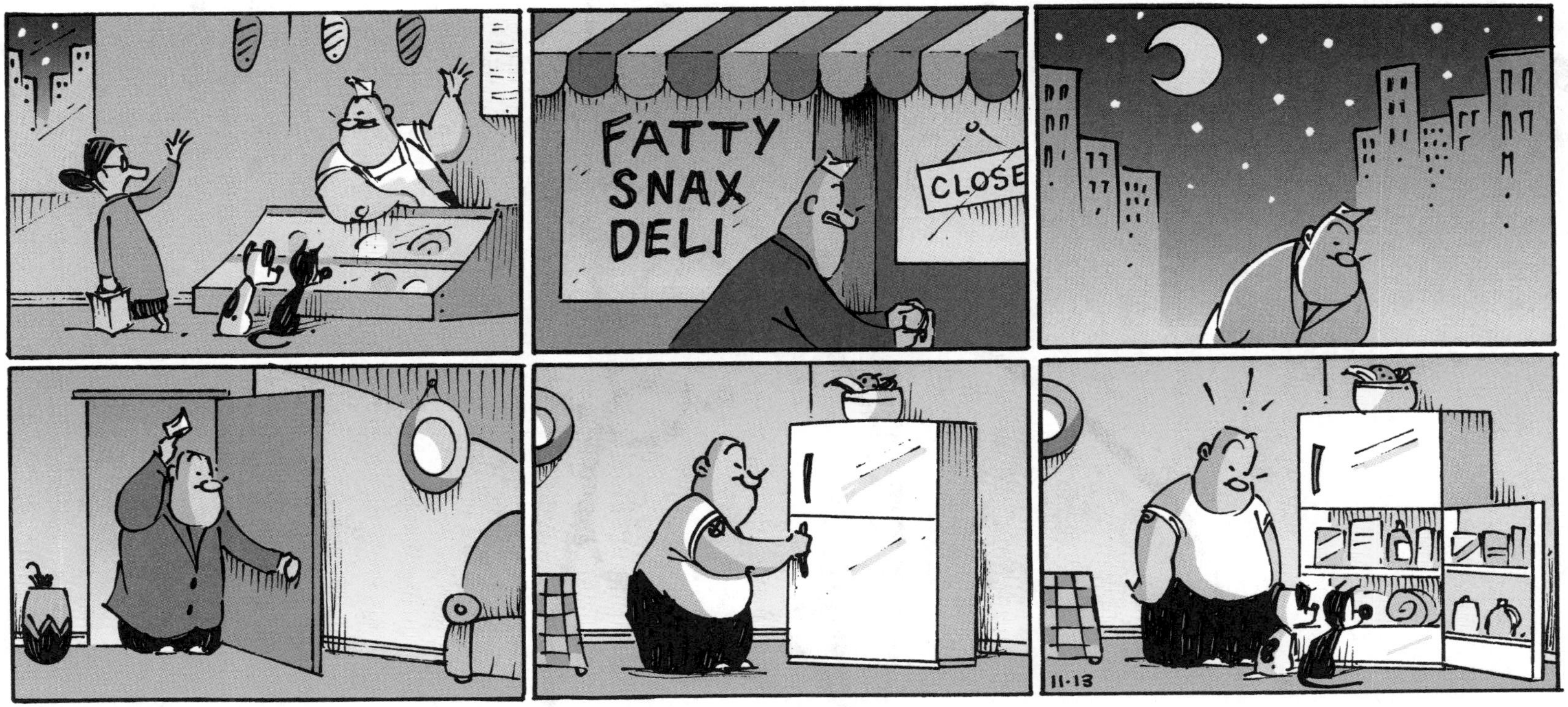
FATTY SNAX DELI
CLOSE
11-13

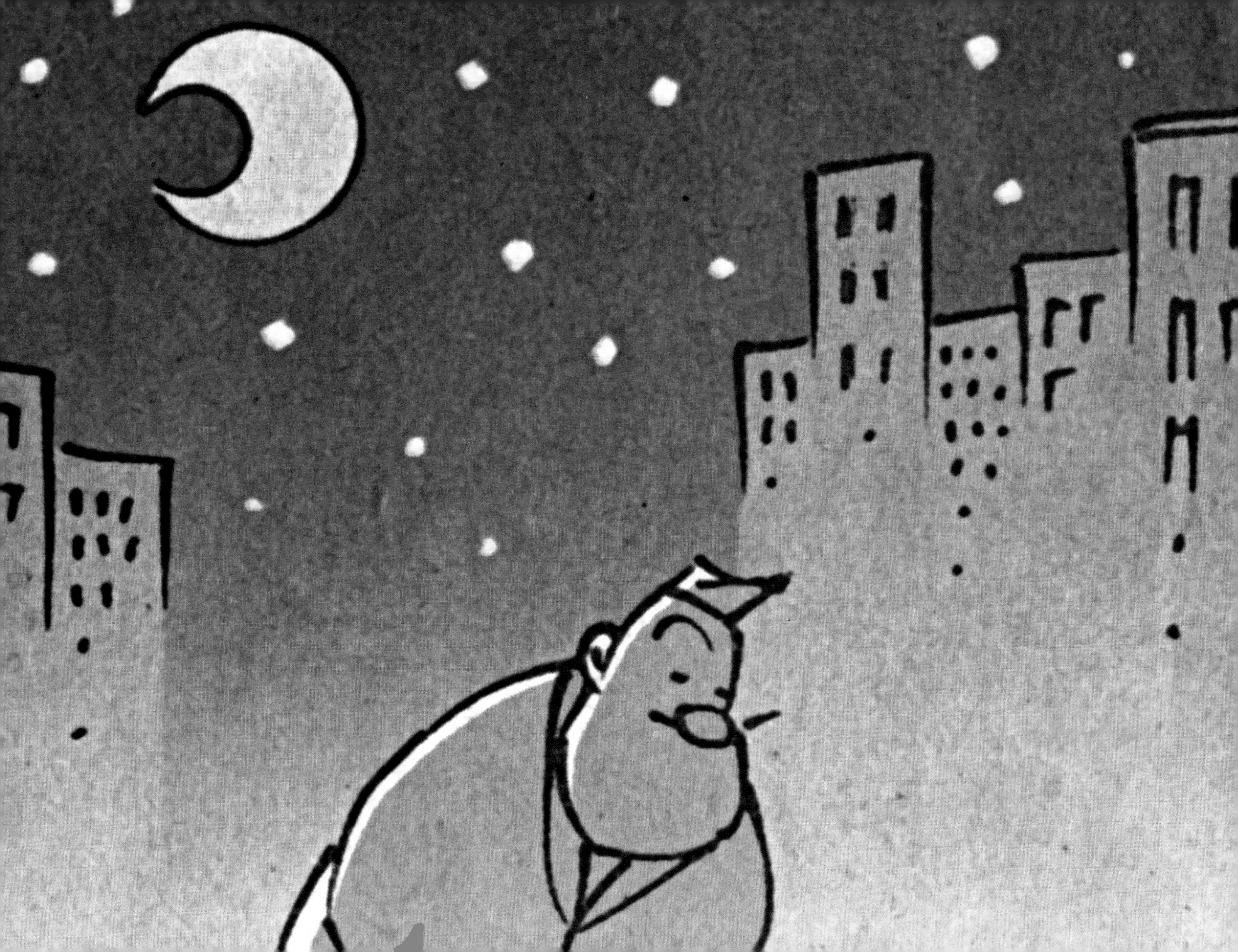

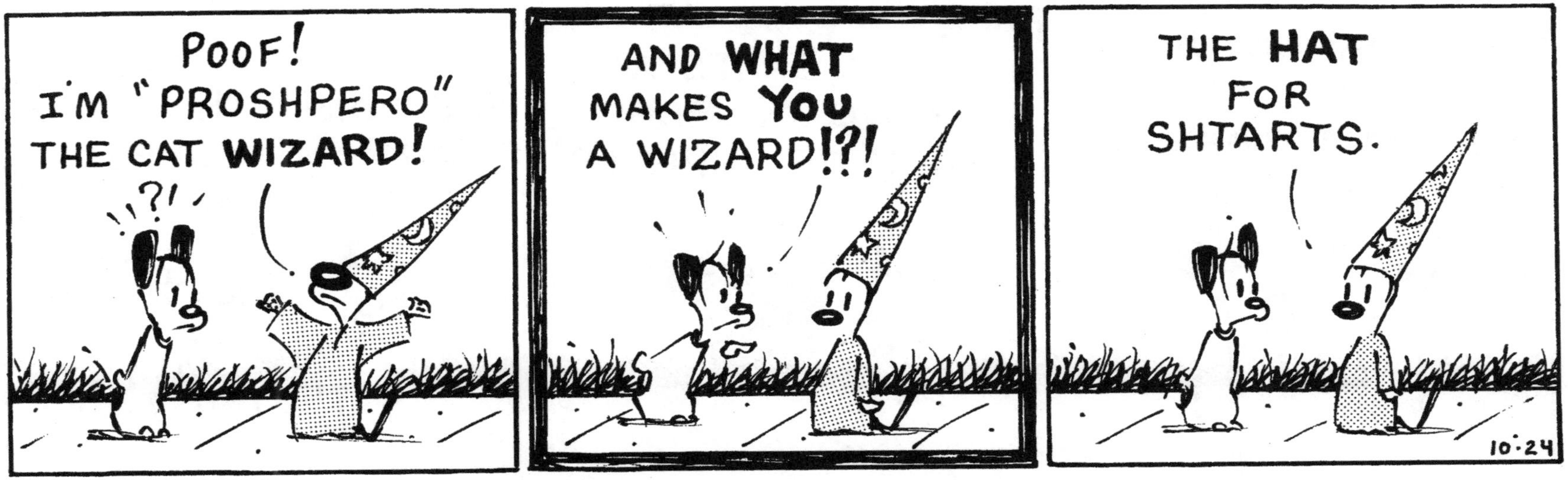
POOF!
I'M "PROSHPERO" THE CAT WIZARD!
?!
AND WHAT MAKES YOU A WIZARD!?!
THE HAT FOR SHTARTS.
10·24

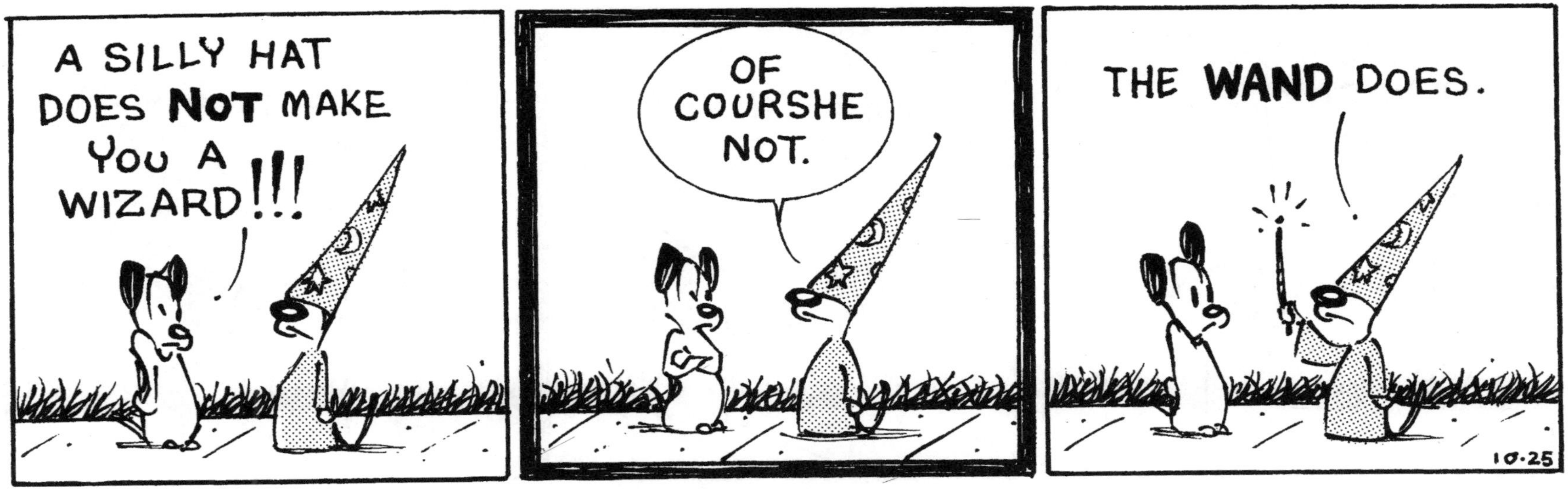
A SILLY HAT DOES NOT MAKE YOU A WIZARD!!!
OF COURSHE NOT.
THE WAND DOES.
10·25

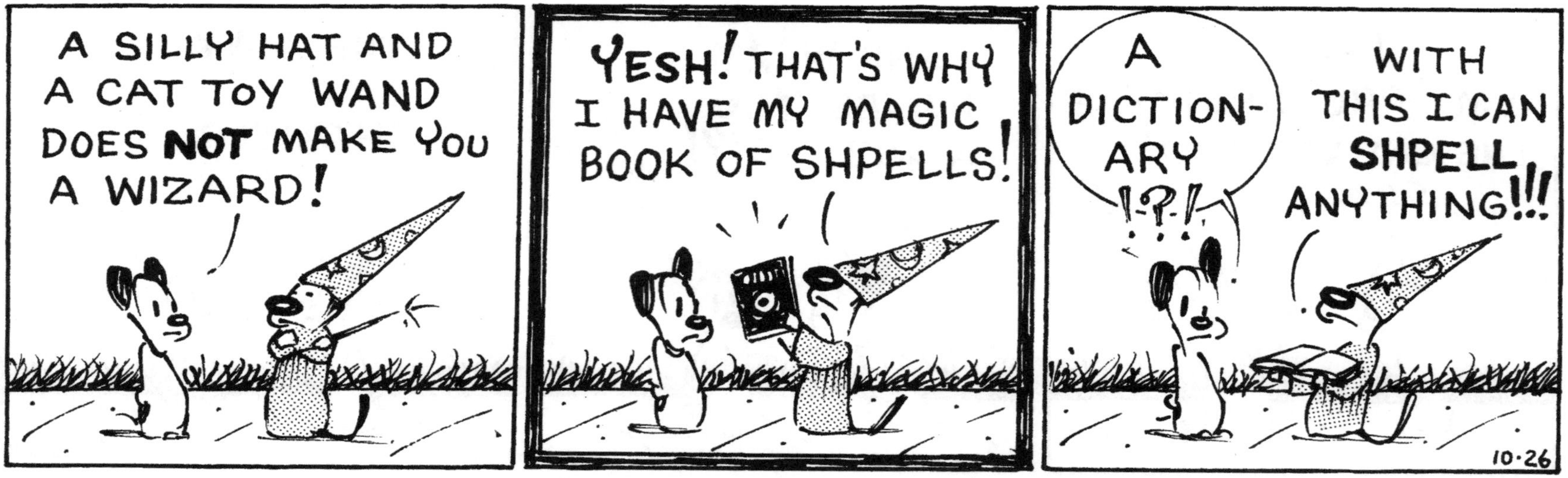
A SILLY HAT AND A CAT TOY WAND DOES **NOT** MAKE YOU A WIZARD!
YESH! THAT'S WHY I HAVE MY MAGIC BOOK OF SHPELLS!
A DICTION-ARY !?!
WITH THIS I CAN **SHPELL** ANYTHING!!!
10·26

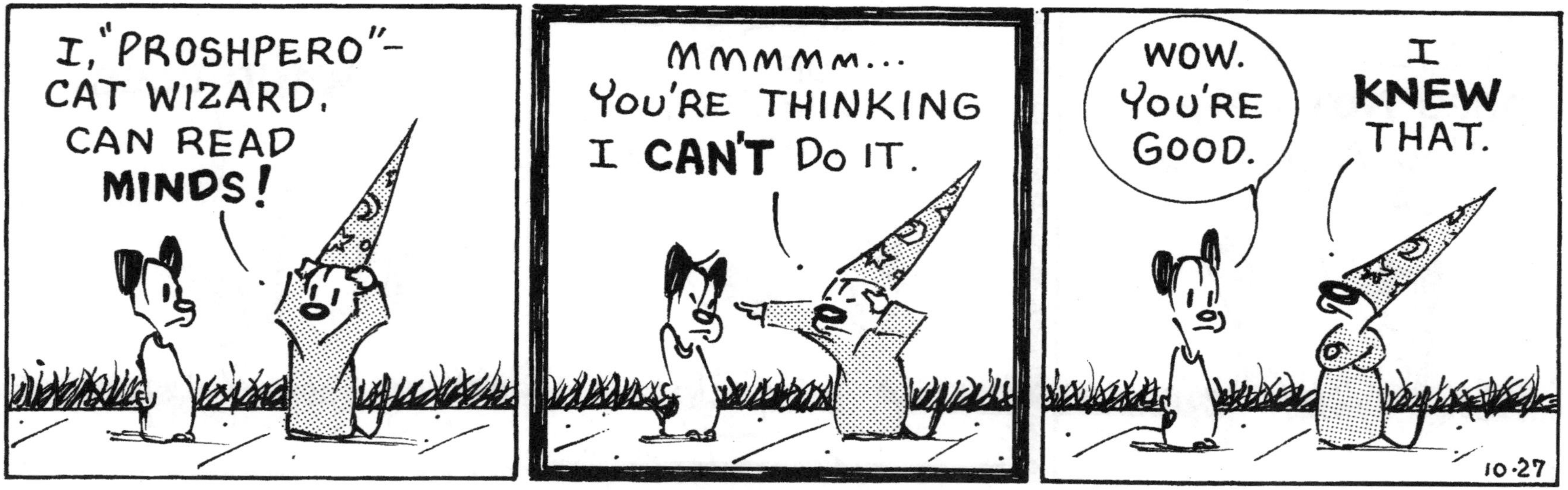
I, "PROSHPERO"– CAT WIZARD, CAN READ **MINDS**!
MMMMM... YOU'RE THINKING I **CAN'T** DO IT.
WOW. YOU'RE GOOD.
I **KNEW** THAT.
10·27

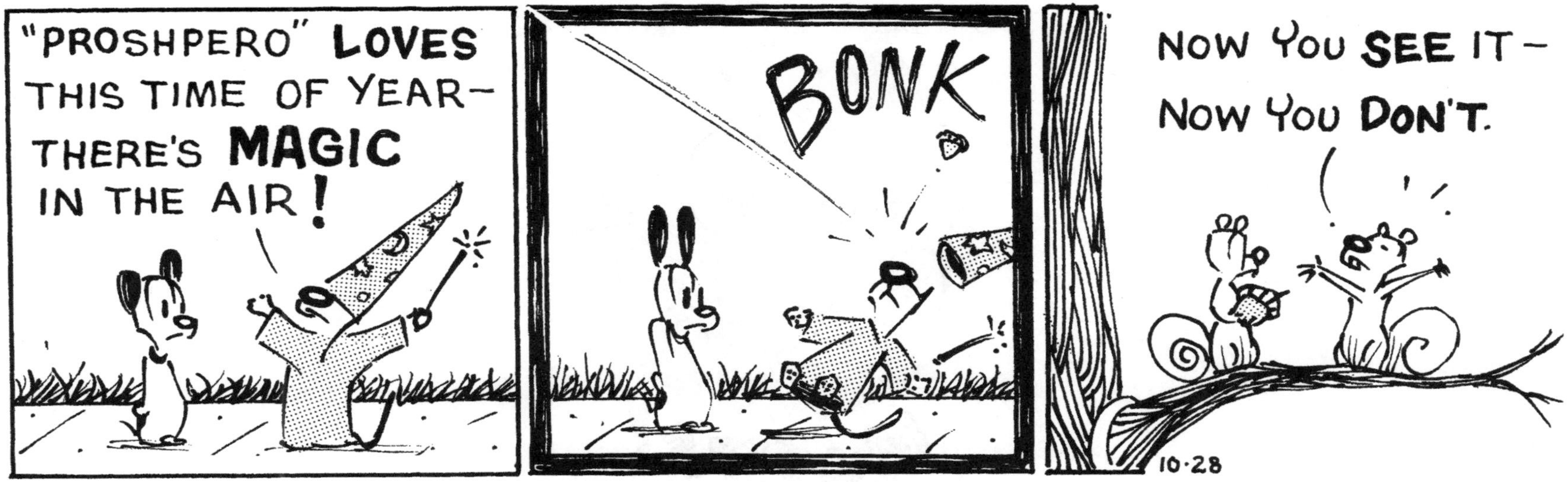
"PROSHPERO" LOVES THIS TIME OF YEAR–THERE'S MAGIC IN THE AIR!
BONK
NOW YOU SEE IT–NOW YOU DON'T.
10·28

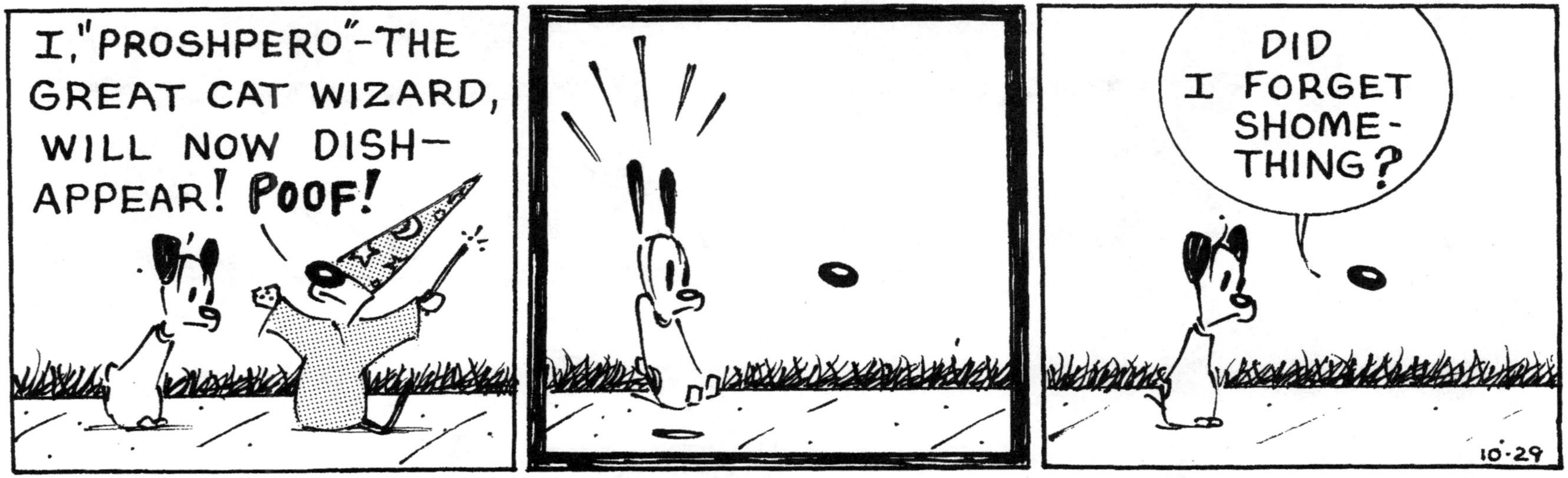
I, "PROSHPERO"–THE GREAT CAT WIZARD, WILL NOW DISH–APPEAR! POOF!
DID I FORGET SHOME-THING?
10·29

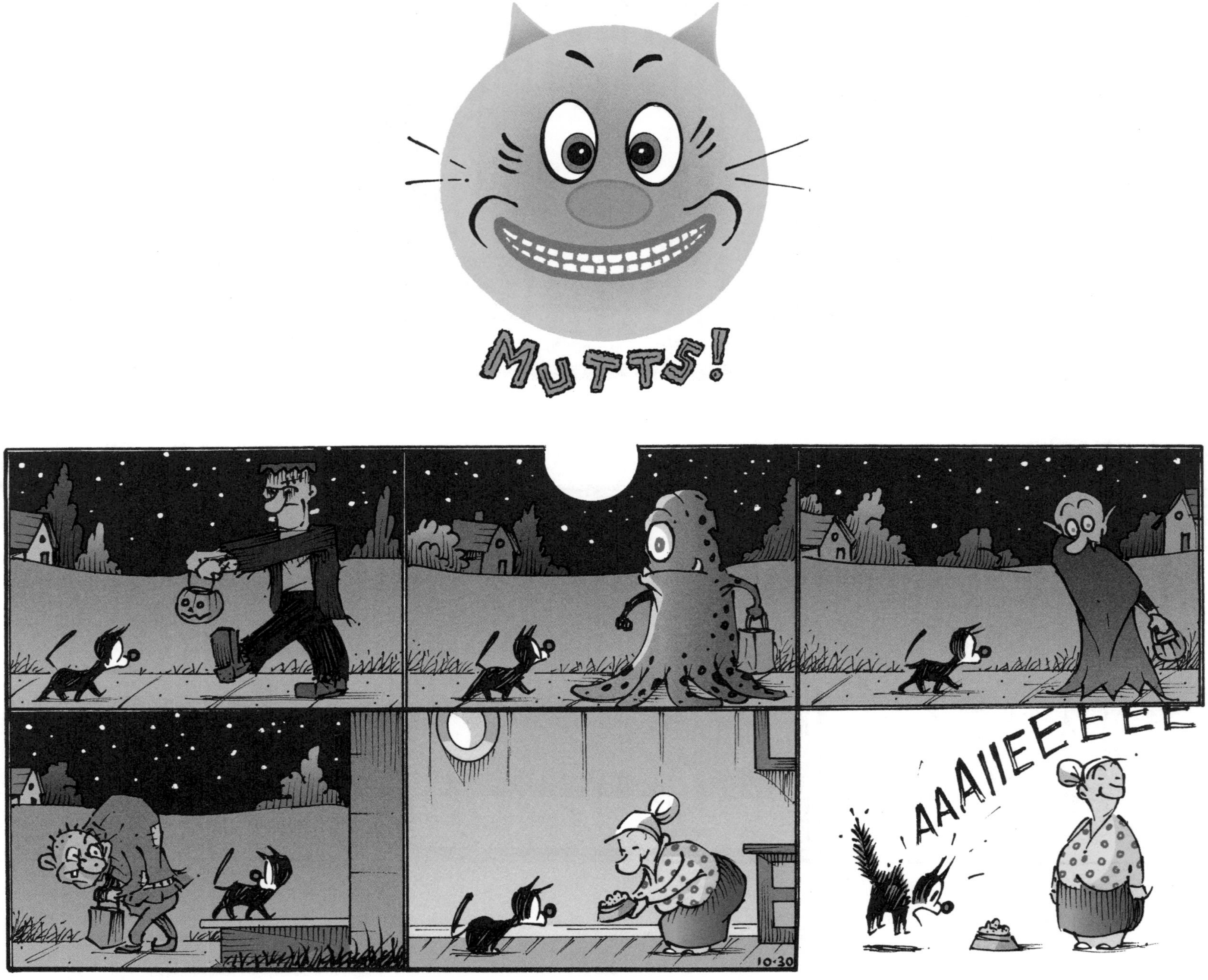
MUTTS!
AAAIIEEEEE
10·30

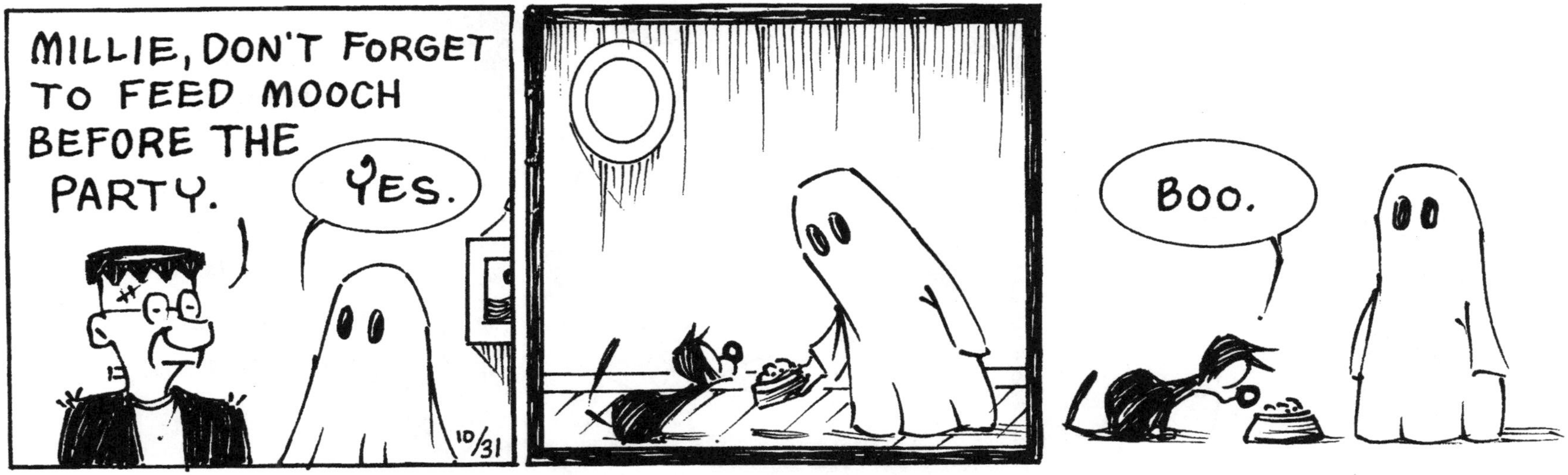
MILLIE, DON'T FORGET TO FEED MOOCH BEFORE THE PARTY.
YES.
BOO.
10/31

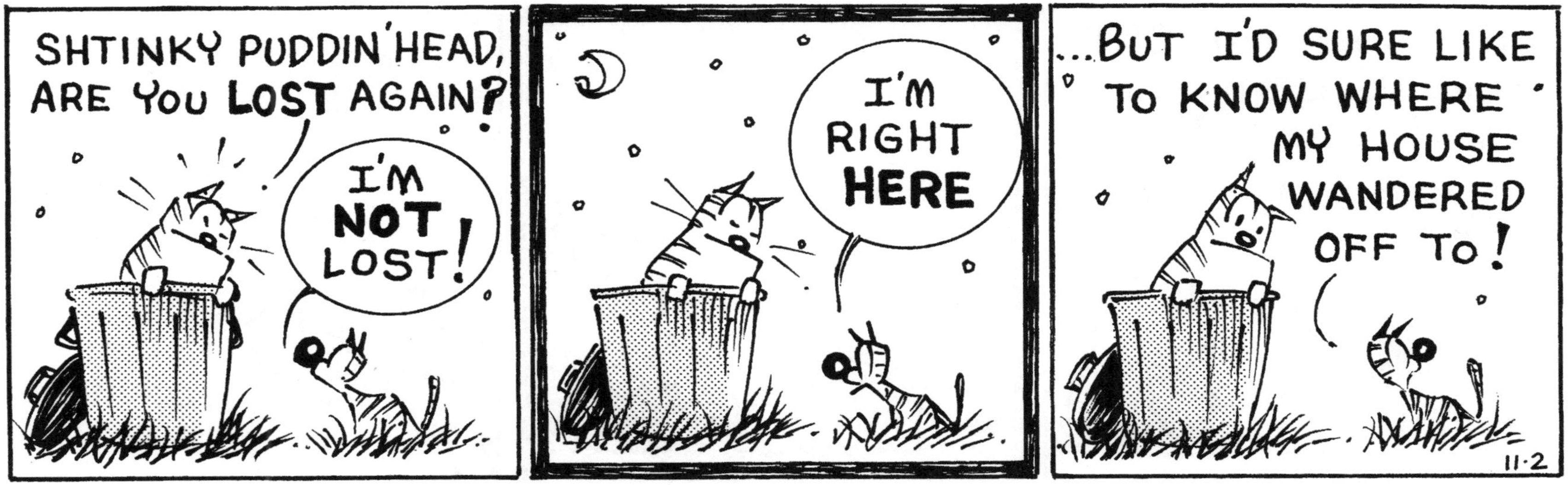
SHTINKY PUDDIN'HEAD, ARE YOU **LOST** AGAIN?
I'M **NOT** LOST!
I'M RIGHT **HERE**
...BUT I'D SURE LIKE TO KNOW WHERE MY HOUSE WANDERED OFF TO!
11·2

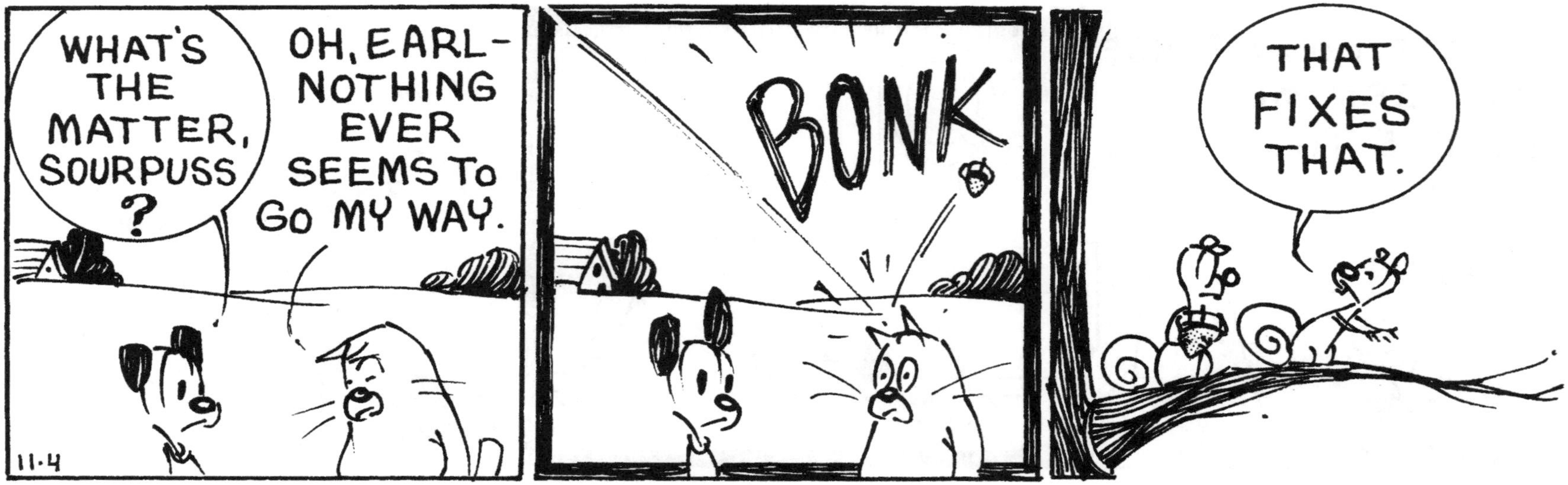
WHAT'S THE MATTER, SOURPUSS?
OH, EARL- NOTHING EVER SEEMS TO GO MY WAY.
11·4
BONK
THAT FIXES THAT.

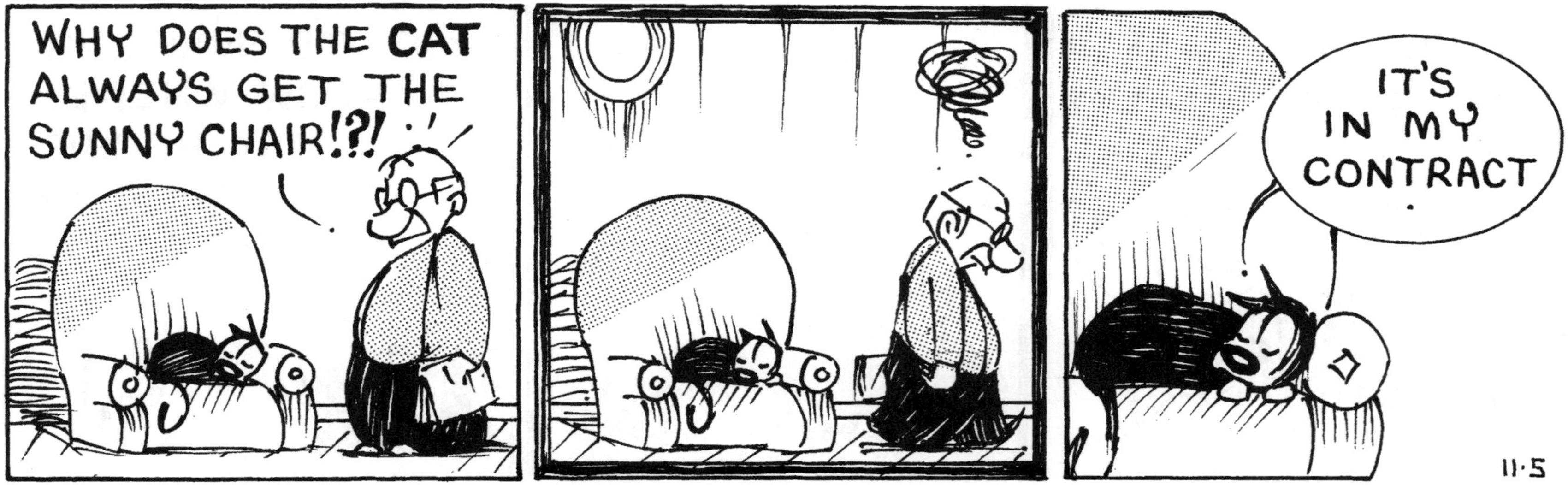
WHY DOES THE **CAT** ALWAYS GET THE SUNNY CHAIR!?!
IT'S IN MY CONTRACT.
11·5

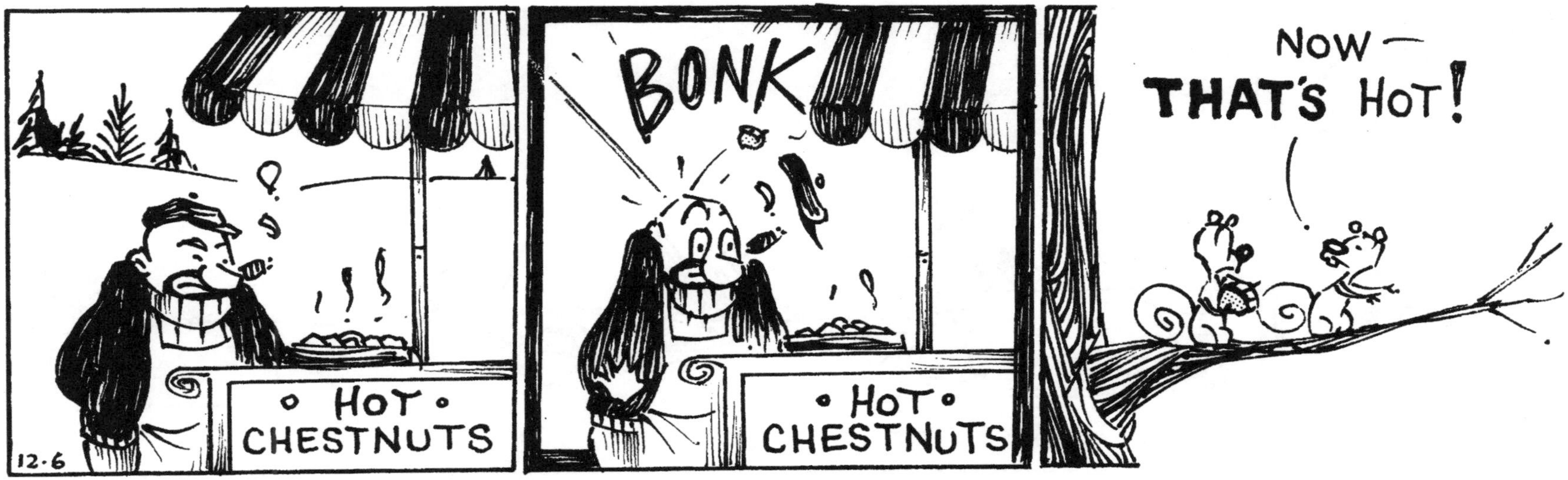
12·6
• HOT •
CHESTNUTS
BONK
• HOT •
CHESTNUTS
NOW —
THAT'S HOT!

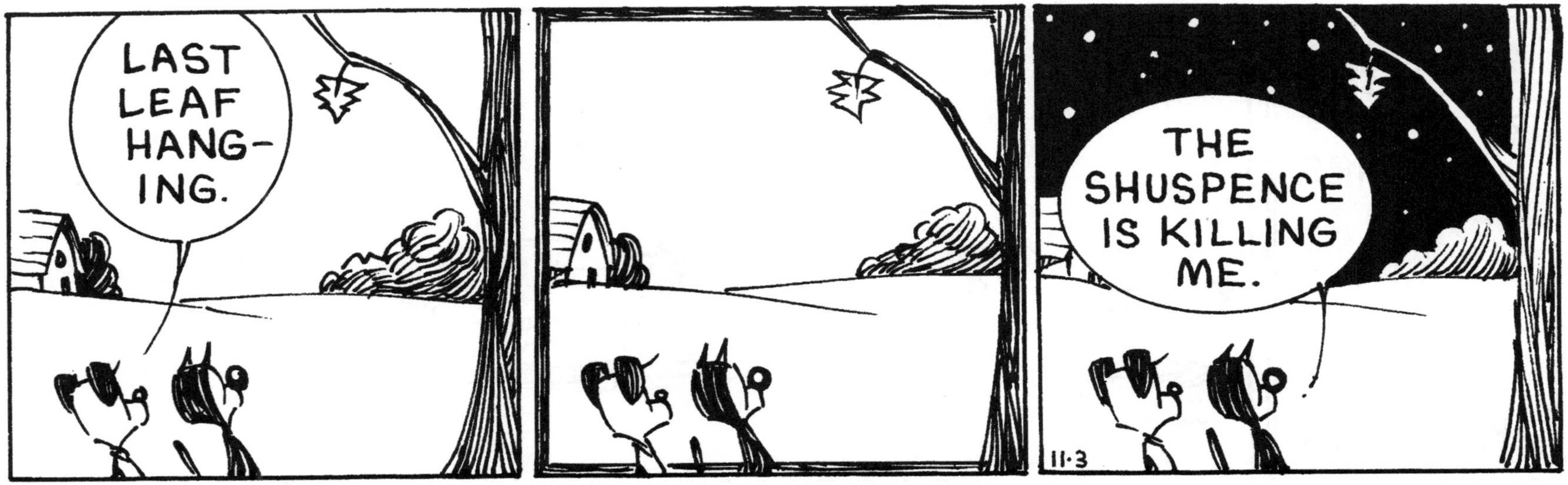
LAST LEAF HANG- ING.
THE SHUSPENCE IS KILLING ME.
11·3

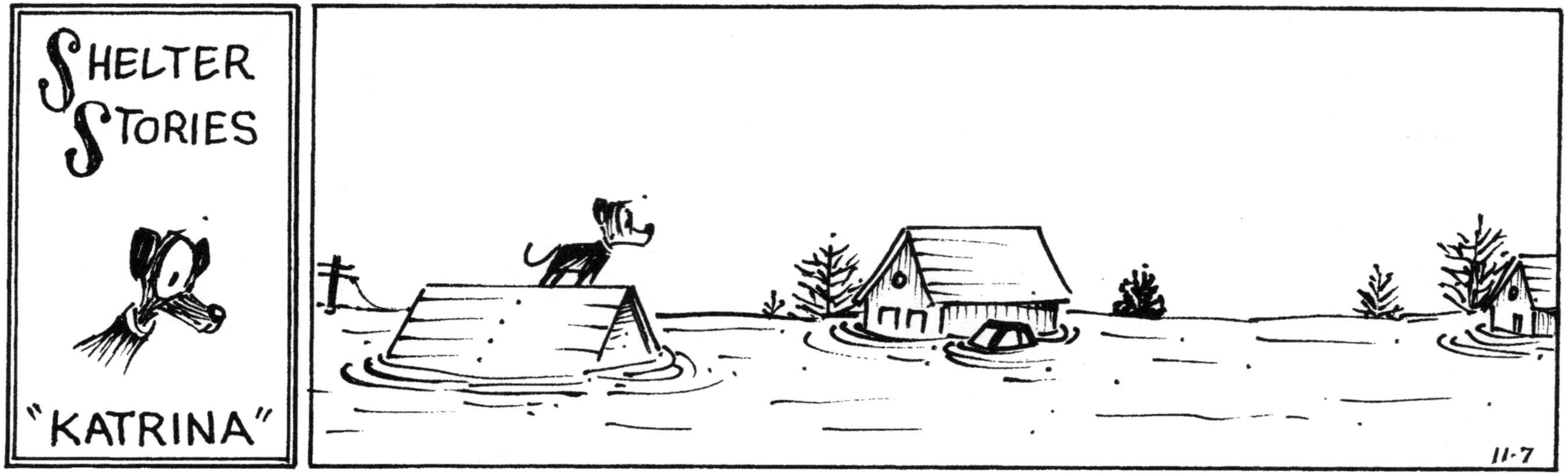
SHELTER STORIES
"KATRINA"
11·7

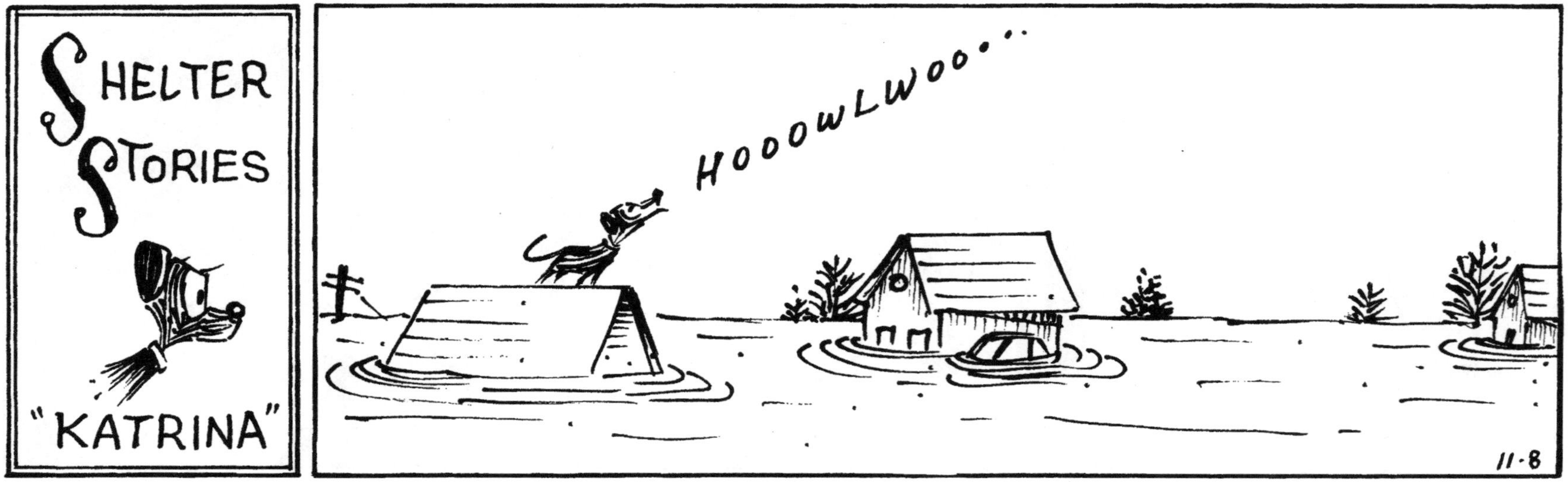
SHELTER STORIES
"KATRINA"
HOOOWLWOO...
11·8

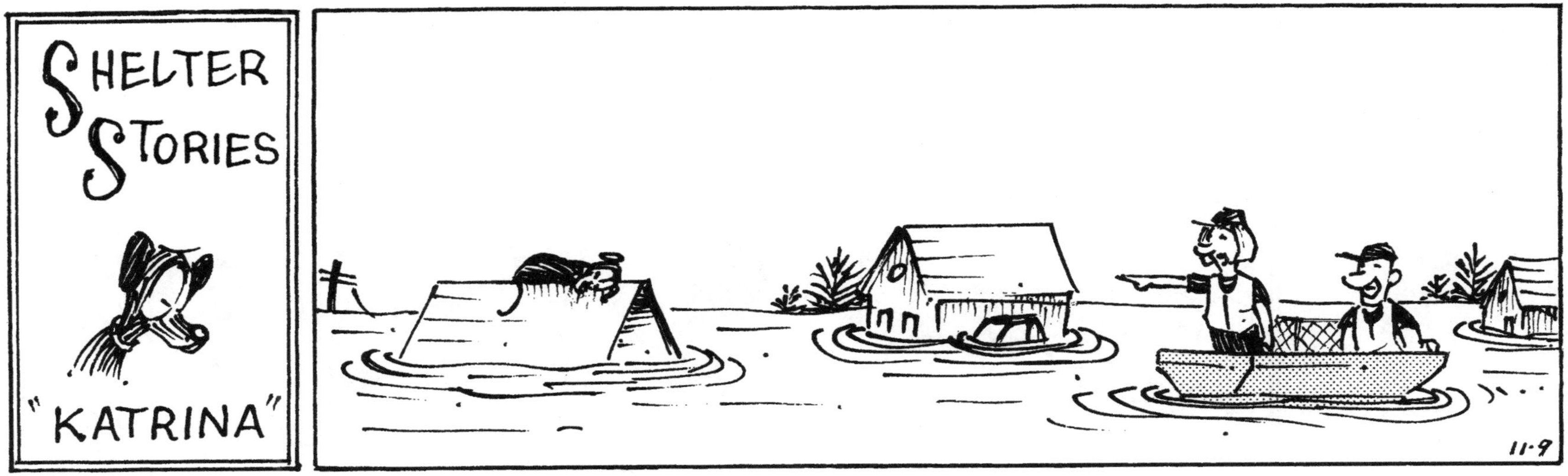
SHELTER STORIES
"KATRINA"
11-9

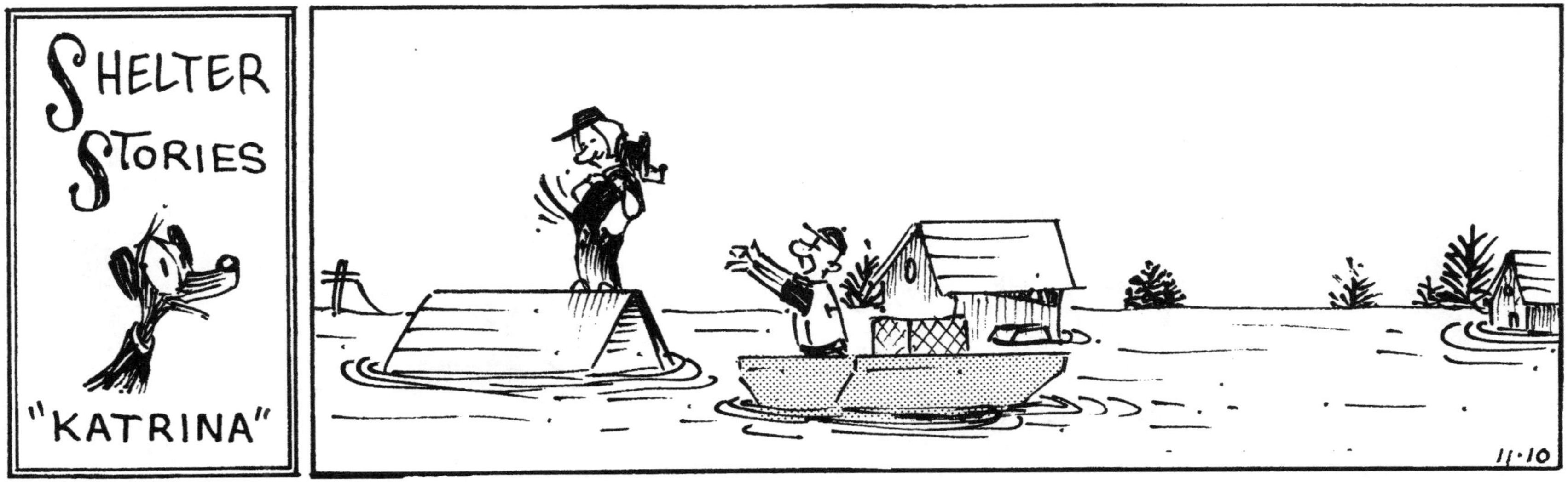
SHELTER STORIES
"KATRINA"
11-10

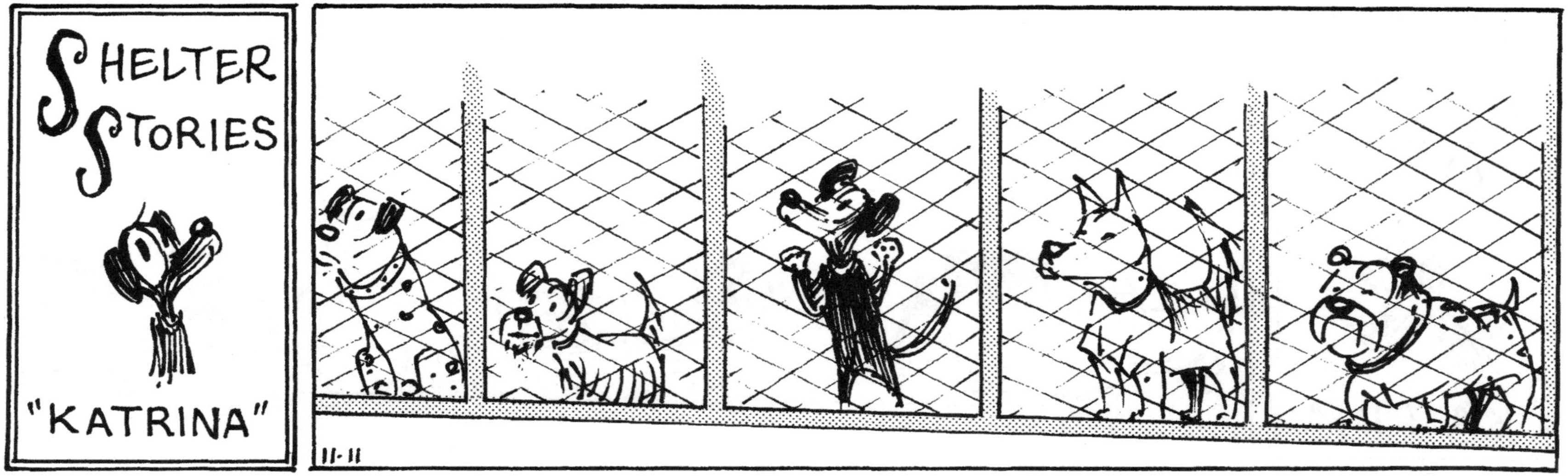
SHELTER STORIES
"KATRINA"
11-11

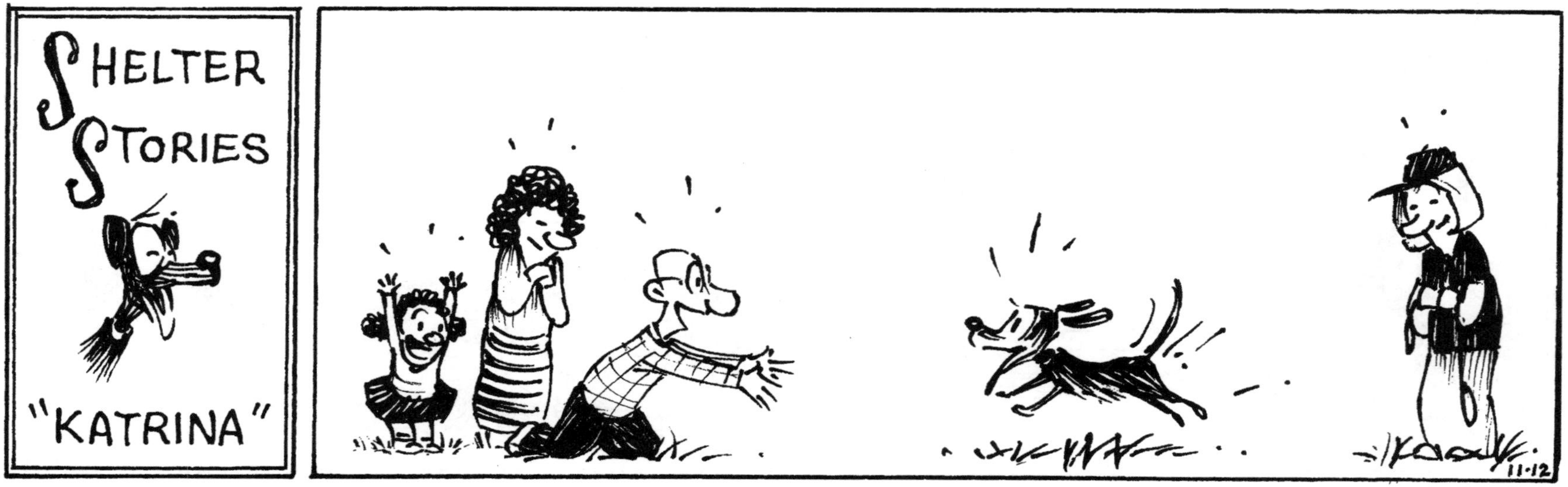
SHELTER STORIES
"KATRINA"
11-12

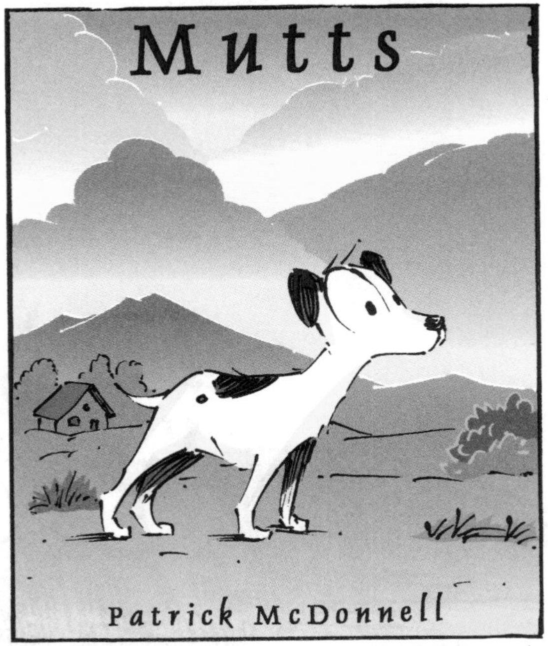
Mutts
Patrick McDonnell

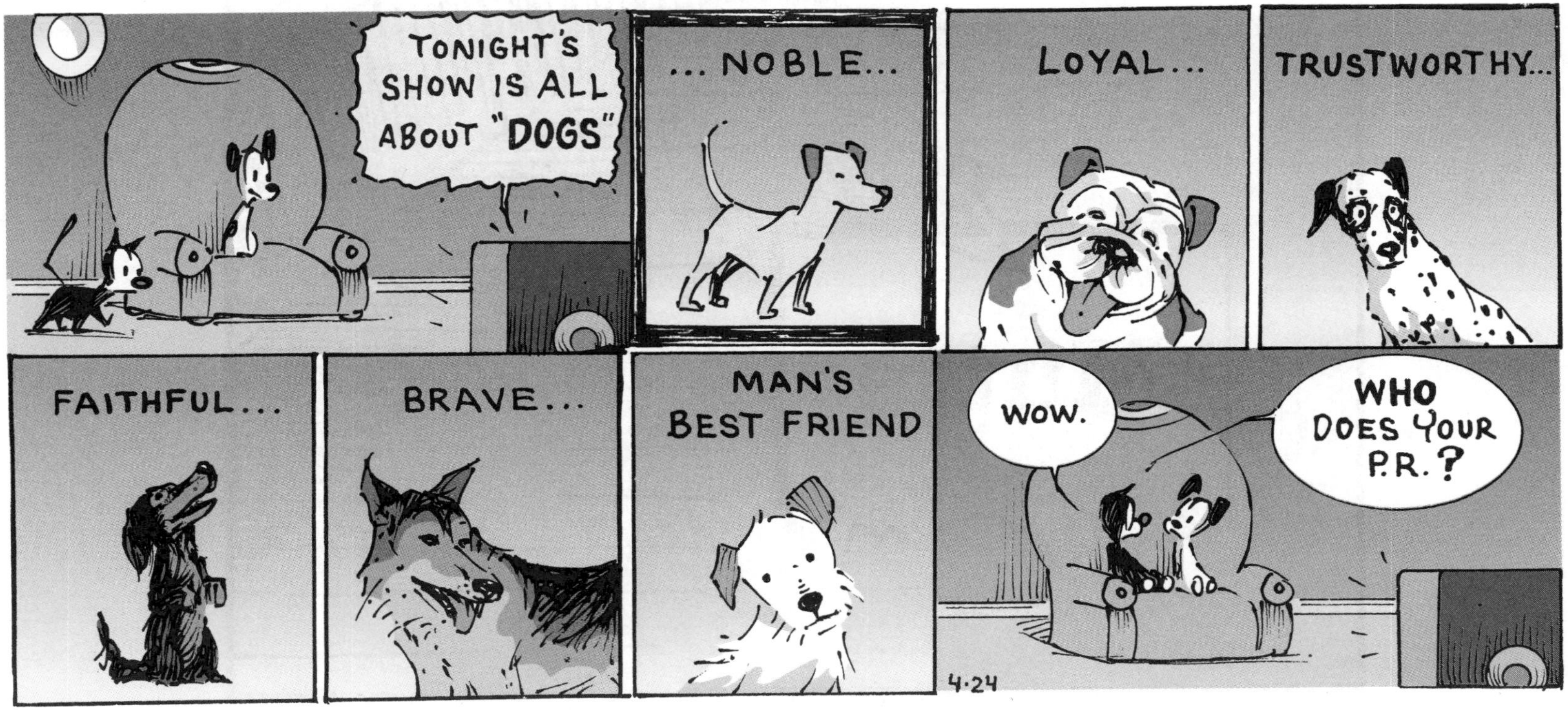
TONIGHT'S SHOW IS ALL ABOUT "DOGS"
... NOBLE...
LOYAL...
TRUSTWORTHY...
FAITHFUL...
BRAVE...
MAN'S BEST FRIEND
WOW.
WHO DOES YOUR P.R.?
4·24

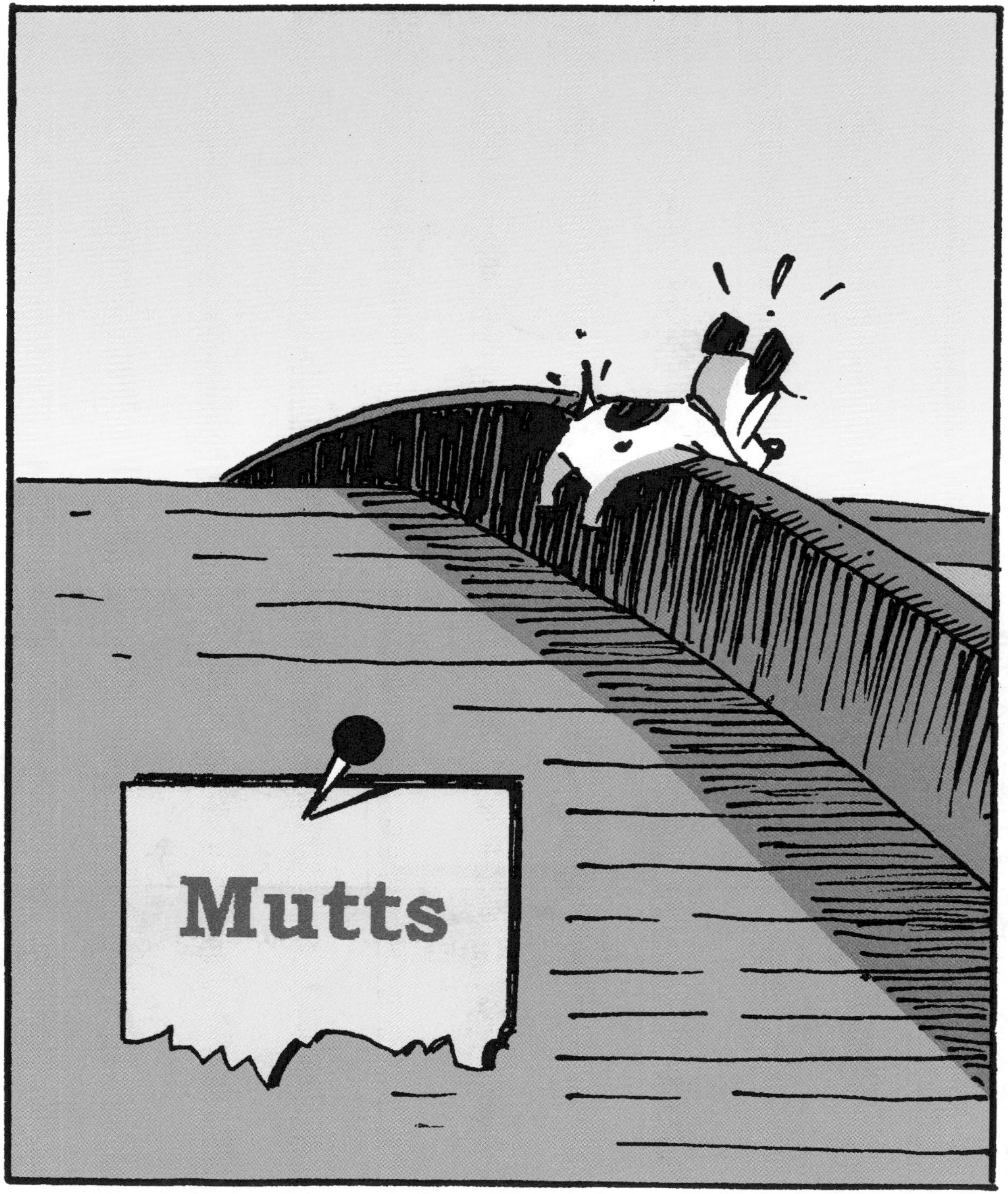
Mutts

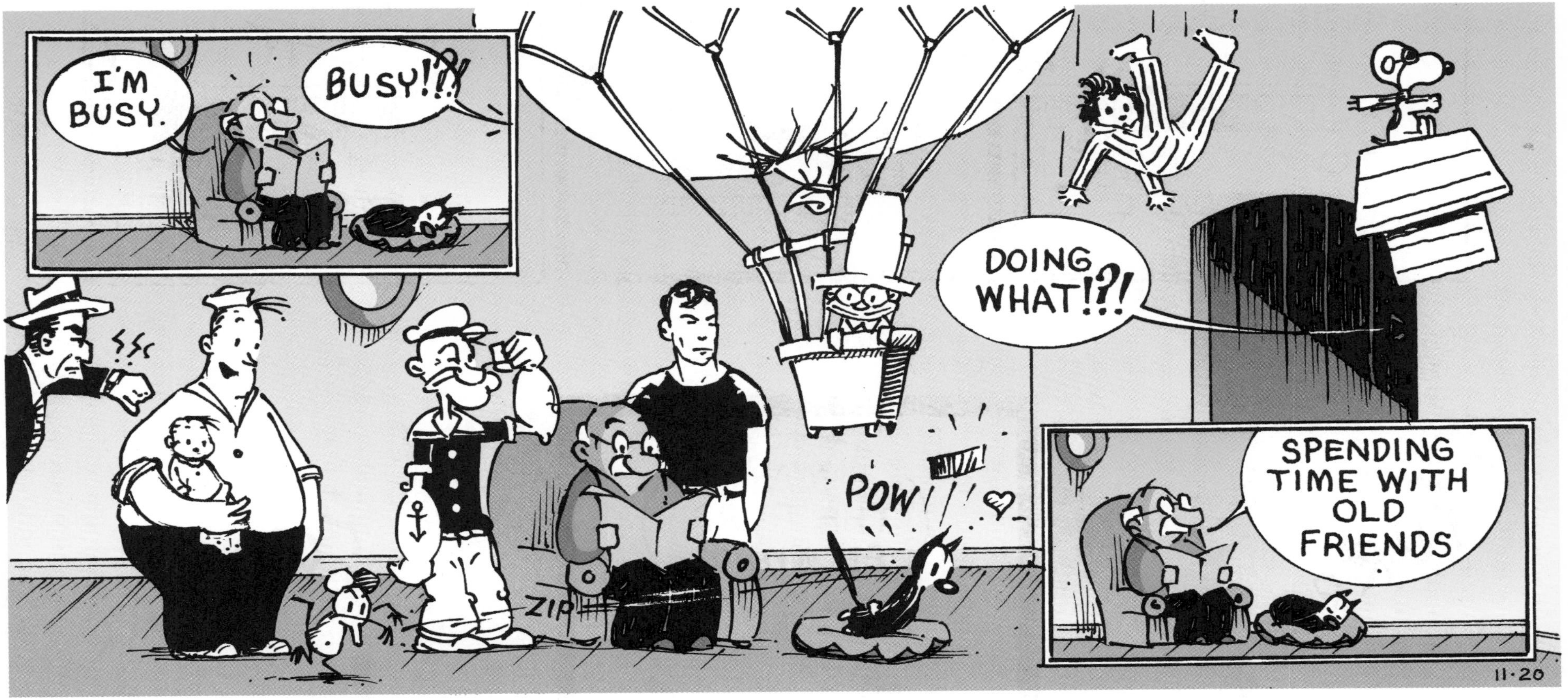
I'M BUSY.
BUSY!?!
DOING WHAT!?!
ZIP
POW
SPENDING TIME WITH OLD FRIENDS
11·20

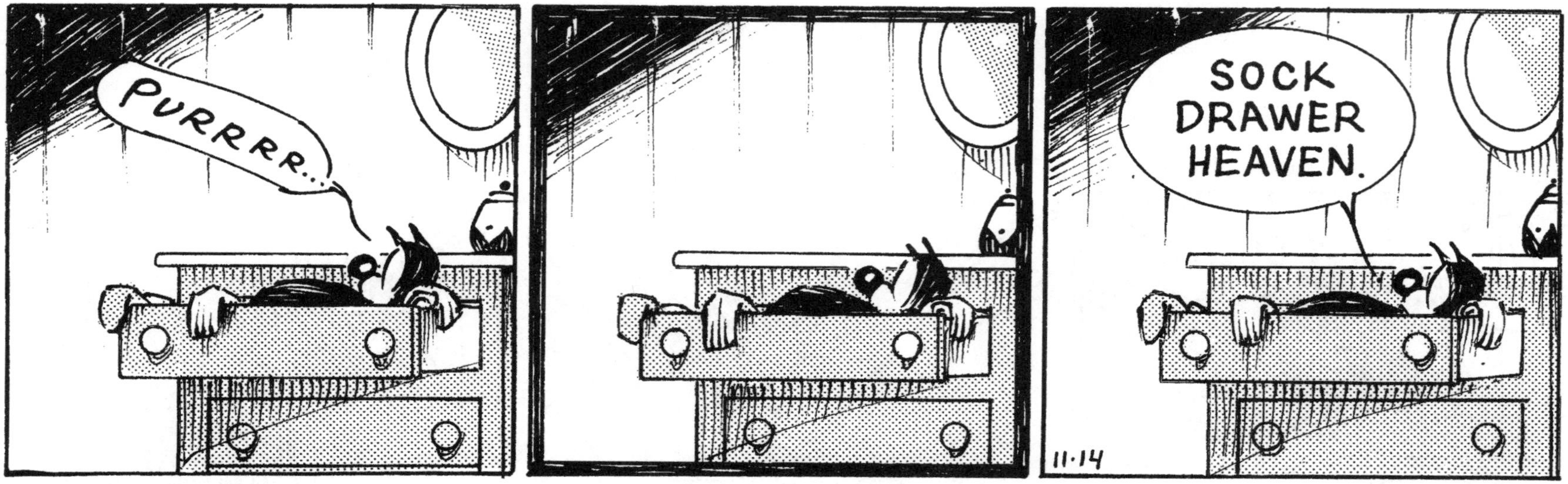
PURRRRR...
SOCK DRAWER HEAVEN.
11-14

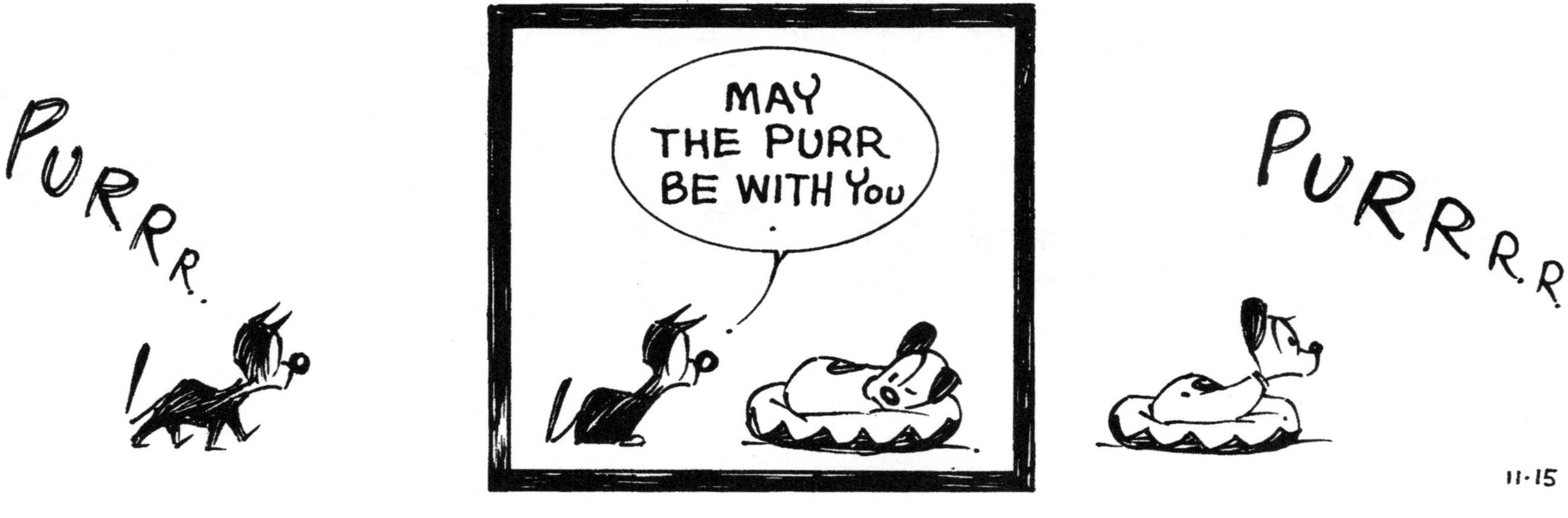
PURRRR.
MAY THE PURR BE WITH YOU.
PURRRRR
11-15

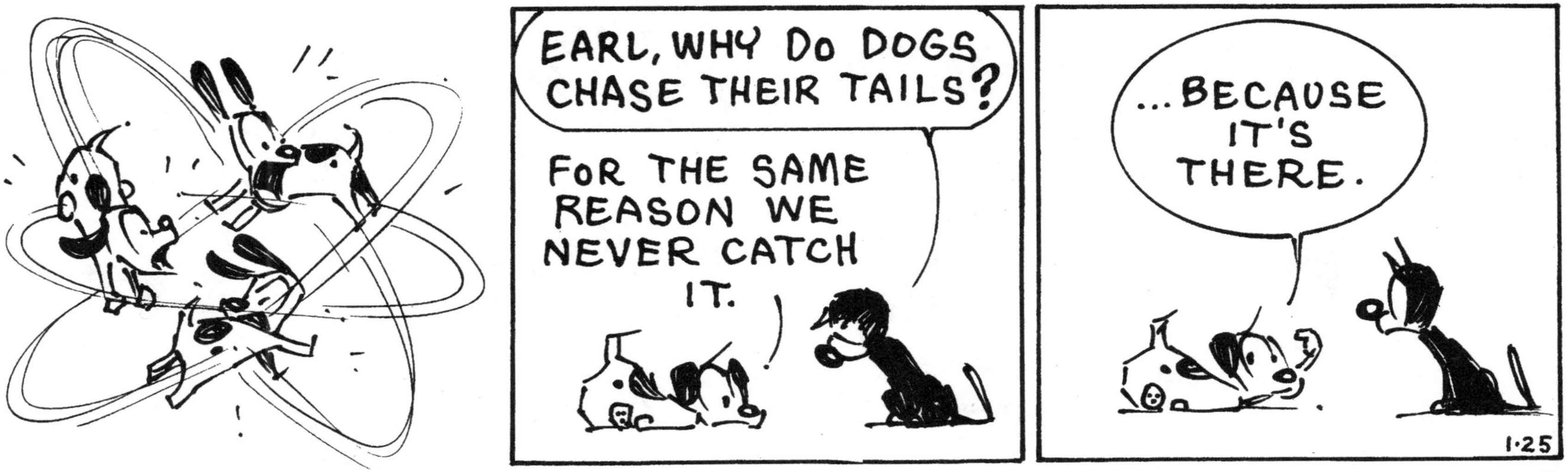
EARL, WHY DO DOGS CHASE THEIR TAILS?
FOR THE SAME REASON WE NEVER CATCH IT.
...BECAUSE IT'S THERE.
1·25

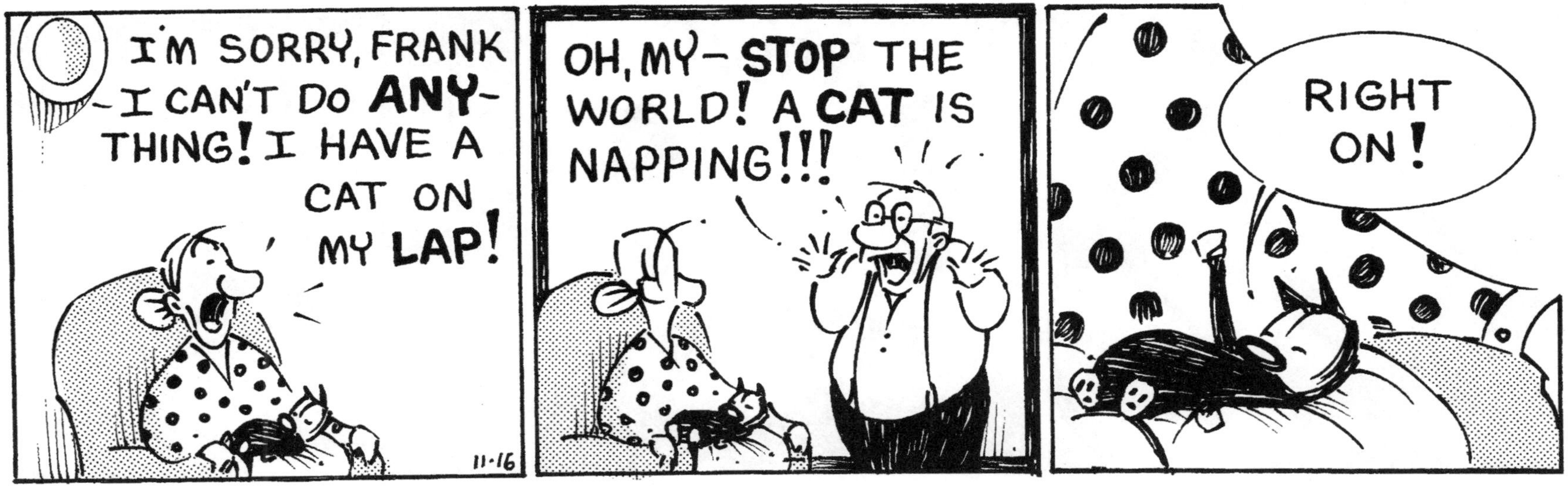
I'M SORRY, FRANK -I CAN'T DO **ANY-THING!** I HAVE A CAT ON MY **LAP!**
11·16
OH, MY- **STOP** THE WORLD! A **CAT** IS NAPPING!!!
RIGHT ON!

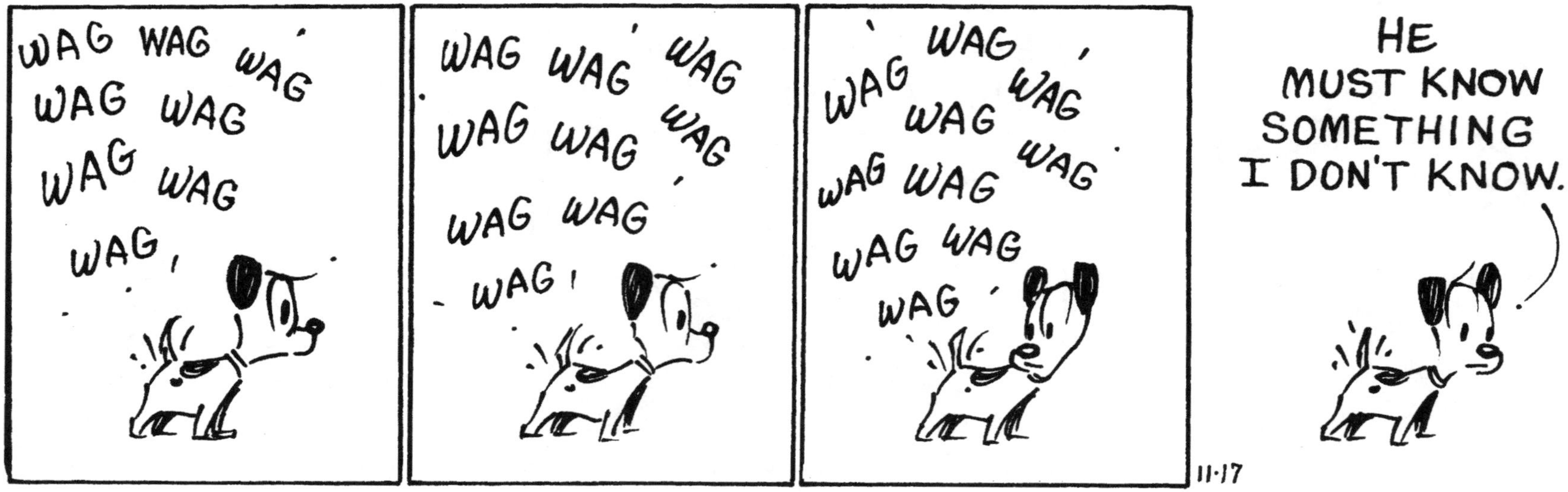
WAG WAG WAG
WAG WAG
WAG WAG
WAG
WAG WAG WAG
WAG WAG WAG
WAG WAG
WAG
WAG WAG
WAG WAG
WAG
WAG WAG
WAG WAG
WAG
HE MUST KNOW SOMETHING I DON'T KNOW.
11·17

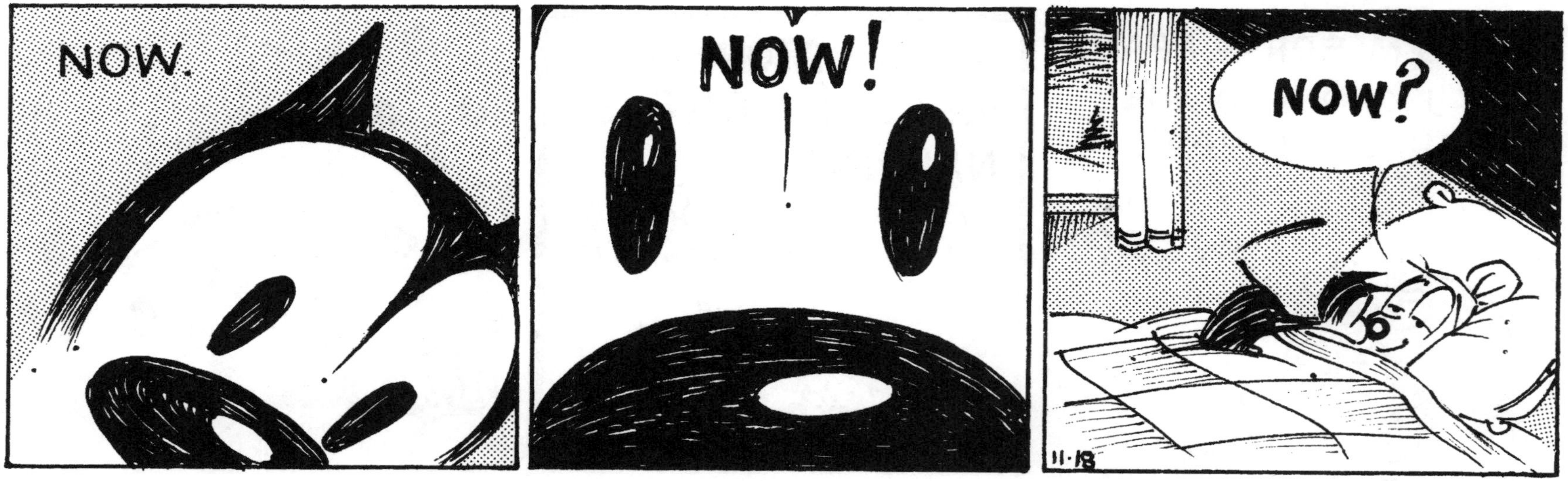
NOW.
NOW!
NOW?
11·18

PAT McDONNELL'S
MUTTS
CARTOON

CAT FORECAST
GOOD DAY FOR A NAP.
GOOD DAY FOR A NAP.
GOOD DAY FOR A NAP.
GOOD DAY FOR A NAP.
11·27

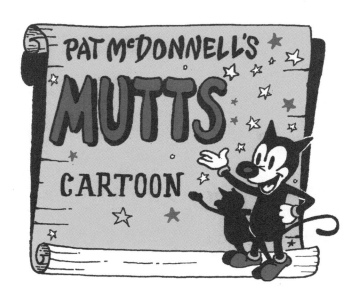

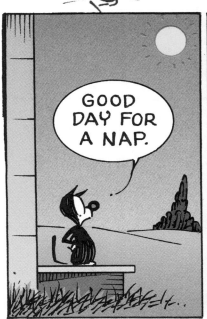

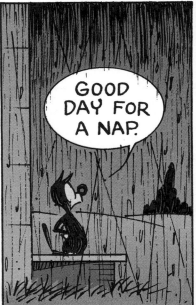

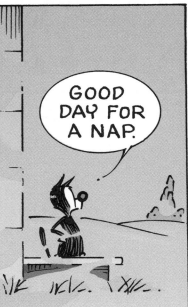

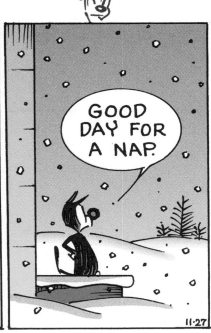

Giving Thanks

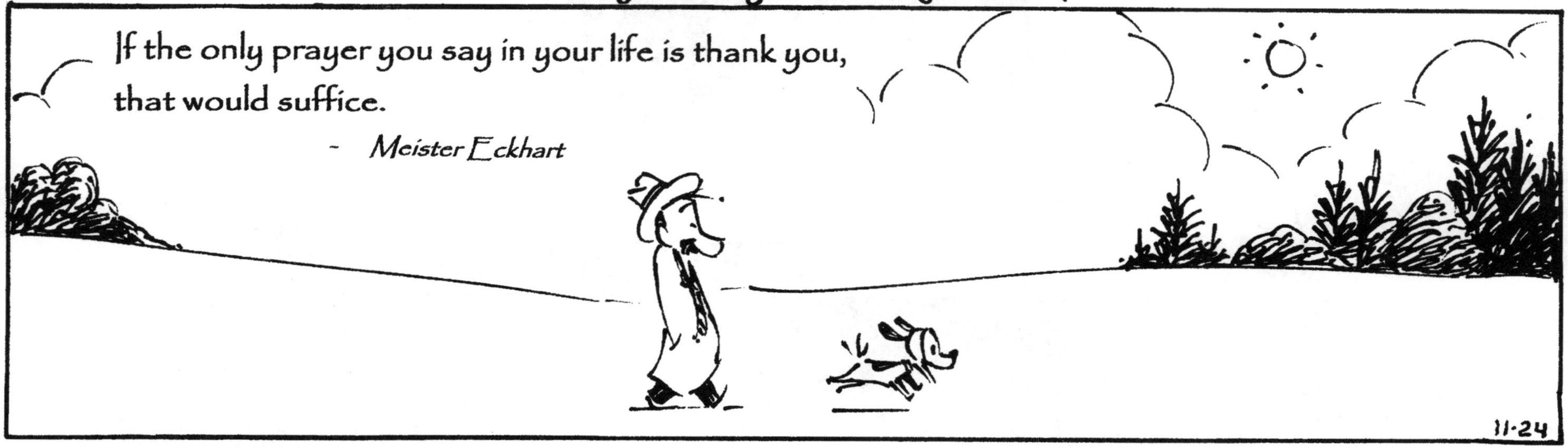
If the only prayer you say in your life is thank you, that would suffice.
- Meister Eckhart
11-24

Giving Thanks

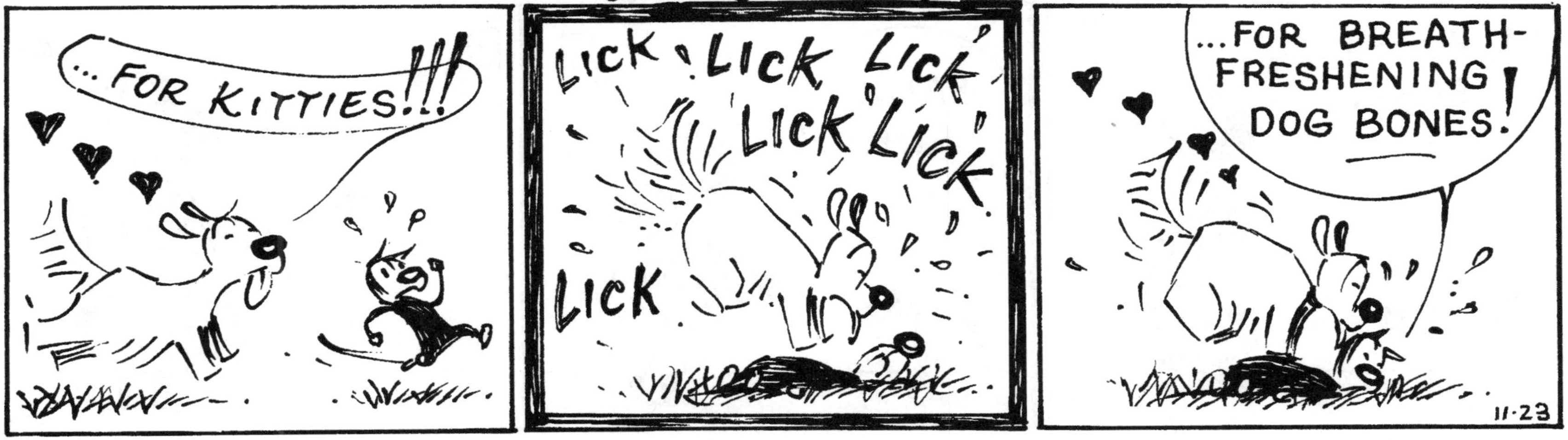

...FOR KITTIES!!!
LICK LICK LICK LICK LICK LICK
...FOR BREATH-FRESHENING DOG BONES!
11·23

Giving Thanks

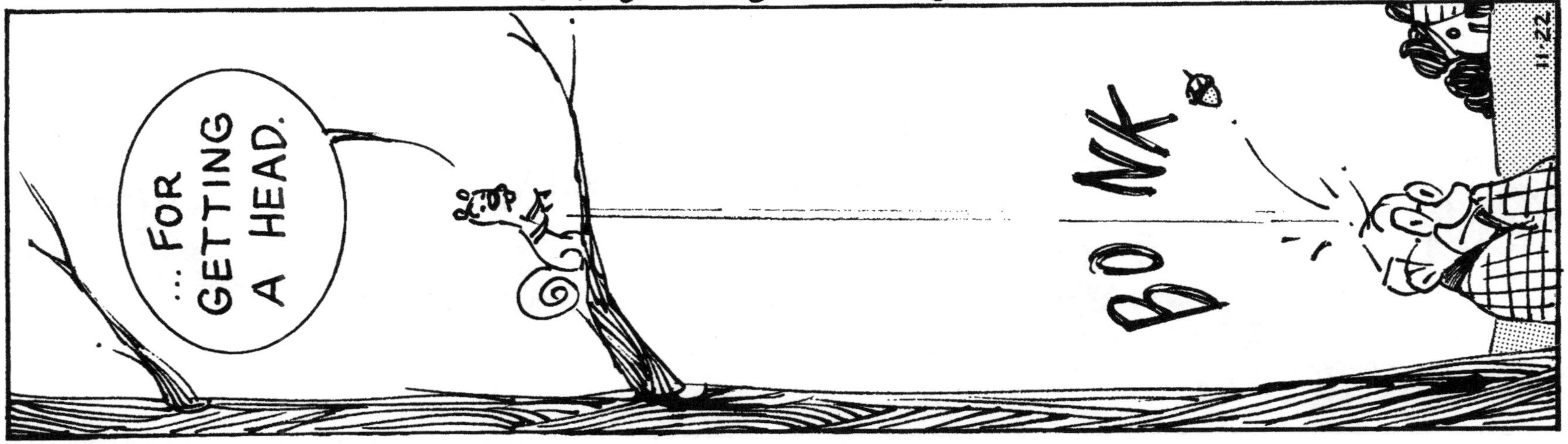

...FOR GETTING A HEAD.
BONK
11·22

Giving Thanks

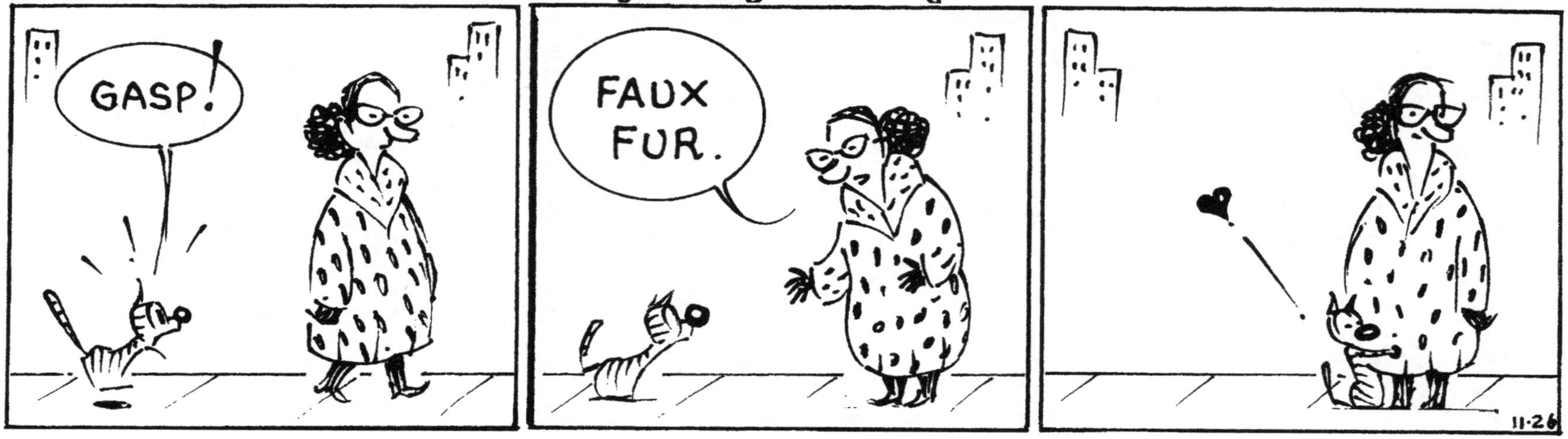
GASP!
FAUX FUR.
11·26

Giving Thanks

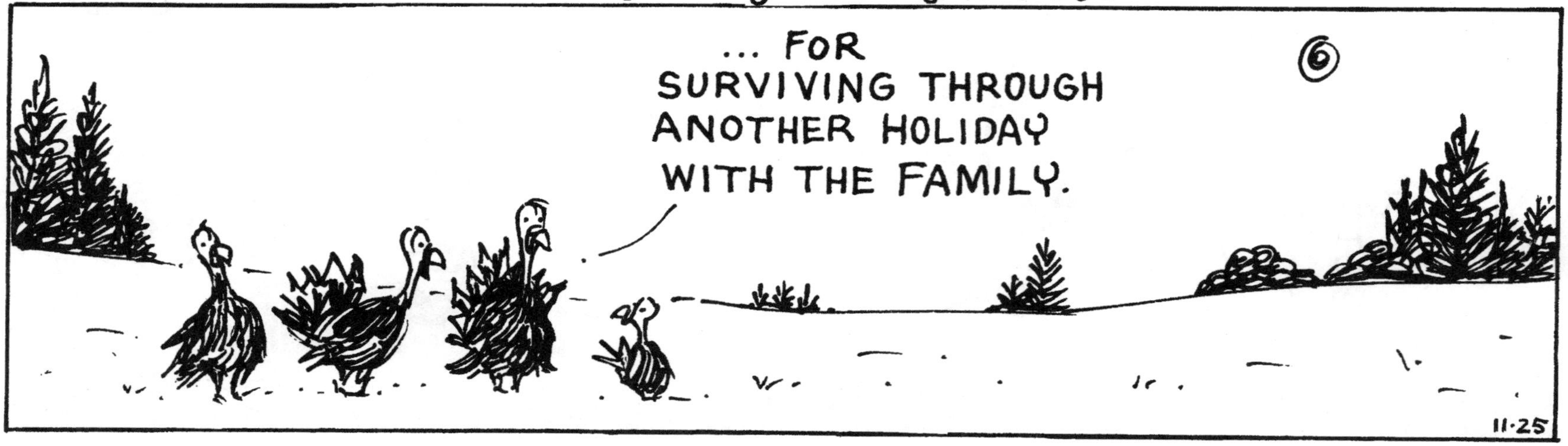
... FOR SURVIVING THROUGH ANOTHER HOLIDAY WITH THE FAMILY.
11·25

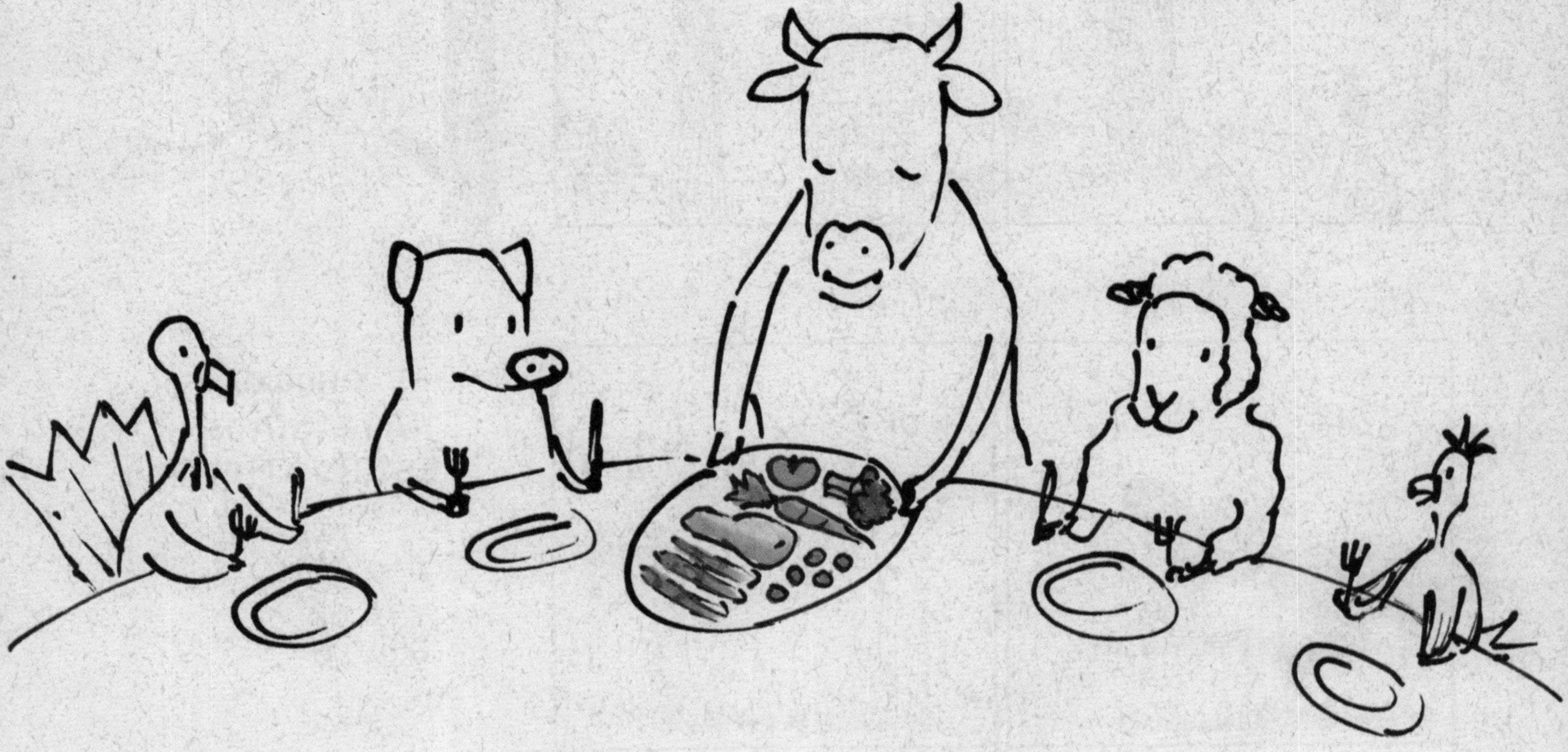

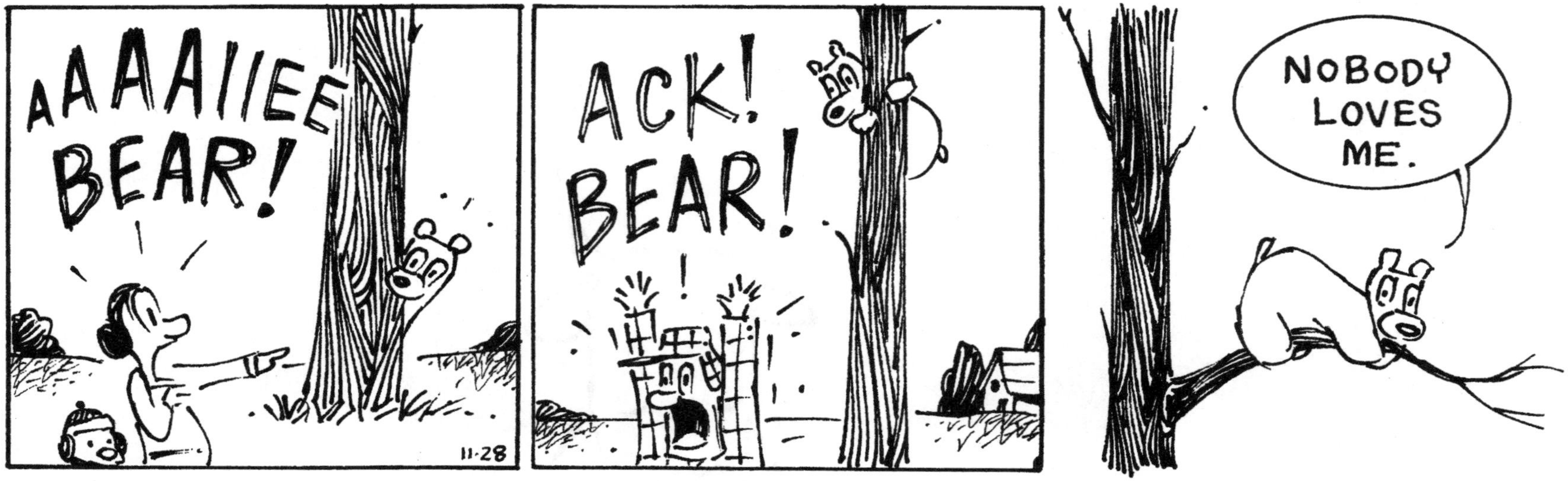
AAAAIIEE BEAR!
11-28
ACK! BEAR!
NOBODY LOVES ME.

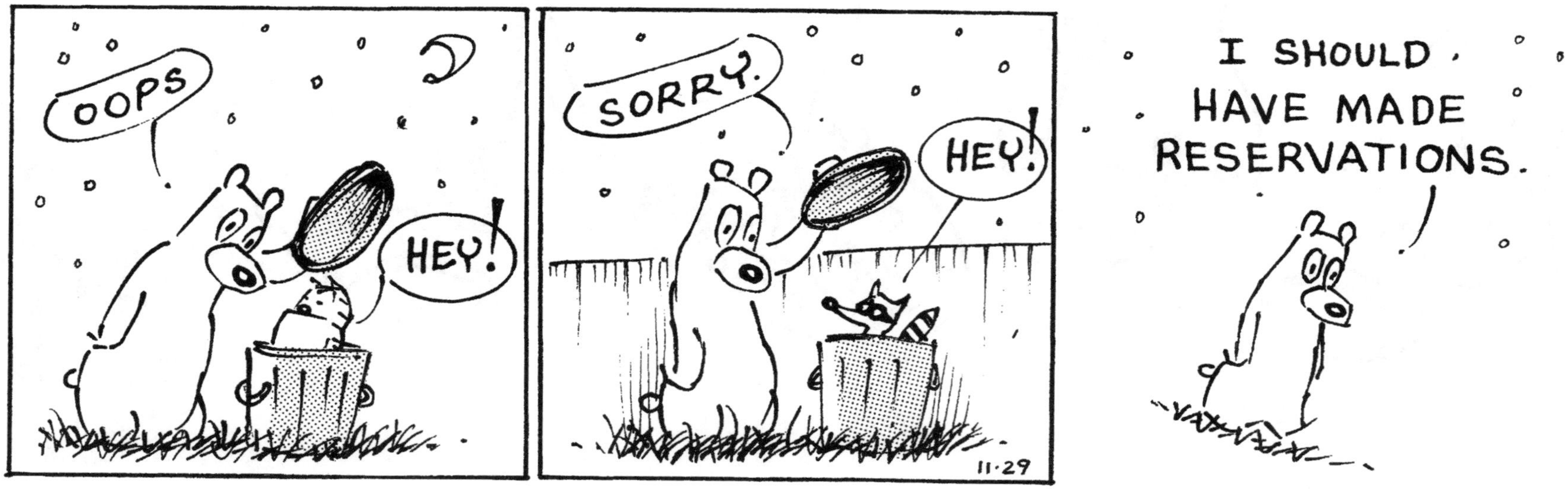
OOPS
HEY!
SORRY.
HEY!
11-29
I SHOULD HAVE MADE RESERVATIONS.

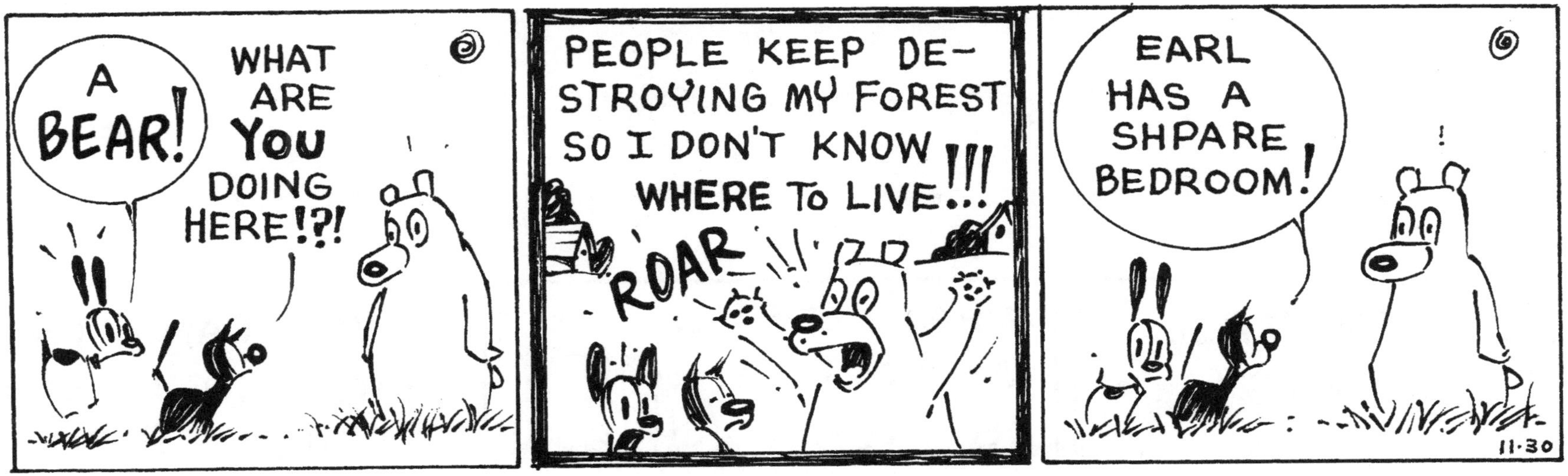
A BEAR!
WHAT ARE YOU DOING HERE!?!
PEOPLE KEEP DE-STROYING MY FOREST SO I DON'T KNOW WHERE TO LIVE!!!
ROAR
EARL HAS A SHPARE BEDROOM!
11-30

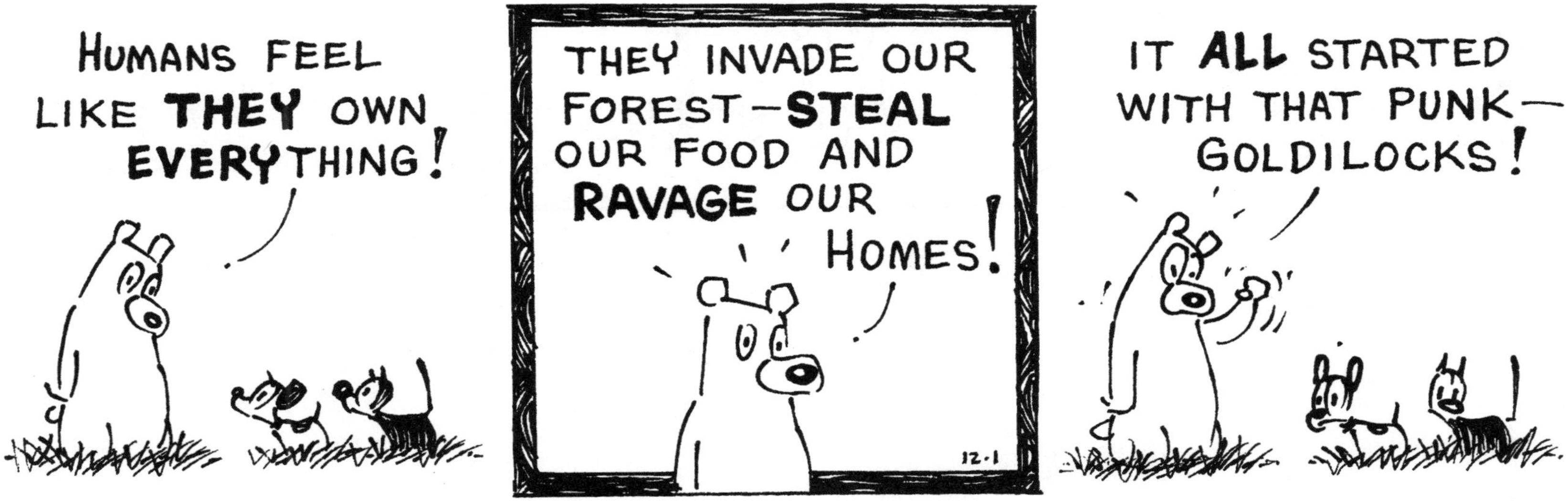
HUMANS FEEL LIKE THEY OWN EVERYTHING!
THEY INVADE OUR FOREST—STEAL OUR FOOD AND RAVAGE OUR HOMES!
12-1
IT ALL STARTED WITH THAT PUNK—GOLDILOCKS!

THE NEW MALL IS "TOO BIG".
12·2
WHAT'S LEFT OF MY FOREST IS "TOO SMALL".
WHY CAN'T THEY FIND SOMETHING "JUST RIGHT"?

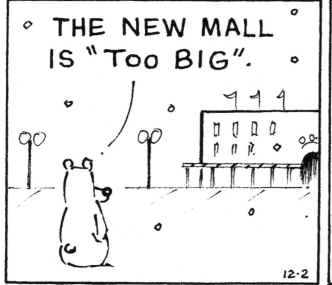

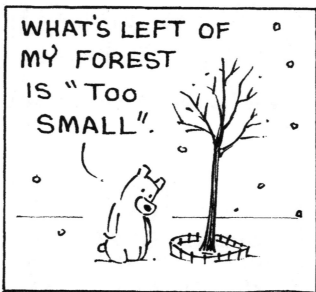

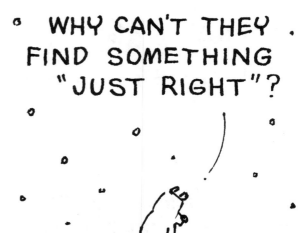

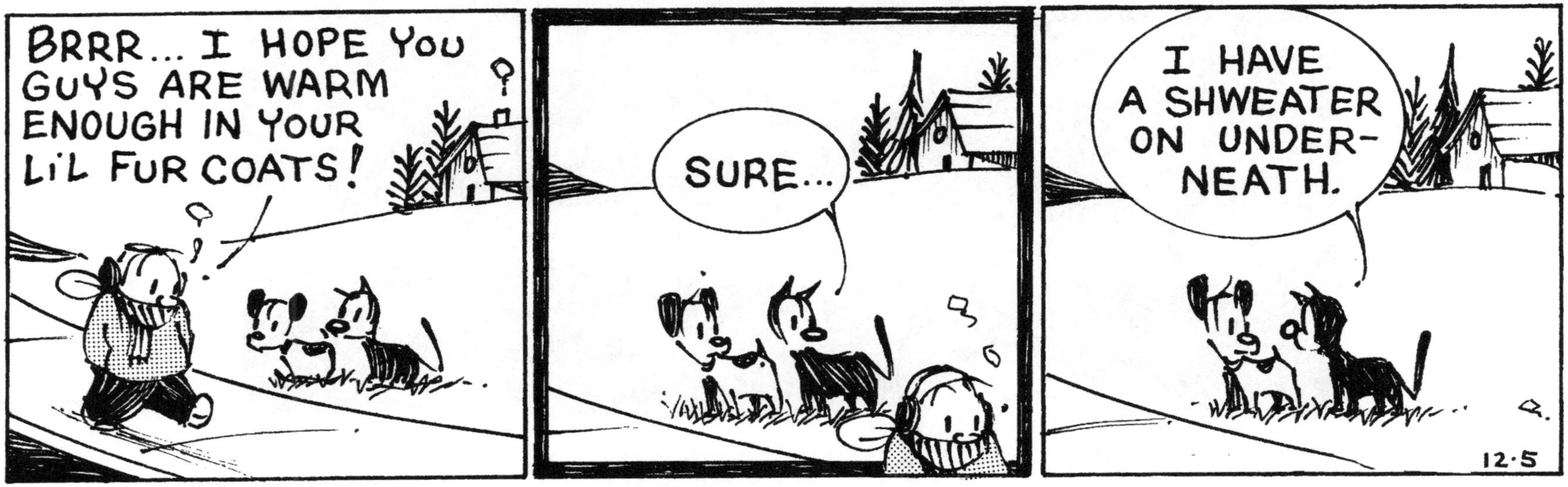
BRRR... I HOPE YOU GUYS ARE WARM ENOUGH IN YOUR LI'L FUR COATS!
SURE...
I HAVE A SHWEATER ON UNDER-NEATH.
12·5

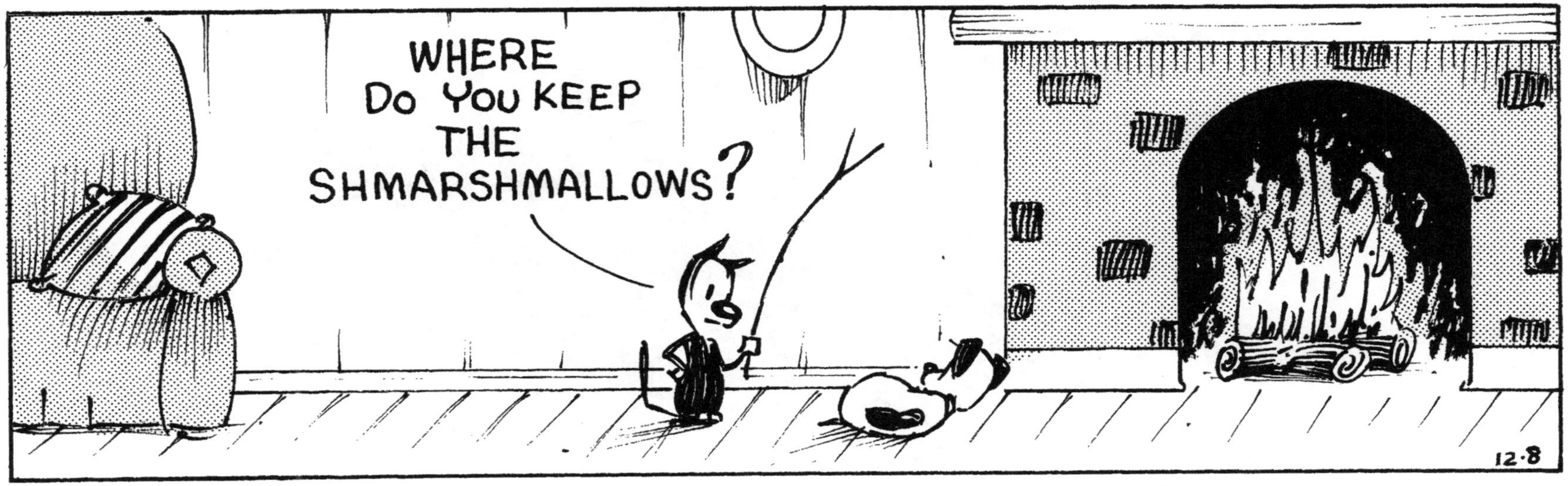
WHERE DO YOU KEEP THE SHMARSHMALLOWS?
12·8

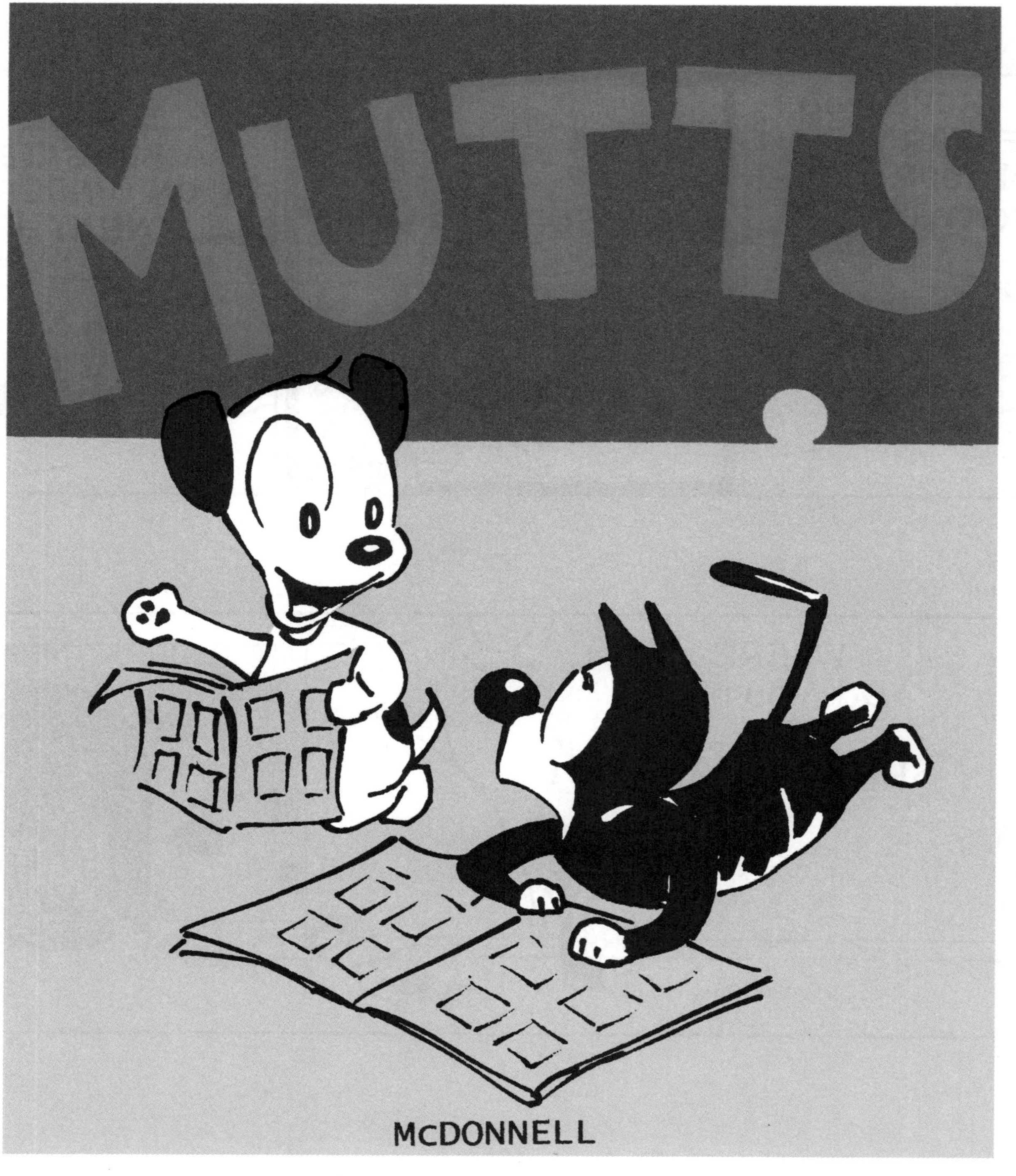
MUTTS
McDONNELL

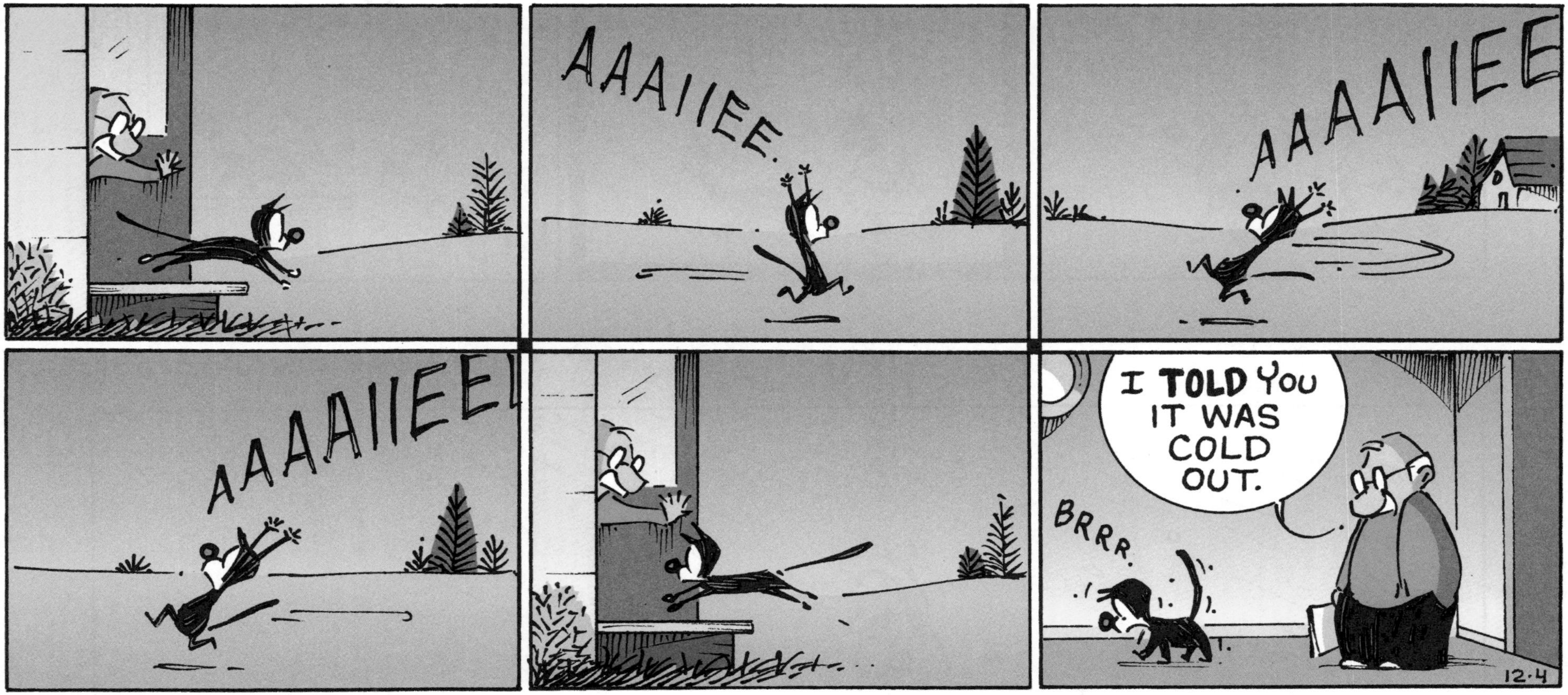
AAAIIEE.
AAAAIIEE
AAAAIIEEE
I TOLD YOU IT WAS COLD OUT.
BRRRR.
12·4

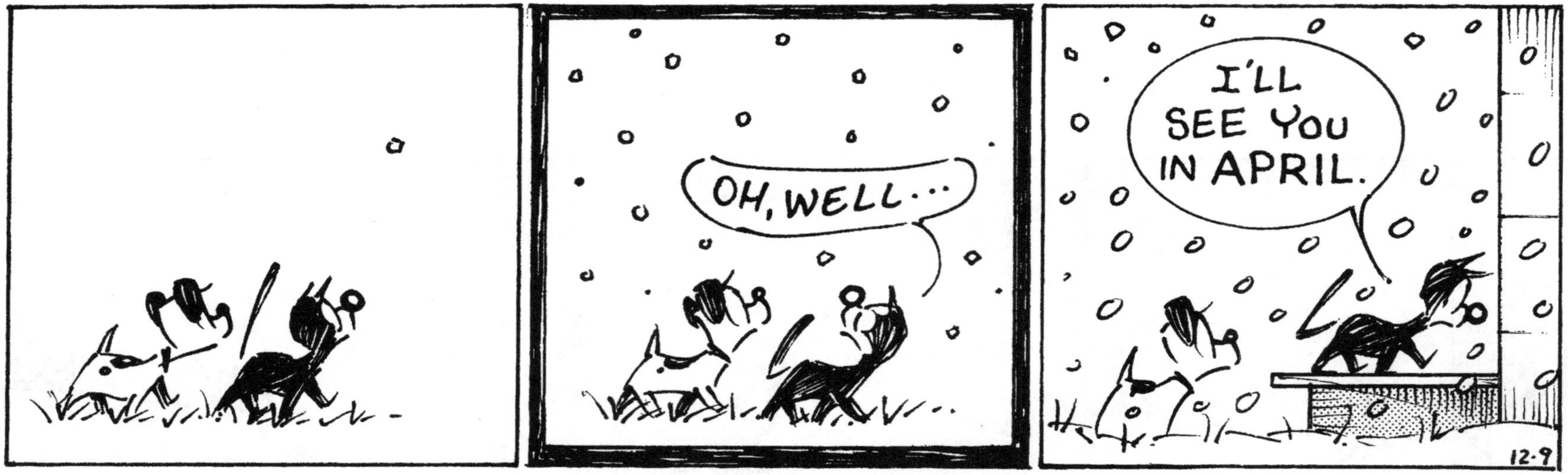
OH, WELL...
I'LL SEE YOU IN APRIL.
12·9

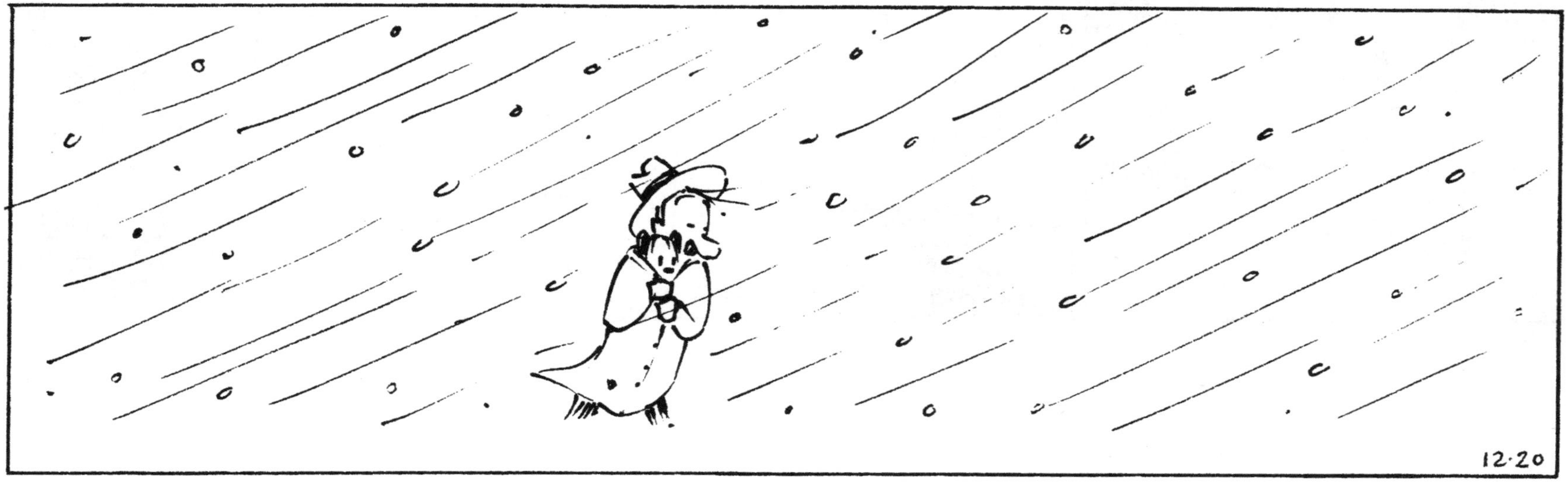
12·20

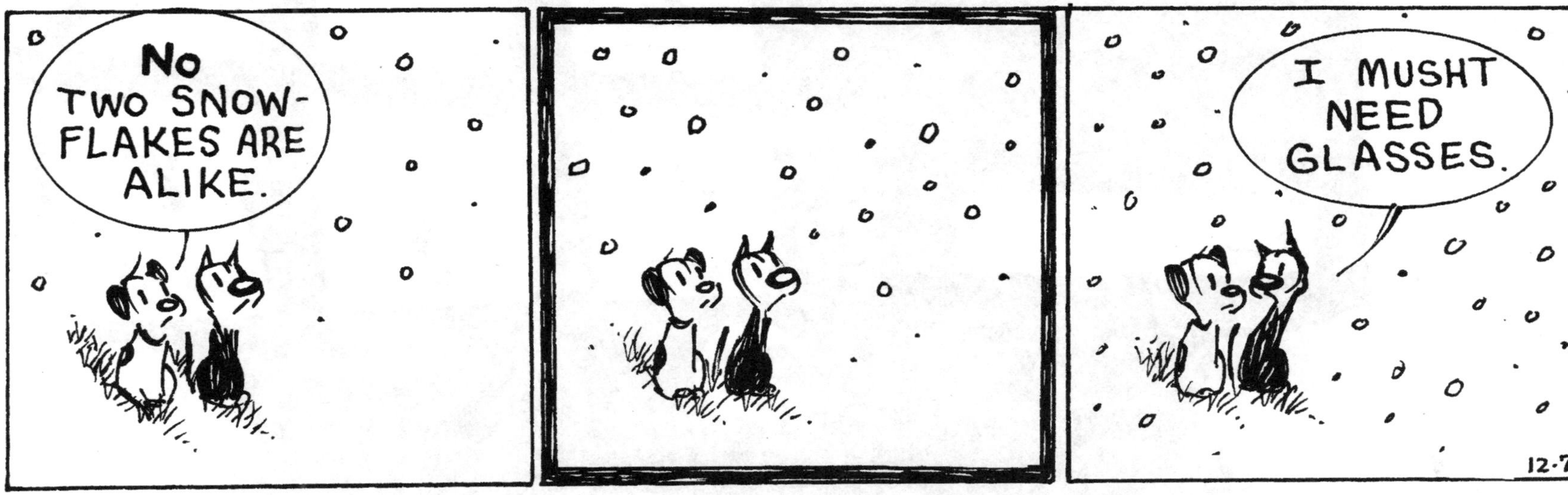
No TWO SNOW-FLAKES ARE ALIKE.
I MUSHT NEED GLASSES.
12·7

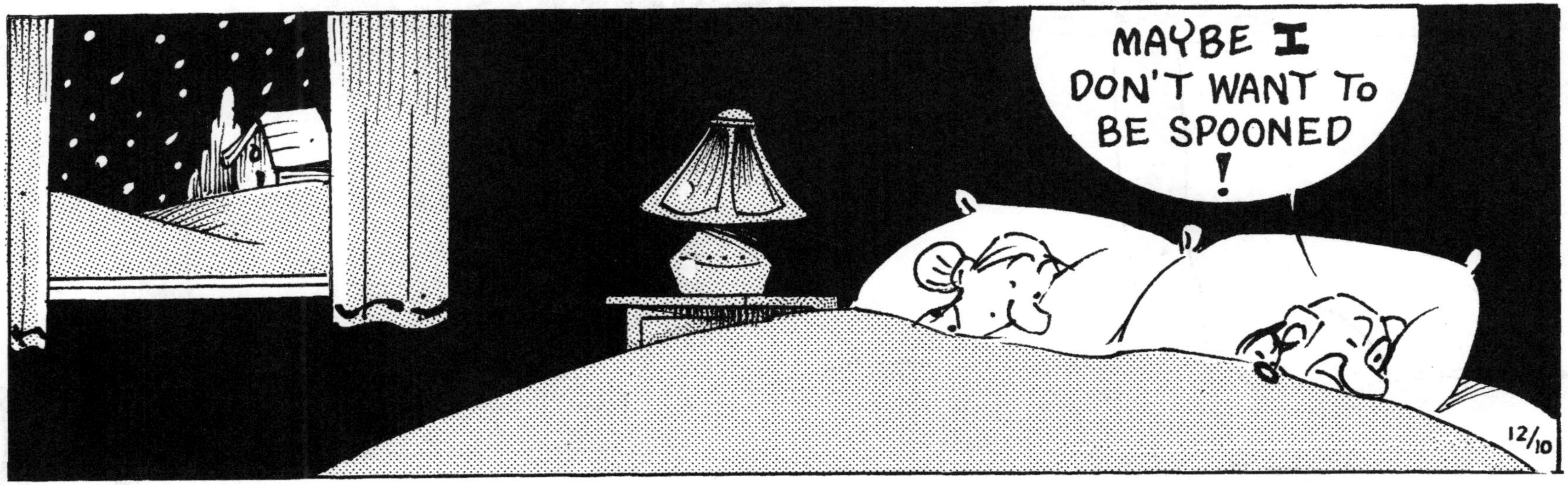
MAYBE I DON'T WANT TO BE SPOONED!
12/10

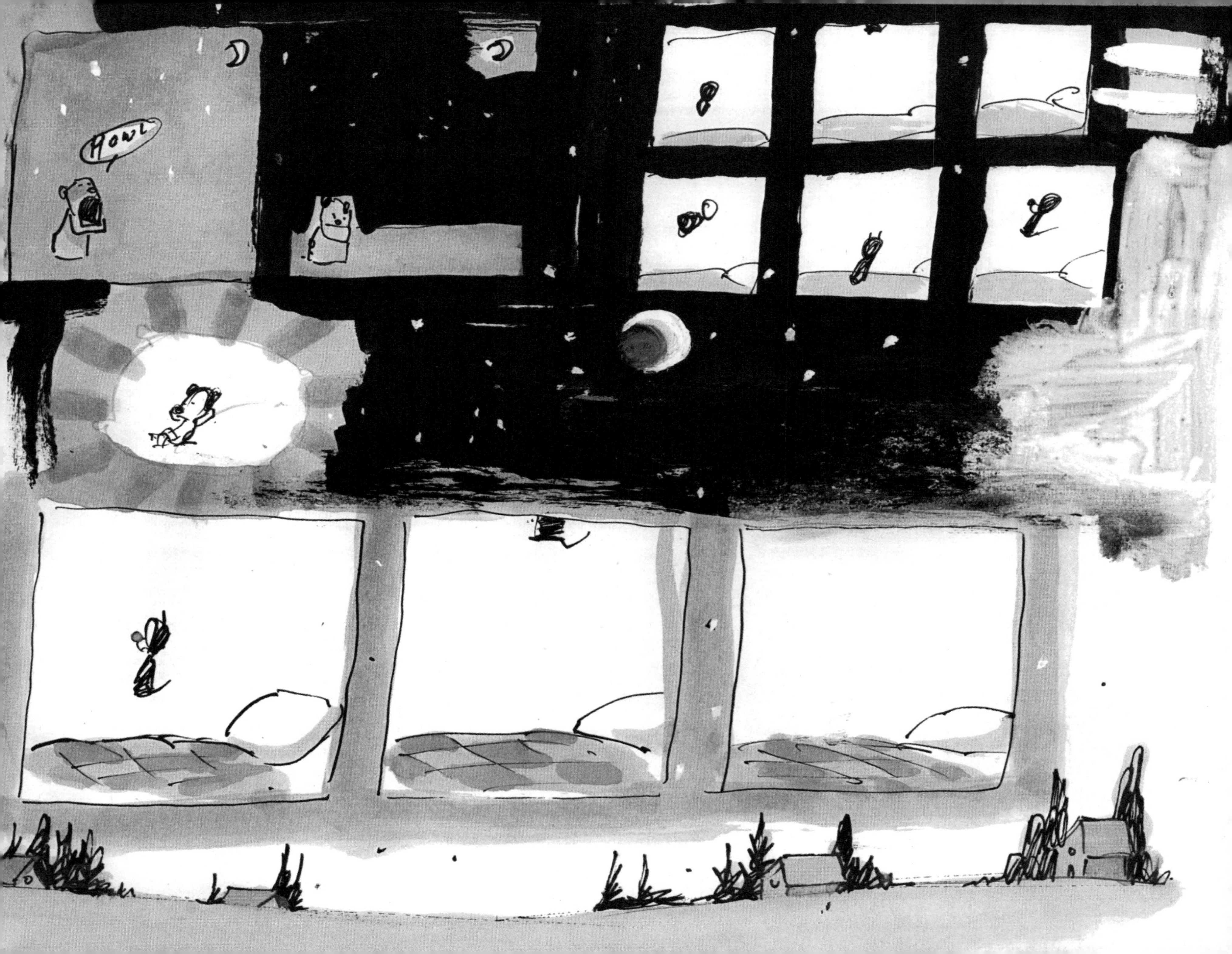
HOWL

MUTTS

PATRICK McDONNELL

OKAY, EARL—I THINK WE WALKED ENOUGH.
12-11

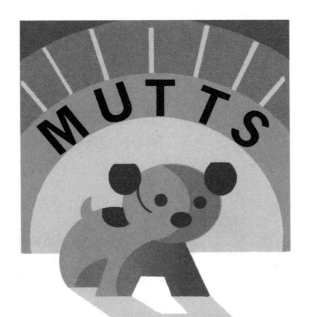

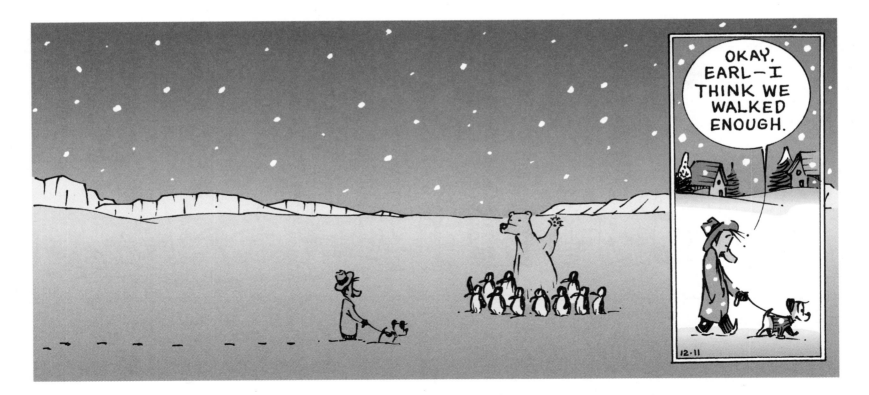

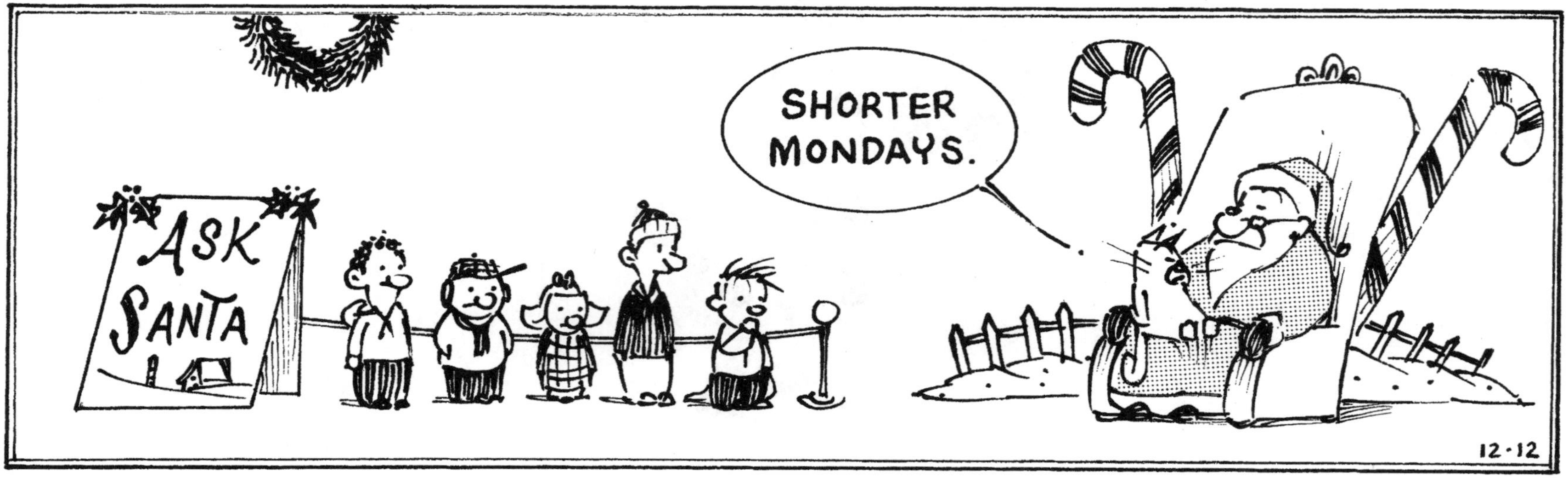
SHORTER MONDAYS.
ASK SANTA
12-12

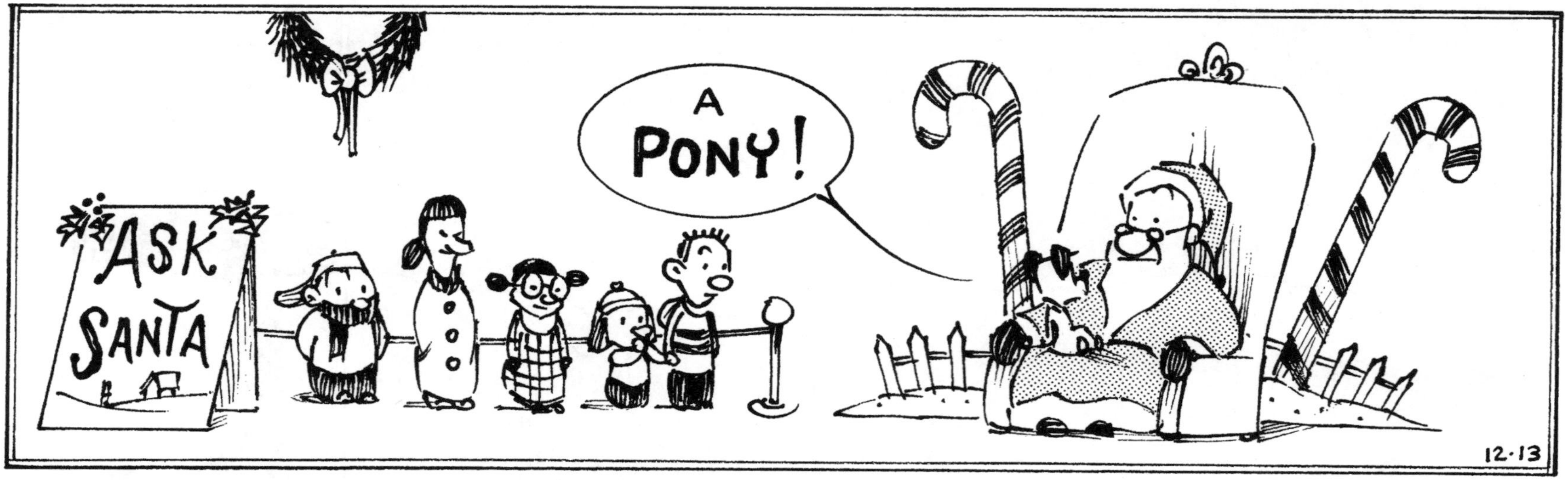
A PONY!
ASK SANTA
12-13

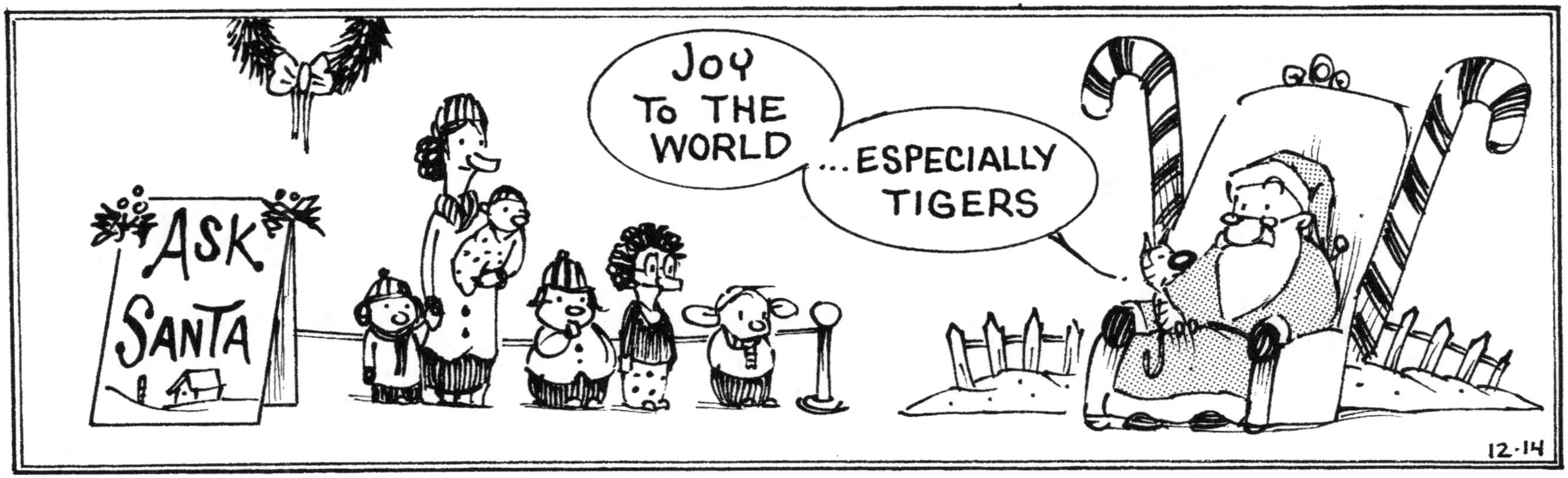
ASK SANTA
JOY TO THE WORLD
...ESPECIALLY TIGERS
12-14

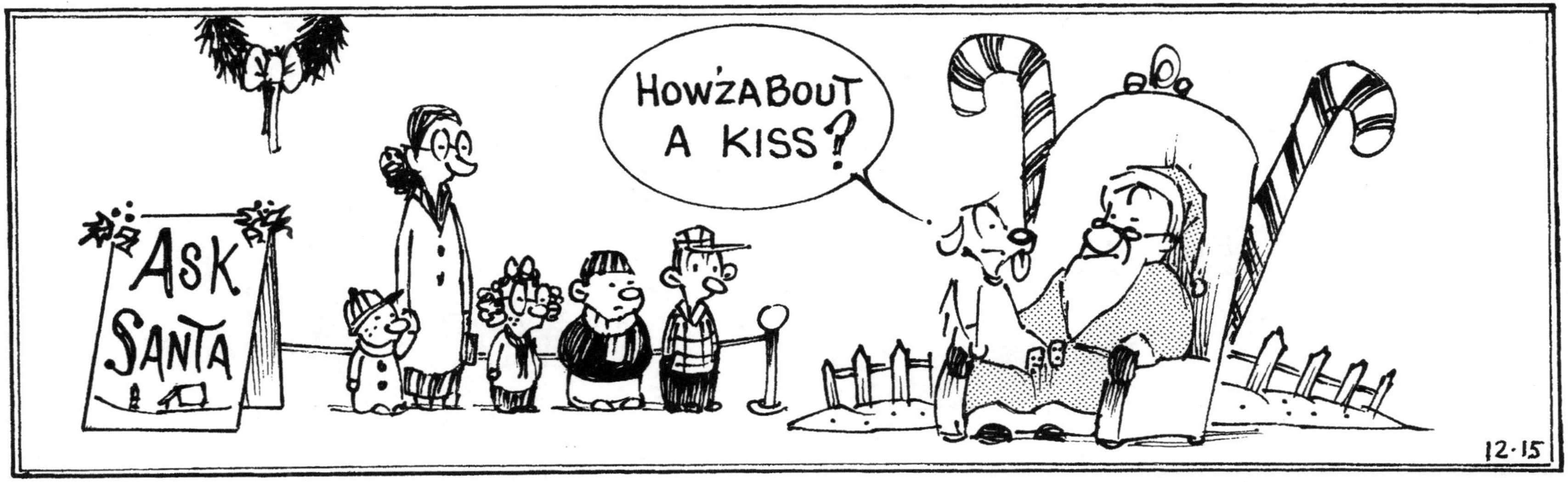
ASK SANTA
HOW'ZABOUT A KISS?
12-15

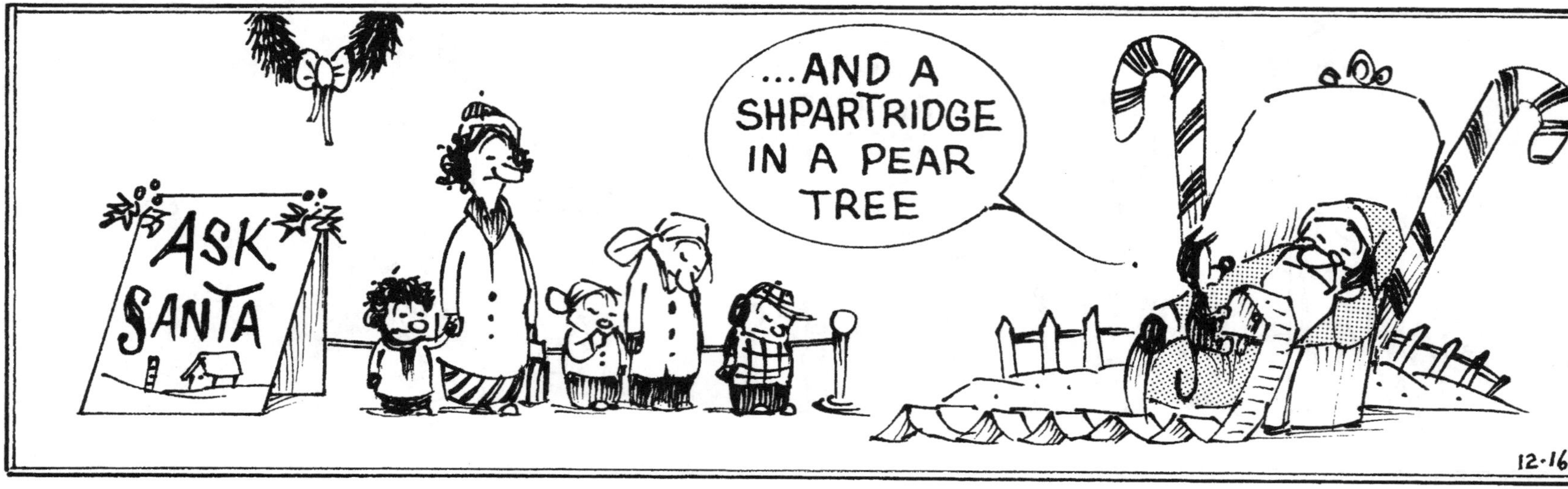
ASK SANTA
...AND A SHPARTRIDGE IN A PEAR TREE
12-16

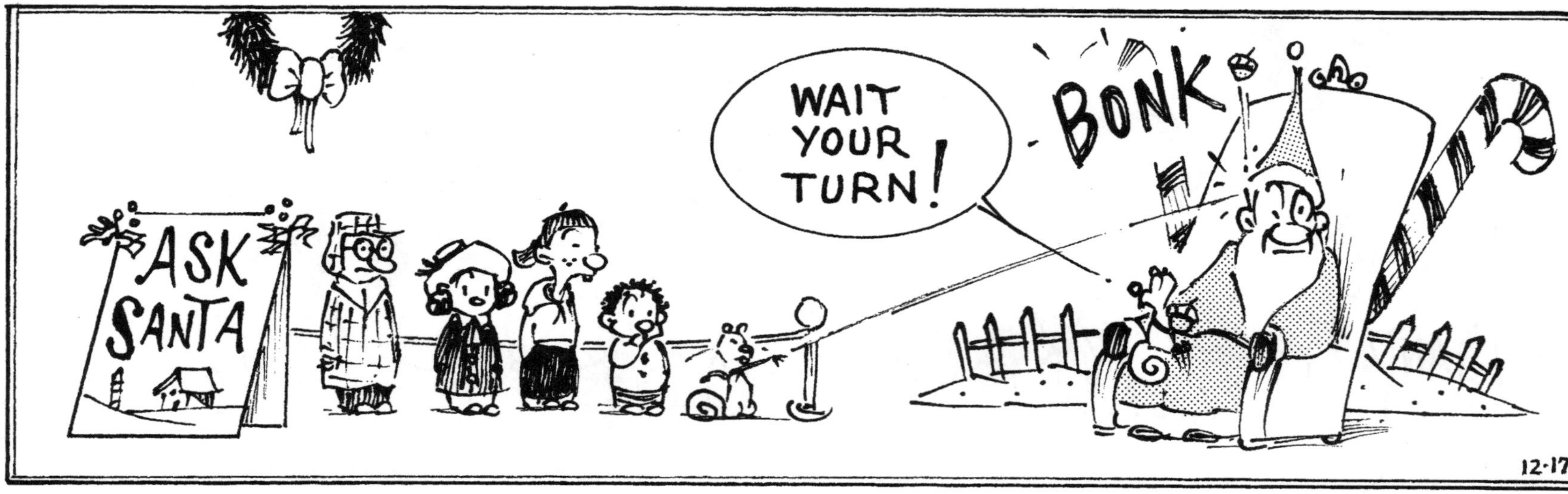
ASK SANTA
WAIT YOUR TURN!
BONK
12-17

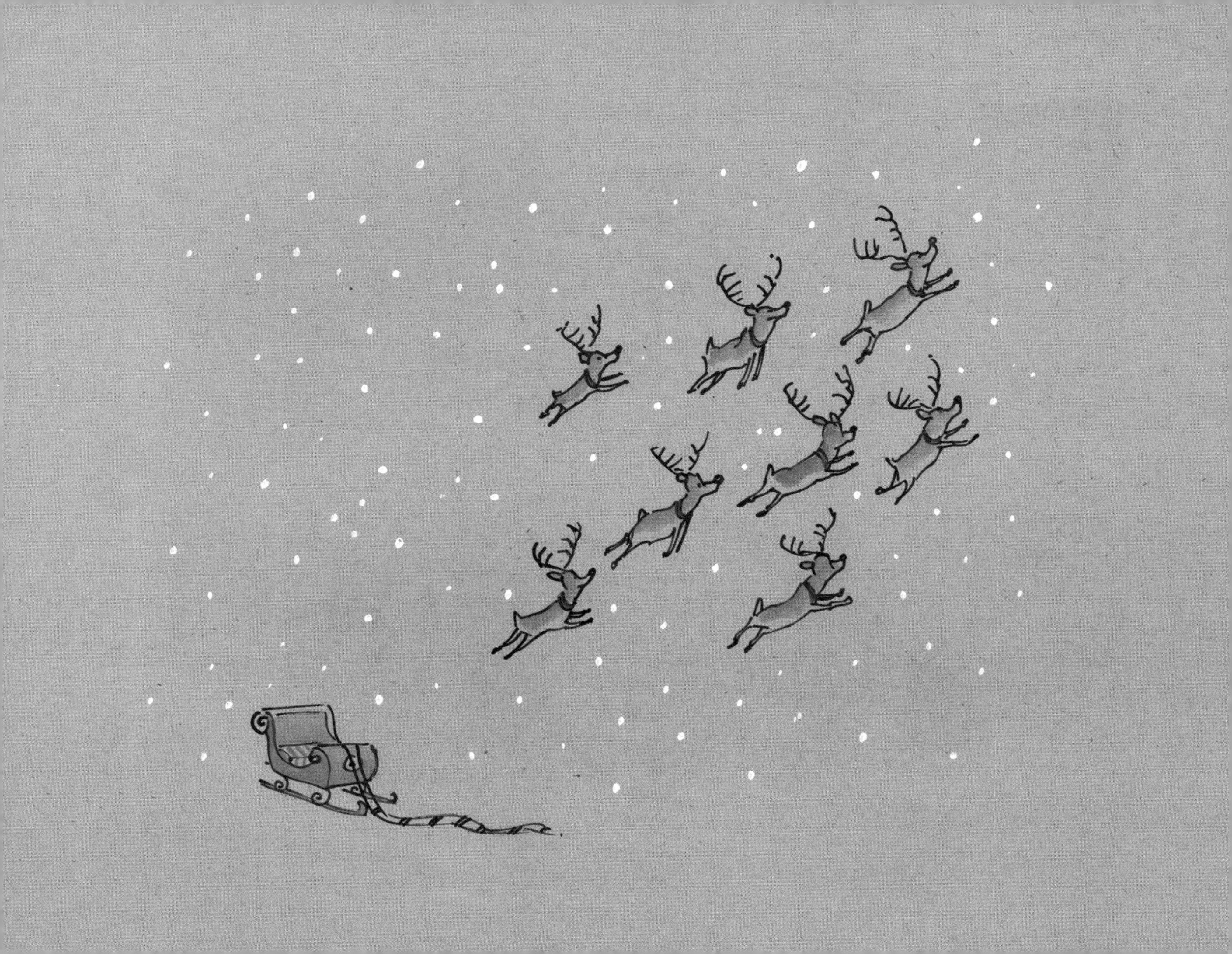

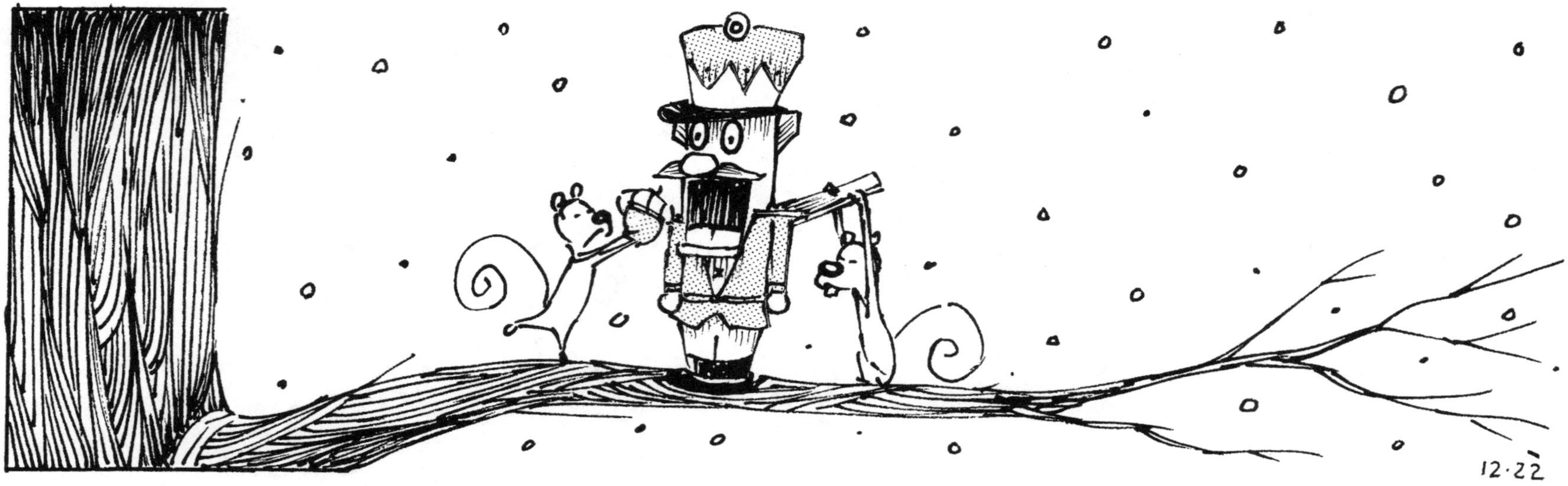
12·22

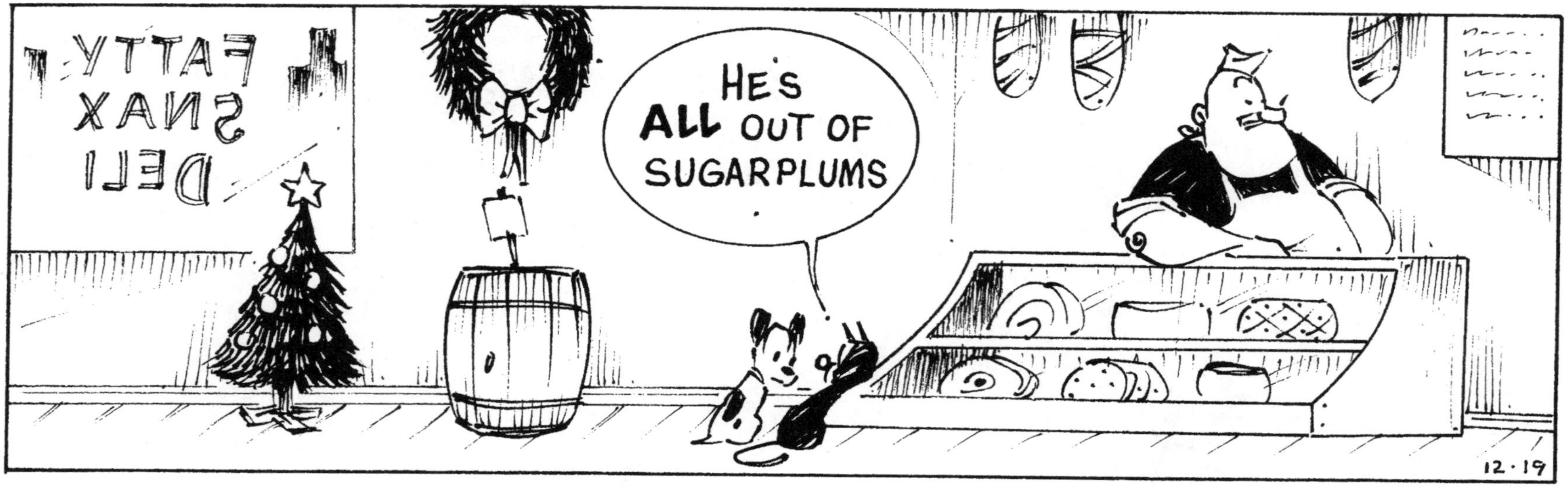
FATTY
SNAX
DELI
HE'S **ALL** OUT OF SUGARPLUMS
12·19

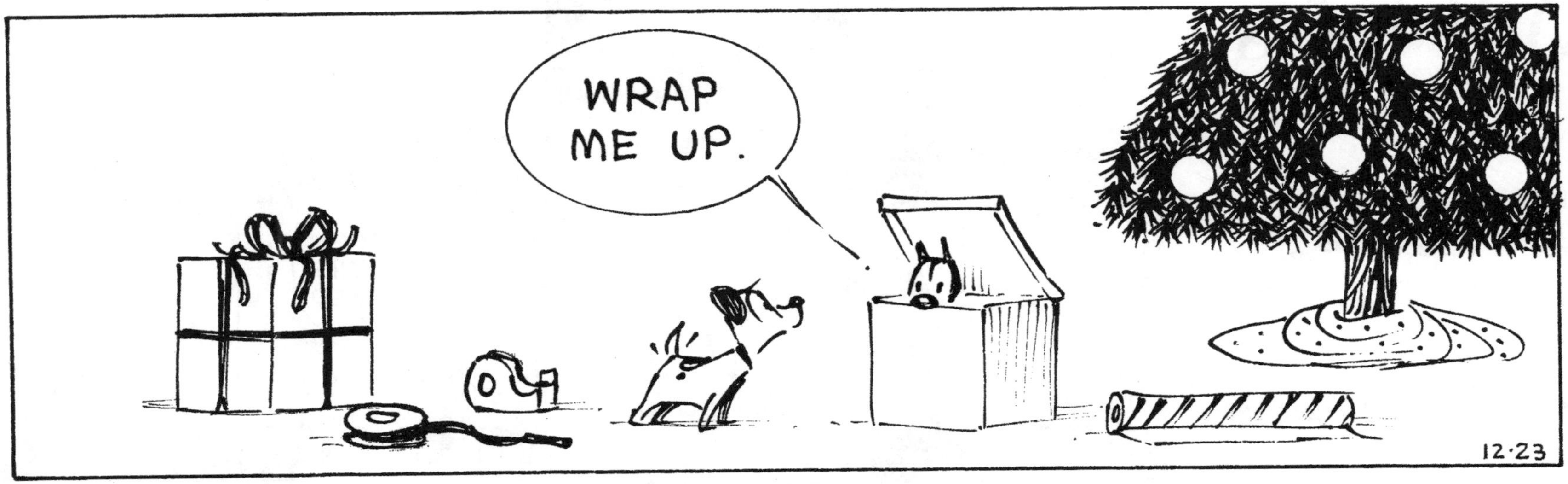
WRAP ME UP.
12·23

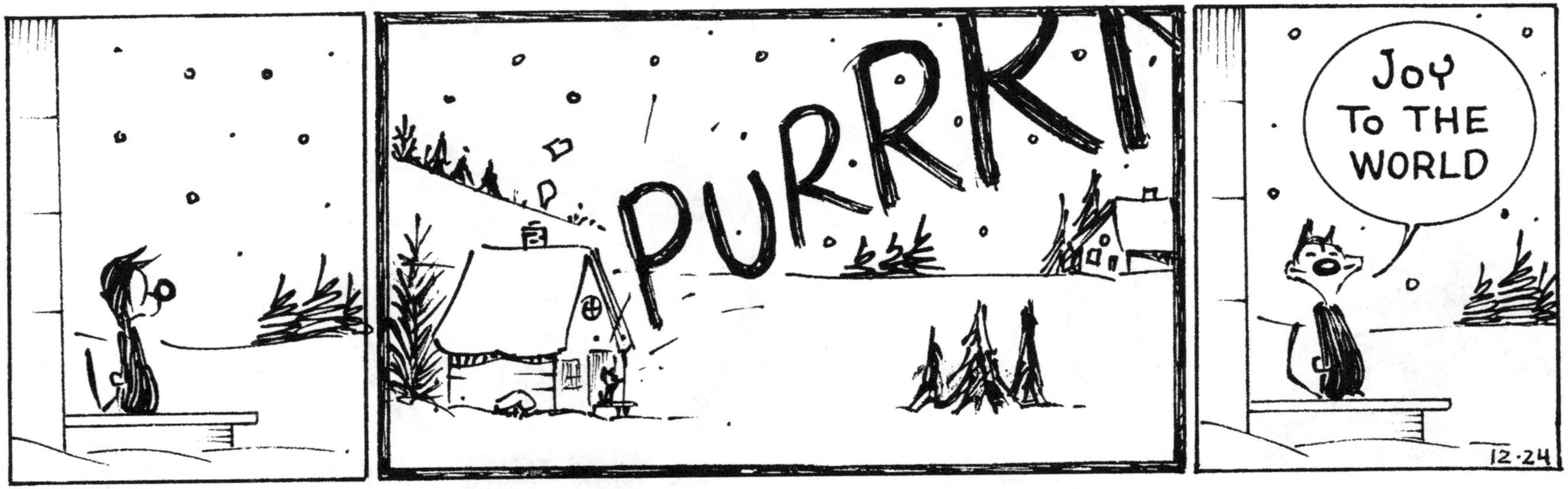
PURRRR
JOY TO THE WORLD
12·24

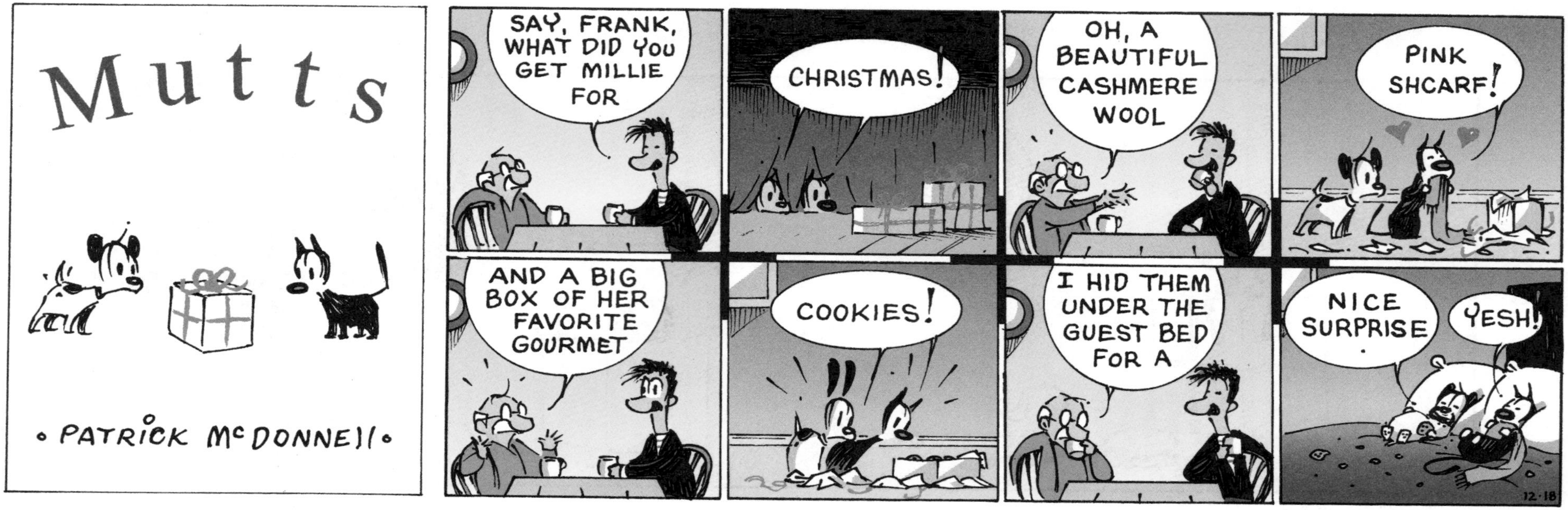
Mutts
• PATRICK McDONNELL •
SAY, FRANK, WHAT DID YOU GET MILLIE FOR
CHRISTMAS!
OH, A BEAUTIFUL CASHMERE WOOL
PINK SHCARF!
AND A BIG BOX OF HER FAVORITE GOURMET
COOKIES!
I HID THEM UNDER THE GUEST BED FOR A
NICE SURPRISE.
YESH!
12·18

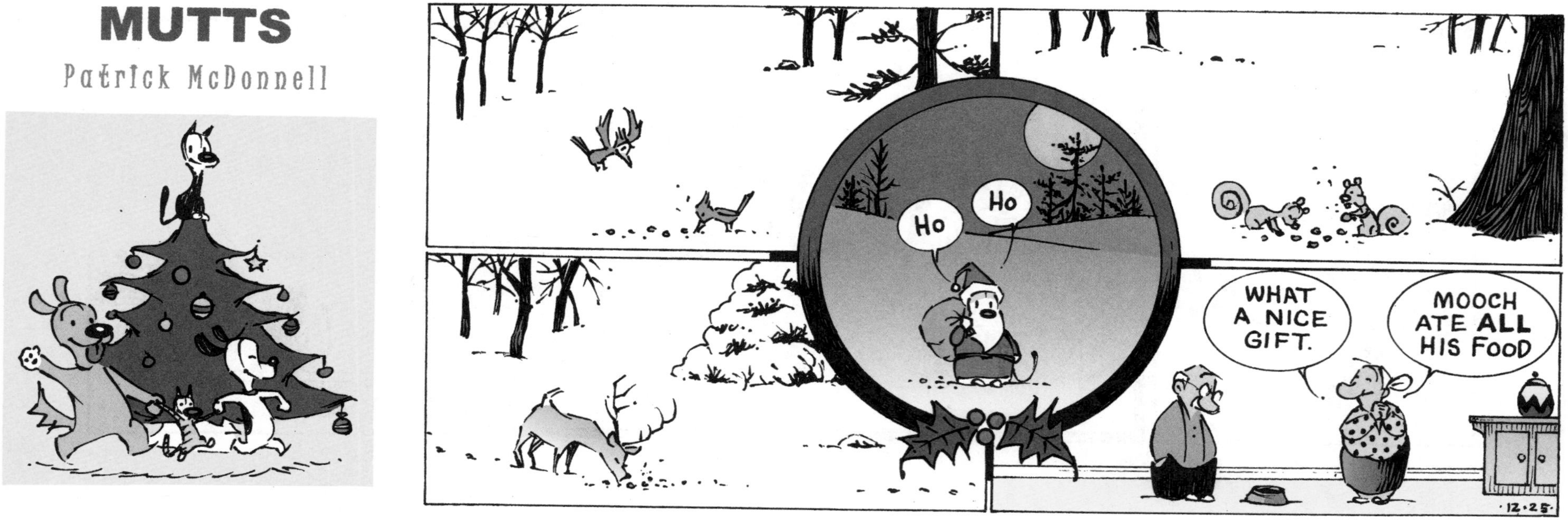
MUTTS
Patrick McDonnell
Ho
Ho
WHAT A NICE GIFT.
MOOCH ATE ALL HIS FOOD
·12·25·

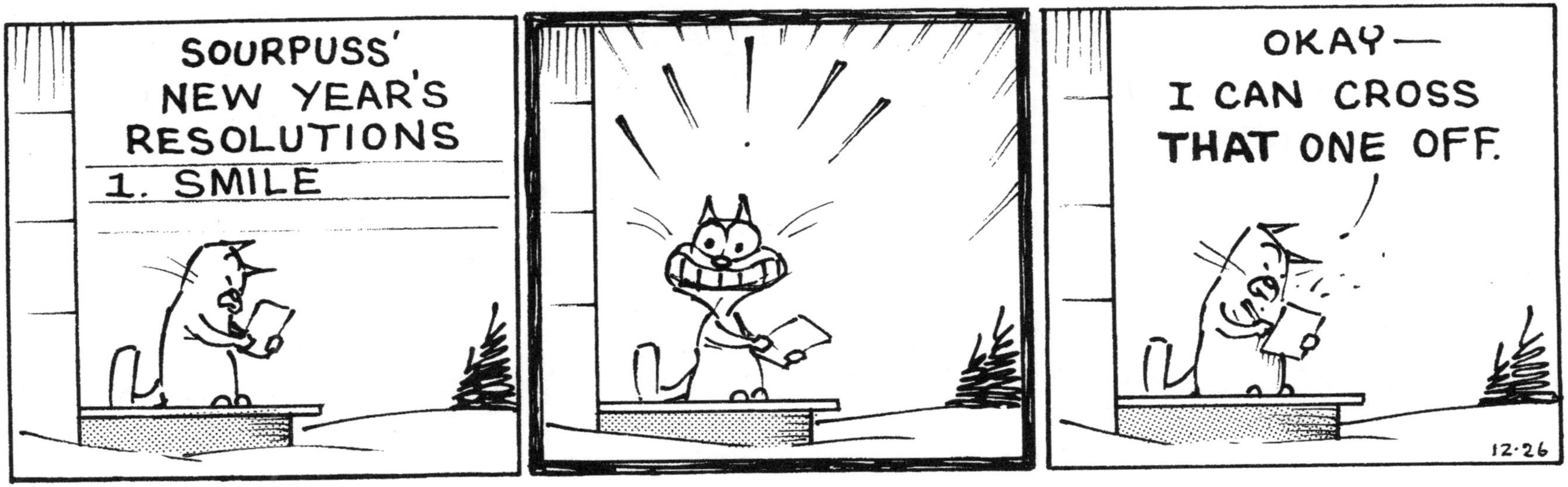
SOURPUSS' NEW YEAR'S RESOLUTIONS
1. SMILE
OKAY— I CAN CROSS THAT ONE OFF.
12·26

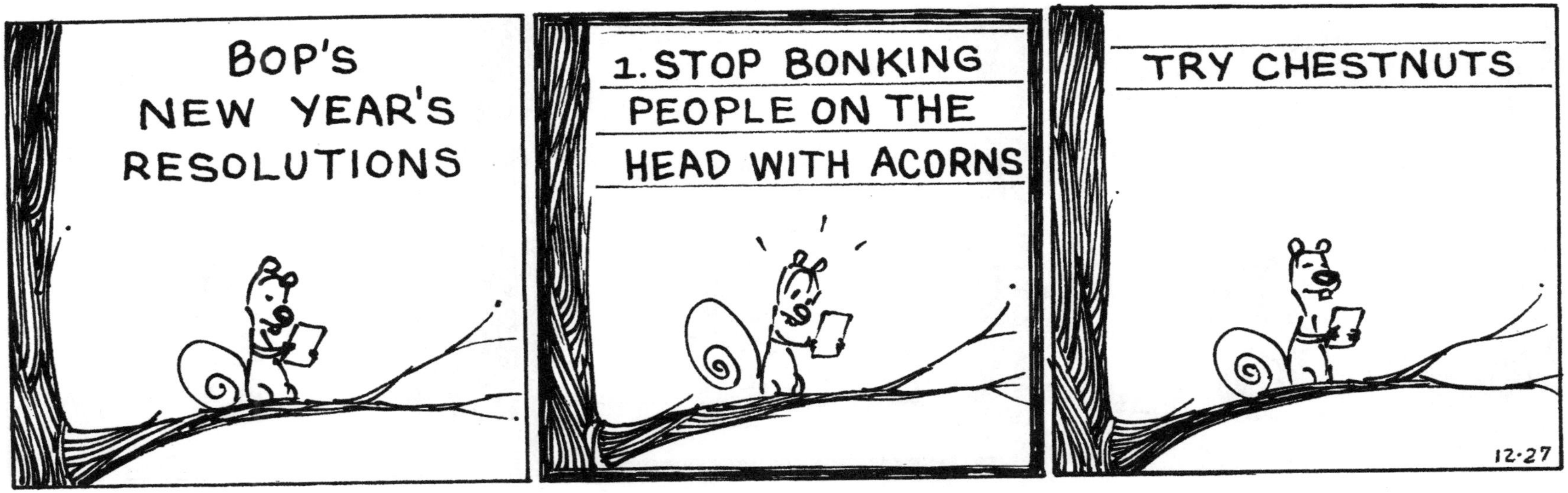
BOP'S NEW YEAR'S RESOLUTIONS
1. STOP BONKING PEOPLE ON THE HEAD WITH ACORNS
TRY CHESTNUTS
12·27

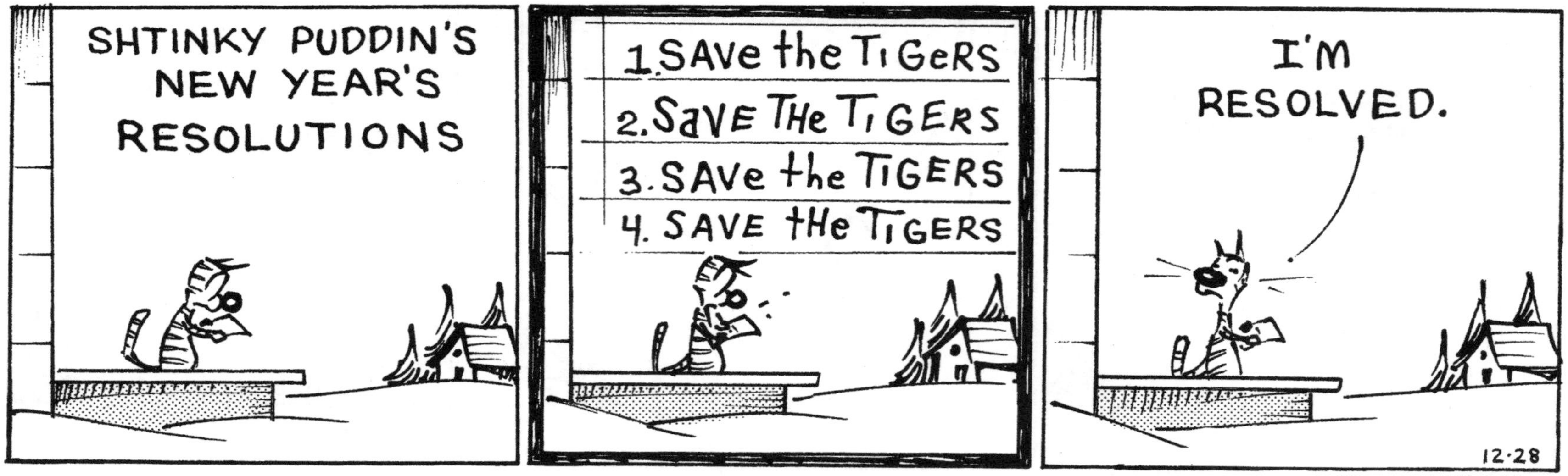
SHTINKY PUDDIN'S NEW YEAR'S RESOLUTIONS
1. SAVE the TIGERS
2. SAVE THE TIGERS
3. SAVE the TIGERS
4. SAVE tHe TIGERS
I'M RESOLVED.
12-28

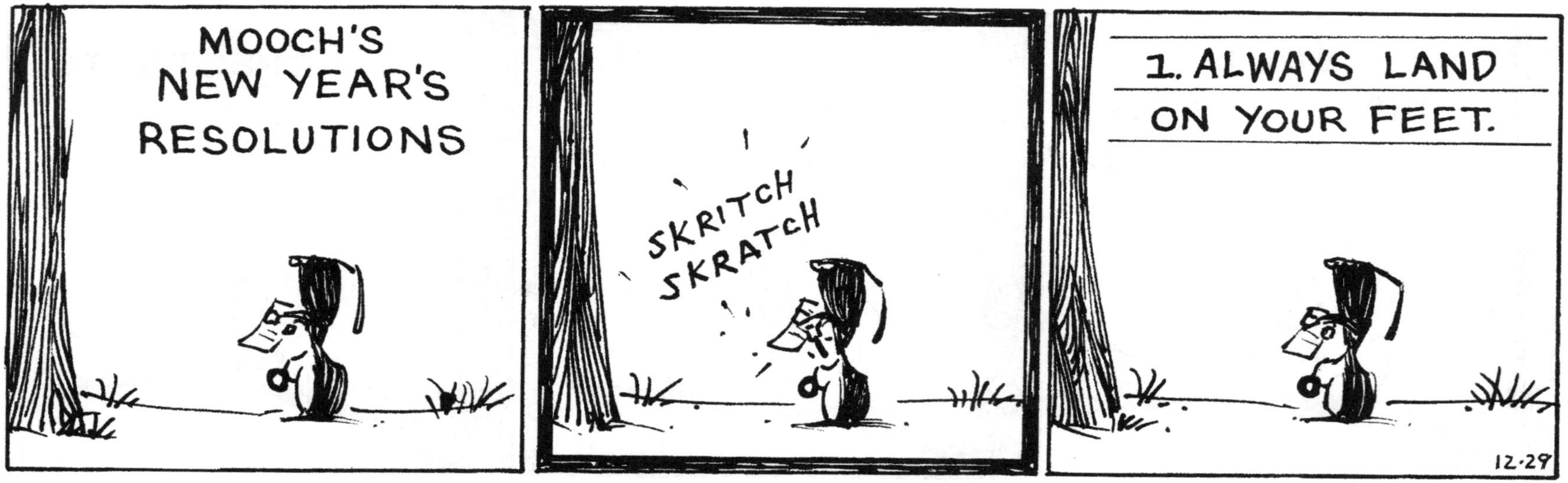
MOOCH'S NEW YEAR'S RESOLUTIONS
SKRITCH SKRATCH
1. ALWAYS LAND ON YOUR FEET.
12-29

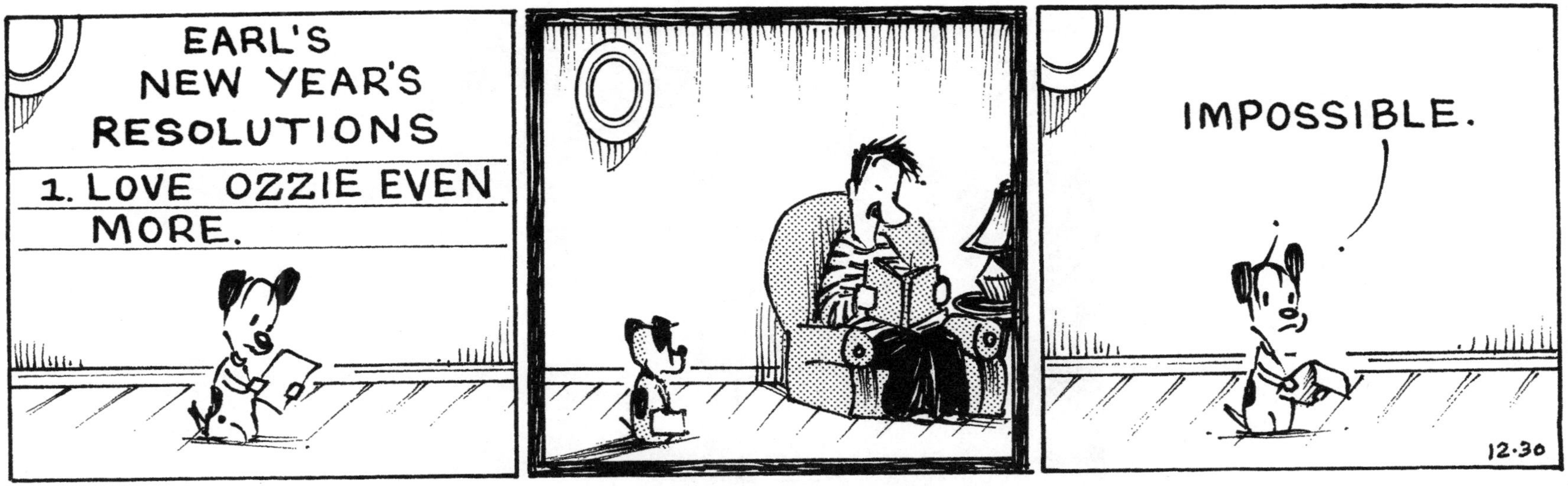
EARL'S NEW YEAR'S RESOLUTIONS
1. LOVE OZZIE EVEN MORE.
IMPOSSIBLE.
12·30

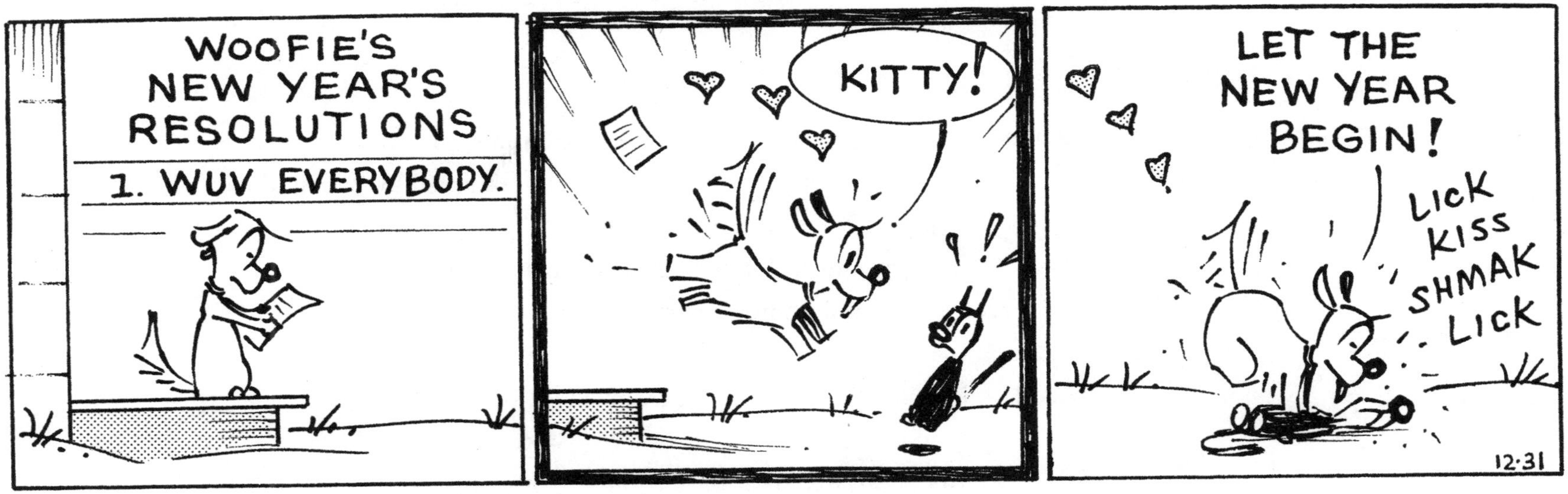
WOOFIE'S NEW YEAR'S RESOLUTIONS
1. WUV EVERYBODY.
KITTY!
LET THE NEW YEAR BEGIN!
LICK KISS SHMAK LICK
12·31

— PICTURE CREDITS —

page 3: Pen and ink drawing for cover of San Diego Comic-Con Guide

page 27: Ink drawing on photograph of Dark Horse Mutts figurines sculpted by Yoe Studios

page 59: Pen and ink sketch

page 72: Ink and watercolor page from sketchbook

page 98: Polaroid photo of Earl and Peanut

page 105: Ink and watercolor, page from sketch book

page 134: Ink and watercolor, page from sketch book

page 187: Back cover illustration for HSUS Guide to Vegetarian Eating

page 196: Ink and watercolor, page from sketchbook

page 201: Illustration for PETA holiday card

page 208: Ink and watercolor preliminary sketch for *The Gift of Nothing*